MW00397229

WriteNow

WriteNow

THIRD EDITION

Karin L. Russell
Keiser University

WRITE NOW, THIRD EDITION

This book is printed on acid-free paper.

1 2 3 4 5 6 7 8 9 LCR 24 23 22 21 20

ISBN 978-1-260-26034-2 (bound edition)
MHID 1-260-26034-8 (bound edition)
ISBN 978-1-260-79904-0 (loose-leaf edition)
MHID 1-260-79904-2 (loose-leaf edition)
ISBN 978-1-260-79905-7 (instructor's edition)
MHID 1-260-79905-0 (instructor's edition)

Portfolio Manager: *Erin Cosyn*
Product Development Manager: *Carla Samodulski*
Marketing Manager: *Byron Kanoti*
Content Project Managers: *Susan Trentacosti (Core), Emily Windelborn (Assessment), Sandra Schnee*
Buyer: *Susan K. Culbertson*
Design: *Debra Kubiak*
Content Licensing Specialist: *Sarah Flynn*
Cover Image: *Front cover: McGraw-Hill Education; Back cover: Artcyclone/DigitalVision Vectors/Getty Images*
Compositor: *SPi Global*

Library of Congress Cataloging-in-Publication Data

Names: Russell, Karin L., author.
Title: Write now / Karin Russell, Keiser University.
Description: Third edition. | New York, NY : McGraw-Hill Education, [2020] | Includes index.
Identifiers: LCCN 2019050144 | ISBN 9781260260342 (hardcover) | ISBN 9781260799040 (loose leaf edition) | ISBN 9781260799057 (annotated instructor's edition) | ISBN 9781260799064 (ebook)
Subjects: LCSH: English language–Rhetoric–Problems, exercises, etc. | Report writing–Problems, exercises, etc. | Academic writing–Problems, exercises, etc. | Critical thinking–Problems, exercises, etc.
Classification: LCC PE1408 .R86823 2020 | DDC 808/.02–dc23
LC record available at https://lccn.loc.gov/2019050144

mheducation.com/highered

BRIEF CONTENTS

Table of Contents

7 > Explaining a Process: Cultures and Traditions 147

12 > Solving a Problem: Crime and Justice 300

Part 3 Research Guide

Preface

WHY *WRITE NOW*?

College students taking the first-year composition course often wonder how what they are learning will benefit them. From the beginning, *Write Now* has been designed to respond to that question by demonstrating that being able to write effectively is essential for achieving success and that writing can be a worthwhile and satisfying experience. Now in its third edition, *Write Now* gives students greater confidence as they approach writing for college, for their careers, or for their everyday lives, while guiding them through the process of exploring ideas, drafting, revising, and editing their work. The third edition offers students plenty of practical, hands-on advice for dealing with any writing situation they might encounter, whether they are writing as college students or as nurses, police officers, office managers, or any other type of professional.

FEATURES OF *WRITE NOW*

A Focus on Writing in Careers—Not only does *Write Now* teach students how to write for college, it shows them how to transfer their skills to other environments, with a focus on professional settings. In Part 1, students learn to recognize their rhetorical situations, to practice writing processes that work for them, and to think, read, and write critically. In Part 2, they learn specific strategies for writing—such as narration, process analysis, and persuasion—through "how to" instruction and career-based selections organized around a theme. For example, in Chapter 9, "Analyzing Causes and Effects: Health and Medicine," students learn how to explain causes and effects and are asked to analyze "An Accident Report" by the Occupational, Safety, and Health Administration (OSHA). This reinforces for students how useful writing strategies and skills will be to their future careers.

Rhetorical Star: A Tool to Reinforce the Writing Situation—*Write Now* guides students through the process of writing, revising, and editing their work with a unique five-point approach—the rhetorical star—that focuses them on their subject, audience, purpose, strategy, and design. Throughout the text, the star reminds students to consider their various rhetorical situations and provides them with a tool for analyzing any type of writing and for composing their own written work.

FIGURE 1.1
The Rhetorical Star

A Wide Variety of Reading Selections—Carefully chosen to reflect the theme of each chapter in Part 2 and to exemplify the qualities of each type of writing, the professional selections and student essays span numerous areas of interest and disciplines, providing opportunities for students to apply critical reading strategies as well as topics and models for their own writing.

STUDENT WRITING

Note: Tracie Ranew used the American Psychological Association (APA 7th edition) format to document her sources. Your instructor may require you to use APA or perhaps the Modern Language Association (MLA) format if you use sources for your paper. Please see Chapters 13–14 for more details about research and documentation methods.

A Glimpse into Four Styles of Rap
by Tracie Ranew

Since the 1970s, rap music has been entertaining audiences all across the United States and beyond. While its origins were representative of the Black community, particularly in the Bronx neighborhood of New York City, rap is now popular among music lovers of many cultures. Some of the most significant categories of rap that have captured the hearts of music fans are oldschool, gansta, crunk, and alternative. 1

The first category, oldschool rap, is pretty straight forward. Rappers tell stories by talking into the microphone, with rhyming lyrics accompanied by 2

Career-Based DESCRIPTIVE NARRATIVE WRITING

[preview] **KRIS BISHOP** has an AA degree in rehabilitating assisting, which combines the fields of occupational and physical therapy, a BS degree in health services administration, and an MBA with a concentration in healthcare management. Her passion is working with older patients, and her career in occupational therapy has provided her with experience working with all age groups and in many practice settings including acute care, rehabilitation hospitals, skilled nursing facilities, and home care. Bishop wrote the following case narrative about a patient she treated, Mrs. Thompson, who was in declining health after the death of her husband and needed rehabilitation to increase her ability to manage several daily living skills.

Case Narrative by Kris Bishop, COTA/L

Each Wednesday the rehabilitation team members of the 120-bed skilled nursing and rehabilitation facility meet to discuss patients' progress and challenges on the sub-acute rehabilitation unit. Attending today's meeting was Mary, a Registered Nurse (RN); Sam, the Registered Physical Therapist (RPT); Renee, a Registered Occupational Therapist (OTR); Jeannie, the Discharge Planner; Betty, the Registered Dietician (RD); Terry, the Speech and Language Pathologist (SLP); and myself, a Certified Occupational Therapy Assistant (COTA). Facilitating the meeting was the Rehabilitation Director, Allison. 1

Patients who were admitted to this unit would be scheduled for daily therapies as prescribed by their Physiatrist, a physician who specializes in physical medicine and rehabilitation, or a Gerontologist, who specializes in aging adults. Most of the patients who were discussed were meeting goals as identified on their individual care plans. Patients' rehabilitative services and skilled nursing care are reimbursed under a prospective payment system which predetermines how much the facility will be paid based upon diagnosis and other factors. This system has a strong influence on when services are provided and the length of time a beneficiary can 2

Career-Based Writing Examples—To emphasize the centrality of writing to the world of work, each chapter in Part 2 includes at least one career-based writing example, as well as a section explaining how students will apply each writing strategy they are learning in school, in their careers, and in their personal lives.

Spotlights on Writing in Professional Settings—**Graduate Spotlights** provide testimonials from real college graduates who emphasize the importance of writing skills in their careers. **Employer Spotlights** give students additional insight into the importance of writing in the work world.

Graduate SPOTLIGHT

Jake Ellis, Media Designer

Jake Ellis is a media designer for a large entertainment and theme park company. He has a BFA degree in sound design. Here's what Ellis has to say about how he uses writing in his career:

©Courtesy of Jake Ellis

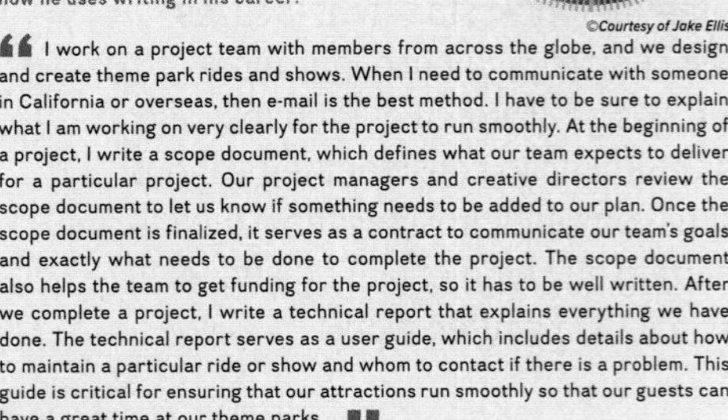

“I work on a project team with members from across the globe, and we design and create theme park rides and shows. When I need to communicate with someone in California or overseas, then e-mail is the best method. I have to be sure to explain what I am working on very clearly for the project to run smoothly. At the beginning of a project, I write a scope document, which defines what our team expects to deliver for a particular project. Our project managers and creative directors review the scope document to let us know if something needs to be added to our plan. Once the scope document is finalized, it serves as a contract to communicate our team's goals and exactly what needs to be done to complete the project. The scope document also helps the team to get funding for the project, so it has to be well written. After we complete a project, I write a technical report that explains everything we have done. The technical report serves as a user guide, which includes details about how to maintain a particular ride or show and whom to contact if there is a problem. This guide is critical for ensuring that our attractions run smoothly so that our guests can have a great time at our theme parks.”

WHAT'S NEW IN THE THIRD EDITION OF *WRITE NOW*?

A New Chapter on Division and Classification—Chapter 6, "Dividing and Classifying: Media and Popular Culture," offers practical guidelines and engaging reading selections that will help students with a type of writing that is essential for analysis and found frequently in academic and workplace writing contexts.

CHAPTER 6 **Dividing and Classifying: Media and Popular Culture**

Peathegee Inc/Blend Images LLC

learning outcomes

In this chapter you will learn techniques for achieving these learning outcomes:

6.1 Identify real-world applications for dividing and classifying. *p. 123*

6.2 Understand the qualities of division and classification writing. *p. 125*

6.3 Interpret images and division and classification readings about media and popular culture. *p. 128*

6.4 Analyze the rhetorical star for dividing and classifying. *p. 142*

6.5 Apply the qualities of division and classification writing. *p. 143*

Blogs and Social Media

Blogs and social media posts can add valuable perspectives to your research paper, but they are not necessarily the best sources for facts. As noted below, the quality of the content depends on authorship, so be sure to evaluate each source carefully. (See pp. 346–347 for advice on evaluating sources.)

Blogs A blog (short for web log) is a personalized online journal, a website or web page that the blogger updates regularly. Bloggers typically write in a conversational style that is less formal than, say, a news article. Blogs often feature advice and opinions. Businesses, organizations, and individuals can create blogs. Typically, almost anyone interested in the discussion at hand can post a comment to a blog.

More Help with Evaluating and Citing Internet Sources—Students need lots of help evaluating and citing the enormous variety of potential sources that are available, including social media sources. We have added a new section in Chapter 13 on blogs and social media. In addition, Chapter 14 has been expanded to include guidelines and models for citing these and other types of online sources in both MLA and APA styles.

Reading and Reflection EVALUATIVE WRITING

Kevin Mazur/Getty Images

[preview] **CRAIG JENKINS** is a pop music critic for *New York Magazine* and *Vulture* (where the following article originally appeared) and has written for *Pitchfork*, *Billboard*, the *New York Times*, *NoisyMusic*, *Spin*, and other publications. He studied English at Gordon College in Massachusetts and is a resident of New York City. The following review is of Ariana Grande's *Sweetener*, her third number one album on the U.S. *Billboard 200*. Grande is a Florida-born singer, songwriter, and actress who performed in the Broadway musical *13*, played the role of Cat Valentine in the Nickelodeon television series *Victorious*, and took numerous other roles on camera and as a voice actress in animated television and films. To learn more about Ariana Grande, go to **arianagrande.com**. If possible, listen to or watch the video for "No Tears to Cry," "R.E.M." or another song on the album before reading the review. Also, think of some of your favorite albums. What criteria do you use to evaluate music?

The Quirky Beauty of Ariana Grande's *Sweetener*
by Craig Jenkins

We've all had a wild year, but Ariana Grande might've had the wildest. Since last spring, the Floridian singer with the outsize voice had her world rocked by a terror attack at her arena show in Manchester. Just two weeks later, she made a brave return to the stage for an uplifting performance at One Love Manchester, a star-studded

2 *Sweetener* is serious enough in its commitment to break with the traditions of Ariana Grande albums to serve three big, weird Pharrell collaborations right up front. "Blazed" is textbook Skateboard P, all funky, ascending keys, and busy percussion. "The Light Is Coming" features a capable Nicki Minaj guest rap and chiptune affectations, and shifting

Compelling New Reading Selections—The new edition includes reading selections on high-interest topics such as balancing college and work, cultural identity and practices, space movies, alternative medicine, and the impact of technology, along with a new work-related selection on massage therapy. The readings are now supplemented by over 80 reading selections, on a wide variety of themes and from a range of disciplines, that are available as part of *Connect Composition for Write Now.*

Multimodal Assignments—Writing situations in both the academic and work worlds now incorporate multimodal elements such as infographics, PowerPoint, and audio clips. To prepare students for these situations and give them practice in responding to them, we have added a multimodal option to the "Options for Writing" box in each chapter in Part 2. In addition, Chapter 15, "Developing an Oral Presentation or a Multimodal Composition," now includes coverage of giving a multimodal presentation.

OPTIONS FOR WRITING A DESCRIPTIVE NARRATIVE ESSAY

Now that you have read one or more examples of descriptive narratives, it's time to write your own. You may choose to write about one of the writing options that follow, the advertisement, the image, or one of the media suggestions. Consider your rhetorical star and the qualities of an effective narrative as you begin to compose your assignment.

Writing Assignment Options

Use one of the following topics to write a descriptive narrative essay recalling a memory.

1. A memorable childhood experience
2. An entertaining pet story
3. A scary or dangerous event you witnessed or experienced
4. Your best (or worst) vacation
5. A lesson you learned as a member of a team or in a club
6. Resisting or succumbing to peer pressure
7. Your worst (or best) day on the job
8. An event that led to a significant decision in your life
9. Meeting someone new or losing someone special
10. A day that changed your life forever

Multimodal Assignment

Using one of the readings, writing assignment options, or another topic, create a multimodal project using the descriptive narrative writing strategy and at least two or more of the options in Table 5.1.

Table 5.1

Multimodal Options		
Artifact	Images	PowerPoint
Artwork	Infographics	Prezi
Audio clip	Journal	Video
Blog	Montage	Website
Digital portfolio	Podcast	Wiki
Graphic organizer	Poster	Writing

(See Chapter 15 for more details about multimodal projects.)

Enhanced Coverage of Documentation—The sections on MLA and APA documentation in Chapter 14 now include models for new types of sources such as social media postings and video. Additionally, more source-based professional and student models are included throughout Part 2, Writing Strategies.

Note: Follow the MLA guidelines for the type of source you are citing, and then add the database information and source URL or DOI to the end of the citation.

Online Audio Recording or Podcast

Sheeran, Ed. "Perfect." *Divide, iTunes* app, Warner/Asylum Records, 2017.

Note: The information that you listened to this song on an app is optional.

MLA Format

Radio Program

Meek, Miki. "Before Things Went to Hell." *This American Life,* Produced by Ira Glass, episode 665, 11 Jan. 2019, WBEZ Chicago, www.thisamericalife.org/665/before-things-went-to-hell. Radio show.

e-Book (Novel)

Angelou, Maya. *Mom & Me & Mom.* Kindle ed., Random House, 2013.

Email, Text Message, or Letter

Record, Michael. "Using the Online Writing Lab." Received by the author, 20 Oct. 2019. Email.

MLA Format

EVEN MORE SUPPORT FOR YOUR COURSE

Connect Composition for Your Course

Connect Composition helps instructors use class time to focus on the highest course expectations by offering their students meaningful, independent, and personalized learning, and an easy, efficient way to track and document student performance and engagement.

The following tools are available within *Connect Composition.*

FEATURE	DESCRIPTION	INSTRUCTIONAL VALUE
Power of Process	An online reader offers nearly 90 professional reading selections and a powerful user interface that guides students through strategies for *Before, During*, and *After Reading* assignments. Additionally, instructors can upload their own readings or the reading selections from each chapter of *Write Now*, including student examples.	Guides students through performance-based assessment activities using the pedagogy of strategies instruction. Students use strategies to read and respond to the text, and instructors can assess students' depth of engagement with the text. Instructors may also choose from pre-built templates for guiding students through Literal and Critical Reading as well as Research and Writing.

FEATURE	DESCRIPTION	INSTRUCTIONAL VALUE
Writing Assignments	Students can engage in peer review through the writing tool, while instructors can create rubrics and assess student writing around specific learning outcomes.	Students draft responses to writing prompts and receive feedback from instructors. Grammar checkers and originality detection alert them to issues before they hand in their work and refer them to learning resources to understand how to correct their errors. An available rubric provides assessment transparency to students, and allows them to see why they got their grade and how to improve. Instructors may also customize this rubric, or create their own.
Adaptive Assessment	Adaptive modules cover critical reading, the writing process, research, argument, paragraph development, and sentence style. Grammar-focused modules are aligned to each section in the Editing Guide.	Provides students with adaptive practice and additional learning resources for important topics, either before or after class, or in a support course.
SmartBook® 2.0	SmartBook 2.0 highlights key concepts and creates a personalized study plan.	SmartBook 2.0 is an adaptive study resource that transforms class time from dull definitions to dynamic debates. Find out more about the powerful personalized learning experience available in SmartBook 2.0 at www.mheducation.com/highered/connect/smartbook.
Handbook	*Connect* includes a complete online handbook for instructors to assign and for students to refer to as needed. The handbook includes chapters on the writing process, argument, research, and documentation as well as grammar, punctuation, mechanics, and help for multilingual writers.	

For more information on any of these features, please e-mail a member of the McGraw-Hill English team at english@mheducation.com.

Custom Options for Using McGraw-Hill Create®

With McGraw-Hill Create, instructors can easily arrange chapters to align with their syllabus, eliminating chapters they do not wish to assign and adding any of the content available only from the McGraw-Hill Create platform to build one or more print or eBook texts— including *Connect Composition* access codes—for their program. Instructors can also add their own material, such as the course syllabus, course rubric, course standards, or specific instruction, from which they want their students to benefit. For more information, go to **https://create.mheducation.com** or contact your McGraw-Hill representative.

Co-requisite Course Support

Write Now also comes with a pre-built Connect course that provides customizable assignments for instructors to choose from, including support for co-requisite models. Within the pre-built course, suggested assignment combinations provide students with plenty of practice in critical reading and writing, as well as choosing correct style, grammar, and punctuation.

In addition, co-requisite course support is now available in the *Write Now* Instructor's Manual. Within this resource, pacing guides for each chapter of the text offer co-requisite class support activities, as well as a chart to help instructors align co-requisite instruction with the goals of the composition course. Please contact your sales representative, or a member of the McGraw-Hill English team, at english@mheducation.com, for more information.

Learning for Everyone

McGraw-Hill works directly with Accessibility Services Departments and faculty to meet the learning needs of all students. Please contact your Accessibility Services office and ask them to e-mail accessibility@mheducation.com, or visit **www.mheducation.com/about/accessibility** for more information.

Teaching Resources

Karin Russell has more than twenty-five years' experience teaching composition, literature, developmental English, and business writing for various Florida schools. She currently oversees curriculum development for a variety of writing, literature, and communication courses. Drawing on her extensive teaching and administrative background, she has prepared the instructor notes for the Annotated Instructor's Edition of *Write Now* as well as the Instructor's Manual, with Heather Burke of Hondros College of Nursing.

ANNOTATED INSTRUCTOR'S EDITION: TEACHING TIPS RIGHT ON THE PAGE

The Annotated Instructor's Edition includes classroom tips, tips for using SmartBook 2.0 and adaptive assessment, as well as classroom tips and answers to activities and Grammar Window exercises. It also provides tips for teaching co-requisite sections of first-year composition.

INSTRUCTOR'S MANUAL

The Instructor's Manual provides a wealth of material to draw on, including the following:

- **Chapter outlines**
- **Lecture notes**
- **Class activities**
- **Pacing Guides for traditional and co-req classes**
- **Sample assignments and writing topics**
- **Connect resources**
- **Discussion questions for online/hybrid classes**
- **Graphic organizers that can be used as handouts**
- **Grading rubrics for each type of writing covered**
- **Peer review worksheets**
- **Co-req support**

Grammar Window
POINT OF VIEW

First person: I, me, my, mine, we, our, ours

Second person: you, yours

Third person: he, she, they, their, theirs

The point of view needs to be consistent within a sentence or paragraph or readers will become confused. Watch for sentences where the point of view shifts for no reason.

Exercise

Correct the shifts in point of view in the following sentences:

1. I looked at the spider and you got really scared.
2. You were driving along and they saw something furry cross the road.

A Word from Karin Russell

For more than twenty-five years, I have taught college-level writing courses and observed students and how they learn to become better writers. I chose to create Write Now *because I felt there was a need for a complete yet concise four-in-one (rhetoric, reader, research guide, and handbook) textbook that incorporates sound pedagogical theory, appeals to students' interests, and demonstrates the relevance of being able to write clear, effective documents.* Write Now *emphasizes a process-oriented approach to writing that focuses on revision and the recursive nature of writing. One of the unique features of* Write Now *is the Rhetorical Star, which I developed to help students analyze their rhetorical situation. Building on Aristotle's rhetorical triangle, the Rhetorical Star guides students through each writing assignment by encouraging them to consider their subject, audience, purpose, strategy, and design.*

In addition to providing students with a variety of engaging readings, images, and activities to stimulate critical thinking and writing skills, I have included Graduate Spotlights, Employer Spotlights, and Career-Based Writing examples to emphasize to students just how important writing is, not only during their college experience but also in their careers and personal lives. Above all, Write Now *sends students the message that being able to write effectively is essential for achieving success and that writing well can be a worthwhile and satisfying experience.*

Acknowledgments

The third edition of *Write Now* would not be possible without the tremendous effort put forth by the McGraw-Hill team. First of all, my thanks go to Mike Ryan, vice president and general manager, and David Patterson, managing director for the skills group, for their leadership. I'm very grateful to Erin Cosyn, portfolio manager for composition, for her wisdom and guidance in shaping this edition. I'm also grateful to Kelly Villella, director, English and College Readiness, for her expert advice and guidance as we finalized the text. Thanks as well go to Ellen Thibault, product developer, for her vast knowledge, attention to detail, high standards, and insightful suggestions for improving every aspect of the text, as well as to Carla Samodulski, product development manager, for her advice and support. I'm grateful as well to Alyssa Ennis for overseeing the Instructor's Manual and PowerPoints for the third edition. Mary Ellen Curley, lead product developer, provided her expertise throughout the development of this edition. I'd also like to thank Byron Kanoti, marketing manager for composition, for expertly marketing the third edition. Susan Trentacosti, lead content project manager, has attended to the many details necessary to get this edition ready. My thanks also go to Sarah Flynn, content licensing specialist, for overseeing the photo research and text permissions, and to Karen Sanatar, photo researcher, for giving me amazing options for the new images that appear in this edition. I'd also like to thank Jessica Cuevas and Debra Kubiak for overseeing the design and cover of the text. They have done wonders with the visual appeal of *Write Now*.

I am grateful to Heather Burke of Hondros College of Nursing for updating the Instructor's Manual and updating the sections on the resources available on Connect.

My thanks also go to the following reviewers, who have provided helpful comments and suggestions as we developed the third edition of *Write Now:*

Atlantic Cape Community College, Cape May County Campus
Vickie Melograno

Bellevue College
Steve Yarborough

Bevill State Community College, Hoover Campus
Jimmy Ellenburg

Bevill State Community College, Sumiton Campus
Stephen Rizzo

Bismarck State College
Erin Price

Blinn College, Schulenburg Campus
Audrey Wick

Casper College
Ben Lareau
Terry Rasmussen

Cecil College
Kathy Weiss

Central Community College
Chyrel K. Remmers

Chattahoochee Technical College
Keith Brooks
Greg Garner

Craven Community College, New Bern Campus
Kyle J. Warner

Crowder College
Janet Reed

Cuyahoga Community College, Western Campus
Amy Cruickshank

Fort Hays State University
Sam Wilks

Georgia Military College, Fairburn Campus
Corey Stayton

Georgia State University
Emory Abbott
Karen Holley
Kirk Swenson

Hondros College of Nursing
Adam Bulizak
Heather Burke
Luann Edwards
Cassie S. Hewitt

Ivy Tech Community College, Marion Campus
Thomas Chester

Ivy Tech Community College, Muncie Campus
Sean Smith

Jackson State University, Main Campus
Monica Granderson
Linda McLemore-Wheeler

Jefferson State Community College, Pell City Campus
Jacob Melvin

Johnson County Community College
Sayanti Ganguly-Puckett

Keiser University, Fort Lauderdale Campus
Hayley Sogren

Keiser University, Tallahassee Campus
Hal Shows
Josephine Yu

Macomb Community College, Center Campus
Linda Brender
Ludger Brinker

Miami Dade College, Wolfson Campus
Victor Uszerowicz
Maria Villar

Midland College, Main Campus
Mary Williams

Midland College, North Campus
Pamela Howell

Miles College, Fairfield Campus
Rachel Pierce

Milwaukee Area Technical College, Downtown Campus
John Allen
Amarilis Martinez

Moberly Area Community College, Columbia Campus
Beth Marchbanks

Moberly Area Community College, Kirksville Campus
Sherry Todd

National American University
Brigit McGuire

Navarro College, Corsicana Campus
Belinda Adams

North Central Michigan College
Dominic Borowiak

Northeast Alabama Community College, Rainsville Campus
Joan Reeves

Northeastern Oklahoma A&M College, Miami Campus
Seonae Ha-Birdsong

Northern Oklahoma College, Stillwater
Tamera Davis
Stephanie Scott
Alicia Sharp
Jeff Tate

North Greenville University
Sarah Bailey
Jenna Garrett
Alicia Looper
Becky Thompson

Saginaw Valley State University
Geof Carter
Kim Lacey

Schoolcraft College, Livonia Campus
Anna Maheshwari

Shelton State Community College, Fredd Campus; Martin Campus
Janice Filer

Shepherd University, Main Campus
Sadie Shorr-Parks

Somerset Community College
Michael Bloomingburg
Erin Stephens

Sowela Technical Community College
Michael Rather

St. Johns River State College
Melody Hargraves

St. Louis Community College
James Sodon
Wei Yan

St. Louis Community College, Florissant Valley Campus
Barbara Wachal

Swedish Institute
Shoba Parasram

Texas State Technical College
Heather Stewart

Tidewater Community College, Virginia Beach Campus
Frances Norge

Washtenaw Community College
Margaret Green

Weatherford College
Diann Ainsworth

Weber State University
Jason Barrett-Fox
Sylvia Newman
Jose Otero

West Kentucky Community and Technical College, Paducah Campus
Tyra Henderson
Tracy Jordan
Bernard Lewis
Sharon Looney
Kelly Paul
Kimberly Russell

West Virginia University
Natalie Updike

Wor-Wic Community College
Dana Burnside
Chuck Porter

New to the Third Edition of *Write Now*

Overall

- A new, smaller trim size and simpler design.

Part 1: Introduction to Writing (Chapters 1–4)

- An article on a topic that working students can relate to has been added in Chapter 1 ("Getting Started with Writing"): "Balancing College and Work Demands" by Robert Feldman.
- An annotated model essay on the fear of failure as a motivator for success has been added in Chapter 3 ("Writing Sentences, Paragraphs, and Essays"): "In Praise of the F Word" by Mary Sherry.
- An annotated model essay on women in the music business has been added to Chapter 4 ("The Critical Thinking, Reading, and Writing Connection"): "Will New Female Rappers Shatter Hip Hop's Glass Ceiling?" by Linda Laban.
- New visual texts for reading and interpreting appear in Chapter 4: including a World War II era poster, "We Can Do It!," and the graph on "The Health Effects of Social Media on Teens."

Part 2: Writing Strategies (Chapters 5–12)

- In each chapter in Part 2, new multimodal assignments give students practice for writing in different modes and genres for varied audiences and purposes, using the skills covered in a given chapter.
- Chapter 5, "Describing and Narrating: Memories," now combines these two strategies that are often used together in essays. Also, Chapter 5 now includes a descriptive narrative on being born into slavery: From *Incidents in the Life of a Slave Girl,* by Harriet Ann Jacobs.
- A new chapter on division and classification has been added: Chapter 6, "Dividing and Classifying: Media and Popular Culture." This chapter includes the following:
    - An essay on patient responses to physical therapy. "Massage: Types of Responses to Treatment" by William Prentice.
    - An essay on popular culture: "Sorry, Your Favorite 'Space' Movie Is Not Actually a Space Movie" by Elahe Izadi.

    - An essay on types of audio storytelling: "Most Popular Podcast Formats" by Christian Cawley.
    - A poem that defines poetry through imagery: "Fragment" by Amy Lowell.
    - A student essay in APA format on types of music: "A Glimpse into Four Styles of Rap" by Tracie Ranew.
    - Visual texts for reading and interpreting: "Playtime Footwear," a Converse advertisement; Buzzle.com, a "Car Types" illustration.
- Chapter 7, "Explaining a Process: Cultures and Traditions," now includes a process essay on the Day of the Dead, written exclusively for this book by the author of *Coco: A Story about Music, Shoes*, an adaptation of the Disney/Pixar film *Coco*. "Picnic with the Dead" by Diana López.
- Chapter 8, "Comparing and Contrasting: Computers and Technology," now includes these new selections:
    - A researched compare/contrast essay on medical practices, written by a registered nurse: "Pros & Cons of Alternative Medicine, Modern Medicine, & Traditional Medicine" by Krystina Ostermeyer.
    - An essay on the value of material things: "Discarded Objects" by Nigel Warburton.
    - A poem in praise of devices and machines: "Technology" by Martin Dejnicki.
- Chapter 10, "Persuading: Relationships," now includes these new selections:
    - A persuasive essay that won *The New York Times* Student Editorial Contest: "I'm a Disabled Teenager, and Social Media Is My Lifeline" by Asaka Park.
    - A persuasive argument on love in the age of social media: "Is Technology Helping or Hurting Your Relationship?" by Melissa Scrivani.
    - A persuasive argument on the relationship between human connection and health: "The Importance of Social Relationships Over the Life Course" by Mark C. Pachucki.
- Chapter 11, "Evaluating: Film and the Arts," now includes these new selections:
    - A review of a blockbuster film: "Review of *Black Panther*" by James Berardinelli.
    - A review of a major pop album: "The Quirky Beauty of Ariana Grande's *Sweetener*" by Craig Jenkins.
    - A poem that evaluates a classic spy thriller: "The James Bond Movie" by May Swenson.
- Chapter 12, "Solving a Problem: Crime and Justice," now includes the following:
    - An excerpt from a researched, problem-solving report in Chapter 12: From "A Comprehensive Technical Package for the Prevention of Youth Violence and

Associated Risk Behaviors" by the National Center for Injury Prevention and Control (NCIPC) and the Centers for Disease Control and Prevention (CDC).

- An argument for reforming the criminal justice system: "Before, During, After Prison: How Florida Should Reform Criminal Justice" by Adrian Moore and Sal Nuzzo.
- An argument for overhauling America's bail system, written by two civil-rights attorneys: "America's Pretrial System Is Broken. Here's Our Vision to Fix It" by Andrea Woods and Portia Allen-Kyle.
- An APA-style researched student argument for preventing crime and taking care of kids: "Combatting Juvenile Delinquency" by Koray Easom.

Part 3: Research Guide (Chapters 13–15)

- Updated, visual coverage of finding library and Internet sources in Chapter 13, "Planning and Writing a Research Paper."
- A new section on working with blogs and social media as sources in Chapter 13.
- Completely updated coverage of APA style—including advice, in-text citations, reference lists, and sample paper—based on the new 7th edition of the *Publication Manual of the American Psychological Association* (2020) in Chapter 14, "Documenting a Research Paper."
- Many new APA and MLA models for in-text citations and references/works cited lists for sources including social media posts, podcasts, games, software, content from YouTube and Netflix, and legal and business documents in Chapter 14.
- A revised chapter on presentations that now includes advice and examples for how to create and deliver a multimodal presentation in Chapter 15, "Delivering an Oral or Multimodal Presentation."

Part 4: Editing Guide

- The Editing Guide has been updated to reflect the evolving nature of language, including the gender-neutral use of the singular *they*.

About the Author

Rhonda Wetherington

Karin L. Russell

Karin Russell is a college English teacher whose experience in helping students achieve success has spanned more than twenty-five years. Russell earned her undergraduate degree in elementary education at Stetson University and her master's degree in reading and language arts education at Florida State University. She continued her education in the English field by earning thirty-six graduate credit hours beyond the master's degree. She has taught composition, literature, humanities, research and writing, technical writing, developmental English, and business writing courses for various Florida schools, including Eastern Florida State College (formerly Brevard Community College), Nova Southeastern University, and several career colleges.

For more than twenty years, Russell has been a full-time English instructor for Keiser University, where she also served as the university department chair for English, humanities, and communications for 12 years. Russell is especially interested in enabling students to develop their writing skills through a process-oriented approach and showing students how writing is applicable to their future careers. She passionately believes that nearly anyone can become a good writer with the right instruction and enough practice.

Rhonda Wetherington

Rhonda Wetherington

PART 1

Introduction to Writing

Why Writing Is Important for Success

Writing effectively is an important skill, one that you can take with you and use for the rest of your life. To be successful in college, in your career, and in your life, you will need to be able to communicate effectively through writing. Whether you are composing a report for your boss, a paper for an instructor, or a letter to resolve a personal matter, being able to write well is essential. The good news is that you don't have to be naturally gifted to learn to become a strong writer. You can develop your writing skills by studying and practicing writing. Whether you are 17 or 77, you have something worthwhile to say that others will be interested in reading. As you read this third edition of *Write Now,* you will learn and practice many valuable techniques that will help you to become a better reader, critical thinker, and writer so that you are able to interpret and communicate messages in an effective manner. Those skills will help you to accomplish your educational, career, and personal goals.

OVERVIEW of Part 1

Chapter 1

You will have an opportunity to create a writing environment that best suits your personality. You will also learn how to assess your rhetorical (or writing) situation.

Chapter 2

You will discover some strategies that work for you as you participate in the steps of the writing process to produce a final, polished document. You will also see how a student writer went through the entire writing process.

Chapter 3

You will learn some methods for writing well-organized sentences, paragraphs, and essays.

Chapter 4

You will gain a better understanding of the connection between critical thinking, reading, and writing, and you will learn some strategies for applying critical thinking skills to analyze written and visual texts as well as websites.

CHAPTER 1

Getting Started with Writing

takayuki/Shutterstock

learning outcomes

In this chapter you will learn techniques for achieving these learning outcomes:

1.1 Create an Ideal Writing Environment. *p. 3*

1.2 Analyze The Rhetorical Situation: The Star Approach. *p. 5*

1.1 Create An Ideal Writing Environment

Even if you haven't had much success with writing in the past, you can become a good writer at school, on the job, and in your personal life. Your academic history doesn't define your future as a writer. Through this course, you will learn and apply many strategies that will strengthen your writing skills so you can say something worthwhile in a way that readers will find interesting. Instead of feeling overwhelmed by writing assignments, you will learn to break them into manageable tasks. Take a moment to visualize yourself writing a strong paper, one that you can proudly submit to your instructor or boss.

One way to help you achieve success is to create a comfortable writing atmosphere that contains everything you need to accomplish your task. Whether you are taking your class on campus or online, here are some steps to help you find your writing groove.

1. Find a Good Place to Write

Try writing in different places to discover where you experience the most success. Do you work better at home, in a library, in an empty classroom, outside, or in a café? Choose a place that won't be too distracting, whether at home or away from home. If you can't find a peaceful place, try listening to something soothing on your iPod to reduce outside interference.

2. Plan Your Time to Write

What time of day are you the sharpest? Do you like to compose first thing in the morning, or does your brain get fired up in the middle of the night? Try to schedule your writing time when you are likely to develop your best work. If your busy life prevents you from writing at the opportune time, then learn to adapt your writing habits to your schedule. Though it may not be ideal, you can write a little bit at a time if necessary. For example, you might be able to write during your commute (if you're not driving) or even while waiting at the dentist's office. With the right attitude, you can be productive in nearly any environment at any time. Instead of making excuses for not having time to write, use the time that you do have wisely. Consider using a paper or digital calendar to plan time to write. Look for gaps in your schedule. If your writing time is on your calendar, you are less likely to fill that time with other, less productive tasks such as hanging out with friends or watching television.

3. Select Your Materials

Before you begin writing, assemble the materials you will need. Some writers like to brainstorm ideas on paper. If that's your style, do you prefer a legal pad, spiral notebook, or fancy journal? Do you have a favorite pencil or pen? Also, you should have a dictionary and thesaurus nearby. *Dictionary.com* and *Thesaurus.com* are excellent Web-based resources.

Other writers are comfortable starting right in with a computer. Make sure you have enough battery strength or a power supply so you won't lose momentum by having to stop writing. Choose a font style, color, and size that make you comfortable during the composing process. You can always change them before you submit your work.

4. Establish a Method for Saving Your Work

What happens if you lose the folder or notebook that has your assignment in it? Whether you are writing on paper or on a computer, you'll need a backup system for situations like this one. Make a copy of written assignments. If you compose your assignment on a computer, then don't just trust your hard drive. Save a copy to a flash drive or another data-storage device. You can even e-mail your assignment to yourself as an extra precaution so that it is stored safely in cyberspace.

For an online class, compose your assignments in a word processing program (such as Microsoft Word or Pages). Then copy and paste them into the online course platform. That way if you lose your Internet connection, or if the course system goes down while you are trying to post your assignment, you won't lose your work.

5. Create an Inviting Atmosphere

Determine what kind of environment most inspires you to write. Do you prefer order or chaos? Do you like bright or soft lighting? Do you prefer complete silence, or does listening to music help you to think clearly? Are you most comfortable sitting at a desk, or are you more creative on the sofa? Try different scenarios to see what kind of ambience helps you produce your best work.

6. Minimize Distractions

If you live with other people, ask them to give you some time for writing without interruptions. If you have children, arrange to have someone else watch them while you write. Turn off your TV and cell phone. Try to focus all of your energy on what you are writing so that you can concentrate and do your best work.

Sometimes you won't have an opportunity to choose your writing environment, such as when you're writing an in-class essay or when you're at work. If that's the case, do what you can to minimize distractions. Try to distance yourself from people with annoying habits, such as pen clicking or humming. Sit away from the door if noises from the hallway are likely to bother you. As you develop your writing skills, also work on learning how to tune out distractions so that you are able to write in a variety of circumstances.

Activity — Imagining Your Ideal Writing Environment

Make a collage that represents your ideal writing environment. Include what you would see, where you would write, the materials you would use, and anything else you would need to create the right atmosphere for you. Write a brief description explaining the collage. You may be asked to share your ideal writing environment with a few classmates.

1.2 Analyze the Rhetorical Situation: The Star Approach

The term **rhetoric** simply refers to the art of communicating effectively through writing or speaking. Whether you are writing an essay for school, a report for your boss, or an e-mail to your friend, your goal is to convey a message to the reader. You want to be sure that your reader understands the intent of your message. Therefore, every time you sit down to write, you need to consider five points of the rhetorical situation: subject, audience, purpose, strategy, and design.

Rhetoric The art of communicating effectively through writing or speaking.

These five points make up the "rhetorical star" (Figure 1.1). Each point of the star is an essential component of your final written product. Using the rhetorical star will help to ensure that you communicate effectively.

Subject

For some writing projects, you will need to determine what **subject** to cover. A subject is a general concept, such as health, technology, or crime. Choose an appropriate subject that fits within the parameters of your assignment (Figure 1.2). After you have selected a broad subject, you will need to narrow it to a specific topic, such as nutritional shakes, tablet features, or home security systems. Make sure your topic is narrow enough that you can adequately cover it in your document. For example, you wouldn't be able to cover the entire subject of "staying fit" in a short paper, but you could adequately cover a few specific fitness techniques.

As you consider what you want to say and how much detail you want to include, keep your purpose and audience in mind. You might think about what your readers will already know about your subject and what they might want to learn. Also, consider whether research is necessary for you to adequately cover your topic. See Chapter 2 for more details about discovering and narrowing a topic for your paper.

FIGURE 1.1
The Rhetorical Star

FIGURE 1.2
Subject

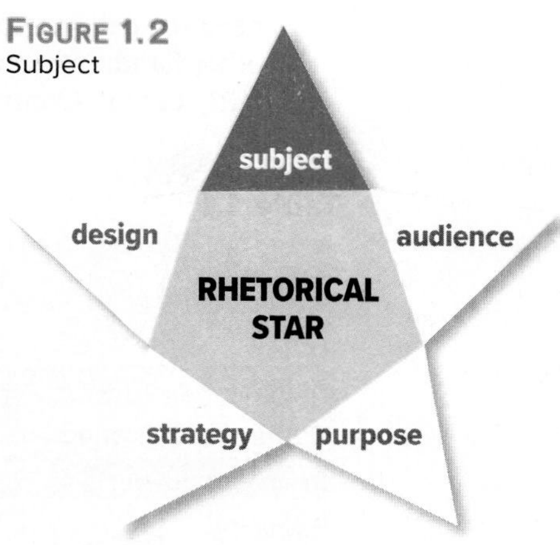

Audience

Consider the readers who make up your **audience** (Figure 1.3). Are you writing for a particular *discourse community* (a group of people who share common interests, knowledge, and values related to a particular subject)? Each of us belongs to a number of discourse communities such as school clubs, social or religious groups, and professional organizations. Each group has its own vocabulary and conventions

FIGURE 1.3
Audience

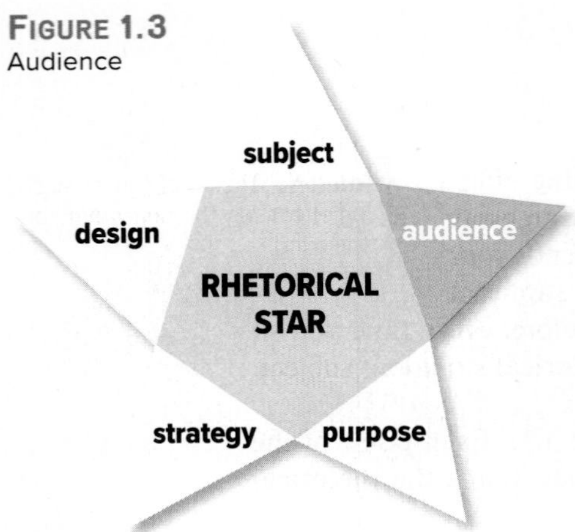

of communication, called *jargon.* For example, if you are writing a software review for members of the computer club, you can probably safely assume that they will understand terms that are specific to the computer world, such as *bits* and *bytes.* Similarly, if you are writing a letter to members of a certain professional field, such as health care or homeland security, you won't need to explain concepts related to that field.

Keep in mind the needs and interests of your primary audience, but realize that others (your secondary audience) might also read your document. See Table 1.1 for audience characteristics to consider when you are writing.

Some audience characteristics will matter more than others depending on your subject and purpose. For example, if you are writing an article about a work-related topic that will be published in your company's newsletter, your readers' interests and knowledge of the subject would be more important than their gender and cultural background. If most of the readers are employees, then you can use the vocabulary that is specific to your career field. If, on the other hand, the newsletter is geared more for your organization's clients, then you may need to explain specialized terms in more detail and consider other audience characteristics.

After you have determined who your audience will be, you will need to consider your tone and level of formality.

Tone The mood or feeling a writer or speaker is trying to create.

- **Tone:** Your **Tone** is the mood or feeling you are trying to create through your writing. Your tone can be businesslike (serious), academic, humorous, or opinionated. Choose a tone that is appropriate for your purpose and audience.
- **Level of formality:** Your writing style can be *formal* or *informal.* Formal writing tends to be more serious than informal writing. The use of contractions (such as *I'm* and *doesn't*) is usually limited. In formal writing you generally need to spell out complete words and choose your words carefully. On the other hand, informal writing, such as the writing in this book, tends to be fairly casual. Contractions are acceptable and can help the writing not to

Table 1.1

Audience Characteristics		
Age	Experience	Opinions
Beliefs	Gender	Political views
Cultural background	Interests	Reading ability
Education level	Knowledge of the subject	Religion
Ethnicity	Occupation	Socioeconomic status

Employer SPOTLIGHT

Tracy Wetrich, Director of Human Resources for the National Aeronautics and Space Administration at Kennedy Space Center

Tracy Wetrich

Tracy Wetrich has a BS degree in industrial organizational sociology with a minor in human resources. As a human resources director, one of Wetrich's responsibilities is to find the best people for the available positions. She reviews résumés and cover letters and provides hiring managers with quality candidates to interview. Here's what Wetrich has to say about the qualities she looks for in a job applicant:

"The résumé is the first opportunity for a candidate to make a good impression. If it clearly and effectively communicates the applicant's education, skills, experience, and knowledge, he or she is likely to fare well in the job search process. If an applicant doesn't write well, then he or she probably doesn't speak well, and the ability to communicate is critical in most aspects of the jobs. For example, written communication is important in everything from e-mail to writing formal proposals, project summaries, performance plans, and evaluations. Written communication also serves as a foundation for preparing materials for presentation. Individuals who are proficient in oral and written communication are often well suited for advancement to lead and supervisory positions, where these skills become even more critical. A candidate who has completed formal college classes in writing, oral communication, and literature is more likely to be able to communicate effectively, have a broad vocabulary, read and interpret materials with critical comprehension, and influence people and decisions. Candidates who possess good communication skills have a strong foundation that will prepare them for many opportunities."

sound too stuffy. You would likely use a more formal approach in a report for your boss than you would in an e-mail to a co-worker. In school, a research essay would be much more formal than a journal entry.

Purpose

Determine your reason, or **purpose,** for writing (Figure 1.4). Why are you writing? What are you hoping to accomplish? What effect do you wish to have on your audience? Whether you are composing a class assignment, workplace document, or personal letter, your writing will have at least one of five main purposes: to inform, to interpret, to persuade, to entertain, and to express feelings.

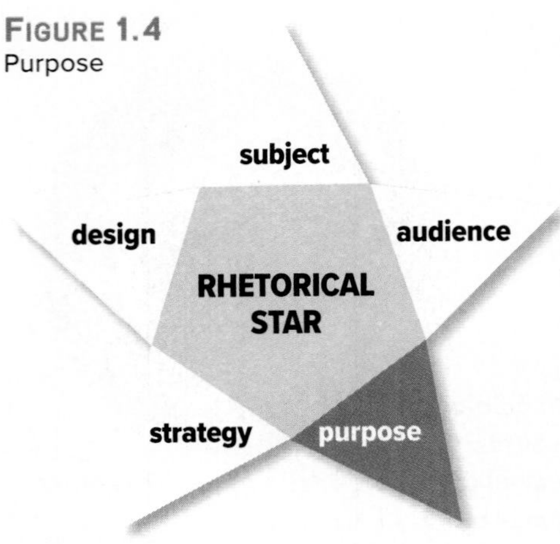

FIGURE 1.4
Purpose

1. Writing to Inform Most writing is informative in some way. When you write to inform, your goal is to provide readers with useful information about your subject or teach them how to do something. For example, you might write an essay summarizing an article or a story you have read, a set of instructions explaining how to perform a workplace procedure, or a recipe for making your grandmother's special chili.

2. Writing to Interpret Sometimes writing can help you or your audience better understand something. For example, you might write an essay interpreting (analyzing) a poem for a literature class, or you may write a comparison of two software packages that your boss is considering implementing. When you write interpretatively, you are giving your opinions about the subject rather than just reporting information. Sometimes your interpretation may include an evaluation of your subject. For instance, you might write an evaluation of an employee or a review of a movie you have seen.

3. Writing to Persuade Although almost any type of writing needs to be convincing, sometimes your main purpose is to argue a point. For example, you might write an essay arguing for or against a proposed law, or you might submit a letter to your boss convincing him or her why you deserve a raise. Other times you may want to persuade your readers to actually do something. For instance, you might challenge your readers to do more than just recycle bottles, cans, and paper products to help preserve the environment for future generations.

4. Writing to Entertain Some types of writing are primarily intended to entertain readers. You might choose to write a story, a poem, a cartoon, or song lyrics to move your readers or make them laugh. Often you can entertain your readers at the same time that you address another purpose. You might want to use humor in an informative or a persuasive paper to help engage your readers in the material being covered.

5. Writing to Express Feelings You can use personal expression in many ways. You might write a note to someone special, an essay about an exciting or a scary event you experienced, a reaction to a magazine or newspaper article, or a letter to your apartment manager expressing your dissatisfaction with the length of time it is taking to get your leaky faucet repaired.

Combined Purposes The five purposes for writing are not mutually exclusive; they overlap. For instance, if you are writing an essay as part of an application for a scholarship, you may address three purposes by informing the readers about your background and situation, expressing your feelings about how much you need the scholarship and how grateful you would be to receive it, and persuading your readers that you are a worthy recipient of the scholarship.

Activity Writing a Professional E-mail

You should always use proper tone and language when communicating with your instructor (or boss or colleague) by e-mail.

1. Use an appropriate screen name (e-mail address) that includes your name.
2. Write a clear subject heading.
3. Address your instructor professionally.
4. Write your message clearly and concisely. If you have questions, make them specific.
5. Use standard grammar, capitalization, and punctuation.
6. Avoid using all capital letters. This can be considered shouting.
7. Maintain a professional tone.
8. End with a polite closing and your name.

Unprofessional E-mail

From: hotsexymamma@email.com
To: mwilliams@starsuniversity.edu
Subject: class

hey teach
i'm confuzed bout the paper cuz i stayed up partyin' 2 late and blew off class what am i sposed to do i can't afford to fail this class again HELP ME!!!!!!!!!
BTW u better not bust me for turning it in late

Professional E-mail

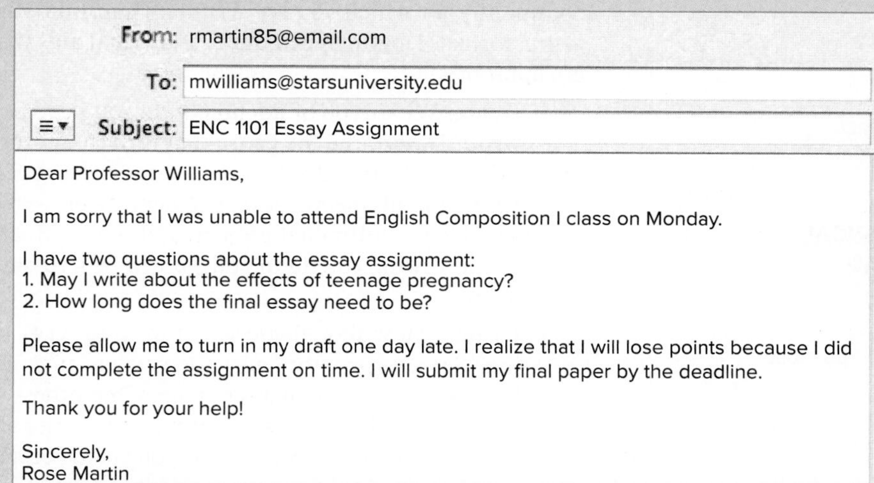

From: rmartin85@email.com
To: mwilliams@starsuniversity.edu
Subject: ENC 1101 Essay Assignment

Dear Professor Williams,

I am sorry that I was unable to attend English Composition I class on Monday.

I have two questions about the essay assignment:
1. May I write about the effects of teenage pregnancy?
2. How long does the final essay need to be?

Please allow me to turn in my draft one day late. I realize that I will lose points because I did not complete the assignment on time. I will submit my final paper by the deadline.

Thank you for your help!

Sincerely,
Rose Martin

—continued

Activity Writing a Professional E-mail (*cont.*)

In pairs or small groups, write a short e-mail to an instructor (or boss or colleague) using unprofessional words and tone. Trade papers with another pair or group, and revise the other paper so that it is a more professional communication.

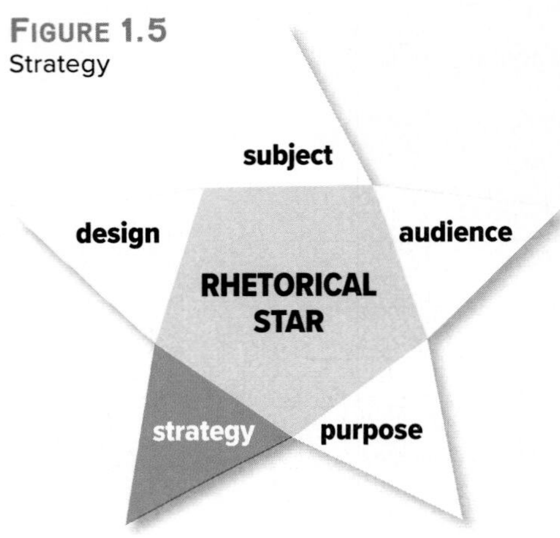

FIGURE 1.5
Strategy

Strategy

You'll need to choose an approach, or **strategy,** that best serves your purpose and audience (Figure 1.5). In this textbook you will learn about eight major writing strategies: describing and narrating, dividing and classifying, explaining a process, comparing and contrasting, explaining causes and effects, persuading, evaluating, and solving a problem. You may be able to combine writing strategies as well. Table 1.2 offers a quick overview of the different strategies.

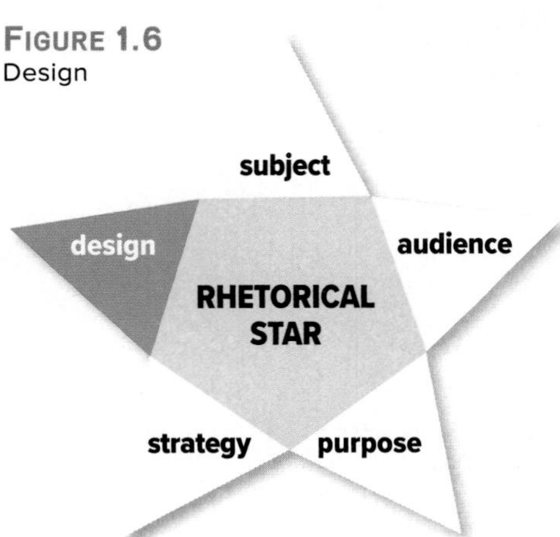

FIGURE 1.6
Design

Design

Finally, think about how you are going to **design** your document (Figure 1.6). Consider the design expectations of your instructor or boss and the discourse community for which you are writing. Determine the genre, format, length, appearance, and visual aids that are appropriate for your document.

- **Genre:** What type of document do you need to write? Determine the genre that is most appropriate for your task: story, essay, research paper, letter, e-mail, memo, advertisement, flyer, website, blog, multimodal project, and so on. Much of the writing you do in college will be in essay form.
- **Format:** How should you structure your writing? Some instructors may allow you to turn in handwritten informal assignments, but others will require that you use a computer to write all assignments. Be sure to follow your instructor's guidelines very closely. Also, you may need to adhere to guidelines provided by the Modern Language Association (MLA) or the American Psychological Association (APA), especially if you are writing a paper based on research.

Table 1.2

Writing Strategies	
Describing and Narrating	Tell a descriptive story about something that happened. Usually you will present the details of the event in chronological order, but occasionally a flashback can be useful. Be sure to cover *who, what, where, when, why,* and *how.* Also, use plenty of sensory appeal (sight, sound, taste, smell, touch) to help your reader envision what happened.
Dividing and Classifying	Divide a concept into groups with common traits or principles and explain the significant elements of each group.
Explaining a Process	Tell how something works or what something does. You may give step-by-step instructions so your reader can perform the task, or you can write an explanation so that your audience is able to understand your subject.
Comparing and Contrasting	Show how two people, places, or objects are similar and/or different. Be sure to make a worthwhile point while using this strategy.
Explaining Causes and Effects	Examine how one event or situation caused another to occur, or determine the effects of an event or situation. Be careful to apply sound logic as you analyze causes and effects.
Persuading	Take a stand about an important or controversial issue, and convince your reader that your position is valid. You may use personal experience or research to support your main idea.
Evaluating	Make a judgment about your subject by determining how well it meets specific standards that you feel are important for that subject.
Solving a Problem	Explain a problem to your reader and offer several solutions. You may evaluate each possible solution before persuading your reader that one specific solution is best.

See Chapters 13 and 14 for more information about writing and documenting research papers.

- **Length:** How long should your document be? Is there a word or page minimum (or limit)? If your instructor does not specify a length, then let the topic guide you. Be sure to fully develop each point that you want to make.
- **Appearance:** How should your document look? Find out if you need to single-space or double-space your papers. Typically, if you single-space a paper, you will begin each paragraph at the left margin. However, if you double-space a paper, you will need to indent each paragraph. Choose a font size, style, and color that are appropriate for your writing situation. Also, determine if you can use headings, bullets, columns, or boxes to emphasize your main points.
- **Visual aids:** Would adding visual aids enhance your paper? Often pictures, diagrams, charts, or graphs will help get your ideas across to your audience.

For example, if you are including a variety of statistics in a research paper, then you may decide to include a chart or graph to help the reader visualize the impact of the concept you are discussing.

Note: For more details on design, see the section on multimodal composition (15.5) in Chapter 15.

Applying the Rhetorical Star Analysis

You can apply the rhetorical star analysis to all types of writing. Whether you are composing a paper for school, writing an e-mail message to your boss, or creating a flyer for an event you are hosting, you will benefit from considering the five points of your rhetorical star: subject, audience, purpose, strategy, and design. Also, being aware of how other writers apply the rhetorical star can help you understand your own rhetorical star as you write. Whether you are reading a textbook for school, a professional journal for work, or a magazine or newspaper for pleasure, understanding the writer's rhetorical star can help you to interpret the material and comprehend it on a deeper level.

Activity Applying the Rhetorical Star to Your Own Writing

Choose three specific hypothetical writing situations that you could encounter (currently or in the future): one for school, one at work, and one in your personal life. For each scenario, determine your rhetorical star:

1. What is your subject?
2. Who is your primary audience? Is there a secondary audience? If so, who? What does your audience expect from your document?
3. What is your primary purpose? Do you intend to inform, to interpret, to persuade, to entertain, or to express feelings? Would you use a combination of purposes? If so, which ones?
4. What primary writing strategy would you use: describing and narrating, dividing and classifying explaining a process, comparing and contrasting, explaining causes and effects, persuading, evaluating, or solving a problem? Would you combine strategies? If so, which ones?
5. How would you design your document? What specific design features related to format, appearance, and visual aids would be appropriate for your document?

article

BALANCING COLLEGE AND WORK DEMANDS

Preview

Robert Feldman is dean in the College of Psychological and Behavioral Sciences at the University of Massachusetts, Amherst. He earned a BA. from Wesleyan University and an MS. and a PhD. from the University of Wisconsin—Madison. He has written more than 100 books, book chapters, and scientific articles. The following is an excerpt from his textbook *P.O.W.E.R. Learning and Your Life: Essentials of Student Success, 4e,* from Chapter 2: "Making the Most of Your Time." As you read, notice the five points of the rhetorical star: subject, audience, purpose, strategy, and design. After you finish reading the article, look at the rhetorical star analysis that follows it.

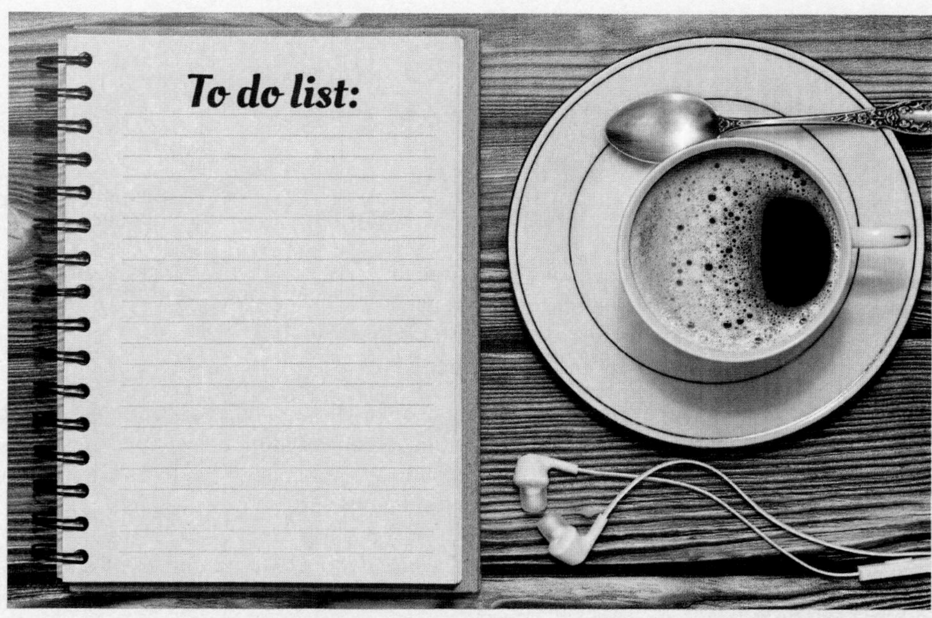

AntonGrachev/Shutterstock

BALANCING COLLEGE AND WORK DEMANDS

Juggling college and a job can be exhausting. Not only must you manage your time to complete your schoolwork, but in many cases, you'll also face time management demands while you are on the job. Here are some tips to help you keep everything in balance:

- *Make to-do lists for work, just as you would for your schoolwork.* In fact, all the time management strategies you use for school can be applied to on-the-job tasks.
- *If you have slack time on the job, get some studying done.* Try to keep at least some of your textbooks, class notes,

—continued

—*continued*

or notecards always with you so you can refer to them. Of course, you should never do schoolwork without your employer's prior agreement. If you don't get permission, you may jeopardize your job.

- *Use your lunch or dinner hour effectively.* Although it's important to eat a nutritious lunch and not to wolf your food down, you may be able to use some of the time allotted to you for lunch to fit in some studying.
- *Ask your employer about flextime.* If your job allows it, you may be able to set your own hours, within reason, as long as the work gets done. If this is an option for you, use it. Although it may create more time management challenges for you than would a job with set hours, it also provides you with more flexibility.
- *Always keep in mind why you're working.* If you're working because it's your sole means of support, you're in a very different position from someone who is working to earn a bit of extra money for luxuries. Remember what your priorities are. In some cases, school should always come first; in others, your job may have to come first at least some of the time. Whatever you decide, make sure it's a thoughtful decision, based on consideration of your long-term priorities.

Source: Robert Feldman. *P.O.W.E.R. Learning and Your Life: Essentials of Student Success.* New York: McGraw Hill, 2020. Used with permission.

Model Rhetorical Star Analysis of "Balancing College and Work Demands"

subject
design
audience
RHETORICAL STAR
strategy
purpose

Subject	The segment covers several specific suggestions to help working college students manage their time and prioritize work and school activities effectively.
Audience	The primary audience consists of college students. A secondary audience may include people who are close to college students, such as a parent, partner, friend, or child. People who are not college students but have busy schedules would benefit from reading the article as well.
Purpose	The main purpose is to inform readers about ways to manage their time.
Strategy	The primary writing strategy is to explain the process of managing time. The author also uses persuasive strategy to convince students to use their time wisely, keep study materials close by, and thoughtfully prioritize job- and school-related obligations.
Design	The text is blocked into paragraphs, with bullet points and italicized headings to make the material easily readable. The images are relevant and appealing, and they serve to enhance the written text.

Activity Applying the Rhetorical Star to the Work of Others

Choose an article or essay in a popular print or online newspaper, magazine, or professional journal. Determine the five points of the rhetorical star by answering the following questions:

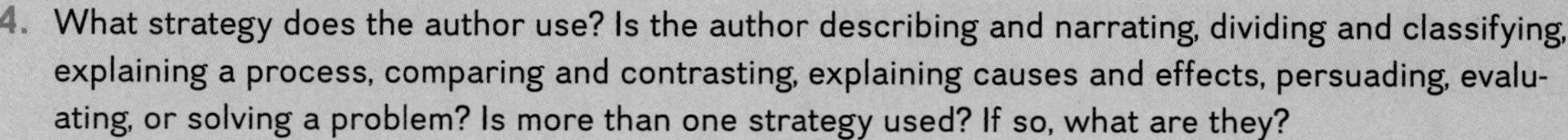

1. What is the subject?
2. Who is the primary audience? Is there a secondary audience? If so, who? What does the audience expect from the document?
3. What is the primary purpose? Does the author wish to inform, interpret, persuade, entertain, or express feelings? Has the author combined purposes? If so, which ones?
4. What strategy does the author use? Is the author describing and narrating, dividing and classifying, explaining a process, comparing and contrasting, explaining causes and effects, persuading, evaluating, or solving a problem? Is more than one strategy used? If so, what are they?
5. How is the article designed? Are headings, bullets, or visual aids included? How effective is the design?

CHAPTER SUMMARY

1. Increase your chances for success by creating an ideal atmosphere for writing.
2. Every time you write, consider the five points of the rhetorical star: subject, audience, purpose, strategy, and design.
3. Choose an interesting and useful subject for your paper.
4. Consider your audience's needs and expectations as you write your document.
5. The five purposes for writing are to inform, interpret, persuade, entertain, and express feelings.
6. Choose a writing strategy that best suits your purpose and audience. Describing and narrating, dividing and classifying, explaining a process, comparing and contrasting, explaining causes and effects, persuading, evaluating, and solving a problem are all popular writing strategies.
7. Use an effective and appealing design for your document.

WHAT I KNOW NOW

Use this checklist to determine what you need to work on to feel comfortable with your understanding of the material in this chapter. Check off each item as you master it. Review the material for any unchecked items.

- ☐ 1. I am ready to create my own **ideal writing environment.**
- ☐ 2. I know the five points of the **rhetorical star.**
- ☐ 3. I can choose an interesting and useful **subject.**
- ☐ 4. I am aware of important **audience** characteristics to consider.
- ☐ 5. I understand the five **purposes** for writing.
- ☐ 6. I know what the eight **writing strategies** are.
- ☐ 7. I am aware that I need to choose an effective document **design.**

Design elements: *Graduate Spotlight:* Ingram Publishing/AGE Fotostock

CHAPTER 2

The Writing Process

Keith Brofsky/Getty Images

learning outcomes

In this chapter you will learn techniques for achieving these learning outcomes:

2.1 Discover ideas about a topic. *p. 18*

2.2 Plan and organize a document. *p. 23*

2.3 Compose a document. *p. 30*

2.4 Get appropriate feedback on a document. *p. 30*

2.5 Revise a document. *p. 33*

2.6 Edit a document. *p. 34*

2.7 Proofread a document. *p. 35*

Following the Writing Process

After you have analyzed your rhetorical star to get a good sense of what you need to do (see Chapter 1), it's time to start writing. Just like you need to find your own ideal writing environment, you will need to find the writing process that works well for you. The seven steps of the writing process are (1) discovering, (2) planning, (3) composing, (4) getting feedback, (5) revising, (6) editing, and (7) proofreading (see Figure 2.1). Learning to apply these seven steps will help you find the methods that work best for your writing process.

Writing can be a messy process, so you won't always follow all of the steps in sequence. Sometimes you might get to the composing step and decide you need more supporting points, which will take you back to the discovering step. Also, the steps are flexible. Some writers are comfortable beginning with the planning or even composing step while others prefer to try a number of discovering techniques before writing. Try different strategies to learn what works well for you. Continue working through the steps of the writing process until you are satisfied with your paper—or at least until your deadline arrives.

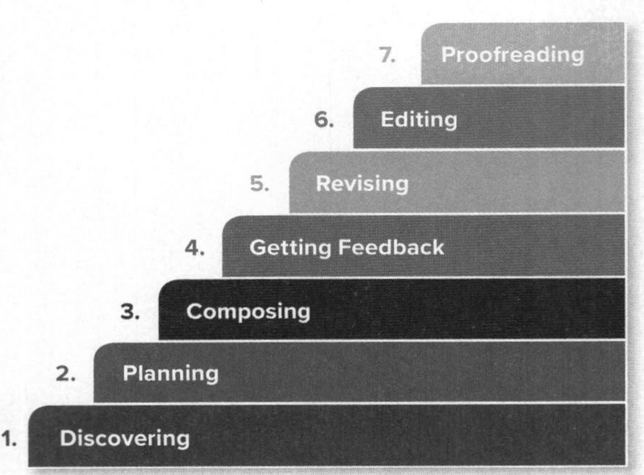

FIGURE 2.1 The Seven Steps of the Writing Process

2.1 Discovering

During this step you will explore your topic. You have several options for going about the discovery process. Your goal is to generate ideas about the topic you have selected. Have you ever experienced writer's block? The following strategies can help you overcome that ominous blank piece of paper or computer screen.

Brainstorming Writing whatever comes to mind about a topic.

Brainstorming

When you **brainstorm,** you write whatever comes to mind about your topic. If you don't have a topic, then use this approach to generate one. You can write all over the page if you like. Use arrows, boxes, question marks, circles, doodles, or whatever you can think of to explore ideas. Don't worry about writing in complete sentences or organizing your ideas. Just let your creativity spill onto the page.

Amanda Laudato chose to write an essay for her English composition class about the influential musician Eminem. Figure 2.2 shows her brainstorming notes.

Listing List all the ideas that you can think of that relate to your topic. **Listing** is different from brainstorming because it's focused on a specific topic. There are no wrong ideas at this point. Keep writing for about 10 minutes. You should then review your list to see which ideas you like and which you want to eliminate. Put an "X" next to items you think won't be useful, but don't cross them out because you may change your mind. Some items on your list may stand out as potential main ideas, whereas others would make good supporting points. If that's the case, your list will also be helpful during the planning stage.

Listing Making a list about ideas related to a specific topic.

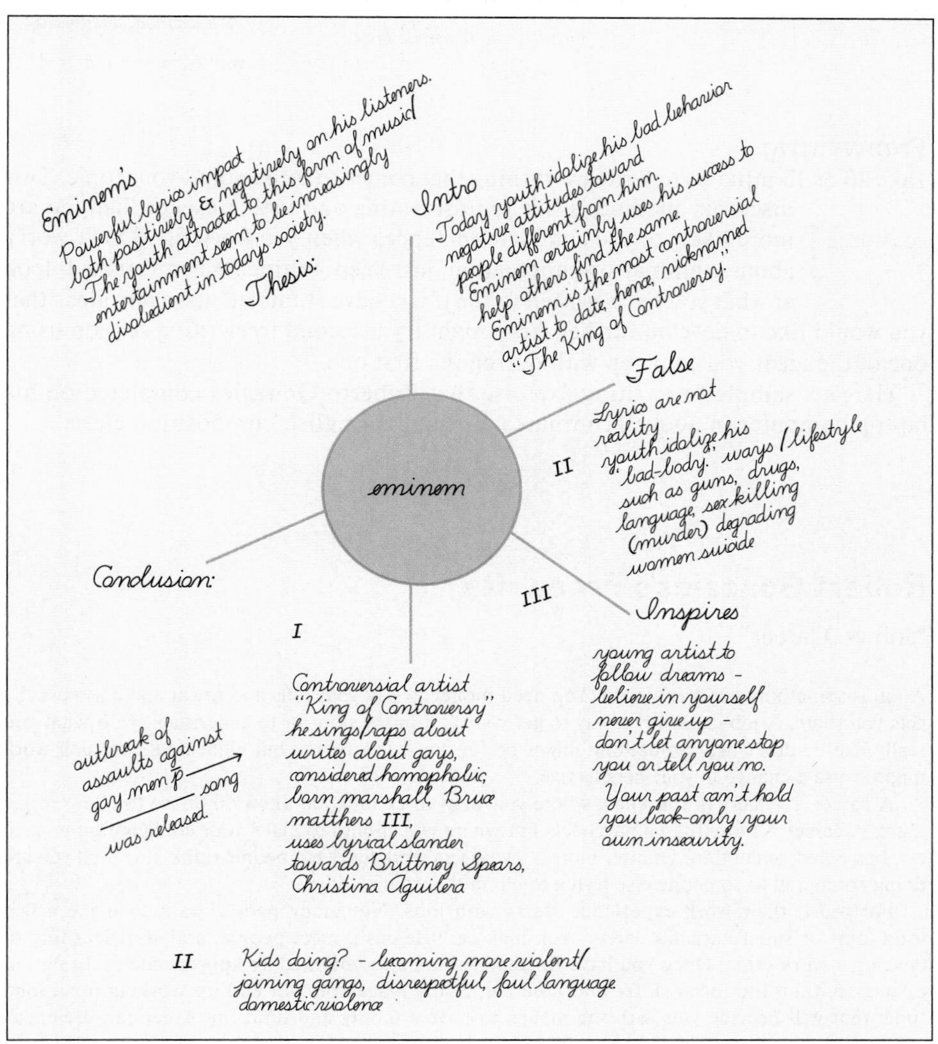

FIGURE 2.2 Brainstorming Notes

ESOL Tip >

If you cannot think of a word in English, write the word in your native language so you do not interrupt your flow of ideas. You can change it to the correct English word later.

Here's a sample list on the subject of having a career rather than just a job:

greater financial reward
higher interest level
greater self-esteem
better potential for development
more required skills and training
more advancement opportunities
higher level of competence required
long term instead of short term
larger contribution to the community
greater sense of satisfaction
using talents to do something well
professionalism necessary
higher education required

Freewriting

Freewriting Unstructured writing for a set amount of time.

Take 10 or 15 minutes to write everything that comes to mind about your topic. This discovery method is like brainstorming and listing except that you are more likely to use complete sentences when you **freewrite.** Don't worry about grammar or punctuation; just keep writing. When finished, look at what you have written to see if you have stumbled upon any ideas that you would like to develop further. You might try a second freewriting session using one of the ideas you came up with during the first one.

Here's a sample freewriting exercise that Roberto Gonzales completed on his laptop computer in about 12 minutes during his English composition class:

Robert Gonzales's Freewrite

"Job vs. Career"

A job is something you have to do. You need money to pay your bills and to eat and a job usually gets you there. A job is usually a way to get your foot in the door or to experiment with what you really like or don't like. Something might be fun for a few hours, but eight hours of such work might cause a change in your perspective.

A career is a ladder. You know where you want to be and you know you have to climb to get there. A career is more than a paycheck, but where you choose to make your contribution to society. In a career small things matter more . . . who you work for, what people think, how well you are doing compared to someone else trying to climb that same ladder.

For most, their work experience starts with jobs. Not many people want to make a fast food joint or supermarket a career. You make a little cash, meet people, and start learning to develop a work ethic. Once you have finished school and obtained an appropriate certification or degree, then the focus shifts into a career. Some place you will end up working for a long time; that will provide you with the means to have a family and fund the American dream. A career is that security blanket that allows you to not worry so much about a job, but gives you the assurance that you're going places and that each step of that ladder equals a better life for you and your family.

Questioning Consider the journalist's questions as you try to discover ideas about your topic. Who? What? When? Where? Why? How? (See Figure 2.3.) Write everything you can think of for each question. Afterward, you can decide which ideas you would like to investigate further. Use your answers as a starting point for your essay. This technique works especially well for informative pieces, narrative writing (storytelling), and problem solving.

Who?
How?
What?
Why?
When?
Where?

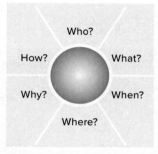

FIGURE 2.3 Journalist's Questions

Journaling Begin keeping a daily writer's **journal** (paper or electronic) where you jot down ideas that pop into your head. These ideas can be related to an assignment you are pondering, or they can be just general thoughts that you might like to explore later. You can use your journal to reflect on your feelings about yourself and your surroundings.

Journal A place to keep track of thoughts and feelings.

You might write about events from your past and consider how these events have affected you or others. You may even want to predict what could happen in the future. When journaling, don't worry about grammar or sentence structure; just let your ideas flow and see where they lead you. Reread your journal entries in search of ideas to expand on for your assignments.

Sketching Even if you don't have an artistic side, you may find that doodling or drawing will help you generate ideas about your topic, especially if you are a visual person. A simple stick figure sketch might help you visualize your subject and give you material you can write about later. You might write captions for your drawings so that when you review them later you'll remember what you had in mind when you were creating them.

Talking You may find it useful to bounce your ideas off classmates, friends, coworkers, or family members. Tell them about your assignment and the ideas you have about approaching the task. You may come up with a brilliant idea while you are talking about your assignment, or someone else may say something that sparks your interest. Either way, just hearing the ideas being spoken can stimulate your creativity. Additionally, you might seek out someone who is familiar with the topic of your paper. Ask the person questions to learn more about your subject. He or she might be able to help you focus your topic.

Reading Sometimes you may find it helpful to read what others have written about your topic. Printed or online books, magazines, newspapers, or professional journals can serve as great resources for an assignment, especially a research essay. Seeing the approach that others have taken can enable you to formulate your own ideas. If you do decide to use someone else's words or ideas in your paper, be sure to cite your sources appropriately to avoid plagiarism. (See Part 3 to learn more about documenting sources.)

Viewing Often you'll find that looking at a photograph, painting, advertisement, television show, film, or website will stir your emotions and inspire you to write. If you are having trouble coming up with a topic for a writing assignment, you might think about

Activity — Discovering Ideas to Write About

Choose one of the following topics:

education	music	computers	television
health	movies	celebrities	video games
pets	commercials	fashion	nature
vacations	sports	musicians	
crime	cuisine	medicine	

Try one or more of the discovery techniques, such as brainstorming, listing, freewriting, questioning, or sketching, to see how many ideas you can come up with in 5 to 10 minutes that relate to your topic. Be prepared to share your findings.

Employer SPOTLIGHT

Murielle Pamphile, Director of Student Services

©Karin Russell

Murielle Pamphile is the director of student services for a private university that offers degrees in a wide variety of majors that prepare students for specific careers. She has a BS in biology, an MS in health management, and a PhD in educational leadership. Here's what Pamphile has to say about the skills graduates need when they enter the workforce in a new career:

“I work with students to ensure they have good employability skills. To determine exactly what skills graduates need to land a good job, I meet with employers in the fields related to students' majors and review comments from advisory board meetings and employer surveys. Employers frequently tell me that, in addition to developing skills related to a specific career field, students need to possess good résumé writing and job interviewing skills. Those skills are important for obtaining a job because employees will need to have good communication skills in the workplace. Also, students need to tailor their résumés to showcase the exact skills, qualifications, and certifications (if applicable) they have to demonstrate that they are a good fit for an employer. For example, a graduate looking for a job in the radiology field needs to include key terminology from that field on his or her résumé. Furthermore, employers often contact me to ask for a list of candidates who are qualified for a specific position. The graduates I recommend are those who have the appropriate job skills as well as strong communication skills. While students are in school, I encourage them to take their composition courses seriously and to visit the writing center so that they will develop the skills they need to be successful in their careers.”

something you have seen recently that caught your attention. Or you could surf the Web to look for an intriguing topic. You might also watch the History Channel or Discovery Channel to get ideas for papers. As with printed sources, you will need to document visual sources if you use specific details from them in your writing (see Part 3).

2.2 Planning

After you have discovered your topic and some supporting ideas, you will want to plan your essay. Having a plan will help you write a better finished product. Begin to organize what you came up with during the discovering stage. Also, remember to keep your rhetorical star (subject, audience, purpose, strategy, and design) in mind. Here are some planning techniques to try.

Narrowing Your Focus Often the ideas that writers generate during the discovery stage of the writing process are too broad to develop fully in a short paper. For example, "cooking" is too broad to write about in a short paper; however, you could focus an essay on "tips for healthy cooking."

Activity Narrowing Your Focus

When you generate potential topics for essays, you will find that many are too broad to adequately cover in a short essay. When that happens, it's time to narrow your focus. When you narrow a topic, you get more specific. You may need to narrow your topic several times before it is narrow enough to cover in your paper.

EXAMPLE

Broad Topic: Computers
Narrower Topic: Computers and writing
Fully Narrowed Topic: How computers influence the writing process

Narrow the focus of several of the following topics to make them suitable for a short essay:

careers
music
entertainment
sports
natural disasters
laws
college
fitness
student organizations
drugs
business
terrorist events
movies
children

Writing a Preliminary Thesis A **thesis** is a statement that identifies your topic and your opinion about that topic. Here's an example: *Joining the Student Government Association (SGA) has many benefits.* Keep your tentative thesis in mind when you are planning your essay. You can revise your thesis later if you change your opinion as you discover more about the topic. See Chapter 3 for more details on thesis statements.

Thesis A statement that identifies the main idea of an essay.

Determining Main Points After your focus is clear and you have a tentative thesis, decide what main points you want to cover in your document. You will need enough main points to fully support your thesis. While there is no "correct" number of main points, having three to five of them in an essay often works well. Choose your main points carefully. The next planning technique can help you determine your main points.

Clustering Write your topic in the center of the page and draw a circle around it. Draw several lines out from your topic. At the end of each line, write a main idea and circle it. Then draw lines radiating out from each main idea. At the end of each line, write supporting ideas that relate to the circled word it connects to. One clustering exercise might lead to another. For instance, you may find that you have a lot to say about one of your main points and decide to shift your focus to just that main point. Then you may cluster again, this time putting the new idea in the center of the page. Clustering is a great way to begin to organize your ideas because it helps you to see the relationships among them. For example, if you are writing an essay about why your trip to the Bahamas was the best vacation you ever went on, your cluster might look like the one shown in Figure 2.4.

FIGURE 2.4 Sample Idea Cluster

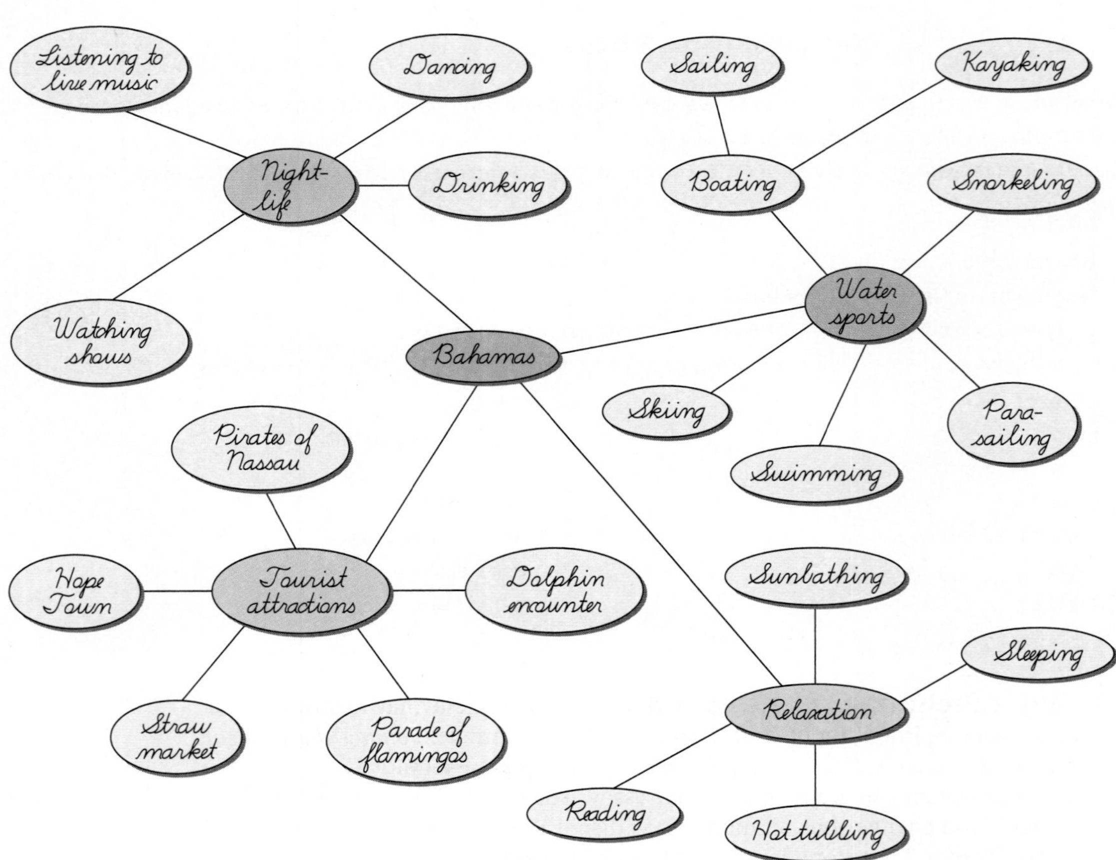

Activity Creating an Idea Cluster

Choose one of the following topics, or one that you used in a previous activity, and narrow it to a more focused topic. For example, if you chose "exercise" as your topic, your subtopic might be "winter sports."

television shows
recreational activities
exercise
tablets
transportation
music artists
hobbies
magazines
video games
computers

Create a cluster diagram for your topic. Make sure that you have at least three or four headings radiating out from your main topic. If you find that you have a lot of ideas for one heading but not the others, you may want to begin again using that one as your main topic.

Creating a Graphic Organizer Developing a **graphic organizer** can help you plan and organize your document. It can enable you to see the relationships among your ideas so that you can put them into a logical order before composing your first draft.

Graphic organizer A visual representation of an abstract idea.

Figure 2.5 shows examples of graphic organizers you can use for the various writing strategies covered in this textbook. You may modify them as needed to fit your specific writing assignments and preferences.

Here are some tips for using each type of graphic organizer.

1. **Describing and Narrating:** When writing a descriptive narrative, answer the journalist's questions about a particular event.
   - *Who* was involved?
   - *What* happened?
   - *When* did the event take place?
   - *Where* did it occur?
   - *Why* did the event happen?
   - *How* did it occur?
2. **Dividing and Classifying:** When writing a division and classification paper, divide a concept into groups with common traits or principles and explain the significant elements of each group.
3. **Explaining a Process:** When writing a "how-to" paper, explain each step of the process in chronological order.
4. **Explaining Causes and Effects:** When writing a cause-and-effect analysis paper, make a list of the causes (reasons) and the effects (results) related to your topic.
5. **Comparing and Contrasting:** When comparing and contrasting two subjects, write ideas that are unique to the first subject in the left-hand side of the first

FIGURE 2.5
Sample Graphic Organizers

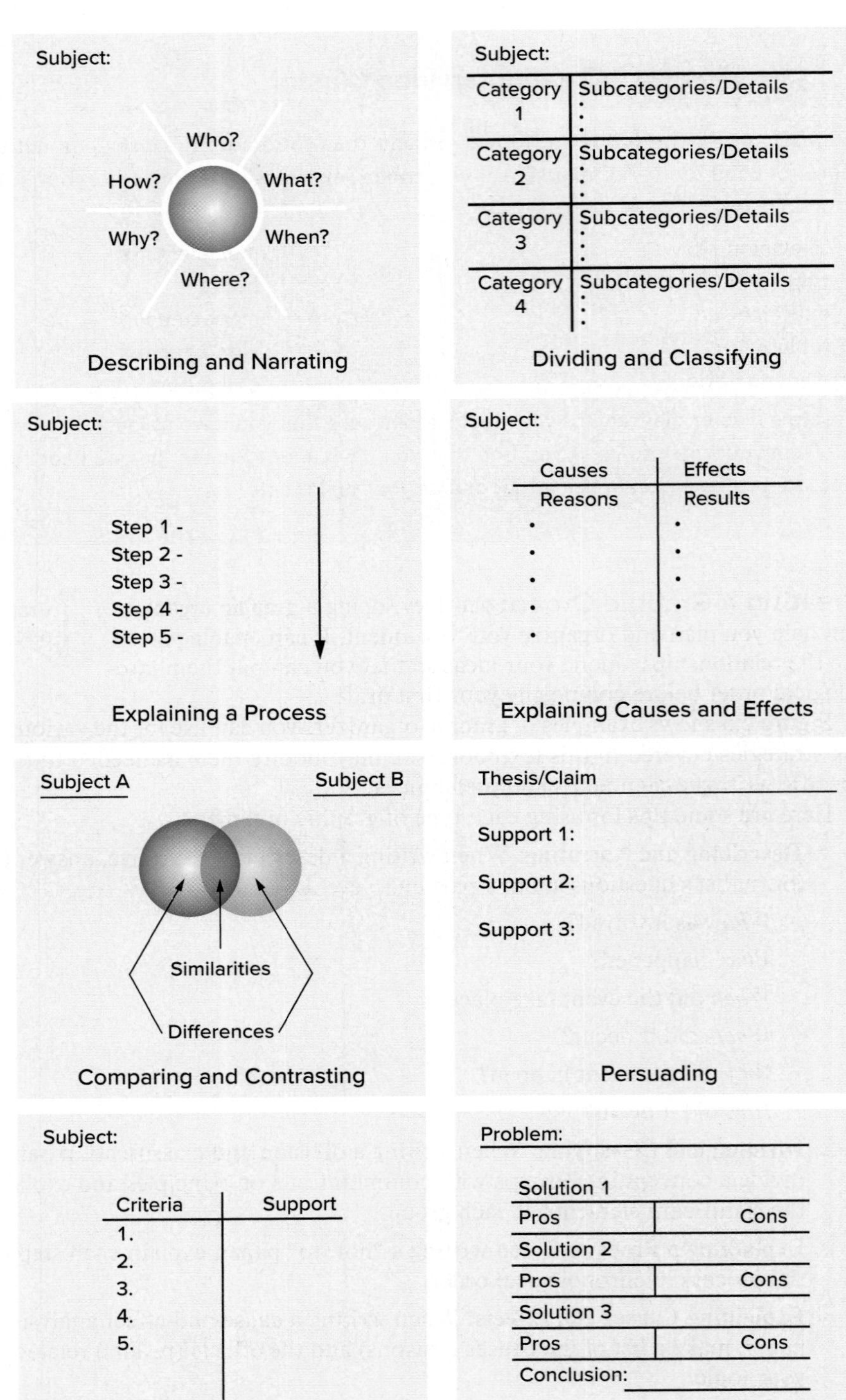
Subject:
Who?
How?
What?
Why?
When?
Where?
Describing and Narrating
Subject:
Category 1
Subcategories/Details
Category 2
Subcategories/Details
Category 3
Subcategories/Details
Category 4
Subcategories/Details
Dividing and Classifying
Subject:
Step 1 -
Step 2 -
Step 3 -
Step 4 -
Step 5 -
Explaining a Process
Subject:
Causes
Effects
Reasons
Results
Explaining Causes and Effects
Subject A
Subject B
Similarities
Differences
Comparing and Contrasting
Thesis/Claim
Support 1:
Support 2:
Support 3:
Persuading
Subject:
Criteria
Support
1.
2.
3.
4.
5.
Evaluating
Problem:
Solution 1
Pros
Cons
Solution 2
Pros
Cons
Solution 3
Pros
Cons
Conclusion:
Solving a Problem

circle, and write ideas that are unique to the second subject in the right-hand side of the second circle. Place ideas that are common to both in the center, where both circles intersect. This is called a *Venn diagram.*

6. **Persuading:** When writing a persuasive or argumentative document, write your thesis (claim) at the top of the page, and then list relevant details for each supporting point.
7. **Evaluating:** When writing an evaluation, make a list of criteria you will use to judge the topic and support for each judgment.
8. **Solving a Problem:** When proposing a solution to a problem, write out the pros and cons for several possible solutions before coming to a final conclusion.

Ordering Ideas After you've completed a cluster or rough graphic organizer, you will need to decide how to arrange your main points logically in your paper. Some writers find that simply listing the main points works best for them. Others prefer to create an informal or a formal outline (see the next section). For example, in the informal outline that follows, it makes sense to cover tourist attractions, water sports, and relaxation before nightlife because that is the order in which the events would likely occur.

Outlining One purpose for creating an **outline** is to help you organize your writing. An outline is a blueprint of the divisions and subdivisions in your paper that illustrates the relationships among the ideas you present. Outlines can be formal or informal. To develop an informal outline, note each main point that you plan to cover in your essay, and then list the supporting ideas that you want to include with each point. An informal outline can help you see the structure of your paper, but it is less detailed than a formal outline. Although you don't necessarily need to include the introduction or conclusion in your outline, you will need them for your final essay. (See Chapter 3 for more details about essay structure.)

Outline A blueprint of the divisions and subdivisions in a paper.

Sample Informal Outline

Attention-Getter: As soon as I stepped into my hotel room and looked out the sliding glass doors that opened right onto the white sand beach and turquoise ocean, I knew this was going to be a trip to remember.

Thesis Statement: My vacation to the Bahamas was the best experience of my life.

Tourist Attractions
- Pirates of Nassau
- Hope Town
- Straw market
- Dolphin encounter
- Parade of flamingos

Water Sports
- Boating: sailing and kayaking
- Parasailing
- Snorkeling
- Skiing

Relaxation
- Reading books about local culture
- Sunbathing
- Sleeping
- Hot tubbing

Nightlife
- Listening to live music
- Watching shows
- Dancing

Some writers prefer to use a formal topic or sentence outline, and some instructors require students to write one. A formal outline has more structure than an informal one. To develop a formal outline, assign each main point in your essay a Roman numeral: I, II, III, and so on. Then break down each idea into at least two parts (supporting points) and label those A, B, C, and so on.

Continue breaking down points as needed (see the basic outline structure), but remember that you always need to have at least two points when you subdivide your ideas. In other words, an "A" must be followed by a "B," and a "1" must be followed by a "2." Capitalize the first word of each line and all proper nouns.

Basic Outline Structure

I. First main point
  A. First supporting point
    1. Major detail or example
      a. Minor detail or example
      b. Minor detail or example
    2. Major detail or example
    3. Major detail or example
  B. Second supporting point
    1. Major detail or example
    2. Major detail or example
II. Second main point (and so on)

Although you do not need to have the same number of supporting points under each heading, your outline should be somewhat balanced. If most of your ideas fit beneath one main point, then you may want to narrow your focus to just that point and break it down further.

Also, be sure to keep like ideas parallel by stating similar ideas in a similar way. (See Part 4 for more on parallel structure.)

Not Parallel: Parasailing, snorkeling, and to water ski are fun activities.

Parallel: <u>Parasailing</u>, <u>snorkeling</u>, and <u>water</u> <u>skiing</u> are fun activities.

Discussion: The second sentence includes a series of words that end with "ing." Lists of nouns, verbs, adjectives, or adverbs should all be in the same form.

Sample Formal Topic Outline

Attention-Getter: As soon as I stepped into my hotel room and looked out the sliding glass doors that opened right onto the white sand beach and turquoise ocean, I knew this was going to be a trip to remember.

Thesis Statement: My vacation to the Bahamas was the best experience of my life.

I. Tourist Attractions
  A. Pirates of Nassau
    1. Brief history
    2. Museum
  B. Hope Town
  C. Straw market
    1. People
    2. Merchandise
  D. Dolphin encounter
  E. Parade of flamingos
II. Water Sports
  A. Boating
    1. Sailing
    2. Kayaking
  B. Parasailing
  C. Snorkeling
  D. Skiing
III. Relaxation
  A. Reading books about local culture
  B. Sunbathing
  C. Hot tubbing
IV. Nightlife
  A. Listening to live music
  B. Watching shows
  C. Dancing

Grammar Window
PARALLEL STRUCTURE

Revise the following sentences to give them parallel structure:

1. This school encourages students to have good attendance, to turn in assignments on time, and displaying a positive attitude.
2. Ray says that when he graduates he will get a great job, purchase a newer car, and he doesn't like his current apartment.

Partial Sample of a Formal Sentence Outline

IV. The nightlife in the Bahamas is amazing.
  A. Many restaurants offer live music featuring Goombay drums that reflect the local culture.
  B. Live shows are abundant, especially during the Junkanoo festival, when costumed people parade through the streets dancing to music played on drums, cowbells, and whistles.
  C. For those who like more active entertainment, dancing is quite popular at the local bars and restaurants.

Activity Outlining

Based on the clustering activity that you completed, write an informal outline or a formal topic or sentence outline. Be sure to organize your ideas logically. You may need to write a draft first and then rework it to make the ideas flow logically.

2.3 Composing

Once you have narrowed your topic and have a plan for organizing your ideas, you are ready to begin composing your essay. Use the ideas that you generated during the discovering and planning stages to help you develop your rough draft. Let your cluster or outline serve as your guide. Also, be sure to focus on the first four points of the rhetorical star: subject, audience, purpose, and strategy. You can determine the design of your document later. As you begin to write, focus more on getting your ideas on the computer screen (or on paper) than on how you present your ideas. Go easy on yourself. You are not aiming for perfection, especially with the first draft.

You may want to write the easiest parts first to help build your confidence. In a short essay, you might write a paragraph about each main point. In a longer assignment, you might need several paragraphs to fully develop each main point. (See Chapter 3 for more details about thesis statements and essay development.)

Keep writing until you feel that you have covered all, or most, of the main points you had planned to address in your paper. Be sure to save your rough draft or put it in a safe place. Now take a well-deserved break! If you have time, let your ideas gel a bit before you continue to the next step of the writing process. If you give yourself a little time off, then you'll be able to review your work from a fresh perspective.

Activity Composing

Write a paper on the topic you have chosen, using the informal or formal outline you developed in the previous activity to guide its organization. Don't worry about grammar and punctuation for your first draft.

2.4 Getting Feedback

After you have written your first draft, you will find that it is helpful to get someone else's advice about your paper. Unless you are writing an essay for an in-class assignment, you should have an opportunity to get feedback from someone who can give you useful tips for revising your paper. Having a conference with your instructor, participating in a peer review activity with a classmate, or working with a campus-based or online writing tutor are all excellent ways to help you improve your writing.

Activity Getting Feedback

Have someone else (such as a classmate, writing tutor, friend, or family member) read the rough draft you composed in your last activity. Read the reviewer's feedback and decide which suggestions you want to accept, ignore, or modify. If you are working with another classmate, then you will need to provide him or her with constructive feedback as well.

Conferences One technique you can use to get feedback on your assignment is to have a conference with your instructor, if possible. He or she should be able to provide you with insightful suggestions for revision. If you're taking an online course, you may be able to e-mail your assignment to your instructor and wait for feedback. Many instructors are willing to provide students with general suggestions for improving their papers. However, don't expect your instructor to correct your paper for you. Your job is to learn how to revise and edit your own papers. You may also have a conference with a peer review partner or a writing lab tutor.

Peer Review Participating in a peer review exercise is a great way to improve your writing. Your instructor may give you an opportunity to complete a peer review activity in class. Usually you will pair up with another student (or a group of students) and provide constructive criticism (ideas for improvement) about each other's drafts. You can also use this method in an online class via e-mail.

You will receive valuable suggestions for revising your paper, and you will be able to offer your peer review partner helpful feedback as well. Additionally, you'll have an opportunity to see how someone else has approached the assignment. Even after you finish your writing course, you can continue to use these peer review strategies. Outside of college, co-workers, family members, and friends often review each other's writing before it reaches its intended audience.

Tips for Peer Reviewers

- **Consider the writer's feelings.** Begin by pointing out something positive in the paper. What do you like best about the paper? Is there a particular part that you find especially interesting or insightful? What details and examples are most useful?
- **Provide constructive criticism.** Even if you are not the strongest writer, you know good writing when you see it. Are there specific areas that could be clearer or that need more explanation? Focus mostly on the larger issues, such as content, organization, and development. Avoid marking every error in grammar, punctuation, or spelling unless the writer has specifically asked you to do so. Be tactful with the comments you make, but don't just say you like everything if there are areas that need improvement.

  Additionally, be sure to give the writer concrete suggestions for how to improve the paper. For example, maybe the paper needs more specific examples to fully support the thesis statement, or perhaps some areas could be clearer.

Tips for Writers

- **Communicate with the reviewer.** Tell your peer review partner what you would like him or her to review. Depending on how rough your draft is, you might not be ready for help with grammar, punctuation, and mechanics. Maybe there are particular parts of your paper that you're not sure about or that seem awkward or undeveloped to you. Ask the reviewer to focus on those areas.
- **Take the suggestions in stride.** Remember that your peer review partner is trying to offer you constructive suggestions for making your paper better. Also, keep in mind that there are many ways (not just a right way and a wrong way)

SAMPLE PEER REVIEW QUESTIONS

1. Which sentence states the main idea (thesis) of the essay? Is it clear? Is its placement appropriate? Why or why not?
2. Are there any additional details that could be included to help you better understand the essay? What is missing or unclear?
3. Are the details covered in a logical sequence? Which ones, if any, seem out of place?
4. What part of the essay is most memorable? Why?
5. Are transitions, such as "furthermore," "for example," and "next," used to help the ideas in the paper flow logically? If not, which ones would be useful?
6. Does the author provide the reader with a sense of completion at the end? If so, how?
7. What kinds of grammatical errors, if any, are evident in the essay?
8. What final suggestions do you have for the author?

to approach a writing assignment. Thank the reviewer for the feedback, and then make your own decision about what to change . . . or not. In the end, you are the author, so the choices you make about your paper are up to you.

Writing Centers and Online Writing Labs Some schools offer an avenue for getting feedback on your papers from a qualified professional through a writing center or online writing lab (OWL). These resources are designed for writers of all ability levels. If you have access to a writing center on campus, find out what kinds of services it provides and when it is open. At the writing center, you may have an opportunity to sit down with a person who can read your rough draft and provide suggestions for revising and editing. Additionally, writing centers often have a wide variety of print and computerized materials to help you with every aspect of the writing process.

If your campus doesn't have a writing center, or if the timing doesn't work with your schedule, you might have an OWL you can utilize. When you use an OWL, you typically submit your draft electronically and then receive feedback from a qualified professional, often within a day or two.

Tips for Working with Writing Tutors

Regardless of whether you use a writing center or an OWL, here are some tips that will help you make the most of it:

- **Have a rough draft ready.** If you haven't put any thought into your assignment, a writing tutor will have difficulty helping you. Even if your draft is extremely rough, you need to have something the writing tutor can read so that you can receive useful feedback.
- **Have your instructor's directions handy.** Often a writing tutor will ask you about the assignment's specifications. That way he or she can help determine if you have met your instructor's requirements or if you have gotten off track. Also, if your instructor provides you with grading criteria (in the form of a rubric or grid), be sure to share that information with your writing tutor.

- **Have specific questions in mind.** Asking a writing tutor simply to tell you what is wrong with your paper isn't the best approach. What specific areas would you like him or her to review? Are you concerned about the organization or development of your paper? Do you need help with any grammar issues? Also, don't expect to have your paper corrected for you. A writing tutor may point out a few errors so that you can see what kinds of issues you need to work on, but it is your responsibility to proofread and correct your paper.
- **Keep an open mind and a positive attitude.** Remember that the writing tutor, like a peer reviewer, wants to help you become a better writer by providing you with constructive criticism. Try not to be too sensitive about your work. Consider the feedback you receive, and make the changes you feel are necessary. Keep in mind that it is your paper. If you disagree with some of the feedback, or if you have additional questions, you can always get a second opinion. Ultimately, you have to decide what strategies work best for your paper.

2.5 Revising

Many writers are tempted to take that first draft, correct the "mistakes," and then turn it in. If you do that, you will be skipping one of the most important steps of the writing process. Good writers typically spend more time revising than working on any other step. The term *revision* literally means to see again. You'll need to read back over your work and make improvements. Here are some higher-order concerns to consider as you revise your paper:

Adding and Deleting Ideas

- Have you included all of the main points you had hoped to cover?
- Will including more ideas strengthen your essay?
- Are any points irrelevant?
- Are any points repetitious?
- Have you included any points that you could delete without weakening your paper?

Developing

- Have you included enough details and examples to support your main points?
- Can you expand on some points to provide greater clarity for your audience?

If you feel your paper needs more development, you can try additional discovery techniques to come up with more details and examples. You want to make sure to have enough support for your paper to convince your audience that the opinion in your thesis is accurate.

Arranging

- Does the order of your main points make sense?
- Can you rearrange main points and details to help your readers better understand the point you are making?

As you are revising your paper, move sentences and paragraphs around to see what flows better and makes more sense. If you are revising on a computer, the cutting and pasting features in your word processing program will simplify this procedure. Be sure to save different versions of your drafts so that you can go back to previous versions if you need to. If you are revising on paper, you can literally cut and paste (or tape or staple) sentences and paragraphs. You may want to make multiple copies of your draft before revising so that you can remember how you originally wrote it. Continue cutting and pasting until you find the arrangement that best fits with your rhetorical star.

2.6 Editing

Once you are satisfied with the large-scale revisions you have made to your paper, you will want to examine it more closely. When you edit a paper, you are looking for lower-order concerns, such as errors in words, sentence structure, grammar, punctuation, spelling, and mechanics. You can use your computer's spell checker as well as a print or digital thesaurus and dictionary to help you edit your paper. Read your paper aloud (to yourself or an audience). Listen to the flow of ideas. Consider the following questions as you edit your paper and make changes accordingly. (See Part 4 for more details about editing.)

Word Choice (Diction)

- Have you chosen precise words that will create a specific picture in your readers' minds?
- Do any important words have a common meaning that readers might think of instead of the meaning you intend?
- Are there any words that could be more interesting or lively?

Sentence Structure

- Do any sentences sound awkward?
- Do the sentences vary in length and style?
- Are any sentences too short and choppy?
- Are any sentences long enough to create confusion for your readers?

ESOL Tip >

Use a standard American dictionary as well as a dictionary written for non-native speakers to help you with diction.

Grammar

- Are there any problems with subject-verb agreement?
- Do all of the pronouns make sense?
- Are there enough adjectives to fully describe the nouns?
- Are all of the adverbs used correctly? For example, is *well* used to modify verbs instead of *good,* which is an adjective?
- Do all of the modifiers make sense?

Punctuation

- Do all sentences end with an appropriate punctuation mark?
- Are quotation marks used correctly?
- Are commas, semicolons, and colons used effectively? Are any of them unnecessary or misplaced?
- Do special punctuation marks, such as dashes and ellipses, fit with the writing?

Spelling/Usage

- Are there any spelling errors that the spell checker might overlook, such as *they're* instead of *their* or *you're* instead of *your?*
- Does the spelling of each word, such as *affect* or *effect,* reflect your intended meaning?

Mechanics

- Are the correct words capitalized?
- Are abbreviations appropriate, or do they need to be spelled out?
- Are numerals and spelled-out numbers used correctly?

2.7 Proofreading

After you have finished revising and editing, be sure to proofread your final paper. As you read your paper this time, you are looking for the really nitpicky details, such as repeated words and typographical errors, that you may have overlooked previously. You might want to read your paper aloud again. Another strategy is to read your paper backward, from the last sentence to the first sentence. That way you can focus on every word. Most writers have difficulty finding all of the errors in their own papers. Therefore, you may want to have another person review your paper again. The more feedback you receive the better.

After you have proofread for the last time, be sure to submit your essay in the correct format. Is your paper supposed to be double-spaced? Are you expected to turn in a hard copy, an electronic version, or both? Have you followed all of the directions for the assignment? Following your instructor's guidelines is an important part of the assignment. Once you submit your final paper, you'll have the satisfaction of having completed an original piece of writing.

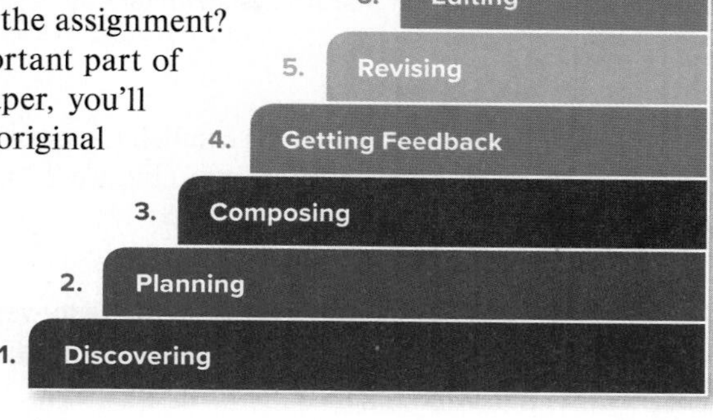

FIGURE 2.6 The Seven Steps of the Writing Process

One Student's Writing Process

Thomas Ryan Gorsuch followed the steps of the writing process (Figure 2.6) as he wrote

Rhetorical Star Analysis Worksheet

Subject	Gaming media's influence of "Rock Band" and "Rock Band 2." How the gaming media have encouraged people to buy and play Rock Band.
Audience	People who might read this paper would range from young teens to late 40's. Might appeal to musicians and males or females.
Purpose	To inform the reader how the media have influenced people to think or feel that purchasing Rock Band they will have a more exciting, healthy happy family life.
Strategy	<u>Cause</u> How we're blinded by the truth about what the media have to say. Appreciation for musicians. <u>Effects</u> Wanting to pursue musical arts, fun family togetherness, and a more fulfilling life.
Design	APA format, 750-word essay, 12 pt font, double spaced, Times New Roman, indented paragraphs, page #s in header, header and title

FIGURE 2.7 Rhetorical Star Analysis Worksheet

his first essay for English Composition 1. He began by completing an analysis based on the rhetorical star (Figure 2.7), and then proceeded with the stages shown here.

1. Discovering

Thomas did much of his discovery work in his head. He also talked with family members and classmates about his topic. He used a clustering exercise for both discovering and planning purposes.

2. Planning

Thomas created a cluster to begin to generate and organize his ideas for his essay about the impact of the *Rock Band* music video game (Figure 2.8).

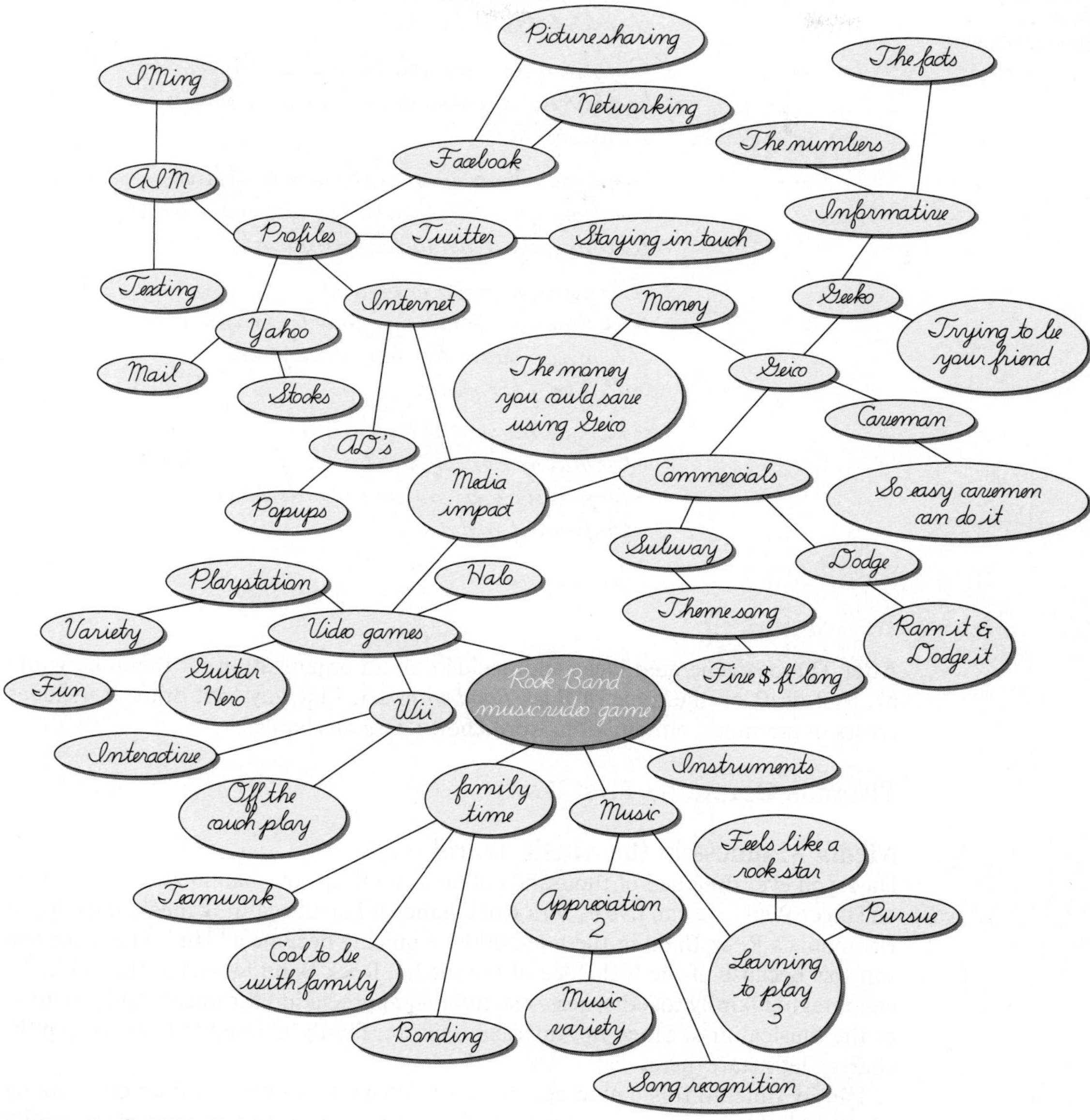

FIGURE 2.8 Thomas Gorsuch's Cluster

Informal Outline Thomas chose not to write a formal outline, but many students do benefit from creating one. Instead, he organized his ideas into the informal outline shown in Figure 2.9.

FIGURE 2.9
Thomas's Informal Outline

The impact of Rock Band or the impact that Rock Band has had.

Thesis { Rock band has impacted the public by family togetherness, appreciation for music & pursuing of musical arts.

Hook { Have you ever dreamed of thousands of fans chanting your band's name as you walk on stage? Well now you can with Rock Band.

Intro { The gaming media introduced Rock Band in 2007 and quickly became a "hit." The main reason has been through the influence of the media.

Body {
- Pursue musical arts
- Bringing family together, for family fun night
- Appreciation for music and interest in the form of media

3. Composing

After Thomas generated ideas and decided on an organization for them, he wrote his first draft on the topic of *Rock Band*'s impact. Like any first draft, it includes errors in grammar, punctuation, word choice, and mechanics.

Thomas Gorsuch's First Draft

Media Madness in the Music World

Have you ever dreamed of thousands of fans chanting your band name as you walk on stage? Well, you can live it, with Rock Band. When the gaming media introduced Harmonix's Rock Band in the mid-2000s, it quickly became a "Hit." The main reason was because of the influence of the media. Rock Band impacted the public by encouraging family togetherness, teaching an appreciation for music, and pursuing of the musical arts. Since in American culture, family is rated "#1 on the top 40 charts," let's start there.

Family time, in this day in age, is rare to come by, so when it does come along I tend to hold on to and appreciate it. When I was younger I remember my family use to have a planned day that we called "family fun night". It was a night that we would all enjoy dinner together followed by a night of playing games. Sadly this is an activity that is rarely seen in family gatherings today. Through the media, the game of Rock Band, since its first iteration, has made this picture more appealing and possible. I have heard many of my friends and family talk of how this game brought them closer together. Since this game succeeds only when everyone works together, or in this case, plays together, this creates an attitude of team work and cooperation. Together, my family, friends and I each play a different instrument making up one Rock Band! Even if I'm not playing an instrument I feel included and involved by being part of the concert, cheering the band on, and becoming like one of the groupies. Music video gaming has replaced rolling dice on a flat game board to picking up an instrument or microphone, moving along as if really standing on stage. This get's my heart pumping, whether from trying to keep up with the beat, listening to cheering fans, or just from making a fool of myself. My family has so much fun, enjoying a wonderful experience that will bond us and probably be talked and laughed about for a long time. If you thought keeping the rhythm was hard, try singing on tune.

In this game, almost without my knowledge of it, it gave me an appreciation for music. Music is hard, and takes a lot of practice to perfect. When playing Rock Band the success of my band and the score shown is based on accuracy of hitting the right notes and the right time. This does not come naturally to everyone and definitely not to me. Although I know the song, listened to it in the car, or have scene it performed live, it is a completely different story to have to play it myself. Another point of music appreciation I learned is through the different styles of music. Rock Band has a variety of genres, of course starting out with Classic Rock turning to Alternative Rock and Country. When I play this game I learn about the different styles of music, how to play it, recognize it, and distinguish it apart from other styles. Suddenly I found that I had a new or renewed interest in music itself which lead to my interest in music lessons.

Now that I have been playing Rock Band, I, and many of my friends and family I have talked to, have wanted to learn to play an instrument for real. Rock Band gave me a taste of what performing music would be like and gave me a beginning level feel for each instrument that makes up a rock band. As Rock Band continues to add things making it even better and more difficult, it made me appreciate musicians and in turn, made me want to become one, at least for fun. I am not the only one, the media's influence in making Rock Band so popular has impacted the world in a way that many others have also taken up or started to pursue either a career or hobby in musical arts. I would say that the media has a pretty powerful influence.

As you can see, the media influences viewers like me, through TV, radio, and online advertisement that Rock Band makes my life more exciting and fun. It tells me that I can have fun with my family, learn about music and its different genres, and also help me to become a better musician, if I chose to pick up an instrument for real. So, if you are not already doing so, let Rock Band bring you together, so you can have your own "family fun night!"

4. Getting Feedback

Peer Review Before revising his essay, Thomas submitted it to two classmates for peer review. The feedback he received from Elizabeth Robson and Lana Darby is shown in Figures 2.10 and 2.11.

FIGURE 2.10 Elizabeth's Peer Review of Thomas Gorsuch's Paper

Author: Thomas Gorsuch
Reviewer: Elizabeth Robson

Peer Review Questions

1. Which sentence states the main idea (thesis) of the essay? Is it clear? Is its placement appropriate? Why or why not?

"Rock Band impacted the public by encouraging family togetherness, teaching an appreciation..."

2. Are there any additional details that could be included to help you better understand the essay? What is missing or unclear?

Source for quote "#1 on top 40 charts"

3. Are the details covered in a logical sequence? Which ones, if any, seem out of place?

Yes, they are starting with family ending w/pursuing of the musical arts.

4. What part of the essay is most memorable? Why?

"My family has so much fun...talked and laughed about for a long time."

5. Are transitions, such as "furthermore," "for example," and "next," used to help the ideas in the paper flow logically? If not, which ones would be useful?

Could use some transitions.
I only found couple, maybe use "As a Result" in the 4th paragraph instead of "now that"

6. Does the author provide the reader with a sense of completion at the end? If so, how?

Yes, he states thesis again and leaves me/w a memorable statement.

7. What kinds of grammatical errors, if any, are evident in the essay?

A few words should be replaced.
"now that" changed to "since" (4th paragraph)
take "it" out of sum sentence "... it, and many of ... family have ... ."

8. What final suggestions do you have for the author?

Use the 3rd person point of view.

FIGURE 2.11 Lana's Peer Review of Thomas Gorsuch's Paper

Author: Thomas Gorsuch
Reviewer: Lana Darby

Peer Review Questions

1. Which sentence states the main idea (thesis) of the essay? Is it clear? Is its placement appropriate? Why or why not?

The 3rd sentence states the main idea. "The gaming media introduced Harmonix's Rock Band in the mid-2000s and quickly became a "Hit" It is clear and is placed well following the opening "attention getter" line.

2. Are there any additional details that could be included to help you better understand the essay? What is missing or unclear?

Explain gaming media. Explain to reader that this is a game that hooks up to XBox or Playstation. Therefore, you and your family get interaction versus your son or daughter sitting in their room alone playing a war or violent video game for hours while the parent watches it.

3. Are the details covered in a logical sequence? Which ones, if any, seem out of place?

Details are O.K.

4. What part of the essay is most memorable? Why?

Parts that emphasize family time and once you spend time as a family you realize what you may have been missing.

5. Are transitions, such as "furthermore," "for example," and "next," used to help the ideas in the paper flow logically? If not, which ones would be useful?

"Since" is used a lot. Find different word.

6. Does the author provide the reader with a sense of completion at the end? If so, how?

Yes. The author recaps ideas in the summary and ends with a positive suggestion.

7. What kinds of grammatical errors, if any, are evident in the essay?

Possible commas missing.

8. What final suggestions do you have for the author?

Detail more the options or features of the game. Also, suggest that he hopes his children will remember the time as he remembered his family tradition.
Also, go in depth about how you can change levels in the singing and instrument. Start on easy move up to beginner then to harder levels. That makes you want to focus and try harder to achieve the goal. From personal experience, I know how hard it is to sing on key with the game.

5. Revising

Thomas made some revisions to his paper based on peer review feedback he received. He focused mainly on higher-order concerns, such as adding, deleting, and rearranging ideas, as he revised his first draft. For example, he switched the third and fourth paragraphs because he decided that it made more sense to discuss specific instruments before mentioning music appreciation in general. He also strengthened his topic sentences and added more transitions. (See Chapter 3 for more details about topic sentences and transitions.)

Thomas Gorsuch's Second Draft In the second draft shown below, all of Thomas's changes appear in angle brackets and red type. Since Thomas was concentrating on higher-order concerns, this draft includes errors in grammar, punctuation, word choice, and mechanics.

Media Madness in the Music World

Have you ever dreamed of thousands of fans chanting your band name as you walk on stage, Well, you can live that dream with <<*Rock Band,* whether you choose its original first version, latest fifth version, or any in between.>>. In the mid-2000s, the gaming media introduced Harmonix's *Rock Band,* which quickly became a "Hit." The main reason was because of the influence of the media. <<The *Rock Band* video games have been wildly popular among gamers of all ages throughout the United States.>> <<*Rock Band*>> has <<affected>> the public by encouraging family togetherness, <<influencing people to pursue>> the musical arts, and teaching an appreciation for music.

<<One way *Rock Band* has influenced families is by giving them an opportunity to spend time together. Today,>> family time is rare to come by, so families should hold on to and appreciate it. When I was younger I remember my family use to have a planned day that we called "family fun night". It was a night that we would all enjoy dinner together followed by a night of playing games. Sadly this is an activity that is rarely seen in family gatherings today. <<The *Rock Band* game has>> made this picture more appealing and possible. I have heard many of my friends and family talk of how this game has brought them closer together. Music video gaming has replaced rolling dice on a flat game board to picking up an instrument or microphone, moving along as if really standing on stage. Since this game is successful only when everyone plays together, this creates an attitude of team work and cooperation. Together, my family, friends, and I play a different instrument, making up one Rock Band! Even if I'm not playing an instrument I feel included and involved by being part of the concert, cheering the band on like groupies. <<*Rock Band* get's the players' hearts>> pumping, whether from trying to keep up with the beat, listening to cheering fans, or just from making a fool of myself. My family has so much fun <<playing *Rock Band* and>> enjoying a wonderful experience that we will probably <<talk and laugh>> about for a long time. If you thought keeping the rhythm was hard, try singing on tune.

<<Another effect of the *Rock Band* game is that it has caused many players to want to play a real instrument. *Rock Band*>> gave me a taste of what performing music

<<as a singer, guitar player or drummer>> would be like and a beginning level feel for each instrument that makes up a rock band. As <<players progress through *Rock Band,* the game>> continues to add <<new levels, songs, and venues, causing the game to be>> even better and more difficult. <<These advancements>> make me appreciate musicians and in turn, want to become one, at least for fun. The media's influence in making Rock Band so popular has <<affected>> the world in a way that <<has likely caused>> many <<people>> to pursue either a career or hobby in musical arts.

Note: Thomas took the advice from Lana, one of his peer reviewers, and added more details about how the game works to his third paragraph.

<<Furthermore, the *Rock Band* game has helped people to develop a stronger>> appreciation for music. Music <<can be difficult to perform>>, and takes a lot of practice to perfect. When playing Rock Band the success of <<the>> band and the score shown is based on accuracy of hitting the right notes and the right time. This does not come naturally to everyone. Although I know the song <<from listening>> to it in the car or <<hearing>> it performed live, it is a completely different story to have to play it myself. <<*Rock Band* also helps gamers to appreciate>> music is through <<introducing them to>> different styles of music. Rock Band has a variety of <<musical>> genres, <<such as>> Classic Rock, turning to Alternative Rock, and Country. When I learn about the different styles of music, how to play it, recognize it, and distinguish it apart from other styles. Suddenly I found that I had a new or renewed interest in music itself which lead to my interest in music lessons.

As you can see, the media has influenced viewers like me, through TV, radio, and online advertisement that by purchasing <<*Rock Band* they>> will have a more exciting and fun life. <<Players>> will have fun with <<their families>> for a change, become <<better musicians, if they choose to pick up an instrument for real>>, and learn <<more>> about music and its different genres, So, if you are not already doing so, let <<*Rock Band*>> bring you together <<with your family and friends>>, so you can have your own "family fun night!"

6. Editing

After Thomas completed his second draft, he began to edit his paper. He focused primarily on lower-order concerns, such as correcting grammar, punctuation, and sentence structure.

Additionally, he took his classmate's peer review suggestion and switched from the first person to the third person point of view, which uses *he, she,* and *they* instead of *I, me,* and *my.*

Thomas Gorsuch's Third Draft All of Thomas's changes appear in angle brackets and red type.

Media Madness in the Music World

Have you ever dreamed of thousands of fans chanting your band name as you walk on stage? Well now you can live it, with *Rock Band.* In the mid-2000s the gaming media introduced Harmonix's *Rock Band,* which quickly became a "Hit." <<The *Rock Band* video games have been wildly popular among gamers of all ages throughout the United States.>> *Rock Band* has <<affected>> the public by encouraging family

Note: Thomas took the advice of Elizabeth, one of his peer reviewers, and changed his point of view from the first person to the third person beginning in his second paragraph.

togetherness, <<influencing people to pursue>> the musical arts, and teaching an appreciation for music.

<<One way *Rock Band* has influenced families is by giving them an opportunity to spend time together. Today,>> family time is rare to come by, so families should hold on to and appreciate it. <<In the past, some families uses to have planned nights when they>> would all enjoy dinner together followed by a night of playing games. Sadly this is an activity that is rarely seen in family gatherings today. <<*Rock Band* game has>> made this picture more appealing and possible. Since this game reached stores, it has brought <<families>> closer together. This new age of technology gaming has now replaced rolling dice on a flat game board to picking up an instrument or microphone, moving along as if really standing on stage. Since this game is successful only when everyone plays together, this creates an attitude of team work and cooperation. <<Each participant plays>> a different instrument making up one Rock Band! Even <<the people who are not>> playing an instrument feel included and involved by being part of the concert. <<They cheer>> the band on like groupies. <<*Rock Band* get's the players' hearts>> pumping, whether from trying to keep up with the beat, listening to cheering fans, or just from making fools of <<themselves>>. <<Families have>> so much fun <<playing *Rock Band* and>> enjoying a wonderful experience that <<they>> probably <<will talk and laugh>> about for a long time. If you thought keeping the rhythm was hard, try singing on tune.

<<Another effect of the *Rock Band* game is that it has caused many players to want to play a real instrument.>> Rock Band <<gives players>> a taste of what performing music <<as a singer, guitar player or drummer>> would be like and a beginning level feel for each instrument that makes up a rock band. As <<players progress through Rock Band, the game>> continues to add <<new levels, songs, and venues, causing the game to be>> even better and more difficult. <<These advancements help players to>> appreciate musicians and, in turn, want to become one, at least for fun. The media's influence in making Rock Band so popular has <<affected>> the world in a way that <<has likely caused>> many <<people>> to pursue either a career or hobby in musical arts.

<<Furthermore, the *Rock Band* game has helped people to develop a stronger>> appreciation for music. Music <<can be difficult to perform>>, and takes a lot of practice to perfect. When playing <<*Rock Band*>> the success of <<the>> band and the score shown is based on accuracy of hitting the right notes and the right time. This does not come naturally to everyone. <<Even if players are familiar with a>> song <<from listening>> to it in the car or <<hearing>> it performed live, it is a completely different story to have to play it <<themselves>>. <<*Rock Band* also helps gamers to appreciate>> music is through <<introducing them to>> different styles of music. Rock Band has a variety of <<musical>> genres, <<such as>> Classic Rock, Alternative Rock, and Country. <<Players>> learn about the different styles of music, how to play it, recognize it, and distinguish it apart from other styles.

As you can see, the media has influenced viewers through TV, radio, and online advertisement that by purchasing Rock Band <<they>> will have a more exciting and fun life. <<Players>> will have fun with <<their families>> for a change, become <<better musicians, if they choose to pick up an instrument for real>>, and learn

<<more>> about music and its different genres, So now let *Rock Band* bring you together <<with your family and friends>>, so you can have your own "family fun night!"

7. Proofreading

Thomas read through his paper one more time, proofreading for errors, awkward sentences, and word choice. He also took out the word *media* in the title because his emphasis shifted from the media to just the *Rock Band* game.

Thomas Gorsuch's Final Draft Thomas's final corrections appear in angle brackets and red type.

Madness in the Music World

Have you ever dreamed of thousands of fans chanting your band <<'s>> name as you walk on stage? Well now you can live it, with *Rock Band I, II, III, IV,* or *V.* In the mid-2000s, the gaming media introduced Harmonix's <<*Rock Band*>>, which quickly became a <<hit>>. <<Since then>> the *Rock Band* video games have been wildly popular among gamers of all ages throughout the United States. *Rock Band* has affected the public by encouraging family togetherness, influencing people to pursue the musical arts, and teaching an appreciation for music.

One way *Rock Band* has influenced families is by giving them an opportunity to spend time together <<and become closer.>> Today, family time is rare to come by, so families should appreciate <<the time they have together by doing something engaging>>. In the past, some families use<<d>> to have planned nights when they would all enjoy dinner together followed by a night of playing games. Sadly this is an activity that is rarely seen in family gatherings today. The new *Rock Band* game has made this picture more appealing and possible. This new age of technology gaming has now replaced rolling dice on a flat game board <<with>> picking up an instrument or microphone <<and playing songs>> as if <<the players are>> really <<performing>> on stage. Since this game is successful only when everyone plays together, <<it>> creates an attitude of <<teamwork>> and cooperation. Each participant plays a different instrument making up one <<r>>ock <<b>>and<<.>> *Rock Band* <<gets>> the players' hearts pumping, whether from trying to keep up with the beat, listening to cheering fans, or just making fools of themselves. Even the people who are not playing an instrument feel included and involved by being part of the concert. <<The observers>> cheer the band on like groupies. Families have so much fun playing *Rock Band* and enjoying a wonderful experience that they probably will talk and laugh about <<it>> for a long time.

Another effect of the *Rock Band* game is that <<it encourages>> many players to want to play a real instrument. *Rock Band* gives players a taste of what performing music <<would be like>> as a singer, guitar player, or drummer and a beginning level feel for each instrument that makes up a rock band. As players progress through *Rock Band,* <<new levels, songs, and venues continue to open>>, causing the game to be even better and more <<challenging>>. These advancements help players to appreciate musicians and, in turn, want to become <<like them>>, at least for fun. The media's influence in making *Rock Band* so popular has affected the world <<by influencing>> many people to pursue either a career or hobby in <<the>> musical arts.

Furthermore, the *Rock Band* game has helped people to develop a stronger appreciation for music. Music can be difficult to perform and takes a lot of practice to perfect. When playing *Rock Band* <<,>> the success of the band and the score shown <<are>> based on accuracy of hitting the right notes and the right time. This does not come naturally to everyone. Even if players are familiar with a song from listening to it in the car or hearing it performed live, <<they find>> it completely different to have to play <<the song>> themselves. *Rock Band* also helps gamers to appreciate music through introducing them to different styles of music. *Rock Band* has a variety of musical genres, such as <<classic rock, alternative rock, and country.>> Players <<can>> learn about the different styles of music, how to play <<them>>, recognize <<them>>, and distinguish <<them>> from other styles.

<<*Rock Band* has revolutionized family fun time.>> Players will have <<a great time>> with their families for a change, become better musicians, if they choose to pick up an instrument for real, and learn more about music and its different genres<<.>> So now let *Rock Band* bring you <<and your family together,>> so you can have your own "family fun night!"

Clean Copy of Thomas Gorsuch's Final Paper

Madness in the Music World

Have you ever dreamed of thousands of fans chanting your band's name as you walk on stage? Well now you can live it, with *Rock Band* I, II, III, IV, or V. In the mid-2000s, the gaming media introduced Harmonix's *Rock Band,* which quickly became a hit. Since then the *Rock Band* video games have been wildly popular among gamers of all ages throughout the United States. *Rock Band* has affected the public by encouraging family togetherness, influencing people to pursue the musical arts, and teaching an appreciation for music.

One way *Rock Band* has influenced families is by giving them an opportunity to spend time together and become closer. Today, family time is rare to come by, so families should appreciate the time they have together by doing something engaging. In the past, some families used to have planned nights when they would all enjoy dinner together followed by a night of playing games. Sadly this is an activity that is rarely seen in family gatherings today. The new *Rock Band* game has made this picture more appealing and possible. This new age of technology gaming has now replaced rolling dice on a flat game board with picking up an instrument or microphone and playing songs as if the players are really performing on stage. Since this game is successful only when everyone plays together, it creates an attitude of teamwork and cooperation. Each participant plays a different instrument making up one rock band. *Rock Band* gets the players' hearts pumping, whether from trying to keep up with the beat, listening to cheering fans, or just making fools of themselves. Even the people who are not playing an instrument feel included and involved by being part of the concert. The observers cheer the band on like groupies. Families have so much fun playing *Rock Band* and enjoying a wonderful experience that they probably will talk and laugh about it for a long time.

Another effect of the *Rock Band* game is that it encourages many players to want to play a real instrument. *Rock Band* gives players a taste of what performing music would be like as a singer, guitar player, or drummer and a beginning level feel for each instrument that makes up a rock band. As players progress through *Rock Band,* new levels, songs, and venues continue to open, causing the game to be even better and more challenging. These advancements help players to appreciate musicians and in turn, want to become like them, at least for fun. The media's influence in making *Rock Band* so popular has affected the world by influencing many people to pursue either a career or hobby in the musical arts.

Furthermore, the *Rock Band* game has helped people to develop a stronger appreciation for music. Music can be difficult to perform and takes a lot of practice to perfect. When playing *Rock Band,* the success of the band and the score shown are based on accuracy of hitting the right notes at the right time. This does not come naturally to everyone. Even if players are familiar with a song from listening to it in the car or hearing it performed live, they find it completely different to have to play the song themselves. *Rock Band* also helps gamers to appreciate music through introducing them to different styles of music. *Rock Band* has a variety of musical genres, such as classic rock, alternative rock, and country. Players can learn about the different styles of music, how to play them, recognize them, and distinguish them from other styles.

Rock Band has revolutionized family fun time. Players will have a great time with their families for a change, become better musicians, if they choose to pick up an instrument for real, and learn more about music and its different genres. So now let *Rock Band* bring you and your family together, so you can have your own "family fun night!"

QUESTIONS FOR REFLECTION

1. Read the first sentence. Does it capture your attention? Why or why not?
2. Based on the introduction, what do you expect from the rest of the essay?
3. Does the essay deliver what Thomas promised in the introduction? Explain.
4. Which supporting details seemed the most helpful? Why?
5. Would you want to play *Rock Band* based on this essay? Why or why not?

CHAPTER SUMMARY

1. Follow the seven stages of the **writing process** to write effective documents.
2. Use different **discovery** methods to help you choose and narrow your subject.
3. Create a cluster or outline to help you **plan** and organize your document.
4. **Compose** your rough draft without worrying too much about grammar and punctuation.
5. **Get feedback** on your paper from someone who can give you suggestions for revision.

6. When **revising** a document, you may add and delete ideas, further develop your concepts, or rearrange your points to make your writing more effective.
7. **Edit** your paper carefully for diction, sentence structure, grammar, punctuation, spelling, and mechanics.
8. **Proofread** your paper and make corrections before submitting your final draft.

WHAT I KNOW NOW

Use this checklist to determine what you need to work on to feel comfortable with your understanding of the material in this chapter. Check off each item as you master it. Review the checklist periodically for any unchecked items.

- [ ] 1. I have found several **discovery methods** I can use to find and explore topics.
- [ ] 2. I am familiar with how to develop a cluster or outline to **plan** my paper.
- [ ] 3. I won't be too hard on myself as I **compose** my first draft.
- [ ] 4. I understand the importance of **getting feedback** from a classmate, a tutor, or an online writing service to help me improve my paper.
- [ ] 5. I am aware that I will need to **revise** my paper by adding, deleting, rearranging, and further developing my ideas.
- [ ] 6. I know that I need to carefully **edit** my paper for diction, sentence structure, grammar, punctuation, spelling, and mechanics.
- [ ] 7. I'll leave time to **proofread** my final paper before turning it in to my instructor.

Design elements: *Graduate Spotlight:* Ingram Publishing/AGE Fotostock

CHAPTER 3

Writing Sentences, Paragraphs, and Essays

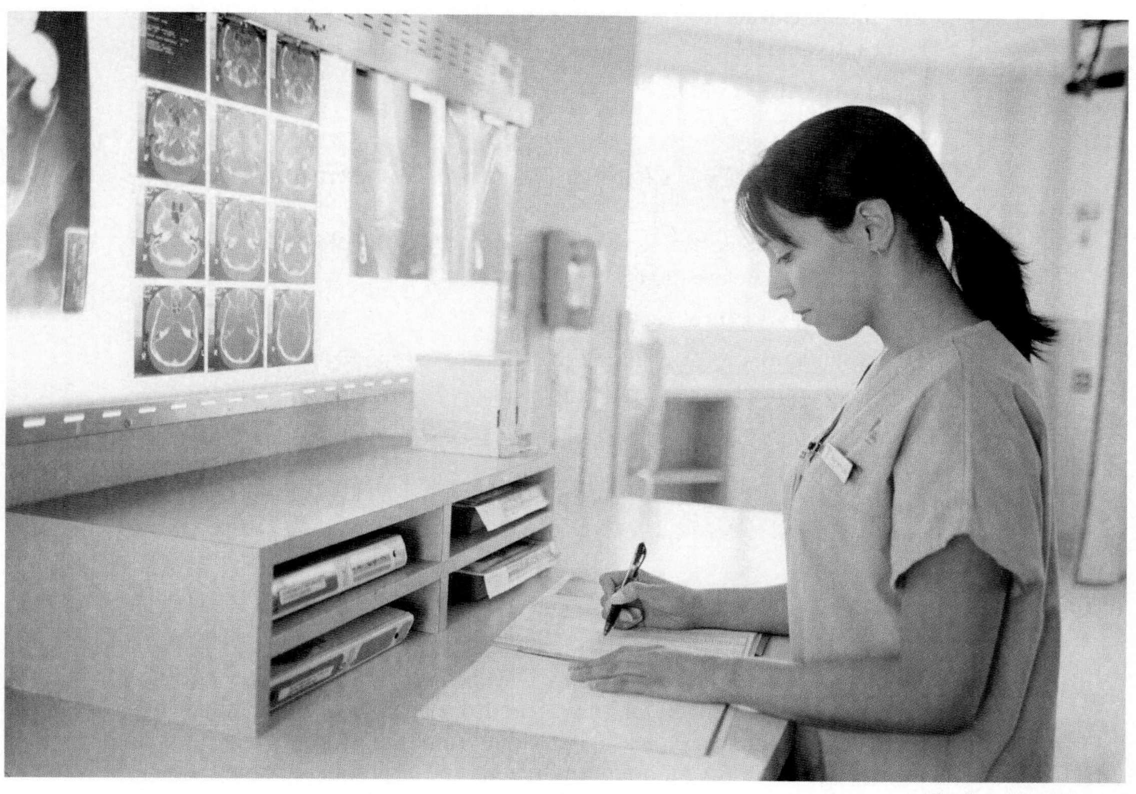

Mike Powell/Getty Images

learning outcomes

In this chapter you will learn techniques for achieving these learning outcomes:

3.1 Write complete sentences, including topic sentences and thesis statements. *p. 50*

3.2 Write and develop paragraphs using transitional words and phrases to create better flow. *p. 52*

3.3 Write and develop multi-paragraph essays that include an introduction, a body, visuals (if appropriate), and a conclusion. *p. 57*

3.1 Writing a Sentence

Sentence Components

Writing an effective sentence requires careful thought. Basically, every sentence needs to have three elements. It needs to have a subject and a verb, and it needs to express a complete thought. The subject is the topic of your sentence; the verb is the action in the sentence; and the complete thought allows the sentence to stand on its own.

Incomplete Sentence: While I was driving to work today.

Complete Sentence: While I was driving to work today, I saw a bobcat.

Discussion: The first sentence has a subject (I) and a verb (was driving), but the word *while* causes it to be incomplete. For more on complete and incomplete sentences, see Part 4.

Activity Writing Complete Sentences

Revise each incomplete sentence below so that it contains a subject and a verb and expresses a complete thought:

1. While I was enrolling in college.
2. Some of the most popular college majors are.
3. Is the best instructor I have had so far.
4. Joining a social or professional organization.
5. The best way to achieve success in college.

Parts of Speech

Reviewing the eight *parts of speech* can strengthen your sentence-writing skills. Table 3.1 lists the parts of speech and describes their functions. Basically, every word in a sentence serves a particular function. Although a complete sentence needs to include only a noun and a verb and express a complete thought, you may use other words, such as adjectives and prepositions, to provide more details for your readers.

Sentence Variety

Whether you are writing a short paragraph or an entire essay, you will need to vary your sentence length and style. If all of your sentences are similar, then your writing style will probably seem dull to your readers. A short, simple sentence can help you to emphasize a key point, whereas a longer, more complex sentence may

Table 3.1

The Eight Parts of Speech		
Part of Speech	**Description**	**Examples**
Nouns	Name a person, place, or thing	Dr. Oz, New York, book
Pronouns	Replace a noun	me, them, herself, it, that, who
Verbs	Show action or a state of being	jump, surfed, has been running, will be swimming, is, was
Adjectives	Modify or describe a noun	cute, sweetest, green, playful, funny, Asian
Adverbs	Modify or describe a verb, an adjective, or another adverb	slowly, carefully, completely, sooner
Prepositions	Link a noun to another word	to, before, on, over, with, beyond
Conjunctions	Join clauses, sentences, or words	for, and, nor, but, or, yet, so, although, unless, because
Interjections	Express a strong feeling	Oh! Cool! Ouch! Wow!

Activity Identifying Parts of Speech

Identify the part of speech of each highlighted word in the sentences below:

1. The friends assembled food, drinks, and fishing gear for the outing.
2. It was a sunny day, and the water was perfectly calm.
3. Sophie said, "Wow! Look at the size of that fish."
4. She tried to get the fish into the boat, but it got away too quickly.
5. The boat rapidly approached the shore.

enable you to illustrate the relationships among the ideas you are presenting. Varying your sentence lengths and patterns creates greater interest for the reader. Read the following:

> ***ESOL Tip >***
>
> When writing in standard American English, place an adjective before, not after, a noun. For example, write "the blue car" instead of "the car blue."

Draft: Some forms of body art have been around for centuries. Body art is growing in popularity. Many men and women are getting tattoos. Some people are also getting a variety of body piercings. Other people are getting implants to change their appearance. Many people who try body art want to make a bold statement.

Read the previous passage aloud. How does it sound? Is it exciting or boring? You probably noticed that the ideas are presented in a short, choppy manner and that some words are repeated unnecessarily. Basically, the sentences are similar in structure and lack variety.

Revised: Although various forms of body art have been around for centuries, today it is growing in popularity. Many men and women are using tattoos, body piercings, and implants to change their appearance and make a bold statement.

The revised passage sounds much better when read aloud because the sentences vary in length and structure, and the ideas flow better together. Notice that some ideas were combined to create more variety in sentence structure and to eliminate repeated words such as *body art* and *people.*

Activity Revising for Better Sentence Variety

Revise the following paragraph by varying the structure of the sentences to make the ideas flow more smoothly. You may reword, reorganize, and combine sentences, but be sure to keep all of the ideas present in the original paragraph. To be effective, your final paragraph will need to have fewer sentences and words without losing any of the details.

Vacationing in Key West

Key West, Florida, is a fun-filled vacation destination. It is an island situated at the southernmost point of the United States. First of all, there are many activities to enjoy in Key West. Some people enjoy water sports in Key West. The fishing is first-class. The dolphin encounters are wonderful for nature lovers. Diving and snorkeling are popular sports in Key West. Additionally, the nightlife in Key West is exceptional and makes it a fun place to visit. Duval Street has great bars. There are numerous bars with live music. Sloppy Joe's is a famous bar. Ernest Hemingway loved to go to Sloppy Joe's. Hog's Breath Saloon is a popular nightspot. Two Friends Bar is a popular evening destination. There is karaoke at Two Friends Bar. Key West provides tourists with opportunities for several other activities as well. There are quaint shops to visit. Visitors can see a live performance at the Tennessee Williams Theatre. Travelers can tour Ernest Hemingway's house. There is so much to do in Key West. As a result, many people enjoy traveling to Key West every year.

3.2 Writing a Paragraph

A **paragraph** is a group of sentences that all relate to one idea. Sometimes a paragraph can stand on its own, and other times a paragraph is part of a larger essay or document. Typically, a stand-alone paragraph consists of three main parts: a topic sentence, several main points with supporting sentences, and a concluding sentence (see Figure 3.1).

Paragraph A group of sentences related to one idea.

Topic Sentence

A **topic sentence** states the main idea of a paragraph.

Topic sentence A sentence that states the main idea of a paragraph.

A good topic sentence has two main components—a topic and an opinion about the topic. It also has to be a complete sentence. Remember, a complete sentence contains a subject and a verb and expresses a complete thought. For example, the following includes all of the necessary components of a good topic sentence: "Even though working and going to school full time can be challenging at times, the advantages far outweigh the disadvantages."

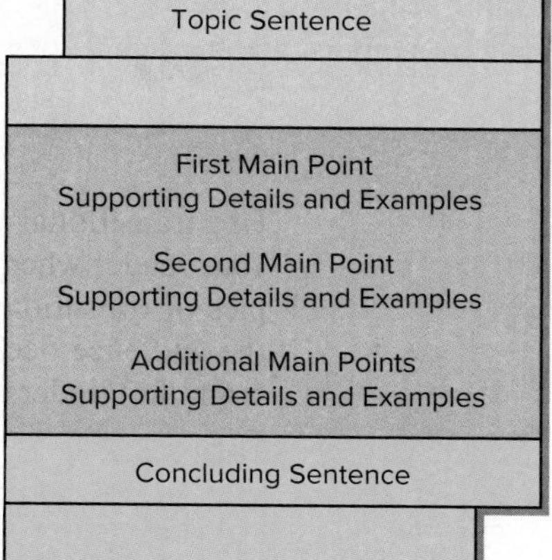

FIGURE 3.1 Basic Paragraph Structure

Poor Topic Sentence: Reasons to learn to write.

Revised Topic Sentence: Learning to become a better writer can help you to be more successful in achieving your educational, career, and personal goals.

Discussion: The poor sentence lacks a verb, an opinion, and a complete thought. The revised sentence has all of the required components.

Activity Writing Topic Sentences

Brainstorm a list of at least five topics to which most college students can relate. The topics can be about music, television, movies, current events, school, careers, or other areas of interest. From that list, choose the two that you like best. Write a topic sentence for each topic you choose. Be sure each topic sentence includes the topic and an opinion and is a complete sentence.

Supporting Sentences

The body of your paragraph will include supporting sentences with points and examples that support the opinion in your topic sentence. While there is no magic number of supporting sentences, you will usually need at least three to five sentences to support each topic sentence in an academic paper. You will want to have enough supporting sentences to fully develop your topic. Keep in mind that college writers are more likely to have too few supporting sentences than too many. Also, make sure that your paragraph is unified. In other words, every idea you include must help support the opinion in your topic sentence.

Activity Writing Supporting Sentences

Choose one of the topic sentences that you created in the Writing Topic Sentences activity. Write four to five supporting sentences to go along with your topic. Be sure that all sentences clearly relate to the opinion expressed in the topic sentence.

Transitions

Use transitional words and phrases throughout your paragraphs to help signal to your reader when you are changing direction or moving to a new point. (See examples of transitions in Table 3.2.) Transitions make your writing more coherent for the audience because they serve to bridge ideas. Without transitions, your readers might not understand the connection you are trying to make between two ideas.

Table 3.2

Transitions	
Type of Transition	**Examples**
To give examples	for example, for instance, such as, that is
To show time or order	about, after, afterward, as soon as, at, before, beforehand, during, finally, first, immediately, in the meantime, later, meanwhile, next, presently, second, soon, subsequently, then, third, today, tomorrow, until, when, without delay, yesterday
To show location	above, across, against, along, alongside, among, around, away from, behind, below, beneath, beside, between, beyond, by, down, in back of, in front of, inside, into, near, nearby, off, on top of, onto, outside, over, throughout, to the left, under, underneath
To compare (show similarities)	also, as, as though, in the same way, like, likewise, neither, both, similarly
To contrast (show differences)	although, but, even though, however, in contrast, in spite of, on the other hand, otherwise, still, yet
To show a cause	another reason, because, one reason, since
To show an effect	as a result, consequently, hence, therefore, thus
To add information	additionally, again, along with, also, and, another, as well, besides, equally important, finally, furthermore, in addition, moreover, next
To show emphasis or repetition	again, even, certainly, emphatically, in other words, in particular, in fact, in the same way, more importantly, more specifically, obviously, of course, to emphasize, truly
To conclude or summarize	all in all, as a result, consequently, finally, for this reason, hence, last, to conclude, to summarize

Activity Using Transitions

Using the words below, fill in the blanks in the following paragraph by adding transitional words or phrases. Be sure that your transitions show the logical relationships among the ideas in the paragraph.

for example	all in all	first of all	also
in addition	another reason	as well	second

See You at the Movies

Going to see a movie at a theater is far superior to viewing one at home. ______, the technology is much better at the theater. ______, the screen is many times larger than home televisions. This causes the characters and events to appear much larger than in real life. The sound system is better ______. The Dolby surround sound and booming volume help viewers to feel as if they are actually on location with the actors. ______, sharing the experience with a large audience adds to the excitement of the movie. Audience members can laugh, gasp, or cheer together when important scenes occur. ______ why the theater is more enjoyable is the vast selection of snacks at the concession stand. ______ to the standard popcorn, chocolate, and cola products, many movie theaters ______ offer nachos with cheese, personal pizzas, cinnamon-glazed nuts, and a variety of other options to satisfy the audience's hunger. ______, watching a movie at the theater beats viewing one at home every time.

Concluding Sentence

If you are writing a stand-alone paragraph, the last sentence should serve as your conclusion. Restate the main idea and opinion you introduced in your topic sentence. Be sure to use different words than you did the first time.

Topic Sentence: Learning to become a better writer can help you to be more successful in achieving your educational, career, and personal goals.

Reworded Concluding Sentence: Strengthening your writing skills will enable you to become more accomplished in school, on the job, and in your personal life.

Depending on the length of your paragraph, you may want to add one more sentence after your reworded thesis. If so, you will want to include something that readers will remember. See the example in the model paragraph that follows. Notice that the transitional words are highlighted.

Activity Writing Concluding Sentences

Write a concluding sentence for the topic sentence and supporting sentences you created in the Writing Topic Sentences (page 53) and Writing Supporting Sentences (page 54) activities. Be sure your concluding sentence uses different words to remind your readers of the opinion in the topic sentence.

Model Paragraph

Internships

Topic Sentence	Working as an intern for a local medical facility is an excellent way to begin your career in the allied health field.
First Main Point	First of all, as an intern you will learn valuable skills that you may not learn in college.
Supporting Details	For example, you will have an opportunity to work with real patients and learn how to meet their needs while they are in the office. Also, you will gain a greater understanding of what doctors and other health professionals will expect from you while you are on the job.
Second Main Point	Another benefit to taking on an internship is that you will have a chance to prove that you are capable of handling the duties that you will be responsible for when you are on the job.
Supporting Details	For instance, you can demonstrate your competence in performing crucial administrative and clinical tasks.
Third Main Point	Finally, the greatest benefit to serving as an intern is that the experience may very well lead to a permanent position.
Supporting Details	If you work hard, know your stuff, and get along well with others, then you are likely to land a job at the intern site.
Reworded Topic Sentence	Consequently, the skills, real-world experience, and job opportunities that an internship provides are extremely advantageous to your career in the allied health field.
Memorable Statement	Even though internships are usually not paid positions, they are well worth their time for the benefits you will receive.

Graduate SPOTLIGHT

MeiLynn D'Alessandro, Sales Representative

©Karin Russell

MeiLynn D'Alessandro has a degree in marketing and works as a sales representative for an educational consulting group. Here's what D'Alessandro has to say about the importance of written communication in her career:

"I do a tremendous amount of writing in my career. First, I write a summary of each school's needs to send to others in my company so they can understand how we can best serve the needs of teachers and students. My summaries have to be detailed and accurate, with specific suggestions that are appropriate because many people depend on the solutions my company develops. Also, every day I write dozens of e-mail messages to my customers to answer questions and explain technology in a clear and concise manner. Additionally, I develop digital sales flyers that I use to showcase our newest products. These flyers must be descriptive and persuasive. Finally, I write a monthly report summarizing the meetings I have had with customers to make the management team aware of my activity in my territory. Having strong writing skills is critical to my success as a sales representative."

3.3 Writing an Essay

An **essay** (also known as a *composition*) is a group of paragraphs related to a particular subject or theme. Essays are usually designed to achieve one of the five purposes for writing: to inform, to interpret, to persuade, to entertain, and to express feelings (see Chapter 1 for more details). An essay with a clear organizational structure is easier for your readers to understand. Like virtually every other type of document that you write, an essay needs to have a beginning, a middle, and an ending (introduction, body, and conclusion). Figure 3.2 illustrates the basic structure of an essay.

Essay A group of paragraphs related to a particular subject.

FIGURE 3.2 Basic Essay Structure

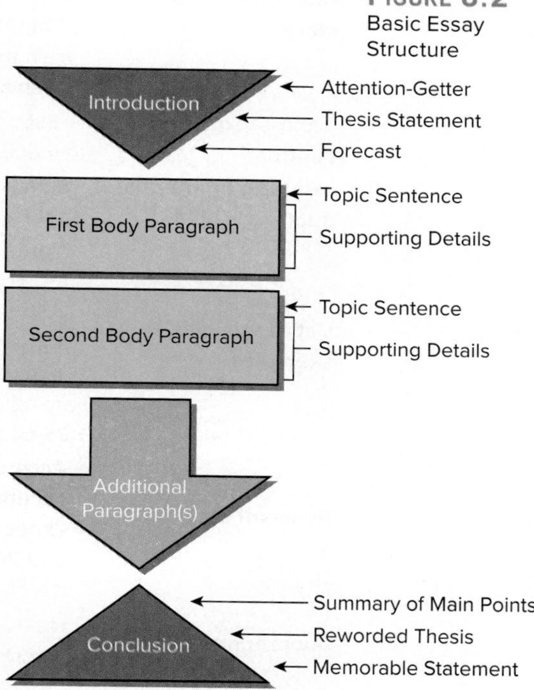

Introductory Paragraph

Your introduction should accomplish three tasks: capture the audience's attention, state your thesis, and provide an overview of the main points you will cover in the body of the essay. Avoid beginning a paper with dull statements such as, "This essay is going to be about . . . " or "I'm going to explain. . . . " Instead, start with something that will capture your audience's interest.

Attention-Getters The first few sentences are some of the most important sentences in your entire essay. This is your one chance to convince the audience that your paper is worth reading. You will need to make the most of this opportunity. Whatever type of lead-in you choose to get your audience's attention, you will want to ensure that it effectively introduces your thesis statement. The idea is to entice your audience to continue reading your paper. Table 3.3 lists examples of attention-getting strategies for introductory paragraphs.

Thesis Statement After you have gained your audience's attention, you'll need to state your **thesis.** Your thesis identifies the main idea of your essay for your audience. Typically, the thesis should appear early in the essay, in the first or second paragraph, depending on the length of the attention-getter and the length of the essay. A thesis statement is just like a topic sentence except that it states the main idea for an entire essay instead of just one paragraph. A thesis has the same two components as a topic sentence: the topic and your opinion. (See Table 3.4 for some sample thesis statements.) A thesis, like any complete sentence, needs to have a subject and a verb and express a complete thought.

Thesis Identifies the main idea of an essay.

Table 3.3

Sample Attention-Getters	
Brief description or story	Two trains were headed toward each other. One was traveling 70 mph, the other 45 mph. The trains collided, causing a loss of 14 lives and injuries to over 100 others. What the passengers didn't know when they boarded the train that fateful day was that one of the engineers had been smoking marijuana before work.
Comparison or contrast	Just as a tiger stalks its prey, serial killers often follow their victims before attacking them.
Inspiring or intriguing quote	Samuel Johnson once stated, "Great works are performed, not by strength, but by perseverance."
List of relevant examples	Many public figures have used their celebrity status to help promote a worthy cause. Bono, the lead singer for the band U2, was nominated for the Nobel Peace Prize for his global humanitarian efforts. Talk show host Oprah Winfrey has inspired hundreds of thousands of people to read classic novels. Actress Angelina Jolie has encouraged people to consider the plight of children in Third World countries.
Relevant statistic	According to the United States Department of Labor, occupations and industries related to health care are expected to add the greatest number of jobs between now and 2026.
Short summary	On October 29, 2012, Hurricane Sandy ripped through the New Jersey shore, New York City, and Long Island, causing massive damage. It flooded subways, destroyed buildings, and left millions of people stranded without electricity.
Surprising statement	I looked into the woods beyond the rocky path and couldn't believe the grotesque creature I saw!
Thought-provoking question	Have you ever been in a situation that you knew would change your life forever?

Poor Thesis: Many people earn a college degree.

Poor Thesis: The benefits of a college education.

Revised Thesis: Obtaining a college education has several benefits.

Discussion: The first "poor thesis" example simply states a fact about the subject without offering an opinion. The second "poor thesis" example has a subject and an opinion, but it lacks a verb and doesn't express a complete thought. The revised thesis is a complete sentence with a subject, a verb, and an opinion.

Be sure your thesis statement makes a significant point that will engage your readers. Also, avoid including absolute terms such as *always* and *will definitely* in your thesis because readers will usually be able to think of exceptions to the point you are making.

Table 3.4

Sample Thesis Statements	
Strategy	**Example**
Describing and narrating	What began as a casual camping trip to the Great Smoky Mountains turned into a near-tragic event for everyone involved.
Dividing and classifying	Most car drivers fall into these six categories: speed demon, slowpoke, distracted, daredevil, nervous, and logical.
Process writing	Landing the perfect job can be easy if you follow five simple steps.
Comparing and contrasting	Providing for the needs of a child is similar to maintaining a vehicle.
Analyzing causes and effects	Americans can help make the planet a greener place by changing a few simple habits at home, at work, and out in the community.
Persuading	The age at which adults can drink alcoholic beverages should be lowered to 18 throughout the United States.
Evaluating	The *Hunger Games* series by Suzanne Collins is an excellent read for teens and adults.
Solving a problem	The best strategy for finding a job in a tough economy is to earn a degree in a rapidly growing career field.

Poor Thesis: People who exercise live longer than those who don't exercise.

Revised Thesis: People who exercise are likely to live longer than those who don't exercise.

Discussion: The qualifier "are likely" tempers the thesis and makes it easier to support.

Overview of Main Points Another function of an introduction is to give the reader an overview of the main points you will cover in the body of the essay. This is called a **forecast.** Similar to a forecast that predicts the weather, a forecast in an essay helps the reader to predict what the main points will be.

Thesis with Forecast: Obtaining a college education is beneficial because it can lead to greater self-esteem, a higher-paying job, and a better style of living.

Activity

Developing a Thesis Statement

Narrow the following topics and write a thesis statement for each one.

1. A reality television show
2. A career field
3. A celebrity
4. A sports figure
5. Professionalism

Forecast Helps the reader predict the main points.

Discussion: This thesis statement suggests that the body paragraphs of the essay will explain each of the benefits mentioned: greater self-esteem, a higher-paying job, and a better style of living.

If the thesis does not contain an overview of the supporting points you will cover in the essay, then you can include another sentence, or a series of sentences, to give the reader an indication of what to expect. Remember, your forecast should not sound mechanical. You do not necessarily need to include a list of your main points; however, you owe it to your readers to give them some idea of what to expect in the body of the essay.

Body Paragraphs

Body paragraphs are similar to stand-alone paragraphs except that they are part of a larger essay. Each body paragraph should focus on one main point that supports the opinion in your thesis. Often they begin with a topic sentence and include several supporting sentences. Be sure to include enough details and examples to fully support your topic sentence. You may develop your ideas by using one or more of the writing strategies covered in this text: describing and narrating, dividing and classifying, explaining a process, comparing and contrasting, analyzing causes and effects, persuading, evaluating, or solving a problem. Also, use transitions within the paragraph to help your ideas flow smoothly and at the end of the paragraph to lead the reader into the next body paragraph. To maintain **unity** in your essay, make sure every idea relates to the overall thesis of the essay.

Unity Ensures every idea relates to the overall thesis of the essay.

Activity Achieving Unity

Identify the sentences that do not support the opinion in the topic sentence of the following paragraph. Explain why those sentences should not be included in the paragraph.

Getting around on Two Wheels

Using a scooter for transportation has many benefits. First of all, riding a scooter saves gasoline. Scooters get anywhere from about 60 to 125 miles per gallon depending on the size of the motor. Riders can feel good about consuming less fuel and enjoy the reward of spending less money at the gas pump. Second, scooters are easy to park. They take up less space, giving riders more parking options. Some scooters have a center stand to use when parked that is difficult to operate. Also, many parking lots have spaces set aside for motorcycles and scooters. This can be extremely convenient, especially at places where parking lots tend to fill up. Finally, riding a scooter is fun. Commuting to work or school doesn't seem like a chore when riding a scooter. On a beautiful day riders can enjoy a great breeze and the soothing warmth of the sunshine. Riding in the rain is a whole different story. There's nothing worse than arriving at your destination soaked or muddy, which is why many scooter riders also own a car.

Incorporating Visuals into Your Essay You may decide that including one or more visual images in your essay will enhance the message you are conveying to your audience. You might incorporate a photograph, artwork, graphic organizer, table, chart, or graph into your essay. If you do so, be sure to refer to the image in your text. Also, if you are not the originator of the visual image, be sure to give credit to the source. At times a web address may be sufficient. However, your instructor may require that you follow APA or MLA guidelines for integrating images. (See Chapter 14 for more details about citing source material in your text.)

Concluding Paragraph

The last paragraph of your essay should wrap up the entire document. Similar to the introduction, the conclusion should accomplish three tasks: reword your thesis statement, summarize your main points, and end with a memorable thought.

Thesis Statement in Introduction: Earning a college degree has several benefits.

Reworded Thesis in Conclusion: Once you have completed your college education, you will enjoy the rewards for the rest of your life.

Avoid introducing new ideas, changing your focus, or upsetting your readers in your conclusion. Also, even though you might be tempted to end with a cliché, such as "and that's the way the cookie crumbles," please resist. Instead, end with a powerful idea that will make a lasting impression on the readers. You may use techniques that are similar to attention-getters (see Table 3.3), such as quotes, surprising statements, or thought-provoking questions.

Reading and Reflection MODEL ESSAY

[preview] **MARY SHERRY** is an adult literacy teacher who writes about a variety of educational concerns. The article that follows, which was originally published in *Newsweek*, has gained a lot of attention, both positive and negative. Is failing students the answer to helping them eventually achieve success? As you read the article, consider this question and pay particular attention to the organizational strategy the author uses and the ideas she presents.

In Praise of the F Word

by Mary Sherry

Introduction

Attention-Getter

Tens of thousands of 18-year-olds will graduate this year and 1
be handed meaningless diplomas. These diplomas won't look any different from those awarded their luckier classmates. Their validity will be questioned only when their employers discover that these graduates are semiliterate.

Eventually a fortunate few will find their way into educational- 2
repair shops—adult-literacy programs, such as the one where I teach basic grammar and writing. There, high-school graduates and high-school dropouts pursuing graduate-equivalency certificates will learn the skills they should have learned in school.

Thesis Statement

They will also discover they have been cheated by our educational system.

First Main Point

As I teach, I learn a lot about our schools. Early in each ses- 3
sion I ask my students to write about an unpleasant experience they had in school. No writers' block here! "I wish someone would have had made me stop doing drugs and made me study." "I liked to party and no one seemed to care." "I was a good kid and didn't cause any trouble, so they just passed me along even though I didn't read and couldn't write." And so on.

Supporting Details

4 I am your basic do-gooder, and prior to teaching this class I blamed the poor academic skills our kids have today on drugs, divorce and other impediments to concentration necessary for doing well in school. But, as I rediscover each time I walk into the classroom, before a teacher can expect students to concentrate, he has to get their attention, no matter what distractions may be at hand. There are many ways to do this, and they have much to do with teaching style. However, if style alone won't do it, there is another way to show who holds the winning hand in the classroom. That is to reveal the trump card of failure.

Second Main Point

5 I will never forget a teacher who played that card to get the attention of one of my children. Our youngest, a worldclass charmer, did little to develop his intellectual talents but always got by. Until Mrs. Stifter.

Supporting Details

6 Our son was a high-school senior when he had her for English. "He sits in the back of the room talking to his friends," she told me. "Why don't you move him to the front row?" I urged, believing the embarrassment would get him to settle down. Mrs. Stifter looked at me steely-eyed over her glasses. "I don't move seniors," she said. "I flunk them." I was flustered. Our son's academic life flashed before my eyes. No teacher had ever threatened him with that before. I regained my composure and managed to say that I thought she was right. By the time I got home I was feeling pretty good about this. It was a radical approach for these times, but, well, why not? "She's going to flunk you," I told my son. I did not discuss it any further. Suddenly English became a priority in his life. He finished out the semester with an A.

7 I know one example doesn't make a case, but at night I see a parade of students who are angry and resentful for having been passed along until they could no longer even pretend to keep up. Of average intelligence or better, they eventually quit school, concluding they were too dumb to finish. "I should have been held back," is a comment I hear frequently. Even sadder are those students who are high-school graduates who say to me after a few weeks of class, "I don't know how I ever got a high-school diploma."

Third Main Point

8 Passing students who have not mastered the work cheats them and the employers who expect graduates to have basic skills. We excuse this dishonest behavior by saying kids can't learn if they come from terrible environments. No one seems to stop to think that—no matter what environments they come from—most kids don't put school first on their list unless they perceive something is at stake. They'd rather be sailing.

Supporting Details

9 Many students I see at night could give expert testimony on unemployment, chemical dependency, abusive relationships. In spite of these difficulties, they have decided to make education a priority. They are motivated by the desire for a better job or the need to hang on to the one they've got. They have a healthy fear of failure.

10 People of all ages can rise above their problems, but they need to have a reason to do so. Young people generally don't have the maturity to value education in the same way my adult students value it. But fear of failure, whether economic

or academic, can motivate both. Flunking as a regular policy has just as much merit today as it did two generations ago. We must review the threat of flunking and see it as it really is—a positive teaching tool. It is an expression of confidence by both teachers and parents that the students have the ability to learn the material presented to them. However, making it work again would take a dedicated, caring conspiracy between teachers and parents. It would mean facing the tough reality that passing kids who haven't learned the material—while it might save them grief for the short term—dooms them to longterm illiteracy. It would mean that teachers would have to follow through on their threats, and parents would have to stand behind them, knowing their children's best interests are indeed at stake. This means no more doing Scott's assignments for him because he might fail. No more passing Jodi because she's such a nice kid.

Conclusion
Reworded Thesis
Memorable Statement

This is a policy that worked in the past and can work today. 11
A wise teacher, with the support of his parents, gave our son the
opportunity to succeed—or fail. It's time we return this choice to
all students.

Source: Mary Sherry, "In Praise of the F Word," *Newsweek*, May 5, 1991.

Activity Annotating an Essay

Choose an interesting article from a printed or online magazine or professional journal. Make a copy of the article or print it out so that you can write on it. Label the essay parts or note any areas that are missing. Being aware of how professional writers organize their essays can help you to become a better writer.

Introduction: Attention-getter, thesis statement, overview of main points.
Body paragraphs: Topic sentences, supporting points, transitions.
Conclusion: Reworded thesis, summary of main points, memorable statement.

After you have labeled the document, determine the effectiveness, or lack thereof, of the article and its organization:

- How effective is the thesis? The introduction as a whole?
- Are the supporting details sufficient?
- Does the conclusion seem sufficient? Why or why not?
- What, if anything, would make the article better?

Writing Attitude Survey

How do you feel about writing? Do you find it to be painful? Or do you get excited about the prospect of creating a new written work? Take this attitude survey to explore your thoughts on writing. There are no right or wrong answers, but you may learn something about yourself as a writer when you review your answers. Figure 3.3 is an example of one student's writing attitude survey.

1. How do you feel about writing in general?
2. What are characteristics of good writing?
3. Why is effective writing important?
4. How confident are you in your writing abilities?
5. What are your strengths and weaknesses with writing?
6. What kinds of writing do you enjoy?
7. What kinds of writing do you dislike?
8. How much time do you spend writing each week for work, school, and yourself?
9. What joys or challenges have you faced as a writer?

Activity Responding to the Writing Attitude Survey

Use some of the ideas from your responses to the writing attitude survey to write an essay about how you perceive yourself as a writer. Your thesis statement should state your overall view of how you see yourself as a writer. To support your main idea, be sure to include specific details about your past writing experiences.

For example, if writing is one of your favorite activities, you might include details about how you have always kept a journal or how you have received recognition for your excellent writing abilities. You may also choose to include what you like about writing and why it is important to you. If your feelings about writing aren't favorable, you might write about some of the experiences you have had that have led to your discomfort with or dislike for writing. You might also explore what it would take for you to become more confident in your writing abilities.

Another option is to focus on a pivotal experience that changed your perception of yourself as a writer. Maybe you always hated (or loved) to write until you encountered a particular teacher, boss, or assignment. Exploring your perceptions of yourself as a writer will help you to make the most out of your composition class.

Matthew Ruffell

Writing Attitude Survey

How do you feel about writing? Do you find it to be painful? Or do you get excited about the prospect of creating a new written work? Take this attitude survey to explore your thoughts on writing. There are no right or wrong answers, but you may learn something about yourself as a writer when you review your answers.

1. How do you feel about writing in general?

I feel that I spend too much time on wording my writing. I also put a lot of effort into writing, making it entertaining.

2. What are characteristics of good writing?

Good characteristics in writing:
- Organization: Thoughts, not random babbling
- Flow: Is it easy to read, no reading twice
- Grammar: Is it written well, does it sound good read out loud?

3. Why is effective writing important?

Effective writing is important to:
- Convey information about a topic
- To catch the reader's interest

4. How confident are you in your writing abilities?

I'm not as confident as I'd like to be. I haven't written a paper since 10th grade of high school. I'm challenged when it comes to choosing my words, using a better choice per se.

5. What are your strengths and weaknesses with writing?

I have the basics of writing down. I'm terrible with the flow of information and spelling.

6. What kinds of writing do you enjoy?

I enjoy poetry. It's kind of like writing lyrics to a song; plus it's easy to put my emotions behind it. I also like writing research papers because I learn a lot from them.

7. What kinds of writing do you dislike?

I don't like to write novels or short stories. I cannot keep the plot going, and I struggle to stay on topic.

8. How much time do you spend writing each week for work, school, and yourself?

I don't write much in my spare time. I do write for my classes. So far, I'm actually enjoying it, but I'm worried about writing in psychology class.

9. What joys or challenges have you faced as a writer?

Poetry is personal expression; I can do that pretty well☺ My challenges are working on patience, organization, and word choice.

FIGURE 3.3 Completed Writing Attitude Survey

STUDENT WRITING

Matthew Ruffell completed a writing attitude survey (see page 65) as part of his discovery process. The following is Matthew's final essay about how he perceives himself as a writer.

A Literary Genius I Am Not

by Matthew Ruffell

When it comes to writing, I'm about as dumb as a bag of hammers. In other words, English composition is not my strongest course of study. I have always dreaded tackling anything that had to do with demonstrating my writing skills. The reason for this is that there are a number of challenges I face when it comes to writing.

The first challenge I face when writing is having the patience to actually sit down and do the assignment. I don't typically write for any other purpose than an assignment for school or work. The truth is, I have never really had an interest in writing. I guess I have always thought of it as boring, just not for me. By nature, I'm more of a visual person. I prefer pictures and movies to written words. As a result, I always procrastinate when I have to write a paper, waiting until the day before the assignment is due to work on it. I always manage to get my assignments completed, but I find it difficult to be patient enough to write them.

The next challenge I face when writing is organizing my thoughts. Finding a topic is easy for me. There are plenty of things that I can rant and rave about. The struggle is collecting my thoughts on a particular subject matter. I have so many thoughts pin-balling around my head at any one given moment. To collectively organize them would take a lifetime to achieve. When writing about a particular subject, I just can't seem to get my thoughts out on paper. They tend to be choppy and not flow well together. I find myself spending much of my time writing and rewriting my thoughts. I spend much of my time trying to get the wording right and making sure I don't go off on a tangent about something unrelated to the topic. The last thing I want to do is confuse the reader by having an unorganized train of thought. In the end, I will eventually end up with a nicely organized and flowing paper that makes sense to the reader although I nearly beat myself blind doing so.

Another obstacle I face when writing is choosing the right words to emphasize my thoughts on a particular topic. I tend to think that much of my writing is boring, not very exciting to read. One reason for this is I don't have a very large vocabulary. I spend so much time searching for words that will add a little pizzazz to my work, which can be somewhat challenging. I often find myself asking questions such as, "Does that sound right?" "Will the readers understand what I mean?" I want to keep the readers interested and not lull them off to sleep. Using the right word combinations and substitutions in order to emphasize the key points and cut down wordiness is essential. There is almost nothing worse than reading a wordy and boring piece of writing.

Overall, I am not a literary genius by any stretch of the imagination. After reading this essay, you'll be sure to agree. I'm praying that by taking this course I will become a better writer, not so that I can go on to write novels, but just so that I can actually write a paragraph or two without sounding like an idiot. To do this, I'll need to become more patient with my writing, get better at organizing my thoughts, and somehow find the right words to communicate my intended message to my audience.

QUESTIONS FOR REFLECTION

1. Which sentence or sentences best state Ruffell's main idea?
2. What three points does the student make to support his main idea?
3. Are his supporting details effective? Why or why not?
4. What is your overall opinion of Ruffell's writing? Is he as bad as he thinks he is? Why or why not?
5. How do your writing experiences compare with Ruffell's?

CHAPTER SUMMARY

1. An effective sentence has a subject and a verb and expresses a complete thought.
2. Vary sentence length and structure to add interest to your writing style.
3. A good paragraph contains a topic sentence, supporting sentences, transitions, and a concluding sentence.
4. An effective essay includes an introduction, a body, and a conclusion.
5. A good introduction captures your audience's attention, states your thesis, and lets the reader know what to expect from the rest of the essay.
6. Well-developed body paragraphs provide enough details and examples to fully support the opinion in your thesis.
7. A solid concluding paragraph restates the thesis in different words, summarizes the main points in the essay, and ends with a memorable thought.

WHAT I KNOW NOW

Use this checklist to determine what you need to work on to feel comfortable with your understanding of the material in this chapter. Check off each item as you master it. Review the checklist periodically for any unchecked items.

- ☐ 1. I understand the three requirements for a **complete sentence.**
- ☐ 2. I am able to **vary the structure** of my sentences.
- ☐ 3. I can write a suitable **topic sentence** and **concluding sentence** for a paragraph.
- ☐ 4. I understand how to develop a **paragraph** using specific **supporting details** and examples.
- ☐ 5. I know the three parts of an **essay.**
- ☐ 6. I understand how to write an **introductory paragraph** with a **clear thesis.**
- ☐ 7. I know how to develop **body paragraphs** in an essay.
- ☐ 8. I can write a solid **concluding paragraph** for an essay.

Design elements: *Graduate Spotlight:* Ingram Publishing/AGE Fotostock

CHAPTER 4

The Critical Thinking, Reading, and Writing Connection

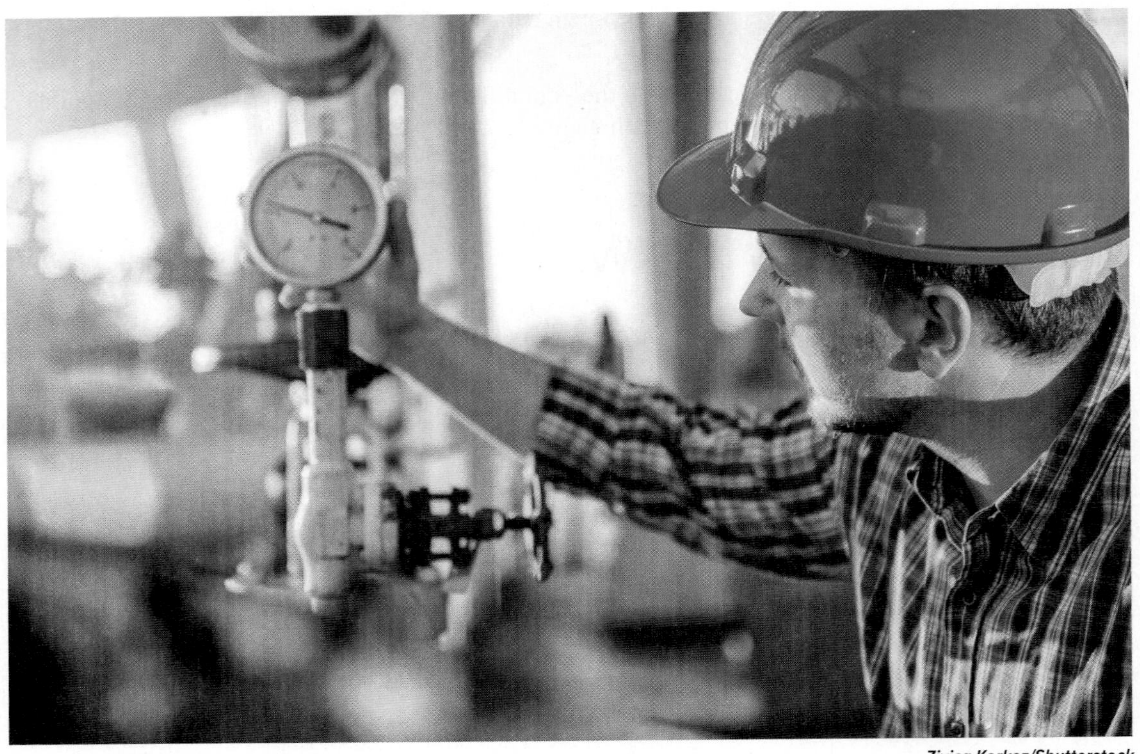

Zivica Kerkez/Shutterstock

learning outcomes

In this chapter you will learn techniques for achieving these learning outcomes:

4.1 Interpret written texts using critical thinking skills. p. 69

4.2 Participate in class discussions about readings. p. 74

4.3 Interpret visual texts, including photographs, graphs, advertisements, and websites. p. 75

4.4 Identify logical fallacies. p. 84

Thinking Critically

You are surrounded by written and visual texts on a daily basis. Whether watching television, surfing the Web, reading an article, viewing a clip on *YouTube.com*, instant messaging with a friend, or studying a textbook, you are being bombarded by different kinds of messages and images. The messages that you encounter are often misleading or contradictory. Therefore, you have to be able to think critically about them to determine what ideas to accept or reject.

Critical thinking is similar to detective work. When you think critically, you interpret (analyze) ideas and reflect on them. You are going beyond your initial impression of a written or visual text to uncover the deeper, less obvious meanings within. To think critically you have to evaluate the credibility of written and visual texts and the logic presented through them to determine if you agree or disagree with the information you are receiving. Being able to think critically will help you to become a better reader, writer, and decision maker. One way to strengthen your critical thinking skills is by learning how to read and interpret written and visual texts.

Critical thinking Interpreting ideas and reflecting on them.

4.1 Reading and Interpreting Written Texts

Reading is one of the best ways to get inspiration for writing. In addition to providing stimulating ideas to respond to, reading helps you strengthen your vocabulary and see how others have approached writing tasks. Becoming a good analytical reader can help you become a good critical thinker and writer. These skills will help you to be successful in school, in your career, and in other areas of your life.

Reading critically is different from reading for pleasure. When you read with a critical eye, you are searching for clues, analyzing details, and making inferences to form your own opinions about the work. Different readers will likely have unique responses to a written text based on their own knowledge, experiences, and interests. While there may not be one "right" way to interpret a particular text, some interpretations are more informed than others. Use this three-step process for a close, critical reading: (1) pre-read and anticipate; (2) read and analyze; (3) reread and annotate.

1. Pre-read and Anticipate

Before reading, look over the work to get an idea of what to expect when you read it.

- **Publication information:** Where and when was the article originally published? Is the content relevant today, or does it provide a glimpse into the past?
- **Biographical information:** If you have access to it, consider the author's biographical information. What is the writer's occupation and education? Does he or she appear to be qualified to discuss the topic at hand? Does the writer seem to have any particular bias about the topic?

- **Title:** Contemplate the title. What do you expect from the work based on the title? Does the title entice you to want to read the material?
- **Overview:** Skim through the text. Look at the headings, visual images, and overall organization to help prepare you for a more careful reading. Read the introductory paragraph and the topic sentence in each supporting paragraph so you have an idea of what you will learn from the material.
- **Predictions:** Based on your preview, identify what you already know about the subject, and make predictions about what you will learn from the text. Keep in mind that your predictions may or may not be accurate.

2. Read and Analyze

After you have skimmed through the text and thought about what you know about the subject and hope to find out, it's time to read the text carefully and analyze it. The term *analyze* means to break something down into its parts. You can examine the parts of an essay to understand it better.

- **Main idea:** As you begin reading, find the author's thesis. What point is the author trying to convey to the reader? Is the thesis stated clearly and effectively?
- **Supporting points:** What specific details and examples does the author use to substantiate his or her thesis? How does the supporting material serve to extend or clarify the author's main point? Is the support sufficient and accurate?
- **Rhetorical star:** Determine the five points of the author's rhetorical star (Figure 4.1). What is the *subject?* What *audience* is the author trying to reach? What was the author's *purpose* in writing (to inform, persuade, analyze, express feelings, or entertain)? What writing *strategy* (or strategies) does the author use to achieve his or her purpose. Is the author describing and narrating, dividing and classifying, explaining a process, comparing and contrasting, explaining causes and effects, persuading, evaluating, or solving a problem? What is the *design* of the text? How is it organized? Are visuals included? (See Chapter 1 for more details about the rhetorical star.)

FIGURE 4.1 The Rhetorical Star

3. Reread and Annotate

After you have carefully read the text, you should read it again to annotate it by highlighting key ideas, making notes in the margins, and recording your thoughts about what you are reading. Annotating the text will help you to process what you have read so that you can use the information later for a test, discussion, or writing assignment.

- **Define:** Note any words you come across that are unfamiliar to you. While you don't have to look up every new word you read, sometimes you may encounter a word that is critical to your understanding of the work. Determine if you need to look up the meanings of words you don't know or if you can figure them out well enough in context.

- **Summarize:** One of the best ways to understand and remember something that you have read is to summarize it in your own words. To write a **summary,** follow these three steps:
  1. Identify the thesis statement (main point) and rewrite it in your own words.
  2. Identify the supporting points and write one or two sentences explaining each supporting point.
  3. Write a one-sentence conclusion that summarizes the main point of the text.

  Be sure to place any exact wording you borrow from the original text in quotation marks so that you can distinguish your words from the author's when you read your summary later.

Summary A shortened version of an original work including only the main ideas.

- **Visualize:** You may find it helpful to create some sort of visual representation of a text you have read, especially if you are a visual learner. Making charts, graphs, and other visual organizers might help you to comprehend the material more readily. This is especially true for textbook material. For example, you might read a chapter in a history book and then create a chart or graph that highlights key events, times, and locations.
- **Synthesize:** The term *synthesize* means to put together. After you have read and broken down the material, then you want to put the ideas together in a meaningful way. When you write a **synthesis,** you connect the ideas you are reading to what you already know about the subject based on other texts and personal experience. When you connect the new material to prior knowledge, you will be better able to comprehend and recall the new material.

Synthesis A combination of ideas from different sources to form a new whole.

- **Question and evaluate:** After you have carefully read and reread the text, critique it by asking a variety of questions:
  - What is the author's tone? Is it straightforward, sarcastic,
  - or pretentious?
  - Is the thesis fully supported?
  - Are the details and examples relevant?
  - Does the author seem biased? If so, how?
  - Which details are based on verifiable facts, opinionated statements, or personal values?
  - Has the author used any logical fallacies? (See the discussion of fallacies on pages 83–86.)
  - Is the text convincing and effective? Why or why not?

ESOL Tip >

Use contextual clues to determine the meaning of words instead of relying too heavily on dictionary definitions.

[preview] **LINDA LABAN** is a freelance writer who has authored numerous articles about arts, entertainment, and travel in a variety of publications, such as *New York Post, Entertainment Weekly, Vulture,* and *The Boston Globe.* This essay was originally published by SXSW (South by Southwest), an organization that hosts an annual festival of media and music in Austin, Texas. Before reading, what do you expect the essay to be about based on the title? What have you heard or read about the concept of a "glass ceiling"? Notice the annotations that accompany the article. How similar or different would your annotations be if you were responding to the essay?

Will New Female Rappers Shatter Hip Hop's Glass Ceiling?

by Linda Laban

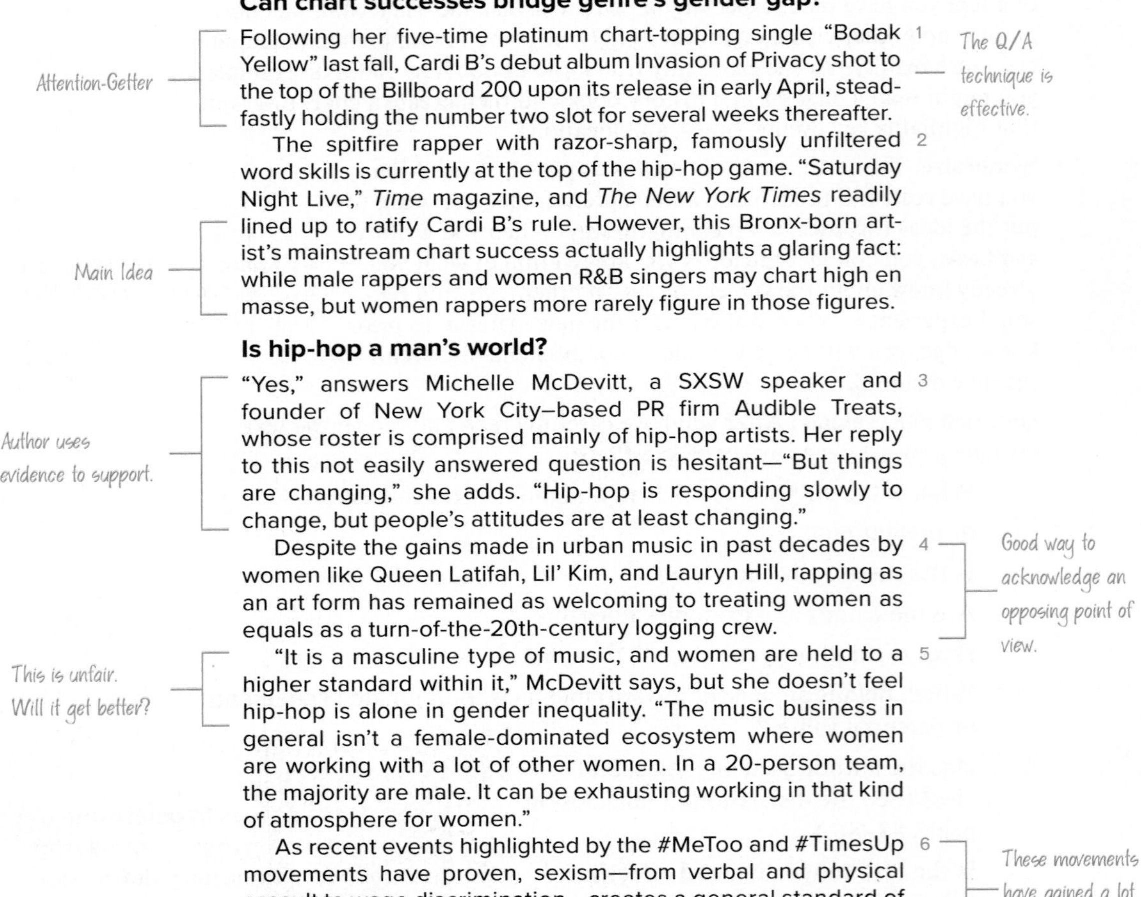
Attention-Getter
The Q/A technique is effective.
Main Idea
Author uses evidence to support.
Good way to acknowledge an opposing point of view.
This is unfair. Will it get better?
These movements have gained a lot of attention.

Can chart successes bridge genre's gender gap?

1 Following her five-time platinum chart-topping single "Bodak Yellow" last fall, Cardi B's debut album Invasion of Privacy shot to the top of the Billboard 200 upon its release in early April, steadfastly holding the number two slot for several weeks thereafter.

2 The spitfire rapper with razor-sharp, famously unfiltered word skills is currently at the top of the hip-hop game. "Saturday Night Live," *Time* magazine, and *The New York Times* readily lined up to ratify Cardi B's rule. However, this Bronx-born artist's mainstream chart success actually highlights a glaring fact: while male rappers and women R&B singers may chart high en masse, but women rappers more rarely figure in those figures.

Is hip-hop a man's world?

3 "Yes," answers Michelle McDevitt, a SXSW speaker and founder of New York City–based PR firm Audible Treats, whose roster is comprised mainly of hip-hop artists. Her reply to this not easily answered question is hesitant—"But things are changing," she adds. "Hip-hop is responding slowly to change, but people's attitudes are at least changing."

4 Despite the gains made in urban music in past decades by women like Queen Latifah, Lil' Kim, and Lauryn Hill, rapping as an art form has remained as welcoming to treating women as equals as a turn-of-the-20th-century logging crew.

5 "It is a masculine type of music, and women are held to a higher standard within it," McDevitt says, but she doesn't feel hip-hop is alone in gender inequality. "The music business in general isn't a female-dominated ecosystem where women are working with a lot of other women. In a 20-person team, the majority are male. It can be exhausting working in that kind of atmosphere for women."

6 As recent events highlighted by the #MeToo and #TimesUp movements have proven, sexism—from verbal and physical assault to wage discrimination—creates a general standard of challenges women everywhere face.

7 "Sexism exists in white-collar and blue-collar jobs in general, and it does also apply to the artistic space," says McDevitt, who has represented female rappers Remy Ma, Kreayshawn, Bhad Bhabie, and Rah Digga.

Powerful statement!

8 "The rap industry is a microcosm of the wider world," agrees Brooklyn-based rapper Miss Eaves (real name Shanthony Exum), who performed at SXSW. "Hip-hop isn't special, it's a reflection of a wider illness."

9 As was seen at SXSW, there is no shortage of talent or enthusiasm as a new generation of women rappers are working hard at their craft, with showcasing artists such as Princess Nokia, Kamaiyah, Bad Gyal, and Rapsody all racking up critical notice.

Why is this happening?

10 "Women and female-identifying rappers have a lot of talent that's ignored by the mainstream," says Miss Eaves. "I love pop music. There is artistry in that. But there is a lot of misogyny and homophobia there."

11 Miss Eaves isn't waiting for the mainstream to offer her a seat at the table. "Why would I want to work so hard to create a space in a place where I'm not welcome? I can create a new space where I can be me," she says.

Her reaction is understandable.

12 That space is on social media, which she uses to communicate directly with her audience. "Social media allows artists to be true to their style—that helped me," the 35-year-old says. "I feel my audience is predominantly female and my music speaks to women. Indie rappers are able to be public and grow their audience and bypass the sexist industry. That's very freeing. I don't know how I would feel if I were not able to market myself."

Social media can be a great tool.

13 24-year-old Californian rapper Saweetie, who is signed to Artistry Worldwide/Warner Bros. Records and also appeared at SXSW, agrees: "Social media opened up the playing field for women to have their voice be heard. My music touched a lot of women who wrote to me saying how inspiring it is to see a woman doing this. It's important for us women to come together and support each other, and collaborate."

14 Miss Eaves agrees: "That's what I hate in hip-hop . . . women going up against each other when they should be supporting each other. We are in an era when females are coming together, and they can get the attention they deserve in a male-dominated industry."

Yes, women should support each other.

15 There's a knock-on effect, with the women rappers who hit the top of the charts bettering the situation for all female hip-hop artists. McDevitt thinks the music industry is much more open to female rappers since Cardi B hit the number one spot, even if it's only for commercial reasons: "Music executives are already looking for the next Cardi B," she explains.

16 Saweetie hopes Cardi B's success helps debunk attitudes toward women rappers in general: "Women can be in the top tier. On that, Cardi B is an inspiration. She's a good performer, her music is good. She deserves to be where she is."

Everyone should have a fair chance at success!

17 Rather than copycat knockoffs, Miss Eaves' individuality will become more widespread, if not mainstream. But, she says, a female figurehead is empowering.

Good point.

“Cardi B and I are not the same, but it is really, really good to see people who look like you being successful,” she emphasizes. “When you see people like yourself continually beat down, it’s harder to reach goals that should otherwise be achievable.” 18

In summary, Laban has pointed out how unfairly some female rappers have been treated, even though many are talented and successful. More work needs to be done so all are given an equal opportunity for achieving success.

Source: Laban, Linda. “Will New Female Rappers Shatter Hip Hop’s Glass Ceiling?” SXSW 2018. Used by permission.

Activity Interpreting an Essay

Choose an interesting article from a newspaper, magazine, or online source that relates to your major or a particular interest or hobby.

Pre-read and anticipate: Preview the article and make predictions about what it will cover.

Read and analyze: Read through the text and determine the main points, supporting points, and rhetorical star.

Reread and annotate: Go through the text more thoroughly and annotate it with your comments. You might circle vocabulary words, write questions, summarize material, create a visual organizer, and write a synthesis.

Note: You may want to choose a reading selection from later in this textbook or a chapter from a textbook for another class.

4.2 Participating in Class Discussions about Readings

Whether you are taking your composition course on campus or online, your instructor will likely have you discuss some of the readings for the course. Here are some tips to follow for live or virtual class discussions:

1. Read the selection carefully, and have your notes and annotations handy during the discussion.
2. Skim through the questions at the end of the selection in case your instructor asks you to discuss some of them in class or in a threaded discussion.
3. Listen to (or read) your classmates’ comments with an open mind.
4. Share your opinions about the work, even if they contradict another classmate’s opinion. However, be tactful with your responses. Also, you will need to support your opinions with specific details and examples from the text. Remember to use quotation marks for exact wording you use from the text.

5. Feel free to ask questions about areas of the text that are confusing or ambiguous (having more than one interpretation). If you have a question about a text, you are probably not the only one in the class who does.
6. Take notes during the discussion. You never know what might show up later on a test or writing assignment.

Graduate SPOTLIGHT

Jake Ellis, Media Designer

Courtesy of Jake Ellis

Jake Ellis is a media designer for a large entertainment and theme park company. He has a BFA degree in sound design. Here's what Ellis has to say about how he uses writing in his career:

" I work on a project team with members from across the globe, and we design and create theme park rides and shows. When I need to communicate with someone in California or overseas, then e-mail is the best method. I have to be sure to explain what I am working on very clearly for the project to run smoothly. At the beginning of a project, I write a scope document, which defines what our team expects to deliver for a particular project. Our project managers and creative directors review the scope document to let us know if something needs to be added to our plan. Once the scope document is finalized, it serves as a contract to communicate our team's goals and exactly what needs to be done to complete the project. The scope document also helps the team to get funding for the project, so it has to be well written. After we complete a project, I write a technical report that explains everything we have done. The technical report serves as a user guide, which includes details about how to maintain a particular ride or show and whom to contact if there is a problem. This guide is critical for ensuring that our attractions run smoothly so that our guests can have a great time at our theme parks. "

4.3 Reading and Interpreting Visual Texts

Visual texts surround you on a daily basis. Sometimes visual texts accompany written texts, and other times they appear alone. You find them in e-mail messages, websites, magazines, television shows, films, billboards, textbooks, and newspapers. Similar to written texts, visual texts are designed to serve a particular purpose and convey a message to the reader. People who are visually literate are best able to make sense of them.

Visual literacy The ability to read and interpret a variety of visual texts.

Visual literacy refers to the skill of being able to read and interpret a variety of visual texts. While visual texts may seem easier to understand than written texts, often they are not. For example, the message is frequently a little more challenging to discern. Understanding the hidden meanings in visual texts requires many of the critical thinking strategies that you use for written texts. You can make annotations to visual images next to the image itself or in the form of interpretation notes. The list that follows provides some ideas to consider when analyzing different images, such as photographs and paintings, charts and graphs, and advertisements.

Reading and Interpreting Visual Texts

1. **Subject:** Does the image focus on people, objects, numbers, a setting, or an event? How is the subject matter portrayed? What kind of action is taking place (if any)?
2. **Purpose:** Is the goal to evoke emotions, persuade the viewer to do something, provide an example of a concept, or visually represent ideas presented in a written text? What message is being conveyed?
3. **Audience:** Who is targeted by the image? Is it geared toward the general public, or is it aimed at people who represent a particular education level, age group, background, ethnicity, attitude, religious affiliation, hobby, or other group?
4. **Writing:** If written text is included, how is it integrated with the visual image? Does the text consist of just a caption, or are more details included? Do the written text and visual image complement each other, or are they contradictory? Which receives more emphasis, the written or the visual aspects of the text?
5. **Logic:** Is the image misleading in any way, or does it fairly and accurately represent the subject?
6. **Effectiveness:** Does the image or advertisement accomplish its purpose? Is it convincing? Why or why not?

Note: See Tables 4.1, 4.2, and 4.3 for examples of interpretation notes for an image (poster), a graph, and an advertisement.

Visual texts surround us every day. They are designed to serve a particular purpose and convey a specific message.
Lars A. Niki

Interpreting an Image

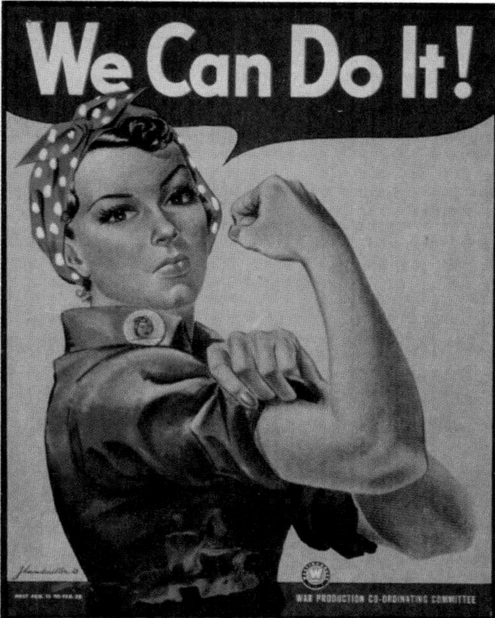

War Production Coordinating Committee, "We Can Do It!" poster.

Source: National Archives and Records Administration

Table 4.1

Image Interpretation Notes	
Subject	"We Can Do It!" The photo is of a poster developed in 1942 by Westinghouse Electrical Company that depicts a strong-looking woman (now known as Rosie the Riveter) flexing her bicep muscles. She is wearing a blue work shirt and a red polka-dotted scarf on her head that mostly hides her brunette hair, other than a few curly locks sticking out. The expression on the woman's face is confident and capable. The background is a dark yellow.
Purpose	To persuade women to join the war effort.
Audience	Women primarily, especially housewives who might consider joining the labor force by working in factories to produce items needed for World War II.
Writing	The title is very catchy. While the picture of a woman stands out the most, the "We Can Do It!" text, which looks like a cartoon bubble to indicate the woman is saying it, is significant. The text sounds very motivational. The signature of J. Howard Miller appears in the lower left corner, giving credit to the artist. The dates to post the sign also appear in the lower left corner of the poster. Finally, the Westinghouse Electrical Company logo and the War Production Co-Ordinating Committee identification are displayed in the lower right corner.
Logic	The poster is presented clearly and effectively. There are no tricks or apparent flaws in logic.
Effectiveness	The poster appears to be very motivational. Many women who would not have ordinarily taken on jobs outside the home during that era did join the workforce. The poster is now considered to be an icon of World War II.

Interpreting a Graph

Social Media = Positive & Negative

Do Social Media Platforms You Use Make These Health-Related Factors Better or Worse?

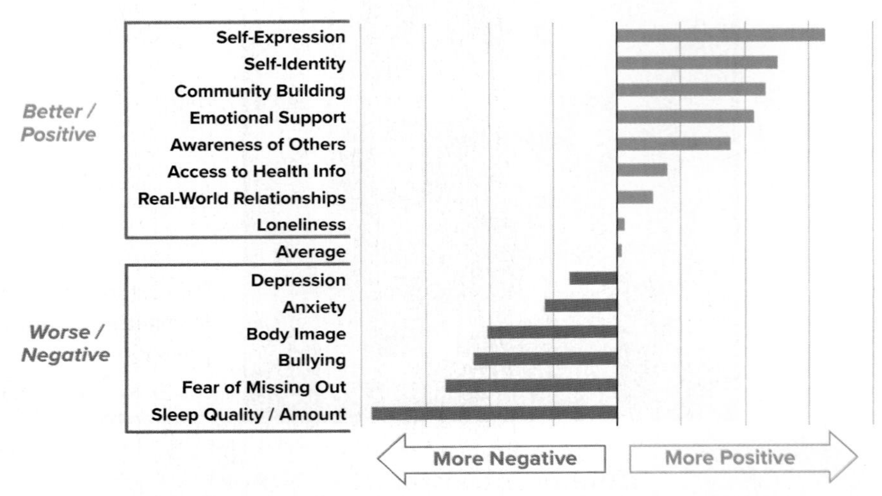

BOND Internet Trends 2019

Source: Royal Society For Public Health Survey of 1,479 British teens in 'early-2017'. Each teen was asked to rate 5 of the most popular social networks (YouTube, Facebook, Twitter, Snapchat & Instagram) on each dimension. Data presented = average of scores for each social netwrok.

The Health Effects of Social Media on Teens

Source: Mary Meeker.

Table 4.2

Graph Interpretation Notes	
Subject	Social media: The bar graph displays British teens' perceptions of the positive and negative effects of social media by considering several health-related factors. The graph indicates that the positive and negative effects are fairly equally balanced. More specifically, the graph indicates which factors are affected positively and which are affected negatively.
Purpose	The purpose of the bar graph is to demonstrate visually that social media (specifically YouTube, Facebook, Twitter, Snapchat, and Instagram) have both positive and negative health-related effects on teenagers.

Audience	The audience is comprised of anyone interested in social media trends, including teenagers who use social media; parents of teenagers; and teachers, psychologists, social workers, and health care providers who work with teenagers.
Writing	To accompany the bar graph and related text, the question the teens were asked was: "Do social media platforms you use make these health-related factors better or worse?" The headings *Better/Positive* and *Worse/Negative* are displayed, as well as the list of positive and negative health-related factors. The arrows with the labels *More Negative* and *More Positive* are also useful. Below the graph is an explanation that 1,479 teens took the survey in early 2017 in response to a question about five specific social media networks, and that the data presented equals the average of scores for each social network platform.
Logic	The graph and text seem to display a reasonably logical cause-and-effect analysis. The source, the Royal Society for Public Health, is reputable. The sample size is fairly large and seems adequate. It's hard to say if the graph's findings would also represent teens from other countries because all of the survey respondents are from Great Britain. Additionally, the graph is based solely on teens' perceptions, which may or may not be accurate.
Effectiveness	The graph is effective at raising awareness of the potential positive and negative health-related factors of teens using social media. It is also effective at showing which specific health factors are affected more positively or negatively for teens who use social media.

Activity Interpreting a Visual Text

Choose an image, a graph, or an advertisement in a printed or an online textbook, magazine, or newspaper. Interpret the image based on its subject, purpose, audience, writing, logic, and effectiveness. You may want to share your chart with another classmate or group. See Tables 4.1, 4.2, and 4.3 for examples of interpretation notes for an image, graph, or advertisement.

Interpreting an Ad

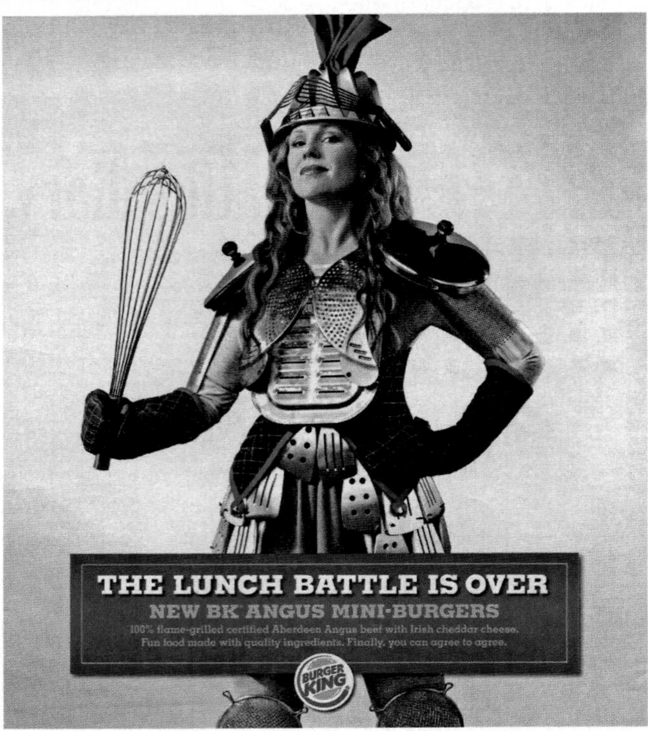

Source: The Advertising Archives

Table 4.3

Advertisement Interpretation Notes	
Subject	Burger King Angus Mini-Burgers: The ad contains an image of a woman wearing armor made of cooking utensils, pot lids, and other kitchen supplies. A small picture of the Burger King logo appears near the bottom of the ad along with more details about the burgers.
Purpose	To persuade the readers that they should go to Burger King and eat angus mini-burgers for lunch.
Audience	People who enjoy hamburgers and like to eat out for lunch.
Writing	The heading near the bottom of the ad states, "THE LUNCH BATTLE IS OVER." Below that in slightly smaller letters appears the subheading, "NEW BK ANGUS MINI-BURGERS." The fine print at the bottom explains the benefits of the new angus burgers and points out that they are flame-grilled, high quality, and enjoyable.
Logic	The image gives the audience the impression that the burgers are made by a motherly person in a kitchen. The woman in armor catches the readers' attention because she looks like a combination of a medieval warrior and mom with a friendly smile.
Effectiveness	The ad is effective because the image of the woman is eye-catching and the Burger King logo is easily recognizable. Many people eat fast food during a break from work or school. Also, many people might like to try something new. Overall, the ad is fairly catchy and persuasive.

Reading and Interpreting Websites

Critical thinking skills are especially important when it comes to analyzing websites. Unlike most books, magazines, television shows, and movies, some websites do not go through a review process. That means anyone with limited computer skills can post something on the Web, no matter how inaccurate it may be. While the Internet is an extremely valuable tool for obtaining information, you want to be sure that the ideas and images presented on a particular site are trustworthy. Use professional websites from reputable organizations. Here are some tips for making sure that the websites you use are useful and credible:

1. **Source:** Notice who posted the information on the Web. Is the author an expert in the field with the appropriate credentials? Is the organization reputable? If you have doubts about the author or organization, then you may want to investigate by searching for a biography of the author or the history of the organization. Also, check the uniform resource locator (URL). Look for clues that tell you about the identity of the website. For example, commercial sites end in "com," government sites end in "gov," educational sites end in "edu," and nonprofit organization sites end in "org."
2. **Date:** Check to see when the information was posted. In many cases you will want to have the most up-to-date information. If the information seems too old, then find a more current source.
3. **Logic:** If the claims seem too good to be true or highly improbable, then you will want to verify the information by consulting another source.
4. **References:** Notice if the website documents its sources. Many reputable sites will include a bibliography to back up the information they present. If there is a list of sources, look to see if they seem appropriate. If no sources are cited, then you should be wary of the information, unless an expert with good credentials provides the ideas.
5. **Visual images:** Use the strategies you read about earlier in this chapter to analyze the visual material included in the website. If you can hardly believe what you're looking at, then it's possible that a photograph has been altered and is intentionally misleading.
6. **Links:** See if the links work and if they lead to useful information. If they don't work or seem inappropriate, then you'll want to try another website.
7. **Effectiveness:** How useful is the content? Is it relevant? Is it presented clearly and logically? Does the material seem accurate? If a website you are viewing seems to be inaccurate, then you can always go to an *anti-hoax site* to check its validity. Two popular anti-hoax sites are **www.nonprofit.net/hoax** and **www.scambusters.org**. If the website you are viewing is listed, then find a new source.

Interpreting a Website

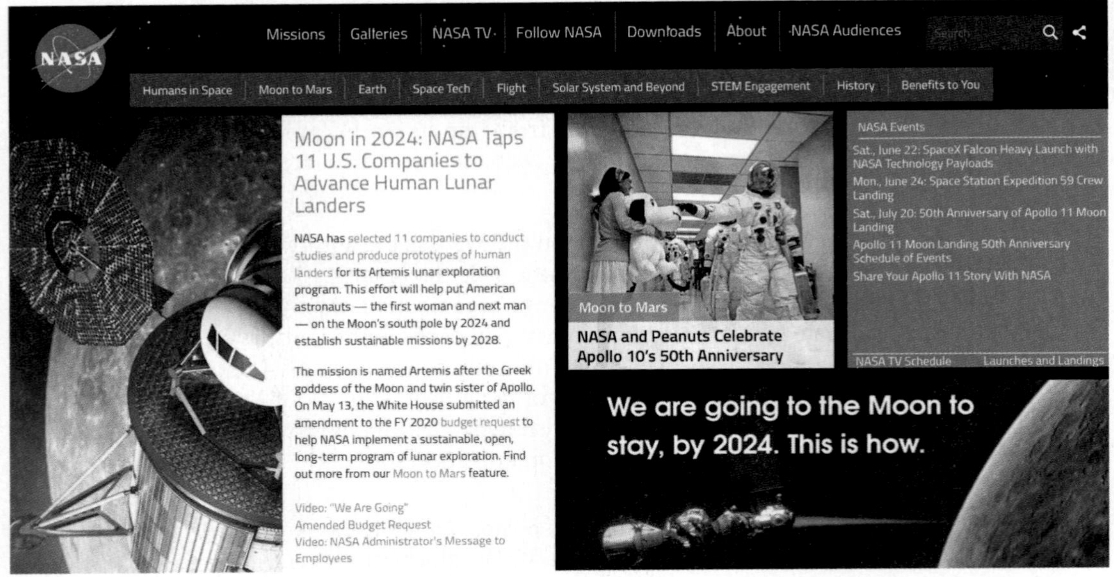

National Geographic, "Explore Today" Web page.

Source: NASA. www.nasa.gov

Table 4.4

Website Interpretation Notes	
Source	NASA: The URL ends in "gov," so the information provided should be reliable and legitimately from NASA.
Date	The material on this website is updated regularly, so the information is always current.
Logic	The website presents factual information in a clear and effective manner. The articles, events, videos, and photographs are designed to create interest in the space program at NASA.
References	The articles on this website include source material and quotes from experts in their respective fields.
Visual Images	The visual images throughout the website are stunning and accurately reflect the content they accompany.
Links	All of the links work, and they lead to useful information from reputable sources.
Effectiveness	The website is quite effective. In addition to the story about human lunar landers in the screenshot, the website covers a wide variety of other subjects related to planets, the solar system, humans in space, and space technology. This would be a useful Web source for a research project on anything related to science and outer space.

Activity Interpreting a Website

Go to **www.malepregnancy.com**, or choose another website that interests you. You might consider a site on a topic that you would like to investigate further. Complete a chart, like the one in Table 4.4, giving your interpretation of the site. You may want to share your chart with another classmate or group.

4.4 Logical Fallacies

Logical reasoning uses sound judgment. **Logical fallacies,** on the other hand, occur when someone draws a conclusion without using sound reasoning. To identify logical fallacies, or flaws in reasoning, you have to think critically about the written and visual texts you read. Sometimes writers purposely employ logical fallacies to try to mislead the reader into seeing things a particular way. For instance, politicians and advertisers may use logical fallacies to try to fool their audiences into believing they are the best candidate or have the best product. Such tactics are not an ethical means of influencing an audience. Other times writers use logical fallacies inadvertently as they try to prove a point because they are not aware of the flawed reasoning they are presenting.

Logical fallacies Occur when someone draws a conclusion not based on sound reasoning.

False authority or testimonial fallacy: James Bond wears an Omega watch, so you should wear one too.

Source: The Advertising Archives

As you read written and visual texts, you need to be familiar with logical fallacies so that you can recognize them and take them into account in your analysis. Also, you will want to avoid using flawed logic in your own writing. Table 4.5 presents a few of the most common types of logical fallacies.

Table 4.5

Logical Fallacies			
Type	**Definition**	**Example**	**Explanation**
Band Wagon Appeal	Implying that an idea must be true if it is popular. Join the crowd.	Everyone knows that holistic medicine is better than traditional medicine.	Even if many people believe it, that doesn't provide scientific proof for the argument.
Card Stacking	Providing evidence for only one side of a case or deliberately omitting essential information that would change the reader's opinion.	Sunni should get a promotion because she has never missed a day at work and she completes all of her tasks in a timely manner.	Supervisors consider many factors when deciding whom to promote. Maybe Sunni often arrives late or does poor work.
Character Attack or *Ad Hominem* Attack	Attacking a person rather than an issue.	Candidate X should not become the next company president because he divorced his wife and married his assistant.	His private life has nothing to do with whether or not he would make a good company president.
Circular Reasoning or Begging the Question	Attempting to support a position by simply restating it in a different way.	Dr. Brilliant is a good instructor because he teaches his students well.	The idea is merely being repeated without offering any specific evidence as to what makes Dr. Brilliant an effective instructor.
Either/Or Reasoning	Suggesting there are only two possible solutions to a problem (one right and one wrong) when, in reality, there could be many potential options for resolving the issue.	Either the government needs to subsidize gas costs or our economy is going to collapse.	First of all, does the entire economy depend on the price of gas? Also, there are several ways to cut down on fuel costs other than having the government help to offset the price.
False Analogy	Comparing things that are not similar in the most important respects.	The governor hit the jackpot with the new property tax increase proposal.	The governor is not gambling, so the analogy doesn't make sense.

Table 4.5 (*cont.*)

Logical Fallacies			
Type	**Definition**	**Example**	**Explanation**
False Authority or Testimonial	Mentioning an authority figure or celebrity as support for arguing a point.	Eric Zane, who plays Dr. Mark Gnome on *Haye's Anatomy,* recommends taking "Cure It All" pills, so they must be effective.	Eric Zane is an actor playing a role, not a real doctor, so he is not qualified to recommend a specific type of treatment.
False Cause or *Post Hoc*	Suggesting that because one thing happened after another, the first event caused the second one.	I ate chocolate and my sore throat disappeared.	The sore throat could have gone away for another reason unrelated to the chocolate.
Glittering Generality	Using emotionally charged words, such as *love, truth, honor, democracy,* and *justice,* to gain the audience's approval.	If you are truly patriotic, you need to do the honorable thing and vote to increase your local sales tax.	The implication is that voting a particular way will determine if someone is (or is not) patriotic and honorable.
Hasty Generalization	Drawing a conclusion without having sufficient evidence.	A child comes home two days in a row without homework, so the parent assumes that the teacher has stopped assigning homework.	The child may have forgotten to bring home the work or may be intentionally misleading the parent.
Non Sequitur	The conclusion does not logically follow the evidence that is provided.	Fast-food chains are very popular in the United States. No wonder obesity is so common.	Many factors contribute to high obesity rate in the United States. One can't assume that there is only one cause or that fast-food chains are the cause of obesity.
Red Herring	Diverting the reader's attention from the main issue by introducing something irrelevant. It comes from the practice of dragging a stinky fish across the ground to distract tracking dogs away from a scent.	The idea of gay marriages is an important issue, but do gay people really want to deal with all of the pressures associated with marriage?	The second part is irrelevant because it has nothing to do with whether gay marriages should be legal or not.

—continued

Table 4.5 (*cont.*)

Logical Fallacies			
Type	**Definition**	**Example**	**Explanation**
Slippery Slope	Suggesting that if one change occurs, then other, unwanted, changes will inevitably occur as well. The analogy is that once someone starts sliding down a "slippery slope," he or she won't be able to stop.	If we allow dogs on the beach, then the next thing you know dogs will be sitting at tables in fine restaurants.	The two events are unrelated, so there's no reason to assume that one event will lead to the other.
Stereotyping	Attaching a trait to people who belong to a particular religious, ethnic, racial, age, or other group.	Old people make terrible drivers, so they shouldn't be allowed to drive.	This is an unfair claim because many senior citizens are fine drivers.
Tradition	If something has always been done a certain way, then it must be the correct way.	Our company has always bought cigars and champagne for our clients during the holidays. We don't need to change to something else.	Just because the tradition is long-standing doesn't mean that it's a good one. Some clients may not like cigars, and some might not be able to tolerate alcohol. Another gift might be more appropriate.

Activity Identifying Logical Fallacies

A. Identify and explain the fallacies in these statements. Note that some statements contain more than one fallacy:
   1. Amalie Dubois speaks English as a second language, so she will never be a good writer.
   2. People who ride motorcycles are all rebellious outlaws who should be locked up in prison.
   3. Dean Meanzie is incompetent because he doesn't know what he is doing.
   4. We should nominate Susie Saucer for president of the Student Government Association because she gets good grades in math class.
   5. Either the college will have to allow students to retake classes for free, or the enrollment is going to seriously decrease.
   6. Everyone eats at Princess Pizza after the game, so that restaurant must have the best pizza in town.

B. Choose five types of logical fallacies and write original examples for each of them. If possible, trade lists with another classmate or group. Identify the fallacies in each other's examples and explain why the reasoning is flawed.

STUDENT WRITING

Stacie Ross wrote the following essay in response to an advertisement for milk, sponsored by America's Milk Processors, that she came across in *Women's Health.* The image shown here contains the original advertisement used with the addition of a person comparing herself to Olympian Dara Torres.

The Body of an Olympian

by Stacie Ross

1 Would you like to have a lean, sculpted, and healthy body? Drinking milk could help you develop the body of an Olympian. Well, that is the message implied in the milk advertisement that appeared in *Women's Health* magazine. It's summer, that time of year when people will wear fewer clothes and want to look their best doing it. Subscribers are reading this magazine in hopes of learning new ways to achieve a healthier lifestyle. The "got milk?" ad is convincing because the images and words inspire readers to want to add nutritious milk to their diets so they can experience the healthful benefits.

Marion Curtis, StarPix/AP Images

2 The purpose of the ad is to convince readers that they too should drink milk after exercising to obtain the same wellness as an Olympic swimmer. The ad never makes any claims that anyone who drinks milk three times a day can look as good as Dara Torres, yet viewers cannot help but wonder if their bodies would look like that. Nor does that ad imply that drinking milk gives Dara the stamina to train hard and achieve picture perfect results. However, when consumers see this ad, they might want to knock back a big cool glass of low-fat or fat-free milk.

3 Additionally, the images in the ad are quite appealing and serve to make the ad more persuasive. There is an ocean of calm, blue water that seems to go on forever. It just about makes the readers want to jump in and go for a swim. Then there are the huge, fluffy, milky white clouds that let the reader almost feel the cool, gentle wind. There stands forty-six-year-old, five-times Olympic swimmer, Dara "Dairy" Torres with all her rippling muscles, wearing a tiny bikini, and sporting a thick milk mustache. On a warm summer day, after a long, exhausting workout, athletes would want a cold, revitalizing drink to help them cool down.

4 Finally, Dara Torres's words in the "got milk?" advertisement add to its credibility. Dara states, "I'm a natural in water. But after a workout, my natural choice is milk." She also gives the readers a few facts about milk: "The protein helps build muscle, plus its unique mix of nutrients helps me refuel. Three glasses of lowfat

or fat free milk a day. Lap it up." Her statements might convince the readers that milk is the logical choice of beverage they need to be strong and healthy. Many of the readers of *Women's Health* magazine are aware that the National Institutes of Health has been advising consumers to drink more milk for years. Furthermore, women have become more aware of the fact that they need to consume enough calcium daily to promote bone health and prevent osteoporosis. Savvy readers will react positively to the ad when they are reminded of these facts.

Most readers realize they will never attain the 5
physique of Dara Torres. However, after viewing the "got milk?" advertisement in *Women's Health* magazine, many might just be persuaded to add a glass or two with their daily meals or after a workout. Why not drink milk if it could possibly help one to obtain the body of an Olympian?

QUESTIONS FOR REFLECTION

1. What kind of attention-getter does Ross use? Is it effective? Why or why not?
2. Identify Ross's thesis. What is her overall opinion of the "got milk?" advertisement? Do you agree or disagree with her position? Why?
3. What are the main points in the essay? Are the body paragraphs in the essay organized effectively? Why or why not?
4. Find examples of transitions in the essay. Are they helpful? Are there enough transitions for Ross's essay to flow smoothly? Explain.
5. The advertisement uses the testimonial of a famous Olympian to help encourage consumers to buy milk. Is it logical for Dara Torres to sell milk? Is she a credible authority figure for this product? Why or why not?

Activity Write a Response to a Text in This Chapter

Use the critical thinking skills you have learned in this chapter to write a response to the "We Can Do It!" poster on page 77 or another visual image, website, or written text. For the subject you choose, fill in an interpretation chart like the one in this chapter for that type of subject (for example, if you are responding to a website, use the chart on page 82).

CHAPTER SUMMARY

1. Strengthening your critical thinking skills will help you to become a better reader, writer, and decision maker.
2. Learning to read written texts, visual texts, and websites with a critical eye will help you to strengthen your reading and writing skills.
3. Applying your critical thinking skills during a live or online class discussion will help you to strengthen your reading and writing skills.
4. Learning to recognize logical fallacies will help you to strengthen your critical thinking, reading, and writing skills.

WHAT I KNOW NOW

Use this checklist to determine what you need to work on in order to feel comfortable with your understanding of the material in this chapter. Check off each item as you master it. Review the material for any unchecked items.

☐ 1. I know what **critical thinking** means.

☐ 2. I am familiar with the **three-step reading process.**

☐ 3. I know how to use an **interpretation chart** to evaluate a written text, image, or website.

☐ 4. I am aware of strategies I can use to communicate in **class discussions.**

☐ 5. I know how to recognize several different types of **logical fallacies.**

Design elements: ***Graduate Spotlight:*** **Ingram Publishing/AGE Fotostock**

PART 2

Writing Strategies

Why Writing Strategies Can Be Combined

Each chapter in Part 2 is based on a writing strategy and a theme, so the readings and images are connected. The writing strategies are addressed one at a time so that you can master the specific skills that each type of writing requires. You may want to practice the strategies individually at first to become proficient with them. As you become more comfortable with each technique, then you may want to begin combining writing strategies as needed.

In many writing situations, writing methods are combined, depending on the circumstances of the writing task. For example, someone writing an article about yoga might begin by describing what yoga is. Then the author may explain the physical and mental benefits (effects) of participating in yoga to convince (persuade) the reader that learning to do yoga is worthwhile. Finally, the writer might explain the steps in the process so that the reader understands what to do. You will notice that many of the readings in this text reflect the common practice of mixing writing strategies. As you go about your writing assignments in Part 2, you will want to choose the writing methods that best suit your rhetorical star.

OVERVIEW of Part 2

CHAPTER 5

Describing and Narrating: Memories

Ariel Skelley/Getty Images+

learning outcomes

In this chapter you will learn techniques for achieving these learning outcomes:

5.1 Identify real-world applications for writing a descriptive narrative. *p. 93*

5.2 Understand the qualities of an effective descriptive narrative. *p. 95*

5.3 Interpret images and descriptive narrative readings about memories. *p. 104*

5.4 Analyze the rhetorical star for describing and narrating. *p. 117*

5.5 Apply the qualities of descriptive narrative writing. *p. 118*

Writing Strategy Focus: Describing and Narrating

Narration is the art of storytelling. When we narrate a story, we retell the event or series of events, based on our memories, so that someone who wasn't there has a good idea of what happened. To make narratives more vivid, include descriptive writing that appeals to the readers' senses. Although narratives can be fiction, this chapter focuses mostly on real, nonfiction narratives. While fictitious stories are fabricated, nonfiction narratives need to be based on events that really occurred.

We are constantly surrounded by stories in the news, documentaries, movies, television programs, commercials, and even Facebook posts. We find others' stories engaging because they allow us to peek into someone else's world. Sometimes we relate to the experiences of the storyteller, and other times we are surprised by the unique situations that others have faced. In this chapter you will have an opportunity to read about others' memories and to write about your own. Storytelling, however, is not limited to your personal life; you can also use descriptive narrative writing in college and in the workplace.

5.1 Real-World Applications for Describing and Narrating

Writing Descriptive Narratives in College

You will have many opportunities to write descriptive narratives in college. You might need to retell what happened during an important historical event. Your humanities instructor may ask you to attend a cultural event, such as a concert or play, and write about the experience. If doing fieldwork is a requirement for your major, your instructor may ask that you keep a narrative journal to document what you observe and do while in the field.

Writing Descriptive Narratives in Your Daily Life

Writing descriptive narratives can also be an important part of your personal life. You may choose to keep a travel journal to document some of the places you visit. You might want to write stories about special occasions and events on your Facebook page. If you have children, you may decide to keep a baby book where you record the details of their most memorable experiences so they can read about them when they're older. Additionally, if you have any special interests or hobbies, you may decide to participate in online forums and contribute to Weblogs (blogs) to retell stories related to your interest to fellow participants.

Writing Descriptive Narratives in Your Career

Being able to write a descriptive narrative can be critical to your career. Before interviewing for a job, you can benefit from writing a cover letter telling about some of your relevant work experiences to supplement your résumé. If you're applying for a promotion, you might write a report for your bosses, telling them about your past accomplishments and describing why you are a worthy candidate for the position. If you notice a problem with a procedure or an employee in your workplace, you may need to write a descriptive narrative retelling the exact details of what occurred so that the problem can be resolved. Including accurate details in a narrative can be crucial because a poorly written narrative can cost a company money, lead to a lawsuit, or cause injury or even death. Here are a few specific applications for writing descriptive narratives on the job:

Health care: patient history, patient care report, accident report, medical narratives.

Law: deposition, court report, letter explaining an event to a client or opposing party, police report.

Education: report card narratives, observations of students or other teachers, newsletters to parents.

Homeland security: recollection of a terrorist event, details about past or current safety plans.

Business: history of financial activities for the IRS, story about a grand opening, explanation of findings for an audit report.

Culinary arts: regional history for a menu, story of how your restaurant got started for a newspaper or a magazine article.

Graduate SPOTLIGHT

Doug Tolliver, Ultrasound Technologist

Doug Tolliver has a degree in diagnostic medical sonography. He works as an ultrasound technologist in a hospital. Here's what Tolliver has to say about the importance of written communication to his career:

©Karin L. Russell

“Writing is really important to my work at the hospital. When a patient's image comes up on the screen, I have to annotate the image for the doctors, describing exactly what I see. After that, I have to write a narrative explaining how I read each scan. For example, if I see a cancerous mass, an aneurysm, or a degenerative fetal condition, I must explain that in my notes. I also have to document in the patient's chart exactly what procedure I performed with the date and time. All of this documentation is important because the doctor will use the information I write to give a diagnosis to the patient. Therefore, writing an accurate narrative is critical to the patient's health and safety.”

Computers: story to accompany a video game being designed, history of how a computer company or program was developed, explanation documenting how a particular program was created.

Activity **Writing Real-World Descriptive Narratives**

On your own, in pairs, or in small groups, brainstorm uses for writing descriptive narratives at school, in your daily life, and on the job. You may want to choose your own career field or the prospective career field(s) of the participants in your group. Be prepared to share your results.

5.2 How to Write an Effective Descriptive Narrative

Before reading professional or student examples of descriptive narrative writing, you will need to understand the qualities involved. Look for these characteristics when you read the selected essays in this chapter, and follow these suggestions when you write your own narrative essays.

1. Establish a Clear Purpose

Your introductory paragraph should include some kind of attention-getter to engage your readers in your descriptive narrative. For instance, you could begin your essay with an intriguing statement, such as, "As I stood at the edge of the hazy woods at dusk, I had the distinct sensation that I was not alone."

State or Imply the Thesis. When writing a descriptive narrative, typically you will want to state your thesis early so readers know what to expect as they continue reading. For example, your thesis might be "Surviving Hurricane Irma helped me to fully appreciate how precious my family is to me." Occasionally, you might save your thesis for the ending of your narrative, as a lesson or moral to your story. This technique is particularly effective when you're trying to surprise your audience. Sometimes it may be appropriate to imply your thesis. When you leave the thesis unstated, you lead your reader to draw a conclusion about your descriptive narrative. In most types of essays, however, the thesis should appear in the introduction.

Develop a Title. Create a title for your descriptive narrative that will entice your readers. It can be fairly precise, such as "Backpacking on the Appalachian Trail," or a little more vague, such as "The Night When Terror Struck My Family's Home."

Even though your title and introduction will come first in your final essay, many writers find success in writing them later. If you use that technique, be sure to have a preliminary thesis in mind as you write the body of your essay.

Grammar Window
POINT OF VIEW

First person: I, me, my, mine, we, our, ours

Second person: you, yours

Third person: he, she, they, their, theirs

The point of view needs to be consistent within a sentence or paragraph or readers will become confused. Watch for sentences where the point of view shifts for no reason.

Exercise

Correct the shifts in point of view in the following sentences:

1. I looked at the spider and you got really scared.
2. You were driving along and they saw something furry cross the road.

2. Identify the Time and Place

Somewhere in the early part of your descriptive narrative you will need to mention when and where the event occurred. If you are writing about a really important event in your life, you may be able to give an exact date and time as well as a precise location of where the action took place. Keep in mind that an essay shouldn't read like a list of diary entries.

- **Time:** If you don't want to date yourself, you might just mention that the event occurred on the eve of your ninth birthday. Mentioning the time of year may also be relevant to your story. For example, hiking in the mountains in winter is quite different from doing so in spring or summer.
- **Place:** Telling where the event took place will help readers better understand your story. Provide the readers with physical descriptions of the setting, including the natural environment, building, room, décor—whatever is necessary for your audience to visualize the events in your story.

3. Keep a Consistent Point of View

Although it is not appropriate in all types of academic and workplace writing, when you write about yourself it is typically best to use the first person point of view. Be careful not to begin too many sentences with *I.* Vary your sentence structure and approach. Also, generally it is better not to shift to the second person point of view; however, sometimes authors use *you* intentionally to make the readers feel as if they are right there in the story. If you do shift your point of view, make sure you are doing so for a reason. A sentence such as "*I* was so scared because *you* didn't know what was going to happen next" can confuse your readers. If you are writing a narrative about someone else, then you should write in the third person point of view, using pronouns such as *he, she,* and *they.*

Activity Shifting Viewpoints

Write a one-paragraph descriptive narrative about yourself in the first person point of view. Revise your narrative using the third person point of view. For example, your first version might start as follows: "When I was in 10th grade, I. . . ." Your second version might start this way: "When Danielle was in 10th grade, she. . . ." Be prepared to share your paragraphs and discuss how each version might affect the audience.

4. Keep the Verb Tense Consistent

You should also be consistent in the verb tense or tenses you use throughout your narrative. You will probably want to retell your story in the past tense to show that the event or events happened previously. For example, you might say, "I went to the edge of the murky river to get a better view and was alarmed when an alligator burst out of the water and looked me straight in the eyes." However, you may prefer to keep the action in the present tense for a more dramatic effect: "As I am standing at the edge of the water to get a better view, I am alarmed when an alligator bursts out of the water and looks me straight in the eyes." Either choice can work, but be careful not to shift verb tenses and write, "While I *stood* at the edge of the murky river an alligator *looks* me straight in the eyes." Whichever tense you choose, make sure that you use it consistently.

5. Include Plenty of Details and Sensory Appeal

When you are writing a story, be sure to consider all of the journalist's questions: *who, what, where, when, why,* and *how.* Also, include ample sensory details to fully engage your readers. What did you see, hear, feel, smell, and taste? You will need to include enough concrete sensory details so that your reader fully grasps what it was like for you during the experience. You want your readers to feel something when they read your essay.

For example, if you are writing a story about a family reunion, let the readers *hear* the loud music playing and the children gleefully laughing in the background; help them *see* the multigenerational family members gathered around picnic tables adorned with colorful arrays of homemade delicacies; make them *feel* the warm, loving embrace of your favorite relative, Grandma Martha. However, be sure to not get so carried away with your details that your narrative loses its focus. Every detail you include should help support the main point of your narrative.

Grammar Window

VERB TENSES

Choose 5 to 10 interesting verbs. Write them in the present tense and then the past tense. For example:

Present Tense Verbs: blast, pass out, rush, startle, sting, trip.

Past Tense Verbs: blasted, passed out, rushed, startled, stung, tripped.

See the Editing Guide for more information on verb tenses.

Activity Writing to Appeal to the Senses

In pairs or small groups, share a few personal objects, drawings, or photographs that have special meaning or reveal something about you. The items should appeal to different senses. Take turns describing the items you chose and explaining why they are significant. As a team, come up with a dominant impression, original similes and/or metaphors, and a specific sensory appeal for each item. A representative from each group will share descriptive ideas about a couple of favorite items with the class. This activity may give you ideas for writing a descriptive essay.

Often you can enhance descriptive narrative writing by using figurative writing, such as similes and metaphors. Similes are comparisons that use *like* or *as*. For instance, if you are describing a dragonfly, you might say, "The dragonfly looks like a mini helicopter hovering over the bow of the canoe." Metaphors are more direct comparisons that do not use *like* or *as*. For example, you could say, "The dragonfly is a fragile mini helicopter hovering over the bow of the canoe."

Similes and metaphors can help you make your descriptions more vivid for the reader. However, be careful to use original similes and metaphors rather than clichés. You don't want to describe someone as being "as cool as a cucumber," because that simile has been used many times and lacks the element of freshness and surprise.

6. Present the Details in a Logical Sequence

When you write a descriptive narrative, you will typically want to present the events in chronological order. Use a variety of transitions to help your reader follow your sequence of events. Transitional expressions, such as *first, next, then,* and *after that,* will help keep your readers on track. (See Chapter 3 for more on transitions.) Experiment with different transitions to see which ones help your writing to flow smoothly. Your essay should not sound like a checklist, nor should it be one long paragraph. Instead, write fully developed paragraphs to get your point across to your audience.

You may even decide to include specific times or dates along the way to help make the flow of ideas clear for the reader. Sometimes it may be appropriate to include a flashback to illuminate an event that occurred before the action in your story. If you choose the flashback method, be sure to signal the change in sequence with a transition so you don't lose your readers. Also, don't overuse flashbacks. Your audience shouldn't have to read your descriptive narrative several times to figure out what happened when.

7. Use Dialogue Effectively

Often in a descriptive narrative you can use dialogue to help make your story more realistic. Including the exact words that someone says is often more effective than just summarizing that person's ideas. For example, it would be much more dramatic to quote your cousin saying "Help, I can't swim! Please save me!" than simply to state that Marisa said she couldn't swim and pleaded for someone to save her. If you do use dialogue, be sure to make the language appropriate for the speakers. Your four-year-old nephew shouldn't sound like a rocket scientist, and your great-grandmother shouldn't sound like a rap star.

8. Include Visual Aids If Appropriate

Pictures, diagrams, or other visual images can help your reader more fully comprehend the story you are retelling. For instance, if you are recalling an experience you had while white-water rafting, you might include a photograph of yourself on a raft. Make sure any images you include support, and don't overshadow, your writing. Your goal is to use your words to help the reader envision what happened.

9. End with a Thought-Provoking Conclusion

Your descriptive narrative needs to make a significant point about something that you learned or came to understand as a result of your experience. While the point doesn't have to be earth shattering, it should strike readers as relevant and interesting. However, don't make your ending sound mechanical by stating, "The point of this story is . . ." or "The lesson I learned is. . . ." Instead, wrap up your descriptive narrative in a natural way and end on a memorable note. For example, if your story is about the horrible calamities you suffered on a primitive camping trip in the wilderness, you might end by writing, "Although I am thrilled to have survived the challenges I faced in the Rocky Mountains, I've decided that my next vacation will be aboard a luxurious cruise ship. Grand Cayman, here I come!"

Career-Based DESCRIPTIVE NARRATIVE WRITING

[preview] **KRIS BISHOP** has an AA degree in rehabilitating assisting, which combines the fields of occupational and physical therapy, a BS degree in health services administration, and an MBA with a concentration in healthcare management. Her passion is working with older patients, and her career in occupational therapy has provided her with experience working with all age groups and in many practice settings including acute care, rehabilitation hospitals, skilled nursing facilities, and home care. Bishop wrote the following case narrative about a patient she treated, Mrs. Thompson, who was in declining health after the death of her husband and needed rehabilitation to increase her ability to manage several daily living skills.

Case Narrative **by Kris Bishop, COTA/L**

Each Wednesday the rehabilitation team members of the 120-bed skilled nursing and rehabilitation facility meet to discuss patients' progress and challenges on the sub-acute rehabilitation unit. Attending today's meeting was Mary, a Registered Nurse (RN); Sam, the Registered Physical Therapist (RPT); Renee, a Registered Occupational Therapist (OTR); Jeannie, the Discharge Planner; Betty, the Registered Dietician (RD); Terry, the Speech and Language Pathologist (SLP); and myself, a Certified Occupational Therapy Assistant (COTA). Facilitating the meeting was the Rehabilitation Director, Allison. 1

Patients who were admitted to this unit would be 2
scheduled for daily therapies as prescribed by their Physiatrist, a physician who specializes in physical medicine and rehabilitation, or a Gerontologist, who specializes in aging adults. Most of the patients who were discussed were meeting goals as identified on their individual care plans. Patients' rehabilitative services and skilled nursing care are reimbursed under a prospective payment system which predetermines how much the facility will be paid based upon diagnosis and other factors. This system has a strong influence on when services are provided and the length of time a beneficiary can

receive those services. Patients must make progress towards established goals, or they may not be eligible to continue with rehabilitation services such as occupational, speech, and physical therapies.

3 The patient who was being discussed was Mrs. Thompson, a 75-year-old widow. Her husband of fifty years had passed away suddenly about a year ago. Prior level of function indicates Mrs. Thompson was in good health with some chronic issues such as high cholesterol, obesity, and hypertension, which were controlled by oral medication and diet. She was independent in her activities of daily living including eating, grooming, bathing, transfers, and mobility. Her instrumental activities of daily living (IADL), which are more complex activities such as driving, community mobility, health management, meal preparation, shopping, financial management, and safety, were all intact. Mrs. Thompson had social support from her married daughter and three grandchildren who live in the same town. Sabrina, Mrs. Thompson's daughter, started to notice her mother was not driving much and was declining visits from her family and friends. Sabrina scheduled a doctor's appointment, and no significant medical problems were noted. Global mental functions such as orientation and temperament were not problematic. Her specific mental functions, such as attention, memory and thought processes, were noted to be within normal ranges. Energy, drive, and sleep quality were the only areas that were described as not at her prior level.

4 Despite this assessment and medical monitoring by her physician as well as the support of her family, Mrs. Thompson continued to decline. She no longer drove, and her daughter had to assist with managing the finances and homemaking. As the weeks passed, Mrs. Thompson rapidly lost her ability to ambulate, requiring the use of a cane, then a walker, and finally a wheelchair. She was unable to get in the shower without help and needed assistance with meals. Sabrina made arrangements for her mother to move in with her family and set up an area for her including a bedroom and bathroom. Mrs. Thompson continued to decline until she became bedridden. A mechanical lift was the only way that she could get out of her hospital bed. Sabrina's home was too small for all this necessary equipment, and her mother needed more care than she could provide. Mrs. Thompson was transported to the hospital for a full medical work up and, when stable, was discharged to the skilled nursing and rehabilitation unit in our skilled nursing facility.

5 When Mrs. Thompson arrived, she was completely bedbound. She was unable to raise her head off the pillow. She could not roll from side to side in the bed and was unable to tolerate the head of the bed being raised past 10 degrees. She was incontinent of bowel and bladder and needed total care for all of her activities of daily living such as bathing, grooming, and dressing. She was even unable to feed herself! The only thing she was able to do was watch television, and she was only able to use the remote control if it was positioned correctly in her hand. If she needed assistance, she required a light touch device to use her call system or she would yell for help. According to her medical history, there was no clear physical reason why the patient was unable to perform any activities. Her cognitive abilities were reassessed utilizing an Allen Cognitive Screening Assessment, and it was determined she would be able to learn new skills, her short term and long term memory were intact, and she verbalized motivation to return home and to her prior level of independence.

6 The rehabilitation team met previously, and it was decided that physical therapy would work with the patient first, with a goal of improving her active range of motion, strength, and endurance. The team established an exercise program that nursing could follow through with to facilitate more rapid progress. The physician decided that occupational therapy was not indicated until Mrs. Thompson could tolerate a higher level of activity. Unfortunately, Sam from physical therapy did not have a lot of success with Mrs. Thompson. She did not like exercising and made many excuses not to participate. Other PT's tried to motivate her without progressing towards goals. The treatment team discussed different options: discharging the patient back to the hospital for an additional medical workup prescribing psychiatric care, or discharging her to long-term custodial care. The consensus of the team was that she was poorly motivated, she had poor rehabilitation potential, and she should be

discharged from skilled services. As the case was being discussed, Renee, the OTR, and I decided to ask once again for orders for an evaluation to see if we could improve Mrs. Thompson's quality of life through adaptation of her environment and assistive devices. Occupational therapy was given an order to evaluate.

7 The occupational therapy evaluation measures many skills that could be utilized to return a patient to more purposeful activity. Strength, endurance, and range of motion are assessed as it relates to a person's ability to participate in an occupation. Manual muscle testing of her bilateral upper extremities revealed poor strength, which is defined as being unable to move an extremity to overcome gravity. The 9 Hole Peg Test was performed to assess fine motor skills, which were determined to be below normal range for her age. Sensory functions such as vision, hearing, balance, sensitivity to touch, smell, taste, pain, and kinesthesia are assessed for their impact on engaging in activity. Cognitive ability and motivational factors are factored into the evaluation. One of the most important aspects of an evaluation is to determine the patient's goals and interests. The patient is the most important member of the treatment team!

8 Upon completion of the evaluation, goals were established for environmental assessment and modifications to accommodate safe wheelchair mobility and use of a mechanical lift by the nursing staff. Development of a positioning program to prevent joint contractures and skin breakdown due to dependent mobility was also a goal. A restorative program was to be established to maintain passive range of motion. The long term goal was for the patient to be discharged to the Residential Care unit.

9 I was assigned to Mrs. Thompson for treatment to address goals as established by the Occupational Therapy evaluation. Part of an initial intervention involves establishing a rapport with the patient. We talked about her family—her late husband, daughter, son-in-law, and grandchildren. We chatted about what she did for work, her leisure interests, and what she wanted to accomplish. She shared her feelings about living in a nursing home for the rest of her life. The longer we worked together the more she opened up. She seemed to be more comfortable with the idea of occupational therapy and what she might accomplish. I gave her the opportunity to decide when she wanted her therapy sessions and on which goals we would focus for the day. I found out two things—she loved the game of Scrabble, and she was embarrassed for her grandchildren to see her in a nursing home. I had a game board at home and brought it in to challenge her to a game. She stated that she played the game regularly with her late husband, and she always won. One of our goals was to change her position to take the pressure off areas that were prone to breakdown. I positioned her on her side with the use of wedges and a pillow for support. Since she was right-hand dominant, I put her on her left side so she could manage the tiles with her right hand. She was so excited to play she cried! The next session she was positioned on her right side to use her left arm. We put light weights on her arms to increase her strength during play. We were making progress. Discussion with the OTR resulted in upgrading our goals to address bed mobility and sitting tolerance. Next, we positioned the board on an over-bed table and increased upright sitting by 10 degrees. She progressed with her sitting tolerance to 30-minute durations at about 75 degrees. This was adequate for her to begin to feed herself meals due to improved sitting tolerance and increased upper extremity strength.

10 At this point the goals need to be upgraded once again. Through occupation-based intervention, we were able to develop her ability to sit without the support of her hospital bed and progress to participation in bathing and grooming at the bedside. The next goal was transfers. Mrs. Thompson was so excited at her progress she agreed to work with Physical Therapy for lower-body strengthening and transfer training. The education on some basic adaptive equipment such as a long reacher, shoe horn, and leg lifter provided some additional motivation and help in regaining independence in lower body dressing.

11 Family education is important to help a patient in progressing with goals and maintaining accomplishments achieved in Occupational Therapy. While Mrs. Thompson's family members were supportive and visited regularly, they had not been involved

with her therapy sessions. With the patient's permission, I spoke with Sabrina and arranged a time she could meet with her mother and me. She was amazed at the progress her mother had made and what she was able to do. This facilitated a discussion with Mrs. Thompson about returning to live in her daughter's home. The patient was motivated to return home, and her family was excited to have her there. A home assessment session was scheduled to determine any environmental barriers to mobility and safety concerns and to provide recommendations.

12 It was determined that Mrs. Thompson would not have much assistance during the day due to her daughter's and son-in-law's work schedules and the children being in school, so there were a few more goals to address. She needed to be able to prepare simple meals for herself. She wanted to walk to the mailbox to get the mail. Her family wanted peace of mind that Mrs. Thompson would be safe during the day. I taught her safety techniques in the kitchen. We recommended that she obtain a personal response system so she could press the panic button if she got in trouble. Home health occupational and physical therapy was ordered so she could transition her skills to her home environment.

13 The final team meeting was her discharge meeting. Mrs. Thompson walked into and out of the meeting with her rolling walker without assistance. She returned home that week with her daughter, her grandchildren, and a profound sense of accomplishment. Her progress was a tribute to all the therapists who were part of her team and those who were able to think outside the box to help her achieve her goals. By the way, she never beat me in Scrabble, but she was clearly the winner.

Source: Kris Bishop.

QUESTIONS FOR REFLECTION

1. Bishop uses the first person point of view when she describes her treatment of Mrs. Thompson. How does this point of view affect the reader?
2. Which specific details from the descriptive narrative give you the clearest idea of what happened? Are the details presented in a logical sequence? Explain.
3. Bishop uses description and narration as her primary writing strategy, but she also uses comparison and contrast. Identify passages where she uses comparison and contrast and explain why those passages are significant to the narrative.
4. This case narrative goes beyond the details of the events that Bishop observed and includes information about the patient's personal life. Why do you suppose an occupational therapist would want to include that in a descriptive narrative? Is it useful information? Why or why not?
5. How do you feel about the ending of the narrative? Is the conclusion effective? Why or why not?

Career-Based DESCRIPTIVE NARRATIVE WRITING

[preview] **JUNIOR HIGH SCHOOL TEACHERS** know that, most of the time, things go smoothly in the classroom; however, occasionally a student needs help remembering basic courtesy. When things go awry, teachers usually have to describe the problem and the consequences on a discipline form to create a record for the school and the student's parent(s) or guardian(s). A junior high instructor completed the following discipline form when an incident occurred in his classroom. The names have been changed to protect the privacy of the individuals involved. Do you remember attending junior high school? What did some of the children do to get into trouble? What were the consequences?

School Discipline Form

Description of Infraction:

1 During today's science class Kenny was loud and unruly. He entered the classroom at the beginning of the period by pushing through the other students who were lined up at the door and then slammed his books down hard on the table. During our opening bell activity, he was turned around in his seat pestering another student to give him a pencil. When asked to turn around, he rudely said, "If I need a dumb pencil, what am I supposed to do?" Finally, during a paired reading activity, Kenny pulled a book out from his partner's hands while she was reading her assigned paragraph and told her to go get another one.

Explanation of Teacher Actions:

2 After Kenny talked back when he was turned around in his seat, I went to his desk and warned him that he needed to settle down and begin following the classroom procedures or he would need to go to the office. Taking his partner's book away from her was unacceptable and required disciplinary intervention.

Student Explanation:

3 Kenny did not provide further explanation, nor did he dispute Mr. Williams's account of the events.

Additional Information:

4 I called and discussed this matter with Kenny's mother on 11/12/2019. Kenny will be serving a 30-minute detention on 11/15/2019, and will write a letter of apology to his reading partner.

QUESTIONS FOR REFLECTION

Considering Writing Strategies

1. Based on the teacher's descriptive narrative, can you envision what happened? Explain.
2. Which words on the form are objective? Which words are subjective?
3. Why did the teacher include dialogue from the student in the report? Is it helpful? Why or why not?
4. Why did the teacher combine description and narration in the report? Is this approach effective? Why or why not?
5. Was Kenny's punishment fair? Why or why not?

Activity: Writing Descriptive Narratives as a Professional

Think about your existing or future career. Create a list of instances in which you might be asked to write a descriptive narrative. Explain the purpose and audience for these career narratives. Who or what would your writing affect? How important would the quality of your writing be? Be prepared to share your answers.

5.3 Describing and Narrating in the Context of Memories

Of all the resources we have as writers, our memories rank among the best. Without our memories, we would have little understanding of where we have been or where we are going. As human beings, we naturally look back over the past and recall experiences to help us make sense of our lives and our world. Some of our most poignant memories revolve around major life events, such as births and deaths, marriages and divorces, joyous occasions and tragedies. Before writing about your own memory, read one or more of the narratives that follow and answer the questions for reflection. Reading and interpreting the stories of others can help you write your own descriptive narratives for your daily life, school, and career.

Reading and Reflection DESCRIPTIVE NARRATIVE WRITING

[preview] **Harriet Ann Jacobs** (1813–97) was an African-American writer who spent 27 years as a slave before she was set free. Once free, she became an abolitionist speaker and reformer. Her book *Incidents in the Life of a Slave Girl,* from which the essay that follows is excerpted, was originally published in Boston, c. 1860 under the pseudonym Linda Brent. Jacobs was one of the first writers to chronicle the struggle for freedom by female slaves. Before reading, try to imagine what it would be like to have your civil liberties taken away from you without just cause. How would you feel? What would you do?

From *Incidents in the Life of a Slave Girl*
by Harriet Ann Jacobs

PREFACE BY THE AUTHOR

1 READER, be assured this narrative is no fiction. I am aware that some of my adventures may seem incredible; but they are, nevertheless, strictly true. I have not exaggerated the wrongs inflicted by Slavery;[1] on the contrary, my descriptions fall far short of the facts. I have concealed the names of places, and given persons fictitious names. I had no motive for secrecy on my own account, but I deemed it kind and considerate towards others to pursue this course.

2 . . . I was born and reared in Slavery; and I remained in a Slave State twenty-seven years. Since I have been at the North, it has been necessary for me to work diligently for my own support, and the education of my children. This has not left me much leisure to make up for the loss of early opportunities to improve myself; and it has compelled me to write these pages at irregular intervals, whenever I could snatch an hour from household duties.

3 When I first arrived in Philadelphia [. . . I was advised] to publish a sketch of my life. [. . .] I have not written my experiences in order to attract attention to myself; on the contrary, it would have been more pleasant to me to have been silent about my own

[1] Note that we have retained Harriet Jacobs's original use of capitalization.

history. Neither do I care to excite sympathy for my own sufferings. But I do earnestly desire to arouse the women of the North to a realizing sense of the condition of two millions of women at the South, still in bondage, suffering what I suffered, and most of them far worse. I want to add my testimony to that of abler pens to convince the people of the Free States what Slavery really is. Only by experience can anyone realize how deep, and dark, and foul is that pit of abominations. May the blessing of God rest on this imperfect effort in behalf of my persecuted people!

I. CHILDHOOD

4 I WAS born a slave; but I never knew it till [I was] six years of [age . . .]. My father was a carpenter, and considered so intelligent and skillful in his trade, that, when buildings out of the common line were to be erected, he was sent for from long distances, to be head workman. On condition of paying his mistress two hundred dollars a year, and supporting himself, he was allowed to work at his trade, and manage his own affairs. His strongest wish was to purchase his children; but, though he several times offered his hard earnings for that purpose, he never succeeded. [. . . My parents] lived together in a comfortable home; and, though we were all slaves. . . I never dreamed I was a piece of merchandise, trusted to them for safe keeping, and liable to be demanded of them at any moment.

5 I had one brother, William, who was two years younger than myself—a bright, affectionate child. I had also a great treasure in my maternal grandmother, who was a remarkable woman in many respects. She was the daughter of a planter in South Carolina, who, at his death, left her mother and his three children free, with money to go to St. Augustine, where they had relatives. It was during the Revolutionary War; and they were captured on their passage, carried back, and sold to different purchasers. [. . .] She was a little girl when she was captured and sold to the keeper of a large hotel.

6 She was much praised for her cooking; and her nice crackers became so famous in the neighborhood that many people were desirous of obtaining them. In consequence of numerous requests of this kind, she asked permission of her mistress to bake crackers at night, after all the household work was done; and she obtained leave to do it. [. . .] The business proved profitable; and each year she laid by [saved] a little, which was saved for a fund to purchase her children.

7 Her master died, and the property was divided among his heirs. The widow had her dower in the hotel, which she continued to keep open. My grandmother remained in her service as a slave; but her children were divided among her master's children. As she had five, Benjamin, the youngest one, was sold, in order that each heir might have an equal portion of dollars and cents. [. . .] His sale was a terrible blow to my grandmother; but [. . .] she went to work with renewed energy, trusting in time to be able to purchase some of her children. She had laid up [saved] three hundred dollars, which her mistress one day begged as a loan, promising to [re]pay her soon. The reader probably knows that no promise or writing given to a slave is legally binding; for, according to Southern laws, a slave, *being* property, can *hold* no property. When my grandmother lent her hard earnings to her mistress, she trusted solely to her honor. The honor of a slaveholder to a slave!

8 [. . .] When I was six years old, my mother died; and then, for the first time, I learned, by the talk around me, that I was a slave. [. . .] I grieved for her, and my young mind was troubled with the thought who would now take care of me and my little brother. I was told that my home was now to be with her mistress; [. . .] Those were happy days—too happy to last. The slave child had no thought for the morrow; but there came that blight, which too surely waits on every human being born to be a chattel.[2]

9 When I was nearly twelve years old, my kind mistress sickened and died. [. . .] I was sent to spend a week with my grandmother. I was now old enough to begin to think of the future; and again and again I asked myself what they would do with me. [My mistress. . .] had promised my dying mother that her children should never suffer for anything; and when I remembered that, and recalled her many proofs of attachment to me,

[2] **Chattel** Property, possession, or object.

I could not help having some hopes that she had left me free. My friends were almost certain it would be so. They thought she would be sure to do it, on account of my mother's love and faithful service. But, alas! we all know that the memory of a faithful slave does not avail much to save her children from the auction block.

After a brief period of suspense, the will of my mistress was read, and we learned that she had bequeathed me to her sister's daughter, a child of five years old. So vanished our hopes. My mistress had taught me the precepts of God's Word: "Thou shalt love thy neighbor as thyself." "Whatsoever ye would that men should do unto you, do ye even so unto them." But I was her slave, and I suppose she did not recognize me as her neighbor. I would give much to blot out from my memory that one great wrong. [. . .]

Source: Harriet Ann Jacobs, *Incidents in the Life of a Slave Girl* (Boston: Thayer & Eldridge, 1861).

QUESTIONS FOR REFLECTION

Considering Ideas

1. Which descriptive details from the narrative are most memorable? Identify specific passages and explain why they stand out.
2. According to Jacobs, she did not know she was a slave until she was six years old. How could she now know? What caused her to find this out about herself? How did she react to this knowledge?
3. Near the end of the story, Jacobs states, "The slave child had no thought for the morrow; but there came that blight, which too surely waits on every human being born to be a chattel." What is the significance of that sentence? What reaction do you suppose the author is hoping to achieve from the reader?

Considering the Rhetorical Star

1. What is the *subject* of the excerpt? Is the specific topic engaging? Why or why not?
2. Who is the intended *audience* for the piece?
3. What is the author's main *purpose* (to inform, to persuade, to entertain, to express feelings) for the essay? Does she use a combination of purposes? How effective is her approach? Explain.
4. What writing *strategies* does the author use in the article? How do these strategies affect the work?
5. What is the *design* of the piece? Is it effective? Why or why not?

ESOL Tip >

Write a descriptive narrative about moving from your homeland to a foreign land. From where did you move? How old were you? What was the reason for your move?

Considering Writing Strategies

1. In the first paragraph, Jacobs specifically addresses the reader, which is unusual in a descriptive narrative. Why she does she do this? What effect does it have on you as the reader?
2. How does the author establish the time and place of her descriptive narrative? Is her approach effective? Why or why not?
3. What is the tone of the essay? Give examples of specific words that reflect the writer's tone.

Writing Suggestions

1. Have you ever been in a situation where you felt extremely uncomfortable or powerless? Write a descriptive narrative telling about your experience. What happened? What did you do? Did anyone help you? How did everything turn out in the end?
2. In the last sentence of the excerpt, Jacobs mentions "a great wrong," Have you ever had someone betray you intentionally or otherwise? What happened? Were you able to make amends with the person? Write a descriptive narrative telling about your experience.

Reading and Reflection DESCRIPTIVE NARRATIVE WRITING

[preview] **NEAL GABLER** has contributed to numerous publications, including the *New York Times* and the *Los Angeles Times.* He also has reviewed movies for PBS on a program called *Sneak Previews* (originally hosted by Gene Siskel and Robert Ebert) and later became a panelist for *Fox News Watch.* In the following essay, which was originally published in the *Los Angeles Times,* Gabler examines our fascination with urban legends, which are modern stories that become widespread even though they have little or no basis in fact. Before reading, think about an urban myth that you have heard from another person. Is the story plausible? How did you react to it? Were you frightened?

How Urban Myths Reveal Society's Fears
by Neal Gabler

1 The story goes like this: During dinner at an opulent wedding reception, the groom rises from the head table and shushes the crowd. Everyone naturally assumes he is about to toast his bride and thank his guests. Instead, he solemnly announces that there has been a change of plan. He and his bride will be taking separate honeymoons and, when they return, the marriage will be annulled. The reason for this sudden turn of events, he says, is taped to the bottom of everyone's plate. The stunned guests quickly flip their dinnerware to discover a photo of the bride *in flagrante*[1] with the best man.

2 At least that is the story that has been recently making the rounds up and down the Eastern seaboard and as far west as Chicago. Did this really happen? A *Washington Post* reporter who tracked the story was told by one source that it happened at a New Hampshire hotel. But then another source swears it happened in Medford, Massachusetts. Then again another suggests a banquet hall outside Schenectady, New York. Meanwhile, a sophisticated couple in Manhattan has heard it happened at the Pierre.

3 In short, the whole thing appears to be another urban myth, one of those weird tales that periodically catch the public imagination. Alligators swarming the sewers after people have flushed the baby reptiles down the toilet. The babysitter who gets threatening phone calls that turn out to be coming from inside the house. The woman who turns out to have a nest of black-widow spiders in her beehive hairdo. The man who falls asleep and awakens to find his kidney has been removed. The rat that gets deep-fried and served by a fast-food outlet. Or, in a variation, the mouse that has somehow drowned in a closed Coca-Cola bottle.

4 These tales are preposterous, but in a mass society like ours, where stories are usually manufactured by Hollywood, they just may be the most genuine form of folklore we have. Like traditional folklore, they are narratives crafted by the collective consciousness. Like traditional folklore, they give expression to the national mind. And like traditional folklore, they blend the fantastic with the routine, if only to demonstrate, in the words of University of Utah folklorist Jan Harold Brunvand, the nation's leading expert on urban legends, "that the prosaic contemporary scene is capable of producing shocking or amazing occurrences."

5 Shocking and amazing, yes. But in these stories, anything can happen not because the world is a magical place rich with wonder—as in folktales of yore—but because our world is so utterly terrifying.

[1] **In flagrante** Caught in the act of being unfaithful.

Here, nothing is reliable and no laws of morality govern. The alligators in the sewers present an image of an urban hell inhabited by beasts—an image that might have come directly from Hades and the River Styx in Greek mythology. The babysitter and the man upstairs exploits fears that we are not even safe in our own homes. The spider in the hairdo says that even on our own persons, dangers lurk. The man who loses his kidney plays to our fears of the night and the real bogymen who prowl them. The mouse in the soda warns us of the perils of an impersonal mass-production society.

6 As for the wedding reception tale, which one hacker on the Internet has dubbed "Wedding Revenge," it may address the greatest terror of all: that love and commitment are chimerical[2] and even friendship is meaningless. These are timeless issues, but the sudden promulgation[3] of the tale suggests its special relevance in the age of AIDS, when commitment means even more than it used to, and in the age of feminism, when some men are feeling increasingly threatened by women's freedom. Thus, the groom not only suffers betrayal and humiliation; his plight carries the hint of danger and emasculation, too. Surely, a legend for our time.

7 Of course, folklore and fairy tales have long subsisted on terror, and even the treacly[4] cartoons of Walt Disney are actually, when you parse them, dark and complex expressions of fear—from Snow White racing through the treacherous forest to Pinocchio gobbled by the whale to Dumbo being separated from his mother. But these crystallize the fears of childhood, the fears one must overcome to make the difficult transition to adulthood. Thus, the haunted forest of the fairy tales is a trope[5] for haunted adolescence; the witch or crone, a trope for the spent generation one must vanquish to claim one's place in the world, and the prince who comes to the rescue, a trope for the adult responsibilities that the heroine must now assume.

8 Though urban legends frequently originate with college students about to enter the real world, they are different from traditional fairy tales because their terrors are not really obstacles on the road to understanding, and they are different from folklore because they cannot even be interpreted as cautionary. In urban legends, obstacles aren't overcome, perhaps can't be overcome, and there is nothing we can do differently to avoid the consequences. The woman, not knowing any better, eats the fried rat. The babysitter is terrorized by the stranger hiding in the house. The black widow bites the woman with the beehive hairdo. The alligators prowl the sewers. The marriage in Wedding Revenge breaks up.

9 It is not just our fears, then, that these stories exploit. Like so much else in modern life—tabloids, exploitalk programs, real-life crime best sellers—urban legends testify to an overwhelming condition of fear and to a sense of our own impotence within it. That is why there is no accommodation in these stories, no lesson or wisdom imparted. What there is, is the stark impression that our world is anomic.[6] We live in a haunted forest of skyscrapers or of suburban lawns and ranch houses, but there is no one to exorcise the evil and no prince to break the spell.

10 Given the pressures of modern life, it isn't surprising that we have created myths to express our malaise. But what is surprising is how many people seem committed to these myths. The *Post* reporter found people insisting they personally knew someone who had attended the doomed wedding reception. Others went further: They maintained they had actually attended the reception—though no such reception ever took place. Yet even those who didn't claim to have been personally involved seemed to feel duty bound to assert the tale's plausibility.

11 Why this insistence? Perhaps the short answer is that people want to believe in a cosmology of dysfunction because it is the best way of explaining the inexplicable in our lives. A world in which alligators roam sewers and wedding receptions end in shock is at once terrifying and soothing—terrifying because these things happen, soothing because

[2] **Chimerical** Fanciful or mythical.

[3] **Promulgation** Publication or dissemination.

[4] **Treacly** Overly sentimental.

[5] **Trope** Figure of speech.

[6] **Anomic** Disoriented or alienated.

we are absolved of any responsibility for them. It is just the way it is.

12 But there may be an additional reason why some people seem so willing to suspend their disbelief in the face of logic. This one has less to do with the content of these tales than with their creation. However they start, urban legends rapidly enter a national conversation in which they are embellished, heightened, reconfigured. Everyone can participate—from the people who spread the tale on talk radio to the people who discuss it on the Internet to the people who tell it to their neighbors. In effect, these legends are the product of a giant campfire around which we trade tales of terror.

13 If this makes each of us a co-creator of the tales, it also provides us with a certain pride of authorship. Like all authors, we don't want to see the spell of our creation broken—especially when we have formed a little community around it. It doesn't matter whether these tales are true or not. What matters is that they plausibly reflect our world, that they have been generated from the grass roots and that we can pass them along.

14 In a way, then, these tales of powerlessness ultimately assert a kind of authority. Urban legends permit us to become our own Stephen Kings, terrorizing ourselves to confirm one of the few powers we still possess: the power to tell stories about our world.

QUESTIONS FOR REFLECTION

Considering Ideas

1. Before reading Gabler's essay, were you familiar with any of the urban legends he mentions? Which ones? What was your initial reaction to them?
2. Why do you think urban myths spread so fast? Why do we find some of them to be fascinating?
3. What fears does Gabler suggest urban myths address? Do you agree or disagree with the author? Why?

Considering the Rhetorical Star

1. What is the main *subject* of Gabler's descriptive essay? Is the specific topic engaging? Why or why not?
2. Who is the intended *audience* for the story? How do you know?
3. What is the author's main *purpose* (to inform, to interpret, to persuade, to entertain, to express feelings) for the essay? Does he use a combination of purposes? How effective is his approach? Explain.
4. The author uses description and narration as the primary *strategy* for the story. Does he employ other strategies? What are they, and how do they affect the piece?
5. What is the *design* of the work? Is it effective? Why or why not?

Considering Writing Strategies

1. Which specific passages in Gabler's essay appeal to the reader's senses? What do these passages add to the piece? Explain.
2. What point is Gabler trying to get across to the reader? How successful is he in making this point? Explain your answer.
3. What specific details caught your attention in the essay? Why are those particular ideas more memorable than others?

Writing Suggestions

1. Have you ever observed (or participated in) something that was stranger than fiction? Write a descriptive narrative about your experience. Make your descriptions vivid by capturing the sensory details and emotions related to the incident.
2. What scares you? Write your own urban myth that addresses one of your fears. Be sure to include enough sensory appeal so that your readers are fully immersed in your creative story.

Reading and Reflection DESCRIPTIVE NARRATIVE WRITING

Library of Congress, Prints and Photographs Division [LC-USZ62-43605]

[preview] **LANGSTON HUGHES** (1902–1967) was an early twentieth-century writer known especially for his poetry. In the following poem, Hughes writes about a mother giving her son advice. He may be recalling an experience he had with his mother. Hughes has captured an endearing moment when a young boy learns about life's challenges. Before reading, think about what kind of advice your mother, or another significant role model, gave you when you were a child. How has the advice affected your life?

Mother to Son by Langston Hughes

Well, son, I'll tell you:
Life for me ain't been no crystal stair.
It's had tacks in it,
And splinters,
And boards torn up,
And places with no carpet on the floor—
Bare.
But all the time
I'se been a-climbin' on,
And reachin' landin's,
And turnin' corners,
And sometimes goin' in the dark
Where there ain't been no light.
So boy, don't you turn back.
Don't you set down on the steps
'Cause you find it's kinder hard.
Don't you fall now—
For I'se still goin', honey,
I'se still climbin',
And life for me ain't been no crystal stair.

Source: Langston Hughes, "Mother to Son" from *The Collected Poems of Langston Hughes* by Langston Hughes.

QUESTIONS FOR REFLECTION

Considering Ideas

1. What advice is the mother passing along to her son?
2. Why do you think the mother has a need to share this information with her son?
3. What is the theme or overall point of the poem?

Considering the Rhetorical Star

1. What is the main *subject* of Hughes's poem? Is the specific topic engaging? Why or why not?
2. Who is the intended *audience* for the poem? How do you know?
3. What is the author's main *purpose* (to inform, to interpret, to persuade, to entertain, to express feelings) for the narrative? Does he use a combination of purposes? How effective is his approach? Explain.
4. The poet uses descriptive narration as the primary *strategy* for the poem. Does he employ any other writing strategies? What are they, and how do they affect the poem?
5. What is the *design* of the poem? Is it effective? Why or why not?

Considering Writing Strategies

1. Notice the dialect and missing letters in the poem. Why does Hughes use this style of writing? What effect does he accomplish in doing so?

2. Identify several of the metaphors (comparisons that don't use *like* or *as*) that Hughes uses in the poem. What do these metaphors represent? How effective are they?
3. What aspects of narration does Hughes incorporate into the poem?

Writing Suggestions

1. Write an essay recalling a time when a parent or other role model gave you some advice. What did he or she say? Why has this memory stuck with you for so long? Was the advice useful to you? Has it changed your life in any way?
2. Write an essay to a younger sibling or child about something you have learned through your experiences. Tell a story to fully illustrate your point.

ESOL Tip >

Is there a particular saying or parable in your home country or culture that has significant meaning to you or that can teach a valuable lesson? Write an essay about this saying or parable. What life lessons can others learn from it?

STUDENT WRITING

Adrenaline Rush

by Claudia Martinez

Skydiving is a wild and amazing experience. 1
Jumping out of an airplane about 15,000 feet in the air and plunging towards the earth at a speed of 160 miles per hour would give anyone an adrenaline rush like no other. The entire skydiving experience takes no more than 30 minutes, but the memory lasts a lifetime. Skydiving is something I would recommend to everyone to try at least once in his or her life. My first and only skydiving experience had my emotions go all the way from fear, to excitement, to relief, making it the most unforgettable day of my life.

Now just because I agreed to jump out of a plane 2
does not mean that I was not scared or nervous. From the moment I promised my friend, Calixto, that we would go skydiving for our birthdays, I would get that roller coaster feeling in my stomach just thinking about it. Once we arrived at the Sebastian Airport, my fear doubled! I could not believe I was actually there. I almost even backed out when I was filling out the 20-page packet filled with insurance waivers and the words "POSSIBLE DEATH" on every other page I signed. After the paperwork was complete, the instructors prepared my friend and me with harnesses and goggles, and shortly afterwards we were loading the plane. The plane had a total of 15 people on it. The plane climbed up at such an angle that I had to put my feet firmly on the floor to keep from sliding off the bench on which I was sitting. It seemed like an eternity before we reached the appropriate height, and all I could see through the window was the Atlantic Ocean down below.

After I jumped out of the plane, the excitement I 3
felt falling straight down made me scream at the top of my lungs. There was no way anyone could hear me though because all I could hear was the air rushing up against my body. My instructor and I fell for a minute straight; it was the most awesome feeling in the world. The air hitting my face made my cheeks flap around, and the air coming in my nose was overwhelming. I had difficulty moving my arms towards my face because of the intensity of the wind. When the parachute opened, we were pulled up suddenly. Then we just slowly cruised down to the ground. The view was absolutely gorgeous. I could see some land now and not just the ocean, which made me feel a little more at ease. We glided down for seven

minutes, and, surprisingly, landed right where we had taken off.

4 When I was safe on the ground again, the relief I felt to have survived and enjoyed skydiving is indescribable. I was glad I had the courage to go through with it. My family and friends seemed to be just as relieved as I was once they saw me again all in one piece after I landed. When the crew took off my equipment, I did not have any particular thoughts in my head. I could not hear much either because of the change in altitude. Everything sounded distant. I was surprised at how different the actual experience was from how I had imagined it. As I walked over to my family and friends, I could see the relief on everyone's faces, especially my parents'. In the end, I think we were all just at ease once my feet were on the ground.

5 Skydiving is something that I plan on doing again in the near future. I do not think it is something that I will ever get tired of doing because it is a wonderful experience like no other. Although I had never considered doing it before Calixto suggested it, I do not regret it at all. All in all, skydiving is an out of this world experience, and I would recommend that anyone, adventurous or not, should try it.

Source: Claudia Martinez.

QUESTIONS FOR REFLECTION

1. Identify Martinez's thesis statement. Is it effective? Why or why not?
2. Are the events narrated in a logical sequence? Why or why not?
3. What is the most memorable part of the essay? What makes it memorable?
4. List several transitions used in the essay. Are there enough to keep the essay flowing smoothly? Why or why not?
5. Would you ever want to go skydiving? Why or why not?

STUDENT WRITING

The Ring

by Danielle Malico

1 People all over the world spend valuable time and cash to see championship fights. Whether it is for boxing, wrestling, or ultimate fighting, crowds gather in bars and around televisions to support their favorite fighters. Many know what it is like to be a spectator, but few know the fighter's experience. I, on the other hand, have first-hand knowledge of what it is like to be in the ring.

2 The first sound I hear is the familiar bell that brings me to reality. All around are my friends, family, and people who want to see women brawl. This is far from a quiet event. The onlookers are comparable to screeching howler monkeys with beer and snacks in their hands. My body feels heavy; I am covered in all the necessary places to prevent injury. The guard in my mouth causes excess fluid to run down my chin. The ring smells like rubber and sweat from previous battles. These conditions are not ideal for the average woman, but for me boxing is my place in the world, my sanctuary, my one talent.

©Karin L. Russell

3 I look over at my competition. She is shorter and thicker than I am, and her stance is impeccable. Immediately I realize that this will be a

memorable occasion. I can tell everything about my opponent by her reaction to the first punch, whether she backs away or comes in closer. I always test the water with a three-punch combination: a jab, a strong right, and a left hook. With each strike I exhale, making the hits more effective. She moves in closer, mainly because of her height, partially because she is confident. This makes me hesitate, but I know I cannot let this stab of fear affect my performance.

I prance around on my tiptoes, and she fol- 4
lows me like a lost puppy. During the first two-minute round, she and I do the well-known first round dance. This is how we figure each other out. Not much damage is done on either end, a couple of simple blows, and soon enough the bell rings signifying our thirty-second break. I stagger over to my corner of the ring. My coach gives me the usual pep talk as I spit my mouth guard into a bowl. He takes a bottle and pours cold water into my mouth, while simultaneously wiping beads of sweat off my head, neck, and chest. He reminds me of a father, very proud of his little girl.

Soon enough, before I am fully rejuvenated, 5
it will be time to go back to the fight for the second round. I am so prepared. Whether I win or lose the fight, I know that I will fight my best and make my coach and myself proud. I will relish every moment of my time in the boxing ring. There is no other place I would rather be.

Source: Danielle Malico

QUESTIONS FOR REFLECTION

1. When you saw a picture of the author and read the title, what kind of ring did you expect to read about in the essay?
2. Identify several examples of sensory details in Malico's essay. What could you see, hear, smell, feel, and so on?
3. What comparison does the author make in the essay?
4. Is the descriptive narrative objective or subjective? Explain.
5. What is the point of Malico's essay? How do you know?

Activity Sharing a Memory

In pairs or small groups, brainstorm a list of events that the members in your group have experienced. These events can be fun, scary, inspirational, exciting, exhilarating, horrifying, and so on. Briefly discuss the list to see which events seem most interesting to the group. Next, each participant will tell a brief descriptive story about one incident so the other students have a good idea what happened during the experience. A representative from each group may share a few of the highlights from the stories with the class. This activity may give you ideas for writing a narrative essay.

OPTIONS FOR WRITING A DESCRIPTIVE NARRATIVE ESSAY

Now that you have read one or more examples of descriptive narratives, it's time to write your own. You may choose to write about one of the writing options that follow, the advertisement, the image, or one of the media suggestions. Consider your rhetorical star and the qualities of an effective narrative as you begin to compose your assignment.

Writing Assignment Options

Use one of the following topics to write a descriptive narrative essay recalling a memory.

1. A memorable childhood experience
2. An entertaining pet story
3. A scary or dangerous event you witnessed or experienced
4. Your best (or worst) vacation
5. A lesson you learned as a member of a team or in a club
6. Resisting or succumbing to peer pressure
7. Your worst (or best) day on the job
8. An event that led to a significant decision in your life
9. Meeting someone new or losing someone special
10. A day that changed your life forever

Multimodal Assignment

Using one of the readings, writing assignment options, or another topic, create a multimodal project using the descriptive narrative writing strategy and at least two or more of the options in Table 5.1.

Table 5.1

Multimodal Options		
Artifact	Images	PowerPoint
Artwork	Infographics	Prezi
Audio clip	Journal	Video
Blog	Montage	Website
Digital portfolio	Podcast	Wiki
Graphic organizer	Poster	Writing

(See Chapter 15 for more details about multimodal projects.)

Interpreting an Advertisement

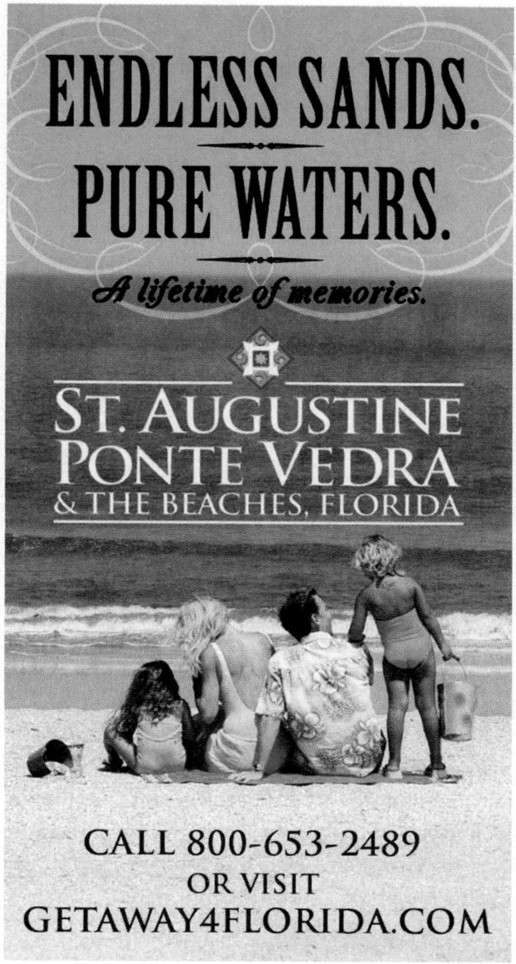

St. Augustine, Ponte Vedra & The Beaches Visitors & Convention

Source: Advertisement from *Arthur Frommer's Budget Travel*, June 2008, p. 134.

This advertisement appeared in *Budget Travel* magazine. Who is the intended audience for the ad? How do the picture and text interact? Why do you suppose the people are facing the other way? Is the advertisement persuasive? Why or why not? What story does it tell? Write a descriptive narrative essay that relates to the ad.

Chris Robbins/Getty Images

Writing about an Image

Look at several of the images in this chapter and consider these questions: What experience does the image represent? What story does it tell? What emotions do the people in the image portray? What ideas about your own memories does the image conjure? Write a descriptive narrative that relates to one of the images in this chapter. You can tell about the people in the photograph and what they are doing. Imagine what happened before or after the snapshot was taken. What other events might have occurred? Another option is to write about an experience of your own that the image reminds you of. For example, you might write a narrative about a time when you went on a camping trip or visited the beach.

Media Connection for Describing and Narrating

You might watch, read, and/or listen to one or more of the suggested media narratives to discover additional examples of this type of writing. Exploring various media may help you to better understand methods for narration. You may also choose to write about one or more of the media suggestions. For example, you might listen to (or watch the music video of) Brad Paisley's song "Letter to Me" and write a letter to yourself in the past, offering advice you have learned as you have gotten older and wiser. Another option is to go to the *This I Believe* website and read others' essays before writing about a belief of your own and the life experiences that led you to this belief.

Table 5.2

Media Chart				
Television	A&E Biography	History Channel	Travel Channel	*Dateline*
Film	*Letters to Juliet* (2010)	*La La Land* (2016)	*Colette* (2018)	*The Secret Life of Walter Mitty* (2013)
Print/ E-Reading	*I Know Why the Caged Bird Sings* by Maya Angelou	*Reader's Digest*	*The Color Purple* by Alice Walker	*Life of Pi* by Yann Martel
Internet	*Adventure Blog* **www .adventureblog.org**	*This I Believe* **thisibelieve.org**	*Diaries & Journals* **www .worldimage. com/diaries**	*Multimedia Storytelling* **www.interactive narratives.org**
Music	"Letter to Me" by Brad Paisley	*Telling Stories* by Tracy Chapman	*Radio Diaries* (NPR)	"Bohemian Rhapsody" by Queen

5.4 Analyzing the Rhetorical Star for Writing a Descriptive Narrative

As you prepare to write your narrative, consider the five points of the rhetorical star (Figure 5.1). You might use some of the questions in the chart as you conduct your rhetorical star analysis.

Subject	Have you had an experience that you have been eager to share with others? Maybe you often tell this story to new acquaintances. If so, that may be the perfect story for you to narrate. You will want to write about a personal experience that has significance for you. Your story could be exciting, humorous, shocking, or terrifying. Maybe you learned something from the experience, or perhaps the experience changed you in some way. If you don't feel like writing about something from your past, you might try going to a café, watching a sporting event, or attending a concert. You can document your experience in your narrative.

FIGURE 5.1 The Rhetorical Star

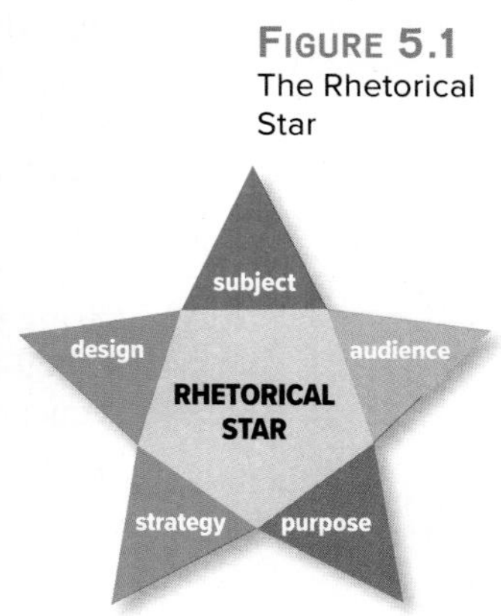

Audience	Who are your readers? What do they need to know about your experience? Will the readers relate to your descriptive narrative? What emotions do you want them to experience as they read your narrative? Will they be amused, surprised, or horrified by the details?
Purpose	What are you hoping to accomplish through your descriptive narrative? Is your main purpose to inform or entertain the reader? Or are you combining purposes? Are you writing objectively (sticking to just the facts), or are you writing subjectively (including your feelings and opinions)? Keep your purpose in mind as you begin narrating your story.
Strategy	Will you include other writing strategies in addition to description and narration to tell your story? For example, do you want to use comparison and contrast, process analysis, or cause and effect to enhance your narrative? If you are using other strategies, is narration your main organizational method, or are you using a brief narrative to introduce an essay that uses another strategy?
Design	How long should your descriptive narrative be? How many details do you need to include to fully explain your story? What other design elements, such as headings, photographs, or diagrams, might help your reader to better understand what happened?

5.5 Applying the Writing Process for Describing and Narrating

After you have completed your rhetorical star analysis, follow the steps of the writing process (Figure 5.2) to compose your paper.

1. **Discovering:** As you begin to explore your topic, you might freewrite everything that comes to mind about your topic, including why it is meaningful to you. Also, you can use the journalist's questions to help you generate ideas about your topic (Figure 5.3) and sensory appeal (Figure 5.4). After you have come up with some ideas, you might tell one of your stories to a classmate or friend to see if he or she becomes engaged in your narrative.
2. **Planning:** Once you have chosen an event or series of events to write about, try listing everything you can remember about your topic. Also, try numbering the events, creating a cluster, or developing an outline (informal or formal) to help you organize your ideas. Remember to follow a chronological sequence for your narrative. You may include flashbacks as well if they are appropriate for your topic.

3. **Composing:** Earlier in this chapter you learned about the nine qualities of an effective descriptive narrative (see pages 95–99). These characteristics are a key part of the writing process:

   1. Establish a clear purpose.
   2. Identify the time and place.
   3. Keep a consistent point of view.
   4. Keep the verb tense consistent.
   5. Include plenty of details and sensory appeal.
   6. Present the details in a logical sequence.
   7. Use dialogue effectively.
   8. Include visual aids if appropriate.
   9. End with a thought-provoking conclusion.

   Write a first draft of your descriptive narrative using these nine qualities. Don't worry too much about grammar and punctuation at this time. Keep focused on retelling the details related to the event. Be sure to keep your overall point in mind as you write.

4. **Getting feedback:** Have at least one classmate or other person read your rough draft and answer the peer review questions that follow. If you have access to a writing tutor or center, get another opinion about your paper as well.

5. **Revising:** Using all of the feedback available to you, revise your descriptive narrative. Make sure that your story is full of specific details and that you have used enough transitions for your reader to easily follow the flow of your ideas. Add, delete, and rearrange ideas as necessary.

6. **Editing:** Read your descriptive narrative again, this time looking for errors in grammar, punctuation, and mechanics. Pay particular attention to your consistency with verb tenses and point of view, as these areas can be tricky for narrative writing.

7. **Proofreading:** After you have thoroughly edited your essay, read it again. This time, look for typographical errors and any other issues that might interfere with the readers' understanding of your descriptive narrative.

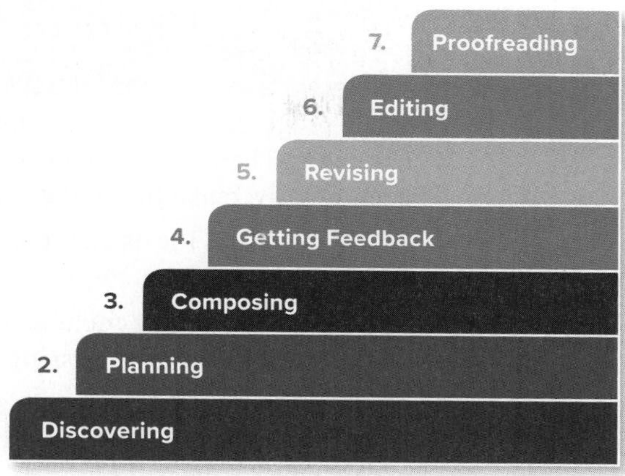

FIGURE 5.2
The Seven Steps of the Writing Process

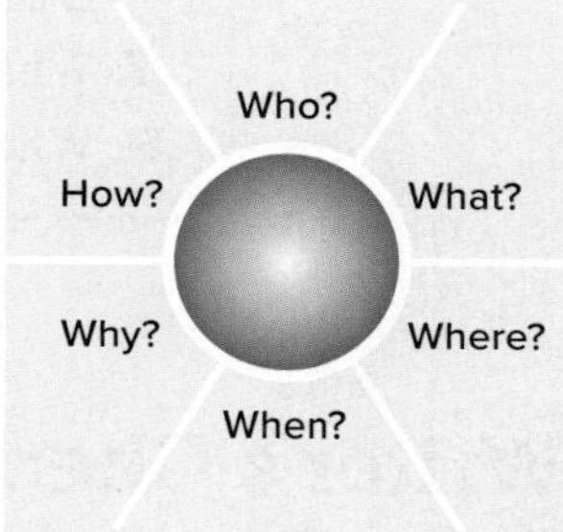

FIGURE 5.3
Journalist's Questions

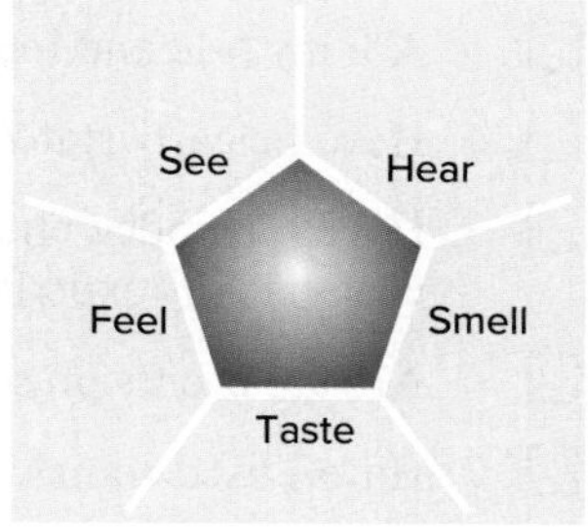

FIGURE 5.4
Sensory Appeal

PEER REVIEW QUESTIONS FOR DESCRIBING AND NARRATING

Trade rough drafts with a classmate and answer the following questions about his or her paper. Then, in person or online, discuss your papers and suggestions with your peer. Finally, make the changes you feel would most benefit your paper.

1. Identify the thesis statement. Is its placement appropriate? Why or why not?
2. Could the author include additional details to help you better understand the story? What is missing or unclear?
3. Are the details covered in a logical sequence? If flashbacks are used, are they clear? Why or why not?
4. What part of the descriptive narrative is most memorable? Why?
5. Does the story include dialogue? If so, does the dialogue flow smoothly and seem appropriate for the speakers?
6. Does the author provide the reader with a sense of completion at the end? If so, how?
7. What kinds of grammatical errors, if any, are evident in the essay?
8. What final suggestions do you have for the author?

Writer's Checklist for Writing a Descriptive Narrative

Use the checklist below to evaluate your own writing and help ensure that your descriptive narrative is complete. If you have any "no" answers, go back and work on those areas.

- [ ] 1. Are my title and introduction enticing?
- [ ] 2. Have I clearly stated or implied my thesis?
- [ ] 3. Have I included enough details and sensory appeal so the reader can visualize my experience?
- [ ] 4. Are the events presented in a logical sequence?
- [ ] 5. Have I used transitions to help the sequence of events flow smoothly?
- [ ] 6. Have I used dialogue to enhance my story?
- [ ] 7. Have I used a consistent point of view and verb tense?
- [ ] 8. Have I ended the story satisfactorily?
- [ ] 9. Have I proofread thoroughly?

CHAPTER SUMMARY

1. Descriptive narrative writing is about retelling a story so that your readers understand what happened during an important event.
2. Descriptive narrative writing is an important part of your education, daily life, and career.
3. Interpreting narrative readings and images can help you to prepare to write a descriptive narrative.
4. Carefully analyze your rhetorical star before writing a descriptive narrative: subject, audience, purpose, strategy, and design.
5. Use these qualities when writing a descriptive narrative: establish a clear purpose; identify the time and place; keep a consistent point of view; keep the verb tense consistent; include plenty of details and sensory appeal; follow a logical sequence; use dialogue effectively; include visual aids if appropriate; and end with a thought-provoking conclusion.

WHAT I KNOW NOW

Use this checklist to determine what you need to work on in order to feel comfortable with your understanding of the material in this chapter. Check off each item as you master it. Review the material for any unchecked items.

- ☐ 1. I know what **descriptive narrative** writing is.
- ☐ 2. I can identify several **real-world applications** for writing descriptive narratives.
- ☐ 3. I can **evaluate** descriptive narrative readings and images.
- ☐ 4. I can analyze the **rhetorical star** for writing a descriptive narrative.
- ☐ 5. I understand the **writing process** for writing a descriptive narrative.
- ☐ 6. I can apply the **nine qualities** of descriptive narrative writing.

Design elements: *Graduate Spotlight:* Ingram Publishing/AGE Fotostock

CHAPTER

6 Dividing and Classifying: Media and Popular Culture

Peathegee Inc/Blend Images LLC

learning outcomes

In this chapter you will learn techniques for achieving these learning outcomes:

Writing Strategy Focus: Dividing and Classifying

The writing strategy of dividing and classifying involves dividing a concept into groups with common traits or principles and then studying the significant elements within the groups. This process is known as classifying. For example, films can be classified into a variety of categories, such as action adventure, horror, drama, and comedy. Sometimes a writer may further divide groups into subgroups. For instance, action movies can be further subdivided into the following types: science fiction, superhero, martial arts, disaster, and chase. Writing to divide and classify concepts allows you to give meaning to a broader topic.

In this chapter, you will learn how other writers have divided and classified topics related to the theme of media and popular culture. You will also create your own division and classification text. Knowing how to divide and classify a subject is useful to you at school, in your daily life, and in your career.

6.1 Real-World Applications for Dividing and Classifying

Writing to Divide and Classify in College

College courses will provide you with ample opportunities to divide and classify. In an anatomy or biology course you may need to categorize systems of the body, such as circulatory, respiratory, nervous, digestive, lymphatic, and so on. For a literature course an instructor may require you to write about different genres of works, such as short stories, novels, plays, and poems. Each category has its own characteristics and subcategories. In your math course you might be tasked with developing different types of graphs, such as line, bar, and pie.

Writing to Divide and Classify in Your Daily Life

You naturally place concepts into categories in your personal life. For instance, when you do laundry you might sort items into different piles, such as whites, darks, bright colors, and light colors to help ensure that your clothing and linens look their best. If you're into exercise you might try to vary your routine for the greatest health benefits by doing cardiovascular training, resistance training, and recreational sports. You may further explain these exercises by considering the characteristics or benefits of each one. You might even subdivide the categories. For example, recreational sports might include the subcategories of swimming, bicycling, and playing tennis.

Writing to Divide and Classify in Your Career

Being able to write using division and classification is also extremely useful in the workplace. In order to analyze productivity at work, a supervisor might ask you to make a list of your responsibilities and divide them into categories according to importance, relevancy, or other significant qualities. If you work in a health care facility you might classify patients according to their health condition or need for interventions, medications, or equipment. If you're a teacher, you will likely need to classify students according to interests, abilities, or special needs. In a business setting you will need to categorize areas of the monthly or annual budget.

Here are a few specific applications for dividing and classifying topics in the workplace:

Health care: types of health care facilities, treatments, equipment, procedures, and medications.

Law: types of crimes, suspects, investigation techniques, legal services, documents, cases, and clients.

Education: kinds of students, learning styles, teachers, teaching methods, assignments, and books.

Computers: types of computers, software, components, training, and technical support.

Business: types of funding options, managerial styles, bosses, employees, communication strategies, and conflict-resolution strategies.

Culinary arts: kinds of knives, regional cuisines, courses of a meal, types of menus, and categories of dining experiences.

Massage therapy: types of therapeutic massages, oils, and additional services.

Graduate SPOTLIGHT

Lisa Fournier, President/Owner

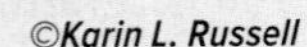
©Karin L. Russell

Lisa Fournier has a degree in business administration. She is the president and owner of Southern Photo, a retail store that specializes in photo restoration, printing services, custom framing, and photography equipment. Here's what Fournier has to say about the importance of written communication in her field:

“Writing is vital to my career. I have to use a variety of media to get my message across to my customers. I write letters, e-mails, blogs, television and newspaper advertisements, and employee training manuals. I have to understand the power of words to influence my customers as well as my employees. One of the writing strategies I use often is division and classification. For example, I work with various categories of cameras, lenses, scanning/printing, framing, and graphic arts. Also, I sell many types of accessories, such as flashes, tripods, bags, batteries, straps, cleaning cloths, and darkroom equipment. Furthermore, photography training is available in three main areas: travel, portrait, and general use. Dividing larger subjects into categories and subcategories makes it easier for employees to help customers in the store and online.”

Activity: Writing a Real-World Division and Classification Text

On your own, in pairs, or in small groups, brainstorm uses for division and classification writing at school, in your daily life, and on the job. You may want to choose your career field or the prospective career field(s) of the participants in your group. Be prepared to share your results with your instructor or the class.

6.2 Qualities of Effective Division and Classification Writing

1. Determine a Purpose for Your Classification

What are you trying to achieve by dividing and classifying your subject? Write an opening paragraph that introduces the subject and categories. Include a thesis statement that makes your goal clear. For example, if you are writing an essay about types of movies, your thesis might be as follows: While moviegoers can enjoy many different types of movies, four of the most popular categories are action, horror, drama, and comedy. The reader would then expect the essay to cover those four categories in the order in which they are presented in the thesis.

2. Choose Distinct Categories Based on Common Traits or Principles

As you are determining what categories to include, try to ensure that each one is unique without having much overlap. For instance, including action adventure and science fiction as separate categories might not work well because many science fiction movies also reflect action adventure. In that case, science fiction could be included as one of the subsets of action adventure. Keep in mind, you don't necessarily have to include all of the possible categories related to your subject, just the ones that are likely to be the most interesting and relevant to your audience. Three to five categories will likely be sufficient for most subjects.

3. Organize the Categories Logically

Determine the best way to organize the categories. You might use chronological order, emphatic order (order of importance), spatial orientation (such as left to right, top to bottom, or front to back), or another logical method for organizing your main categories. For instance, if you are writing about some of the different types of music, such as jazz, rock, and punk, you might cover them chronologically from the oldest to the newest form of music.

Grammar Window
ADJECTIVES

Adjectives are words that describe nouns (people, places, or things). The adjectives are highlighted in the following sentence:

Thunderous applause broke out as the sweaty musician smashed his fiery red guitar onto the dark, dusty stage.

Write a sentence for each of the following topics using three or more adjectives that create a precise image in the minds of your readers. Be sure to appeal to your readers' senses.

1. A football game (or other sporting event)
2. A skateboard, surfboard, or snowboard
3. A specific tattoo
4. A famous person's face
5. A photograph, a painting, or an advertisement in this chapter

ESOL Tip >

In many languages, such as Spanish, the adjective follows the noun, but in English, the adjective precedes the noun.

4. Use Relevant Details and Examples to Explain Each Category and Support Your Thesis

Analyze each category in the order in which you presented it in the thesis. Begin each body paragraph with a topic sentence that clearly identifies one category. Discuss the distinguishing traits or principles of each category. For example, the goal of action adventure movies might be to excite the audience and get their adrenaline pumping. A horror movie might be created to scare the viewers. Movies that are more dramatic might be geared toward making the audience feel something, such as love, sorrow, or empathy. Of course, comedies are generally created with the idea of getting the audience to laugh and feel at ease. Additionally, give specific examples that illustrate each category. In this case, when writing about the category of horror films, some examples that might be included are *Frankenstein* (1931), *Psycho* (1960), *Alien* (1979), *Get Out* (2017), and *Venom* (2018).

5. As You Analyze Each Category, Make Comparisons to Other Categories for Clarification

When writing about each category in the body of the essay, explain the ways in which each one is similar to and different from other categories. For instance, while explaining horror movies, you might say that a horror film may get the audience's adrenaline pumping like an action adventure movie, but the ultimate goal is to scare the viewers. Making comparisons between categories can help you transition from one category to the next.

6. Conclude Your Essay Effectively

End the essay by summarizing the main categories and rewording the thesis statement. You might also draw some sort of conclusion about the material. Perhaps one category is most important, or possibly all are equally valuable. The type of conclusion you draw depends on the purpose of the essay and the needs and expectations of the audience.

Activity Classifying Candy

On your own, in pairs, or in small groups, make a list of as many different specific types of candy as you can think of. Review the list and create at least three possible classification systems based on the criteria you choose. Be prepared to share your results with the class.

Career-Based DIVISION AND CLASSIFICATION WRITING

[preview] **WILLIAM PRENTICE** is a professor in the Department of Exercise and Sports Science and coordinator of the Post-Professional Athletic Training Program at the University of North Carolina. He holds several degrees, including a PhD in sports medicine and applied physiology from the University of Virginia. He has authored more than 100 journal articles and abstracts and written at least 10 textbooks, including *Principles of Athletic Training,* from which the following article has been excerpted. Before reading, have you ever had a professional massage or wanted to schedule one? Did you know that different types of massage bring about different responses?

Massage: Types of Responses to Treatment by William Prentice

1 Massage is the systematic manipulation of the soft tissues of the body. The movements of gliding, compressing, stretching, percussing, and vibrating are regulated to produce specific responses in the patient.

2 Massage seems to be regaining popularity among athletic trainers as a treatment modality. Manipulation of the soft tissue by massage is a useful adjunct to other modalities. Massage causes mechanical, physiological, and psychological responses.

Mechanical Responses

3 Mechanical responses to massage occur as a direct result of the graded pressures and movements of the hand on the body. Such actions encourage venous and lymphatic drainage and mildly stretch superficial and scar tissue. Connective tissue can be stretched effectively by friction massage, which helps prevent rigidity in scar formation. When a patient is forced to remain inactive while an injury heals or when edema surrounds a joint, the stagnation of circulation may be prevented by using certain massage techniques.

Physiological Responses

Massage can increase circulation and, as a result, increase metabolism to the musculature and aid in the removal of metabolites. It also helps overcome venostasis and edema by increasing circulation at 4 and around the injury site, assisting in the normal venous blood return to the heart.

5 The reflex effects of massage are processes that, in response to nerve impulses initiated through rubbing the body, are transmitted to one organ by afferent nerve fibers and then back to another organ by efferent fibers. Reflex responses elicit a variety of organ reactions, such as body relaxation, stimulation, and increased circulation.

6 Relaxation can be induced by slow, superficial stroking of the skin. It is a type of massage that is beneficial for tense, anxious patients who may require gentle treatment.

7 Stimulation is attained by quick, brisk action that causes a contraction of superficial tissue. The benefits derived by the patient are predominantly psychological. He or she feels invigorated after intense manipulation of the tissue.

8 Increased circulation is accomplished by mechanical and reflex stimuli. Together they cause the capillaries to dilate and be drained of fluid as a result of firm outside pressure, thus stimulating cell metabolism, eliminating toxins, and increasing lymphatic and venous circulation. In this way, the healing process is aided.

Psychological Responses

9 The tactile system is one of the most sensitive systems in the human organism. From earliest infancy, humans respond psychologically to being touched. Because massage is the act of laying on of hands, it can be an important means for creating a bond of confidence between the athletic trainer and the patient.

Source: William Prentice, *Principles of Athletic Training: A Guide to Evidence-Based Clinical Practice,* 16th ed. Copyright ©2017. Used by permission of McGraw-Hill.

QUESTIONS FOR REFLECTION

1. What is the primary purpose of the article? Does the article achieve its purpose? Why or why not?
2. What categories of responses to massage are featured in the article? Are any categories subdivided? Explain.
3. Compare and contrast the design of the article to a typical college essay. Which type of design is more effective for this type of writing? Why?
4. Why does the writer include headings? Are they useful? Why or why not?
5. Which type(s) of response would you want to achieve if you received a massage? Why?

6.3 Dividing and Classifying in the Context of Media and Popular Culture

Pop culture is all about the way we live, what we do, where we go, how we communicate, what we buy and wear, and what we believe. Various media reflect what is popular in our culture today. The articles and books we read, the movies and television programs we watch, the music and talk shows we listen to, the websites we visit, the video games we play, and the advertisements we observe all reveal our popular culture. The subjects of media and pop culture offer ample material for division and classification writing. Read one or more of the following sample essays. Doing so can help you with your own division and classification writing for school, at work, and in your daily life.

Reading and Reflection DIVISION AND CLASSIFICATION WRITING

[preview] Award-winning journalist **ELAHE IZADI** writes about pop culture for the *Washington Post,* where the article that follows originally appeared in 2018. She earned two bachelor's degrees from University of Maryland, in journalism and African-American history. Although she was born in and currently resides in Washington, DC, she grew up mainly in rural Maryland. She is also a stand-up comic and has performed at numerous locations, including DC Improv and Kennedy Center. To learn more about the author, visit her web page at **https://elaheizadi.com.** Before reading the article, think about any space movies you have seen. What are some of their traits and features?

Sorry, Your Favorite "Space" Movie Is Not Actually a Space Movie

by Elahe Izadi

1 Thanks to *First Man,* the Damien Chazelle film starring Ryan Gosling as Neil Armstrong that was released Friday, we have yet another space movie.

2 People love space movies. There's something about watching humans struggle in the unforgiving, mysterious and undiscovered realms of the universe that satiates a particular craving.

3 But what, exactly, makes a movie a space movie? Is it merely the location? What if only a few scenes are in space? What about the involvement of aliens? Is it a space movie if the movie title has a space-y word, like "galaxy" or, say, "space"?

4 Space movies cross genres—some are action flicks while others are more meditative dramas—but they all have a similar appeal. Perhaps it's how they're the most extreme man vs. nature story, in which the harshness of space exposes the best and worst of the human spirit. Or maybe it's the enjoyment of witnessing the grit, hard work and scientific genius needed to get to space and survive there. And you can't forget those iconic scenes showing our home planet from the heavens and how this inspires us to be better to each other, and to the Earth itself.

5 Space movies, like space itself, spark introspection about humanity's place in light of the expansiveness of the universe.

Sci-Fi

6 We've eliminated Sci-fi from consideration. These movies, which are immensely enjoyable, undermine crucial characteristics that make space movies appealing. Technological advances totally outside of the realm of possibility are treated as givens, afterthoughts. In sci-fi, traveling at the speed of light, *which is not possible,* is just chop-chop, smack that button on our space jet panel and let's get moving, I got places to go and warp drive to get me there.

7 Also, space ain't so bad in science-fiction movies. Watching them doesn't make you feel the fear that the celestial environment should provoke in your heart, like how if you're in space without a proper suit, your body will expand to twice its size and you'd suffocate pretty instantly. Also, it's crazy cold.

8 By freeing sci-fi from the expectations we have from space movies, you can enjoy them even more. No more "Whoa! Bombs falling in zero gravity in *The Last Jedi?* That's not possible!"

9 "We did all go, 'How do bombs drop in space?'" Ben Morris, visual effects supervisor for *The Last Jedi,* told Nerdist. "And we sat there for ages. And then [director] Rian [Johnson] said, 'They're Maglev

[magnetic] bombs. It's *Star Wars*. Let's not worry. Let's move on.'"

10 Sorry, the *Star Wars* movies aren't space movies.

Aliens

11 The presence of aliens is usually a clear signal that we're deep in sci-fi territory, in which case, refer to the section above. If aliens are walking, talking characters in the movie, it's not a space movie. If the aliens seem realistically scary and real and shriek or chase you around, then it's an alien movie, not a space movie. This includes aliens invading Earth.

Based on a True Story

12 If it's based on a true story about people trying to get to space and we see at least one or two scenes in space, it's a space movie. Any realistic movie about space travel should contain some essential space-movie elements, such as how difficult it is to get there and how harsh a place it is. *Apollo 13* is the quintessential space movie.

13 But we'd also argue that *Hidden Figures* is a space movie. It's about NASA and the ordinary people needed to get to space. But more importantly, the entire plot is about solving the complicated puzzle of orbiting the Earth and returning, in addition to how ignorance (racism) holds us all back. We get the climactic scenes of John Glenn in space and humans looking up at the sky from Earth. And *Hidden Figures* makes space math look thrilling, which should count for something.

Space as Merely a Backdrop

14 In true space movies, space itself is a character and essential to the story, not merely a setting. The characteristics of space prompt all of the other drama or action. The entirety of *Gravity* is about how awfully difficult space can be. While *The Martian* is about something that hasn't happened yet, *it could maybe one day,* and the story—both on Mars and on Earth—is driven by the attributes of space and our desire to explore beyond Earth. Both space movies!

The Close Calls

15 You could argue either way with a handful of movies.

16 *Interstellar* has sci-fi elements, but the most outlandish (spoiler!) are reserved for the end of the film. Much of the movie is about the science of black holes and exploring space-time, and to get the needed visual effect, a famous astrophysicist helped create "the most accurate simulation ever of what a black hole would look like." (Likewise, *Contact,* from what I've read, appears to be a borderline space movie. But I haven't seen it, so feel free to @ me.)

17 *Armageddon,* it can be argued, is a space movie. Sure, the idea that NASA would send oil drillers to bore into an asteroid propelling toward Earth may seem insane. But it's all about sending some guys to space and them trying to blow up a space thing. *Deep Impact,* while more scientifically accurate, is more of a the-world-is-ending movie.

Is Space Involved at All?

18 Despite its misleading title, *Space Jam* is not a space movie. It has nothing at all to do with space. It did, however, give us an incredibly catchy space song.

Source: Elahe Izadi, "Sorry, Your Favorite 'Space' Movie Is Not Actually a Space Movie," From *The Washington Post.*

QUESTIONS FOR REFLECTION

Considering Ideas

1. From just reading just the title, what did you expect the article would be about? Did it live up to your expectations? Why or why not?
2. Have you seen any of the movies Izadi describes in the article? Do you agree or disagree with her explanations? Why?
3. What are some of the movie examples included in the essay? Do you agree that they are not really space movies? Why or why not?

Considering the Rhetorical Star

1. What is the *subject* of the article?
2. Who might the *audience* be for this article, which was originally published in the *Washington Post?*

3. What is the author's main *purpose* (to inform, to interpret, to persuade, to entertain, to express feelings) for the article?
4. Izadi uses classification as the primary *strategy* for the piece. Does she employ any other writing strategies? What are they, and how do they affect the work?
5. What *design* features does this article include? Are they effective? Why or why not?

Considering Writing Strategies

1. Although Izadi's thesis does not appear in the first paragraph, as is often the case, she does have a thesis. Which sentence is her thesis? Why does she delay stating it until a few paragraphs into the article?
2. What is the tone (serious, academic, sarcastic, humorous, etc.) of the article? Identify a few sentences that illustrate this tone. How does the writer's tone affect you as a reader?
3. What categories does Izadi include in her essay? Do they serve to divide and classify space movies? How do you know?

Writing Suggestions

1. Watch *First Man* or another movie mentioned in the article, and write a division and classification essay about the characters, settings, or other elements present in the film. Discuss the features of the film that illustrate the point you are making in your essay.
2. Write a division and classification essay about a different type of movie, other than those that deal with space. For example, you might write about monsters, zombies, or superheroes. Choose logical categories for the subject, based on logical traits and principles.

Reading and Reflection DIVISION AND CLASSIFICATION WRITING

[preview] **CHRISTIAN CAWLEY**, a resident of Cleveland, United Kingdom, is a freelance podcaster, writer, and editor who has authored numerous articles and books on topics such as information technology, consumer electronics, and entertainment media. He is a frequent contributor to makeuse.com, where the article that follows originally appeared. Before reading the article, consider your own experience. Have you ever listened to a podcast, audio book, or radio show? Why do you think auditory content is so popular? Why might some people prefer that delivery format to written articles?

Most Popular Podcast Formats

by Christian Cawley

Your podcast could probably be better. Perhaps you followed our guide to launching a successful podcast. You might have picked up our tips for streamlining your podcast post-production. But you've noticed the podcast is flagging, and you don't know what to do about it. 1

Perhaps you should put an end to it and put your solitary remaining listener out of their misery. Then again, if you still have a listener who isn't your mom, perhaps the best option is to keep going. After all, you're clearly doing something that someone likes. But how can you rebuild the audience? 2

George Rudy/Shutterstock

3 The smart option is to reformat the podcast. This means looking at the podcast you have now, assessing just what it is, and introducing some new concepts.

4 No matter which format you settle on, be sure to encourage your listeners to rate and review your podcast.

5 So which podcast type are you currently using? There are, strictly speaking, five podcast types.

1. The Solo Podcast

6 This might be the podcast you started off with. Basically, you and the listener, chatting away, sharing your thoughts on whatever your podcast topic might be. These days, the solo podcast is limited to very particular niches. For instance, you might be a comedian or a musician. The solo podcast, therefore, is ideal for you to share your unique slant on the world.

7 While it might seem like an easy solution (and it is when it comes to production), the solo podcast isn't for everyone. If you're unsure of your point of view on a subject, for instance, then you might find yourself drying up (that is, running out of things to say, or losing your thread). It's a good idea, therefore, to have a plan: a format. For a solo show, that might be:

1. Introduction
2. Topic A
3. Transition
4. Topic B
5. Etc.
6. Summary
7. Outro

8 When it comes to production, all you need to do is grab a microphone, find an audio recording app, hit record, and start talking. This is possible on virtually any device, which means you could conceivably publish podcasts on a daily basis (although this is perhaps too regular in most cases).

2. The Podcast Interview

9 Talking to yourself on a weekly basis can be dull. Even if you liven things up with radio show–style sound effects, just chatting on and on, even with a plan, can prove somewhat limiting.

10 But if you're talking on a specialist topic, it's always a good idea to get input from a fellow expert. To begin with, it gives the audience another voice to listen to. You might well have silky tones that rival Morgan Freeman himself, but there should always be room for someone else.

11 How do you bring a guest into the podcast? Several options are available:

1. Telephone—Record the interview on your smartphone using a call recording app. You'll need to sync the data to your computer for editing (unless you have the tools to edit and upload on your phone).
2. Skype—If you don't have a smartphone, you can use Skype on your desktop to call other Skype accounts and telephones. With a Skype call recording tool, the audio will be captured and you'll be able to package it into your podcast later.
3. One-on-One—The final option is to make sure you can get a microphone under the nose of the person you're interviewing. This may require you to spend money on additional hardware, but the end results should be good. Just remember to check the sound levels before recording commences.

12 The format for a podcast interview would look something like this:

1. Introduction
2. Introduce guest
3. Discussion
4. Summary
5. Outro

13 Clearly, an interview scenario has greater time overheads than a solo podcast. It can also require more software, sound hardware, or both. However, the results can be superb.

3. The Multi-Host Show

14 For a more varied collection of voices and opinions on a regular basis, the multi-host show is the way to go. Indeed, many podcasters use this option to start with. After all, if you dry up, there's always someone else available to take up the slack. Execution of a multi-host show can be tricky, however.

15 You basically have two options: online (which means embracing Skype, Google Hangouts, or another VOIP option), while recording the call (preferably at both ends, just in case one of the recordings fails), and offline. The latter can potentially have a travel overhead for one or more hosts, however. You should also consider transportation of hardware: multiple microphones and a mixer for your laptop or tablet will be required.

16 Many podcasts use the multi-host format; it's especially useful if one of the hosts must take a timeout. Typically, a multi-host podcast format follows this structure:

1. Introduction
2. Catch-up
3. Topic A
4. Transition (optional as conversation may move organically)
5. Topic B
6. Etc.
7. Summary
8. Outro

17 As a podcaster with 10 years of experience, I've found that the multi-host format works well. It's also possible to combine it with the previous format, and have one or more guests to interview in the show.

4. The Round Table

18 A variation of the above two formats, this is an approach whereby a single host introduces three or more (perhaps as many as ten) semi-regular guests to discuss a topic.

19 Commonly found in technology and gaming podcasts (as well as those looking at politics), round tables are typically longer than a standard podcast (perhaps two or three times as long). This is usually because of the range of opinions, so it can help to keep the focus of the podcast quite narrow if you want to keep the duration to manageable levels. After all, you need to consider whether your audience will have time for the whole thing!

20 Like multi-host shows, round table podcasts will need to be conducted via your preferred VOIP solution, or in person. Organizing a round table podcast can be time-consuming; however, the format makes it suitable for a live broadcast via Facebook or Google Hangouts/YouTube, in addition to audio-only live broadcasts. In fact, you could even invite a live studio audience!

21 A round table podcast format would typically run as follows:

1. Introductions and profiles of each guest
2. Topic discussion
3. Audience questions
4. Summary
5. Outro

5. The Audio Magazine

22 The final format for a podcast is an eclectic mix of news, interviews, discussions, and perhaps a few gags. It might have a single host or multiple hosts—it's up to you.

23 As most podcasts undergo post-production (that is, editing and mixing), having an audio magazine approach means you can collate your content over the course of a week, edit it together with some links, and publish.

24 All this approach really needs is you and a microphone. If you want to chat to someone remote, you can either hop on a train or Skype them, then record the conversation. All the audio should be synced to your computer, edited together, and published. For one-man podcasts, this is a great way to bounce the format—it's basically a ready-made pivot!

25 Here's how an audio magazine podcast format might look:

1. Introduction and rundown of features
2. Feature 1
3. Feature 2
4. Etc.
5. Listener emails/social network comments
6. Summary
7. Outro

26 Listener feedback is always important for podcasts, but in a show where you might be accused of being low on content, it is particularly useful to involve the audience.

How to Pivot Your Podcast Format

27 You're no doubt using one of these five podcast formats already. If you're looking for a way to refresh things, you have two main options.

28 The first is to do a straightforward pivot to another format. Beware: this may not be straightforward. Perhaps you're quite set in your ways, perhaps your preferred format isn't possible with your hardware or circumstances. Pivoting will also require some planning, perhaps even long-term planning if you're uncomfortable with the change.

29 A second option is to simply incorporate elements of the other formats, perhaps one at a time, over a matter of weeks. This is far easier to manage and lets you drop and add features based on how you think they went.

30 Importantly, reformatting your podcast isn't going to take five minutes. It requires some thought and planning. Take the leap, by all means, but don't rush in! You might also want to give your podcast a new cover design; you can create a podcast cover from scratch with Photoshop.

Make Sure Your Podcast Is Fully Planned

31 We've looked at podcast formats above, but planning your podcast requires a bit more detail.

32 After selecting your format (or a combination thereof), a second set of choices needs to be made. These will help in the long-term development of your podcast, and they'll also prove invaluable for each show you do.

33 Consider questions such as:

- What is the podcast about? What is the ongoing theme?
- Will you have the same segments each week? How many?
- How will you transition between segments? Talking, or a sound effect?
- How frequently will you publish your podcast? How long will they be?

34 Take time to consider and plan for all possibilities—5–10 minutes of planning will give you enough detail to plan for all eventualities, and ultimately help you to produce interesting podcasts week in, week out.

QUESTIONS FOR REFLECTION

Considering Ideas

1. Which type of podcast do you think would be most interesting to listen to? Why?
2. If you were to conduct your own podcast, do you feel you would have enough information to get started based on this article? Explain your response.
3. According to Cawley, what is an advantage to doing a podcast interview?

Considering the Rhetorical Star

1. What is the main *subject* of the article?
2. Who is the *audience* for the work? How do you know?
3. What is the main *purpose* (to inform, to interpret, to persuade, to entertain, to express feelings) for the article?
4. The article uses classification as the primary *strategy* for the first half of the piece. What writing strategy does the author shift to halfway through the article? Why does he do this? How does the shift affect the work?
5. What is the *design* of the work? Is it effective? Why or why not?

Considering Writing Strategies

1. What categories does the article use for classifying podcasts? Are these categories effective? Why or why not?

2. Are the headings and bulleted lists helpful? Why or why not?
3. Do you feel the article uses good sentence variety? Explain. Choose a few sentences to illustrate your point.

Writing Suggestions

1. Choose a series of podcasts and write a classification essay about the content, guests, or style. Be sure your categories are reasonably distinct and based on common traits or principles.
2. Write an essay in which you develop your own classification system for genre of writing, such as novels, poems, or comics. Be sure to use your own principles and traits for dividing and classifying that particular type of writing. Give examples of specific works to further define and illustrate each category.

Reading and Reflection DIVISION AND CLASSIFICATION WRITING

[preview] **AMY LOWELL (1874–1925)** was born in Brookline, Massachusetts, to a prominent New England family. Although her career lasted only a little over a decade, she published more than 650 poems during that time. Lowell's writing style, which reflects elements from American and British poetry, is called "imagism" because it is pure and direct. In 1926 she was posthumously awarded the Pulitzer prize for her collection *What's O'Clock.* Before reading the poem that follows, consider the significance of a rainbow. How do you feel when you see one? What is special about a rainbow?

Archive PL/Alamy Stock Photo

Fragment by Amy Lowell

What is poetry? Is it a mosaic
Of coloured stones which curiously are wrought
Into a pattern? Rather glass that's taught
By patient labor any hue to take
And glowing with a sumptuous splendor, make
Beauty a thing of awe; where sunbeams caught,
Transmuted fall in sheafs of rainbows fraught
With storied meaning for religion's sake.

QUESTIONS FOR REFLECTION

Considering Ideas

1. In the first two lines, the speaker in the poem asks if poetry is a mosaic. In what ways is the poem itself like a mosaic?
2. Does Lowell's "Fragment" change your perception of what a poem is? Why or why not?
3. What do the last two lines of the poem mean to you personally?

Considering the Rhetorical Star

1. What is the *subject* of Lowell's poem? Is its topic engaging? Why or why not?
2. Who is the intended *audience* for the poem?

3. What is Lowell's main *purpose* (to inform, to persuade, to entertain, to express feelings) for the poem? Does she use a combination of purposes? How effective is her approach? Explain.
4. What writing *strategies* (such as description or comparison and contrast) does Lowell use in the poem? How do these strategies affect the work?
5. What is the *design* of the poem? Is it effective? Why or why not?

Considering Writing Strategies

1. The primary writing strategy that Lowell uses to write "Fragment" is definition. How does defining poetry as poetry help to make this category distinct from other categories of literature, such as novels, short stories, and plays?
2. As noted in the preview to "Fragment," Lowell uses "imagism" in her poem. This means that she includes a variety of images to get her point across. How does this approach affect the meaning of the poem?
3. What is the tone of the poem? Which words in the poem indicate the mood or feeling the poet is trying to convey?

Writing Suggestions

1. Write a division and classification essay using the colors of the rainbow to categorize something, such as types of people. You might use the standard colors (red, orange, yellow, green, indigo, and violet) or your own unique version of a rainbow. For example, perhaps people who are indigo (blue) have a cool and mellow personality and people who are red are energetic and easily excitable. You might include examples of well-known personalities as examples to support the categories you selected.
2. Write a division and classification essay about some of the different types of music. Avoid sticking to standard types, such as rock, rap, country, and blues. Instead, come up with your own categories, based on traits and principles you feel are interesting or important. Include examples of specific poems to support your classification system.

STUDENT WRITING

Note: Tracie Ranew used the American Psychological Association (APA 7th edition) format to document her sources. Your instructor may require you to use APA or perhaps the Modern Language Association (MLA) format if you use sources for your paper. Please see Chapters 13–14 for more details about research and documentation methods.

A Glimpse into Four Styles of Rap

by Tracie Ranew

1 Since the 1970s, rap music has been entertaining audiences all across the United States and beyond. While its origins were representative of the Black community, particularly in the Bronx neighborhood of New York City, rap is now popular among music lovers of many cultures. Some of the most significant categories of rap that have captured the hearts of music fans are oldschool, gansta, crunk, and alternative.

2 The first category, oldschool rap, is pretty straight forward. Rappers tell stories by talking into the microphone, with rhyming lyrics accompanied by

beat boxing, which is the "musical expression of the body through the innovation of sounds and the crafting of music by only using the mouth, throat, and nose" (Park & Huynh, 2017). Michael Winslow, known as The Man of 10,000 Sound Effects, has been wowing audiences with his amazing beat boxing skills for many years. Although Coke La Rock and DJ Kool Herc may be the founding fathers of hip hop, "Rapper's Delight" by the Sugarhill Gang made its debut in 1979 and is the first song to make rap music popular around the world (Mize, 2014). Even those who are not into rap might remember the Sugarhill Gang's catchy lyrics about hip hop and rock (Rodgers & Edwards, 1979). Much of America was bebopping to the beats of "Rapper's Delight" and that song paved the way for other oldschool rap artists, such as Run DMC, Whodini, Beastie Boys, and Grandmaster Flash and the Furious Five to get their start in the early 1980s. As a true art form, rap continued to evolve.

3 The second type of rap, which became popular in the mid-1980s, is gansta. Like the name implies, it depicts the gangster lifestyle and the "crime and violence in the inner city" (Gilmore, 2017). The style of gansta rap includes less rhyme and more repetition than oldschool rap. Some well-known gansta rappers are Ice Cube, Snoop Dog, and 50 Cent. Ice-T (Tracy Marrow) is one of the best-known gansta rappers, and the song "O.G. Original Gangster," from his fourth album with the same name, alludes to the rivalry between the east coast and west coast, two subcategories of gansta rap. The lyrics at the end of the song, which are about how he hand writes the lyrics with pen and paper and tries to focus on fun times, clearly show his place in the rivalry, which is Los Angeles (Marrow, 1991). The east coast west coast rivalry that erupted in the 1990s was far more than exchange of words and tragically led to the murder of two prominent gansta hip hop artists: west coast rapper Tupac Shakur in 1996 and east coast rapper The Notorious B.I.G. (Biggie Smalls) in 1997. Both artists were from New York, but Tupac moved to Los Angeles when he was 17. To put it simply, the west coast rappers resented the lack of attention they got as compared to east coast rappers because New York was the birthplace of hip hop music (Giannotta, 2018).

4 Crunk, a newer form of rap from the 1990s, is a bit different from oldschool and gansta rap. "An amalgamation of 'crazy' and 'drunk,' crunk developed in the southern United States in the 1990s under the wider Dirty South umbrella" (Gilmore, 2017). This music is about getting crazy and having fun. Crunk songs tend to be high-pitched and drum-based, which make them great for parties and clubs. Some of the more popular crunk rappers are Salt-N-Pepa, DJ Unk, Three 6 Mafia, Crime Mob, Young Bloodz, and the Ying Yang Twins. The Atlanta-based group Lil Jon & The Eastside Boyz recorded a song called "Get Crunk" which appeared on their album called *Get Crunk, Who U Wit: Da Album*. The group's pride in the South is evident in their lyrics about people from Georgia representing where they are from by raising their hands (Crump, Franklin, Simmons, McDaniels, Smith, & Butler, 1997). This sounds a bit more friendly than the gansta rap rivalry between the East and the West.

5 Finally, as a break in style from the previous types, alternative rap became more mainstream in the mid-2000s. Alternative rap blurs the lines between many different types of music, such as rock, pop, jazz, reggae, soul, country, and others. Artists such as Eminem, Outkast, Kanye West, Jurassic Five, and De La Soul fit into this category (Gilmore, 2017). This non-conformist style of music pushes the boundaries of rap and escapes stereotypes. Rappers are teaming up with other types of artists to produce alternative forms of music. For example, T-Pain joined Taylor Swift, to produce a rap video (which aired on the 2009 Country Music Television Awards) called "Thug Story" which is "obviously a parody of Swift's then-enormous 'Love Story'" (Whitmer, 2017). Hip hop artist Hoodie Allen paired up with Ed Sheeran to record a rap song called "All About It" in 2014. More recently, Post Malone's music is a blend of rap, rock, grunge, folk, country, and rhythm and blues. His album Beerbongs & Bentleys features a number of hit songs, including "Rockstar," "Better Now," and "Ball for Me," which features Nicki Minaj.

6 As rappers continue to engage audiences all around the globe, it seems that rap music is more popular than ever. From the early days of beatboxing and the depiction of the gangster lifestyle to party beats and the more recent blending of mainstream musical forms, clearly oldschool, gansta, crunk, and alternative rap are important genres of the hip hop culture that will influence what is to come in the world of music. Only time will tell how the artform of rap will progress in the future.

REFERENCES

Crump, L., Franklin, B., Simmons, J., McDaniels, D., Smith, L., & Butler, C. (1997). Get crunk. [Song recorded by Lil John & the Eastside Boyz]. On *Get crunk: Who u wit: Da album.* Mirror Image.

Gilmore, J. (2017, September 15). Types of rap music. https://ourpastimes.com/types-of-rap-music-12257641.html

Giannotta, M. (2018, September 23). East coast vs. west coast rivalry: A look at Tupac and Biggie's infamous hip-hop feud. www.amny.com/entertainment/east-coast-vs-west-coast-rivalry-a-look-at-tupac-and-biggie-s-infamous-hip-hop-feud-1.13742586

Marrow, T. (1991). O.g. original gangster. [Song recorded by Ice-T). On *O.g. original gangster.* Sire.

Mize, C. (2014, September 23). History of rap: The true origins of rap music. http://colemizestudios.com/how-did-rap-start/

Park, J., & Huynh, A. (2017, March 21). A beginner's guide to beatboxing. www.humanbeatbox.com/articles/a-beginners-guide-to-beatboxing/

Rodgers, N., & Edwards, B. (1979). Rapper's delight [Song recorded by Sugarhill Gang]. On *The Sugarhill Gang*. Rhino.

Whitmer, P. (2017, November 15). Taylor Swift once rapped with T-Pain and she was never the same. https://noisey.vice.com/en_us/article/kz3533/taylor-swift-once-rapped-with-t-pain-and-she-was-never-the-same

Source: Tracie Ranew.

QUESTIONS FOR REFLECTION

1. What categories does Ranew use to divide and classify rap music? Are they distinct enough for readers to understand? Why or why not?
2. How does Ranew organize the categories in her essay? Does that organizational scheme work well for her topic? Why or why not?
3. Look closely at the category of old-school rap. Does the writer give enough details and examples to fully explain that category? Explain your answer.
4. Find examples of comparisons among the categories. How do they help you, as a reader, better understand each category?
5. What is Ranew's purpose in writing this essay? Does she achieve her purpose? Explain.

Activity Developing Categories

On your own, in pairs, or small groups, choose a subject, such as movies, music, art, or sports, and develop a classification system. Be sure to have a purpose in mind and to develop categories that are fairly distinct. Select one of the categories and determine what subcategories, details, and examples would be appropriate for that topic. A representative from each group will share your group's work with the class. This activity may give you ideas for writing a division and classification essay.

Now that you have read one or more examples of division and classification writing, it's time to write your own. You may choose to write about one of the options that follow, the multimodal assignment, the advertisement, an image, or one of the media suggestions. Consider your rhetorical star and the qualities of an effective division and classification essay as you begin to compose your assignment.

Writing Assignment Options

Use one of the following topics to write a division and classification essay.

1. Types of music, concerts, or instruments
2. Types of novels, poetry, films, or television series
3. Styles of dance, yoga, or exercise
4. Styles of martial arts
5. Kinds of sports or leisure activities
6. Kinds of vacations, weekend getaways, or tourists
7. Types of diets, restaurants, cuisines, or beverages
8. Types of students, family members, or friends
9. Types of bosses, coworkers, or employees
10. Types of dates, boyfriends, girlfriends, partners, or spouses

Multimodal Assignment

A multimodal text uses two or more modalities: visual, audio, linguistic, spatial, or gestural. Use one of the readings or writing assignment options in this book to identify a topic; then, create a classification multimodal project using at least two or more of the options shown in Table 6.1.

Table 6.1

Multimodal Options		
Artifact	Images	PowerPoint
Artwork	Infographics	Prezi
Audio clip	Journal	Video
Blog	Montage	Website
Digital portfolio	Podcast	Wiki
Graphic organizer	Poster	Writing

(See Chapter 15 for more details about multimodal assignments.)

Interpreting an Advertisement

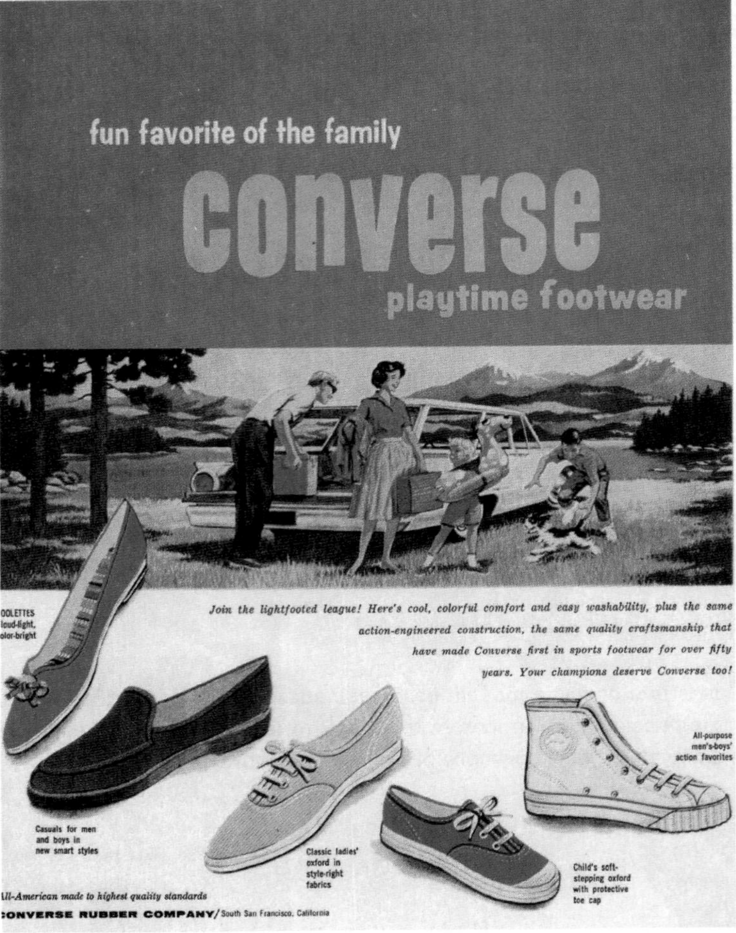

Courtesy of The Advertising Archives

While shoes can be divided into many different categories, this advertisement from the 1960s takes one category of footwear and subdivides it. What is the overall category? What are the subcategories? Who is the intended audience for the ad? How do the image and text interact? Would you consider buying Converse shoes based on the ad? Why or why not? What does the ad suggest about popular culture from the 1960s? Write a division and classification essay related to the Converse advertisement. Remember to break your ideas into various categories and/or subcategories and to explain the qualities of each type.

Writing about an Image

Micro/Electric

SUV

Hatchback

Wagon/Minivan/MPV

Sedan

MuchMania/Shutterstock

Choose one of the images in this chapter, such as the one above, and explain how it reflects the concepts of division and classification. For example, you might write about different categories of cars and explain who might be interested in driving each type and why. What does our choice of vehicle say about identity, consumerism, and pop culture? For example, are gas-guzzling muscle cars as popular as they once were? In the 21st century, is it more socially acceptable to drive a more economical vehicle, such as a microcar or hybrid? Explain.

Media Connection for Dividing and Classifying

You might watch, read, and/or listen to one or more of the media products or outlets listed in Table 6.2 to discover additional examples of division and classification and/or the theme of media and popular culture. Exploring different media may help you to better understand methods for dividing and classifying. You may also choose to write about one or more of the media suggestions. For example, you might watch the *Star Trek* movie and classify some of the different types of characters in the film.

Table 6.2

Media Chart				
Television	*Entertainment Tonight*	*The Walking Dead*	*Stranger Things*	*Game of Thrones*
Film	*Star Trek: Beyond* (2016)	*Star Wars: Episode IX* (2019)	*Toy Story 4* (2019)	*First Man* (2018)
Print/ E-reading	*People*	*National Geographic*	*Vanity Fair*	*Scientific American*
Internet	art.com	https://medium.com/giglue/top-10-genres-of-music-industry-7f19cdb177cb	www.filmsite.org/genres.html	www.topendsports.com/sport/categories.htm
Music	"Beam Me Up" by P!nk	"Categories" by UmConscience	"Pop Culture" by Icon for Hire	"Genres" by PBH & Jack Shizzle & AFISHAL

6.4 Analyzing the Rhetorical Star for Dividing and Classifying in Writing

As you prepare to write your division and classification assignment, consider the five points of the rhetorical star (Figure 6.1). You may use some of the questions in the chart as you conduct your rhetorical star analysis.

FIGURE 6.1
Rhetorical Star

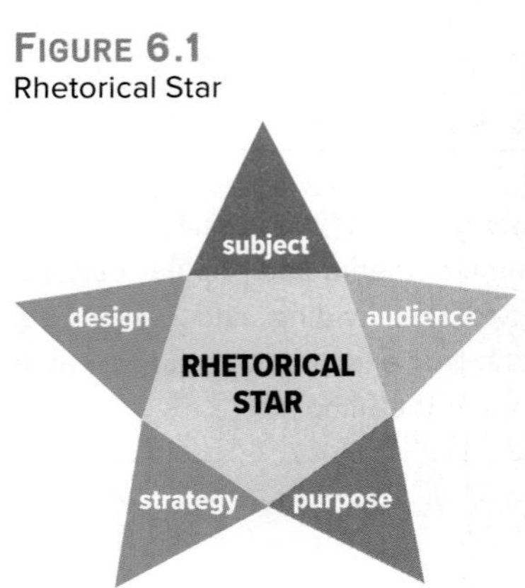

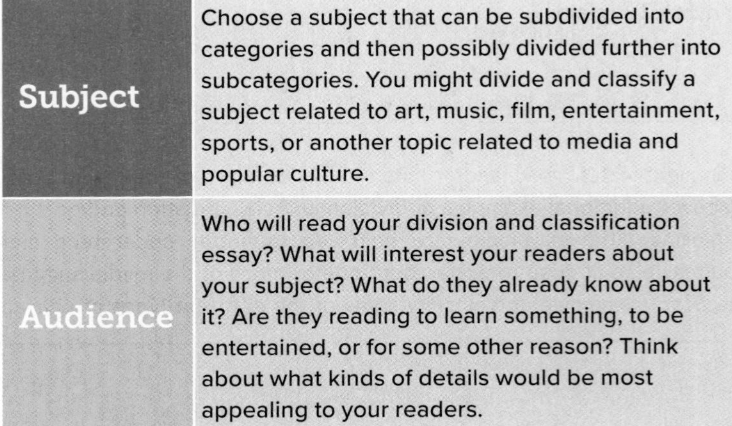

Subject	Choose a subject that can be subdivided into categories and then possibly divided further into subcategories. You might divide and classify a subject related to art, music, film, entertainment, sports, or another topic related to media and popular culture.
Audience	Who will read your division and classification essay? What will interest your readers about your subject? What do they already know about it? Are they reading to learn something, to be entertained, or for some other reason? Think about what kinds of details would be most appealing to your readers.

Purpose	What are you trying to accomplish through your division and classification writing? Are you informing your readers of various categories related to your subject? Do you want to persuade them to believe something? Perhaps your purpose is to divide video games into various categories for examination. Keep focused on your purpose as you write.
Strategy	Dividing and classifying a subject is a writing strategy that can be used on its own, or in combination with other writing strategies. For example, you might describe different types of monsters in movies, or compare and contrast categories of cars based on specific qualities and principles. Choose the strategies that will best suit your purpose.
Design	How lengthy should you make your division and classification essay? How many details do you need to convey to your audience? What other design elements, such as a photograph, drawing, or infographic, might aid your readers? If you decide to include visuals, be sure they don't overshadow your words.

6.5 Applying the Writing Process for Dividing and Classifying

After you have completed your rhetorical star analysis, follow the steps of the writing process (Figure 6.2) to compose your division and classification assignment.

1. **Discovering:** As you begin to explore your topic, you might make a list of possible categories and subcategories, freewrite everything that comes to mind about your topic, explain it to someone else, or complete a graphic organizer, like the one shown in Figure 6.3. If you are writing about an unfamiliar topic, then you may need to conduct research. If you do, be sure to document your sources in your paper. (See Chapters 13–14 for more details about research and documentation.)
2. **Planning:** Narrow down your list of possible categories and subcategories. Decide what order you want to use to

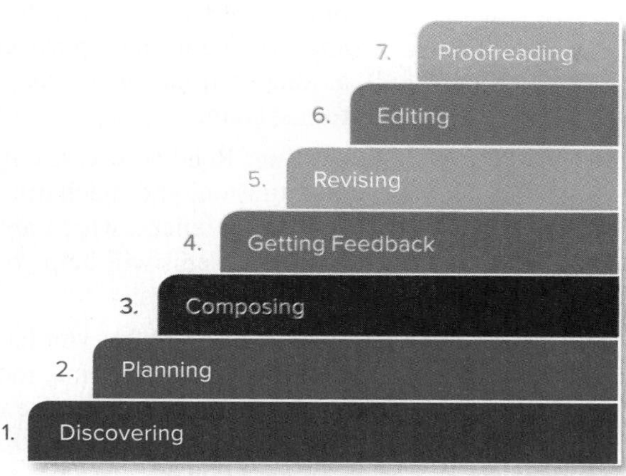

FIGURE 6.2 The Seven Steps of the Writing Process

Subject:

Category	Subcategories/Details
Category 1	Subcategories/Details • • •
Category 2	Subcategories/Details • • •
Category 3	Subcategories/Details • • •
Category 4	Subcategories/Details • • •

Dividing and Classifying

FIGURE 6.3 Dividing and Classifying: Graphic Organizer

present the categories, such as chronological, spatial (left to right, top to bottom, or front to back), or emphatic (order of importance). You might try creating a cluster or an outline to determine how you want to organize your essay.

3. **Composing:** Write a first draft of your essay using the six qualities of division and classification writing described earlier in the chapter:
   1. Determine a purpose for your classification.
   2. Choose distinct categories based on common traits or principles.
   3. Organize the categories logically.
   4. Use relevant details and examples to explain each category and support your thesis.
   5. As you analyze each category, make comparisons to other categories for clarification.
   6. Conclude your essay effectively.

   Don't worry too much about grammar and punctuation at this time. Focus on having clear categories and subcategories that you support with details. Stay focused on your purpose as you write.
4. **Getting Feedback:** Have at least one classmate or other person read your rough draft and answer the peer review questions that follow. If you have access to a writing tutor or center, get feedback from that source, too.
5. **Revising:** Using all of the feedback available to you, revise your essay. Make sure that your categories are distinct and presented in a logical order. Confirm that the details you provide fit with your overall purpose and organizational approach. Ensure that the comparisons you make among your categories help readers to better understand your classification system.
6. **Editing:** Read your essay again, this time looking for errors in grammar, punctuation, and mechanics. Look carefully for comma splices and run-on sentences, which are common in this type of writing. Avoiding these problems will help you to communicate your ideas more clearly to your audience.
7. **Proofreading:** After you have edited your essay one or more times, read it again. This time, look for typographical errors and any other issues that might interfere with the readers' understanding. Check your writing again to make sure that you have eliminated any run-ons or comma splices.

PEER REVIEW QUESTIONS FOR DIVIDING AND CLASSIFYING

Trade rough drafts with a classmate and answer the following questions about your peer's essay. Then, in person or online, discuss your essay with your peer. Finally, make the changes you feel would most benefit your purpose and audience.

1. What is the writer's purpose for composing this division and classification essay? Do the ideas and details in the paper support the overall purpose? Why or why not?
2. Do the categories seem to be distinct enough? What common traits or principles determine the categories? Are there subcategories? If so, are they distinct and useful to readers?
3. What organizational pattern does the writer use? Are the categories (and any subcategories) organized logically? If not, how might they be rearranged?
4. Identify the writer's thesis. Does the writer give enough relevant details and examples to explain each category and support the thesis? If not, what else might be included?
5. What specific comparisons does the author make to help readers understand the distinction among categories? Are there enough comparisons? Why or why not?
6. Does the essay have an effective conclusion? Why or why not? If not, what would make it better?
7. What grammatical errors, if any, are evident in the essay?
8. Overall, how satisfying is the essay to you, as a reader? What final suggestions do you have for the author?

Writer's Checklist for Writing a Division and Classification Essay

- ☐ 1. Is my purpose for writing my division and classification essay clear?
- ☐ 2. Are my categories and subcategories distinct and based on common traits or principles?
- ☐ 3. Have I organized my categories and subcategories logically?
- ☐ 4. Is my thesis clear? Are my details and examples relevant, and do they help to support my thesis?
- ☐ 5. Have I made comparisons among my categories that help readers better understand them?
- ☐ 6. Have I concluded my essay effectively?
- ☐ 7. Did I proofread carefully?

CHAPTER SUMMARY

1. Division and classification writing is about breaking a broad subject into smaller categories and subcategories.
2. Division and classification writing—whether you are the author or reader—can be an important part of your education, daily life, and career.
3. Interpreting texts in which writers use the strategy of dividing and classifying their subjects can help you prepare to write your own.
4. It's crucial to analyze your rhetorical situation before writing a division and classification essay. As you write, pay close attention to your subject, audience, purpose, strategy, and design.
5. When you write a division and classification essay, be sure to follow these steps: Determine a purpose for your classification; choose distinct categories and subcategories based on common traits or principles; organize your categories logically; use relevant details to explain your categories and to support your thesis; as you analyze each category, make comparisons to other categories for clarification; and conclude your essay effectively.

WHAT I KNOW NOW

Use this checklist to determine what you need to work on in order to feel comfortable with your understanding of the material in this chapter. Check off each item as you master it. For any unchecked items, review the chapter to improve your understanding.

- ☐ 1. I know what **division and classification writing** is.
- ☐ 2. I can identify several **real-world applications** for division and classification writing.
- ☐ 3. I can **interpret** division and classification images and readings.
- ☐ 4. I can analyze the **rhetorical star** and apply this to writing a division and classification essay.
- ☐ 5. I understand the **writing process** for dividing and classifying.
- ☐ 6. I can follow the **six steps** for division and classification writing.

Design elements: *Graduate Spotlight:* Ingram Publishing/AGE Fotostock

CHAPTER 7

Explaining a Process: Cultures and Traditions

Jenny Acheson/Getty Images

learning outcomes

In this chapter you will learn techniques for achieving these learning outcomes:

Writing Strategy Focus: Explaining a Process

Process writing explains how to do something, how something works, what something does, or how something was done. Writing about a process, sometimes called *process analysis,* involves breaking a procedure into its component steps. Processes can be instructional or informative. If the readers need to be able to perform the process, then the writing is instructional. For example, a step-by-step explanation of how to conduct a business meeting with an executive from an Asian country would be instructional. If the readers just want to understand the basic sequence of steps or events, then the writing is informative. A news article explaining what happened during a recent event on campus or in your community would be informative. In that case, the readers would not try to replicate the process. Instead they would just want to understand what took place. You will have opportunities to write about processes in college, in your personal life, and in your career.

7.1 Real-World Applications for Explaining Processes

Writing to Explain Processes in College

You will have many opportunities for writing about processes in college. You might need to explain a process, such as mitosis or meiosis, on a biology exam or explain for a history paper what happened during a particular battle. For classes in your major, your instructor may ask you to write step-by-step instructions for performing a particular procedure to demonstrate your understanding of the process.

Writing to Explain Processes in Your Daily Life

Writing about processes will also be a necessary part of your personal life. You may need to write instructions for someone taking care of your home, pets, or children while you are away. You might want to write out a dessert recipe to share with a friend or family member. Maybe you'll need to explain a step-by-step process to the police or insurance company if you witnessed or experienced an accident or natural disaster.

Writing to Explain Processes in Your Career

Every career field includes processes that need to be explained or performed. You might need to leave instructions for someone who will be filling in for you when you are on vacation or away at a seminar, or you may need to write an explanation of how to perform your job for the person replacing you because of your promotion. Here are a few specific applications for process writing on the job:

Health care: admitting a patient, drawing blood, dressing a wound, diagnosing an illness, recording medical exam findings, taking an X-ray.

Massage therapy: creating ambience, using Swedish techniques, working with hot stones.

Computers: installing a program, utilizing a new software application, designing a three-dimensional illustration.

Criminal justice: investigating a crime scene, handling evidence, documenting findings in a report.

Business: opening or closing for the day, keeping the books, tracking inventory, dealing with customer service issues.

Culinary arts: sharpening knives, baking a casserole, cleaning up the kitchen.

Education: lesson plans, written assignments, learning activities, projects, classroom management.

Graduate SPOTLIGHT

Deborah Buza, Caterer

©Karin L. Russell

Chef Deborah A. Buza is a caterer with an AS degree in culinary arts. She owns her own company, Buza's Catering, and is currently writing a cookbook. Here's what Buza has to say about the importance of writing in her career:

"In the catering business, everything relies on possessing good communication skills. I have to be able to explain my menu to potential clients over the phone and in writing in order to get their business. I have to write in clear, complete sentences, or the client will think I am incompetent. Because my parents are from different cultures, Polish and Italian, I enjoy deconstructing recipes from each culture and then combining them to create something totally different. I have to be able to explain how to perform the procedures and techniques that each culture uses during the cooking process. Also, my grandmother always said to put in a pinch of this or a handful of that, but our culture today is much more technical. I have to be precise with the measurements and ingredients. Overall, writing is imperative to my career as a caterer."

Activity Writing about Processes in the Real World

On your own, in pairs, or in small groups, brainstorm uses for process writing at school, in your daily life, and on the job. You may want to choose your own career field or the prospective career field(s) of the participants in your group. Be prepared to share the results with your instructor or the class.

7.2 Qualities of Effective Process Analysis Writing

1. Begin with a Clear Introduction

Your introduction should include some kind of attention-getter to engage your readers in the process. For instance, an essay could begin with a question, such as "Have you ever dreaded having your in-laws come to stay with you for the holidays?" Of course the most important part of your introduction is your thesis statement. State your thesis clearly so readers know what to expect. For example, "If you are trying to throw the best birthday bash ever, then you need to plan a great menu, invite the right people, organize some fun activities, and decorate appropriately."

Create an informative title for your process. It can be straightforward, such as "How to Throw the Perfect Themed Party," or catchy, such as "Surviving a Week with the In-Laws."

2. Include a List of Materials

If your reader is going to perform the process you are explaining, you will need to list all of the materials (ingredients, tools, equipment) necessary to complete the process. Be sure to include specific details and amounts. For example, if you are explaining how to create a costume for a Mardi Gras parade, you would include the types, colors, and quantities of fabrics, sequins, beads, feathers, and makeup that are needed. You would need to mention useful tools for making and assembling the costume, such as scissors, a stapler, and a tape measure. You would also need to include types and quantities for materials needed to hold the costume together, such as staples, glue, elastic, and thread. Try to think of every essential detail.

3. Explain Each Step in Chronological Order

As you write your steps, keep in mind your main purpose, which is either to instruct or inform the audience. Include every necessary step, even if it seems insignificant, to ensure that your reader will be able to perform or understand the process. Make sure to place your steps in chronological order so as not to confuse the reader. At times, you may need to explain why a particular step is performed, especially if you feel the reader may try to skip it. To help your reader understand the flow of steps in the process, use transitions, such as *first, next, then, after that,* and *meanwhile.* Also, be sure to use a variety of action words (verbs) to guide your reader through the process. For example, if you are instructing your readers on how to bake a traditional Mardi Gras king cake, you might use verbs such as *preheat, combine, decorate,* and *bake.* Finally, be sure you cover everything you promised the reader in the thesis.

4. Define Special Terms

If you are using a term that your reader may not know, then be sure to define the word the first time you mention it. Most of the time, you won't need to include a dictionary definition. Instead, explain the term in your own words based on your own experiences. For example, if you are writing about your family's Kwanzaa traditions, you might define *Kwanzaa* by saying it is a tradition celebrated from December 26 through January 1 in African communities around the world that has its origins in the ancient first fruit harvest ceremonies in Africa. You may include additional details about the significance of the holiday, such as the seven principles of Kwanzaa, in your explanation of your family's customs.

5. Give Helpful Tips and Warnings as Needed

You may find that you need to mention useful tips or safety warnings, especially if the process you are explaining is instructional. Include tips or warnings just before or right along with the step they relate to because many readers won't read all of the instructions before trying to complete the process (even if the directions tell them to do so). For example, if you are explaining how to make the most of an Independence Day celebration, you might need to include a cautionary note about handling the grill safely. You could use a symbol, such as a skull and crossbones, to indicate a potential danger.

6. Include Visual Aids as Needed

You may want to include pictures, diagrams, or other visual images to help your reader more fully comprehend the process you are explaining. For instance, if you are explaining how to make a Japanese origami lion, pictures illustrating each step would be of great value to the reader. You would likely want to include a picture of the finished product as well.

7. End with a Decisive Conclusion

Let the reader know when the process is complete. For example, if you are explaining the steps for making potatoes au gratin, you might mention that the dish

Grammar Window
PARALLEL STRUCTURE

In a sentence, ideas that are parallel, or have the same level of importance, should be expressed in parallel grammatical constructions. Presenting sentence elements, such as nouns, verbs, and phrases, in the same way helps to make sentences flow more smoothly.

Examples

Not Parallel: Enthusiastic fans at a football game are notorious for painting their faces, holding up signs for the cameras, and sometimes become quite loud.

Parallel: Enthusiastic fans at a football game are notorious for painting their faces, holding up signs for the cameras, and becoming quite loud.

Discussion: The underlined verbs are of equal importance, so they all need to be in the same form, or parallel.

Exercise

Write five sentences that contain nouns, adjectives, or verbs that are not in parallel form. Trade sentences with another classmate or group. Revise each sentence to make the ideas parallel.

is ready when the cheese on top turns golden brown. Finally, end with any additional suggestions you have for the readers. If you explain the steps for preparing a traditional Mexican dish, you might suggest serving it with margaritas or mojitos (or nonalcoholic versions of those beverages).

Career-Based PROCESS WRITING

[preview] **WHILE THEY** are in college, most people learn the information and skills they need to be successful in their careers; however, sometimes they do not get training in how to be polite in the workplace. Calvin Sun designed the following poster to hang on a wall in the workplace to provide employees with some tips for being considerate of their colleagues. Have you ever had an annoying co-worker? What did he or she do to get on your nerves?

10 Ways to Improve Your Office Etiquette by Calvin Sun

We spend one-third of our working lives at the office. The people we work with can affect our productivity and our careers, and vice versa. Practicing office etiquette makes the place and the workday just a bit more bearable.

1 Watch the volume of your voice

Keep your voice at a reasonable level. Other people are trying to work, and your voice may distract them. Besides, do you really want them to overhear what you're saying? If you have something personal or otherwise sensitive to discuss, consider doing it in a private office or conference room.

2 Use speakerphones with care

If you're on hold and waiting for someone to pick up, then yes, a speakerphone can save you time. Just keep the volume as low as possible. On the other hand, if you're planning to have a regular conversation with the other person, do it behind closed doors. Your co-workers in the area will not appreciate your disturbing them with a conference call.

3 Be sensitive about what you bring for lunch

We're supposed to be inclusive and accepting of people from different backgrounds and cultures, I know. And those other people are supposed to behave likewise. Nonetheless, be aware of how others may react to the lunch you bring. If you think about it, any reaction it causes can't be good for you. They'll either hate the smell and complain about you, or they'll love the smell, assassinate you, and eat your lunch. Either way, you lose out. If you have food with a distinctive aroma, consider either eating it outside or in the lunchroom, rather than at your desk. And some foods probably shouldn't be brought in at all, even to the lunchroom, such as stinky tofu or durian.

4 Respect people's privacy

Because you're most likely in a cubicle or other open office area, you inevitably will overhear snippets of conversations other people are having. Maybe you'll hear something about a project you're involved with or a problem you've encountered before, and you believe you have something to contribute. Yes, if you go over and join the conversation, you could save the day or provide valuable insight. However, you might also be viewed as a busybody.

Think carefully before joining that conversation. One consideration might be the amount of desperation you sense in their voices. The more desperate, the more willing they might be to hear from others.

If you do choose to join them, I suggest you go to their office or cubicle, let them see you as you're listening to them. Then, at a break, casually mention that it sounds like there is a problem, and that if you can help, you'd be happy to. This approach is better than rushing over and telling them you overheard their conversation.

5 Fix, or attempt to fix, what you break

How many times have you gone to the photocopier to find that it was either out of toner, out of paper, or experiencing a paper jam? The problem was still around when you arrived because the previous person did nothing about it and simply left the copier in its problem condition.

Don't be that person. If you can clear the paper jam safely and according to procedure, try to do so. Most photocopiers have diagrams to show you how. If you can't fix the jam or the other problem, leave a signed dated note describing the issue and what you are doing to fix it or have it fixed. Those actions could be a call to the maintenance vendor or to an administrative department. Your co-workers will appreciate your efforts, and signing your name to the note demonstrates your willingness to take ownership.

6 Keep the lunchroom clean

Neither the refrigerator nor the microwave should resemble the Queens Botanical Garden. If you spilled something in either place, clean it up. If you forgot to eat something from the refrigerator, and it's starting to mold, throw it out yourself. Don't leave it for someone else.

7 Be punctual for meetings

If you're an attendee, be on time. If you can't make a meeting or you're going to be late, let someone know. Don't arrive late and ask for a recap. Doing so wastes everyone else's time. If you're the one who's running the meeting, start it on time and resume it on time after a break. To do otherwise (for example, to start late to accommodate latecomers) is unfair to those who showed up on time and only encourages more lateness in the future.

8 Be careful about solicitations

Even if your company has no strict prohibition against solicitations (for example, selling candy for a child's sports team fundraiser), be careful about doing so. Your co-workers may not appreciate being put on the spot. If you do anything at all, the best approach is to display the merchandise in a central location, with a notice about the reason, and an envelope to receive checks or cash.

9 Avoid borrowing or lending

The rich rule over the poor, and the borrower is servant to the lender.

We've heard, in the past few weeks, more than we want to about issues with borrowing and lending. Those issues still apply even at the office level, even between individuals. Any borrowing that occurs can jeopardize a relationship if the repayment is slow, late, less than expected, or nonexistent. No matter how small the amount, the lender may feel resentment. In fact, a small amount might cause resentment precisely because the lender feels embarrassed about asking about repayment.

Avoid borrowing or lending if you can. If you absolutely must borrow, write the lender an IOU with the amount and sign it. Then, pay it back as soon as you can.

10 Don't ask co-workers how to spell

Microsoft Word has a spell checker. Use it. Don't bother your co-workers with such questions. It hampers their productivity and lowers their opinion of you. Some probably won't even want to answer, because doing so makes them feel stupid. When I get such questions, my response is, "Wait a minute while I check the dictionary" or "Wait while I use the Word dictionary."

Source: Calvin Sun, "10 Ways to Improve Your Office Etiquette," **www.scribd.com/doc/12589359/10-Things-for-Office-Etiquette.**

QUESTIONS FOR REFLECTION

1. What is the purpose of the poster? Is the poster helpful? Why or why not?
2. Make a list of the action verbs in each heading. Which ones are most effective? Why?
3. Discuss the design of the poster. Is it appealing? Which features are the strongest? Do you think employees would take the time to read it? Why or why not?
4. Which office etiquette tips are the most important? Which are the least important? Why?
5. Have you ever violated any of the tips on the poster? Which ones? How did your co-workers react?

Career-Based PROCESS WRITING

[preview] **ROSE FARHAT** is a registered medical assistant and a registered phlebotomy technician. She has served as an instructor at Keiser University for more than twenty years. Farhat has taught medical assisting students many skills including how to draw blood, as the instructions that follow explain. As you are reading them, imagine that you are following the steps or that someone is drawing your blood.

Steps in Venipuncture **by Rose Farhat**

There are many steps in the venipuncture process that must be followed to ensure the integrity of the results. Following these steps will also safeguard you as well as your patient from injury.

Step 1: Identify yourself. Patients have the right to know who is providing their care.

Step 2: Verify patient identification by asking the patient to state his or her full name and date of birth. If the patient is in an inpatient facility, check the ID band. If necessary, inquire if the patient is fasting and on any medications.

Step 3: Wash your hands using the proper medical aseptic procedure and put on non-latex gloves.

Step 4: Select and check your equipment ensuring that you have the correct tubes, needle size, and other necessary items to complete the draw successfully. Assemble your needle and syringe.

Step 5: Palpate for a viable vein. The most common vein used is the median cubital, which runs across the antecubital fossa.

Step 6: Clean the draw site in a circular motion from the inside out with alcohol. Allow to air dry for 30 seconds. Do not retouch the site.

Step 7: Apply the tourniquet two to four inches above the site. Enter the site quickly with the bevel of the needle facing up. You should feel a slight "give" into the vein.

Step 8: Complete your collection using the correct order of draw and invert the tubes as required within thirty seconds.

Step 9: Release the tourniquet, remove the needle, and apply pressure to the site with gauze. Immediately discard your needle.

Step 10: Label the tubes with the patient's name, date, time of the collection, and your initials. Always label the tubes in front of your patient.

Step 11: Recheck the patient's site for bleeding, apply a bandage, and discard your used equipment in the proper waste receptacles.

Step 12: Wash your hands using the proper medical aseptic procedure.

Step 13: Document the procedure accordingly.

In conclusion, following the proper steps will not always guarantee that you will "hit" the vein. However, following the proper steps will guarantee your safety, your patient's safety, and the integrity of your specimen results.

Source: "Steps in Venipuncture" by Rose Farhat.

QUESTIONS FOR REFLECTION

1. Who is the audience for the instructions? Do the instructions effectively meet the needs of the audience? Why or why not?
2. Which steps are the clearest? Do any steps need further explanation? Elaborate on your answers.
3. Make a list of the major action verbs in each step. Which ones are the most effective? Why?
4. Would this set of instructions be as effective if it had been written in paragraph form instead of in numbered steps? Why or why not?
5. If you have never drawn blood before, would you be able to do so after simply reading these steps? Why or why not?

Career-Based PROCESS WRITING

[preview] **MARISSA SCOTT** worked in a nursing home while she was attending college. She wrote the following essay for her English Composition I course. Have you ever cared for someone who was ill? How does your experience compare to Scott's?

How to Feed a Nursing Home Resident by Marissa Scott

1 Working in a nursing home with different residents can be difficult at times, especially when it comes to feeding a resident who is in bed. While working in a nursing home, you will encounter people from different cultures, backgrounds, and languages. You will also have to deal with residents who are confused or suffering from dementia. There are a few important steps to remember that can help to simplify the feeding process.

2 The first step is to greet the resident. You should knock on the door to show the patient respect. As you enter the room, greet the resident and identify yourself. Next, explain to the resident that you are there for a feeding, and obtain his or her consent to continue. At this time if the patient is confused or speaks a different language, try to point or use gestures or pictures to help explain the procedure to him or her. If the resident just does not want to be bothered, you should encourage him or her and be supportive. Keep in mind that the patient may come from a culture or background that causes him or her to feel embarrassed that another person has to help with feeding. However, if the resident is confused or combative, just leave him or her alone for a few minutes, and then go back and try it again.

3 The second step, after the resident agrees to the feeding procedure, is to raise the head of the bed, making sure that the resident is sitting in an upright position. Adjust the bed to where you will be able to sit at the resident's eye level. While doing this, you should make sure the resident is aware that you are moving the bed to a different position; otherwise he or she might become frightened. Once you start adjusting the bed, make sure the patient is conscious of what you are about to do because, as previously stated, you need to respect the cultural background of the resident.

4 Once you have the bed adjusted, make the final preparations for feeding the patient. Be sure resident's hands are clean. Additionally, place the food tray over the bed table at a comfortable position for the resident to see the food on the tray. Next, ask the resident if he or she would like a clothing protector. Some people consider a clothing protector to be too similar to a child's bib and would not like to have one on while eating. You don't want to offend the patient and interrupt the feeding process. Next, tell the resident what foods are on the tray and ask what he or she would like to eat first. You shouldn't just choose for the resident. Now you are ready to feed the patient.

5 Begin feeding the resident with fairly small amounts of food on a fork or spoon. Give the patient time to chew and swallow before offering another bite. Look for cues from the resident to help you determine the pace. After every few bites, you should ask if the patient wants a sip of the drink. During the feeding, you should try to make conversation with the resident to help him or her feel more comfortable. Be sure to speak only English. For example, if another person walks into the room and you hold a conversation with that person in Spanish or another language that the resident does not speak, the resident may become offended, confused, or scared and think he or she is in a foreign country. Continue feeding until the patient says he or she is full or until the tray of food is empty. Then you can remove the tray and make sure the patient, the bed, and the tray are clean.

6 While working in a nursing home with residents or patients from different cultures and backgrounds, you need to make sure you give them respect during the feeding process because someone could easily get offended and feel like you are not being considerate of his or her feelings. As you greet the patients, get them ready for a meal, and feed them, always keep these steps in mind to help the nursing home residents feel as comfortable as possible.

Source: Marissa Scott.

QUESTIONS FOR REFLECTION

1. Which sentence in the first paragraph introduces the process that will be described? Is it clear? Why or why not?
2. Does the order of the steps make sense? Why or why not?
3. Which steps are explained the best? Why?
4. Which transitions seem to work best in the essay? What effect do they have on the explanation of the process?
5. Does Scott identify any special tips that the reader should consider before performing the process? If so, what are they?

7.3 Explaining Processes in the Context of Cultures and Traditions

In the readings that follow, you will have an opportunity to examine cultures from different perspectives. The term *culture* refers to the way people in a particular group behave based on their beliefs and values. Groups can have a multitude of cultural orientations. They can be based on social interests, attitudes, hobbies, values, ethnicity, educational goals, work endeavors, or a variety of other characteristics. People from various cultures all around the world have traditions that they like to uphold. Whether these traditions are for sports, holidays, birthdays, entertainment, religious ceremonies, work, or everyday life, they all have specific procedures that the participants or observers follow. For example, fans at a heavy metal concert behave very differently than the audience at a symphony orchestra concert.

As human beings we need to be aware of and sensitive to different cultures and traditions. One reason for this sensitivity is that we are likely to encounter people from many different cultures in the workplace. Additionally, each work environment has its own culture (beliefs, values, and guidelines). These principles guide the behavior of the employees. How employees dress, communicate, perform their tasks, and interact with their clients, customers, or patients all depends on the culture of the organization. The readings in this chapter relate to a variety of different types of cultures and include some of the processes that go along with membership in those cultures. Reading and interpreting what others have written can help you see the structure and style of a process analysis and learn how to write about processes for school, work, and your daily life.

Reading and Reflection PROCESS WRITING

[preview] **DIANA LÓPEZ** is an associate professor of creative writing at the University of Houston–Victoria. She has authored several novels for middle-grade children, including *Lucky Luna* and *Coco, a Story About Music, Shoes, and Family*

Sollina Images/Blend Images/Getty Images

(an adaptation of the Disney/Pixar film *Cocoa*). For more information about the author, visit **www.dianalopezbooks.com.** Before reading the essay that follows, which was written for this textbook, consider these questions: Are you familiar with the Day of the Dead festival or have you seen the Disney/Pixar movie *Coco*? Perhaps you've observed other holidays, such as Mardi Gras or Carnaval. If so, what did you learn from the experience, and how did it affect you?

A Picnic with the Dead
by Diana López

In 2013 when Disney tried to trademark the title *Día de los Muertos* for an animated film set in Mexico, it didn't anticipate the controversy that followed. Cartoonist, Lalo Alcaraz, led the protest, creating a poster with "Muerto Mouse," a skeletal Mickey terrorizing a city beneath the headline, "It's coming to trademark your cultura!" Disney took a step back by dropping its request for the trademark, but then it took a step forward by researching and witnessing what makes Día de los Muertos (Day of the Dead) such an important holiday for the Mexican people. 1

This holiday, celebrated annually on November 2nd, has its roots with the Aztecs. Once a year, it is believed, the spirits of the dead are granted passage to the land of the living, and altars and gravesites laden with ofrendas (offerings) welcome them when they arrive. These offerings are a perfect illustration of how the holiday merges the traditions of the Aztecs and of the Roman Catholic Spanish who colonized the area, for they include rosaries, crosses, and candles featuring la Virgen de Guadalupe alongside sugar skulls, papel picado, and cempasúchil (marigolds), whose fragrance and bright orange color attract the spirits. But the ofrendas also feature items unique to the person being honored—a cigar, for example, for someone who liked to smoke; a baseball or fútbol jersey for an athlete; or a stuffed animal for a child. 2

Many people picnic at the gravesites so that they can share a meal with their departed loved ones. These picnics often include tamales and pan de muerto, a sweet bread topped with bone-shaped impressions. But like the ofrendas, the meals are unique, designed to entice the spirits, for what better way to welcome them than to serve their favorite foods and drinks? While they eat, the living tell stories about the deceased, often funny memories as there is much laughter, but it's also common for people to talk directly to the spirits by sharing the latest news, asking for advice, or introducing new family members. 3

While Día de los Muertos has its roots in Mexico, the holiday has been adopted by many communities in the United States as well. These celebrations tend to be more public. A common practice is for schools and places of business to set up communal altars, inviting students or employees to place photos of those who have passed away—family members, friends, and even pets. In Texas, the Centro Cultural Hispano de San Marcos organizes a 5K fundraiser in the name of a recently deceased community leader. It is a great honor for the family to have their loved one chosen, 4 and the proceeds are used for college scholarships. Corpus Christi hosts a citywide event that includes music, dance, and Día de los Muertos–themed art exhibits. Many cities celebrate with parades, inviting people to participate by dressing up as calacas (skeletons). All celebrations—the traditional and the new—seek to welcome the spirits of the dead, to honor their memories, and in that way, to keep them alive.

After the trademark controversy, Disney 5
regrouped. It moved forward with the project, changing the name to *Coco*. The result was an award-winning film praised by the Mexican community for authentically portraying its culture, especially its reverence for Día de los Muertos, the day that allows entire families, both living and dead, to meet once again and celebrate each other's lives.

Source: Used by permission of Diana Lopez.

QUESTIONS FOR REFLECTION

Considering Ideas

1. Why was Disney's original approach to the film greeted with such hostility? How was the company able to make amends after making a huge cultural error?
2. What is the significance of the Día de los Muertos festival? What are the participants hoping to accomplish and why?
3. What are some of the customs associated with the Day of the Dead celebration?

Considering the Rhetorical Star

1. What is the *subject* of the article? Is the specific topic engaging? Why or why not?
2. Who is the intended *audience* for the piece?
3. What is the author's main *purpose* (to inform, to persuade, to entertain, to express feelings) for the essay? Does she use a combination of purposes? How effective is her approach? Explain.
4. What writing *strategies* does López use in the article? How do these strategies affect the work?
5. What is the *design* of the piece? Is it effective? Why or why not?

Considering Writing Strategies

1. Identify several paragraphs where the author explains processes. Is her approach more informative or instructional? How do you know?
2. In the article, López includes Spanish words, which are translated into English. Why does she do that? What effect does this approach have on the reader?
3. What is the tone of the article? Give examples of specific words that reflect the writer's tone.

Writing Suggestions

1. What kinds of celebrations do you participate in as part of your culture? Based on your personal experiences, write an essay explaining one of your customs. Include plenty of details so that your reader has an understanding of the significance of the celebration and the festivities associated with it.
2. Does your family have a special holiday recipe that has been passed down through the generations? Write an explanation of how to make the special dish. You may want to begin with an introduction explaining a little history about your family's recipe, such as who usually makes the dish and when it is typically served. Also, be sure to include a list of ingredients with specific amounts along with the detailed procedure so that your reader can follow your instructions to make the dish.

Reading and Reflection PROCESS WRITING

Jasmine Tan

[preview] **CHRISTINE NG**, born in Singapore, earned a degree in English with a minor in religious studies from the University of California at Berkeley. She has done technical writing and marketing for several companies, including Sephora, eBay, Omnicell, and PopSugar. In the following essay, Ng offers step-by-step instructions for anyone interested in the art of flirtation. Before reading, think about a time when you have flirted with someone. What did you do? What was the other person's response? Were you sucessful, or did you crash and burn?

Bringing Out the Flirt in You

by Christine Ng

1 Have you ever felt an overpowering urge to make yourself known to another individual? From women's fluttering coy eyelids to men's prowling advances, subtle cues have grown into sexual signals. Why does the desire to use small physical and verbal cues to attract the opposite sex still persist? Simple. People enjoy flirting—the healthy, harmless, usually sexual banter between individuals—and it serves an important, if not necessary, role in socializing. As such, people strive to become experts at the art of flirtation, a process rooted in physical appearance and mannerisms.

2 Attracting attention and finding a mate in the animal kingdom entails the art of flirtation based largely on physical beauty and strength. The male lion bristles his proud mane, and the lionesses work tirelessly to do his bidding and attract his attention. Similarly, the confident male peacock struts about, with his beautiful tail of blue-green feathers spread out, hoping to attract the plain brown female. Unlike other animals, however, humans are much more discerning about their appearance prior to flirtatious acts. Though the animal mating ritual requires only one mate to preen excessively during a limited time period, humans—both male and female—often spend hundreds of dollars a year making sure they always look attractive. One of the best-selling products on **Sephora.com** is *Lip Fusion*, a lip-gloss that contains marine collagen micro-spheres that are absorbed into lips and create a beautiful pout, all without the aid of surgery. At thirty-six dollars, this best-selling wonder product costs much more than conventional lip-gloss, yet stores can't seem to keep it in stock! Similarly, with their obsession for designer jeans and expensive hair treatments, men also find themselves drawn to artifice and activities that might help enhance their appearance. Unquestionably, the dawn of the metrosexual has arrived. As a male co-worker jokingly told me while discussing diets and his Lucky Brand jeans, "Hey, it takes a lot of work to look this good!" With all these men and women trying their best to look good, it is clear that in this society, starting to enhance one's finer physical qualities before attempting to flirt is vital.

3 In addition to physical appearance, physical mannerisms also become important, effective tools—or potential liabilities—during the flirting process. Snorting while laughing, burping the national anthem, and spewing beer out of noses are turn-offs, and few want their other halves (well, at least people who enjoy social etiquette) to practice these behaviors when eating dinner with their families. People need to realize that the skills and behavior they would expect to view on *Jackass*, a crude television show, are not necessary in order to become the center of attention. Flirting between couples should consist of lighthearted, civil interaction with one another that may give the impression of sexual interest, not a locker-room gross-out

contest. Once you realize what is or isn't a flirtatious act, using physical appearance and mannerisms to your best advantage, you will be ready to study and implement the rules of flirtation.

4 First, when flirting, remember to establish eye contact rather than looking at the ground. However, do not overdo eye contact while talking. I've seen people stare so intensely they look like crazed stalkers, so tone down if you know your eyes can blaze holes into concrete. Sometimes looking into another's eyes and then turning away will be enough! You have to make the person know you are interested—but certainly not desperate. Also, remember to listen to the object of your flirtation. If you allow your mind to wander, you may miss significant verbal cues requesting a response. Flirting involves a lot of friendly smiles, giggles, and gestures that a person does not share with just anyone. According to Catherine Yumul, a college student, "You can begin flirting by fluttering eyelids, flipping hair, laughing politely, and winking. The inattentive flirt may remain oblivious to the dynamic potential of a situation. That being said, if someone laughs out loud at your jokes, establishes eye contact and comes within the three foot circle of personal space, success is probably close at hand."

5 Second, allow flirtation to flourish by knowing how to reciprocate flirting cues, whether at an intimate dinner for two, or in a large social setting. First impressions can make or break a successful flirt. This brings to mind a chat I had with my cousin. He asked me for my opinion about a girl he liked, and we began by analyzing her behavior and body language. Time after time, she had laughed at his jokes, established eye contact with him, and hit him on the knee, and she often told him he was funny. Based on her flirtatious overtures, and assuming he would respond mutually—given a chance—I told him to go ahead and ask her out to dinner, confident that the date would go well. I could not have been more wrong. The next day, he revealed to me that he had been half an hour late, showed up dressed in disheveled athletic gear, and even let his female friend tag along! At this point, I slapped myself on the forehead, and called him stupid. It was bad enough to be late and look unconcerned about his appearance, but bringing a female friend was the worst thing he could have done on a date with another woman. Overnight, he seemed to have forgotten that flirting requires "give and take" to thrive. Instead, his looks and actions displayed apparent lack of interest in his date. Successful flirtation, therefore, requires the essential ability to interpret cues and act accordingly

6 Third, besides avoiding inappropriate behavior, refrain from embracing advice gleaned from superficial flirtation guides. Though they might raise self-esteem or build self-confidence temporarily, magazines like *Cosmopolitan* often fall short of bringing out the true flirt in you, opting instead for sensational headlines that scream, "How to Get Your Man" and telling women that wearing a short skirt with a matching plunging neckline and heels will do the trick. Magazines for men are no better either. In *FHM,* famous for its "100 Sexiest Women" countdown, there is an abundance of articles about "beer, babes and fast facts" that teach men how to get a woman to do a variety of things. These sexist magazines can't teach people anything they don't already know about flirting. An extremely unattractive trait, desperation, can be smelled a mile away. Desperate times do not call for desperate measures in this case, for such tactics will only make one feel cheap.

7 Fourth, since no best place to flirt exists, select a location that's right for you. Social situations may cause anxiety for many people, but technology has remedied that situation with the introduction of cyber flirting. With the meteoric rise of social networks in the last several years and the increasing acceptance of online dating sites like **Match.com** and OK Cupid, you may even find a friend of a friend you find attractive and ask her or him out. My aforementioned cousin who "struck out" in a conventional flirting situation even has asked a girl out based on seeing her profile on Facebook, and through a series of messages, managed to find his way into a successful dating situation. By testing the waters by looking at profiles and pictures, we now have various avenues and means to initiate flirting on the Internet.

8 These days, many lonely, insecure people venture into an Internet chat room, flirt, and establish relationships without having ever seen the other person. This increasingly popular method

of flirtation liberates people from the confines of conformity and a physical ideal—at least, until they exchange photos. Now, with all the upgrades on instant messenger software, dozens of ways to express flirtatious thoughts and actions exist through icons. A representative list includes:

;-) represents **"a wink"**
*requests* **"don't tell anyone"**
:) or :-) *symbolizes* **"the smile"**
:-$ *indicates* **"embarrassed"**
(YN) *reveals* **"fingers crossed"**
:-0 *projects* **"surprise"**
:\ conveys **"the worried face"**
LOL *means* **"laughing out loud"**
XOXO *expresses* **"love & kisses"**
g* stands for* **"giggle"
;-(*denotes* **"sadness"**
:P *suggests* **"joking face"**

9 Clearly, the Internet has answered dreams for want-to-be flirts afraid of social situations.

10 Fifth, whenever and wherever you flirt, remember to behave within social bounds. This applies to all occasions, although when you are in a bar or club, the loud music may never let you exchange eloquent banter. In that case, the combination of desperate intoxicated people and cheesy pickup lines (a very lousy attempt at flirting) might go unnoticed or actually work. Otherwise, remember to stick to being polite and engaging, and let your natural effervescence shine through. Whether face-to-face or online, focus on common interests during conversation, and be enthusiastic when the other half begins to open up. Though some people are not conversationalists, focusing on the other individual and his/her interests is always helpful.

11 Finally, no matter what forum you chose for playful repartee, keep in mind that flirting is natural and should not be forced. When taken to extremes, "over the top" flirting undermines any healthy intent. Indeed, sometimes a fine line exists between innocent flirtation and aggressive behavior that could be considered pornographic. Paris Hilton's infamous Carl's Jr. Spicy BBQ Burger commercial offers a perfect example of this. Considered by many as "too hot for television," Hilton spent only *seven* seconds out of a *sixty* second commercial holding a Spicy BBQ Burger. The rest of the time she sensuously washed a car, taking time to suggestively soap down her own body, tracing her considerable assets with suds. Did she connect with her target audience? No doubt. Did her "over the top" mannerisms befitting a wet t-shirt contest tastefully promote Spicy BBQ Burgers? Probably not.

12 Thus, although the media attempt to turn flirting into women wearing garments that leave little to the imagination or ogling men with pickup lines penned by clueless minds, we need to ignore such superficial, demeaning stereotypes and trite—possibly offensive—behavior. Instead, focus on self-improvement. Makeover shows that don't rely on plastic surgery such as *What Not to Wear* on TLC constantly demonstrate how a bit of blush on the cheeks or a new outfit can transform one's appearance and improve self-confidence instantly. So go ahead and do the same. Improve your posture, shave your *Unabomber* beard, and let the transformation begin.

13 As concluded by novelist Victor Hugo, "God created the flirt, as soon as he made the fool." Though we are oftentimes fools, flirts or even both, we can try to avoid compromising situations where playful intentions send conflicting messages. Reject the desire to wear that smutty top so you can get a free drink, and resist wearisome pickup lines such as inquiring whether a person's tired because he or she has been running through your mind all night. Be yourself; enjoy the natural pleasures of flirting, and more than anything else, allow your natural confidence and personality to shine through. That way, flirting will make you nobody's fool.

Source: C. Ng, "Bringing Out the Flirt in You." In C. Ng, *Visions Across the Americas* (Canada: Cengage Learning, 2007).

QUESTIONS FOR REFLECTION

Considering Ideas

1. What are some of the best suggestions for flirting in Ng's essay? What do people need to do to be good at flirting? How does culture play a part in the flirting process? Explain your answers.
2. In addition to telling readers what to do, Ng also tells them what not to do. Why

does she do this? What effect does it have on the reader? Include specific examples from the essay to explain your answers.

3. The author discusses using Internet sites, such as **Match.com** and Facebook, to help with the flirting process. Have you ever participated in online flirting or dating, or do you know someone who has? What were the results?

Considering the Rhetorical Star

1. What is the *subject* of Ng's essay? Is this an appealing subject? Why or why not?
2. Who is the intended *audience* for the article? How do you know?
3. What is Ng's primary *purpose* in the essay? Does she effectively achieve her purpose? Why or why not? Is there a secondary purpose as well? If so, what is it?
4. In addition to process analysis, what other writing *strategies* does the author employ? Identify specific passages from the essay to illustrate your point.
5. As part of her *design,* Ng begins with an attention-getter that is separate from the introduction. How does this approach affect the reader?

Considering Writing Strategies

1. Ng uses process writing as her primary writing strategy. Identify several sentences that clearly indicate that this is a process analysis essay. Is process analysis the most effective strategy for her topic? Why or why not?
2. What examples does the author give to support her main points? Are they effective? Why or why not?
3. Ng saves her most important point for last. What is it? What effect does that placement have on the reader?

Writing Suggestions

1. Choose a particular scenario for flirting, such as on campus, online, at a bar, or in another country. Write an essay explaining how to be successful with flirting in that particular environment. You might include specific tips for success and cautions for the readers to consider when flirting.
2. Think about a task that you are particularly adept at performing related to school, a hobby, or your job. Write an essay explaining how to perform the process. Be sure to include specific tips and/or warnings as needed to help the reader to succeed at performing the process.

Reading and Reflection PROCESS WRITING

[preview] **JACK NORWORTH** wrote the famous song "Take Me Out to the Ball Game" on a piece of scrap paper when he was riding a train to Manhattan, New York, in 1908. He gave the lyrics to Albert Von Tilzer, who composed the music to accompany the song. The New York Music Company published the song, which became an instant hit before the year ended. Today baseball fans still sing this classic song, which took Norworth only fifteen minutes to write, during the seventh inning stretch at nearly every baseball game in the United States. You can listen to the song at **www.youtube.com/watch?v=5OdLsiq6F6k.** Before reading, think about sporting events you like to attend with friends or family. What do you find to be exciting about those events?

"Take Me Out to the Ball Game" Lyrics
by Jack Norworth,
Music
by Albert Von Tilzer

Katie Casey was base ball mad.
Had the fever and had it bad;
Just to root for the home town crew,
Ev'ry sou Katie blew.
On a Saturday, her young beau
Called to see if she'd like to go,
To see a show but Miss Kate said,
"No, I'll tell you what you can do."

"Take me out to the ball game,
Take me out with the crowd.
Buy me some peanuts and cracker jack,
I don't care if I never get back,
Let me root, root, root for the home team,
If they don't win it's a shame.
For it's one, two, three strikes, you're out,
At the old ball game."

Katie Casey saw all the games,
Knew the players by their first names;
Told the umpire he was wrong,
All along good and strong.
When the score was just two to two,
Katie Casey knew what to do,
Just to cheer up the boys she knew,
She made the gang sing this song:

"Take me out to the ball game,
Take me out with the crowd.
Buy me some peanuts and cracker jack,
I don't care if I never get back,
Let me root, root, root for the home team,
If they don't win it's a shame.
For it's one, two, three strikes, you're out,
At the old ball game."

Source: Lyrics by Jack Norworth, Music by Albert Von Tilzer.

QUESTIONS FOR REFLECTION

Considering Ideas

1. Have you ever known a baseball fan, or are you one? To what extreme might fans go to see their favorite players?
2. What traditions does Norworth emphasize through his lyrics?
3. What other traditions might be considered American?

Considering the Rhetorical Star

1. What is the main *subject* of the song?
2. Who is the intended *audience?* Is there also a secondary audience? Who else might the song reach besides the primary audience?
3. What is the Norworth's main *purpose* for the song? Does he achieve his purpose? Explain.
4. The author uses process analysis as the primary writing *strategy* for the song. What other strategies does he use?
5. Is the *design* of the song effective? Why or why not?

Considering Writing Strategies

1. Where does Norworth explain a process in the song? How effective is his explanation?
2. What is the tone (mood) of the song? Identify several words that influence the tone.
3. Find several examples of rhyming words in the song. How does Norworth's use of rhyme affect the song?

Writing Suggestions

1. Write an essay explaining a family tradition that a parent or other family member has passed along to you. You might explain what this tradition entails and why it holds special meaning for you, or you may give the reader how-to instructions for following your family's tradition.

2. Write an explanation related to your favorite sport or hobby. One option is to write a step-by-step explanation of how to perform a process, such as the steps for effectively swinging a golf club or blocking a goal in a soccer game. Another option is to explain the process so that your readers will have an understanding of what is involved in the activity, such as what it is like to go skiing or skydiving.

ESOL Tip >

Write about a tradition followed at sports events in your native country. Why is this tradition important to you and the people of your country? When did it begin?

STUDENT WRITING

Cooking Oxtails, Jamaican Style!

by Karen Ebanks

1 Jamaica is a beautiful island located in the Caribbean Sea, south of Cuba and west of the Dominican Republic. It is known for its beautiful beaches, reggae music and slow, relaxed pace and has long been a favorite tourist destination. Jamaica's population is made up of many different races, resulting in a multifaceted culture that is as diverse as its people. Food is one of the most important aspects of Jamaican culture.

2 Jamaicans love to cook, and many of the island's popular dishes contain meat that is not traditionally eaten in the United States. Some of those meats include goat, cow's feet, tripe, and oxtails. All of these dishes are standard fare in a Jamaican home and are also served at various traditional events, such as wedding receptions, celebrations, funeral repast services, and the like. Serving a Jamaican dish is a great way to add something different to one's traditional weeknight dinner, and by following the instructions listed below for Jamaican oxtails, it should not be too difficult. Jamaican oxtails are especially tasty as many seasonings are used to create this dish, and although a few hours are required, it is well worth the time.

3 The following ingredients are necessary to cook this dish:

- ☐ 3 lbs. beef oxtail
- ☐ 2 green onion stalks, chopped
- ☐ 1 cup vinegar
- ☐ 4 cloves garlic, chopped
- ☐ 3 tsp. salt
- ☐ 3 pcs. fresh thyme, chopped
- ☐ ¼ tsp. cayenne pepper
- ☐ ½ green pepper
- ☐ 1 tbsp. onion powder
- ☐ 6 pimento berries (also called allspice)
- ☐ 1 tbsp. garlic powder
- ☐ 2 tbsp. vegetable oil
- ☐ 1 tsp. paprika
- ☐ 1 can butter beans, drained
- ☐ 1 tbsp. browning sauce (optional)
- ☐ 2 carrots sliced thinly
- ☐ 1 onion, chopped
- ☐ water

4 First, trim the fat from the meat and then wash the pieces in a solution of water and vinegar. Next, season the meat with the dry seasonings (salt, pepper, onion powder, garlic powder, and paprika) followed by the browning sauce. If you can, let the meat sit for a few hours or possibly overnight in the refrigerator, which will allow it to season more thoroughly. After that, heat the vegetable oil in a large frying pan and transfer the meat to the pan in order to "brown" it, which means to cook the meat for a short time over medium heat to give it a brown color.

5 When the meat has browned, transfer the pieces of meat into a pressure cooker pot, along with the remaining seasonings, such as the onions, garlic, thyme, green pepper, and pimento berries. Cooking the meat in a pressure cooker will allow it to cook much faster, as oxtail meat can be somewhat tough and take a long time to become tender. Next, pour 4½ cups of water into the pot and cook at high pressure for 20 minutes. High pressure is considered the period in which the pressure regulator on the top of the pressure cooker begins to jiggle gently. Remove the pot from the heat and then allow it to cool completely. Running cold water over the pot lid will help it to cool faster. Only when it is fully cooled should you remove the lid from the pressure cooker.

6 At this point, taste the oxtails to determine if more seasonings are required. If so, add salt, pepper, or other seasonings accordingly. Next, add the carrots and cook for an additional 15 minutes over medium heat, stirring occasionally. Finally, add the butter beans, and after cooking for 5 more minutes, your oxtail dish will be done. This recipe takes about 2½ hours to prepare and serves four people.

7 Jamaican oxtails make a wonderful, tasty meal that is best served over another popular Jamaican dish called rice and peas. (Of course, it never hurts to serve it with a bit of Jamaican rum as well.) You can find oxtails at any typical Jamaican restaurant here in the U.S., or you can choose to be adventurous and attempt to cook your own. Either way, you will enjoy a delicious Jamaican dish that might make you consider taking a trip to the island itself. Yah Mon!

QUESTIONS FOR REFLECTION

1. What does Ebanks accomplish in the first paragraph? She delays the thesis until the second paragraph. Is this approach effective in this essay? Why or why not?
2. The author provides the reader with a list of ingredients. Would the essay be stronger or weaker if the ingredients were in paragraph form? Why?
3. Based on these instructions, would you be able to cook Jamaican oxtails if you had all of the necessary ingredients? Why or why not?
4. What transitions does the author use to help guide the reader? Which ones are the most useful? Why?
5. Which parts of the concluding paragraph leave you with a lasting impression? Why?

STUDENT WRITING

How to Make a Traditional Hawaiian Lei

by Alexander Gehring

1 Lei making is a very rich and time-honored tradition of Hawaii. Leis were first introduced to the islands from early Polynesian settlers traveling across the Pacific from Tahiti. Traditional leis can be made from just about anything you can find in nature. Flowers, leaves, shells, feathers, and even bone and teeth of various animals can be used. Early Hawaiians constructed and wore leis as a way to beautify and to distinguish themselves from others.

2 The most significant of all leis is the Maile lei. The Maile lei is known as the "lei of royalty" and is given as a sign of respect and honor. In the past they were used as an offering during times of war. The two opposing chiefs would intertwine the Maile vine, officially establishing peace between the tribes. Today, they are reserved for special and memorable occasions such as weddings, birthdays, graduations, and elections. In a traditional Hawaiian wedding the Kahuna (Hawaiian priest) will use the Maile lei and tie the hands of the bride and groom together signifying their commitment to one another. When students in Hawaii graduate from school, they receive so many leis that sometimes it is hard to see their faces.

3 The fringed ti leaf lei is one of the oldest and simplest leis to make. To make one, all you need are two large ti leaves. If you are lucky enough to live in an area where ti plants are native, then all you need to do is pick your leaves and wash them. If not, you can order them on the Internet. Ti leaves come in two colors: green and red. Traditionally, green leaves are used when making leis, but the choice is yours.

4 Before making the lei, you need to remove the stiff center vein of the leaf. To do this, make a shallow cut on the backside of the leaf along the vein, being careful not to cut all the way through the leaf. After you have made your cut, strip off the vein with your fingers. Next, tie the two leaves together at the stems using a square knot. Finally, fringe the leaves by making small strips in them. You now have an authentic Hawaiian lei that you can wear or give to a friend.

5 There are, however, a few unspoken rules to keep in mind when receiving a lei from someone. The giving of a lei is a friendly celebration and should never be refused. Also, it is considered disrespectful to remove a lei when in the presence of the person who gave it to you. To wear a lei, gently drape it over your shoulders, allowing it to hang down in both the front and back.

6 Hawaiian leis are a fun part of any celebration. Most people appreciate them and greet them with a smile. Leis are universal and can be given at almost any event. The next time you want to make someone feel special, make him or her an authentic Hawaiian lei.

QUESTIONS FOR REFLECTION

1. Look back through the essay and identify some of the different writing strategies that Gehring uses to explain how to make a Hawaiian lei. Why does this combination approach work well for this topic?
2. Does the author use any words that are new to you? Do you think he defines them sufficiently? Why or why not?
3. Do you have enough information to actually make a lei? Explain.
4. Could any parts of the essay be illustrated with a graphic? Which parts would benefit most? What would you include?
5. Which part of the essay is most interesting or memorable? Why?

Activity Sharing a Familial or Cultural Tradition

In pairs or small groups, brainstorm to create a list of family traditions and cultural traditions the members in your group have experienced. Next, each participant will explain one of his or her cultural traditions in detail so the other students have a good idea of its significance. A representative from each group will then share a few ideas with the class. This activity may provide you with ideas for a writing assignment.

Activity Writing Simple Instructions

In pairs or small groups, write an explanation of a short, easy process that can be performed in a classroom setting. Give your instructions to another student or group to see if they can perform the process. Likewise, you or your group will attempt to perform the instructions from another group. Discuss any steps or details that were lacking in either set of directions. How could the instructions be improved? Share your results with the class.

Now that you have read one or more examples of process analysis, it's time to write your own. You may choose to write about one of the writing options that follow, the advertisement, the image, or one of the media suggestions. Consider your rhetorical star and the qualities of an effective process paper as you begin to compose your assignment.

Writing Assignment Options

Use one of the following topics to write an informative or instructional essay. Remember to consider your rhetorical star as well as the steps for writing about a process as you compose.

1. How to manage time or stress
2. How to study for an exam or how to pass a class, such as English Composition
3. How to achieve success (or failure) in college, on the job, or in life
4. How to perform a process on the job
5. How to make the most of a vacation to a particular location
6. How to construct or assemble a small item
7. How a piece of machinery or equipment works
8. How to plan the perfect wedding or other celebration
9. How to eat right or get in shape
10. How an event occurred

Shutterstock / emka74

OPTIONS FOR WRITING A PROCESS ESSAY

Interpreting an Advertisement

While most advertisements appear in magazines or newspapers or on billboards, sometimes people use their cars to advertise their views. What do you think about the "Coexist" bumper sticker on page 168? What message does the artist convey and why? Write a response to this bumper sticker or another one. For example, you might write an essay suggesting ways that people can get along (coexist) better with others.

Multimodal Assignment

Using one of the readings, writing assignment options, or another topic, create a multimodal project using the process analysis writing strategy and at least two or more of the options in Table 7.1.

Table 7.1

Multimodal Options		
Artifact	Images	PowerPoint
Artwork	Infographics	Prezi
Audio clip	Journal	Video
Blog	Montage	Website
Digital portfolio	Podcast	Wiki
Graphic organizer	Poster	Writing

(See Chapter 15 for more details about multimodal compositions.)

Writing about an Image

George Tiedemann/Sports Illustrated/Getty Images

OPTIONS FOR WRITING A PROCESS ESSAY

Look at the images throughout this chapter and consider these questions: What cultural tradition does the image represent? What process is being performed? What tone does the image portray? How do the artist's techniques affect the image? What ideas about your own culture and traditions does the image conjure? Choose one of the images in the chapter, such as the NASCAR photo, that depicts a process you are familiar with, and write an essay relating to it. You might respond to the image, tell what is happening in the image, or explain how to perform a process that relates to the image in some way. For example, you might choose to write an essay giving instructions for how to perform a particular soccer kick or move, or you may decide to explain how to play a musical instrument.

Media Connection for Explaining Processes

You might watch, read, and/or listen to one or more of the media products or outlets listed in Table 7.2 to discover additional examples of process analysis. Exploring various media may help you to better understand methods for explaining processes. You may also choose to write about one or more of the media suggestions. For example, you might watch an episode of *Legendary Locations* with Josh Gates or *Bizarre Foods* with Andrew Zimmern on the Travel Channel and then write an essay explaining the best way to experience the culture and take in the sights in a particular city, such as Paris. Be sure to give credit to the source you use in your essay.

Table 7.2

Media Chart				
Television	*Hell's Kitchen*	Home and Garden (HGTV)	Travel Channel	DIY Network
Film	*How to Train Your Dragon: The Hidden World* (2019)	*How to Lose a Guy in Ten Days* (2003)	*Annihilation* (2018)	*How to Survive a Plague* (2012)
Print/ E-Reading	*The World of Chinese*	*Bon Appétit*	*Hispanic Lifestyle*	*Ebony*
Internet	**essortment.com**	**guitarvision.com**	**howstuff works.com**	**origami-instructions .com**
Music	"50 Ways to Say Goodbye" by Train	"How to Save a Life" by The Fray	"How to Love" by Lil Wayne	"How to Be a Heartbreaker" by Maria and The Diamonds

7.4 Analyzing the Rhetorical Star for Explaining a Process in Writing

As you prepare to write your process paper, consider the five points of the rhetorical star (Figure 7.1). You might use some of the questions in the chart as you conduct your rhetorical star analysis.

Subject	Choose a topic appropriate for a college-level audience. It should be a process you are very familiar with but your readers may not understand or know how to do. Make sure that the process isn't too simple or too complicated.
Audience	Who are your readers? What do they need to know about the process? Do you want your readers to be able to perform the process? Or do you just want them to have an understanding of how something was done or how something works? How much detail do you need to include based on the characteristics and needs of the audience? You are better off giving too much detail than not enough detail if you are not sure how familiar your audience is with the process.
Purpose	Is your main purpose to instruct or inform? An instructional process tells the readers how to make or do something. An informative process tells the readers how something works, how a process was done, or how something was made. What additional goals do you have? Is your explanation meant to entertain the reader? Are you trying to convince your readers that a particular method works better than another? Are you combining purposes? Keep your purpose in mind as you begin writing.
Strategy	Will you include other writing strategies in addition to explaining the process? For example, do you want to use definition, description, or narration to enhance your explanation?
Design	Do you want to explain the process in paragraph form? Or would numbered steps be more effective? How long should your explanation be? What other design elements, such as headings, pictures, or diagrams would help your reader to better understand the process? See Figure 7.2 for an example of process writing with numbered steps and photographs.

FIGURE 7.1 The Rhetorical Star

FIGURE 7.2 Sample Design for Instructions

Below is an explanation for the process of transferring a patient from a bed to a stretcher using the "draw sheet transfer" method. What features are especially helpful to the design? Do you think you could be successful doing a draw sheet transfer using these instructions? Why or why not?

Draw Sheet Transfer

STEP 1

- ☐ Loosen the draw sheet on the bed, and form a long roll to grasp.
- ☐ Prepare the stretcher by unbuckling the straps, adjusting the height of the stretcher so that it is even with the bed, and lowering the side rails.
- ☐ Set the brakes on the stretcher (if so equipped) to the ON position.
- ☐ Position the stretcher next to and touching the patient's bed.

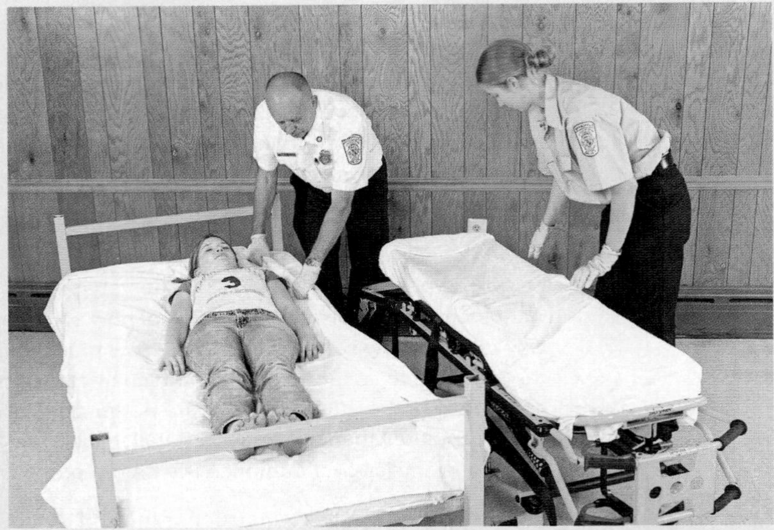

Rick Brady/McGraw-Hill Education

STEP 2

- ☐ Both rescuers should stand on the same side of the stretcher and then reach across it to grasp the draw sheet firmly at the patient's head and hips.

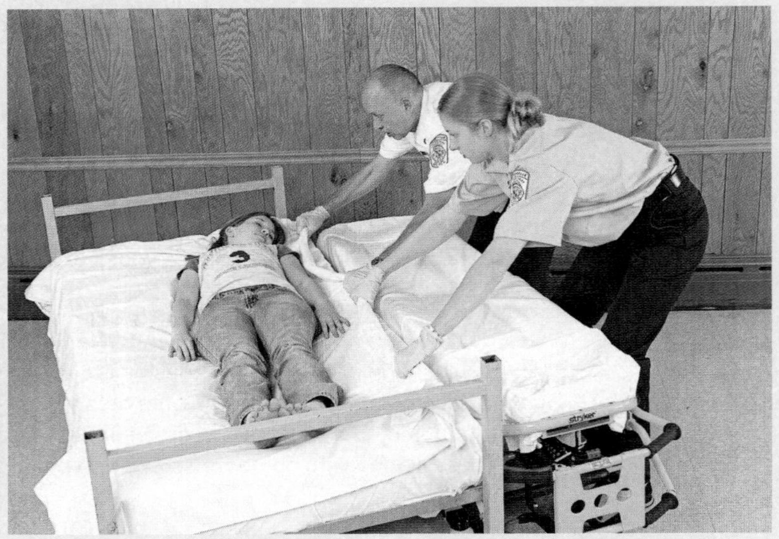

Rick Brady/McGraw-Hill Education

STEP 3

☐ On a signal from the rescuer at the patient's head, both rescuers gently slide the patient from the bed to the stretcher.

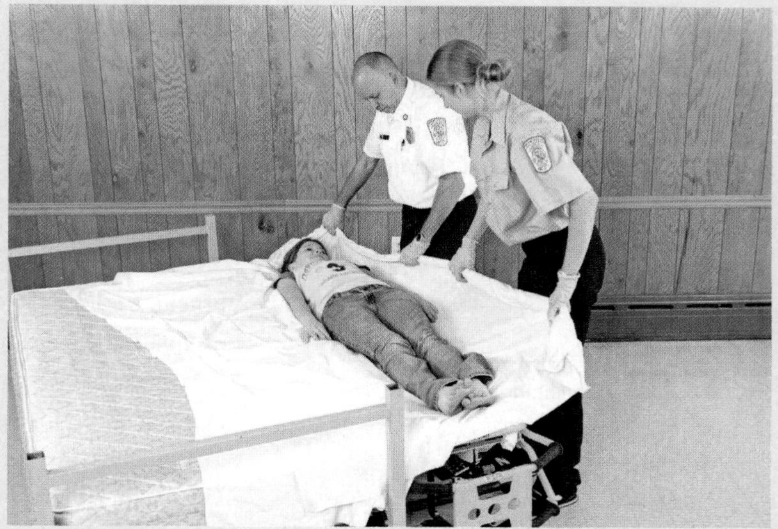

Source: Aehlert, *Emergency Medical Responder,* McGraw-Hill, 2011. *Rick Brady/McGraw-Hill Education*

7.5 Applying the Steps for Writing about a Process

After you have completed your rhetorical star analysis, follow the steps of the writing process (Figure 7.3) to compose your process paper.

1. **Discovering:** When you have chosen a topic, you may want to make a rough sketch of the process or procedure to help aid your writing process. Next, you might brainstorm to determine what materials are needed to complete the process. Additionally, you may want to develop a rough list of the steps you think will be important to include and then put the steps into chronological order by numbering them. Using the Explaining a Process graphic organizer (Figure 7.4) may help you with this.
2. **Planning:** Try creating a list or an outline (informal or formal) to help you organize your ideas. Remember to follow a chronological sequence for your process. Go through the process step-by-step in your mind to make sure that the way you have ordered ideas is clear and logical.

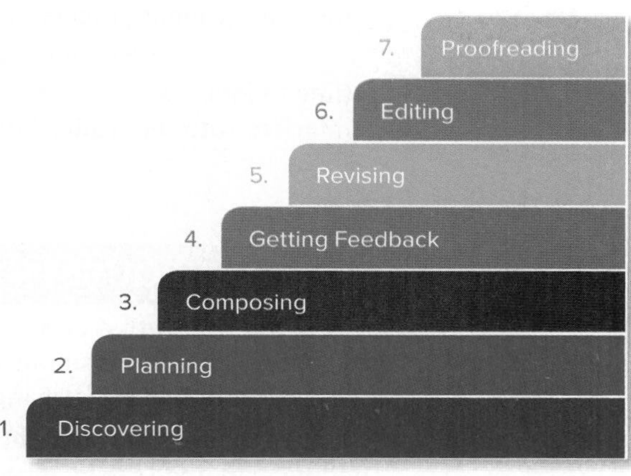

FIGURE 7.3 The Seven Steps of the Writing Process

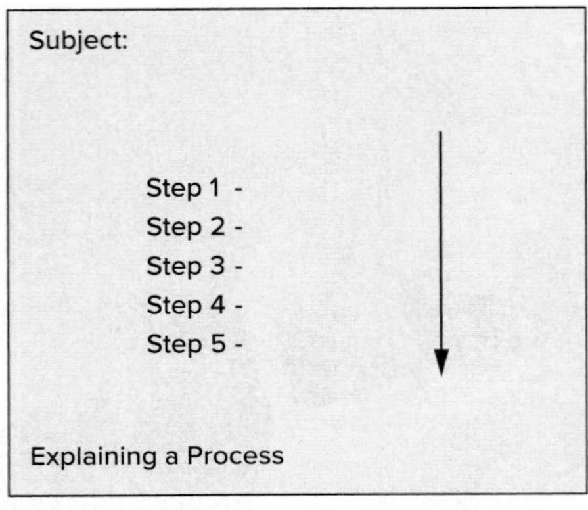

Subject:
Step 1 -
Step 2 -
Step 3 -
Step 4 -
Step 5 -
Explaining a Process

FIGURE 7.4 Explaining a Process

3. **Composing:** Write a first draft of your process analysis. Don't worry too much about grammar and punctuation at this time. Focus on retelling the details related to the process. Be sure to keep your overall point in mind as you write.

   Use the seven qualities of effective process writing you learned earlier in this chapter. These characteristics are a key part of the writing process:

   1. Begin with a clear introduction.
   2. Include a list of materials as needed.
   3. Explain the steps in chronological order.
   4. Define special terms as needed.
   5. Give helpful tips and warnings as needed.
   6. Include visual aids as needed.
   7. End with a decisive conclusion.

4. **Getting Feedback:** Have at least one classmate, or other person, read your rough draft and answer the peer review questions that appear below. If you have access to a writing tutor or center, get another opinion about your paper as well. If possible, ask your reviewer to explain which parts are most clear and which steps, if any, need more explanation.
5. **Revising:** Using all of the feedback available to you, revise your process analysis. Make sure that the steps of your process are clear and follow a chronological order. Additionally, check to see that you have kept your audience's needs in mind throughout your explanation of the process. Try going though the process in your head using your explanation to make sure that you haven't left out any important steps or warnings.
6. **Editing:** Read your process analysis again, this time looking for errors in grammar, punctuation, and mechanics. Pay particular attention to your use of transitions and action verbs because these areas are especially important for writing about processes.
7. **Proofreading:** After you have carefully edited your essay, read it one last time to look for typographical errors and any other issues that might interfere with the readers' understanding of your explanation.

PEER REVIEW QUESTIONS FOR EXPLAINING A PROCESS

Trade rough drafts with a classmate and answer the following questions about his or her paper. Then, in person or online, discuss your papers and suggestions with your peer. Finally, make the changes you feel would most benefit your paper.

1. Identify the thesis statement. Does it effectively let you know what process will be explained? Why or why not?

2. Are there any additional materials that need to be included or terms that need to be defined? What are they?
3. Do the steps flow logically and smoothly? Why or why not?
4. Which part do you think is explained best? Why?
5. Do you feel that you fully understand the process the author is explaining? If not, which parts could use more details or clarification?
6. Does the author provide the reader with a sense of completion at the end? If so, how?
7. What kinds of grammatical errors, if any, are evident in the explanation?
8. What final suggestions do you have for the author?

Writer's Checklist for Explaining a Process

Use the checklist below to evaluate your own writing and help ensure that your explanation of the process is complete. If you have any "no" answers, continue working on those areas.

- ☐ 1. Is my title suitable?
- ☐ 2. Does my thesis statement clearly identify the process I am explaining?
- ☐ 3. Does my introduction give the reader an indication of the points I make in the body of my essay or instructions?
- ☐ 4. If they are necessary, have I identified the materials and quantities effectively?
- ☐ 5. Have I included all of the necessary steps for the reader to understand or perform the process?
- ☐ 6. Are all of my steps in chronological order?
- ☐ 7. Have I used transitions to increase readability?
- ☐ 8. Have I used active verbs to emphasize each step?
- ☐ 9. Have I clearly defined terms that my reader may not understand?
- ☐ 10. Have I indicated when the process is complete?
- ☐ 11. Have I proofread thoroughly?

CHAPTER SUMMARY

1. Use the process writing strategy to explain how to do something or describe how something works or was done.
2. Process writing is an important part of your education, daily life, and career.

3. Every culture in the world has traditions and procedures that it follows. Being sensitive to the processes associated with various cultures will help you to be more successful in the workplace.
4. Interpreting readings and images that relate to processes can help you to prepare to write a process analysis essay.
5. Carefully analyze the rhetorical star before explaining a process in writing: subject, audience, purpose, strategy, and design.
6. Use these qualities when writing about a process: Begin with a clear introduction; include a list of materials as needed; explain the steps in chronological order; define special terms as needed; give helpful tips and warnings as needed; include visual aids as needed; end with a decisive conclusion.

WHAT I KNOW NOW

Use this checklist to determine what you need to work on to feel comfortable with your understanding of the material in this chapter. Check off each item as you master it. Review the material for any unchecked items.

- ☐ 1. I know what **process writing** is.
- ☐ 2. I can identify several **real-world applications** for process writing.
- ☐ 3. I can evaluate **readings and images** that explain a process.
- ☐ 4. I can analyze the **rhetorical star** for writing about a process.
- ☐ 5. I understand the **writing process** for explaining a process.
- ☐ 6. I can apply the **seven qualities** of writing about a process.

CHAPTER

8 Comparing and Contrasting: Computers and Technology

Source: Mr. Gerald Sonnenberg/U.S. Air Force

learning outcomes

In this chapter you will learn techniques for achieving these learning outcomes:

Writing Strategy Focus: Comparing and Contrasting

When you compare and contrast subjects, you are looking at similarities and differences between them. People often use comparison and contrast to better understand one subject in terms of another. Furthermore, the comparison and contrast strategy is useful for making decisions. For example, when you decided to enroll in your current college or university, you probably compared it to one or more other schools to determine which one would best fulfill your needs as a student.

When you compare and contrast subjects, you must use specific points, or criteria, for your comparison. When you were comparing schools, you probably considered some of the following criteria to help make your decision: location, programs offered, class size, facilities, accreditation, and so on. Weighing the relevant criteria is essential to the comparison and contrast process. Being able to write an effective comparison and contrast paper will be useful in school, in your daily life, and in your career.

8.1 Real-World Applications for Comparing and Contrasting

Writing to Compare and Contrast in College

You will often be asked to identify similarities and differences between two or more subjects in college courses. You might need to compare and contrast characters in a literature class. Your psychology instructor may ask to you compare and contrast two theories or learning styles. In a history class, you may need to compare and contrast significant events, people, or places. Similarly, an instructor in your major course of study may require that you compare and contrast two or more methods for accomplishing a task or performing a skill.

Writing to Compare and Contrast in Your Daily Life

You make comparisons on a daily basis: Deciding what to wear, what to eat, where to go, and what to do all require comparisons. When you decide to make a major purchase, such as an entertainment system, a car, or a home, you'll need to compare the options to see which item best suits your needs and fits within your budget. Additionally, if you need someone to fix your car, babysit your child, or repair your home, then you'll need to compare and contrast your options to make the best possible decision.

Writing to Compare and Contrast in Your Career

Being able to write an effective comparison is also extremely useful in the workplace. When you look for a job you will need to compare the offers you get based on a number of factors, such as salary, location, benefits, and work environment. You might need to compare and contrast two software packages or pieces of equipment to decide which one would be more effective to use at your place of employment. Or you may need to compare candidates for a position within your organization to decide which one is most qualified for the job. Here are a few specific applications for comparison and contrast writing in your career:

Health care: symptoms, treatments, office procedures, or record-keeping methods.

Law: case studies, witnesses' testimonies, or legal procedures.

Education: teaching and learning methods, models, and styles.

Computers: hardware, software, applications, or designs.

Massage therapy: massage techniques, equipment, and lubricants.

Culinary arts: ingredients, cooking styles, menu designs, knives, or cleaning methods.

Business: business models, lending sources, locations, products, and services.

Graduate SPOTLIGHT

Carlos Felix, Software Engineer

©Karin L. Russell

Carlos Felix has a degree in computer engineering. He is currently a software engineer for Harris Corporation, which is an information technology and communications company that serves government and commercial markets internationally. Here's what Felix has to say about the importance of written communication in his career:

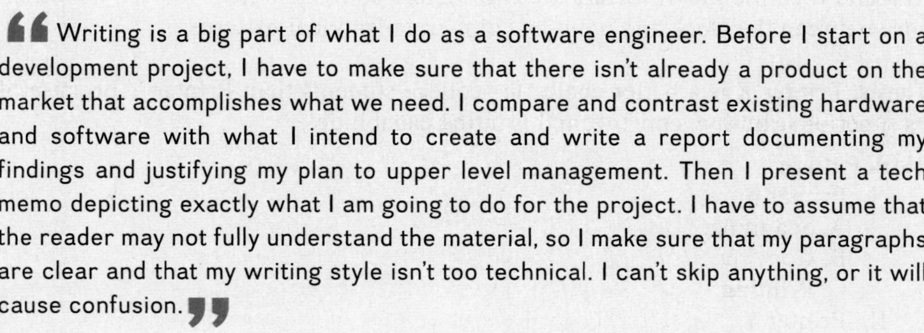

"Writing is a big part of what I do as a software engineer. Before I start on a development project, I have to make sure that there isn't already a product on the market that accomplishes what we need. I compare and contrast existing hardware and software with what I intend to create and write a report documenting my findings and justifying my plan to upper level management. Then I present a tech memo depicting exactly what I am going to do for the project. I have to assume that the reader may not fully understand the material, so I make sure that my paragraphs are clear and that my writing style isn't too technical. I can't skip anything, or it will cause confusion."

Activity Brainstorming Real-World Comparison and Contrast Writing

On your own, in pairs, or in small groups, brainstorm uses for writing comparisons at school, in your daily life, and on the job. You may want to choose your career field or the prospective career field(s) of the participants in your group. Be prepared to share your results with your instructor or class.

8.2 Qualities of Comparison and Contrast Writing

1. Begin by Identifying the Elements You Are Comparing

Somewhere in the first paragraph, mention the items you are comparing. Depending on your subject, you may decide to emphasize similarities, differences, or both. You will want to make your approach clear in your thesis and introduction. For example, if you are comparing two printers, you might focus on differences and write a thesis like this: Printer X is a better choice for college students than Printer Y because of its superior scanning, copying, and printing capabilities.

2. Use a Block or Point-by-Point Approach

There are two basic patterns for organizing a comparison and contrast essay. When you use the *block pattern,* you explain your points of comparison for one item, and then you explain your main points about the second one. If you use the *point-by-point pattern,* you focus on each point you are making and tell about both items as they relate to that point.

Choose the method that seems to work best for your topic. For example, if you are writing an essay comparing two video game systems, the point-by-point method might work best because you can easily highlight the features of each system. However, if you are writing about how technology has changed the way you spend your leisure time, you might use the block pattern to write about the past first and then the present. Here are two sample outlines to help you see the difference between the block and point-by-point organizational patterns:

Thesis: Printer X is a better choice for college students than Printer Y because of its superior scanning, copying, and printing capabilities.

Block Pattern

I. Printer X
  A. Scanning
  B. Copying
  C. Printing
II. Printer Y
  A. Scanning

B. Copying
C. Printing

Point-by-Point Pattern

I. Scanning
  A. Printer X
  B. Printer Y
II. Copying
  A. Printer X
  B. Printer Y
III. Printing
  A. Printer X
  B. Printer Y

3. Describe Your Subjects Fairly and Accurately

Use vivid descriptions so that your reader can imagine the subjects you are comparing and contrasting. Choose the details that your readers will most need to understand. Also, you will want to balance your coverage of the subjects you are comparing and contrasting. If you focus mostly on just one of the items, you may have difficulty convincing the readers that your points are valid.

Furthermore, you will need to ensure that your comparisons are ethical. You don't want to unfairly skew the details and examples you provide about one subject so that you undermine the other. For example, if you are comparing cable and satellite television services, it would be unethical to point out that satellite reception is sometimes interrupted by stormy weather, but neglect to mention that cable reception is also interrupted on occasion for various reasons.

4. Consider Using an Analogy

Often you can enhance your comparisons by using some sort of analogy. Typically, an analogy compares something unfamiliar to something familiar. For example, if you are comparing your experience playing two new video games, you might say that one is as exciting as leaping out of an airplane at 30,000 feet, while the other is about as stimulating as reading all of the ingredients on a cereal box. If you do use an analogy, be careful to avoid clichés. Comparing your life to a ride on a roller coaster isn't exactly going to "wow" your readers. You are better off coming up with a fresh, original analogy.

ESOL Tip >

Analogies are especially helpful if your topic is unfamiliar to readers who are unacquainted with your culture.

5. Use Transitions to Help Your Writing Flow Smoothly

If you choose the right transitions, your comparison and contrast essay will be more coherent for your audience. When you are emphasizing similarities, transitions such as *also, similarly,* and *both* can be useful. When you focus on differences, you might try transitional devices such as *however, unlike,* and *on the other hand.* Using transitional expressions can also help you to keep your essay from sounding like a tennis match, where you awkwardly bounce back and forth between the two subjects. Varying your word choice and sentence structure will also help you to avoid the monotony of the tennis ball effect.

6. Conclude Logically

Typically, the conclusion is a good place to restate your main idea and summarize your main points. When writing a comparison, you might come to a logical conclusion that wasn't obvious from the thesis. For example, if you are comparing two video games or movies, you might determine which one you would recommend. If you include your recommendation in the introduction, your readers might not bother reading your complete comparison.

Activity Making Analogies

Analogies are useful when writing to compare something unfamiliar to something familiar.

EXAMPLE

In the movie *Forrest Gump*, the title character says, "Life is like a box of chocolates. You never know what you're gonna get."

In pairs, groups, or on your own, come up with an analogy for each of the following subjects. Be careful to avoid clichés. Instead, create original comparisons.

1. Life or happiness
2. A computer, a camera, or another electronic device
3. A joyous occasion, such as a wedding, the birth of a child, or a school graduation
4. A specific messy situation, such as a breakup, job loss, or property foreclosure
5. A specific person or animal from a television show or movie

8.3 Comparing and Contrasting in the Context of Computers and Technology

We are relying more and more on technological devices for work, school, and entertainment. Most of us use computers, smartphones, and a variety of other gadgets on a daily basis. When we get a break from our hectic schedules, many of us enjoy surfing the Internet, watching movies or television, listening to digital music, or playing video games. Additionally, technology has revolutionized the way we communicate with one another. Through e-mail, text messaging, and smartphones, we are able to be in virtually constant contact with our co-workers, classmates, friends, and families. We feel lost when the computer network goes down or our smartphone service is interrupted.

With all of the high-tech products available on the market, we have to make careful decisions about which ones we want to purchase. To make those choices, we need to compare and contrast the items we are considering to determine which ones have the best design, features, and price to meet our needs most effectively. As you analyze the readings and images in this chapter, consider the following questions: How is the technology portrayed? How does it impact people? Has technology simplified or complicated our lives? What does the future of technology have in store for us? Additionally, seeing how other writers have structured their comparison and contrast essays will help you to organize your own essays.

Grammar Window
ADVERBS

You will need to choose precise words when you describe items you are comparing or contrasting. In doing so, you may find adverbs to be quite useful. Adverbs modify (or explain) verbs, adjectives, or other adverbs and typically tell how, when, where, or why. Writers commonly use adverbs incorrectly, so you will want to be careful when writing them. The adverbs are highlighted in the following sentences:

Incorrect example: Drive careful when traveling during treacherous weather.

Correct example: Drive carefully when traveling during treacherous weather.

Activity: Choose a paragraph in a magazine, online article, or this textbook. Add at least three adverbs to the paragraph.

Career-Based COMPARING AND CONTRASTING

[preview] **PETER CARDON** is an associate professor of clinical management communication for the school of business at the University of Southern California Marshall. He has an MBA and a PhD from Utah State University. He has published numerous articles on the topics of intercultural communication and social networking. The two readings that follow are excerpts from Cardon's book titled *Business Communication: Developing Leaders for a Networked World.* Cardon has documented his sources using the *Chicago Manual of Style* (CMS) format, with raised numbers and endnotes. This style of citing sources is common in book publishing and is often used by and in disciplines including business, fine art, and history. The first reading illustrates the block pattern of comparison; the second reading reflects the point-by-point pattern of comparison. Read both comparisons before answering the questions for reflection that follow the second one.

Block Pattern The Evolving Workplace by Peter Cardon

Industrial Age	Information Age	Social Age
Command-and-control (Little communication between teams and units)	Mass two-way communication (Extensive communication between teams and units)	Networked communication (Extensive communication between individuals with shared interests)
Respect for position	Respect for expertise and position	Respect for expertise and contributions to the network
Holding authority is power	Holding knowledge is power	Sharing knowledge is power
Efficiency, competitiveness, and authority are key values	Autonomy, innovation, and achievement are key values	Transparency, honesty, and camaraderie are key values

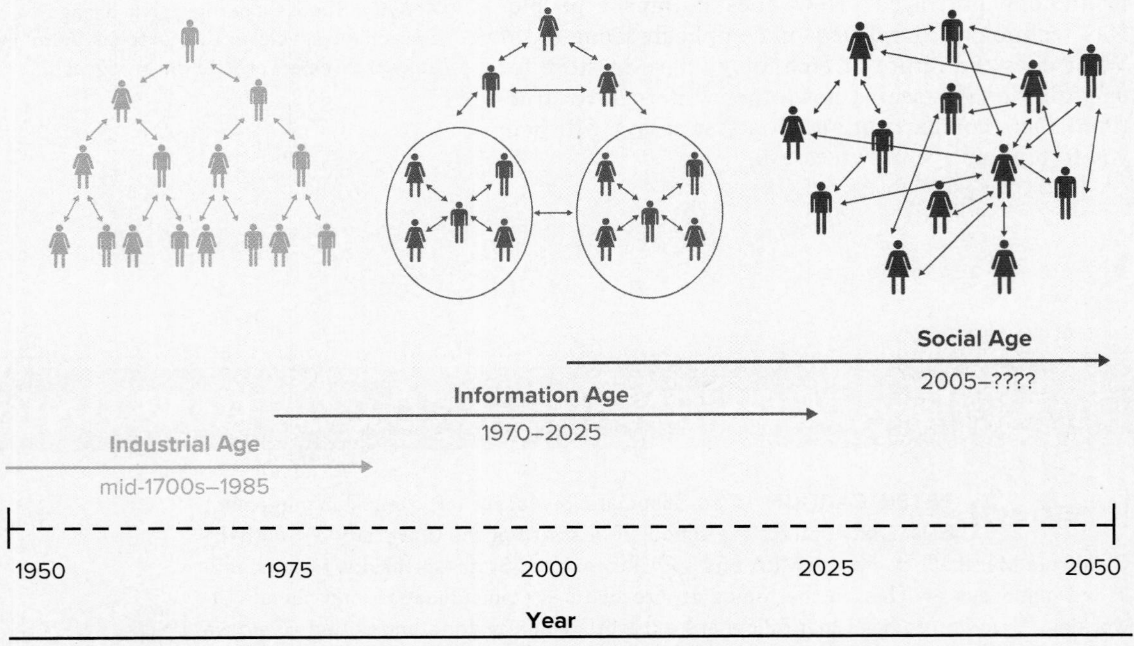

Source: Peter Cardon, *Business Communication: Developing Leaders for a Networked World,* McGraw-Hill, 2018.

Point-by-Point Pattern Characteristics of the Social Age by Peter Cardon

1 The evolution of the Internet . . . from Web 1.0 to Web 2.0 platforms is the primary driver of the Social Age. In the original Internet, referred to as **Web 1.0,** most web pages were read-only and static. As the Internet evolved, referred to as **Web 2.0,** what emerged was the read-write web,

where users interact extensively with web pages—authoring content, expressing opinions, and customizing and editing web content among other things. Web 2.0 communication tools, often referred to as **social media,** include social networks, blogs, wikis, gaming, podcasts, and information tagging. In simple terms, Web 1.0 communication tools are primarily passive and static. By contrast, Web 2.0 communication tools are interactive, customizable, and *social.*[1] **User 1.0** refers to an individual who primarily uses and prefers Web 1.0 tools, whereas **User 2.0** refers to an individual who primarily uses and prefers Web 2.0 tools (see Table 1).[2] The emerging Social Age is adopting many workplace norms and values from users of Web 2.0 tools.

Increasingly, companies are adopting social networking platforms that contain Web 2.0 communication tools (also called *enterprise social software* and *Enterprise 2.0*) in the workplace. These platforms contain many of the features available on social networking websites: user profiles, microblogs, blogs, wikis, and file uploading. They often include a variety of other communication and collaboration tools as well, including online audio and video calls, shared work spaces, calendars, and private messaging (or e-mail) systems. Thus, most companies—especially medium- to large-sized businesses—are increasingly moving toward corporate intranets that contain both Web 1.0 and Web 2.0 tools.

The emerging work culture associated with the Social Age presents many benefits to companies and business professionals in the context of team and networked communication (see Table 2).[3] When social media are used for professional purposes, teams can communicate more efficiently; companies can interface more responsively to customers, clients, and suppliers; customers and other interested individuals can be directly involved in the development of products and services; and anyone with shared professional interests can communicate easily, not needing to travel to see one another.

Notes

1. Michael Chui, Andy Miller, and Roger P. Roberts, "Six Ways to Make Web 2.0 Work," *McKinsey Quarterly,* (July 2009): www.mckinsey.com/
2 business-functions/mckinsey-digital/our-insights/six-ways-to-make-web-20-work. no. 1.

2. Simon Wright and Juraj Zdinak, *New Communication Behaviors in a Web 2.0 World—Changes, Challenges and Opportunities in the Era of the Information Revolution* (Paris: Alcatel-Lucent, 2008): 10.

3. Wright and Zdinak, *New Communication Behaviors in a Web 2.0 World;* Andreas M. Kaplan and Michael Haenlein, "Users of the World, Unite! The Challenges and Opportunities of Social Media," *Business Horizons* 53, no. 1 (2010): 59–68; AON Consulting, *Web 2.0 and Employee Communications: Summary of Survey
3 Findings* (Chicago: AON Consulting, March 2009); Jacques Bughin, Michael Chui, and Andy Miller, "How Companies Are Benefiting from Web 2.0,"

Table 1

Comparisons between User 1.0 and User 2.0

User 1.0	User 2.0
Passively reading and searching for content	Actively creating and sharing content online
Depends on content creator; does not express own opinion	Can express opinions and even change the content presented
Getting the web as is	Customizing web pages and content
Email is the main communication tool	Peer-to-peer programs are the main communication tools
The computer is the main access point	Connects from various devices
Connected online for time-limited sessions	Connected online all the time

Table 2

Benefits and Challenges of Social Media in the Workplace	
Benefits of Social Media	**Challenges and Risks of Social Media**
To Companies: • Team communication and collaboration • Succession planning • Recruitment and on-boarding • Idea sharing/knowledge management • Skills development and training • Interfacing with customers, suppliers, and partners • Decreased time to market for new products and services • More innovative, creative, effective, and profitable approaches to work problems • Less time and fewer resources needed for business travel	*To Companies:* • Lack of adoption and penetration • Lack of permanence • Confusion over which communication channels to use • Distraction from work, too much socializing • Lack of control of information provided externally and internally • Lack of systems for rewarding networked and team communication and collaboration
To Business Professionals: • Build professional networks internally and externally • Access business expertise and knowledge more rapidly • Enhance camaraderie with peers	*To Business Professionals:* • Lack of boundaries between professional and private lives • Lower productivity due to multitasking • Excessive opportunism and self-promotion • Mistakes and incompetence broadcast to larger audiences

McKinsey Quarterly 17, no. 9 (2009); Andrew McAfee, *Enterprise 2.0: New Collaborative Tools for Your Organization's Toughest Challenges* (Boston: Harvard Business Press, 2009); Avanade, *CRM and Social Media: Maximizing Deeper Customer Relationships* (Seattle, WA: Avanade, 2008); Jennifer Taylor Arnold, "Twittering and Facebooking While They Work," *HR Magazine* 54, no. 12 (December 1, 2009); Soumitra Dutta, "What's Your Personal Social Media Strategy?" *Harvard Business Review* (November 2010): 127–130.

QUESTIONS FOR REFLECTION

1. In the first reading, how effectively do the visuals illustrate the lists above them? Explain.
2. What points does Cardon make in the second reading?
3. Should the second reading include more visual images to support the written text? Why or why not?
4. Which comparison do you find to be more useful? Why?
5. Based on both of these readings, how do you feel about the Social Age? Which aspects of the Social Age and social media do you identify with most and/or least? Explain.

Reading and Reflection COMPARING AND CONTRASTING

[Preview] **KRYSTINA OSTERMEYER** has worked with patients of all ages as a registered nurse in different types of clinical settings such as a telemetry and stepdown unit, an allergy and immunotherapy clinic, and a diabetes education office. In her spare time, she writes freelance articles for a variety of online publications including *Nurse Guidance* and *Elite Learning,* where the article that follows was originally published. In the article, Ostermeyer compares and contrasts modern and traditional medicine. Before reading, consider different types of medicine with which you are familiar or have experienced. Which do you prefer? Why?

Pros & Cons of Alternative Medicine, Modern Medicine, & Traditional Medicine

by Krystina Ostermeyer

1 Imagine this scenario: You're a long-time migraine-sufferer. You've been shuttled around from doctor to doctor, handed prescription after prescription after prescription. Your medicine cabinet is filled with medications—both prescription and over-the-counter. Your purse sounds like a pharmacy—every time you set it down, a pill bottle rattles. After a while, you wonder, "I wonder if there are other ways to treat my migraines?" In conjunction with all of these prescriptions, you begin to make appointments with massage therapists, chiropractors, apply essential oils to your skin, and take supplements. And wonder of all wonders—your migraines actually begin to improve! This, my fellow nurses, is a very brief summary of the past twenty years of my life.

2 As a patient or a health care provider, it can be difficult to wade through the various options of medicine available to patients with chronic conditions, especially when we must consider that what works for one patient may not work for another patient.

Modern Medicine

3 **What is it?** If you've ever gone to an urgent care clinic because you had strep throat or pink eye and left with a prescription for an antibiotic, you've been the recipient of modern medicine.

4 Modern medicine, or standard medical care, is practiced by a medical doctor (an MD) or a doctor of osteopathy (a DO). It is also practiced by the healthcare team: ". . . physical therapists, physician assistants, psychologists, and registered nurses."

5 **Pros:** The rate at which modern medicine is advancing is astonishing. You can sit on your couch and watch TV and see commercials for new medications at an alarming pace—and these new medications have reduced our death rates for stroke, heart disease, and cancer. In fact, due to modern medicine, the death rate from heart disease has decreased by 60% since 1970. The death rate from HIV/AIDS has dropped more than 75% since 1995, when it was at its peak.

6 **Cons:** However, critics of modern medicine are quick to point out that there is a pill for everything. Yes, we are quick to create more drugs, and yes, we are living longer due to said drugs—but are we living better?

7 Medicine has evolved, and we now have surgeons who are able to p
cally. We have cardiovasc
perform open-heart surg
invasive approach. We ha
specialties such as oncolo
ogy, podiatry, and urology.

8 But critics point out that medicine has evolved to the point that we're treating disease instead of preventing it.

Alternative Medicine

9 **What is it?** Alternative medicine is a treatment that is used in place of a conventional medical treatment. For example, if your physician prescribed you a blood pressure medication and you opted instead to overhaul your diet completely in hopes of reducing your blood pressure, this could be an example of an alternative medicine.

10 **Pros:** Often, alternative medicine is considered "natural." Most people who opt for alternative medicine are choosing these treatments because they are seeking a more natural approach to healing their chronic conditions.

11 Examples of alternative medicine include:

- Acupuncture.
- Chiropractic care.
- Reiki, which is an energy therapy that relies on the practitioner to use healing energy to mend imbalances by placing their hands gently over the body.
- Herbal medicine—the World Health Organization estimates that 80% of the world's population use some type of herbal medicine, and studies show that herbal preparations are effective at treating allergies, chronic fatigue, and premenstrual syndrome, amongst other health maladies.
- Ayurvedic medicine, which is a 3,000-year-old Indian medical system that is still in use today. It utilizes herbs, diets, and specific health practices to treat illness.

12 **Cons:** Certain alternative medicine practices have been studied and have been deemed to be safe, and even effective. Others have not been heavily studied—and some have even been found to be harmful. For example, the products used in Ayurvedic medicine may contain toxic minerals, such as lead.

13 In addition, just because something is "natural" does not always mean it is *safe*. A prime example is the herb kava kava; this herb is often used to [illegible]eat anxiety, but it can also cause liver damage.

14 [illegible]good practice would be to discuss alternative [illegible]nts with your physician. You may also want to consider complementary medicine, which is utilizing alternative treatments along with standard medicine. For example, I take prescription medicine daily to prevent migraines. I also go to a chiropractor once weekly, because these therapies complement each other.

Traditional Medicine

15 **What is it?** According to the World Health Organization, traditional medicine is "the knowledge, skills and practices based on the theories, beliefs and experiences indigenous to different cultures, used in the maintenance of health and in the prevention, diagnosis, improvement or treatment of physical and mental illness."

16 Although there are various forms of traditional medicine, one of the most prevalent and most commonly used is traditional Chinese medicine (TCM), as it dates back over 3,000 years and is still in practice today.

17 TCM uses yin, ". . . the earth, cold, and femininity" and yang, "the sky, heat, and masculinity." Yin and yang must be in balance for good health.

18 **Pros:** Although TCM is 3,000 years old, it is still evolving, and its prevalence and practice is growing throughout the world. It is used to prevent and treat disease.

19 TCM relies heavily on a variety of practices, but it uses herbal medicine. Three of its most commonly used herbs are gingko biloba, garlic, and ginseng.

20 **Cons:** The herbs used in TCM can be unsafe in certain individuals. In addition, fewer regulations are in place to ensure the safety of herbs. For example, when you pick up a prescription at the pharmacy, you can be assured that it has been tested to ensure its safety and its efficacy. You cannot be as certain regarding your herbals.

21 As such, taking an herb that has been untested can lead to toxicity, especially in people who are ill and the elderly.

The Bottom Line . . .

22 Regardless of which branch of medicine you prescribe to, you should make sure that any medications, supplements, or treatments you are utilizing are safe—discuss them with your healthcare provider.

References

Kiefer, D. (2016, November 1). *What exactly is alternative medicine?* https://owl.english.purdue.edu/owl/resource/560/01/

National Cancer Institute. (2015, April 10). *Complementary and alternative medicine.* www.cancer.gov/about-cancer/treatment/cam

Sullivan, T. (2018, May 6). *Modern medicine vs alternative medicine: Different levels of evidence.* www.policymed.com/2011/08/modern-medicine-vsalternative-medicine-different-levels-of-evidence.html

Wachtel-Galor, S., & Benzie, I.F.F. (2011). *Herbal medicine: A growing field with a long tradition.* www.ncbi.nlm.nih.gov/books/NBK92773/

Note: The author of this article chose to use the APA (7th edition) format for listing her sources, but chose to omit in-text parenthetical citations. Your instructor may ask you to use the APA or MLA format for writing a research-based assignment.

QUESTIONS FOR REFLECTION

Considering Ideas

1. What are some of the pros and cons of modern medicine?
2. What are some of the pros and cons of traditional medicine?
3. List some examples of technological advances in medicine discussed in the article. How would you feel about having a robot perform an operation on you? Why?

Considering the Rhetorical Star

1. What is the *subject* of the article? Is the specific topic engaging? Why or why not?
2. Who is the intended *audience* for the piece?
3. What is the author's main *purpose* (to inform, to persuade, to entertain, to express feelings) for the essay? Does she use a combination of purposes? How effective is her approach? Explain.
4. What writing *strategies* does Ostermeyer use in the article? How do these strategies affect the work?
5. What is the *design* of the piece? Is it effective? Why or why not?

Considering Writing Strategies

1. Does Ostermeyer's article use the block or point-by-point pattern for organizing the essay? Is this approach effective? Why or why not?
2. The author highlights pros and cons for the three types of medicine. Is this writing strategy helpful for the reader? Explain.
3. How would you describe the writer's style? Is the article more formal or informal. Why do you think the author chose this style?

Writing Suggestions

1. Research two specific types of medical practices that could be used to help treat a particular condition. Write a comparison and contrast essay explaining the details of each approach. You may choose also to recommend one approach over the other. Be sure to document your sources according to the method your instructor requires. (See Chapter 14 for more details about documenting sources.)
2. Write a comparison and contrast essay explaining how technology has changed something other than medicine. What are the advantages and disadvantages of the old and new ways? What might the future hold? If you use research, be sure to document your sources using your instructor's preferred method. (See Chapter 14 for more details about documenting sources.)

ESOL Tip >

In what ways is An
similar to and diffe
cal practices in an
which you are fam
prefer? Why?

Reading and Reflection COMPARING AND CONTRASTING

[preview] **Nigel Warburton** is a British philosopher, podcaster, and freelance writer. He is best known for popularizing philosophy and for writing several bestselling books. He has a BA from the University of Bristol and a PhD from Darwin College, Cambridge. The article that follows originally appeared in the magazine *New Philosopher*. Before reading, have you ever come across a piece of old technology, such as a computer, video game system, or other device? What was your reaction?

Discarded Objects
by Nigel Warburton

1 My mother died earlier this year. In going through her possessions, amongst the school reports, the letters, and old photograph albums, I found my father's early pocket calculator—a Sharp Elsi Mini. A relic from the 70s, chunky brushed steel and plastic, with red light-emitting diodes, it had a heavy retro feeling in my hand. I was transported back to my early teenage years, when this machine represented the height of technology. It had been a gift from clients—a valuable one since it cost the equivalent of a laptop today. I remember as a child testing it to its limits: Multiplying numbers until the eight place screen overflowed, which it signaled with a row of red dots; dividing 100 by 3 to see the 33.333333 stream across the screen; turning it upside down, to type in the magical number 0.7734 which in the simple font of the calculator read "hello." Now, its soft leather case was missing, and it sat at the bottom of a cupboard, no longer a valuable tool to work out expense accounts—just a discarded piece of junk from long ago.

2 I didn't expect it to still work. Over 40 years on, that would have been too much to ask—it's almost an antique. But I bought four AA batteries anyway and switched it on. A little red zero appeared on the screen. All four of its simple functions worked. I searched the Internet and discovered that whereas many early calculators drained batteries in no time, this particular one had been a breakthrough as it was relatively economical in its power use. So why, I wondered, was it at the bottom of a cupboard? Why had we as a family gone through so many cheaper calculators when we had a fully functioning machine in the house? At school I'd needed a scientific calculator to replace the log tables and slide rule I'd begun to master just as they became obsolete. But since then, I've only used a calculator to add, subtract, multiply, and divide.

3 Meanwhile, like many people, I have a drawer in which I keep a range of discarded smart phones, most of which had a life of two years or less and should really have been recycled. None of them could do what my current phone does; the cameras in particular seem incredibly primitive and the memories tiny by comparison. I'm no longer sure why I'm keeping them.

4 But my father's calculator does everything I need a calculator to do and has a more appealing design than any of the cheap plastic calculators available today. For me at least, it is not a piece of obsolete technology and it has a personal history. Modern calculators are cheaper and no doubt more energy-efficient, but this one still does the job it was made for. Yet I wonder how many people still use such machines. Calculators don't get passed on between generations.

They're throwaways and scarcely valued at all because the technology in them is so cheap. In a few years, they may, like slide rules, become almost completely obsolete as free-standing objects, as they are so easily integrated as apps on a smart phone or computer.

5 Children of my generation didn't anticipate that the objects we grew up with would be transitory: no one told us that technology would evolve at such a rate that the devices imagined in the science fiction of our childhood would be surpassed and made to look outdated by real innovations by the time we reached adulthood. When I went to the public library as a child, there was no talk of electronic books or digital technology that would allow someone to carry the equivalent of a small library on a device in their handbag. Typewriters seemed here to stay in one form or another, as did pay phones and pagers. We recognized that technology would change gradually, of course, but didn't anticipate the accelerating pace of such change in our lifetimes.

6 The machines that we create are supposed to help us. They're functional objects, not merely decorative, and are to be judged on their success or failure at performing what they were designed to do. New technologies either perform old functions better than existing technologies, or serve new ends. But in a world that is changing so swiftly, businesses have a vested interest in hooking us into technology brands that need constant upgrading. We easily fall into the consumer traps that have been set for us, forever trying to fulfill new desires for new products, never quite achieving a state of contentment with the technology we have acquired because someone, somewhere has just come up with a faster, more streamlined, more efficient machine than the one we bought last year. Meanwhile, as a result of this cycle of unfulfilled desires, we leave an ever-growing heap of discarded objects behind us, obsolete and semi-obsolete machines that once seemed to answer our needs, but now appear dated and clunky.

7 This might sound as if there is an easy way out: simply stick with something that works well enough and refuse to be seduced by technological novelty, no matter what it promises in terms of efficiency. But try holding on to old technology: it's just not that easy. True, a few idiosyncratic writers have, for example, continued to use their manual typewriters, but that forces them to stockpile ribbons and replacement parts, and to hunt down the few surviving typewriter-technicians when something goes wrong. A machine without a supply of parts and the people who know how to fit them can leave you high and dry. Like it or not, we are all caught up in the flow of new technologies, and opting out will only leave us isolated and shut out from the world our children inhabit.

8 So my father's calculator is really exceptional. It's a machine from another age that carries on working without requiring a service, and the only parts that ever have to be replaced are still easily available: standard batteries. What's more, I haven't acquired new mathematical needs, needs that this calculator can't meet; adding, subtracting, dividing, and multiplying are not functions that can be better performed by a newer machine—you either get the right answer or you don't. Unlike so many technological objects I use, this one has been around long enough to acquire some personal history for me. I remember my father's delight when he came home with this very calculator, how carefully we had to handle it because of its value, the now-lost snug leather zip-up case that it was kept in, exactly where it was stored in the cupboard under our newly-acquired and almost miraculous color television.

9 Yet, I'm fairly sure that I'll stop using this calculator quite soon, even though its performance has, incongruously, passed the test of time, and even though it carries memories from my childhood. It's just easier to use the calculator on my smart phone or laptop than to stop what I'm doing and pick up a different piece of equipment. Digital technology is quickly applying its own form of Occam's Razor—the medieval injunction not to multiply entities beyond necessity—to the objects around me. Although the technological imperative has cluttered my life with the shells of once-useful objects, one promise that it seems to be fulfilling is to reduce the number of technological objects that I need to

perform the functions that once required a portfolio of machines.

10 The pocket calculator, along with the pocket camera and the address book, will soon be consigned to history as separate physical objects; they're now just functions of another digital machine. I suppose that's progress. But when I look at my father's calculator, I still feel we might be losing something along the way.

Source: Nigel Warburton, "Discarded Objects," *New Philosopher*, pp. 91–92. Used by permission of The Bull Media Company Ltd.

QUESTIONS FOR REFLECTION

Considering Ideas

1. How does Warburton feel about finding the calculator? Are his feelings mixed? Explain.
2. Is the calculator a piece of "junk," or does it still have some sort of value? What point is the author making about technology?
3. Do you agree or disagree with the closing statement that ". . . we might be losing something along the way"? Explain.

Considering the Rhetorical Star

1. What is the *subject* of the article? Is the specific topic engaging? Why or why not?
2. Who is the intended *audience* for the piece?
3. What is the author's main *purpose* (to inform, to persuade, to entertain, to express feelings) for the essay? Does the author use a combination of purposes? How effective is this approach? Explain.
4. What writing *strategies* does the article reflect? How do these strategies affect the work?
5. What is the *design* of the piece? Is it effective? Why or why not?

Considering Writing Strategies

1. Identify several passages where the author uses the compare and contrast writing strategy. What does he compare and contrast? Is the author's approach effective? Why or why not?
2. How would you describe the author's writing style? Is it more formal or informal? Is this approach effective? Why or why not?
3. In the article, Warburton recalls when his father first brought home the calculator. Is this an effective approach for the subject matter? Why or why not?

Writing Suggestions

1. Write a creative essay in which you compare and contrast life in the present or past with life in the future. Focus on several known or imagined technological advances to illustrate your points. You may choose ideas that reflect good or not-so-good potential changes.
2. Write a comparison and contrast essay about two different types of technology or about doing something with and without technology. Be sure to document any sources you use. (See Chapter 14 for more details about documenting sources in the MLA and APA formats.)

Reading and Reflection COMPARING AND CONTRASTING

[Preview] **Martin Dejnicki** is the creator of a website called AnitaPoems, dedicated to his wife Anita. As he explains his story in the introduction to his website, one day he presented his wife with a beautiful bouquet of flowers and a love poem that he had printed in a spiral booklet. Anita barely noticed the flowers, but the heartfelt poem brought tears to her eyes. This event inspired him to create the website so that others could experience the same kind of joy. Visit **anitapoems.com** to read more of his poetry on a wide range of subjects. Before reading, think about how technology has affected you. What kinds of technology do you make use of on a daily basis? Is it more of a help or a hindrance?

Technology
by Martin Dejnicki

I wake up each morning,
when my android makes noise.
Technically speaking,
he's just one of my toys.

Call me lazy,
but I try to save time.
Microwaving my breakfast,
is not a real crime.

Before I dance,
with my electric toothbrush.
Straight for the inbox,
I dive in a rush.

With the click of a mouse,
I outsource my work.
Through Amazon reviews,
I search for my perk.

I won't wait for weeks,
demand it today.
Another PS3 game,
I can't wait to play.

I attempt to snap out,
from my wired realm.
It seems like technology,
is right at the helm.

I drive half a block,
to the grocery store.
Technology is friendly,
and opens the door.

I finally use
my dry mouth to speak.
I'm definitely rusty,
and sound like a freak.

Why can't they get a robot,
to slice the meat.
My disappointment,
I eagerly tweet.

At the checkout,
I have a clear choice.
Use a human
or a machine with a voice.

I return to my office,
my game has arrived.
My ancestors were truly,
technology deprived.

Source: AnitaPoems.com: www.anitapoems.com/blog/technology-poem.

QUESTIONS FOR REFLECTION

Considering Ideas

1. What is Dejnicki's view of technology? How do you know?
2. At a store, do you prefer to check out with a live person at a cash register or using "a machine with a voice"? Why?
3. The poet mentions his ancestors in the last line. Compare and contrast how his life might be different from that of his ancestors.

Considering the Rhetorical Star

1. What is the *subject* of the poem?
2. Who might the *audience* be for this poem?

3. What is the author's main *purpose* (to inform, to interpret, to persuade, to entertain, to express feelings) for the poem?
4. What is the main writing *strategy* for the poem? Does Dejnicki employ any other writing strategies? What are they, and how do they affect the work?
5. What *design* features does this poem include? Are they effective? Why or why not?

Considering Writing Strategies

1. How does the author's use of rhyme affect the poem?
2. What is the tone (serious, sarcastic, humorous) of the poem? Identify a few lines that illustrate this tone. How does the writer's tone affect the reader?
3. What comparisons does the author state or imply in the poem?

Writing Suggestions

1. Think about a new electronic device, such as a laptop, tablet, smartphone, or gaming system, that you obtained. Write an essay comparing and contrasting how things were before and after you got the new item.
2. Can you imagine what it would be like to have a personal robot to do your chores? Write a comparison and contrast essay about life with and without a robot.

Reading and Reflection COMPARING AND CONTRASTING

Johnny Louis/Getty Images

[preview] **GEORGE SAUNDERS,** who was born in Amarillo, Texas, is a professor at Syracuse University, where he earned his MFA degree in creative writing. He is an award-winning author of fiction and nonfiction. *Tenth of December: Stories, Congratulations, by the Way: Some Thoughts on Kindness,* and *Lincoln in the Bardo: A Novel,* three of his more recent works, have been well received along with his numerous prior publications. In the futuristic short story that follows, Saunders explores the role of advertising in consumerism as a grandfather attempts to take his grandson to see a Broadway show in New York City. Before reading, consider the effect that today's advertising has on you. What influences your purchasing decisions? Do you ever feel overwhelmed by the advertisements you encounter?

My Flamboyant Grandson
by George Saunders

1 I had brought my grandson to New York to see a show. Because what is he always doing, up here in Oneonta? Singing and dancing, sometimes to my old show-tune records, but more often than not to his favorite CD, "Babar Sings," sometimes even making up his own steps, which I do not mind, or rather I try not to mind it. Although I admit that once, coming into his room and finding him wearing a pink boa while singing, in the voice of the Old Lady, "I Have Never Met a Man Like That Elephant," I had to walk out and give it some deep thought and prayer, as was also the case when he lumbered into the parlor during a recent church couples dinner, singing "Big and Slow, Yet So Very Regal," wearing a tablecloth spray-painted gray, so as to more closely resemble Babar.

2 Being a man who knows something about grandfatherly disapproval, having had a grandfather who constantly taunted me for having enlarged calves—to the extent that even today, when bathing, I find myself thinking unkind thoughts about Grandfather—what I prayed on both occasions was: Dear Lord, he is what he is, let me love him no matter what. If he is a gay child, God bless him; if he is a non-gay child who simply very much enjoys wearing his grandmother's wig while singing "Edelweiss" to the dog, so be it, and in either case let me communicate my love and acceptance in everything I do.

3 Because where is a child to go for unconditional love, if not to his grandfather? He has had it tough, in my view, with his mother in Nevada and a father unknown, raised by his grandmother and me in an otherwise childless neighborhood, playing alone in a tiny yard that ends in a graveyard wall. The boys in his school are hard on him, as are the girls, as are the teachers, and recently we found his book bag in the Susquehanna, and recently also found, taped to the back of his jacket, a derogatory note, and the writing on it was not all that childish-looking, and there were rumors that his bus driver had written it.

4 Then one day I had a revelation. If the lad likes to sing and dance, I thought, why not expose him to the finest singing and dancing there is? So I called 1-800-culture, got our Promissory Voucher in the mail, and on Teddy's birthday we took the train down to New York.

5 As we entered the magnificent lobby of the Eisner Theatre, I was in good spirits, saying to Teddy, The size of this stage will make that little stage I built you behind the garage look pathetic, when suddenly we were stopped by a stern young fellow (a Mr. Ernesti, I believe) who said, We are sorry, sir, but you cannot be admitted on merely a Promissory Voucher, are you kidding us, you must take your Voucher and your Proof of Purchases from at least six of our Major Artistic Sponsors, such as AOL, such as Coke, and go at once to the Redemption Center, on Forty-fourth and Broadway, to get your real actual tickets, and please do not be late, as latecomers cannot be admitted, due to special effects which occur early, and which require total darkness in order to simulate the African jungle at night.

6 Well, this was news to me, but I was not about to disappoint the boy.

7 We left the Eisner and started up Broadway, the Everly Readers in the sidewalk reading the Everly Strips in our shoes, the building-mounted miniscreens at eye level showing images reflective of the Personal Preferences we'd stated on our monthly Everly Preference Worksheets, the numerous Cybec Sudden Emergent Screens outthrusting or down-thrusting inches from our faces, and in addition I could very clearly hear the sound-only messages being beamed to me and me alone via various Kakio Aural Focussers, such as one that shouted out to me between Forty-second and Forty-third, "Mr. Petrillo, you chose Burger King eight times last fiscal year but only two times thus far this fiscal year, please do not forsake us now, there is a store one block north!," in the voice of Broadway star Elaine Weston, while at Forty-third a light-pole-mounted Focusser shouted, "Golly, Leonard, remember your childhood on the farm in Oneonta? Why not reclaim those roots with a Starbucks Country Roast?," in a celebrity rural voice I could not identify, possibly Buck Owens, and then, best of all, in the doorway of PLC Electronics, a life-size Gene Kelly hologram suddenly appeared, tap-dancing, saying, "Leonard, my data indicates you're a bit of an old-timer like myself! Gosh, in our day life was simpler, wasn't it, Leonard? Why not come in and let Frankie Z. explain the latest gizmos!" And he looked so real I called out to Teddy, "Teddy, look there, Gene Kelly, do you remember I mentioned him to you as one of the all-time great dancers?" But Teddy of course did not see Gene Kelly, Gene Kelly not being one of his Preferences, but instead saw his hero Babar, swinging a small monkey on his trunk while saying that his data indicated that Teddy did not yet own a Nintendo.

8 So that was fun, that was very New York, but what was not so fun was, by the time we got through the line at the Redemption Center, it was ten minutes until showtime, and my feet had swollen up the way they do shortly before they begin spontaneously bleeding, which they have done ever since a winter spent in the freezing muck of Cho-Bai, Korea. It is something I have learned to live with. If I can sit, that is helpful. If I can lean against something,

also good. Best of all, if I can take my shoes off. Which I did, leaning against a wall.

9 All around and above us were those towering walls of light, curving across building fronts, embedded in the sidewalks, custom-fitted to light poles: a cartoon lion eating a man in a suit; a rain of gold coins falling into the canoe of a naked rain-forest family; a woman in lingerie running a bottle of Pepsi between her breasts; the Merrill Lynch talking fist asking, "Are you kicking ass or kissing it?"; a perfect human rear, dancing; a fake flock of geese turning into a field of Bebe logos; a dying grandmother's room filled with roses by a FedEx man who then holds up a card saying "No Charge."

10 And standing beneath all that bounty was our little Teddy, tiny and sad, whose grandfather could not even manage to get him into one crummy show.

11 So I said to myself, Get off the wall, old man, blood or no blood, just keep the legs moving and soon enough you'll be there. And off we went, me hobbling, Teddy holding my arm, making decent time, and I think we would have made the curtain. Except suddenly there appeared a Citizen Helper, who asked were we from out of town, and was that why, via removing my shoes, I had caused my Everly Strips to be rendered Inoperative?

12 I should say here that I am no stranger to innovative approaches to advertising, having pioneered the use of towable signboards in Oneonta back in the Nixon years, when I moved a fleet of thirty around town with a Dodge Dart, wearing a suit that today would be found comic. By which I mean I have no problem with the concept of the Everly Strip. That is not why I had my shoes off. I am as patriotic as the next guy. Rather, as I have said, it was due to my bleeding feet.

13 I told all this to the Citizen Helper, who asked if I was aware that, by rendering my Strips Inoperative, I was sacrificing a terrific opportunity to Celebrate My Preferences?

14 And I said yes, yes, I regretted this very much.

15 He said he was sorry about my feet, he himself having a trick elbow, and that he would be happy to forget this unfortunate incident if I would only put my shoes back on and complete the rest of my walk extremely slowly, looking energetically to both left and right, so that the higher density of Messages thus received would compensate for those I had missed.

16 And I admit, I was a little short with that Helper, and said, Young man, these dark patches here on my socks are blood, do you or do you not see them?

17 Which was when his face changed and he said, Please do not snap at me, sir, I hope you are aware of the fact that I can write you up?

18 And then I made a mistake.

19 Because as I looked at that Citizen Helper—his round face, his pale sideburns, the way his feet turned in—it seemed to me that I knew him. Or rather, it seemed that he could not be so very different from me when I was a young man, not so different from the friends of my youth—from Jeffie DeSoto, say, who once fought a Lithuanian gang that had stuck an M-80 in the ass of a cat, or from Ken Larmer, who had such a sweet tenor voice and died stifling a laugh in the hills above Koi-Jeng.

20 I brought out a twenty and, leaning over, said, Look, please, the kid just really wants to see this show.

21 Which is when he pulled out his pad and began to write!

22 Now, even being from Oneonta, I knew that being written up does not take one or two minutes, we would be standing there at least half an hour, after which we would have to go to an Active Complaints Center, where they would check our Strips for Operability and make us watch that corrective video called "Robust Economy, Super Moral Climate!," which I had already been made to watch three times last winter, when I was out of work and we could not afford cable. And we would totally miss "Babar Sings"!

23 Please, I said, please, we have seen plenty of personalized messages, via both the building-mounted miniscreens at eye level and those suddenly outthrusting Cybec Emergent Screens, we have learned plenty for one day, honest to God we have—

24 And he said, Sir, since when do you make the call as far as when you have received enough useful information from our Artistic Partners? And just kept writing me up.

25 Well, there I was, in my socks, there was Teddy, with a scared look in his eyes I hadn't seen since his toddler days, when he had such a fear of chickens

that we could never buy Rosemont eggs, due to the cartoon chicken on the carton, or, if we did, had to first cut the chicken off, with scissors we kept in the car for that purpose. So I made a quick decision, and seized that Citizen Helper's ticket pad and flung it into the street, shouting at Teddy, Run! Run!

26 And run he did. And run I did. And while that Citizen Helper floundered in the street, torn between chasing us and retrieving his pad, we raced down Broadway, and glancing back over my shoulder I saw a hulking young man stick out his foot, and down that Helper went, and soon I was handing our tickets to the same stern Mr. Ernesti, who was now less stern, and in we went, and took our seats, as the stars appeared overhead and the Eisner was transformed into a nighttime jungle.

27 And suddenly there was Babar, looking with longing toward Paris, where the Old Lady was saying that she had dreamed of someone named Babar, and did any of us know who this Babar was, and where he might be found? And Teddy knew the answer, from the Original Cast CD, which was Babar is within us, in all of our hearts, and he shouted it out with all the other children, as the Old Lady began singing "The King Inside of You."

28 And let me tell you, from that moment everything changed for Teddy. I am happy to report he has joined the play at school. He wears a scarf everywhere he goes, throwing it over his shoulder with what can only be described as bravado, and says, whenever asked, that he has decided to become an actor. This from a boy too timid to trick-or-treat! This from the boy we once found walking home from school in tears, padlocked to his own bike! There are no more late-night crying episodes, he no longer writes on his arms with permanent marker, he leaps out of bed in the morning, anxious to get to school, and dons his scarf, and is already sitting at the table eating breakfast when we come down.

29 The other day as he got off the bus I heard him say, to his bus driver, cool as a cucumber, See you at the Oscars.

30 When an Everly Reader is reading, then suddenly stops, it is not hard to trace, and within a week I received a certified letter setting my fine at one thousand dollars, and stating that, in lieu of the fine, I could elect to return to the originating location of my infraction (they included a map) and, under the supervision of that Citizen Helper, retrace my steps, shoes on, thus reclaiming a significant opportunity to Celebrate My Preferences.

31 This, to me, is not America.

32 What America is, to me, is a guy doesn't want to buy, you let him not buy, you respect his not buying. A guy has a crazy notion different from your crazy notion, you pat him on the back and say hey pal, nice crazy notion, let's go have a beer. America to me should be shouting all the time, a bunch of shouting voices, most of them wrong, some of them nuts, but, please, not just one droning glamorous reasonable voice.

33 But do the math: a day's pay, plus train ticket, plus meals, plus taxis to avoid the bleeding feet, still that is less than one thousand.

34 So down I went.

35 That Citizen Helper, whose name was Rob, said he was glad about my change of heart. Every time a voice shot into my ear, telling me things about myself I already knew, every time a celebrity hologram walked up like an old friend, Rob checked a box on my Infraction Correction Form and said, isn't that amazing, Mr. Petrillo, that we can do that, that we can know you so well that we can help you identify the things you want and need?

36 And I would say, Yes, Rob, that is amazing, sick in the gut but trying to keep my mind on the five hundred bucks I was saving and on all the dance classes that would buy.

37 As for Teddy, as I write this it is nearly midnight and he is tapping in the room above. He looks like a bird, our boy, he watches the same musical fifteen times in a row. Walking through the mall he suddenly emits a random line of dialogue and lunges off to the side, doing a dance step that resembles a stumble, spilling his drink, plowing into a group of incredulous, snickering Oneontans. He looks like no one else, acts like no one else, his clothes are increasingly like plumage, late at night he choreographs using plastic Army men, he fits no mold and has no friends, but I believe in my heart that someday something beautiful may come from him.

Source: G. Saunders, "My Flamboyant Grandson," *The New Yorker*, Jan. 28, 2002, **www.newyorker.com/archive/2002/01/28/020128fi_fiction.**

QUESTIONS FOR REFLECTION

Considering Ideas

1. How does the grandfather feel about his grandson, Teddy, in Saunders's story? Give specific details from the story to illustrate your point.
2. What are some of the obstacles that the grandfather and his grandson face as they make their way toward the Broadway show? How do the characters overcome these obstacles?
3. Compare and contrast Saunders's futuristic view of society with today's reality. Give several specific examples from the story as points for your comparison. Also, do you feel Saunders's view of the future is possible? Why or why not?

Considering the Rhetorical Star

1. What is the main *subject* of Saunders's short story? Is the specific topic engaging? Why or why not?
2. Who is the intended *audience* for the story? How do you know?
3. What is the author's main *purpose* (to inform, to interpret, to persuade, to entertain, to express feelings) for the story? Does he use a combination of purposes? How effective is his approach? Explain.
4. What is Saunders's primary writing *strategy*? What other strategies does he use? Give specific examples to illustrate your point.
5. What is the *design* of the story? Is it effective? Why or why not?

> **ESOL Tip >**
> You may want to compare advertising in the United States to advertising in your home country.

Considering Writing Strategies

1. Identify several passages in which the grandfather compares and contrasts his current situation to that of his past. What role do these passages play in the story? Explain.
2. The author includes several references to people in the story who presumably work for the government. Identify these characters and explain what purpose they serve in the story. What might Saunders be saying about the government by including them?
3. Many of Saunders's paragraphs begin with the word "and." Why do you suppose the author uses this technique? What effect does this technique have on the reader?

Writing Suggestions

1. In Saunders's story, the grandfather decides to rebel and run away from the Citizen Helper with Teddy because he probably feels that the interrogation and treatment of being written up was unjust. Write an essay comparing and contrasting the grandfather with another literary figure or with someone real, such as a politician or an activist. What do they believe in? What challenges do they face? What do they do to try to accomplish their goals?
2. What do you think the world will be like in fifty years? Will we go back to a simpler lifestyle? Will robots do everything for us? Write an essay comparing and contrasting today's world with what you imagine for the future. You might consider how you believe technology will affect transportation, lifestyle, education, work, and entertainment.

STUDENT WRITING

Kindle vs. iPad

by James Ingram, Amanda Laudato, and Daniel Volpe

1 If you are looking for an electronic book (e-book) reader, two of the choices available to you are the Amazon Kindle Paperwhite and the Apple iPad Mini. Both devices have a similarly sized screen (6.6" and 7.9", respectively), allow users to surf the Internet, and, most importantly, provide access to literally millions of books and periodicals. Both the iPad and Kindle offer a reasonably pleasant digital reading experience; however, they vary substantially in terms of their overall capabilities.

2 First, let's look at the reading capabilities of the Amazon Kindle Paperwhite. When you pick it up, it feels very light (at 5.7 ounces) and comfortable in your hands. The Kindle offers consumers the ability to download a book from virtually anywhere using Wi-Fi or 4G LTE service. Once you have downloaded a book, which takes about one minute, you can read the pages in black and white or listen to the book using the text-to-speech feature. The pages look very similar to those in a paperback book, and turning the pages requires only the swipe of a finger. If you need to look up a word, the built-in dictionary is right there at your fingertips. Because the lighting is adjustable, you are able to read the Kindle outside in direct sunlight, and reading the pages for long periods of time will not strain your eyes any more than reading an actual paperback book. The latest models are even waterproof, which is great for the beach, bathtub, or poolside. Even so, you might decide to move on to another activity.

3 If you get tired of reading the book or want to further investigate a concept in the book you are reading, you might want to sample some of the other features on your Kindle. For example, you can conduct a Google search to get the information you need. Even though scrolling through the dull, black and white Web pages on the Kindle is a bit awkward, it is functional. You may also decide to shop for more books at the Amazon store. Furthermore, you can download documents from your computer and read and store 8–32 GB of books and data on the Kindle, depending on which model you choose. If you run out of storage, you have the option to archive books and periodicals and retrieve them later to make room for more downloads. Finally, the battery life on the Kindle will last up to six weeks with minimal use.

4 Similar to the Kindle Paperwhite, the Apple iPad Mini is quite nice to hold, although at 10.4 ounces it feels slightly heavier than the Kindle. Downloading a book from the iBooks application takes less than a minute, like the Kindle. To download a book, you need to have Wi-Fi access or a 4G data plan. When you read a book on the iPad, the full color palette really comes to life, especially in a magazine or children's book. However, the backlit screen can strain your eyes after a while, and you can barely see the screen in direct sunlight—so much for reading by the pool or on the beach. The methods for turning pages and looking up words are just as easy on the iPad as they are on the Kindle. Furthermore, like the Kindle, the iPad also has a text-to-speech feature so you can listen instead if you like. If you need to take a break from reading, the iPad, unlike the Kindle, offers a number of options.

5 The major differences between the Kindle and the iPad are most evident when it comes to the other capabilities of the devices besides book reading. On the iPad you can search the Internet in full color using Safari. On the iPad you have the full range of the Internet, just as you would on a computer. But there's more! An iPad provides you access to hundreds of thousands of Web applications (apps) that are fun and functional. You can read and send e-mail, FaceTime with friends and family, create and

export documents, take photos and videos, watch movies and television shows, play games, and listen to music. The apps give the iPad virtually limitless capabilities. Furthermore, you have 128 GB of storage and can archive books and store documents on the Internet to save space on your iPad. While the battery lasts only about 10 hours during constant use, that is enough to get most people through an entire day before needing to plug in.

6 The final verdict comes down to how you want to use your device. If your main goal is to have a reader that most resembles a book, then the Amazon Kindle Paperwhite is for you. The free 4G service (on some models), easy-on-the-eyes features, and ability to read outside make the Amazon Kindle the clear winner as simply an e-book reader. However, if you are looking for an all around, full-color device that is aesthetically pleasing and more versatile than just an electronic reader, then the Apple iPad is the best choice. The expanded capabilities of the iPad are virtually limitless.

QUESTIONS FOR REFLECTION

1. Is the essay organized using the block or point-by-point pattern? Would the essay be more or less effective if the authors had used the other approach? Explain.
2. Which parts of the essay are the most useful? Why?
3. What are some of the similarities and differences between the Kindle and the iPad?
4. Which features are better on the Kindle? Which features are better on the iPad?
5. Based on this comparison, which device would you purchase? Why?

Activity Comparing Media Perspectives

In pairs or small groups, compare two magazine, newspaper, or Web-based articles from different sources that cover the same story or topic. (Another option is to use two online videos on the same topic.) Find similarities in the message, organization, intended audience, and so on between the articles or videos. A representative from each group will share a few of the highlights from the comparison with the class. This activity may give you ideas for writing a comparison and contrast essay.

OPTIONS FOR WRITING A COMPARISON AND CONTRAST ESSAY

Now that you have read one or more examples of comparison and contrast writing, it's time to write your own comparison and contrast. You may choose to write about one of the writing options that follow, the advertisement, the image, or one of the media suggestions. Consider your rhetorical star and the qualities of an effective comparison and contrast as you begin to compose your assignment.

Writing Assignment Options

Use one of the following topics to write a comparison and contrast essay.

1. Two musicians, actors, comedians, or sports figures
2. Two paintings, photographs, posters, or sculptures
3. Two essays, short stories, songs, poems, plays, movies, or television shows
4. Two pieces of technology, such as computers, smartphones, or MP3 players
5. Two advertisements, commercials, or infomercials
6. Two people, such as parents, siblings, friends, teachers, employers, or health care workers
7. Two buildings, monuments, or other landmarks
8. A Mac vs. a PC
9. A "then and now" comparison of an opinion, attitude, or belief that has changed
10. A "now and then" comparison of a person, place, or thing that has changed over time

Multimodal Assignment

Using one of the readings, writing assignment options, or another topic, create a multimodal project using the comparing and contrasting writing strategy and at least two or more of the options in Table 8.1.

Table 8.1

Multimodal Options		
Artifact	Images	PowerPoint
Artwork	Infographics	Prezi
Audio clip	Journal	Video
Blog	Montage	Website
Digital portfolio	Podcast	Wiki
Graphic organizer	Poster	Writing

(See Chapter 15 for more details about multimodal compositions.)

Interpreting an Advertisement

The Advertising Archives

As you can see from this Apple advertisement, iPad users can open up to nine windows at a time. How might this feature be useful for making comparisons? What kinds of comparisons would you make if you were using an iPad? Does the advertisement compel you to want to purchase an iPad? Why or why not? Write an essay comparing and contrasting two tablets, smartphones, computers, or other pieces of technology. You might make a recommendation for the reader regarding which one is more useful or a better value.

Writing about an Image

AF archive/Alamy Images

Write a comparison and contrast essay that relates to one of the pictures or advertisements in this chapter. You may write about the image itself, or you may choose to write about something the image reminds you of. For example, if you write about the Apple advertisement, you might compare and contrast two iPad applications. If you write about this image from the film *Robot & Frank*, you might compare the human character to the robot.

Media Connection for Comparing and Contrasting

You might watch, read, and/or listen to one or more of the suggested media outlets or products listed in Table 8.2 to discover additional examples of comparison and contrast and/or the theme of computers and technology. Exploring various media may help you to better understand methods for comparing and contrasting. You may also choose to write about one or more of the media suggestions. For example, you might watch the news coverage of a specific topic or event on both FOX and CNN and then compare and contrast the coverage given. Or you may decide to listen to Zapp's song "Computer Love" and write an essay that compares and contrasts traditional and online dating techniques. Be sure to give credit to any sources you use in your essay.

Table 8.2

Media Chart				
Television	*The Blacklist*	*The Bachelor*	FOX vs. CNN	*The Big Bang Theory*
Film	*Ready Player One* (2018)	*Her* (2013)	*The Social Network* (2010)	*Robot & Frank* (2012)
Print/ E-Reading	*Mother Jones*	*Consumer Reports*	*Wired*	*PC Magazine*
Internet	**amazon.com**	**shopper.cnet.com**	**gizmodo.com**	**pcworld.com**
Music	"Nothing Compares 2 U" by Sinead O'Connor	"According to You" by Nicki Bliss	"Online" by Brad Paisley	"Computer Love" by Zapp

8.4 Analyzing the Rhetorical Star for Writing a Comparison and Contrast Essay

As you prepare to write your comparison and contrast paper, consider the five points of the rhetorical star (Figure 8.1). You might use some of the questions and suggestions in the chart as you conduct your rhetorical star analysis.

FIGURE 8.1 The Rhetorical Star

Subject	Although you could compare several items, it is usually best to begin with just two items for a comparison and contrast essay as you are developing your skills with this writing strategy. You may choose two items that seem similar but are different, or you may choose two items that seem drastically different but have something in common. Be sure that you can make a worthwhile point through your comparison. While you could compare apples and oranges, think about what the reader will gain from the comparison. If you are analyzing the nutritional value of each fruit and making a recommendation about which one provides the most health benefits, then you might be able to make it work. However, there is no need to simply point out the similarities and differences between apples and oranges without having a specific purpose in mind.
Audience	Who will read your comparison? What will interest your readers about your subject? Do they already know something about the items you are comparing? Are they reading to make a decision, such as whether to buy a PC or a Mac? Or are they just curious about your topic? Think about what kinds of details would be most appropriate for your readers.
Purpose	Think about what you are trying to accomplish through your comparison. You need to have a clear reason for making a comparison. Maybe you want to purchase a new laptop for school, and you've narrowed it down to two brands or models. Or possibly you want to determine which organization would provide you with the best career opportunities. Keep focused on your purpose as you write your comparison.
Strategy	Your main goal may be simply to explore the similarities and/or differences between two people, places, or things. However, you may decide to combine strategies. For example, you might be comparing two smartphones and evaluating which one is the better value or has the most useful features.
Design	How many points do you need to include about each item to make your comparison and contrast clear to the reader? What other design elements, such as photographs or illustrations, might enable your readers to better understand the items you are comparing? Although it wouldn't necessarily be appropriate for a school assignment, if you were creating a brochure for a product you were selling, you might use a chart or bullets to emphasize the similarities and differences between your product and the competition. That way the audience could easily discern why your product is better.

Activity Comparing and Contrasting Jobs

Research two specific jobs in your career field. Compare and contrast them according to several points and determine which one would better suit you. You might use a list or chart to help organize your thoughts. This comparison could be the basis for an essay.

8.5 Applying the Qualities of Comparison and Contrast Writing

After you have completed your rhetorical star analysis, follow the steps of the writing process (Figure 8.2) to compose your paper.

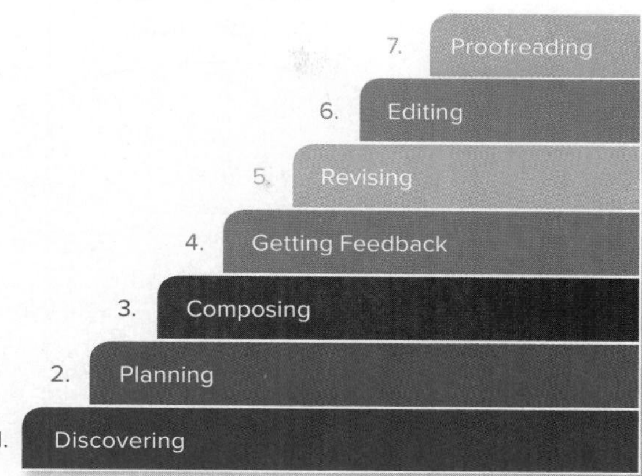

FIGURE 8.2 The Seven Steps of the Writing Process

1. **Discovering:** After you have chosen your specific topic and two suitable items to compare and contrast, you might brainstorm ideas that relate to each item. You might also make a list of possible points for comparing and contrasting and then complete a free-writing exercise about the items.
2. **Planning:** Once you have decided which subjects to compare, list the similarities and/or differences between the items. Go through the list and determine which ideas would be most interesting and beneficial to your audience. You might also try making a Venn diagram to help you organize your thoughts (Figure 8.3). Draw one large circle for each main point, making sure the circles overlap in the middle. The similarities go in the center part that overlaps, and the differences go on the outside areas.

   Once you have your main points worked out, you will need to create your thesis. Make sure the thesis states a significant point. Next, decide whether the block or point-by-point pattern will work best for your essay. Then create an outline using the block or point-by-point method. If you change your mind later, you can easily reorganize your essay to follow the other method.
3. **Composing:** Write a first draft of your comparison and contrast essay using the qualities outlined earlier in the chapter.
   1. Identify the elements being compared.
   2. Use the block or point-by-point method.
   3. Describe the subjects fairly and accurately.
   4. Consider using an analogy.
   5. Include transitions.
   6. End with a logical conclusion.

   As usual, don't focus on grammar and punctuation at the composing step. Instead, work on fully developing the details related to each subject you are comparing or contrasting.
4. **Getting Feedback:** Have at least one classmate or other person read your rough draft and answer the peer review questions on page 207. If you have access to a writing tutor or center, get another opinion about your paper as well.

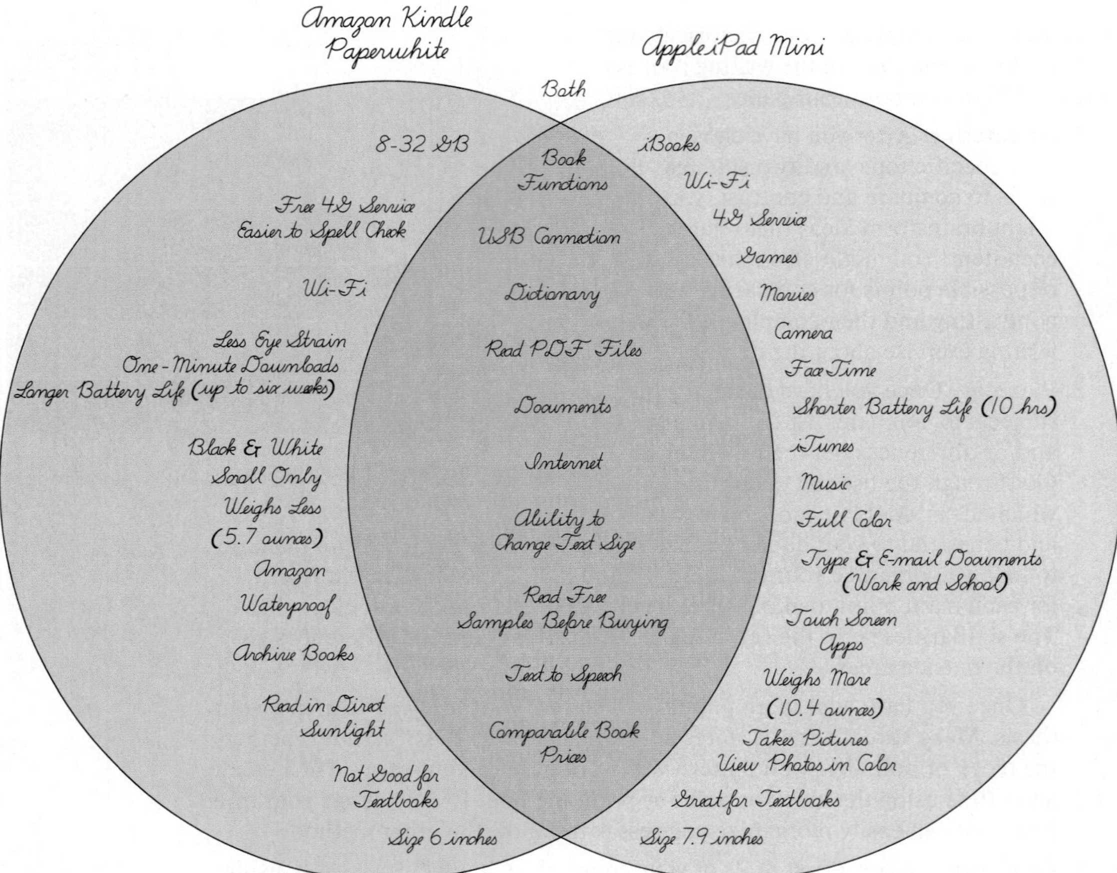

FIGURE 8.3 Student Venn Diagram

If possible, ask your reviewer(s) if your overall approach (block or point-by-point) works well.

5. **Revising:** Using all of the feedback available to you, revise your comparison and contrast essay. Make sure that you have given fairly equal attention to each subject in your paper and that your points flow smoothly. Add, delete, and rearrange ideas as needed. Additionally, if you have used the block method, and encountered problems with it, you might rearrange it to see if the point-by-point method will work better for your topic. Likewise, if you have used the point-by-point method, and have noticed problems, you might reorganize it to see if the block method would work better.

6. **Editing:** Read your essay again, this time looking for errors in grammar, punctuation, and mechanics. Pay particular attention to precise diction (word choice) because the way you describe each subject as you compare and/or contrast will help to give your audience a clear picture of the similarities and differences between them.
7. **Proofreading:** After you have carefully edited your essay, read it one last time. Look for typographical errors and any other issues that might interfere with the readers' understanding of your essay.

PEER REVIEW QUESTIONS FOR COMPARING AND CONTRASTING

Trade rough drafts with a classmate and answer the following questions about his or her paper. Then, in person or online, discuss your papers and suggestions with your peer. Finally, make the changes you feel would most benefit your paper.

1. What elements are being compared in the essay? Are they clearly stated in the thesis?
2. Does the author use the block or point-by-point organizational pattern? Does that pattern seem to be effective? Why or why not?
3. Are the subjects being compared described fairly and accurately, or does the comparison seem to be skewed more in favor of one subject?
4. What analogies, if any, has the author used? How effective are they?
5. What part of the essay is most memorable? Why?
6. Is the conclusion effective? Why or why not?
7. What kinds of grammatical errors, if any, are evident in the essay?
8. What final suggestions do you have for the author?

Writer's Checklist for Comparison and Contrast

Use the checklist below to evaluate your own writing and help ensure that your comparison and contrast essay is complete. If you have any "no" answers, go back and work on those areas if necessary.

- ☐ 1. Have I identified the elements I am comparing and contrasting in my thesis?
- ☐ 2. Have I organized my ideas logically using the block or point-by-point method?
- ☐ 3. Have I described the subjects I am comparing and contrasting fairly and accurately?
- ☐ 4. Have I used analogies to enhance my comparison?
- ☐ 5. Have I used enough transitions to help my writing flow smoothly?
- ☐ 6. Is my conclusion effective?
- ☐ 7. Have I proofread thoroughly?

CHAPTER SUMMARY

1. The comparison and contrast writing strategy focuses on the similarities and differences between subjects.
2. Comparison and contrast writing is an important part of your education, daily life, and career.
3. Interpreting readings and images that include comparisons and contrasts can help you to prepare to write your own comparison and contrast essay.
4. Carefully analyze the rhetorical star before writing a comparison and contrast essay: subject, audience, purpose, strategy, and design.
5. Use these qualities when writing a comparison and contrast essay: identify the elements being compared; use the block or point-by-point method; describe the subjects fairly and accurately; consider using an analogy; include transitions; end with a logical conclusion.

WHAT I KNOW NOW

Use this checklist to determine what you need to work on in order to feel comfortable with your understanding of the material in this chapter. Check off each item as you master it. Review the material for any unchecked items.

- [ ] 1. I know what **comparison and contrast writing** is.
- [ ] 2. I can identify several **real-world applications** for comparison and contrast writing.
- [ ] 3. I can evaluate **readings and images** that reflect comparisons and contrasts.
- [ ] 4. I can analyze the **rhetorical star** for comparison and contrast writing.
- [ ] 5. I understand the **writing process** for comparison and contrast writing.
- [ ] 6. I can apply the **six qualities** of writing about comparisons and contrasts.

Design elements: *Graduate Spotlight:* Ingram Publishing/AGE Fotostock

CHAPTER 9

Analyzing Causes and Effects: Health and Medicine

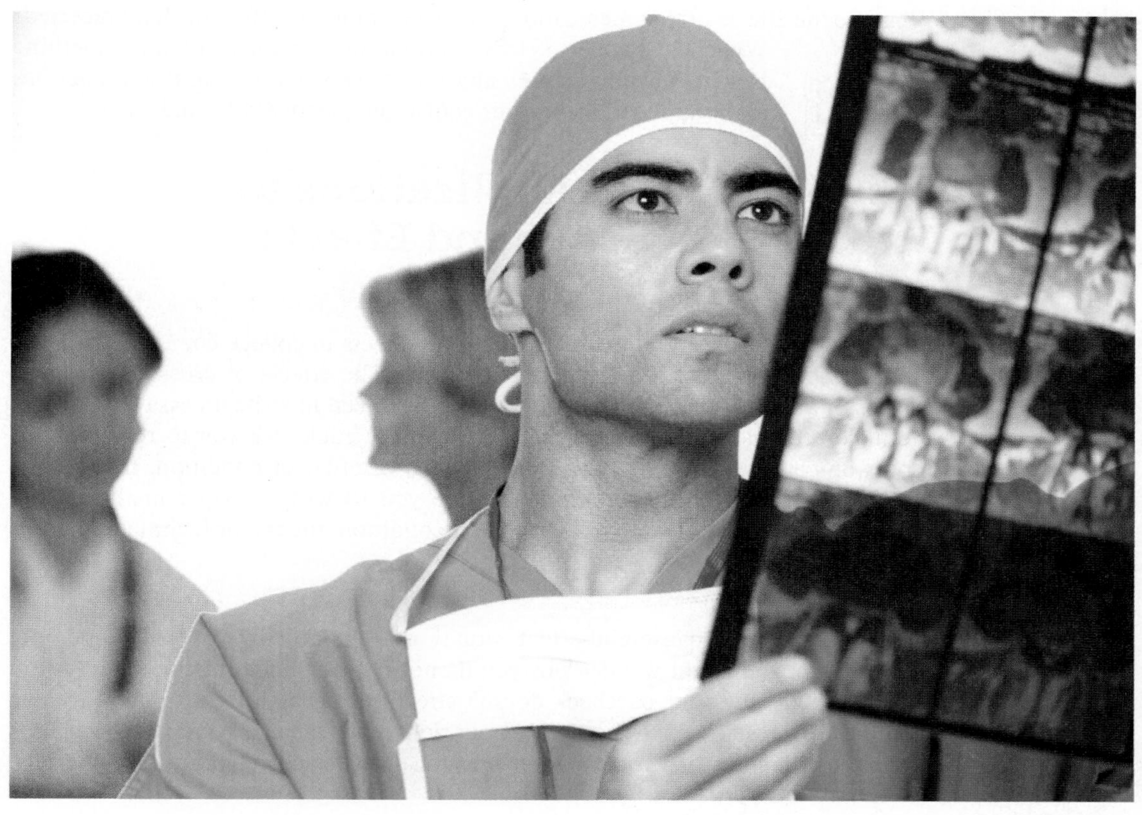

Tetra Images/Corbis

learning outcomes

In this chapter you will learn techniques for achieving these learning outcomes:

Writing Strategy Focus: Explaining Causes and Effects

Because human beings are so curious, we often wonder why something has occurred. Why do I feel better today than yesterday? Why is my back sore? Why did I lose (or gain) five pounds last month? Why haven't I been sleeping well? Why don't I have the complete health coverage I need? When we ask "why," we are looking for reasons (causes) that have led to a particular result (effect).

Other times we might wonder about the effects of a particular situation or event. What are the effects of that medication, massage, or physical therapy that I received? What will happen if I discontinue my treatment or try something new? Analyzing causes and effects (known as **causal analysis**) has many applications in your education, personal life, and career.

Causal analysis Analyzing reasons and results

9.1 Real-World Applications for Explaining Causes and Effects

Writing to Explain Causes and Effects in College

You will often be asked to identify causes and effects in college courses. Your biology instructor may ask you on a test to discuss the effects of crossbreeding two species of animals. In a history course you might need to write an essay explaining the major causes for a war. A psychology teacher could ask you to research and report on causes for a particular psychological disorder or condition. In a course in your major, your instructor may require you to write a paper analyzing the cause-and-effect relationship of a particular condition, theory, or technique.

Writing to Explain Causes and Effects in Your Daily Life

You probably face cause-and-effect situations regularly in your personal life. For example, you might wonder why you do not have as much time to study as you feel you need, why your paycheck doesn't stretch as far as it used to, or why your relationship doesn't seem to be working out right now. You can search for the causes of these problems so that you can implement changes to achieve your desired results.

Writing to Explain Causes and Effects in Your Career

Being able to write about causes and effects is essential to your career. Your boss might ask you to write a feasibility study to determine if a new product, service, or procedure is going to meet your needs. You may need to write a report analyzing the possible causes for a work-related problem regarding patients, clients, or customers. Perhaps you will need to investigate the causes for decreased profits or inefficient methods. Here are some additional cause-and-effect relationships you may need to write about on the job:

Health care: causes of symptoms or conditions, effects of medications and other treatments.

Law: causes for an accident or dissolution of a marriage, effects of negligence or a violent act.

Education: causes for student achievement or failure, effects of trying a new teaching method or learning tool.

Computers: causes for computer crashes or software freezes, effects of implementing a new software program or network.

Business: causes for business growth or decline, effects of streamlined office procedures or a new marketing strategy.

Culinary arts: causes of kitchen accidents or food-borne illness, effects of using high-quality ingredients and cookware.

Massage therapy: causes for creating a peaceful ambience, effects of applying too much or too little pressure.

Graduate SPOTLIGHT

Jamie Wheeler, RN

Jamie Wheeler is a registered nurse (RN) with an AS degree in nursing. She currently manages patient care at a subacute rehabilitation center. Here's what Wheeler has to say about the importance of written communication in her career:

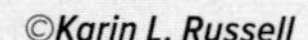
©Karin L. Russell

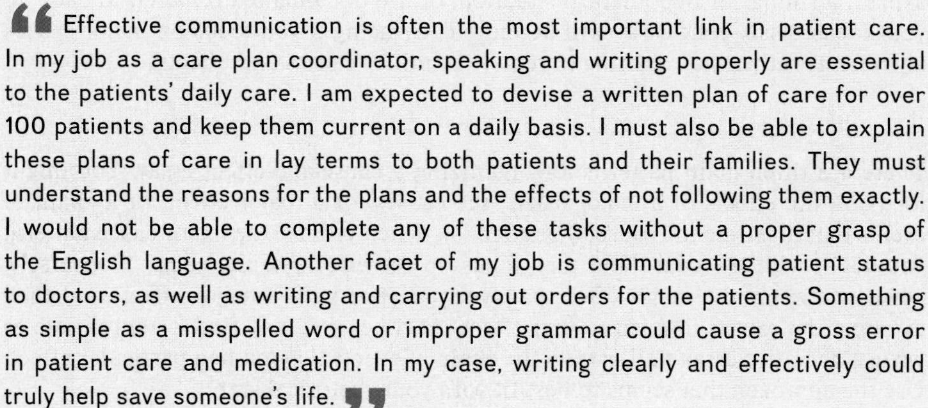

“Effective communication is often the most important link in patient care. In my job as a care plan coordinator, speaking and writing properly are essential to the patients' daily care. I am expected to devise a written plan of care for over 100 patients and keep them current on a daily basis. I must also be able to explain these plans of care in lay terms to both patients and their families. They must understand the reasons for the plans and the effects of not following them exactly. I would not be able to complete any of these tasks without a proper grasp of the English language. Another facet of my job is communicating patient status to doctors, as well as writing and carrying out orders for the patients. Something as simple as a misspelled word or improper grammar could cause a gross error in patient care and medication. In my case, writing clearly and effectively could truly help save someone's life.”

Activity: Brainstorming Real-World Cause-and-Effect Writing

On your own, in pairs, or in small groups, brainstorm uses for analyzing causes and effects at school, in your daily life, and on the job. You may want to choose the prospective career field(s) of the participants in your group. Be prepared to share your results.

9.2 Qualities of Effective Cause-and-Effect Writing

1. Begin by Identifying the Cause or Effect You Are Analyzing

Start with an attention-getter that relates to your main topic. For instance, if you are writing an essay about the effects of diet and exercise, you might begin by citing statistics, telling a brief story, or asking a question such as this: "Have you ever wished that you had more energy to accomplish all of the tasks you face on a daily basis?"

Next, your thesis statement should give the readers a clear indication of the focus of your essay. For example, a thesis focused on effects might go like this: "Improving your diet and exercise habits can drastically enhance your life." Make sure that you will be able to adequately support your thesis statement in the body of your essay. For instance, you might support the previous thesis statement about health and exercise with details about feeling, performing, and looking better.

2. Explain the Cause-and-Effect Relationship Convincingly

Don't assume that your readers will automatically accept the cause-and-effect relationship you suggest in your essay. You have to illustrate that the connection exists by presenting your ideas logically and fully supporting your thesis. For instance, you might describe a specific example, provide a testimonial from a credible source, explain a similar or hypothetical situation, or use documented research to back up your ideas. Also, your essay will be more convincing if you focus on major causes and effects rather than shifting to remote or minor causes and effects.

3. Organize the Causes and/or Effects Effectively

There are three main patterns for organizing a cause-and-effect essay. You might focus on the effects of a major cause, the causes for a major effect, or a chain of events that illustrate the cause(s) or effect(s). When you use the major cause pattern, you begin with the cause and then focus on the effects of the cause. Conversely, when you apply the major effect pattern, you start with a major effect, and then examine the causes that led to that effect. At times you may find it appropriate to write a narrative essay to illustrate the chain of events that led to a particular effect. Use the approach that seems to best fit with your rhetorical star.

On the pages that follow are sample outlines illustrating the three different organizational patterns for a causal analysis essay.

Outline Showing the Effects of a Major Cause

Thesis: Improving your diet and exercise habits can drastically enhance your life.

I. Feel better
  A. More restful sleep
  B. More energy
II. Perform better
  A. Physically
  B. Mentally
III. Look better
  A. Healthier skin
  B. Less body fat
  C. Toned muscles

Outline Showing the Causes for a Major Effect

Thesis: Thousands of people regularly suffer from sleepless nights, not realizing that they might be able to minimize their problem if they identify and address some of the factors that lead to insomnia.

I. Environmental factors
  A. Loud noises
  B. Bright lights
  C. Uncomfortable temperature
II. Physical factors
  A. Illness
  B. Pain
  C. Drug or alcohol use
III. Psychological factors
  A. Stress
  B. Anxiety
  C. Depression
IV. Dietary factors
  A. Too much caffeine
  B. Too many carbohydrates

Causal Chain of Events

Thesis: My mother's breast cancer was the major reason I decided to become an oncology nurse.

I. Mom diagnosed with breast cancer
  A. Bad news on November 11, 2018
  B. Family felt scared and helpless
II. Attended doctor's appointments with Mom
  A. Observed the medical staff in action
  B. Impressed with medical equipment
III. Mom survived and lives life to the fullest
  A. Mom grateful to medical staff
  B. Inspiration for joining the medical profession

4. Use Sound Logic

Be sure to avoid using logical fallacies in your causal analysis. You don't want to jump to an erroneous conclusion about a cause-and-effect relationship. For example, if someone works out every day for one week without losing weight, that doesn't mean exercise isn't an effective method for weight loss. Other factors could be present, such as diet and the intensity level of the workout.

Additionally, the fact that one event precedes another doesn't mean the first event caused the second one. For instance, if a student always drinks a diet cola and eats a candy bar before passing an exam, that doesn't mean the cola and candy were the cause of the success. A more likely cause would be that the student read the textbook, paid attention in class, and studied the material to achieve a passing test score. Double-check the claims that you make to ensure that you present a cogent cause-and-effect relationship. (See Chapter 4 for more details about logical fallacies.)

Grammar Window

PRONOUN AGREEMENT

Sometimes pronoun agreement issues arise when writing about causes and/or effects. Pronouns need to agree with their *antecedents* (the nouns to which they refer). If the noun is singular, the pronoun also needs to be singular. Likewise, if the noun is plural, the pronoun needs to be plural as well. Avoid using a pronoun unless it refers to a specific antecedent mentioned previously.

Singular noun/pronoun example: James decided to take the "biggest loser" weight loss challenge at his office, so he has given up cheeseburgers and French fries.

Discussion: *James* is singular, so *he* is the correct singular pronoun.

Plural noun/pronoun example: The school administrators are concerned about the flu, so they want to be sure that all students have an opportunity to be vaccinated.

Discussion: *Administrators* is plural, so *they* is the correct plural pronoun.

Faulty pronoun agreement: Each of the blood donors wanted to know their blood type.

Discussion: *Each* is singular and *their* is plural, so the pronouns lack agreement. Ignore the nouns in a prepositional phrase (such as *of the blood donors*) when determining pronoun agreement.

Correction: Each of the blood donors wanted to know his or her blood type.

Activity: Correct the pronoun agreement error in each of the following sentences. Change the verb tense if necessary.

1. Ashley uses hand sanitizer because they want to kill as many germs as possible.
2. Vishnu and Stewart wear lab coats in the lab because he wants to stay clean.
3. The student needs to wear shoes in the lab to protect their feet from chemicals and other hazards.
4. Kevin knows not to eat in the microbiology lab because they want to remain healthy.
5. In the medical laboratory, Rose and Tina always place used syringes in the hazardous materials containers because she wants to follow the appropriate safety procedures.

5. Conclude Effectively

As usual, it's a good idea to restate your main idea and summarize your main points in your final paragraph. When writing causal analysis, you will need to be careful not to overgeneralize in your conclusion. You are probably better off saying that a particular cause *may* lead to several effects than claiming that it *will* absolutely lead to those results. Your thesis will be more plausible if you temper your language in anticipation of potential objections to your claim. Finally, end with a memorable statement that will linger in the minds of the readers.

Career-Based CAUSE-AND-EFFECT WRITING

[preview] **THE OCCUPATIONAL SAFETY AND HEALTH ADMINISTRATION (OSHA)** is a division of the U.S. Department of Labor. Established in 1970, OSHA's purpose is to prevent workplace injuries and keep employees safe by enforcing a code of safety standards. However, when accidents happen, a report must be completed that details the contexts and causes for the accident. The following is a real accident report filed by OSHA. Have you ever experienced or witnessed an accident on the job? What were the causes? What were the effects?

Accident Report **by the Occupational Safety and Health Administration (OSHA)**

Accident Summary No. 69

Accident Type: Death due to burns
Weather Conditions: Unknown
Type of Operation: Excavating for building a road
Size of Work Crew: 2
Competent Safety Monitor on Site: No
Safety and Health Program in Effect: No
Was the Worksite Inspected Regularly: No
Training and Education Provided: No
Employee Job Title: Bulldozer Operator
Age & Sex: 44-Male
Experience at this Type of Work: 15 years
Time on Project: 2 days

Brief Description of Accident

A bulldozer operator was preparing a road bed 1
by using the machine to lift trees out of the way. A hydraulic line to the right front hydraulic cylinder ruptured, spraying hydraulic fluid onto the engine manifold and into the operator's compartment. Upon contact with the hot manifold, the hydraulic fluid ignited, engulfing the operator in flames. The operator died from the burns he received.

Inspection Results

Following an inspection, OSHA issued citations 2
for two serious violations of OSHA standards:

1. Frequent and regular inspections of equipment were not made by competent persons designated by the employer in accordance with 29 Code of Federal Regulations (CFR) 1926.20(b)(2). It was determined that the hydraulic hose had been installed backward so that a bend in the fitting connection made contact with the body of the bulldozer, resulting in wear and abrasion of the hose at the connection. This was not discovered during inspection of the machine.
2. The employees doing inspections were not instructed to examine the hoses for signs of wear and abrasion as required by 29 CFR 1926.21(b)(2).

Accident Prevention Recommendations

- Train maintenance and operating personnel to recognize potential problems with the operation of the machinery.
- Have competent persons perform periodic inspections of all operating equipment.
- Ensure that the employer initiates and maintains a safety and health program, in accordance with 29 CFR 1926.20(b)(1).

Sources of Help

OSHA Construction Standards [29 CFR Part 1926], 3
which include all OSHA job safety and health rules and regulations covering construction, may be purchased from the Government Printing Office, phone (202) 512-1800, fax (202) 512-2250, order number 869022-00114-1, $33.

OSHA-funded free consultation services are 4
listed in telephone directories under U.S. Labor Department or under the state government section where states administer their own OSHA programs.

OSHA Safety and Health Training Guidelines for 5
Construction, Volume III (available from the National Technical Information Service, 5285 Port Royal Road, Springfield, VA 22161; phone (703) 487-4650; Order No. PB-239-312/AS, $25) can help construction employers establish a training program.

Courses in construction safety are offered by 6
the OSHA Training Institute, 1555 Times Drive, Des Plaines, IL 60018, 847/297-4810.

OSHA regulations, documents and technical 7
information also are available on CD-ROM, which may be purchased from the Government Printing Office, phone (202) 512-1800 or fax (202) 5122250, order number 729-13-00000-5; cost $79 annually; $28 quarterly. That information also is on the Internet World Wide Web at **www.osha.gov/**.

NOTE: The case here described was selected 8
as being representative of fatalities caused by improper work practices. No special emphasis or priority is implied nor is the case necessarily a recent occurrence. The legal aspects of the incident have been resolved, and the case is now closed.

Source: United States Department of Labor (Occupational Safety and Health Administration), **www.osha.gov/OshDoc/data_FatalFacts/f-facts69.html**.

QUESTIONS FOR REFLECTION

1. Discuss the cause-and-effect relationship in the accident report.
2. Review the design of the report, such as the list of details at the beginning and the headings throughout. Is the design effective for this type of report? Why or why not?
3. What could have been done to prevent the accident?
4. Although the details of the settlement are not included in the report, what kind of compensation do you feel the family of the victim should receive? Why?
5. Are you currently employed, or have you ever been? What precautions does your current or former company take to ensure the safety of its employees? What additional measures could the company take to be even more careful?

9.3 Analyzing Causes and Effects in the Context of Health and Medicine

Although cause-and-effect analysis has applications in virtually every career field, in this chapter you will have an opportunity to examine a few of the cause-and-effect relationships that occur in health and medicine. This theme is useful to explore whether you are going into a health-related field or not. Every human being has to deal with health-related issues at one time or another. Reading and interpreting what others have written can help you see the structure and style of a cause-and-effect analysis and to write your own causal analysis for school, work, and your daily life.

Reading and Reflection CAUSE-AND-EFFECT WRITING

[preview] **SHIRLEY VANDERBILT** is a staff writer for *Body Sense* and *Massage & Bodywork* magazines. She has written numerous articles on massage therapy, reflexology, nutrition, and other health-related issues. In the following essay, Vanderbilt examines the critical role that food plays in our overall health and explains some of the effects of an alternative medicine technique called nutritional cellular cleansing. In her article, Vanderbilt highlights a few of the main points from a book called *The 28-Day Cleansing Program: The Proven Recipe System for Skin and Digestive Repair* by Scott Ohlgren, a holistic health practitioner, and Joann Tomasulo, a whole foods expert. Before reading, consider your own eating habits. How does what you eat affect how you feel?

Food: Your Body's Natural Healer by Shirley Vanderbilt

1 Your body can heal itself from skin and digestive disorders, as well as a host of other maladies,[1] if you just give it a chance. What does it take?

2 According to Scott Ohlgren, holistic health practitioner and proponent of nutritional cellular cleansing, it's as easy as changing what goes from hand to mouth. What's difficult, he says, is living with the diseased state your diet has created and the rounds of pharmaceuticals that never quite cure what ails you.

3 If you're filling your body's fuel tank with processed,[2] or even fake foods, the machinery will eventually clog up and break down. The symptoms that result, whether a mildly annoying acne or more life-threatening colon condition, are a reaction to this toxic overload and dysfunction. Ohlgren says the first thing you need to look at is your diet. Change to a clean, nutritional intake and you can eliminate the symptoms.

4 To get started on that path, Ohlgren has published, along with coauthor and whole foods expert Joann Tomasulo, a user-friendly guide for nutritional cellular cleansing—*The 28-Day Cleansing Program* (Genetic Press, 2006).

5 At the heart of this approach is the principle of cellular regeneration,[3] a process our bodies go through on a continual basis. Cells are constantly renewing themselves, sloughing off used-up matter and regenerating with fresh matter. The materials they use for replacement are derived directly from what you ingest. What have you been giving them to work with lately?

Unwrapping Our Habits

6 The evolution of our eating habits from a nutrient-rich diet to processed grocery foods has led to a genetic breakdown, Ohlgren says, with each generation influencing the next. It's not likely your body will have the same fortitude and disease resistance as that of your great grandparents, or even your next-door neighbor who comes from different stock. But rather than pointing a finger at someone in the past, he says, we need to focus on personal responsibility in the present. "I am in trouble. I have these conditions. Now what are the steps I need to take in order to strengthen my genetics, my well-being, my immune system?"

7 Ohlgren suggests we start with "unwrapping our habits of eating." The cleansing foods he recommends are basically what our ancestors ate—foods in a more natural state. Each has an important role in allowing the body to regenerate as nature designed and, in turn, support its innate healing power.

[1] **Maladies** Diseases of the body.

[2] **Processed foods** Foods that have been altered from their natural states.

[3] **Cellular regeneration** The body's ability to restore or replace cells.

Get With the Program

8 Ohlgren's first rule of thumb for cellular cleansing is to stop the body's toxic load by eliminating processed food items and replacing them with a variety of grains, beans, vegetables, nuts, and fruits, along with healthy oils, soy products, and, of course, lots of water. To maintain hydration, divide your body weight in half and drink that amount of ounces of pure water every day. Eliminating animal protein is a personal issue, depending on your level of physical activity, but dairy products are out because of their mucus-forming properties.

9 Next come the three Rs—remineralize, rebacterialize, and reenzymize. Organic vegetables and sea algae grown in mineral-rich environments can provide these essential nutrients. Maintaining a healthy level of friendly bacteria is important to proper digestion and impacts other functions such as immunity and detoxification of harmful substances. Restock your gut-friendly bacteria with fermented cultured foods such as kimchi, sauerkraut, tempeh, and miso, but make sure the products are not pasteurized (a process that kills the bacteria and enzymes you need). Ohlgren's guidebook offers two hundred recipes, but as he points out, if you don't have time to cook you can still find much of what is needed at your local whole foods deli. Flexibility is the key, and he'll be the first to tell you there's no dogma in this approach.

10 To complement the diet, Ohlgren encourages including what he calls "physical transformers" such as skin brushing, saunas, alkalinizing baths, and colon hydrotherapy. He also recommends getting a few sessions of cleansing bodywork—deep tissue, Thai massage, and acupuncture, for example—and adding a cardiovascular workout three times a week. These active supplements will support the internal and external cleansing process, aid in lymph system circulation, and revitalize your energy level.

11 After completing the four-week program, you can go back to eating as you did before, Ohlgren says, but chances are you won't want to. The results of the cleansing program will give you cause to pause and consider the direct relationship between your food choices and your health. "It really comes down to self-empowerment," Ohlgren says. "I want to get people to pay attention to an incredibly powerful action that we do every day and have done since the first day of our life."

Source: S. Vanderbilt, "Food: Your Body's Natural Healer," *Body Sense*, Spring/Summer 2007, pp. 36–37.

QUESTIONS FOR REFLECTION

Considering Ideas

1. What health issues does the author address in her essay?
2. What suggestions does Vanderbilt offer for helping to resolve those health issues?
3. Have you ever paid attention to how you feel when you vary your diet? What effects have you noticed?

Considering the Rhetorical Star

1. What is the *subject* of the article?
2. Who is Vanderbilt's intended *audience?* How do you know?
3. What is the author's *purpose* for writing the article? Does she achieve her purpose? Why or why not?
4. In addition to cause-and-effect analysis, what other writing *strategies* does Vanderbilt use? Give specific examples from the article to illustrate your point.
5. What specific *design* features does the author use to make her writing appealing to the audience?

Considering Writing Strategies

1. Does Vanderbilt focus more on causes or effects? Which organizational pattern has she employed?
2. What techniques does the author use to try to convince the reader that the cause-and-effect relationship is valid? Is her approach effective? Why or why not?
3. Why does Vanderbilt include headings in her essay? Are they useful? Why or why not?

Writing Suggestions

1. Identify a health issue with which you are familiar. Write an essay explaining the causes or effects that relate to that issue. You might also make suggestions for the reader to follow, as Vanderbilt does in her essay.
2. Have you ever tried a trendy diet, such as South Beach or Atkins? Write an essay explaining why you tried it and/or the effects of doing so.

Reading and Reflection CAUSE-AND-EFFECT WRITING

[preview] **SUSAN BORDO** was born in Newark, New Jersey, and is a professor of philosophy and the Otis A. Singletary Chair in the Humanities at the University of Kentucky. She has written a number of works, including *The Creation of Anne Boleyn* and her best-known book, *Unbearable Weight: Feminism, Western Culture, and the Body,* which was named a Notable Book by the *New York Times,* was nominated for a Pulitzer Prize, and received a Distinguished Publication Award from the Association for Women in Psychology. To learn more about Susan Bordo and see a complete list of her works go to **www.cddc.vt.edu/feminism/bordo.html**. In the following essay, Bordo looks at how the Western media portray women and how this is affecting various cultures across the globe. Before reading, think about how you feel about your own body image. How does the media affect your self-concept about your appearance?

The Globalization of Eating Disorders **by Susan Bordo**

1 The young girl stands in front of the mirror. Never fat to begin with, she's been on a no-fat diet for a couple of weeks and has reached her goal weight: 115 lb., at 5′4—exactly what she should weigh, according to her doctor's chart. But in her eyes she still looks dumpy. She can't shake her mind free of the "Lady Marmelade" video from *Moulin Rouge*. Christina Aguilera, Pink, L'il Kim, and Mya, each one perfect in her own way: every curve smooth and sleek, lean-sexy, nothing to spare. Self-hatred and shame start to burn in the girl, and envy tears at her stomach, enough to make her sick. She'll never look like them, no matter how much weight she loses. Look at that stomach of hers, see how it sticks out? Those thighs—they actually jiggle. Her butt is monstrous. She's fat, gross, a dough girl.

2 As you read the imaginary scenario above, whom did you picture standing in front of the mirror? If your images of girls with eating and body image problems have been shaped by *People* magazine and Lifetime movies, she's probably white, North American, and economically secure. A child whose parents have never had to worry about putting food on the family table. A girl with money to spare for fashion magazines and trendy clothing, probably college-bound. If you're familiar with the classic psychological literature on eating disorders, you may also have read that she's an extreme "perfectionist" with a hyper-demanding mother,

and that she suffers from "body-image distortion syndrome" and other severe perceptual and cognitive problems that "normal" girls don't share. You probably don't picture her as Black, Asian, or Latina.

3 Read the description again, but this time imagine twenty-something Tenisha Williamson standing in front of the mirror. Tenisha is black, suffers from anorexia, and feels like a traitor to her race. "From an African-American standpoint," she writes, "we as a people are encouraged to embrace our big, voluptuous bodies. This makes me feel terrible because I don't want a big, voluptuous body! I don't ever want to be fat—ever, and I don't ever want to gain weight. I would rather die from starvation than gain a single pound."[1] Tenisha is no longer an anomaly. Eating and body image problems are now not only crossing racial and class lines, but gender lines. They have also become a global phenomenon.

4 Fiji is a striking example. Because of their remote location, the Fiji islands did not have access to television until 1995, when a single station was introduced. It broadcasts programs from the United States, Great Britain, and Australia. Until that time, Fiji had no reported cases of eating disorders, and a study conducted by anthropologist Anne Becker showed that most Fijian girls and women, no matter how large, were comfortable with their bodies. In 1998, just three years after the station began broadcasting, 11 percent of girls reported vomiting to control weight, and 62 percent of the girls surveyed reported dieting during the previous months.[2]

5 Becker was surprised by the change; she had thought that Fijian cultural traditions, which celebrate eating and favor voluptuous bodies, would "withstand" the influence of media images. Becker hadn't yet understood that we live in an empire of images, and that there are no protective borders.

6 In Central Africa, for example, traditional cultures still celebrate voluptuous women. In some regions, brides are sent to fattening farms, to be plumped and massaged into shape for their wedding night. In a country plagued by AIDS, the skinny body has meant—as it used to among Italian, Jewish, and Black Americans—poverty, sickness, death. "An African girl must have hips," says dress designer Frank Osodi. "We have hips. We have bums. We like flesh in Africa." For years, Nigeria sent its local version of beautiful to the Miss World Competition. The contestants did very poorly. Then a savvy entrepreneur went against local ideals and entered Agbani Darego, a light-skinned, hyper-skinny beauty. (He got his inspiration from M-Net, the South African network seen across Africa on satellite television, which broadcasts mostly American movies and television shows.) Agbani Darego won the Miss World Pageant, the first Black African to do so. Now, Nigerian teenagers fast and exercise, trying to become "lepa"—a popular slang phrase for the thin "it" girls that are all the rage. Said one: "People have realized that slim is beautiful."[3]

7 How can mere images be so powerful? For one thing, they are never "just pictures," as the fashion magazines continually maintain (disingenuously) in their own defense. They speak to young people not just about how to be beautiful but also about how to become what the dominant culture admires, values, rewards. They tell them how to be cool, "get it together," overcome their shame. To girls who have been abused they may offer a fantasy of control and invulnerability, immunity from pain and hurt. For racial and ethnic groups whose bodies have been deemed "foreign," earthy, and primitive, and considered unattractive by Anglo-Saxon norms, they may cast the lure of being accepted as "normal" by the dominant culture.

8 In today's world, it is through images—much more than parents, teachers, or clergy—that we are taught how to be. And it is images, too, that teach us how to see, that educate our vision in what's a defect and what is normal, that give us the models against which our own bodies and the bodies of others are measured. Perceptual pedagogy: "How To Interpret Your Body 101." It's become a global requirement.

[1]From the Colours of Ana website (**http://coloursofana.com/ss8.asp**). [This and subsequent notes in the selection are the author's.]

[2]Reported in Nancy Snyderman, *The Girl in the Mirror* (New York: Hyperion, 2002), p. 84.

[3]Norimitsu Onishi, "Globalization of Beauty Makes Slimness Trendy," *The New York Times*, Oct. 3, 2002.

9 I was intrigued, for example, when my articles on eating disorders began to be translated, over the past few years, into Japanese and Chinese. Among the members of audiences at my talks, Asian women had been among the most insistent that eating and body image weren't problems for their people, and indeed, my initial research showed that eating disorders were virtually unknown in Asia. But when, this year, a Korean translation of *Unbearable Weight* was published, I felt I needed to revisit the situation. I discovered multiple reports on dramatic increases in eating disorders in China, South Korea, and Japan. "As many Asian countries become Westernized and infused with the Western aesthetic of a tall, thin, lean body, a virtual tsunami of eating disorders has swamped Asian countries," writes Eunice Park in *Asian Week* magazine. Older people can still remember when it was very different. In China, for example, where revolutionary ideals once condemned any focus on appearance and there have been several disastrous famines, "little fatty" was a term of endearment for children. Now, with fast food on every corner, childhood obesity is on the rise, and the cultural meaning of fat and thin has changed. "When I was young," says Li Xiaojing, who manages a fitness center in Beijing, "people admired and were even jealous of fat people since they thought they had a better life. . . . But now, most of us see a fat person and think 'He looks awful.'"[4]

10 Clearly, body insecurity can be exported, imported, and marketed—just like any other profitable commodity. In this respect, what's happened with men and boys is illustrative. Ten years ago men tended, if anything, to see themselves as better looking than they (perhaps) actually were. And then (as I chronicle in detail in my book *The Male Body*) the menswear manufacturers, the diet industries, and the plastic surgeons "discovered" the male body. And now, young guys are looking in their mirrors, finding themselves soft and ill defined, no matter how muscular they are. Now they are developing the eating and body image disorders that we once thought only girls had. Now they are abusing steroids, measuring their own muscularity against the oiled and perfected images of professional athletes, body-builders, and *Men's Health* models. Now the industries in body-enhancement—cosmetic surgeons, manufacturers of anti-aging creams, spas and salons—are making huge bucks off men, too.

11 What is to be done? I have no easy answers. But I do know that we need to acknowledge, finally and decisively, that we are dealing here with a cultural problem. If eating disorders were biochemical, as some claim, how can we account for their gradual "spread" across race, gender, and nationality? And with mass media culture increasingly providing the dominant "public education" in our children's lives—and those of children around the globe—how can we blame families? Families matter, of course, and so do racial and ethnic traditions. But families exist in cultural time and space—and so do racial groups. In the empire of images, no one lives in a bubble of self-generated "dysfunction" or permanent immunity. The sooner we recognize that—and start paying attention to the culture around us and what it is teaching our children—the sooner we can begin developing some strategies for change.

[4] Reported in Elizabeth Rosenthal, "Beijing Journal: China's Chic Waistline: Convex to Concave," *The New York Times*, Dec. 9, 1999.

Source: Susan Bordo, "The Globalization of Eating Disorders."

QUESTIONS FOR REFLECTION

Considering Ideas

1. According to Bordo, what factors contribute to the body image problem that some people, especially young women, face? Are these reasons feasible? Why or why not?
2. What comparison does the author make in paragraph 10? Is this a valid comparison? Why or why not?
3. In the concluding paragraph, the writer suggests that eating disorders are a cultural problem. Do you agree or disagree with her claim? Explain your answer.

Considering the Rhetorical Star

1. What is the *subject* of Bordo's essay?
2. Is the intended *audience* limited to people with eating disorders, or would others be interested as well? Explain.
3. What is the author's *purpose* for writing the essay? Does she achieve her purpose? Why or why not?
4. In addition to cause-and-effect analysis, what other writing *strategies* does Bordo use? Give specific examples from the essay to illustrate your point.
5. Does the *design* of the essay seem better suited to academic writing or magazine writing? Explain.

Considering Writing Strategies

1. What type of attention-getter does Bordo use? What purpose does it serve? How effective is the introductory paragraph of the essay?
2. Does the author focus more on the causes or effects of eating disorders? What specific examples does she use to support her position?
3. Although most of the essay is written from the third person point of view, the author occasionally shifts to the first and second person points of view. Identify passages where these shifts occur. Why does she change points of view in those areas? What effect do the shifts have on the reader?

ESOL Tip >

Instead of focusing on American culture, write about how people from your culture perceive body image.

Writing Suggestions

1. Write an essay focusing on the effects of young Americans' obsession with their appearance. You might consider how having a distorted body image will affect them at school, on the job, and in their personal lives.
2. Have you ever known someone with an eating disorder or other psychological condition, such as panic attacks, schizophrenia, or obsessive compulsive disorder? Write an essay explaining the causes or effects of the disorder. Include details about the person you know to provide support for your main points. You may want to use a different name to protect the person's identity. Be sure to cite any resources you use in your paper.

Reading and Reflection CAUSE-AND-EFFECT WRITING

[preview] **CHARLES "CHUCK" CORBIN** is a professor in the Department of Exercise Science and Physical Education at Arizona State University and holds a PhD from the University of New Mexico. Corbin has co-authored more than thirty books, published hundreds of papers, and developed dozens of physical activity videos and computer software packages. The excerpt that follows is from a textbook titled *Concepts in Fitness and Wellness: A Comprehensive Lifestyle Approach,* which Chuck Corbin co-authored with Gregory J. Welk, William R. Corbin, and Karen A. Welk. To learn more about the U.S. government's dietary guidelines, visit **www.health.gov/dietaryguidelines/**. Before reading, consider your own views about carbohydrates. Are carbs a big part of your diet, or do you try to limit your intake of them?

Dietary Recommendations for Carbohydrates by Charles B. Corbin

1 **Complex carbohydrates should be the principal source of calories in the diet.** Carbohydrates have gotten a bad rap in recent years due to the hype associated with low-carbohydrate diets. Carbohydrates have been unfairly implicated as a cause of obesity. It is true that they cause insulin to be released and that insulin, in turn, causes the body to take up and store excess energy as fat. However, this is overly simplistic and doesn't take into account differences in types of carbohydrates. Simple sugars (such as sucrose, glucose, and fructose) found in candy and soda lead to quick increases in blood sugar and tend to promote fat deposition. Complex carbohydrates (e.g., bread, pasta, rice), on the other hand, are broken down more slowly and do not cause the same effect on blood sugar. They contribute valuable nutrients and fiber in the diet and should constitute the bulk of a person's diet. Distinguishing between simple and complex carbohydrates is important, since they are processed differently and have different nutrient values.

2 A number of low-carb diet books have used an index known as the glycemic index (GI) as the basis for determining if foods are appropriate in the diet. Foods with a high GI value produce rapid increases in blood sugar, while foods with a low GI value produce slower increases. This may seem to be a logical way to categorize carbohydrates, but it is misleading, since it doesn't account for the amount of carbohydrates in different servings of a food. A more appropriate indicator of the effect of foods on blood sugar levels is called the glycemic load. Carrots, for example, are known to have a very high GI value, but the overall glycemic load is quite low. The carbohydrates from most fruits and vegetables exhibit similar properties.

3 Despite the intuitive and logical appeal of this classification system, neither the glycemic index nor glycemic load have been consistently associated with body weight. Diets based on low glycemic index diets also don't have advantages for weight loss. There is some evidence linking glycemic load to a higher risk for diabetes so it is wise to still minimize simple carbohydrates.

4 **Reducing dietary sugar can help reduce risk of obesity and heart disease.** Minimizing sugar consumption is a good goal, since people who consume high amounts of sugar also tend to consume excess calories. The dietary guidelines specifically recommend decreasing consumption of added sugars to reduce excess calorie consumption and weight gain. The World Health Organization suggests limiting sugars to 5 to 10 percent of total calories consumed.

5 A variety of foods contribute to daily sugar intake, but soft drinks and sugar-sweetened beverages are the primary sources of added sugars in the American diet. A typical 12-ounce sweetened soft drink contains 150 calories, mostly sugar. Soft drink makers have responded by making smaller sizes and providing alternatives, but personal restraint is still needed to minimize consumption. Reducing consumption of sugar-sweetened beverages is a simple, but important, diet modification.

6 **Increasing consumption of dietary fiber is important for overall good nutrition and health.** Diets high in complex carbohydrates and fiber are associated with a low incidence of coronary heart disease, stroke, and some forms of cancer. Long-term studies indicate that high-fiber diets may also be associated with a lower risk for diabetes mellitus, diverticulosis, hypertension, and gallstone formation. However, it is not known whether these health benefits are directly attributable to high dietary fiber or other effects associated with the ingestion of vegetables, fruits, and cereals.

7 It has proven difficult to isolate the effects of dietary fiber, but there is no debate about the benefits. Past guidelines distinguished soluble fiber (typically found in fruits and oat bran) from insoluble fiber (typically found in grains), but this was an oversimplification of the different types of fiber as well as how they are processed in the body. From a technical perspective, dietary fibers are defined as carbohydrate molecules that escape digestion in the small intestine and pass into the large intestine, where they are slightly or nearly completely fermented. The fermentation products actually

contribute to the many physiological benefits of dietary fiber since they can be absorbed into the bloodstream.

8 The National Academy of Medicine (formerly the Institute of Medicine) currently distinguishes natural fibers in food from "functional fibers," which are extracted, modified, or synthesized forms of fibers. However, new recommendations have sought to create a more integrated index of dietary fiber. The combination of fibers that we eat interacts to produce health benefits, so the goal is to consume a diverse array of dietary fibers. From this perspective, the additional functional fibers that are added to food are analogous to vitamin-fortified foods that supplement our diets to ensure that we have sufficient amounts and types of fiber in our diet.

9 Currently, few Americans consume the recommended amounts of dietary fiber. The average intake of dietary fiber is about 15 g/day, which is much lower than the recommended 25 to 35 g/day. Foods in the typical American diet contain little, if any, dietary fiber, and servings of commonly consumed grains, fruits, and vegetables contain only 1 to 3 g of dietary fiber. Therefore, individuals have to look for ways to ensure that they get sufficient fiber in their diet. Manufacturers are allowed to declare a food as a "good source of fiber" if it contains 10 percent of the recommended amount (2.5 g/serving) and an "excellent source of fiber" if it contains 20 percent of the recommended amount (5 g/serving). Because fiber has known health benefits, the dietary guidelines encourage consumers to select foods high in dietary fiber, such as whole-grain breads and cereals, legumes, vegetables, and fruit, whenever possible.

10 **Fruits and vegetables are essential for good health.** Fruits and vegetables are a valuable source of dietary fiber, are packed with vitamins and minerals, and contain many beneficial phytochemicals, which may have positive effects on health. The current guidelines recommend that adults eat 2½ cups of a wide variety of vegetables from all the subgroups of colors and starches a day. A major advantage of this suggestion is that it can make you feel full without eating a lot of calories. The guidelines also suggest that adults eat 2 cups of fruit a day, with half coming in the form of whole fruit. Fruit provides many essential vitamins and most are a good source of fiber as well.

11 Numerous studies have confirmed the many benefits from fruits and vegetables, but the most powerful documentation is in the detailed report provided by the Dietary Guidelines Advisory Committee. The committee examined numerous health associations with various eating patterns and food groups and provided the following conclusion: *"Vegetables and fruit are the only characteristics of the diet that were consistently identified in every conclusion statement across the health outcomes."* These conclusions clearly contributed to the increased emphasis being placed on a plant-based diet in the dietary guidelines.

12 The popularity of farmers' markets reflects broader interest in fresh fruits and vegetables. However, a challenge in promoting fruit and vegetable consumption is the higher relative cost. Many public health advocates have lobbied for subsidies that would help lower costs of fresh fruits and vegetables. Considerable research is now also focused on understanding factors that influence fruit and vegetable consumption in different segments of the population.

Source: C. B., Corbin, G. J., Welk, W. R., Corbin, and K.A. Welk, (2018). *Concepts in fitness and wellness: A comprehensive lifestyle approach.* New York: McGraw-Hill Higher Education.

QUESTIONS FOR REFLECTION

Considering Ideas

1. What is Corbin's view about carbohydrates? Is his view consistent with other recent literature on the subject? Explain.
2. What are the effects of reducing added dietary sugar? Explain.
3. According to Corbin, what are some of the benefits of eating fruits and vegetables? Give several specific examples.

Considering the Rhetorical Star

1. What is the *subject* of Corbin's text and why is it relevant?

2. Who is the intended primary *audience* for the piece? How do you know? Who might be a secondary audience for the work?
3. What is the *purpose* of the excerpt? Does the author achieve his purpose? Why or why not?
4. In addition to analyzing causes and effects, what other writing *strategies* does Corbin use? Give several specific examples.
5. What is the *design* of the work? Is it effective? Why or why not?

Considering Writing Strategies

1. How would you characterize the tone of the excerpt? Is it more formal or informal? Explain.
2. How are Corbin's ideas organized? Is this organizational strategy effective? Why or why not?
3. Corbin cites numerous sources to support his views on carbohydrates. What effect does this technique have on the reader?

Writing Suggestions

1. What are some of the reasons people change their eating habits? Write an essay focusing on several different causes for modifying one's diet. If you use outside research, be sure to cite your sources.
2. Have you tried modifying your diet for health reasons? Were you successful? If so, were the results lasting? Were you unsuccessful? If so, why didn't the diet work for you? Write a cause-and-effect essay about your experience with dieting.

Reading and Reflection CAUSE-AND-EFFECT WRITING

[preview] **WILLIAM SHAKESPEARE (1564–1616)** was born in Stratford-upon-Avon, England. Known as "the bard" (storyteller), Shakespeare is considered by many to be the greatest writer in the English language or possibly even the world. His works, which consist of 38 plays, 154 sonnets, and several other poems, have been translated into every major living language. In addition to being a writer, Shakespeare was an actor, producer, and part owner in the Lord Chamberlain's Men playing company. Many of his plays, such as *Romeo and Juliet, Hamlet, Othello,* and *Macbeth,* were presented in the famous Globe Theatre in Southwark, England. Visit **www.shakespeare.org.uk/home.html** to learn more about Shakespeare's life and works. In the sonnet that follows, the speaker in the poem tells how he feels about his love. Before reading, consider these questions: Have you ever been in love? How did it make you feel? Did the feelings last, or did something cause a change of heart?

GL Archive/Alamy Images

Sonnet 147: My Love Is As a Fever Longing Still by William Shakespeare

My love is as a fever longing still,
For that which longer nurseth the disease;
Feeding on that which doth preserve the ill,
The uncertain sickly appetite to please.
My reason, the physician to my love,
Angry that his prescriptions are not kept,
Hath left me, and I desperate now approve
Desire is death, which physic did except.
Past cure I am, now Reason is past care,
And frantic-mad with evermore unrest;
My thoughts and my discourse as madmen's are,
At random from the truth vainly express'd;
For I have sworn thee fair, and thought thee bright,
Who art as black as hell, as dark as night.

QUESTIONS FOR REFLECTION

Considering Ideas

1. Which words in the poem does Shakespeare borrow from the medical field? Why do you think he has chosen those words? What effect do they have on the reader?
2. How does the speaker in the sonnet feel about his love? What causes him to feel that way?
3. What message is Shakespeare trying to convey to the reader? Explain.

Considering the Rhetorical Star

1. What is the *subject* of the sonnet?
2. What kind of *audience* might Shakespeare have had in mind as he wrote the poem?
3. What is the author's *purpose* for writing the poem? Does he achieve his purpose? Why or why not?
4. In addition to cause-and-effect analysis, which other writing *strategies* does Shakespeare use? Give specific examples from the poem.
5. What specific *design* features does Shakespeare use to add interest to his poem?

Considering Writing Strategies

1. Which lines create the most vivid images for the reader? What do you envision?
2. Notice Shakespeare's use of rhythm and rhyme in the sonnet. What effect do these elements of poetry have on the reader?
3. What is the tone or mood of the sonnet? Which specific words emphasize this tone?

Writing Suggestions

1. Have you ever been in love? What effect did that feeling have on you? Write an essay explaining your reasons for falling in love with someone or the effects that falling in love had on you.
2. Have you ever had a romantic relationship not work out? Write an essay explaining what led to the demise of your relationship or how the breakup has affected you (positively or negatively).

STUDENT WRITING

Get Fit with Wii

by Olivia Covey

1 For busy students, parents, and professionals, trying to fit in a workout in the middle of a hectic day can be difficult. Luckily, Nintendo Wii has come up with a great way for people to get fit and lose inches off their waistlines in the comfort of their own homes. *Wii Fit* is an interactive game designed to help people of all ages and skill levels target specific areas they need to improve by following an individual fitness routine. Exercising with *Wii Fit* will provide gamers with a fun, convenient, and personalized regimen for getting in shape and losing weight.

2 *Wii Fit* has become popular in the health and fitness world because it has turned the traditional boring fitness routine into a fun and relaxing game for people of all ages. The game is broken down into various stimulating activities that are geared toward different experience levels. One example is an activity called the "hula hoop," which requires the user to balance on the balance board included with the game, while virtually hula hooping. This simple but stimulating activity provides a great aerobic workout. During a workout, the human body releases a hormone called endorphins. Endorphins are neurotransmitters found in the brain that have been linked to psychological feelings of pleasure. The combination of the natural release of these endorphins and the assortment of fun and challenging activities give the user the ultimate workout experience.

3 With the vast amount of technology available today, some people may find the idea of having a video game help them with fitness to be too difficult. On the contrary, not only is *Wii Fit* easy to use, it is extremely convenient. *Wii Fit* gives flexible options for the intensity of each session. It also provides interactive feedback and step-by-step instructions on how to do each activity, making it simple for anyone to pick up a controller and get moving. With this technology, people can exercise in their own living rooms anytime they need to without having to make a trip to the gym. The convenience of the *Wii Fit* increases the probability of commitment to a fitness regimen, resulting in a healthier, happier person.

4 Finally, owning a *Wii Fit* system is like having a personal trainer at home. The system has great features including a program that allows gamers to input information about specific foods they consume through the day to get an estimated calorie intake number. The *Wii Fit* program then takes this number and matches it with an activity with a corresponding MET level. An MET level simply represents the intensity of an activity. For example, if someone is planning to attend a birthday party later in the day, he or she can add a piece of birthday cake to the calorie calculator. The program then comes up with an estimated calorie number for that cake and matches it with activities to burn those calories right off. *Wii Fit* is also great for targeting specific areas of the body. For instance, if someone is particularly concerned with toning mostly the buns and thighs, the *Wii Fit* program can design a series of activities to focus on those specific areas. The *Wii Fit* program then combines and tracks this information on a progress calendar that helps the individual to see goals that have been accomplished and areas in need of improvement. After working out with the *Wii Fit* system for just a few weeks, participants will start to see results.

5 In closing, exercising with a *Wii Fit* is one of the most innovative ways to get in shape and lose unwanted pounds. It is fun and has a variety of activities to choose from, so players will never get bored doing the same routine over and over again. Furthermore, it is convenient and flexible, providing a variety of activities and instant feedback for everyone from beginners to people who work out

regularly. Most importantly, *Wii Fit* is ideal because it is completely personalized. It utilizes a variety of programs to help participants set and achieve specific fitness and weight loss goals. With strong willpower and the help of *Wii Fit,* many gamers can achieve their desired workout results.

QUESTIONS FOR REFLECTION

1. Identify Covey's thesis statement. Is it effective? Why or why not?
2. According to the author, what are the effects of using *Wii Fit?* What do you suppose are the causes for someone wanting to use *Wii Fit?*
3. What three reasons does the author give for using a *Wii Fit* program?
4. Are the author's reasons convincing? Why or why not?
5. Have you ever tried using the *Wii Fit* program? How does your experience compare to the ideas in Covey's essay?

Activity Creating a Cause-and-Effect Chart

Sometimes you may find it challenging to decide whether to write about the causes or effects for a particular subject. If that's the case, creating a chart can help you to make a choice.

Make a chart of causes and effects for one of the following topics (or the topic about which you are going to write an essay). Draw a line down the center of the page and list causes on the left side and effects on the right side.

Dropping out of school
Choosing the right career
Good or poor self-concept
Peer pressure
Drug use
Enrolling in college
Beginning a new job
Exercising more or less
Gaining or losing weight
Alcohol use or abuse

Be prepared to share a few of the highlights with the class. This activity may give you ideas for writing a cause-and-effect essay.

OPTIONS FOR WRITING A CAUSE-AND-EFFECT ESSAY

Now that you have read one or more examples of cause-and-effect writing, it's time to write your own causal analysis. You may choose to write about one of the writing options that follow, the advertisement, the image, or one of the media suggestions. Consider your rhetorical star and the qualities of effective cause-and-effect writing as you begin to compose your assignment.

Writing Assignment Options

Use one of the following topics to write an essay that emphasizes causes, effects, or both.

1. A decision that has changed the direction of someone's life
2. A person, place, object, or experience that is special
3. A contest, sporting event, or hobby
4. Being on a team or in a club or other organization
5. A mistake that someone you know has made
6. The responsibilities of a new job
7. Gaining or losing a family member or friend
8. A law, policy, or ruling that affects people positively or negatively
9. A fortunate (or an unfortunate) experience, event, or diagnosis
10. Peer pressure to do something bad (or good)

Multimodal Assignment

Using one of the readings, writing assignment options, or another topic, create a multimodal project using the cause-and-effect writing strategy and at least two or more of the options in Table 9.1.

Table 9.1

Multimodal Options		
Artifact	Images	PowerPoint
Artwork	Infographics	Prezi
Audio clip	Journal	Video
Blog	Montage	Website
Digital portfolio	Podcast	Wiki
Graphic organizer	Poster	Writing

(See Chapter 15 for more details about multimodal compositions.)

Interpreting an Advertisement

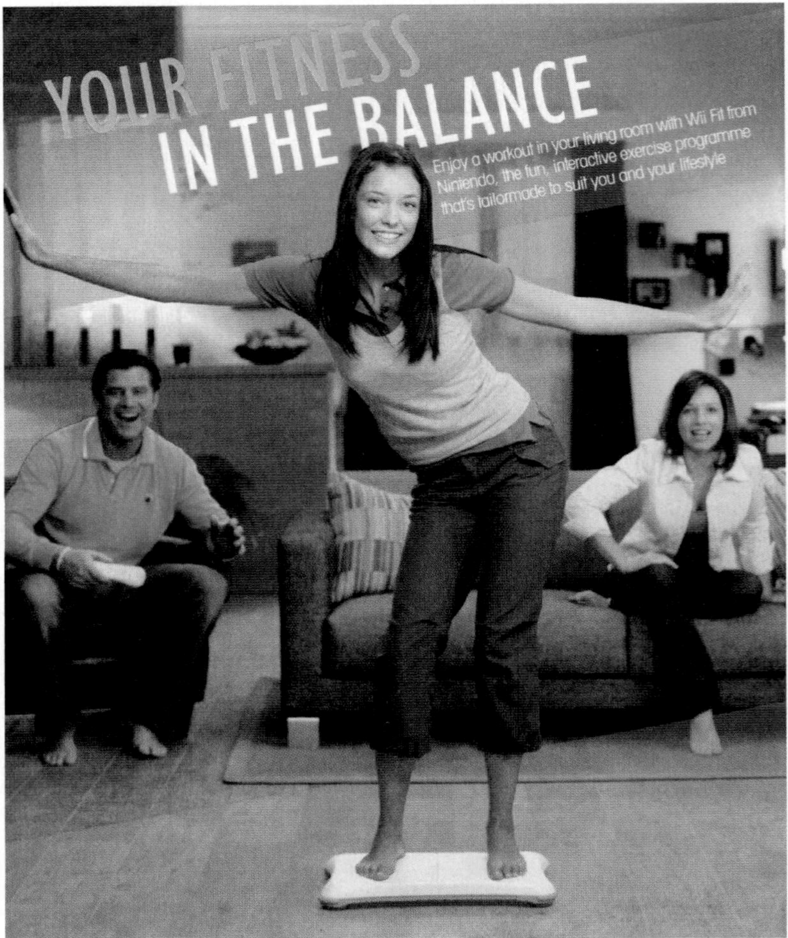

The Advertising Archives

Who is the audience for the advertisement? The image and words in the ad suggest that one's fitness depends on purchasing a *Wii Fit* game and balance board. Is the cause-and-effect relationship logical? Why or why not? Is the advertisement persuasive? Why or why not? Write a cause-and-effect essay related to the *Wii Fit* game or another exercise video game. For this assignment, focus primarily on the effects of the game on its users.

Writing about an Image

ABC/Everett Collection

Write a cause-and-effect essay that relates to one of the images in this chapter. You may write about the image itself, or you may choose to write about something the image reminds you of. For example, you might write a creative essay about the scenes from *Grey's Anatomy*. Or you might write about the photograph of the medical staff in the chapter opening photo using the causal chain pattern to explain the events that led to the x-ray.

Media Connection for Explaining Causes and Effects

You might watch, read, and/or listen to one or more of the suggested media in Table 9.2 to discover additional examples of cause-and-effect analysis. Exploring various media may help you to better understand methods for explaining causes and effects. You may also choose to write about one or more of the media suggestions. For example, you might watch an episode of *Grey's Anatomy* and write an essay explaining the causes or effects for a situation that occurs on the show. Be sure to give credit to any sources you use in your essay.

Table 9.2

Media Chart				
Television	*The Human Body on* Discovery	*Grey's Anatomy*	*The Mindy Project*	*The Doctors*
Film	*Sicko* (2007)	*Supersize Me* (2004)	*What the Health* (2017)	*Side Effects* (2013)
Print/ E-Reading	*Fitness*	*Women's Health*	*Men's Health*	*Natural Health*
Internet	**webmd.com**	**howhealthworks.com**	**www.health.com/fitness**	**everydayhealth.com**
Music	"Hospital" by Counting Crows	"Panic on the Streets of Health Care City" by Thursday	"Medicine" by Kelly Clarkson	"The A-Team" by Ed Sheeran

FIGURE 9.1
The Rhetorical Star

9.4 Analyzing the Rhetorical Star for Writing a Cause-and-Effect Essay

As you prepare to write your cause-and-effect essay, consider the five points of the rhetorical star (Figure 9.1). You might use some of the questions in the chart as you conduct your rhetorical star analysis.

Subject	Be sure to select a topic that is narrow enough to adequately cover within the parameters of your assignment. If you are writing a longer essay or research paper, then you may be able to cover both causes and effects. However, you will probably want to focus on causes or effects (not both) for a shorter paper. For instance, while you could reasonably focus on the causes or effects of staying fit, you probably wouldn't be able to cover the entire history of fitness in America effectively in a brief paper.

Audience	Who will read your essay? Are you aiming at a particular audience, such as college students, parents, or health care workers? Once you have a specific audience in mind, focus on the details that will be most useful to your readers. Is your audience reading just for information, or do the readers need to be able to do something as a result of your essay?
Purpose	Think about what you are trying to accomplish as you write your cause-and-effect essay. Do you want to simply inform the readers about a specific cause-and-effect relationship? Are you writing mainly to persuade your readers that a cause-and-effect relationship exists? Maybe your primary goal is to express your feelings about the serious consequences of a tragic illness or accident that someone you know suffered with a secondary goal of helping others to prevent it from happening to them.
Strategy	Even if your main approach is to explore the causes and/or effects of a particular topic, you may find it useful to combine strategies as well. For example, if you are writing about the effects of your friend's drug use, you might include a description of the behaviors your friend exhibits, compare and contrast your friend's life before and after the drug use began, or offer instructions for someone seeking help to escape a drug addiction.
Design	How should your essay look when you are finished? Do you need to include any photos, illustrations, or graphic organizers to help your reader fully comprehend your ideas? Will other design strategies help your readers to better understand the causes and/or effects you are explaining?

9.5 Applying the Writing Process for Explaining Causes and Effects

After you have completed your rhetorical star analysis, follow the steps of the writing process (Figure 9.2) to compose your cause-and-effect paper.

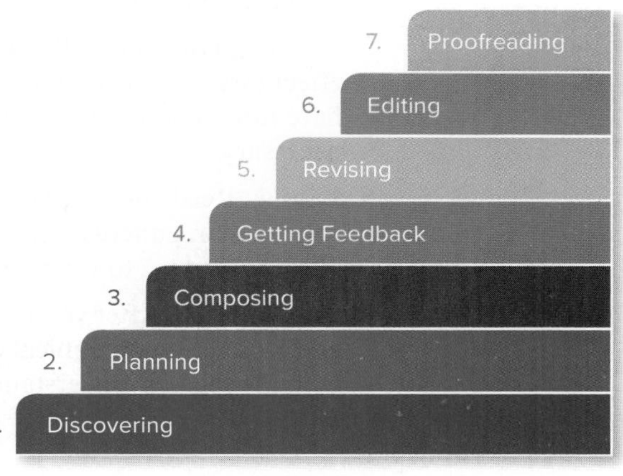

FIGURE 9.2 The Seven Steps of the Writing Process

1. **Discovering:** Once you have chosen a topic, you might try making a chart of causes and effects to help you

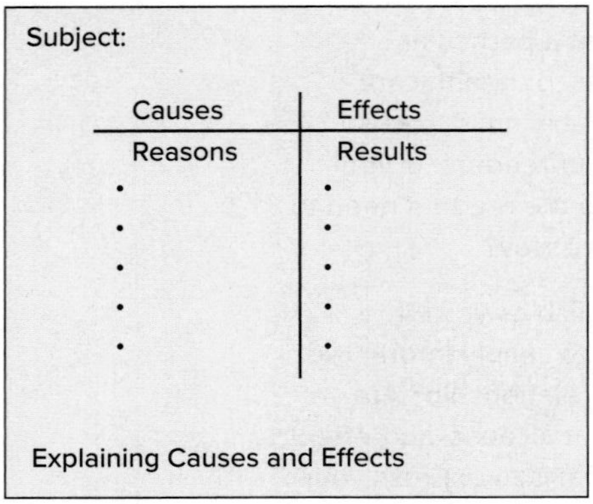

Subject:

Causes	Effects
Reasons	Results
•	•
•	•
•	•
•	•
•	•

Explaining Causes and Effects

FIGURE 9.3 Explaining Causes and Effects

determine which you want to cover in your essay (see Figure 9.3). Next, you may want to complete two freewriting exercises, writing first about causes and then about effects to see which side you can more effectively develop. If you are basing your paper on research, you might want to find some reliable sources on the topic to see which approach will work best for your assignment.

2. **Planning:** Create a cluster or an outline (informal or formal) to help you organize your ideas. Remember to follow one of the cause-and-effect organizational strategies for your essay: the effects of a major cause, the causes for a major effect, or a chain of events that illustrate the cause(s) or effect(s). (See pages 212–213 for more details about these organization patterns.)
3. **Composing:** Write a first draft of your cause-and-effect analysis using the qualities outlined earlier in the chapter. Don't worry too much about grammar and punctuation at this time. Keep focused on the causes or effects you are explaining.
    1. Identify the cause or effect being analyzed.
    2. Explain the cause-and-effect relationship convincingly.
    3. Organize the causes and/or effects effectively.
    4. Use sound logic.
    5. Conclude effectively.
4. **Getting feedback:** Have at least one classmate or other person read your rough draft and answer the peer review questions on page 235. If you have access to a writing tutor or center, get another opinion about your paper as well. You will need to decide which suggestions to accept, reject, or modify.
5. **Revising:** Using all of the feedback available to you, revise your cause-and-effect essay. Make sure that your causal analysis is logical and that you have fully supported your main points. Add, delete, and rearrange ideas as necessary.
6. **Editing:** Read your cause-and-effect essay again, this time looking for errors in grammar, punctuation, and mechanics. You might try reading your essay aloud to "listen" to your word choice and sentence structure.
7. **Proofreading:** After you have carefully edited your essay, read it one last time and look for typographical errors and any other issues that might interfere with the readers' understanding of your essay.

PEER REVIEW QUESTIONS FOR EXPLAINING CAUSES AND EFFECTS

Trade rough drafts with a classmate and answer the following questions about his or her paper. Then, in person or online, discuss your papers and suggestions with your peer. Finally, make the changes you feel would most benefit your paper.

1. What cause-and-effect relationship is being analyzed? Is it clearly stated in the thesis?
2. Has the author convincingly explained the cause-and-effect relationship? Why or why not?
3. Are the causes and/or effects organized logically? Is there a better way to organize them? Explain.
4. Has the author included any logical fallacies? Explain.
5. What part of the essay is most memorable? Why?
6. Is the conclusion effective? Why or why not?
7. What kinds of grammatical errors, if any, are evident in the cause-and-effect essay?
8. What final suggestions do you have for the author?

Writer's Checklist for Causes and Effects

Use the checklist below to evaluate your own writing and help ensure that your explanation of the causes and/or effects is complete. If you have any "no" answers, go back and work on those areas if necessary.

- ☐ 1. Have I identified the cause or effect I am analyzing in my thesis?
- ☐ 2. Have I explained the cause-and-effect relationship convincingly?
- ☐ 3. Have I organized my causes and/or effects effectively?
- ☐ 4. Have I used sound logic?
- ☐ 5. Have I concluded my essay effectively?
- ☐ 6. Have I proofread thoroughly?

CHAPTER SUMMARY

1. The cause-and-effect writing strategy focuses on reasons and results.
2. Cause-and-effect writing is an important part of your education, daily life, and career.

3. Interpreting readings and images that reflect causes and effects can help you to prepare to write a cause-and-effect essay.
4. Carefully analyze the rhetorical star before writing a cause-and-effect essay: subject, audience, purpose, strategy, and design.
5. Use these qualities when writing a cause-and-effect essay: identify the cause or effect being analyzed; explain the cause-and-effect relationship convincingly; organize the causes and/or effects effectively; use sound logic; conclude effectively.

WHAT I KNOW NOW

Use this checklist to determine what you need to work on in order to feel comfortable with your understanding of the material in this chapter. Check off each item as you master it. Review the material for any unchecked items.

- ☐ 1. I know what **cause-and-effect writing** is.
- ☐ 2. I can identify several **real-world applications** for cause-and-effect writing.
- ☐ 3. I can evaluate **readings and images** that reflect causes and effects.
- ☐ 4. I can analyze the **rhetorical star** for cause-and-effect writing.
- ☐ 5. I understand the **writing process** for cause-and-effect writing.
- ☐ 6. I can apply the **five qualities** for writing about causes and effects.

Design elements: *Graduate Spotlight:* Ingram Publishing/AGE Fotostock

CHAPTER

10 Persuading: Relationships

Fuse/Corbis/Getty Images

learning outcomes

In this chapter you will learn techniques for achieving these learning outcomes:

10.1 Identify real-world applications for persuading. *p. 238*

10.2 Understand the qualities of persuasive writing. *p. 240*

10.3 Interpret images and persuasive readings about relationships. *p. 251*

10.4 Analyze the rhetorical star for persuasive writing. *p. 268*

10.5 Apply the qualities of persuasive writing. *p. 270*

Writing Strategy Focus: Persuading

Persuasion is all about swaying your audience to see things your way. To encourage others to see your point of view about an opinion or belief requires you to be convincing. When you write for the purpose of persuading your audience, you may present a position, defend a belief, attack a point of view, or encourage someone to take action. To convince readers to agree with you, you will need to support your **argument** with sound, logical reasons. You may also appeal to your audience's emotions or ethics. The art of persuasion is an important skill to have in college, in your personal life, and in your career.

Argument A communication in which writers or speakers present a position/make a claim with the goal of convincing their audience to agree with their view—or to at least consider its validity.

10.1 Real-World Applications for Persuading

Writing to Persuade in College

You will often be asked to write persuasively in your college courses. For example, your political science instructor might ask you to write an argument for or against changing election laws in your city or state. Your literature instructor may require you to write a persuasive essay about a character in one of Shakespeare's plays or Hemingway's novels. You might decide to e-mail an instructor requesting an extension for an assignment because of a personal situation you are experiencing. An instructor in your major may ask you to write a report arguing why one theory or procedure works best for a particular situation.

Writing to Persuade in Your Daily Life

You use persuasion often in your personal life. You might write a persuasive letter to your property manager requesting that repairs be made in a timely manner. You may decide to write a letter to the editor of a newspaper or magazine disagreeing with an article you read. Or maybe you'll design a flyer convincing people in your community to donate money or volunteer to help clean up a park or build a playground.

Writing to Persuade in Your Career

Being able to write persuasively is also extremely useful in the workplace. To get the job you desire, you will need to write a persuasive cover letter and résumé. You might want to persuade your boss to give you a promotion and a raise or some time off for an important out-of-town event you want to attend. You'll also need to convince your clients, patients, or customers that your organization offers the best product or service in your community. Here are some additional ways to use persuasive strategies in the workplace.

Health care: persuading patients to come in for preventive treatments, to follow prescribed treatments, and to take better care of their bodies.

Graduate SPOTLIGHT

Dat Nguyen, Information Technology Administrator

©Karin L. Russell

Dat Nguyen earned his associate's degree in information technology. He currently works in the IT department for a large company. Here's what Nguyen has to say about the types of writing he uses in his career:

"Taking an English composition class helped prepare me for the kinds of writing I do on the job. One of my main tasks is to make sure that we have the most up-to-date firewall in place to keep intruders out of our system. My company handles highly classified information, so it is essential that my research is thorough. I test and evaluate firewall software to make sure that it is secure. Sometimes I write e-mails to software companies to learn more about the weak points of various firewalls. When I make a final decision, I write a report for my boss persuading him which software provides the best protection. New software comes out just about every month, so I have to stay current with the latest technology and keep convincing my boss that we are using the best system for our network."

Law: persuading potential clients that you can help them, presenting opening and closing arguments for a trial, arguing for or against a proposed law or amendment.

Education: persuading the administration to provide more materials, equipment, or books; persuading parents to become more involved in their children's education.

Computers: persuading customers that you can meet their needs so they will purchase hardware, software, or services.

Business administration: persuading clients that your company is reliable and convincing them to purchase products or services.

Massage therapy: persuading clients to use exercise techniques at home and to get more massages to improve their health.

Culinary arts: persuading customers to purchase menu items or catering services and to visit your establishment more often.

Activity Writing Persuasively in the Real World

In pairs or small groups, brainstorm uses for writing persuasively at school, in your daily life, and on the job. You may want to choose the prospective career field(s) of the participants in your group. Each group may share its results with the class.

10.2 Qualities of Effective Persuasive Writing

1. Introduce the Issue You Are Debating

When you are arguing for your perspective on an issue, hold off a bit before stating your thesis so that readers who disagree with your opinion are more likely to keep an open mind and read further to see what you have to say. Instead of jumping right in with a claim, begin with an explanation of the situation. Provide your readers with enough information to get a basic understanding of the subject. For example, if you are attempting to persuade the reader that younger siblings are sometimes less responsible than older siblings, you might begin by discussing the psychology of birth order. You may need to do some research to adequately explain the issue if you are not completely familiar with the subject from firsthand experience. As always, cite any outside sources you use in your paper.

After you have introduced the subject, then you may want to pose a question to get your reader to think about the issue. However, keep in mind that a question is not a thesis. A question might hint at where you intend to go with your thesis, but it should not replace your thesis. Here are a few examples of thought-provoking questions:

- Should an employee always outwardly agree with his or her boss?
- Should motorists be allowed to talk on cell phones while driving?
- Should a boy be allowed to join the girls' volleyball team if there is no comparable boys' team?
- Do school uniforms help promote a positive learning environment for students?

2. Make a Claim about Your Subject

Claim A debatable assertion.

A **claim** is a debatable assertion. In argumentative writing, the claim serves as the thesis statement. In a persuasive essay, you should state your claim either near the end of the introduction or at the beginning of the conclusion. Whether you are making an assertion about an issue or demanding that something be done, your claim should definitively state your opinion about the issue. You want to make sure your reader knows exactly where you stand.

Avoid using phrases such as "I think, "I believe," and "I feel" because that will make you sound tentative and weaken your argument. Keep a third person point of view and make a strong claim. For example, in a paper about stay-at-home fathers, your thesis might be, "Men who serve as the primary caregivers for their children deserve to be treated with the same respect as women who choose that role."

3. Support Your Claim with Evidence That Appeals to Your Audience

To persuade your audience that your claim is valid, you will need to support it fully. Whether you relate a personal experience, create your own primary source information, or introduce research based on the findings of others, you can use appeals to convince your audience that your argument is credible. **Appeals** are persuasive strategies used to support claims. Three types of appeals are used in argument: ethical (from the Greek word *ethos*), emotional (from the Greek word *pathos*), and logical (from the Greek word *logos*). These appeals can be used individually or in combination. See Table 10.1 for more on these three appeals.

Appeals Persuasive strategies used to support claims.

Table 10.1

Persuasive Appeals		
Type of Appeal	**Definition**	**Example**
Ethical appeal (*ethos*)	Persuade readers by establishing that you are a trustworthy and credible writer. This is sometimes called *character appeal* because you are demonstrating that you are fair in your approach to the issue. Show that you understand the issue, that you are sensitive to it, and that you have considered all sides of it. If you are an expert on the subject, you can mention your profession, experience, or knowledge. Bringing in the opinion of an authority can help you to establish your credibility if you are writing about a topic with which you have little or no firsthand experience. Use an appropriate tone and correct grammar to help demonstrate your good character.	Now, more than ever before, dual-income families are struggling with how to balance jobs, children, and household tasks. Parents need to work out a fair system for handling these responsibilities. As a counselor, I have helped hundreds of families to deal with these pressures using three simple techniques.

—*continued*

Table 10.1 (cont.)

Persuasive Appeals		
Type of Appeal	**Definition**	**Example**
Emotional appeal (*pathos*)	Persuade readers by appealing to their emotions. You can use emotionally charged words to stir the reader's feelings as long as you use them ethically. You might try to gain the sympathy or empathy of the audience about a particular cause for which you are arguing. Using vivid descriptions and narratives of emotional events can help you to appeal to your readers' emotions.	Juanita, age 17, is 5 feet tall, weighs just 88 pounds, and suffers from anorexia. She feels fat in comparison to the women on the covers of fashion magazines. The media need to be more responsible with the wafer-thin images of women they display, or more girls are going to fall prey to serious eating disorders.
Logical appeal (*logos*)	Persuade readers by appealing to their sense of logic with reasons, facts, statistics, and examples. Citing sources from experts on your subject can help you to convince your audience that your evidence is sound. You can also use inductive and deductive reasoning to support your premise logically. (See Figure 10.1 and Table 10.3 for more information about induction and deduction.)	While you and your colleagues may not always agree on important issues, both parties may benefit from working together to resolve conflicts that arise. According to psychologist Joy Peters, learning how to compromise on important issues can lead to better communication, a more productive work environment, and greater job satisfaction.

Activity Brainstorming Persuasive Appeals

On your own, in pairs, or in small groups, choose one (or more) of the claims listed below. Make a list of ethical, emotional, and logical appeals that a writer might use to support and/or refute the claim.

- The lottery and other forms of gambling should be illegal in every state.
- Actors and professional athletes are paid too much.
- Beauty pageants are exploitive.
- People who talk on cell phones while driving, or even walking, are a danger to others.
- People are too dependent on computers.
- The election process is unfair.
- Everyone should be concerned about global warming.

A representative from each group may share a few of the highlights with the class.

4. Use Your Supporting Evidence Logically and Ethically

While you do want your argument to be convincing, you don't want to win over your readers by deceiving them. Furthermore, you don't want to mislead them by using logical fallacies or leaving out pertinent information that would shed a different light on your subject. For example, if you are attempting to persuade your readers that the company that employs you is sexist because it doesn't have any women in upper management, then it would be unfair to leave out the fact that one of the key executives is a woman who happens to be temporarily out on maternity leave. See Table 10.2 for more on logical fallacies.

Basically, your audience will be more likely to agree with your claim if your argument seems reasonable. To do that, you will need to maintain an appropriate tone and give fair treatment to other positions on the issue. To give fair treatment to your subject, you need to acknowledge that an opposing point of view exists. You may bring up a counterargument, find the common ground between the two points of view, and then refute the counterargument. For example, your claim might be that participating in extracurricular activities helps build leadership skills. A valid counterargument is that extracurricular activities take time away from study and sleep, both of which are necessary to succeed in college. You may acknowledge the counterargument, yet refute it by stating that if students manage their time wisely, they will have time for schoolwork, sleep, and extracurricular activities. Furthermore, you may add more credibility to your argument by citing reliable statistics or an expert to support your position that extracurricular activities do help students develop leadership skills that are necessary for success in college and beyond.

When you accommodate a counterargument, your argument becomes stronger. However, your readers need to understand *your* position in the debate. While you do need to deal with significant information that may cast doubt on your perspective, most of your comments need to support the opinion in your thesis. Otherwise, you will confuse your readers or, even worse, defeat your own argument.

Note: If you use outside sources, you must cite them. See Chapters 13 and 14 for specific details about finding and documenting sources using the MLA and APA formats.

Table 10.2

Logical Fallacies			
Logical Fallacy	**Definition**	**Example**	**Explanation**
Bandwagon	Implying that an idea must be true if it is popular. Join the crowd.	Everyone knows that holistic medicine is better than traditional medicine.	Even if many people believe it, that doesn't provide scientific proof for the argument.

—*continued*

Table 10.2 (*cont.*)

Logical Fallacies			
Logical Fallacy	**Definition**	**Example**	**Explanation**
Card stacking	Providing evidence for only one side of a case, deliberately omitting essential information that would change the reader's opinion.	Sunni should get a promotion because she has never missed a day at work and she completes all of her tasks in a timely manner.	Supervisors consider many factors when deciding whom to promote. Maybe Sunni often arrives late or does poor work.
Character attack or *ad hominem* attack	Attacking a person rather than an issue.	Candidate X should not become the next company president because he divorced his wife and married his assistant.	His private life has nothing to do with whether or not he would make a good company president.
Circular reasoning or begging the question	Attempting to support a position by simply restating it in a different way.	Dr. Brilliant is a good instructor because he teaches his students well.	The idea is merely being repeated without offering any specific evidence as to what makes Dr. Brilliant an effective instructor.
Either/or reasoning	Suggesting there are only two possible solutions to a problem (one right and one wrong) when, in reality, there could be many potential options for resolving the issue.	Either the government needs to subsidize gas costs or our economy is going to collapse.	First of all, does the entire economy depend on the price of gas? Also, there are several ways to cut down on fuel costs other than having the government help to offset the price.
False analogy	Comparing things that are not similar in the most important respects.	The governor hit the jackpot with the new property tax increase proposal.	The governor is not gambling, so the analogy doesn't make sense.
False authority or testimonial	Mentioning an authority figure or celebrity as support for arguing a point.	Eric Zane, who plays Dr. Mark Gnome on *Haye's Anatomy,* recommends taking "Cure It All" pills, so they must be effective.	Eric Zane is an actor playing a role, not a real doctor, so he is not qualified to recommend a specific type of treatment.
False cause or *post hoc*	Suggesting that because one thing happened after another, the first event caused the second one.	I ate chocolate and my sore throat disappeared.	The sore throat could have gone away for another reason unrelated to the chocolate.
Glittering generality	Using emotionally charged words, such as *love, truth, honor, democracy,* and *justice,* to gain the audience's approval.	If you are truly patriotic, you need to do the honorable thing and vote to increase your property taxes.	The implication is that voting a particular way will determine if someone is (or is not) patriotic and honorable.

Logical Fallacies

Logical Fallacy	Definition	Example	Explanation
Hasty generalization	Drawing a conclusion without having sufficient evidence.	A child comes home two days in a row without homework, so the parent assumes that the teacher has stopped assigning homework.	The child may have forgotten to bring home the work or may be intentionally misleading the parent.
Non sequitur	The conclusion does not logically follow from the evidence that is provided.	Fast-food chains are very popular in the United States. No wonder obesity is so common.	Many factors contribute to the high obesity rate in the United States. One can't assume that there is only one cause or that fast-food chains are the cause of obesity.
Red herring	Diverting the reader's attention from the main issue by introducing something irrelevant. It comes from the practice of dragging a stinky fish across the ground to distract tracking dogs away from a scent.	The idea of gay marriages is an important issue, but do gay people really want to deal with all of the pressures associated with marriage?	The second part is irrelevant because it has nothing to do with whether gay marriages should be legal or not.
Slippery slope	Suggesting that if one change occurs, then other, unwanted changes will inevitably occur as well. The analogy is that once someone starts sliding down a "slippery slope," he or she won't be able to stop.	If we allow dogs on the beach, then the next thing you know dogs will be sitting at tables in fine restaurants.	The two events are unrelated, so there's no reason to assume that one event will lead to the other.
Stereotyping	Attaching a trait to people who belong to a particular religious, ethnic, racial, age, or other group.	Older people make terrible drivers, so they shouldn't be allowed to drive.	This is an unfair claim because many senior citizens are fine drivers.
Tradition	If something has always been done a certain way, then it must be the correct way.	Our company has always bought cigars and champagne for our clients during the holidays. We don't need to change to something else.	Just because the tradition is long standing doesn't mean that it's a good one. Some clients may not like cigars, and some might not be able to tolerate alcohol. Another gift might be more appropriate.

Activity Recognizing Logical Fallacies

Label the fallacies in the following sentences. Some sentences contain more than one fallacy.

1. Tristan didn't get the job, so the company must not really be hiring.
2. If we allow employees to dress down on Fridays, then soon they will look sloppy every day.
3. Taylor Swift wears that perfume, so it must smell really good.
4. That new movie is going to be a big hit or a complete flop.
5. If people have to wear helmets when they ride bicycles, then they should have to wear helmets when they ride motorcycles.

5. Organize Your Supporting Evidence Effectively

You can organize the evidence in an argumentative or a persuasive essay in a number of ways. For example, you might begin with your second strongest point, then move to your weaker points, and then end with your strongest point. You may also use *deductive* or *inductive* reasoning in persuasive writing. College writers often organize their essays deductively. They introduce a thesis early in the paper and then support it with specific details, examples, and facts in the body paragraphs. The purpose of deductive reasoning is to apply what you already know to a new situation. However, you may want to try inductive reasoning, where you give specific details, examples, and facts to lead your readers to a conclusion, which is your main point. The purpose of inductive reasoning is to discover something new. Figure 10.1 illustrates both types of reasoning. Table 10.3 provides a definition and example for each one.

FIGURE 10.1 Deductive and Inductive Reasoning Patterns

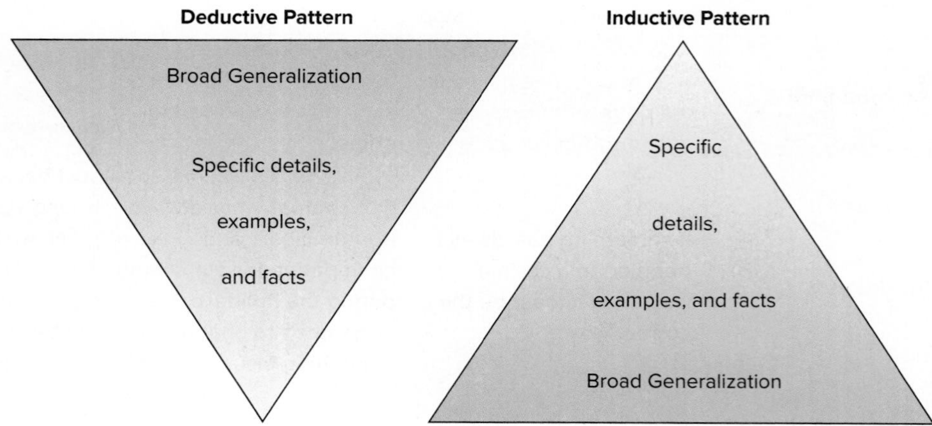

Table 10.3

Deductive and Inductive Reasoning		
Organizational Strategy	**Definition**	**Example**
Deduction	To organize an argument deductively, begin with a generalization of the most important idea, which is your *major premise,* or claim. Then provide more specific details and examples of that major premise, which is your *minor premise*. You can move from a major premise to a minor premise and then draw a plausible conclusion. A classic deductive argument has a conclusion that follows with certainty. No other conclusion is possible based on the evidence.	**Topic:** Polygamy **Major premise (claim):** In 1878, the U.S. Supreme Court ruled that polygamy violates criminal law and is not protected by the notion of religious freedom. This ruling has not been overturned. **Minor premise:** While he was living in the United States, Fred married his second wife without divorcing his first wife or nullifying his marriage to her. **Conclusion:** Fred has broken the law.
Induction	To organize an argument inductively, start with specific details, examples, or observations and then progress to a more general idea that the evidence supports. When you use this strategy, you should examine the evidence carefully before drawing a conclusion. An inductive argument has a conclusion that follows with some degree of probability, but not certainty. Other conclusions are possible.	**Topic:** Class discussions **Observed evidence:** During my last eight classes at Genius University, the male students have contributed more to class discussions than female students. **Generalization (claim):** Male college students are more talkative than female students.

6. End Your Essay Effectively

There are several ways to conclude an argumentative or a persuasive essay. One method is to use the traditional approach of restating your thesis and summarizing your main points. Other strategies are to suggest the implications of the issue or to encourage your readers to take some sort of action. Whatever you do, be sure to leave your reader feeling satisfied with your conclusion.

Grammar Window

RUN-ON SENTENCES

When you write to persuade, you may have a lot to say to your readers. If you are not careful, this can lead to run-on sentences. A run-on sentence, also known as a fused sentence, occurs when two complete sentences (independent clauses) run together without a proper punctuation mark or coordinating conjunction.

Run-on sentence: My friend Leslie loves watching football on Sunday however, her husband, Steve, isn't interested in sports.
Corrected sentence: My friend Leslie loves watching football on Sunday; however, her husband, Steve, isn't interested in sports.
Discussion: A semicolon needs to be placed before the conjunctive adverb *however* to avoid the run-on.
Activity: Correct the following run-on sentences by adding a comma and a coordinating conjunction *(for, and, nor, but, or, yet, so)*. In some cases, you can correct a run-on sentence by inserting a period or a semicolon between two complete sentences or adding a subordinating conjunction *(because, so that)*.

1. Some parents and students feel that school uniforms are beneficial others find them to be too restrictive.
2. The school is having a meeting tonight parents can weigh the pros and cons of school uniforms.
3. Raul likes not having to argue with his daughter about what is appropriate to wear to school he also likes not having to buy a lot of expensive clothes for her.
4. Ai-shi doesn't like wearing a school uniform she feels they are unflattering.
5. Gabriel prefers to wear a uniform to school he never has to worry about getting picked on for wearing something out of style.

See the Editing Guide for more information on run-on sentences.

Career-Based PERSUASIVE WRITING

[preview] **KRISTIN STARR** is a recent (fictitious) college graduate. She knows that, as a new professional, her résumé is one of the most important documents she will ever write. The same is true for you. Keep in mind that the goal of your résumé is to persuade a potential employer to invite you to a face-to-face or phone interview. If your résumé doesn't catch the reader's eye, then you may never get the chance to explain how great you are in person. Your résumé needs to clearly and concisely convey the message that you are qualified for the job that you seek and would be a valuable asset to the organization. When you write your résumé, emphasize your best qualifications, organize your strengths logically, and avoid errors in spelling, grammar, punctuation, and mechanics. With the right qualifications and a well-written résumé, you are likely to land the job you desire. Kristin Starr's résumé illustrates the properties of persuasive writing.

Résumé of Kristin Starr

	123 Beach View Street	**954-555-5555 (cell)**
Kristin Starr	**Ft. Lauderdale, FL 33309**	**kstarr@e-mail.net**

Objective: Position as a medical assistant in a fast-paced physician's office

Education: Associate of Science in Medical Assisting, June 2019, GPA 3.5
Keiser University, Ft. Lauderdale, Florida

Key Strengths:
- Proficient with EKG, phlebotomy, and radiology
- Familiar with electronic health records
- Quick to learn office procedures
- Adept at multitasking
- People oriented/team player
- Excellent oral and written communication skills

Certifications: Registered Medical Assistant, 2019
CPR, 2018

Experience: Receptionist, Harmony Medical Center
Ft. Lauderdale, Florida, August 2017 to present
- Manage multiple phone lines
- Handle insurance claims
- Schedule appointments for multiple physicians
- Write office newsletter

Intern, Healing Hands Medical Associates
Hollywood, Florida, January–May 2017
- Administered injections
- Conducted EKGs efficiently
- Obtained patients' vital signs
- Maintained and filed medical records
- Handled multiple phone lines
- Scheduled patient appointments

Honors and Activities: Phi Theta Kappa Honor Society, Secretary 2019
Dean's List, Three Semesters
Leadership Distinction Award 2019

Volunteer Work: Serenity Rehabilitation Center
Community Animal Shelter

References: Available upon request

QUESTIONS FOR REFLECTION

1. What are some of Starr's key strengths?
2. What part of speech is the word that begins each bullet under "Experience:"? Why?
3. Why did Starr list her volunteer work on her résumé?
4. Why did she list her education first?
5. If you were an employer with a job opening in this field, would you hire Starr? Why or why not?

Career-Based PERSUASIVE WRITING

[preview] **BRYAN DIK** is a professor, researcher, and writer who works in the psychology department at Colorado State University. He is interested in the significance of how and why people choose their careers. In addition to numerous other publications, Dik co-authored a book with Ryan Duffy titled *Make Your Job a Calling: How the Psychology of Vocation Can Change Your Life at Work.* The following article, which was originally published in the Vocation, Vocation, Vocation section of *Psychology Today,* addresses the challenges people face when deciding on a career path. Before reading, consider what factors you considered in choosing a career.

Career Choice: Easy for Superheroes, Hard for Us: Spider-Man and the Power of Person-Environment Fit **by Bryan Dik**

The proliferation of Superhero flicks, popularity of Comic-Con, and the expanding reach of Marvel and DC Comics all testify to the obvious: People love superheroes. There are many reasons for this, but one of them has to be envy. Seriously, who among us hasn't imagined how great it would be to wake up one morning with superpowers? One accidental chemical bath and you're stretching your body into any imaginable form. One newly activated mutant gene and you're able to manipulate the weather. One brief exposure to cosmic radiation and you find yourself with superhuman strength, stamina, and a very helpful resistance to physical injury. This would make choosing a career path easy. Many people spin their wheels for years trying to figure out the right line of work for them. But find yourself with a useful superpower, and it isn't a stretch to see that a lifetime of fighting crime is a career choice that just makes good sense. 1

Psychologists point out that one of the most critical factors in making a wise career choice is "person-environment fit." People have unique patterns of interests, abilities, personality, values, etc., and jobs are unique too, in terms of what needs to get done, what skills are required, what kinds of rewards are offered, etc. The challenge is figuring out what career path is the best fit for the kind of person you are. This is not a complicated concept, but the task is much easier for superheroes than for the rest of us. 2

To illustrate, take Peter Parker. A fateful spider bite spawned his transformation from skinny, clumsy teen one day to web-shooting, wall-climbing Spider-Man the next. Once he understood that "with great power comes great responsibility," it wasn't a leap for Peter to conclude that fighting New York's evil villains was a vocation that fit his strengths extremely well. Now imagine that Peter had squashed the offending spider before its bite, never to enjoy the benefits (or endure the drawbacks) of life as Spider-Man. Peter may have wondered, as most of the rest of us did (or do), 3 what kind of career path he ought to pursue. Given what we know about Peter, he likely would have scored high on trait measures of abilities having to do with science. He also might have scored high on Investigative and Artistic interests, given his enjoyment of science and photography. A personality test might have shown Peter to be reasonably conscientious and open to experience. This pattern of characteristics may have led Peter to choose a career as a reporter, a research scientist, an engineer, or perhaps a college professor. *Daily Bugle* photographer probably was a good fit, but we can assume that Peter would have worked a lot harder to capture Spider-Man shots for page 1 without his double-identity in place.

4 Career counselors generally assume that work-related traits can be measured using psychological tests, and that scores on these tests predict real-life outcomes like happiness on the job. Research has generally supported these assumptions, but because there are so many human traits relevant for choosing a best-fitting career, because we are still learning about how all these traits interact, and because multiple occupations (not just one) usually are available to satisfy any one person's unique combination of traits, choosing a career remains as much an art as it is a science—at least for us non-superheroes.

Source: Bryan Dik, "Career Choice: Easy for Superheroes, Hard for Us," *Psychology Today*, **www.psychologytoday.com/blog/vocation-vocation-vocation/201211/career-choice-easy-superheroes-hard-us.** Reprinted by permission of the author.

QUESTIONS FOR REFLECTION

1. Who is the primary audience for Dik's article? How do you know?
2. What is the author's claim? Does he state it clearly? Explain.
3. How does Dik support his claim? Is the support convincing? Why or why not?
4. How important is the "person-environment fit" when determining a career? Explain.
5. What are some important factors that people should consider when choosing a career according to Dik? Do you agree or disagree with the author's assertions? Explain.

10.3 Persuading in the Context of Relationships

Relationships can be challenging. Disputes between friends, roommates, neighbors, siblings, parents, spouses, partners, and co-workers are quite common. To say that human beings don't always understand each other would be an understatement. People tend to disagree about everything from politics, laws, and finances to values, morality, and religion. A number of factors can contribute to these disagreements, including gender, cultural differences, and experience.

Too often these disputes lead to arguments at home, at school, in the community, or in the workplace. However, instead of arguing over who's right and who's wrong, we can study the issues to gain acceptance, or at least tolerance, of a different perspective. In the following readings, you'll explore a variety of issues. Some are presented as formal arguments while others are designed to give you something to gently debate with classmates and in writing. Reading what others have written can help you write persuasively for school, your personal life, or the workplace.

Paired Readings

The first two readings in this section reveal opposing viewpoints on the use of social networking sites, such as Facebook. Read both articles before answering the questions for reflection that follow the second one. Consider the following questions before you read the articles: Do you regularly participate on Facebook or another social networking website? If so, what positive or negative experiences have you had with it? If you don't use an online social network, have you ever considered joining one? What has kept you from joining?

Reading and Reflection PERSUASIVE WRITING

[preview] **ASAKA PARK** is a bright, talented individual who has autism. She wrote the essay that follows when she was a 17-year-old high school student and became one of the top 12 winners out of 10,509 entries of *The New York Times* Student Editorial Contest. In her winning essay, she argues for the use of social media and explains why social media is such a beneficial part of her life.

I'm a Disabled Teenager, and Social Media Is My Lifeline by Asaka Park

1 I'm keenly attuned to the unwritten rules of social interaction. I can identify the subtle variations in people's facial expressions, and I'm quick to read between the lines. And my discernment is not just on an intellectual level, but also at an intuitive level: I'm intimately familiar with the dance of social interaction.

2 The information that I just provided sounds like a mundanity, until I tell you I was diagnosed with autism. I defy the stereotypes of someone who can't possibly "get it" socially.

3 No one knows that I can. I can "get it."

4 Of course, people don't see that. I struggle with impulsivity. My physical clumsiness makes it hard for me to maintain appropriate facial expressions and tone of voice. While I easily grasp abstract concepts, I often can't convert them into tangible, step-by-step actions, making it difficult to communicate gracefully. Even the untrained eye notices these challenges, and they confound my social faux pas as a failure to understand or share other people's expectations.

5 I'm depleted. Every day at school, I isolate myself from most of my peers: it's a matter of time before they make these assumptions, before they postulate how my brain works. On social media, though, I'm a completely different person. I'm dynamic. I'm assertive. I'm people-oriented.

6 Many claim that social media distracts teens from meaningful, genuine interactions. My experiences, however, are the total opposite of that. Cultivating my own space on the Internet helped me thrive outside the pigeonhole. Namely, I use my blog to explain the real reason why I act the way I do. Even though not everyone will understand, I know some people will, and it gives me tremendous hope.

7 I know I'm not the only one. For many disabled people, social media gives them access to a social life and community involvement in an otherwise inaccessible world (Ryan). Not only does social media give me the platform to correct assumptions, people don't assume things about me in the first place, because it's a level playing field. For example, when I Tweet, my addled movements

are replaced by various emojis and reaction GIFs, which gives me a vaster palette to express myself.

8 Furthermore, I've learned to extend the conversation on disability from my own personal circumstances to the broader issue of ableism. Don Tapscott, a media consultant, remarked, "[Teens] didn't grow up being the passive recipients of somebody else's broadcast" (Parker-Pope). This definitely resonated with me. I used to feel alone, not seeing girls like me on the magazine covers, but not anymore. In a click, I can create my own media where people with disabilities are seen and heard, rather than pliantly consuming the media that routinely devalue people with disabilities.

Works Cited

Parker-Pope, Tara. "Are Today's Teenagers Smarter and Better Than We Think?" *The New York Times,* 30 March 2018, nytimes.com/2018/03/30/well/family/teenagers-generation-stoneman-douglas-parkland-.html.

Ryan, Frances. "The Missing Link: Why Disabled People Can't Afford to #DeleteFacebook." *The Guardian,* 4 April 2018, theguardian.com/media/2018/apr/04/missing-link-why-disabled-people-cant-afford-delete-facebook-social-media.

Note: Park uses the MLA format for her essay. Your instructor may ask you to follow MLA or APA guidelines if you cite sources in your paper. See Chapters 13–14 for more details about citing sources in the MLA and APA formats. While MLA does not require writers to include the URL of online sources, we recommend doing so to allow readers to gain easy access to them.

Reading and Reflection PERSUASIVE WRITING

[preview] **MELISSA SCRIVANI** is the associate life editor, writer, copy editor, and designer for *The Daily Campus,* a newspaper produced by the University of Connecticut. She is completing her degree in elementary education with a concentration in English. Scrivani writes about topics related to student interests and campus life. The following article presents a different viewpoint from the previous article, "I'm a Disabled Teenager, and Social Media Is My Lifeline." Where do you stand on the issue? Are social networking sites helpful or harmful to your relationships? Will you agree more with Parks or Scrivani by the time you finish reading the next article?

Is Technology Helping or Hurting Your Relationship? by Melissa Scrivani

1 Being in a relationship in the 21st century means that technology plays a factor in your relationship whether you want it to or not. There has been a lot of debate over whether technology brings us closer together or drives us apart and, honestly, it really depends on the situation. Our generation has been exposed to a whole new form of socialization, and since it has been around for most of our lives we are more accustomed to it than anyone else. Whether you are in a long-distance relationship or in the same room right at this minute, your phone is affecting your relationship in ways you may not even be aware of.

2 If you are involved in a long-distance relationship, technology will be the main source of communication between you and your significant other. Skype, texting, phone calls, and even Snapchat can all help you feel closer to your partner. This is

definitely a plus, and a huge step up from what was available to couples 20 years ago, but it still has its drawbacks. Nonverbal communication lacks the emotion you get while having a face to face conversation. This can lead to miscommunication and eventually could create conflict. When you're reading a text, you can't pick up on the tone or any other subtle clues that allow you to gauge the person's intent or feelings. This makes it pretty easy to take things the wrong way.

3 Texting can also make people more confrontational because they can hide behind their phones. It can be easier to say whatever you want when you don't have to deal with the consequences in person.

4 According to Dr. Alex Lickerman, a former Director of Primary Care at the University of Chicago, "Our 'emotional invisibility' on the Internet perhaps also explains so much of the vitriol we see on so many websites. People clearly have a penchant for saying things in the electronic world they'd never say to people in person because the person to whom they're saying it isn't physically present to display their emotional reaction."

5 Even couples who are physically together can feel the effects of technology. Being on your phone can take away time with your significant other, as well as cause an array of other problems. Social media and technology have created all new "rules" and etiquette to be aware of, such as texting back within a timely manner. Breaking these rules can cause issues within relationships that never used to exist.

6 Despite the drawbacks, there are still benefits to technology. It allows you to stay more connected to your partner than ever before. It can also help relationships develop deeper and more quickly since there is more time to talk and get to know one another. "Our findings are very clear and consistent, that users of social networks tend to have more close relationships, not just online, but in real life," Dr. Keith Hampton, a communications professor at Rutgers University says.

7 So how can you stop technology from hurting your relationship? When together, try to reserve some phone-free time that can allow you to spend time together without the distraction of a cell phone. When apart, don't say anything over text that you wouldn't say in person. If you feel like you are misunderstanding a text, don't get angry and instead ask your partner to clarify. If you feel like you are about to fight, step back and think about what you want to say, or think about calling the person so you can at least hear the emotion in their voice.

8 Technology can be an amazing tool if you use it correctly. Just be sure to take your partner's feelings into consideration and treat them the same way you would in person.

Source: Melissa Scrivani, "Is Technology Helping or Hurting Your Relationship?" *The Daily Campus*, 14 February, 2018, http://dailycampus.com/stories/2018/2/14/is-technology-helping-or-hurting-your-relationship.

QUESTIONS FOR REFLECTION

Compare and contrast the articles by Park and Scrivani.

Considering Ideas

1. What is each author's claim?
2. Which article presents a more convincing argument? Why?
3. Based on these articles, as well as your own experiences, what effects, if any, do Facebook and other social networking sites have on relationships? Why?

Considering the Rhetorical Star

1. What is the specific *subject* of each article?
2. What is the *purpose* of each article? Does each author achieve her goal? Explain.
3. Who is the intended *audience* for the articles? How do you know?
4. What primary writing *strategy* do Park and Scrivani use for their articles? Do they use any other strategies? Explain.
5. Describe the *design* of each article. Which design is more appealing to you? Why?

Considering Writing Strategies

1. Describe the writing styles of each author. Which author do you connect with more? Why?
2. Which types of appeals (logical, emotional, and/or ethical) does each author use? Give specific examples from the articles.
3. Describe the tone (mood) of each article? Which one has a stronger tone? Identify several words from each article to illustrate your point.

Writing Suggestions

1. Has a social networking site, such as Facebook, ever enhanced or harmed one of your relationships? Write an essay persuading readers that the website is beneficial or detrimental to relationships. Use your own experience (and possibly other research as well) to support your position. Be sure to cite any sources you use. See Chapters 13 and 14 for more details about citing sources.
2. If you have never used a social networking site, would you consider using one now? Why or why not? Write an essay persuading readers that using a social networking website has positive or negative effects on relationships. Use one of the previous articles (and possibly other research as well) to support your point of view. Be sure to cite any source you use. See Chapters 13 and 14 for more details about citing sources.

Reading and Reflection PERSUASIVE WRITING

[preview] **DEBORAH TANNEN,** born in Brooklyn, New York, has published more than 20 books and 100 articles. Her best-selling book, *You Just Don't Understand,* has been translated into 31 languages. Her more recent book, *You're the Only One I Can Tell: Inside the Language of Women's Friendships,* has also been quite successful. She has appeared on numerous radio and television shows, and she has given lectures around the world. She is a university professor in the linguistics department at Georgetown University. You can read more about her and watch some of her interview clips at **www.deborahtannen.com.** Before reading, think about a friendship or romantic relationship you have had with someone of the opposite sex. What difficulties, if any, did you experience when trying to communicate with one another?

Sex, Lies and Conversation: Why Is It So Hard for Men and Women to Talk to Each Other? **by Deborah Tannen**

1 I was addressing a small gathering in a suburban Virginia living room—a women's group that had invited men to join them. Throughout the evening, one man had been particularly talkative, frequently offering ideas and anecdotes, while his wife sat silently beside him on the couch. Toward the end of the evening, I commented that women frequently complain that their husbands don't talk to them. This man quickly concurred. He gestured toward his wife and said, "She's the talker in our family." The room burst into laughter; the man looked puzzled and hurt. "It's true," he explained. "When I

come home from work I have nothing to say. If she didn't keep the conversation going, we'd spend the whole evening in silence."

2 This episode crystallizes the irony that although American men tend to talk more than women in public situations, they often talk less at home. And this pattern is wreaking havoc with marriage.

3 The pattern was observed by political scientist Andrew Hacker in the late '70s. Sociologist Catherine Kohler Riessman reports in her new book *Divorce Talk* that most of the women she interviewed—but only a few of the men—gave lack of communication as the reason for their divorces. Given the current divorce rate of nearly 50 percent, that amounts to millions of cases in the United States every year—a virtual epidemic of failed conversation.

4 In my own research, complaints from women about their husbands most often focused not on tangible inequities such as having given up the chance for a career to accompany a husband to his, or doing far more than their share of daily life-support work like cleaning, cooking, social arrangements and errands. Instead, they focused on communication: "He doesn't listen to me," "He doesn't talk to me." I found, as Hacker observed years before, that most wives want their husbands to be, first and foremost, conversational partners, but few husbands share this expectation of their wives.

5 In short, the image that best represents the current crisis is the stereotypical cartoon scene of a man sitting at the breakfast table with a newspaper held up in front of his face, while a woman glares at the back of it, wanting to talk.

Linguistic Battle of the Sexes

6 How can women and men have such different impressions of communication in marriage? Why the widespread imbalance in their interests and expectations?

7 In [an] issue of *American Psychologist,* Stanford University's Eleanor Maccoby reports the results of her own and others' research showing that children's development is most influenced by the social structure of peer interactions. Boys and girls tend to play with children of their own gender, and their sex-separate groups have different organizational structures and interactive norms.

8 I believe these systematic differences in childhood socialization make talk between women and men like cross-cultural communication, heir to all the attraction and pitfalls of that enticing but difficult enterprise. My research on men's and women's conversations uncovered patterns similar to those described for children's groups.

9 For women, as for girls, intimacy is the fabric of relationships, and talk is the thread from which it is woven. Little girls create and maintain friendships by exchanging secrets; similarly, women regard conversation as the cornerstone of friendship. So a woman expects her husband to be a new and improved version of a best friend. What is important is not the individual subjects that are discussed but the sense of closeness, of a life shared, that emerges when people tell their thoughts, feelings, and impressions.

10 Bonds between boys can be as intense as girls', but they are based less on talking, more on doing things together. Since they don't assume talk is the cement that binds a relationship, men don't know what kind of talk women want, and they don't miss it when it isn't there.

11 Boys' groups are larger, more inclusive, and more hierarchical, so boys must struggle to avoid the subordinate position in the group. This may play a role in women's complaints that men don't listen to them. Some men really don't like to listen, because being the listener makes them feel one-down, like a child listening to adults or an employee to a boss.

12 But often, when women tell men, "You aren't listening," and the men protest, "I am," the men are right. The impression of not listening results from misalignments in the mechanics of conversation. The misalignment begins as soon as a man and a woman take physical positions. This became clear when I studied videotapes made by psychologist Bruce Dorval of children and adults talking to their same-sex best friends. I found that at every age, the girls and women faced each other directly, their eyes anchored on each other's faces. At every age, the boys and men sat at angles to each other and

looked elsewhere in the room, periodically glancing at each other. They were obviously attuned to each other, often mirroring each other's movements. But the tendency of men to face away can give women the impression they aren't listening even when they are. A young woman in college was frustrated: Whenever she told her boyfriend she wanted to talk to him, he would lie down on the floor, close his eyes, and put his arm over his face. This signaled to her, "He's taking a nap." But he insisted he was listening extra hard. Normally, he looks around the room, so he is easily distracted. Lying down and covering his eyes helped him concentrate on what she was saying.

13 Analogous to the physical alignment that women and men take in conversation is their topical alignment. The girls in my study tended to talk at length about one topic, but the boys tended to jump from topic to topic. The second-grade girls exchanged stories about people they knew. The second-grade boys teased, told jokes, noticed things in the room and talked about finding games to play. The sixth-grade girls talked about problems with a mutual friend. The sixth-grade boys talked about 55 different topics, none of which extended over more than a few turns.

Listening to Body Language

14 Switching topics is another habit that gives women the impression men aren't listening, especially if they switch to a topic about themselves. But the evidence of the 10th-grade boys in my study indicates otherwise. The 10th-grade boys sprawled across their chairs with bodies parallel and eyes straight ahead, rarely looking at each other. They looked as if they were riding in a car, staring out the windshield. But they were talking about their feelings. One boy was upset because a girl had told him he had a drinking problem, and the other was feeling alienated from all his friends.

15 Now, when a girl told a friend about a problem, the friend responded by asking probing questions and expressing agreement and understanding. But the boys dismissed each other's problems. Todd assured Richard that his drinking was "no big problem" because "sometimes you're funny when you're off your butt." And when Todd said he felt left out, Richard responded, "Why should you? You know more people than me."

16 Women perceived such responses as belittling and unsupportive. But the boys seemed satisfied with them. Whereas women reassure each other by implying, "You shouldn't feel bad because I've had similar experiences," men do so by implying, "You shouldn't feel bad because your problems aren't so bad."

17 There are even simpler reasons for women's impression that men don't listen. Linguist Lynette Hirschman found that women make more listener-noise, such as "mhm," "uhuh," and "yeah," to show "I'm with you." Men, she found, more often give silent attention. Women who expect a stream of listener-noise interpret silent attention as no attention at all.

18 Women's conversational habits are as frustrating to men as men's are to women. Men who expect silent attention interpret a stream of listener-noise as overreaction or impatience. Also, when women talk to each other in a close, comfortable setting, they often overlap, finish each other's sentences and anticipate what the other is about to say. This practice, which I call "participatory listenership," is often perceived by men as interruption, intrusion and lack of attention.

19 A parallel difference caused a man to complain about his wife, "She just wants to talk about her own point of view. If I show her another view, she gets mad at me." When most women talk to each other, they assume a conversationalist's job is to express agreement and support. But many men see their conversational duty as pointing out the other side of an argument. This is heard as disloyalty by women, and refusal to offer the requisite support. It is not that women don't want to see other points of view, but that they prefer them phrased as suggestions and inquiries rather than as direct challenges.

20 In his book *Fighting for Life,* Walter Ong points out that men use "agonistic" or warlike, oppositional formats to do almost anything; thus discussion becomes debate, and conversation a competitive sport. In contrast, women see conversation as a ritual means of establishing rapport. If Jane tells

a problem and June says she has a similar one, they walk away feeling closer to each other. But this attempt at establishing rapport can backfire when used with men. Men take too literally women's ritual "troubles talk," just as women mistake men's ritual challenges for real attack.

The Sounds of Silence

These differences begin to clarify why women and men have such different expectations about communication in marriage. For women, talk creates intimacy. Marriage is an orgy of closeness: you can tell your feelings and thoughts, and still be loved. Their greatest fear is being pushed away. But men live in a hierarchical world, where talk maintains independence and status. They are on guard to protect themselves from being put down and pushed around. 21

This explains the paradox of the talkative man who said of his silent wife, "She's the talker." In the public setting of a guest lecture, he felt challenged to show his intelligence and display his understanding of the lecture. But at home, where he has nothing to prove and no one to defend against, he is free to remain silent. For his wife, being home means she is free from the worry that something she says might offend someone, or spark disagreement, or appear to be showing off; at home she is free to talk. 22

The communication problems that endanger marriage can't be fixed by mechanical engineering. They require a new conceptual framework about the role of talk in human relationships. Many of the psychological explanations that have become second nature may not be helpful, because they tend to blame either women (for not being assertive enough) or men (for not being in touch with their feelings). A sociolinguistic approach by which male-female conversation is seen as cross-cultural communication allows us to understand the problem and forge solutions without blaming either party. 23

Once the problem is understood, improvement comes naturally, as it did to the young woman and her boyfriend who seemed to go to sleep when she wanted to talk. Previously, she had accused him of not listening, and he had refused to change his behavior, since that would be admitting fault. But then she learned about and explained to him the differences in women's and men's habitual ways of aligning themselves in conversation. The next time she told him she wanted to talk, he began, as usual, by lying down and covering his eyes. When the familiar negative reaction bubbled up, she reassured herself that he really was listening. But then he sat up and looked at her. Thrilled she asked why. He said, "You like me to look at you when we talk, so I'll try to do it." Once he saw their differences as cross-cultural rather than right and wrong, he independently altered his behavior. 24

Women who feel abandoned and deprived when their husbands won't listen to or report daily news may be happy to discover their husbands trying to adapt once they understand the place of small talk in women's relationships. But if their husbands don't adapt, the women may still be comforted that for men, this is not a failure of intimacy. Accepting the difference, the wives may look to their friends or family for that kind of talk. And husbands who can't provide it shouldn't feel their wives have made unreasonable demands. Some couples will still decide to divorce, but at least their decisions will be based on realistic expectations. 25

In these times of resurgent ethnic conflicts, the world desperately needs cross-cultural understanding. Like charity, successful cross-cultural communication should begin at home. 26

QUESTIONS FOR REFLECTION

Considering Ideas

1. What is Tannen's overall claim? Where does she most clearly state her thesis?

2. According to the author, how do men and women communicate differently? What kinds of problems can arise in a relationship because of these different communication styles?

3. What can men and women do to try to overcome their communication obstacles?

Considering the Rhetorical Star

1. What is the main *subject* of Tannen's article? Is the specific topic engaging? Why or why not?
2. Who is the primary *audience* for the article? Is there a secondary audience? Explain.
3. What is the author's main *purpose* for the article? Does she convey her purpose clearly? Explain.
4. Tannen uses persuasion as the primary *strategy* for the piece. What other writing strategies does she use, and how do they affect the article?
5. What *design* features does the author use? Are they effective? Why or why not?

Considering Writing Strategies

1. How does the author establish herself as an authority figure on the subject? Is her approach convincing? Why or why not?
2. Does Tannen use inductive or deductive reasoning in her essay? What other methods does she use to support her argument? Identify several specific examples. Which ones seem to be the most effective? Why?
3. In the concluding paragraph, the writer compares cross-cultural communication to charity. How effective is this simile?

Writing Suggestions

1. In her essay, Tannen draws several conclusions about the different communication styles of men and women. Write an essay arguing for or against her perceptions of the ways in which men and women communicate. Be sure to back up your claim with specific supporting evidence.
2. Tannen suggests that once couples understand the types of problems they have communicating, they will be able to improve their relationships. Do you agree or disagree with the author's assertion? Write an essay arguing for or against her claim.

ESOL Tip >

How do men and women communicate in your home country? Is it different from the way in which they communicate in the United States? If so, write a persuasive essay about which communication style works better.

Reading and Reflection PERSUASIVE WRITING

[preview] **MARK C. PACHUCKI** was born in Schenectady, New York, and earned his doctorate in sociology from Harvard University. He has served as an instructor at several universities and is currently an assistant professor at the University of Massachusetts. His research focuses on a variety of subjects, including social networks, culture, nutrition, and health. Before reading the article, consider the social relationships you have. How important is it for you to have close friends to spend time with and talk to? Would your life be as meaningful without them? Why or why not?

The Importance of Social Relationships Over the Life Course
by Mark C. Pachucki

1 The World Health Organization now recognizes social relationships as an important social determinant of health throughout our lives. Yet, the acknowledgement that social ties can shape our morbidity and mortality has been at times an uphill struggle. This is because the analysis of the effects of human relationships on our health sometimes requires either large or unusually complete datasets, and often, analytic techniques that make complicated demands on causal inference.

2 However, a rapidly expanding body of research shows how examining interdependencies between two individuals who know one another can provide insights into how human health changes at an individual, small-group, and population scale. As such, a growing number of investigators are pursuing inquiry in this and related areas of complex systems science. As part of the University of Massachusetts, Amherst Department of Sociology and Computational Social Science Institute, Mark C. Pachucki, Ph.D., investigates how social relationships shape health throughout the life course.

Acknowledging That Social Ties Can Shape Our Morbidity and Mortality Has Been at Times an Uphill Struggle

3 The transition to adolescence marks an especially formative stage of human development wherein interpersonal awareness and changes in social interactions are happening at the same time as immensely complex hormonal, cognitive, and behavioral transformations. Because of this simultaneity, identifying mechanisms that may produce ill health can be difficult.

4 In a recent study in *Social Science & Medicine,* Pachucki, Emily J. Ozer, Ph.D., Alain Barrat, Ph.D., and Ciro Cattuto, Ph.D., investigated the role of changing social relationships in early adolescent depressive symptoms and self-esteem. In the longitudinal network-behavior research design, we gathered information on simultaneously changing social structure and individual attributes among a bounded community of 6th grade participants (11–12 years). Then, we analyzed the resulting data using a sophisticated class of statistical social network model.

5 One of the novel aspects of this study was the dynamic measurement of children's interaction patterns during a three-month period. We chose the school lunchroom as the site to observe networks, because, by and large, students tend to sit with their closest friends during their limited free times during the day. We identified social interactions using an unobtrusive electronic proximity-sensing radio frequency identification (RFID) tag worn on a neck lanyard. Tags sent data back to small wall-mounted receivers that tracked which tags were in close proximity every twenty seconds. Thus, given students' propensity to switch tables (and thus lunch partners), we were able to observe who spent time with whom in fine detail. To these data we added information on children's socioeconomic background, health attributes, and health behaviors.

A Novel Aspect of This Study Was the Dynamic Measurement of Children's Interaction Patterns during a Three-Month Period

6 We observed that girls who had more interaction partners tended to have fewer depressive symptoms and greater self-esteem within measurement periods, but no parallel trend for boys. However, after controlling for socioeconomic and demographic background as well as changes in network structure, socially connected study participants did not become more similar in terms of

depressive symptoms nor self-esteem over time. This was an important finding because of the rigorous analytic methods employed, yet somewhat surprising because this stage of the life course is thought to be ripe for evidence of interpersonal social influence among peers. Scrutiny of network tie changes found that almost two-thirds of 6th-graders' interaction partners changed each month, which is more turnover in this age group than has been shown using more traditional means of enumerating networks. We also found, as others have, that gender similarity and similar levels of popularity play important roles in friendship formation among this age cohort, and that friends of a given child tend to become friends as well (transitive closure).

Girls with More Interaction Partners Had Fewer Depressive Symptoms, Greater Self-Esteem. There Was No Parallel Trend for Boys

7 We are unambiguously living in an era of computational social science, where massive streams of real-time data on human behavior are increasingly amenable to analysis to improve our understanding of how social processes contribute to health from birth until our twilight years. This example of research on objective measurement of minute-by-minute socialization behaviors is one way to illustrate the subtleties of adolescent relationship dynamics.

8 Yet given the ubiquity of portable devices and advances in Bluetooth and RFID technologies, conducting this type of research is becoming more feasible and widespread. Reliance upon social network data to construct relational datasets that reflect who people actually interact with—rather than simply who people state their friends are—has great potential to clarify how socialization processes unfold and moreover, how social processes interact with biological processes of human development.

9 For instance, Pachucki, in collaboration with Lindsay T. Hoyt, Ph.D., is currently integrating information on changes in human relationships with information on pubertal development during adolescence and disparities in cardiovascular diseases during adulthood. Identifying how relationships matter to future health, but critically—at what stages of life they may matter the most—are worthwhile questions to pursue because they may help us to identify appropriate interpersonal levers for intervention to improve health and well-being.

Source: Mark C. Pachucki, https://obssr.od.nih.gov/the-importance-of-social-relationships-over-the-life-course/. Used by permission of the author.

QUESTIONS FOR REFLECTION

Considering Ideas

1. What is Pachucki's overall claim? Where does he best state his thesis?
2. According to the author, during what stages in human development is it especially important for a person to make changes in interpersonal awareness and social interactions? Why?
3. What is the correlation between interaction and self-esteem for girls and for boys? Why do you suppose the results differ?

Considering the Rhetorical Star

1. What is the *subject* of Pachucki's essay? How thoroughly does he cover the subject?
2. Who might the *audience* be for this article, which was originally published on the website for the National Institute of Health: Office of Behavioral and Social Sciences Research, a government organization?
3. What is the author's main *purpose* (to inform, to interpret, to persuade, to entertain, to express feelings) in writing the article?

4. Pachucki uses persuasion as the primary *strategy* for the piece. Does he employ any other writing strategies? What are they, and how do they affect the work?
5. What *design* features does this article include? Are they effective? Why or why not?

Considering Writing Strategies

1. How does the author establish himself as an authority figure on the subject? As you probably noticed, he refers to himself in the third person in several places in the article. How does that strategy affect his authority? Is his approach convincing? Why or why not?
2. Does Pachucki use inductive or deductive reasoning in the essay? What other methods does he employ to support his argument? Identify several specific examples from the text. Which ones seem to be the most effective? Why?
3. In the concluding paragraph, the author suggests questions to consider for future research. How effective is this approach? Explain.

Writing Suggestions

1. Write a persuasive essay explaining how mobile devices, such as cell phones, have affected people's social interaction. Be sure to cite any sources you use. (See Chapters 13 and 14 for details about citing sources using the MLA and APA formats.)
2. How might communication and social interaction change in the future? Write a creative essay in which you persuade readers about how people will relate to one another in a future decade, such as the year 2040, 2050, or 2100.

STUDENT WRITING

Mursing

by Thomas James "TJ" Pinkerton

1 Not many people are used to seeing a male nurse or "murse" walk into their room in the hospital due to the fact that there are not many males in the nursing profession. In fact, only about 10% of all nurses in the United States are male (Kronsberg, et al., 2018). However, nursing is a great profession for men to get into, and men can make significant contributions to the nursing field. The physical strength of being a man, the power of male camaraderie, and sensitive issues unique to men are significant factors making nursing a logical career choice for men.

2 One reason for men to get into the nursing field is the physical requirements of a nursing position. "In situations that demand nurses to do heavy lifting, or handling of aggressive patients, male nurses find themselves at an advantage" (Dzaher, 2016). For instance, a nurse might have to move patients who cannot move themselves. One example of this would be if a patient needed to use the restroom but could not find the strength to get out of bed. A male nurse would have the strength to lift most patients off of a bed without needing to call for additional help. Furthermore, during a patient's hospital stay, he or she will often need to be moved from one room to another for testing. In that case a nurse needs to be able to lift the patient out of bed, place him or her into a wheelchair, push

the wheelchair to the test site, lift the patient out of the wheelchair, and place him or her on one of the numerous machines used for testing. When the testing is complete, the nurse must repeat this whole process in reverse to return the patient to his or her room. Most men are strong enough to accomplish these tasks on their own, without calling for backup.

3 Another reason why men may want to consider getting into the nursing field is the rapport they can build with male patients. Of course many of the patients in a hospital are going to be male, and some of them are going to be more comfortable if the nurse attending to them is male also. "Some men may feel more comfortable talking openly with another man" (Miller & Fremson, 2018). Some male patients, especially those from an older generation or from a male-dominated culture, are not used to taking orders or advice from women. If that is the case, it is best to assign the patient a male nurse simply as a way to comfort the patient.

4 Additionally, some male patients may prefer a male nurse because they may be embarrassed about why they are in the hospital, especially if it is for a male-related problem. For example, a male patient may prefer to have a male insert a catheter (Miller & Fremson, 2018). While the preference for a male nurse may be discriminatory toward women, the hospital is not the place to fix this type of ailment. Getting the patient healthy enough to return to everyday life should always be the first goal of the hospital, and the comfort of the patient while in the care of the hospital should be a close second. No matter how silly the reason for the patient's request for a male nurse is, his or her needs should be met.

5 Overall, many career fields that have traditionally been reserved mainly for women, including nursing, are opening their doors to men. While in the past it may have seemed a little awkward for a man to pursue a career as a nurse, today the need for men in the nursing field is evident. Men can provide beneficial services for the nursing industry such as physical strength, male companionship, and sensitivity for male patients.

REFERENCES

Dzaher, A. (2016, June 20). 5 reasons for increasing demand for male nurses. *MIMS Today.* https://today.mims.com-5-reasons-for-incresing-demand-for-male-nurses

Kronsberg, S., Bouret, J. R., & Brett, A. L. (2018). Lived experiences of male nurses: Dire consequences for the male profession. *Journal of Nursing Education and Practice,* 8(1), 46–53. www.sciedu.ca/journal/index.php/jnep/article/view/11897/7446

Miller, C. C., & Fremson, R. (2018, January 4). Forget about the stigma: Male nurses explain why nursing is a job of the future for men. *The New York Times*. www.nytimes.com/interactive/2018/01/upshot/male-hurses.html

Note: Pinkerton uses the APA format for his essay. Your instructor may require that you use MLA or another format for your paper. Please see Chapters 13–14 for more on integrating and documenting sources into your writing.

QUESTIONS FOR REFLECTION

1. Identify Pinkerton's claim (thesis). Is it stated clearly?
2. According to the author, why do some men prefer a male nurse? Do you agree with this point? Why or why not?
3. Which types of appeals (logical, emotional, or ethical) does the author use in his essay to support his claim? Are they effective? Why or why not?
4. Is Pinkerton's argument convincing? Why or why not?
5. Do you think men should be a part of the nursing field? Why or why not?

Activity Taking Part in the Great Debate

On your own, in pairs, or in small groups, choose one (or more) of the claims listed below. Make a list of arguments for and against the claim. Determine which side seems to have the best support. If possible, share your list with another classmate or other group and discuss your lists. Where do you agree? Where do you disagree? Avoid getting into a heated debate. The point is to discuss different perspectives rather than draw a conclusion about which side is "right."

- The lottery and other forms of gambling should be illegal in every state.
- Actors and professional athletes are paid too much.
- Beauty pageants are exploitive.
- People who talk on cell phones while driving, or even walking, are a danger to others.
- We are too dependent on computers.
- Our election process is unfair.
- Everyone should be concerned about global warming.

A representative from each group may share a few of the highlights with the class. This activity may give you ideas for writing a persuasive essay.

Persuasion and Marketing

One of the most noticeable forms of persuasion is marketing. Virtually every type of organization—whether it sells a product or provides a service—needs to promote itself to increase revenues. As with other types of persuasion, advertisements need to appeal to the audience using logic, emotions, and/or ethics.

Advertising messages are everywhere:

- "Have your surgery at Healthy Hospital, the number one facility in the region."
- "Ace Accounting Associates will provide you with the most accurate audit or tax return."
- "Come to Crazy Carl's Computers for all of your computer networking needs."
- "Dustin's Divine Delicacies is the most exquisite eatery in the East."
- "Support your local friendly fire department or sheriff's office with a donation."
- "Do your part to reduce carbon dioxide emissions; buy a hybrid car from Gregg's Green Garage."

Activity Identifying and Using Appeals in Advertising

On your own or in pairs or groups, identify the types of appeals used in the fictitious advertising messages listed above. Now, write six one-sentence ads of your own using a variety of appeals. If possible, have another student or group determine which types of appeals you have used in your ads.

OPTIONS FOR WRITING A PERSUASIVE ESSAY

Now that you have read one or more examples of persuasive writing, it's time to write your own argument. You may choose to write about one of the writing options that follow, the advertisement, the image, or one of the media suggestions. Additionally, keep your ears open for hot topics at school or work; you may hear a conversation that sparks your interest. You might also read an online newspaper or magazine to find a controversial topic. Remember to keep track of any sources you use in case you need to cite them in your paper. Consider your rhetorical star and the qualities of effective persuasive writing as you begin to compose your assignment.

Writing Assignment Options

Use one of the following topics to write a persuasive essay.

1. Division of labor for household chores, earning an income, and/or raising children
2. Environmental issue, such as going green, recycling, or avoiding pesticides
3. Laws about smoking cigarettes in public places
4. Health care issue, such as benefits, mandatory vaccinations, or alternative medicines
5. Animal testing for research
6. Cell phone usage while driving or walking
7. Helmet laws for bicyclists and/or motorcyclists
8. The legal drinking age
9. Gun control laws
10. The death penalty

Multimodal Assignment

Using one of the readings, writing assignment options, or another topic, create a multimodal project using the persuasive writing strategy and at least two or more of the options in Table 10.4.

Table 10.4

Multimodal Options		
Artifact	Images	PowerPoint
Artwork	Infographics	Prezi
Audio clip	Journal	Video
Blog	Montage	Website
Digital portfolio	Podcast	Wiki
Graphic organizer	Poster	Writing

(See Chapter 15 for more details about multimodal compositions.)

Interpreting an Advertisement

The Advertising Archives

The Advertising Archives

Who is the specific audience for this advertisement? How do you know? Do you think the target audience would want to purchase beauty products from MAC? Why or why not? Is the ad persuasive? Why or why not? The MAC cosmetics advertisement uses celebrities in an attempt to sell the product. How effective is this practice? Is it fair or misleading? Write a persuasive essay arguing for or against the use of celebrity testimonials. You may want to combine purposes and incorporate a cause-and-effect writing strategy along with persuasion. Be sure to cite any sources you use to support your argument.

Who is the audience for the Carlsberg advertisement? What effect do the images and text suggest that drinking Carlsberg has on friendships among men and women? Do you agree? Why or why not? Is the ad persuasive? Why or why not? Can drinking beer be a catalyst for bringing people together? Conversely, can drinking too much beer create problems in relationships? Write a persuasive essay related to the Carlsberg advertisement and how drinking beer can affect relationships. Make a positive or negative claim about drinking beer and support your thesis convincingly. If you use outside sources, be sure to cite them.

Activity Writing an Advertisement

Create an advertisement for a fictitious product on your own, in pairs, or in groups. Include text and images to help convince your audience to purchase your product.

Note: You'll find an extended group project called "Sales Pitch" as well as suggestions for preparing and presenting group presentations in Chapter 15.

Writing about an Image

Write a persuasive essay about an image in this book or from another source. Make a claim about the image itself, or you may choose to write about something that relates to it. For example, you might write an essay about the Carlsberg advertisement on p. 266, arguing that beer companies glamorize the use of their products. Or you may choose to write about the MAC ad and discuss the ways advertisers use sex appeal to market their products.

Media Connection for Persuading

You might watch, read, and/or listen to one or more of the suggested media in Table 10.5 to discover additional examples of persuasion in the context of relationships. Exploring various media may help you to better understand methods for persuading. For example, you might watch the movie *Endless Love* or listen to (or watch the video of) Taylor Swift's song "Love Story" and write an essay arguing for or against parents telling their children whom they can date.

Table 10.5

Media Chart				
Television	*The Good Place*	*Modern Family*	*The View*	*The Real*
Film	*The Lottery Ticket* (2010)	*Love, Simon* (2018)	*A Star Is Born* (2018)	*Endless Love* (2014)
Print/ E-Reading	*O* (The Oprah Magazine)	*Super Charm*	*Psychology Today*	*The 5 Love Languages* by Gary Chapman (2015)
Internet	**www.createhealthyrelationships.com**	**www.psychologytoday.com/topics/relationships**	**www.savemymarriage.com**	**www.yourtango.com/relationships**
Music	"Girls Like You" by Maroon 5	"Love Story" by Taylor Swift	"Perfect" by Ed Sheeran	"Shallow" by Lady Gaga and Bradley Cooper

FIGURE 10.2 The Rhetorical Star

10.4 Analyzing the Rhetorical Star for Writing Persuasively

As you prepare to write your persuasive paper, consider the five points of the rhetorical star (Figure 10.2). You might use some of the questions in the chart as you conduct your rhetorical star analysis.

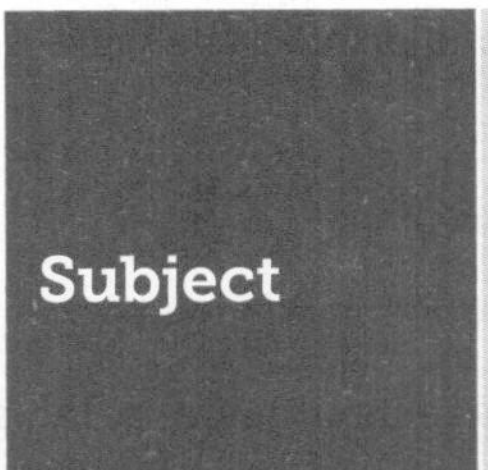

Choose a debatable topic as the focus for your essay. You should have strong feelings about the issue or controversy. You might want to write about a subject that is currently in the news or one that you have experienced on a personal level. For example, you might write about a law or policy that seems unfair or insufficient. Be sure that your topic is neither too narrow nor too broad for the length of your assignment.

Audience	Who will read your persuasive essay? How much does your audience know about the issue you are addressing? What audience characteristics can you appeal to in your argument? Are you aiming at readers who are personally involved with the issue, or are they just interested in learning more about it? How do your readers feel about the issue? Are they likely to be supportive of your position, hostile toward your stance, or unsure of their own perspective on the issue? Include details that will appeal to your specific audience. For instance, you might write an article for your campus newspaper in an attempt to persuade your readers that more students should take leadership roles in school organizations, such as student government or honorary fraternities, because they will gain leadership skills and strengthen their résumés. In that case your primary audience would be college students.
Purpose	Think about what you are trying to accomplish through your persuasive essay. Are you trying to convince the readers to change their minds about a controversial issue? Do you want the audience to take some sort of action? Maybe you just want the readers to understand your position, even if they have a different stance. Keep your purpose in mind as you carefully craft your argument.
Strategy	Even if your primary goal is to persuade your reader, you may also employ other writing strategies. For example, if you are writing an essay persuading the readers that depression should be taken more seriously, then you might define what depression is, describe the symptoms that occur, give a brief narrative or anecdote of someone who suffers from it, and then argue why people need to pay more attention to it and suggest where to go for help.
Design	How many points do you need to make about your subject to fully support your argument? Also, what other design details, such as a photographs or charts, might enhance your persuasive document? Do you want to include headings to help your reader clearly identify your main points? Will including a list of bulleted examples add credibility to your claim? Design your document to be as persuasive as possible.

10.5 Applying the Writing Process for Persuading

After you have completed your rhetorical star analysis, follow the steps of the writing process (see Figure 10.3) to compose your paper.

1. **Discovering:** Once you have decided on a topic, make a list of ideas that support your argument as well as a list of ideas from the opposing point of view (see Figure 10.4). You may also try completing a freewriting exercise to help get the ideas flowing. You may also want to talk with classmates, friends, or family members to learn about opposing viewpoints related to your topic.

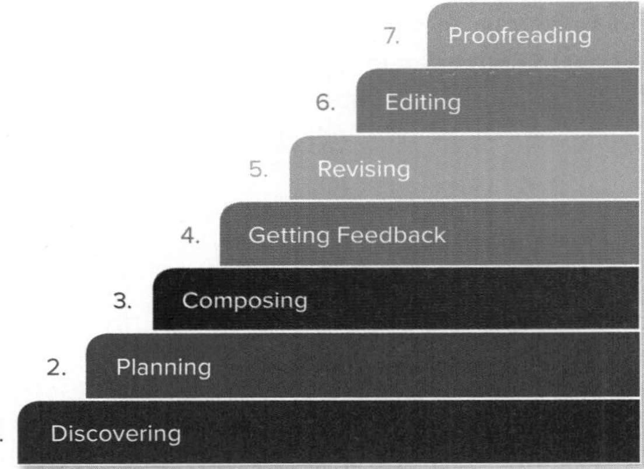

FIGURE 10.3 The Seven Steps of the Writing Process

2. **Planning:** As you plan your draft, list the main points you would like to use to support your persuasive essay. Number your supporting points from most to least persuasive. Then reorder the ideas by putting the second most important supporting point first and the most persuasive supporting point last. Ending with your most persuasive point will usually make the strongest impression on your reader. To help you visualize your organization, create a cluster, an outline (informal or formal), or a graphic organizer (see Figure 10.4).
3. **Composing:** Write a first draft of your persuasive essay. Don't worry too much about grammar and punctuation at this time. Be sure to keep in mind the qualities of persuasive writing outlined earlier in the chapter:
    1. Introduce the subject you are debating.
    2. State a claim about your subject. (This is your thesis.)
    3. Support your claim with evidence that appeals to your audience.
    4. Use supporting evidence ethically and logically.
    5. Organize supporting evidence effectively.
    6. End with a logical conclusion.
4. **Getting feedback:** Have at least one classmate or other person read your rough draft and answer the peer review questions on page 271. If you have access to a writing tutor or center, get another opinion about your paper as well.

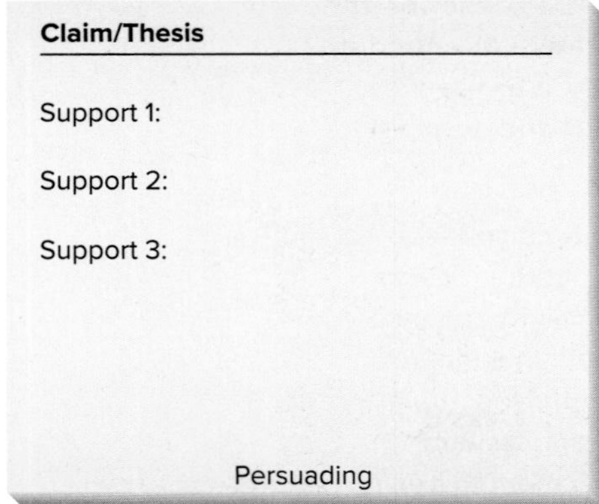

FIGURE 10.4 Graphic Organizer for Persuasion

5. **Revising:** Using all of the feedback available to you, revise your persuasive essay. Make sure that your main supporting point is the strongest evidence for your claim or thesis. Add, delete, and rearrange ideas as necessary.
6. **Editing:** Read your persuasive essay again, this time looking for errors in grammar, punctuation, and mechanics. Make sure you are using transitions effectively to help your reader follow your logic as you work to persuade your audience.
7. **Proofreading:** After you have carefully edited your essay, read it one last time, looking for typographical errors and any other issues that might interfere with the readers' understanding of your essay.

PEER REVIEW QUESTIONS FOR PERSUADING

Trade rough drafts with a classmate and answer the following questions about his or her paper. In person or online, discuss your papers and suggestions with your peer. Finally, make the changes you feel would most benefit your paper.

1. Has the author introduced the issue clearly and effectively? What is the issue?
2. Is the author's claim (thesis) clear? What is the author's overall opinion?
3. Identify examples of ethical, emotional, and/or logical appeals that the author has used. Which appeals are most effective? Which appeals could be more effective?
4. Is the supporting evidence presented ethically and logically? Why or why not?
5. Is the essay organized deductively or inductively? Is this organizational pattern clear and effective? Why or why not?
6. What part of the essay is most memorable? Why?
7. Is the conclusion effective? Why or why not?
8. What kinds of grammatical errors, if any, are evident in the essay?
9. What final suggestions do you have for the author?

Writer's Checklist for Persuading

Use the checklist below to evaluate your own writing and help ensure that your persuasive essay is effective. If you have any "no" answers, go back and work on those areas if necessary.

- ☐ 1. Have I introduced the issue clearly and effectively?
- ☐ 2. Does my claim (thesis) clearly state my opinion about the issue?
- ☐ 3. Have I provided ample supporting evidence to persuade the reader that my perspective is valid?

- [ ] 4. Have I used my supporting evidence ethically and logically?
- [ ] 5. Have I organized my supporting evidence effectively?
- [ ] 6. Is my conclusion sufficient?
- [ ] 7. Have I proofread thoroughly?

CHAPTER SUMMARY

1. Use the persuasive writing strategy to prove a point.
2. Persuasive writing is an important part of your education, daily life, and career.
3. Carefully analyze the rhetorical star before writing a persuasive essay: subject, audience, purpose, strategy, and design.
4. Interpreting persuasive readings and images can help you to prepare to write a persuasive essay.
5. Use these qualities when writing a persuasive essay: introduce the subject; state a claim; give supporting evidence; include ethical, emotional, and/or logical appeals; use supporting evidence ethically and logically; organize supporting evidence effectively; end with a logical conclusion.

WHAT I KNOW NOW

Use this checklist to determine what you need to work on in order to feel comfortable with your understanding of the material in this chapter. Check off each item as you master it. Review the material for any unchecked items.

- [ ] 1. I know what **persuasive writing** is.
- [ ] 2. I can identify several **real-world applications** for persuasive writing.
- [ ] 3. I can evaluate **persuasive readings and images.**
- [ ] 4. I can analyze the **rhetorical star** for persuasive writing.
- [ ] 5. I understand the **writing process** for persuasive writing.
- [ ] 6. I can apply the **six qualities** of persuasive writing.

Design elements: *Graduate Spotlight:* Ingram Publishing/AGE Fotostock

CHAPTER 11

Evaluating: Film and the Arts

WENN Rights Ltd/Alamy Stock Photo

learning outcomes

In this chapter you will learn techniques for achieving these learning outcomes:

11.1 Identify real-world applications for evaluating. *p. 274*

11.2 Understand the qualities of evaluative writing. *p. 276*

11.3 Interpret images and evaluative readings about film and the arts. *p. 280*

11.4 Analyze the rhetorical star for evaluating. *p. 295*

11.5 Apply the qualities of evaluative writing. *p. 296*

Writing Strategy Focus: Evaluating

When you evaluate a subject, you make an overall judgment about it. An effective evaluation needs to be based on several specific criteria or standards for judging the subject. To make an evaluation convincing, you need to support it with specific details and examples. You probably make informal evaluations quite often. For example, if you turn on the television and catch the beginning of a new situation comedy, you will probably decide within a few minutes whether you like the show or not. Your evaluative criteria might include the premise of the story line, the quality of the acting, and the use of humor. Knowing how to structure a formal written evaluation is useful to you at school, in your daily life, and in your career.

11.1 Real-World Applications for Evaluating

Writing to Evaluate in College

You will often be asked to evaluate subjects in your college courses. If you work in collaborative groups, you may be asked to evaluate the experience or your teammates. You might need to evaluate two different programs of study to determine which one will provide you with the most satisfying career in the long run. In a course in your major, you may need to evaluate a method or procedure for accuracy or effectiveness. Near the end of the term you will likely evaluate the course, your textbook, and your instructor.

Writing to Evaluate in Your Daily Life

You evaluate various subjects on a daily basis. If you eat at a restaurant, you are likely to evaluate the meal, service, and overall dining experience. When you see a movie, you probably judge whether it was worth your time and money or if you were satisfied with the characters, plot, or ending. As a consumer you make judgments every time you purchase something. Was it worth the price? Did you receive the service or product that you were promised? In elections, you evaluate each candidate and decide who you feel will do the best job in the position.

Writing to Evaluate in Your Career

Having strong evaluation skills is extremely useful in the workplace. You may need to write a self-evaluation to get a raise or a promotion. When you are offered several positions, you will need to evaluate which one is the best fit for your needs. Once you are on the job, you will likely need to use your evaluation skills regularly. Which vendor can provide you with the best products and services? What plan will have the most positive results? What is the most efficient and cost-effective way for you to reach your goals?

Health care: evaluations of patients, equipment, and procedures.

Occupational therapy: evaluations of a patient's mobility, life skills, and needs.

Law: evaluations of cases, clients, crime scenes, and who is at fault in an accident.

Education: evaluations of students, faculty, classrooms, lessons, and programs.

Computers: evaluations of hardware, software, personnel, and procedures.

Culinary arts: evaluations of cooking techniques, meals, and ingredients.

Business: evaluations of business plans, facilities, employees, products, and services.

Graduate SPOTLIGHT

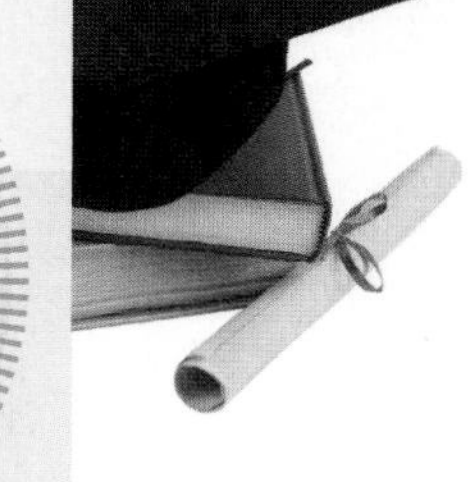

Tawana Campbell, Occupational Therapy Assistant

©Karin L. Russell

Tawana Campbell earned a degree in occupational therapy assisting. She currently works as an occupational therapy assistant for a pediatric outpatient facility. Here's what Tawana has to say about the importance of writing in her career:

"I take careful notes about each session I have with a patient and write a case study. I document everything that happens because the philosophy where I work is, 'If it isn't written down, it didn't happen.' When I meet with a patient, I write out an evaluation of his or her condition and needs, and I determine ways to get effective treatment. Written proof of my evaluation is necessary to persuade the insurance company that special adaptive equipment, such as a wheelchair, splint, or orthotic insert, is necessary.

Because I work with children, I have to be very creative with how I go about treatment. For example, one child had a deficiency in communication skills, so I showed him a movie and asked him to retell the plot. Another child was having problems with sensorimotor skills, so I taught her to dance using her favorite songs from *High School Musical.* Also, I frequently use arts and crafts with children because something as simple as gluing a bead on a piece of construction paper is a useful task. These techniques work great for helping me to establish a good rapport with the children and evaluate their progress. They think we are just playing, but they are really working to overcome the challenges that they face."

Activity Brainstorming Real-World Evaluative Writing

In pairs or small groups, brainstorm uses for writing evaluations at school, in your daily life, and on the job. You may want to choose the prospective career field(s) of the participants in your group. Each group may share its results with the class.

11.2 Qualities of Effective Evaluative Writing

1. Describe the Subject You Are Evaluating

You will need to provide your readers with enough information to understand your subject. For example, if you are evaluating a movie, you might want to explain the premise of the film. That description might include what type of film it is (documentary, comedy, action adventure, and so on) as well as where and when the events in the film take place. You may also decide to introduce the main characters and actors briefly. Be careful to avoid merely summarizing the plot of the movie. In fact, if you include too much summary, then your readers probably won't want to see the movie you are evaluating. If you are evaluating a work of art, you may want to include a picture of the work along with your review. Include just enough details for your readers to be able to grasp your meaning.

2. Make a Claim about the Subject You Are Evaluating

Your thesis should state your overall opinion of the subject you are evaluating. Is the movie a great piece of cinema or a ridiculous waste of time? Does the painting leave you awed and inspired or unmoved? Keep in mind that an evaluation must do more than simply express your overall like or dislike for your subject. You will need to be able to support your claim in the body of your essay. Your reader should have a strong sense of your attitude toward the subject right from the beginning of your essay.

3. Choose Several Criteria for Your Evaluation

For your evaluation to seem valid to your readers, you will need to base your overall opinion on several specific **criteria.** Criteria are principles or standards writers use to judge or evaluate something. If you are evaluating a movie, you might consider criteria that fit with the type of movie you are reviewing. For example, for an action adventure film, you might consider the special effects, sound track, and intensity level. If you're evaluating a play, you might judge the actors, costumes, dialogue, and stage props.

Criteria Principles or standards used to evaluate something.

4. Make a Judgment about Each Criterion

Most of your essay should focus on your evaluative criteria, and your topic sentences should each make a claim about one criterion. For example, if you are evaluating a film, one of your topic sentences might be something like this: Another reason the Imax film *The Hobbit: An Unexpected Journey 3D* (2012) is worth seeing is that the actors Ian McKellen and Martin Freeman give stunning performances as Gandalf and Bilbo Baggins.

5. Support Your Judgments with Specific Evidence

Once you have determined how successfully your subject fulfills each criterion, you will need to support your judgments with specific details. These details should help you back up the overall claim in your introduction. For example, if you are recommending *The Hobbit* to your readers, then your supporting material will come from the movie. If one of your judgments is that the acting is superb, you might support it with specific details about what Ian McKellen and Martin Freeman do to bring their characters vividly to life.

Grammar Window

PRESENT TENSE VERBS

Use present tense verbs when writing about a creative work, even if the author, musician, filmmaker, or artist who created it is deceased. The work lives on even if the creator does not.

Incorrect past tense verbs: Through his song "Imagine," John Lennon *inspired* his fans to envision a peaceful world where everyone *shared.*

Corrected present tense verbs: Through his song "Imagine," John Lennon *inspires* his fans to envision a peaceful world where everyone *shares.*

Discussion: Lennon's song still inspires his fans, even though he was assassinated in 1980. Therefore, present tense verbs are more appropriate than past tense verbs.

Activity: Revise the following sentences, changing the past tense verbs to present tense verbs.

1. Michael Jackson's video *Thriller* was the most popular video of all time.
2. *ET, Transformers,* and *Indiana Jones* were all Steven Spielberg movies with corresponding amusement park attractions in Orlando, Florida.
3. Viewers could look at Leonardo da Vinci's famous painting *Mona Lisa* for hours, wondering why she had that expression on her face.
4. William Faulkner's novel *As I Lay Dying* was much more humorous than the title implied.
5. The 2018 remake of the musical *A Star Is Born* was entertaining.

6. Be Fair with Your Judgments

You want your evaluation to seem reasonable to your audience. For example, if you dislike a television show that you are reviewing, you might acknowledge that it has one redeeming quality. If your overall claim about the television show *My Big Fat Redneck Wedding* is that it is condescending to the viewers, you might show that you are open-minded by mentioning that there are some funny lines in the show. However, you don't want to provide your reader with a completely balanced view of your subject. If you merely tell what you liked and didn't like about the subject, then your reader might be confused about your overall opinion. The majority of your comments need to support the judgment in your thesis.

7. End with a Final Claim about Your Subject

In addition to restating your thesis and summarizing your main points, you might also make a broader judgment that wasn't stated in the thesis. For example, you might end your movie review with a star rating or other general comment so your readers will know for sure your judgment about the movie. If you give the movie four and a half out of five stars, then your readers will know for sure how strong your recommendation is.

Career-Based EVALUATIVE WRITING

[preview] **JOHN SMITH** is an talented (fictitious) professional whose work was evaluated by his employer. Performance evaluations, which are common in the workplace, are often used to determine raises and promotions. Your employer may ask you to complete a self-evaluation in addition to the one your manager completes. Furthermore, as you advance in your career, you may need to evaluate employees you supervise. When writing an employee evaluation, be sure to include specific details to support the judgments you make. Also, be objective and accurate when writing an evaluation.

Sample Employee Evaluation Form

Name: John Smith	Department: Customer Service
Date of Hire: January 5, 2017	Date of Review: September 1, 2019
Supervisor: Jill Johnson	Date of Last Review: April 6, 2018

Rating System

1 = Unsatisfactory	4 = Exceeds Expectations
2 = Needs Improvement	5 = Significantly Exceeds Expectations
3 = Satisfactory	

1. **Quality of employee's work** 4

Comments John does very good work for the company. His attention to detail and ability to provide quality support for his projects and co-workers meet expectations.

2. **Exercise of good judgment** 5

Comments John has shown exceptional judgment, particularly in regard to prioritizing key accounts and customers.

3. **Attendance** 3

Comments While John has not missed an excessive number of days, his absences and shorter days are higher than we would normally like to see. John needs to plan ahead a bit better so that his absences can be anticipated and kept to a minimum.

4. **Employee involvement/participation in team effort** 5

Comments John is an exceptional team player. He strives to work collaboratively with co-workers, and his projects often utilize input from multiple departments. He spearheaded an initiative to better utilize company-wide resources.

5. **Attention to company policies and procedures** 4

Comments John always maintains strict adherence to company guidelines and is quick to verify any new idea or procedure. He does occasionally require a reminder when procedures change, but he is quick to learn new workflows.

6. **Interpersonal relationships and communication with co-workers** 5

Comments One of John's key strengths is his ability to work well with others. He is a natural leader and communicates clearly with others.

7. **Taking initiative to achieve goals and complete assignments** 4

Comments John has good ideas and innovations, but they tend to be at the direction of others. Some of his biggest successes were the implementation of others' ideas. I would like to see John suggest more projects. I know from meetings that he has excellent vision, but he is often hesitant to share it with others.

8. **Responsiveness to changing work requirement** 4

Comments There were two instances this year in which John used outdated forms and, in one case, an outdated workflow. He was quick to rectify the situation, but he should pay closer attention to interoffice memos and trainings.

9. **Work ethic** 5

Comments John has an excellent work ethic. He is attentive to project details and deadlines. His ability to meet or exceed date expectations has helped his projects run successfully.

10. **Overall performance rating** 4.3

Comments John has expressed an interest in continued career growth within the company and he is on track for promotion and greater responsibility. I encourage him to double-check details and be a bit more consistent in minor areas of performance. Overall, John's performance has exceeded expectations for the year.

Areas of Strength:
John works very well with others and strives for the best possible outcomes for everything he takes on. His professionalism and willingness to work toward innovation are excellent. He communicates effectively and collaborates with others.

Areas of Improvement:
I would like to see John take on more responsibility this year. He has natural leadership skills and tends to bring out the best in others. I would encourage him to continue doing this in a more strategic way. By his next review I would like to see him initiate and complete a project on his own.

Employee's Comments:
I think the assessment of my performance is a good reflection of my skills and areas of improvement. During my review I discussed strategies for taking on leadership roles and being a more consistent presence in the overall process. I am committed to my continued communication with all members of my team. I also discussed plans to launch monthly employee information-sharing sessions that will help with consistency.

Date: *September 1, 2019*

Employee's Signature

QUESTIONS FOR REFLECTION

1. What are John's strengths?
2. What are his weaknesses?
3. Which comments need more explanation? What is missing?
4. What specific criteria does the supervisor use to evaluate John? Which ones are most important? Why?
5. Using this same form, how would you rate yourself as an employee? How would you rate your boss?

11.3 Evaluating in the Context of Film and the Arts

What would the world be like without film and the arts? Today we have easy access to more types of fine arts than ever before. Through film, television, the Internet, and other media, we can watch a Broadway play, visit the Louvre museum in Paris, take in a hip-hop concert, or listen to an author read her own poetry aloud without ever leaving the comfort of our own homes. We can use the arts to explore ourselves and our beliefs, learn about the world and other cultures, and escape from reality. With so many options available, how do we decide what is worth our precious time? How do we evaluate the arts when personal preference plays a big part in our perceptions of artistic expressions? We have to base our judgments on clear criteria and specific supporting evidence. The skills you use to evaluate film and the arts will translate to a variety of other areas in your life. Read and discuss one or more of the following evaluations. Doing so will help you to write your own evaluations.

Reading and Reflection EVALUATIVE WRITING

[preview] **KENNETH TURAN,** who has an MS degree from Columbia University, is the film critic for the *Los Angeles Times* and NPR's *Morning Edition.* He has written several books, including *Not to Be Missed: Fifty-Four Favorites from a Lifetime of Film.* In the following article, Turan evaluates the final film based on the hugely successful series of Harry Potter books written by J. K. Rowling. You may want to check out **www.jkrowling.com** to learn more about Rowling's books and characters.

Before reading the article, consider the qualities that make a good movie. What elements are required for a movie to earn a high rating from you?

Movie Review: *Harry Potter and the Deathly Hallows—Part 2*
by Kenneth Turan

1 After seven previous films over a 10-year span, $2 billion in domestic box office and still more treasure overseas, Warner Bros. has unwrapped the Harry Potter advertising line it hoped it would never have to use: "It all ends."

2 In a classic storybook finish, however, *Harry Potter and the Deathly Hallows—Part 2* turns out to be more than the last of its kind. Almost magically, it ends up being one of the best of the series as well.

3 The Harry Potter films, like the boy wizard himself, have had their creative ups and downs, so it's especially satisfying that this final film, ungainly title and all, has been worth the wait. Though no expense has been spared in its production, it succeeds because it brings us back to the combination of magic, adventure and emotion that created the books' popularity in the first place.

4 It also succeeds because the franchise has stuck to its conservative creative guns and seen them pay off. With occasional exceptions like Alfonso Cuarón's *Prisoner of Azkaban* adventure, the Potter films have rarely been daring, valuing superb craftsmanship and care over cutting-edge audacity. Now that we've come to the much-anticipated finale, that expert husbanding of a once-in-a-lifetime franchise has had a cumulative effect that is not to be denied.

5 Not only did the series' three leads—Daniel Radcliffe, Rupert Grint and Emma Watson—turn out to be expertly cast, the production has been able to retain their services through all eight films. And they've been supported by such a deep bench of top-flight British acting talent (Ciarán Hinds is the latest to be added, playing Dumbledore's brother) that when Bill Nighy joined the cast for *Deathly Hallows—Part 1,* he said he'd feared he'd be the only English actor of a certain age who wasn't in a Harry Potter film.

6 All that talent couldn't have come cheap, and the other consistent factor in the Potter universe is the production's refusal to skimp or pinch pennies. That willingness to do whatever it took to bring Stuart Craig's exceptional production designs to life no matter how painstaking the task is central to the new film's success as well.

7 To give just two examples, more than 200,000 golden coins and thousands of other pieces were created to convincingly fill a vault at Gringotts bank, and so much furniture and objects were bought to make Hogwarts' enormous Room of Requirement look more crowded than Charles Foster Kane's storehouse that the set dressing department was busy for months buying up bric-a-brac. Nothing's too good for our Harry.

8 *Deathly Hallows—Part 2* also benefits from sticking with experienced and capable people at the top. Screenwriter Steve Kloves has scripted seven of the eight Potter films, and David Yates has directed four of them. All this practice has allowed the creative team, including returning cinematographer Eduardo Serra, to relax into its best self without having to learn the territory all over again.

9 Splitting the final Potter volume into two films was also to the advantage of Part 2, as was the fact that this film deals only with roughly the final third of the book. This enables it to avoid the tiresome teen angst that hampered Part 1 and devote almost all its time to action and confrontation, starting with the film's initial image of the dread Voldemort (Ralph Fiennes) pointing the all-powerful Elder Wand to the sky and creating . . . the Warner Bros. logo.

QUESTIONS FOR REFLECTION

Considering Ideas

1. What is Turan's overall opinion of *Harry Potter and the Deathly Hallows—Part 2?* If you have seen the movie, do you agree or disagree with his judgment? Why?
2. According to the author, what are some of the best features of the film? Are his reasons compelling? Why or why not?
3. Which details in the essay are most convincing for you as the reader? If you haven't seen the film, would you see it based on Turan's review? Why or why not?

Considering the Rhetorical Star

1. What is the *subject* of the essay? Is it an engaging subject? Why or why not?
2. What is Turan's *purpose* for writing the essay? Does he effectively achieve his purpose? Why or why not?
3. Who is the intended *audience* for the piece? Explain.
4. What is Turan's primary writing *strategy?* Does he use any other writing strategies? Which ones? Give examples to illustrate your point.
5. What is the *design* of the essay? Is the design effective? Why or why not?

Considering Writing Strategies

1. What evaluative criteria does Turan use in his review? Does he fully support the judgments he makes? Explain your answer with examples from the essay.
2. As part of his evaluation, Turan compares this movie to other Harry Potter films, such as *The Prisoner of Azkaban* and *Deathly Hallows—Part 1.* Why does he use this technique? Is it effective? Why or why not?
3. Rather than summarizing his main points in a traditional manner, the author concludes by mentioning the image of Voldemort "pointing the all-powerful Elder Wand to the sky and creating . . . the Warner Bros. logo." Is this an effective conclusion for the article? Why or why not?

Writing Suggestions

1. Write a review of one of the Harry Potter movies. Select several criteria for your evaluation, such as the characters, acting, setting, musical score, special effects, and dialogue. Use specific details and examples from the movie to support the judgments you make about each criterion.
2. For a longer project, read one of the Harry Potter books and write an evaluative essay comparing it to the movie based on the book. You might consider some of the following questions as you write your essay: Which medium is more captivating for the audience? Which version is more satisfying? Would you recommend either one to your readers? Why or why not?

ESOL Tip >

As an alternative writing suggestion, write a review of a movie or book that is famous in your native country. Be sure to translate the title to English for your instructor.

Reading and Reflection EVALUATIVE WRITING

[preview] **JAMES BERARDINELLI**, born in New Brunswick, New Jersey, is a Rotten Tomatoes–approved film critic and writes a blog called *ReelThoughts.* He has bachelor's and master's degrees in electrical engineering from the University of Pennsylvania. He is also the author of a fantasy trilogy titled *The Last Whisperer of the Gods.* Marvel comics date all the way back to 1939 with the publication of *Marvel Comics* no. 1 by Timely Comics. Since then, notable characters, such as Captain America, the Fantastic Four, Spider-Man, the Incredible Hulk, and the X-Men, have been entertaining readers and moviegoers alike. Are you a fan of the Marvel brand? If so, what are some of your favorite characters? Before reading the review, consider the qualities that you find important in a comic-based, action-packed movie. What elements do you need to be satisfied at the box office?

Review of *Black Panther*

by James Berardinelli

1 During the past year, several of the studios releasing superhero movies have upped their game, moving into new territory without tossing aside the tropes that differentiate comic book–inspired fare from its traditional action/adventure cousin. 20th Century Fox started things with *Logan,* a stylish meditation on sacrifice and mortality. DC followed with *Wonder Woman,* a celebration of kick-ass femininity. Now, along comes *Black Panther.* Although seen by some as the final lead-in to the ultimate Avengers story, this movie is much, much more. In fact, save for some plot linkage at the outset, *Black Panther* never lets on that it's even in the same universe as *Iron Man, Hulk, Thor,* and the rest. This is the closest Marvel has come to making a stand-alone tale in many years. Even *Doctor Strange* felt more connected to the larger MCU.

2 In agreeing to co-write and direct *Black Panther,* Ryan Coogler, who previously made *Fruitvale Station* and *Creed,* ensured that he would have carte blanche about how he presented T'Challa's story. While remaining faithful to the character's comic book backstory, Coogler takes the film in some unexpected directions. There's action aplenty but it's intermingled with more serious-minded and thought-provoking material. If there has ever been a more political superhero movie, I can't think of it. *Black Panther* is in-your-face with its political perspective, neither soft-peddling its allegorical aspects nor shying away from an ideology that may be controversial in some circles. The movie embraces the philosophy of inclusion, rejecting competing notions of isolation, nationalism, and imperialism. It goes so far as to use the word "fool" when describing those who would "build barriers." *Black Panther* isn't content with characters in cool costumes pummeling each other in a special effects–laden setting.

3 Although this represents the first full outing for the *Black Panther* character (who made his debut in *Captain America: Civil War*), it's more of an "introduction story" than an "origin story." Coogler's approach is similar to the one Tim Burton used in 1989's *Batman*—don't waste the audience's time

with a blow-by-blow description of how the *Black Panther* got his powers and what he initially does with them. Instead, tell a real story and sprinkle in the details along the way. It's a more satisfying method of storytelling than what we sometimes have to slog through with initial forays.

4 After a prologue, which provides background, context, and an establishing scene set in 1992, the action shifts to the modern-day. The setting is the small (fictional) East African country of Wakanda. To the rest of the world, Wakanda is mired in the third-world and, like its neighbors, struggling with poverty and a lack of resources. That image is a sham, however—an illusion maintained by Wakanda's superior technology to hide the nation's true nature from those who would plunder its most valuable resource, the mineral vibranium. The wonders of Wakanda are known only to its residents.

5 T'Challa (Chadwick Boseman) assumes the throne after the events of *Captain America: Civil War* (in which his father is killed in a terrorist bombing). Armed with technology developed by his super-scientist sister, Shuri (Letitia Wright), and accompanied by his former lover, Nakia (Lupita Nyong'o), and the head of the military, Okoye (Danai Gurira), T'Challa travels to South Korea to capture an amoral mercenary named Ulysses Klaue (Andy Serkis), who is selling vibranium on the black market. On this mission, he encounters CIA agent Everett Ross (Martin Freeman), who previously appeared in *Captain America: Civil War.* The mission to bring Klaue back to Wakanda ends in failure. T'Challa returns home not with a criminal in tow but with the critically injured Ross, who takes a bullet to save Nakia. A short time later, a stranger, Erik Killmonger, appears at Wakanda's border with an unconventional gift and a shocking story—one that allows him to challenge T'Challa in mortal combat for the right to lead Wakanda.

6 *Black Panther* is the first MCU movie to feature a black superhero as the title character. (It is not, however, the first Marvel movie with that distinction. Wesley Snipes' *Blade,* who made three appearances in the late 1990s and early 2000s, broke the "color barrier," although the cinematic superhero landscape of that era was much different.) *Black Panther* celebrates its blackness, ensuring that nearly every role—big, small, and in-between—is played by a black actor. On some level, *Black Panther* is a pushback against a Hollywood culture that shies away from "black films" made for mainstream audiences. The director takes things a step further by employing a reversal of a typical stereotype. Many white-dominated movies feature a token black character (an inclusion that allows them to claim "racial diversity"). Coogler flips this by making Martin Freeman the token white character. Aside from Freeman and Andy Serkis (old buddies from their Peter Jackson days), the only non-black actor with any noteworthy screen presence is Stan Lee, making his expected cameo. (Lee, along with Jack Kirby, created *Black Panther* in 1966.)

7 The film's chief villain, the angry and revenge-minded Killmonger, is a different sort of bad guy than what we're accustomed to getting in superhero movies. Unafflicted by megalomania, Killmonger is motivated by a personal animus and a desire to use violence and chaos to redress the worldwide oppression of black people. He intends to use the resources of Wakanda to achieve that. He is perhaps the most nuanced antagonist ever to emerge from the MCU tapestry. He is not demonized; in fact, the screenplay goes to great lengths to emphasize the tragedy of his genesis and how, were it not for the misguided actions of "good" people, he might never have become the man he became. In keeping with superhero movie expectations, there is a climactic battle between Killmonger and T'Challa but, unlike the resolution of *Wonder Woman,* it's not an anticlimax and the conclusion of the struggle is not by-the-numbers.

8 In casting *Black Panther,* the filmmakers have assembled a group of today's best young black actors, with a veteran or two thrown in for good measure. Chadwick Boseman's T'Challa is a fine addition to the MCU (something we can see now that he has more than a supporting part)—a versatile performer whose previous roles include Jackie Robinson (*42*), James Brown (*Get on Up*), and Thurgood Marshall (*Marshall*). Michael B. Jordan makes his third appearance for Coogler, following leads in *Fruitvale Station* and *Creed.* Lupita

Nyong'o, Danai Gurira, and Letitia Wright play the three strong, self-assured women who fight alongside T'Challa. Angela Bassett, as T'Challa's mother, and Forest Whitaker, as his mentor, represent an older generation. Martin Freeman and Andy Serkis help connect Black Panther to the MCU.

9 *Black Panther* is arguably the most audacious movie to emerge from the MCU to date and has to be in the conversation when considering the all-time best comic book–inspired stories. Although the structure is rooted in the superhero tradition, the production rarely feels limited by that classification. It takes us to new places and sloughs off the generic label that adheres to many films of the genre, providing an experience that is by turns exciting, emotional, and funny. This is a great motion picture—a title that will surely be remembered.

Source: James Berardinelli, "Black Panther (United States, 2018)." ReelViews, February 14, 2018, www.reelviews.net/reelviews/black-panther. Used by permission of the author.

QUESTIONS FOR REFLECTION

Considering Ideas

1. What is Berardinelli's claim (thesis) for the review of *Black Panther?* If you have seen the movie, do you agree or disagree with the claim. Why?
2. Which ideas from the review have the greatest impact on you as the reader? Why? Quote specific passages to explain your point.
3. Whether you have seen the movie or not, would you want to see it based on this review? Why or why not?

Considering the Rhetorical Star

1. What is the *subject* of the review? How thoroughly does Berardinelli cover the subject?
2. Who might the *audience* be for this review, which was originally published in *The Conversation?*
3. What is the author's main *purpose* (to inform, to interpret, to persuade, to entertain, to express feelings) for the article?
4. Berardinelli uses evaluation as the primary *strategy* for the piece. Does he employ any other writing strategies? What are they, and how do they affect the work?
5. What *design* features does this article include? Are they effective? Why or why not?

Considering Writing Strategies

1. What specific criteria does Berardinelli use to evaluate the movie? Are the criteria logical? Does he support his judgments with enough evidence to be convincing? Explain your answer using several examples from the essay.
2. At times the author compares *Black Panther* to other films. Why is that? What effect do these comparisons have on the reader?
3. Does Berardinelli provide enough supporting details for the reader to have a good concept of what the movie is? Why or why not?

Writing Suggestions

1. Write a review of another popular Marvel film. What is significant about the movie? Why is it so popular? Do you feel it will be popular for many years to come, or is it just a passing trend?
2. Find a current image of popular art, such as an album cover, video game cover, or movie poster that you find appealing (or unappealing). Write an essay evaluating why it is appropriate (or inappropriate). Judge the image using several criteria. You might consider how well it fits with the media it is intended to support. Does it make consumers want to buy the product or see the movie? Or is it a turn-off. You will need to include a copy of the image with your essay so your readers can judge it for themselves.

Reading and Reflection EVALUATIVE WRITING

Kevin Mazur/Getty Images

[preview] **CRAIG JENKINS** is a pop music critic for *New York Magazine* and *Vulture* (where the following article originally appeared) and has written for *Pitchfork, Billboard,* the *New York Times, NoisyMusic, Spin,* and other publications. He studied English at Gordon College in Massachusetts and is a resident of New York City. The following review is of Ariana Grande's *Sweetener,* her third number one album on the U.S. *Billboard 200.* Grande is a Florida-born singer, songwriter, and actress who performed in the Broadway musical *13,* played the role of Cat Valentine in the Nickelodeon television series *Victorious*, and took numerous other roles on camera and as a voice actress in animated television and films. To learn more about Ariana Grande, go to **arianagrande.com**. If possible, listen to or watch the video for "No Tears to Cry," "R.E.M." or another song on the album before reading the review. Also, think of some of your favorite albums. What criteria do you use to evaluate music?

The Quirky Beauty of Ariana Grande's *Sweetener*
by Craig Jenkins

We've all had a wild year, but Ariana Grande might've had the wildest. Since last spring, the Floridian singer with the outsize voice had her world rocked by a terror attack at her arena show in Manchester. Just two weeks later, she made a brave return to the stage for an uplifting performance at One Love Manchester, a star-studded benefit for victims of the bombing and their families. Her romance with the rapper Mac Miller fizzled out, and she later revealed that she was dating *Saturday Night Live*'s Pete Davidson, and that the new romance had quickly bloomed into an engagement. Just a few months later, the singer is back with album number four. On this month's new *Sweetener,* Grande spices up the expected array of Max Martin, ILYA, and TB Hits productions that netted platinum certifications for *Yours Truly, My Everything,* and *Dangerous Woman* with a half-dozen quirky beats from Pharrell. The shift in personnel lends the new album a deeper R&B cred than the three before it, and that gives the singer ample opportunity to gush about falling in love.

2 *Sweetener* is serious enough in its commitment to break with the traditions of Ariana Grande albums to serve three big, weird Pharrell collaborations right up front. "Blazed" is textbook Skateboard P, all funky, ascending keys, and busy percussion. "The Light Is Coming" features a capable Nicki Minaj guest rap and chiptune affectations, and shifting tempos reminiscent of the last N.E.R.D. album, *No One Ever Really Dies.* "R.E.M." remakes a five-year-old Beyoncé demo, keeping the original song's gorgeous doo-wop vocals but easing off of the hip-hop verses. It's a bold sequence of songs because Ari albums have a tendency of dropping two megaton hit records by track four (and because the last person to schedule this many Pharrell beats on the same album was Justin Timberlake, who didn't do such a great job of it). *Sweetener* is an exercise in world-building. It's as interested in piecing together a breezy, gregarious mood as it is in crafting hits. There's no EDM banger until "No Tears Left to Cry" at track ten, and it's the only one on the album. As a lead single, it's a delectable fakeout, a promise

of dance-floor heat the record has very little intention of delivering. A few fans of Ariana Grande's dance-pop hits are seething this week.

3 Anchoring this album in the jazzy chords, wonky synth tones, and offbeat samples Pharrell favors gives it a more playful and adventurous energy than the mechanized radio pop Ariana usually gets from all the in-demand pop and EDM beatmakers. The singer's voice is a joy in this setting—in any setting. Elastic vocal runs and delightful harmonies make this batch of lyrics about the ups and downs of a whirlwind romance seem all the more lived in, and Pharrell matches the energy on cuts like the title track, which outfits Ariana's food/sex double entendres with an ad-lib track that sounds like someone scoffing at them in real time, and "Successful," whose drum programming includes a track of sensual, rhythmic breathing. Other collaborators match his methodology. On "God Is a Woman," "Better Off," and "Goodnight n Go," ILYA, Hit-Boy, and TB Hits use kick drums as melodic instruments in the same way P's production on the title track (and a few on the Timberlake album) does. Working with producers who have very specific signature sounds, like Pharrell and the mid-tempo disco-beat tactician Max Martin, sometimes means struggling to come out with a product greater than the sum of its highly recognizable parts; Ariana, a bubbly singer with chops beyond her years, doesn't have this problem.

4 The baking metaphor—of becoming sweeter after life brings you the bitter taste of salt—powering the title track serves as a mission statement for the whole album. Ariana's happy, and she intends to pass the feeling along to anyone who'll listen. The album's not all confections and kisses though; cohabitation and companionship are rewarding, but they also require work. *Sweetener*'s flow between songs about desire and songs about the attendant stresses of making a relationship work feel natural to the dizzying sensation of falling for someone and finding a routine for living that appeases both parties. The album's not afraid to talk about working out the kinks: "Everytime" perches on the point where attraction threatens to become obsession; in "Breathin" and "Get Well Soon," the singer coaches herself through anxiety attacks and fears about her future.

5 This is a confessional album when it comes to matters of the heart, but if you dive into *Sweetener* thinking the calm-after-the-storm conceit of "No Tears Left to Cry" suggested an album about overcoming tragedy, that's not the spirit of the thing. We hear a lot about Ariana being in a good place and working hard to stay there, but not so much about how she got there. *Sweetener* offers gourmet parfait, when some listeners might have expected steak. This isn't a knock against the quality of the music; it's perhaps unfair to make the soul-searching honesty of albums like Bey's *Lemonade* or Kesha's *Rainbow* the bar for how a pop star processes trying times and approaches the business of returning to work afterward. What counts is that Ariana Grande seems at peace after what looked like a rough patch, and *Sweetener* lives up to its name as a heartening dip into the sights, tastes, and smells of blossoming romance.

Source: Craig Jenkins, "The Quirky Beauty of Ariana Grande's *Sweetener*," *Vulture*, August 20, 2018, www.vulture.com/2018/08/review-ariana-grande-sweetener-album.html.

QUESTIONS FOR REFLECTION

Considering Ideas

1. Jenkins compares Ariana Grande's music to that of other artists. Do these comparisons help the reader to understand his assessment of Ariana Grande? Why or why not?
2. The author includes several song titles in his essay. How does this affect you as the reader? Are you familiar with any of them? Could you hear the lyrics in your head as you read the song titles?
3. What is Jenkins's overall evaluation of Ariana Grande's album *Sweetener?* Is his claim convincing? Why or why not?

Considering the Rhetorical Star

1. What is the *subject* of Jenkins's review? How thoroughly does he cover the subject?
2. Who might the *audience* be for this review, which was originally published in *Vulture?*

3. What is the author's main *purpose* (to inform, to interpret, to persuade, to entertain, to express feelings) for the review?
4. Jenkins uses evaluation as the primary *strategy* for the piece. Does he employ any other writing strategies? What are they, and how do they affect the work?
5. What *design* features does this article include? Are they effective? Why or why not?

Considering Writing Strategies

1. Which sentence is his thesis? Is it effective? Why or why not?
2. What set of criteria does Jenkins use to evaluate the album. Are these criteria effective? Why or why not?
3. Does the author provide enough supporting details for the reader to have a good concept of what the album is? Why or why not?

Writing Suggestions

1. Write a review of a new album by one of your favorite artists or groups. You may want to compare it with a previous album by the same group to give your audience a clearer understanding of the new one. Be sure to base your evaluation on clear criteria and include specific supporting examples from the songs on the album to back up your judgments.
2. Find a review of a concert or other performance that you have attended. Write an essay agreeing or disagreeing with the author's evaluation. Support your view with specific details from the performance. Be sure to cite the original source as appropriate. (See Chapters 13–14 for details about citing sources using the MLA and APA formats.)

Reading and Reflection EVALUATIVE WRITING

[preview] **MAY SWENSON (1913–1989),** for whom English was a second language, was born in Logan, Utah, to parents who were Swedish immigrants. She earned a degree from Utah State College before moving to New York, where she wrote and published extensive volumes of poetry and held several positions including stenographer, ghost writer, and manuscript reader. She received numerous honors and fellowships throughout her career and served as a Chancellor of the Academy of American Poets. The following poem is a critique of James Bond movies in general, rather than a formal review of a specific one. Before reading, think about any James Bond movies you have seen. What do they have in common with one another? Also, what is their appeal to a mainstream audience?

The James Bond Movie
by May Swenson

The popcorn is greasy, and I forgot to bring a Kleenex.
A pill that's a bomb inside the stomach of a man inside

The Embassy blows up. Eructations of flame, luxurious
cauliflowers giganticize into motion. The entire 29-ft.

screen is orange, is crackling flesh and brick bursting,
blackening, smithereened. I unwrap a Dentyne and, while

jouncing my teeth in rubber tongue-smarting clove, try
with the 2-inch-wide paper to blot butter off my fingers.

A bubble-bath, room-sized, in which 14 girls, delectable
and sexless, twist-topped Creamy Freezes (their blond,

red, brown, pinkish, lavendar or silver wiglets all
screwed that high, and varnished), scrub-tickle a lone

male, whose chest has just the right amount and distribution
of curly hair. He's nervously pretending to defend

his modesty. His crotch, below the waterline, is also
below the frame—but unsubmerged all 28 slick foamy boobs.

Their makeup fails to let the girls look naked. Caterpillar
lashes, black and thick, lush lips glossed pink like

the gum I pop and chew, contact lenses on the eyes that are
mostly blue, they're nose-perfect replicas of each other.

I've got most of the grease off and onto this little square
of paper. I'm folding it now, making creases with my nails.

Source: May Swenson, "The James Bond Movie" from *New and Selected Things Taking Place* (Boston: Atlantic/Little Brown, 1978). Copyright © 1978 by May Swenson. Reprinted with the permission of The Literary Estate of May Swenson; www.poetryfoundation.org/poems/48376/the-james-bond-movie.

QUESTIONS FOR REFLECTION

Considering Ideas

1. Swenson writes about her experience in the movie theater as well as the movie itself. Why does she do that? What effect does it have on the reader?
2. The author includes several examples of scenes from James Bond movies. What do these scenes reveal?
3. What is Swenson's overall evaluation of James Bond movies? Is her interpretation convincing? Why or why not?

Considering the Rhetorical Star

1. What is the *subject* of Swenson's poem? Is this topic engaging? Why or why not?
2. Who is the intended *audience* for this poem?
3. What is the author's main *purpose* for the poem? How do you know?
4. Swenson uses evaluation as the primary *strategy* for the poem. Does she employ any other writing strategies? What are they, and how do they affect the work?
5. What is the *design* of this poem? Is it effective? Why or why not?

Considering Writing Strategies

1. Which lines from the poem provide the reader with visual imagery? How effective are these lines?
2. What is the tone of the poem? How do you know? Provide examples of words from the poem that affect the tone.
3. Does the poet provide enough supporting details for the reader to have a good concept of what the movie is about? Is it necessary for her to do so? Why or why not?

Writing Suggestions

1. Watch any James Bond movie and write a review on it. Base your review on specific criteria and back up your claims with specific details and examples from the film.
2. Write a review of a poem that has special meaning to you. You might focus on the ideas in the poem as well as the author's techniques. Be sure to support your opinions with specific examples from the poem.

STUDENT WRITING

Adventures in Crime

by Amanda Archer

1 *The Incredibles,* a Pixar Animated Studios production, is an action adventure movie filled with excitement. Although *The Incredibles* may be great fun for a family's movie and popcorn Friday night, its PG rating is perhaps not strong enough. The film opens with the local superheroes revealing their previous thoughts and feelings about their work in candid interviews. As the story progresses the audience learns that these characters have been forced into a protection program that keeps what seemed like good deeds at bay. This introduces the characters to average working class lives where the Parr family has been relocated with middle-class employment; however, underneath their average suburban life they are superheroes, or "supers" as they call themselves. The Parr family members struggle with normal everyday challenges and conceal their above average abilities from the public's eyes. The film portrays many positive values that a mature audience can glean. However, be warned that there are plenty of adult situations and undertones. Furthermore, many good deeds are accomplished with violence that will amuse adults but can negatively influence younger viewers.

2 *The Incredibles* can have educational value for the right age group; adults can interpret the characters' comments and understand what messages lie underneath. The Parr family goes through events that help them cope with their skills and find constructive outlets that help them lead as normal a life as possible. Mr. and Mrs. Parr revive their struggling marriage, and family members discover new abilities, which they use to promote teamwork and strengthen their family ties. This movie can remind viewers that it is possible to teach children morals and values through events that the family encounters. Robert Parr, who is Mr. Incredible, tries to keep his gifted wife Helen, known as Elastigirl, and their children in a recreational vehicle to keep them safe while he attempts to destroy an enemy. He tells them that he cannot let them join him because he is afraid of losing them and would not know what to do without them. Helen tells him that she will not let him fight alone and she explains that together as a family they can accomplish more. Through events that arise, each character is able to learn about the special abilities he or she possesses and use these abilities as a cooperative team. This demonstrates the value of providing support for family members.

3 From the beginning of the movie, the adult content can be overwhelming for younger viewers. The humor and sexual innuendos are definitely created to amuse and entertain an older age group. For example, in one of the opening scenes, Mr. Incredible and Elastigirl are up on a rooftop trying to determine who will receive the credit for defeating a criminal when Elastigirl makes a remark to Mr. Incredible that he needs to be more "flexible." While her comment may seem harmless, her tone of voice has a strong sexual connotation. Additionally,

the language and actions of the adult characters are constantly geared toward adults and the ability to see through what is said and read into the stereotyping of each character they meet.

4 Furthermore, the numerous acts of violence are impossible to miss. The superheroes are seemingly regular people who have taken it upon themselves to intercede for the greater good where they see fit. This involves participating in a large number of violent situations. For example, as Mr. Incredible wraps up his first good deed in the movie, to assist an elderly woman retrieve her cat from a tree, he jumps into his car and is shocked to find a child in his passenger seat. The child exclaims that he is Mr. Incredible's biggest fan and aspires to be his sidekick, Incrediboy. Mr. Parr, who dislikes the annoying boy, ejects the child from the seat, sending him into the air and over the top of the vehicle before crashing onto the ground. This scene reinforces the acceptable use of violence for amusement. Toward the end of the film, Elastigirl tries to sneak into a facility wherein she gets her body stuck in a electronic door and then uses her body as a weapon to knock out several guards and stuff them into a panel in the wall. The continual use of violence toward children as well as "bad guys" is entertaining but not beneficial for young, impressionable viewers. Young children sometimes mimic the superheroes they see on television, but these role models do not set a good example.

5 Overall, *The Incredibles* portrays several positive family values that audience members sometimes forget. However, the rating of this movie should be PG13 so that people are aware that young children should not view it without parental supervision. The humor is enjoyable for viewers who can understand the adult content and undertones throughout the script. As a result, this would be a great movie to view after young children have gone to bed for the night. So sit back, pop some popcorn, and enjoy the comic stereotyping of characters and the superheroes' zany reactions to the situations that occur.

QUESTIONS FOR REFLECTION

1. What is Archer's overall claim about the movie?
2. Is her description of the premise of the film sufficient? Why or why not?
3. What criteria does she use to evaluate the film?
4. Are her judgments fully supported? Explain.
5. What is your reaction to Archer's review? Would you watch the movie? Would you show it to a child under the age of thirteen? Why or why not?

Activity Writing an Artistic Evaluation

In pairs or small groups, choose a work of art to review. You might consider using a painting, photograph, sculpture, song, poem, comic strip, or other work that you can evaluate in a reasonably short amount of time. Work together to choose criteria for your evaluation, make a judgment about each criterion, and present an overall opinion of your subject. Your group members may share your results with the class. If possible, provide your audience with a visual image or copy of the poem or song as appropriate. This activity may give you ideas for writing an evaluative essay.

Now that you have read one or more evaluations, it's time to write your own evaluation. You may choose to write about one of the writing options that follow, the advertisement, the image, or one of the media suggestions. Additionally, keep your ears open for hot topics at school or work; you may hear a conversation that sparks your interest. You might also read through an online newspaper or magazine to find a subject to evaluate. Remember to keep track of any sources you use in case you need to cite them in your paper. Consider your rhetorical star and the qualities of effective evaluative writing as you begin to compose your assignment.

Writing Assignment Options

Use one of the following topics to write an evaluative essay.

1. A book, short story, play, poem, or website
2. A movie, documentary, or television show
3. A song, music video, or album
4. A performance, such as a concert, musical, play, opera, or ballet
5. A work of art, such as a painting, sculpture, or photograph
6. A college course or teacher
7. A job, boss, or co-worker
8. A parent, friend, or significant other
9. A weekend trip or vacation
10. The dining experience at a particular restaurant

Multimodal Assignment

Using one of the readings, writing assignment options, or another topic, create a multimodal project using the evaluative writing strategy and at least two or more of the options in Table 11.1.

Table 11.1

Multimodal Options		
Artifact	Images	PowerPoint
Artwork	Infographics	Prezi
Audio clip	Journal	Video
Blog	Montage	Website
Digital portfolio	Podcast	Wiki
Graphic organizer	Poster	Writing

(See Chapter 15 for more details about multimodal compositions.)

Interpreting an Advertisement

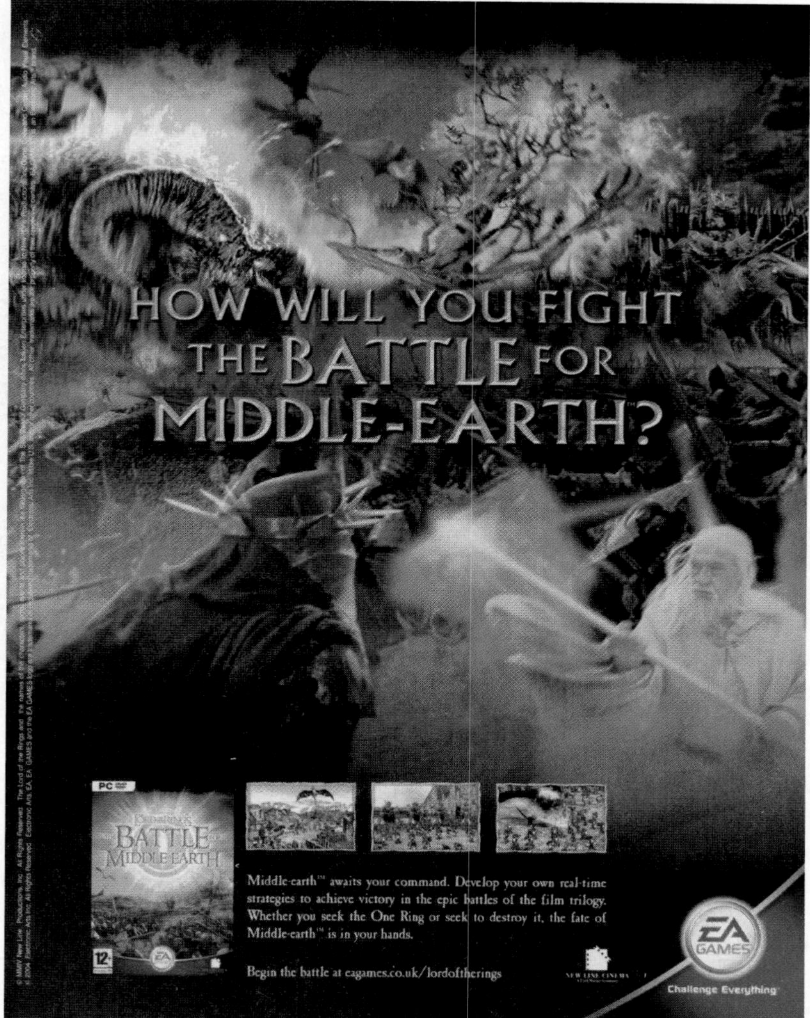

The Advertising Archives

This advertisement depicts "The Lord of the Rings: The Battle for Middle-earth" video game. What effect does the artwork have on you? Is it intriguing? Repulsive? What kind of audience might be interested in the game? If you are a gamer, would you consider buying this game based on the advertisement? Why or why not? Write an essay evaluating this advertisement or another video game advertisement. Base your evaluation on several specific criteria. Consider what needs to be included in an effective advertisement to persuade a gamer to purchase the game.

Writing about an Image

Starry Night by Vincent van Gogh
Antiquarian Images/Alamy Images

Write an essay evaluating an image from this book or from another source. You might start by describing the photograph or painting. Rather than merely focusing on likes and dislikes, evaluate your subject using several criteria that make sense for it. You might consider whether the subject has value as a work of art and why it is worthy of being called art. For example, you might listen to Josh Groban's version of the song "Vincent," look at Vincent van Gogh's painting *Starry Night,* and write your own evaluation of the painting based on specific criteria, such as use of color, shading, and composition.

Media Connection for Evaluating

You might watch, read, and/or listen to one or more of the suggested media listed in Table 11.2 to discover additional examples of evaluation. Exploring various media may help you to better understand methods of evaluating. You may choose to write about one or more of the media suggestions. For example, you might watch an episode of *The X Factor* and evaluate one of the contestants for musical ability, showmanship, and rapport with the audience. Be sure to give credit to any sources you use in your essay.

Table 11.2

Media Chart				
Television	*The X Factor*	*Dancing with the Stars*	*The Voice*	*America's Got Talent*
Film	*Rock of Ages* (2012)	The *Harry Potter* series (2001–2011)	*No Time to Die* (2020)	*Incredibles 2* (2018)
Print/ E-Reading	*Consumer Reports*	*Entertainment Weekly*	*Rolling Stone*	*The Artist's Magazine*
Internet	**metacritic.com**	**nybooks.com**	**rottentomatoes .com**	**music-critic.com**
Music	"Performance Evaluation" by Cocoa Tea	"Vincent (Starry, Starry Night)" by Josh Groban	"Mona Lisa" by Grant-Lee Phillips	"Skyfall" by Adele

11.4 Analyzing the Rhetorical Star for Writing an Evaluation

As you prepare to write your evaluation, consider the five points of the rhetorical star (Figure 11.1). You might use some of the questions in the chart as you conduct your rhetorical star analysis.

FIGURE 11.1 The Rhetorical Star

Subject	Choose a topic that interests you to evaluate. You might write a review related to film and the arts, such as a review of a movie, television show, book, song, or piece of art. If you choose a movie or television show to evaluate, you will want to record it, if possible, so that you can watch it more than once if necessary. You could also look through an art book or online art museum to find a suitable topic. You may choose to evaluate something school related, such as a class or textbook. Another option is to write an evaluation of a work-related subject, such as your boss or work environment. Be sure to select a topic that you feel qualified to evaluate.

Audience	Who will read your evaluation? What will interest your readers about your subject? Are you offering your readers advice about what to watch, read, or listen to? Do you intend for your audience to do something based on your evaluation, or do you just want your readers to understand your position? Think about what kinds of details would be most appropriate to share with your audience.
Purpose	Determine what you are trying to accomplish through your evaluation. If you saw a movie or show that you loved, you might write a review convincing others to view it. Maybe your goal is to simply inform others about a fantastic website that is educational or entertaining. On the other hand, you might want to persuade your audience to take a particular class or go to a specific concert or play.
Strategy	Even if your primary goal is to evaluate your subject, you may decide to use additional writing strategies as well. For example, if you are evaluating a new movie, you might compare and contrast it with an older version of the movie or with a similar movie. If you are evaluating a problem, you may come up with possible solutions for the problem and argue that a particular solution is the most effective.
Design	How many criteria do you need to use to fully support your evaluation of your subject? Also, what other design details, such as photographs or charts, might enhance your evaluation? Will you use some kind of symbol or rating system to make your evaluative criteria clear for the reader?

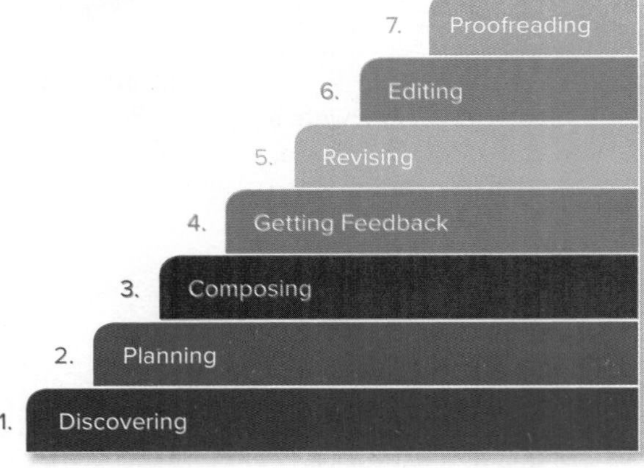

FIGURE 11.2 The Seven Steps of the Writing Process

11.5 Applying the Writing Process for Evaluating

After you have completed your rhetorical star analysis, follow the steps of the writing process (Figure 11.2) to compose your evaluation.

1. **Discovering:** Once you have chosen a topic, you might make a list of criteria to consider for your evaluation. You could even create a checklist or graphic organizer to help you analyze your subject. (See Figure 11.3.)
2. **Planning:** Decide which criteria you want to use for your evaluation.

Create a cluster or an outline (informal or formal) to help you organize your ideas. Because evaluative writing needs to be persuasive, you might save your strongest point for last. Doing so will make your most convincing criterion more memorable for your audience.

3. **Composing:** Write a first draft of your evaluation. Remember to focus each body paragraph on one main criterion that relates to your overall opinion about your subject. Don't worry too much about grammar and punctuation at this time. Use the qualities outlined earlier in the chapter:
    1. Describe the subject being evaluated.
    2. Make a claim about the subject.
    3. Use several specific criteria for the evaluation.
    4. Make a fair judgment about each criterion.
    5. Support each judgment with specific evidence.
    6. End with a final claim about your subject.

Subject:

Criteria	Support
1.	
2.	
3.	
4.	
5.	

Evaluating

FIGURE 11.3 Graphic Organizer for Evaluation

4. **Getting feedback:** Have at least one classmate or other person read your rough draft and answer the peer review questions on page 298. If you have access to a writing tutor or center, get another opinion about your paper as well.
5. **Revising:** Using all of the feedback available to you, revise your evaluation. Make sure that your evaluation is based on specific criteria and that you have fully supported each judgment that you make. Additionally, make sure that your essay is unified. In other words, every judgment you make needs to help support the opinion in your thesis (your claim). Add, delete, and rearrange ideas as necessary.
6. **Editing:** Read your evaluation again, this time looking for errors in grammar, punctuation, and mechanics. Pay particular attention to your consistency with verb tenses. Generally it is best to use the present verb tense when discussing your subject. For example, write that the artist, filmmaker, or author "captivates" the audience rather than "captivated" the audience.
7. **Proofreading:** After you have carefully edited your essay, read it one last time. Look for typographical errors and any other issues that might interfere with the readers' understanding of your evaluation.

PEER REVIEW QUESTIONS FOR EVALUATING

Trade rough drafts with a classmate and answer the following questions about his or her paper. Then, in person or online, discuss your papers and suggestions with your peer. Finally, make the changes you feel would most benefit your paper.

1. Has the author described the subject being evaluated clearly and effectively without giving away too much?
2. Is the author's claim (thesis) clear? What is the author's overall opinion about the subject?
3. What are the author's criteria for evaluating the subject? Do these criteria seem appropriate? Why or why not?
4. Has the author stated a clear judgment about each criterion? What are the judgments? Are they fair? Why or why not?
5. Is each judgment supported with specific details and examples? Is there enough support?
6. Is the concluding paragraph effective? Why or why not?
7. What kinds of grammatical errors, if any, are evident in the evaluation?
8. What final suggestions do you have for the author?

Writer's Checklist for Evaluating

Use the checklist below to evaluate your own writing and help ensure that your evaluation is effective. If you have any "no" answers, go back and work on those areas if necessary.

- ☐ 1. Have I included a clear description of the subject I am evaluating?
- ☐ 2. Does my thesis clearly state my opinion of the subject I am evaluating?
- ☐ 3. Have I used effective criteria to evaluate my subject?
- ☐ 4. Have I made a clear and fair judgment about each evaluative criterion?
- ☐ 5. Have I supported each judgment with specific details and examples?
- ☐ 6. Have I ended with an effective conclusion?
- ☐ 7. Have I proofread thoroughly?

CHAPTER SUMMARY

1. Use the evaluative writing strategy to make a judgment about one or more subjects.
2. Evaluative writing is an important part of your education, daily life, and career.
3. Carefully analyze the rhetorical star before writing an evaluation: subject, audience, purpose, strategy, and design.
4. Interpreting evaluative readings and images can help you to prepare to write an evaluation.

5. Use these qualities when writing an evaluation essay: describe the subject being evaluated; make a claim about the subject; use several specific criteria for the evaluation; make a fair judgment about each criterion; support each judgment with specific evidence; end with a final claim about the subject you are evaluating.

WHAT I KNOW NOW

Use this checklist to determine what you need to work on to feel comfortable with your understanding of the material in this chapter. Check off each item as you master it. Review the material for any unchecked items.

- ☐ 1. I know what **evaluative writing** is.
- ☐ 2. I can identify several **real-world applications** for writing evaluations.
- ☐ 3. I can evaluate **readings and images** about film and the arts.
- ☐ 4. I can analyze the **rhetorical star** for writing an evaluation.
- ☐ 5. I understand the **writing process** for writing an evaluation.
- ☐ 6. I can apply the **six qualities** of an evaluation.

Design elements: *Graduate Spotlight:* Ingram Publishing/AGE Fotostock

CHAPTER 12 Solving a Problem: Crime and Justice

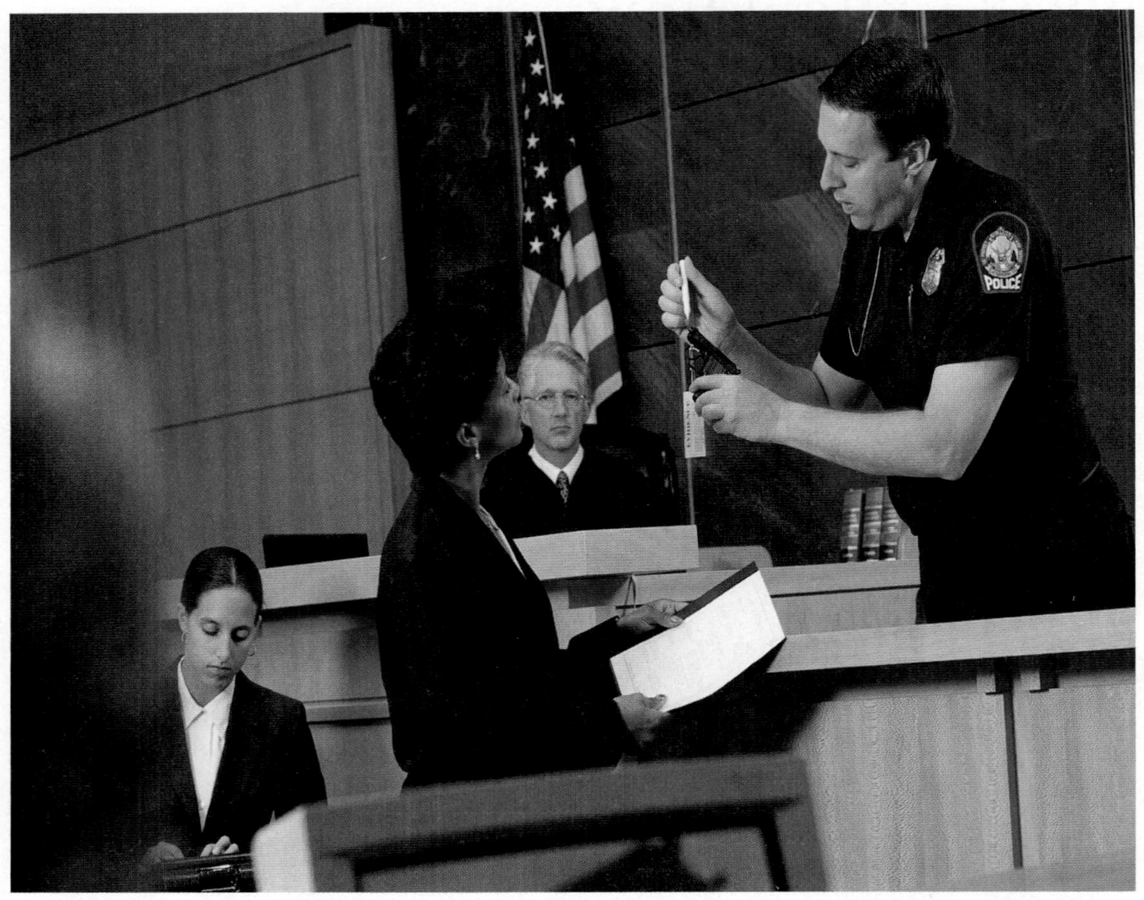

Digital Stock/Corbis/Getty Images

learning outcomes

In this chapter you will learn techniques for achieving these learning outcomes:

12.1 Identify real-world applications for solving a problem. *p. 301*

12.2 Understand the qualities of problem-solving writing. *p. 303*

12.3 Interpret images and problem-solving readings about crime and justice. *p. 307*

12.4 Analyze the rhetorical star for solving a problem. *p. 332*

12.5 Apply the qualities of problem-solving writing. *p. 334*

Writing Strategy Focus: Solving a Problem

You don't have to look far to find problems that need to be solved. Instead of just complaining about a problem, you can attempt to do something about it. What can you do to help mitigate a problem? One way to initiate change is to write about the problem and offer one or more solutions. If you don't know the answer to a problem, then you can investigate to see what you can learn about the situation. You might conduct research to find an answer to the problem. As always, you will need to document any sources that you use for your paper.

12.1 Real-World Applications for Solving a Problem

Writing to Solve a Problem in College

You may be asked to write problem-solving papers in your college courses. In an environmental science course, your instructor may ask you to propose solutions for reducing our dependency on gasoline. Your sociology instructor might assign a paper requiring you propose a solution for a social issue, such as juvenile delinquency or domestic violence. In a course in your major, you may need to write about solutions for improving the public's awareness of an important issue, such as breast cancer, computer piracy, or identity theft.

Writing to Solve a Problem in Your Daily Life

Proposing solutions to problems is also important in your personal life. You might need to come up with a solution for managing your time if you are working and going to school full-time. If you and your roommate or significant other have difficulty in deciding who is responsible for certain tasks at home, then you might solve the problem by writing a proposal for an equitable way to divide the chores. If you are having trouble making your finances stretch as far as they need to, then you might solve the problem by drafting a proposed budget for covering all expenses.

Writing to Solve a Problem in Your Career

Being able to write an effective **proposal** is extremely useful in the workplace. You could suggest solutions to upper-level management that would improve working conditions and morale. Your employer may assign you to write a proposal for solutions that would cut expenses, increase profits, and save jobs. Furthermore, you might need to write a problem-solving report proposing to implement a new program or procedure in your office. Here are some additional ideas for problem-solving writing on the job:

Proposal A plan put forward for consideration by others.

Health care: proposals for purchasing new equipment, implementing a new clinical procedure, or providing better health care coverage.

Graduate SPOTLIGHT

Ken Prosper, Corrections Officer

Ken Prosper is a corrections officer for a county jail. He is a graduate of the corrections academy at a community college. Here's what Prosper has to say about the significance of writing in his career:

Ken Prosper

"In my career, I have to write on a daily basis. The most critical reports are incident reports because they are public record and can be used in a court of law. For example, if the state presses charges against an inmate for criminal activity, the report has to be extremely detailed to win the case. Conversely, if an inmate accuses an innocent officer of using undue force, the report can help to prove the officer's innocence. I also write daily logs, witness statements, and other documents. Writing is so important in this field that officers earn extra compensation for completing college level writing courses. Being an effective writer is crucial to my job security and advancement."

Law: proposals for reducing crime, improving security, or changing crime scene investigation procedures.

Business: proposals for increasing productivity, personnel, and profits.

Education: proposals for increasing student retention or raising funds for a field trip or a new computer lab.

Computers: proposals for updating software, strengthening network connectivity, or upgrading hardware.

Massage therapy: proposals for gaining more clients, improving supplies and equipment, or creating a more appealing ambience.

Culinary arts: proposals for increasing the customer base, changing the menu, or improving sanitation.

Activity Writing to Solve a Problem in the Real World

In pairs or small groups, brainstorm uses for problem-solving writing at school, in your daily life, and on the job. You may want to choose the prospective career field(s) of the participants in your group. Each group may share its results with the class.

12.2 Qualities of Effective Problem-Solving Writing

1. Identify a Problem and Demonstrate That It Exists

Because solutions to problems are often intended to be persuasive, you might delay your claim a little bit so that your reader will be more likely to believe that there is a problem that needs to be addressed. First, you will need to explain what the problem is and prove that it is real. Provide details, examples, a brief narrative, or statistics to convince your audience that there really is a problem. For example, if you are writing about the vandalism in your apartment complex, you might begin by describing specific incidents that have occurred. Maybe Mr. Montana in apartment 27B discovered graffiti on his front door last week, and Ms. Lively in apartment 35C found broken beer bottles and rotten eggs on her terrace yesterday.

2. Appeal to Your Audience

Make the problem relevant to the audience so that they will care about the situation. For instance, if your audience is the other tenants in the complex, then you could point out that they could be targeted next if they don't help to solve the problem. If your audience consists of leaders in the community, you might suggest that if they ignore the vandalism, then the crimes may escalate into something more serious or become more widespread.

3. State Your Claim

Your thesis might claim that a problem exists and assert that something needs to be done about it. Another option is to claim that a particular solution or combination of solutions is the way to solve the problem. For example, your claim might be that your apartment complex needs to implement a better security system because of all the crime that has been occurring lately.

4. Propose One or More Solutions to the Problem

You might focus on one main solution, several potential solutions, or a combination of solutions. By analyzing several potential solutions, you can show the readers that you have thoroughly investigated ways to solve the problem. Even if you settle on one primary solution, you should acknowledge that other possible solutions exist. For example, one way to help prevent vandalism from occurring in your apartment complex is to hire more security. Another possible solution is to organize a neighborhood watch program. A third solution might be to set up surveillance cameras in an attempt to discourage vandals and catch anyone who causes trouble. You can weigh the pros and cons of each solution and then propose the best one(s).

George Doyle & Ciaran Griffin/Superstock

By considering alternative solutions, you can show readers that you have carefully considered a variety of options. You can then refute options except for the solution or combination of solutions you feel would best solve the problem. For instance, although hiring additional security guards might be effective, maybe that solution would be too expensive. Additionally, even though setting up a neighborhood watch system sounds like a good idea, maybe that wouldn't work well for your neighborhood because the vandalism happens during the day when most of the residents are at work or school. Finally, you might argue that setting up surveillance cameras is the best solution because it is fairly cost effective, and visible cameras would deter potential vandals from causing trouble. If an incident occurs, the apartment supervisor could easily review a video recording and provide it to the police.

5. Organize Your Solution(s) Effectively

You have several options for organizing your paper. Table 12.1 outlines two possibilities. Option A takes an inductive approach, where you state your proposal up front and then support it. On the other hand, Option B uses the deductive method, where you explain the problem and possible solutions before proposing a final solution. You may apply these options in various ways.

Grammar Window

COLONS

Sometimes writers use colons incorrectly when providing a list for the reader. The general rule is that a complete sentence must precede a colon that introduces a list.

Incorrect colon usage: Three ways to help prevent home invasions are: to install an alarm system, use deadbolt locks, and get a guard dog.

Correct colon usage: Three ways to help prevent home invasions are as follows: install an alarm system, use deadbolt locks, and get a guard dog.

Discussion: In the incorrect example, an incomplete sentence precedes the colon. Another option is to simply remove the colon between the words *are* and *to install.*

Activity: Insert colons where appropriate in the following sentences. Some sentences may not need a colon.

1. Writing research papers helps students to use higher-level critical thinking skills such as application, analysis, and synthesis.
2. The following items are needed for research paper writers to avoid plagiarism direct quotes for exact wording, in-text citations, and a reference or works-cited page.
3. A few of the details that typically need to be included on a reference or works-cited page are the author's name, the title of the work, and the publication date.
4. Students who get caught plagiarizing usually receive one or more of the following consequences failure of the assignment, failure of the class, and/or expulsion from school.
5. The following are suggestions to help students to avoid plagiarism following their instructor's directions, writing their own papers, and properly documenting all sources used.

6. Persuade Your Audience That Your Solution or Solutions Are Feasible and Worthwhile

Once you have made your claim about the best solution or combination of solutions for the problem, you will need to persuade your reader that your solution is necessary and workable. Illustrate how the proposal will work and/or suggest what could happen if nothing is done about the problem. If it is appropriate for your subject and assignment, you may be able to use personal knowledge and experience to support your essay.

Most proposals to solve problems, however, need to be backed up with evidence that you obtain by conducting research. Citing specific statistics, details, and examples will help to make your proposal more credible for the readers. For example, if one of your solutions is to install security cameras in your apartment building, then you might include statistics about the effectiveness of using security cameras from a reliable source. If you do use outside sources, you will need to document them appropriately. Be sure to avoid logical fallacies (see Chapter 10) in your reasoning.

7. End with a Call to Action

You might conclude your essay by summarizing the problem and solution(s). You may also want to encourage your readers to take action to help solve the problem. Your call to action can take several forms. You might ask the readers to write a letter, get involved, or donate money to help solve the problem.

You might even suggest what the consequences might be if nothing is done to alleviate the problem. However, avoid making idle threats or exaggerating the possible implications of inaction.

Table 12.1

Organizational Patterns for Solving a Problem	
Option A	**Option B**
Introduction and claim (thesis)	Introduction and explanation of problem
Explanation of problem	Solution one—evaluate pros and cons
Proposed solution	Solution two—evaluate pros and cons
Support for proposed solution	Solution three—evaluate pros and cons
Conclusion	Conclusion and final recommendation

Career-Based PROBLEM-SOLVING WRITING

[preview] **THE NATIONAL CENTER FOR INJURY PREVENTION AND CONTROL (NCIPC) AND THE CENTERS FOR DISEASE CONTROL AND PREVENTION (CDC)** authored the following excerpt from a 61-page technical package about juvenile crime. The report is based on 10 years of research and 260 cited sources.

Have you ever wondered what to do about juvenile crime? Teens may turn to violence and crime for a number of reasons. Perhaps criminal activity among today's youth can be decreased by developing a plan of action. Go to **www.cdc.gov/violenceprevention/pdf/yv-technicalpackage.pdf** if you would like to see the entire report.

From A Comprehensive Technical Package for the Prevention of Youth Violence and Associated Risk Behaviors
by the NCIPC and the CDC

Contextual and Cross-Cutting Themes

The strategies and approaches included in this technical package represent different levels of the social ecology, with efforts intended to impact individual behaviors and also the relationships, families, schools, and communities that influence risk and protective factors for youth violence. The strategies and approaches are intended to work in combination and reinforce each other to prevent youth violence in a comprehensive and long-term way (see box below). While individual skills are important and research has demonstrated the preventive effects of many youth skill development programs, approaches addressing relationships with parents, peers, and other caring adults as well as approaches that influence school and community environments are equally important to have the greatest public health impact.

Preventing Youth Violence

Strategy	Approach
Promote family environments that support healthy development	• Early childhood home visitation • Parenting skill and family relationship programs
Provide quality education early in life	• Preschool enrichment with family engagement
Strengthen youth's skills	• Universal school-based programs
Connect youth to caring adults and activities	• Mentoring programs • After-school programs
Create protective community environments	• Modify the physical and social environment • Reduce exposure to community-level risks • Street outreach and community norm change
Intervene to lessen harms and prevent future risk	• Treatment to lessen the harms of violence exposures • Treatment to prevent problem behavior and further involvement in violence • Hospital-community partnerships

The social and cultural context of communities and organizations is critically important to take into account when selecting strategies and approaches for implementation. Practitioners in the field may be in the best position to assess the needs and strengths of their communities and work with partners to make decisions about the combination of approaches included here that are best suited to their context. Data-driven strategic prevention planning models, such as *Communities That Care (CTC)*, *PROmoting School-community-university Partnerships to Encourage Resiliency (PROSPER)*, and the *Cardiff Violence Prevention Partnership*, can support communities in using data to assess local risks and protective factors to inform the selection and ongoing monitoring of evidence-based programs. These data-driven partnerships and activities can contribute to significant reductions in violence, violence-related injuries, and crime as well as cost savings for the medical, educational, and justice systems.

Source: Centers for Disease Control and Prevention.

QUESTIONS FOR REFLECTION

1. What problem is identified? Is the problem significant? Why or why not?
2. Who is the primary audience for the report? How do you know? Who else might be interested in reading it?
3. What solutions does the technical packet propose? Which solution or solutions do you feel would work best to solve the problem? Why?
4. Problem solving is the primary writing strategy of the report. What other writing strategies are used?
5. What do you think of the design of the report? Is it appealing and effective? Why or why not?

12.3 Solving a Problem in the Context of Crime and Justice

If you pay any attention to the news media, you are constantly reminded of problems related to crime and injustice in our society. When you go online, listen to the radio, watch television, or read a newspaper or magazine, you will often come across stories about criminal activity, such as murders, domestic violence, drug trafficking, and home invasions. You will also be exposed to reports of injustices, such as people being treated unfairly because of their race, gender, beliefs, or values. As you are discussing the readings and images in this chapter, think about what is right or fair as you work toward proposing solutions to problems. In the words of Dr. Martin Luther King Jr., "Injustice anywhere is a threat to justice everywhere."

Reading and Reflection PROBLEM-SOLVING WRITING

[preview] **LEE E. BERLIK** is the founder of the award-winning firm BerlikLaw in Virginia. In the following article, from the *Virginia Defamation Law Blog*, Berlik discusses a problem experienced by employees at a sheriff's office in Virginia because

of what they "liked" on Facebook. After this article was published, the federal court ruled that Facebook "liking" is protected free speech. Before reading the article, consider the following: Are you a Facebook user? Do you sometimes hit the "like" button to show your support for a site or cause? Would it seem fair to you to be penalized at work for something you "liked" on Facebook?

Facebook "Likes" Not Protected Speech, Says Virginia Court by Lee E. Berlik

1 Think twice before clicking that Facebook "like" button. You may think you're expressing a constitutionally protected right to express support for a political candidate, for which you cannot be terminated, but Judge Raymond A. Jackson of the Eastern District of Virginia recently ruled that merely "liking" a candidate on Facebook is not sufficiently substantive to warrant First Amendment protection. Expect this ruling to get appealed.

2 Sheriff B.J. Roberts of the Hampton sheriff's office was up for re-election when he learned that several of his employees were actively supporting one of his opponents, Jim Adams. The employees alleged that Sheriff Roberts learned of their support of Adams because they "liked" Adams's Facebook page. They also attended a cookout with Adams and told others of their support, but there was no evidence that the sheriff was aware of these activities. One employee sported a pro-Adams bumper sticker on his car and used choice words to describe the sheriff's campaign literature in speaking with a colleague at the election booth.

3 After winning re-election, Sheriff Roberts did not retain the employees. Sheriff Roberts claimed various benign reasons for the firings, including a reduction in force and unsatisfactory work performance. The employees sued Sheriff Roberts alleging that the firings were in retaliation for exercising their right to free speech and that the sheriff had violated their right to free political association. Sheriff Roberts argued that plaintiffs had not alleged protected speech or political association and that he was entitled to qualified and sovereign immunity[1] even if plaintiffs' speech was protected.

4 To state a claim under the First Amendment for retaliatory discharge, public employees must prove that they were terminated on the basis of "speech" on a matter of public concern. Here, the court concluded that merely "liking" a Facebook page is insufficient speech to merit constitutional protection. The court examined holdings in which constitutional speech protection extended to Facebook posts, and it noted that in those cases, actual statements existed within the record. Conversely, it found, simply clicking the "like" button on a Facebook page is not the kind of substantive statement that warrants constitutional protection. Likewise, the court found that the presence of a bumper sticker supporting Adams did not constitute protected speech without any evidence that the sheriff was aware of the bumper sticker. The court also found that statements describing the sheriff's campaign literature, regardless of expletives, did not constitute protected speech because they did not address a matter of public concern but were instead descriptive of personal opinion.

5 The court also held that even if the plaintiffs' First Amendment arguments had merit, their claims would have failed anyway because the sheriff was entitled to both qualified and sovereign immunity.

[1] **Qualified and sovereign immunity** Legal doctrines that protect government officials from liability and criminal prosecution if they have unknowingly broken a law without malice.

6 As several commentators have already pointed out, this ruling seems contrary to Supreme Court precedent affording First Amendment protection to such acts as saluting a flag, refusing to salute, and wearing an armband. But I disagree with Professor Eugene Volokh, who writes that "the whole point" of the "like" button is to convey "a message of support for the thing you're liking." When you "like" a Facebook page, you get updates from the page you liked in your news feed. Therefore, "liking" a person's Facebook page may be intended as nothing more than a means of monitoring that person's public statements; it doesn't necessarily mean you like or support those statements. It will be interesting to see how the Fourth Circuit deals with this.

Source: Lee E. Berlik, "Facebook 'Likes' Not Protected Speech, Says Virginia Court," *The Virginia Defamation Law Blog*, May 6, 2012, **www.virginiadefamationlawyer.com**.

QUESTIONS FOR REFLECTION

Considering Ideas

1. What problem does Berlik identify in his blog? Do you think this is a genuine concern? Why or why not?
2. Should people who post comments or hit the "like" button on Facebook expect their information to be confidential? Why or why not?
3. Should law enforcement, school officials, or employers have the authority to punish someone for what he or she posts online under any circumstances? Explain.

Considering the Rhetorical Star

1. What is the *subject* of Berlik's article?
2. Who is the intended *audience* for the article? Explain.
3. What is Berlik's *purpose* for writing the article? Is it more informative or persuasive? Identify specific passages from the article that indicate the author's purpose.
4. What is the author's primary writing *strategy?* What other strategies does he use?
5. What is the *design* of the article? Is it effective? Why or why not?

Considering Writing Strategies

1. Although much of Berlik's blog focuses on the facts of the case, he does state his position on the issue. What is his position? Where does he most clearly state that position?
2. What is the author's purpose for writing the article? Rather than proposing solutions to the problem, he uses another tactic. What is it? Is it effective? Why or why not?
3. What evidence does Berlik give to support his point in the concluding paragraph? Is his evidence convincing? Explain.

Writing Suggestions

1. Write an essay proposing a solution for the issue that Berlik describes in his article. Is the solution to consider Facebook posts as private and off-limits to employers? Is the solution to hold employees accountable for everything they post online? Is there a compromise between the different points of view? Take a stand on the issue and convince your readers your proposed solution will work. You may want to include additional research in your essay. If you do so, be sure to cite your sources.
2. If you have your own Facebook page, think about what you have posted there. Have you included anything that would embarrass you if your classmates, instructors, or employers read it? Write an essay proposing a way to self-monitor Facebook posts. You might create hypothetical scenarios to support your thesis.

Reading and Reflection PROBLEM-SOLVING WRITING

Normana Karia/Shutterstock

[preview] **ADRIAN MOORE** is vice president at Reason Foundation, a nonprofit think tank, and lives in Sarasota, Florida. He holds a PhD in economics from the University of California and received a World Outstanding Achievement Award. **Sal Nuzzo** is the vice president of policy and director at the Center for Economic Prosperity at The James Madison Institute in Tallahassee, the state capital of Florida. Nuzzo earned his BS degree in economics with a concentration in public policy from Florida State University. Before reading, what are your thoughts on the effectiveness of detaining criminals in prison? Is prison an effective deterrent for those considering committing a crime?

Before, During, After Prison: How Florida Should Reform Criminal Justice

by Adrian Moore and Sal Nuzzo

1 In Florida, about one of every four people in prison will wind up back in prison soon after being released. We Floridians bear the cost of their new crimes, as well as the roughly $20,000 per year it costs to keep them in prison again. With almost 100,000 people in Florida prisons, this ends up making a big impact on lives and state budgets.

2 Dealing with recidivism is a serious challenge, one closely tied to figuring out who should and should not go to prison in the first place. A brilliant University of Michigan study followed criminals in the Texas system and found that time in prison actually increases the odds a criminal will commit crime again, and also increases the odds they will be unemployed and on public assistance.

3 And a Vera Institute of Justice study concluded that, at some point, more incarceration stops working and "continued growth in incarceration will prevent considerably fewer, if any, crimes than past increases did and will cost taxpayers substantially more to achieve." As well, the longest sentences result in an aged prison population, which costs taxpayers astronomically more, as many of these inmates have chronic health problems that are exacerbated by age.

4 If Florida wants to reduce crime and not just punish criminals after the fact, we have to address every facet of how we approach criminal justice. There is no silver bullet that will solve recidivism. It requires first a "continuum of care" approach that evaluates those going into the criminal-justice system right at the beginning, and works throughout their time in the system to match them with the right interventions, programs and support most likely to solve their particular problems and meet their particular needs to avoid going back to crime. In other words, you have to work with them before, during and after their time in prison. The vast majority will exit prison at some point; whether they succeed or fail to become productive members of society depends to a large extent on how well-prepared they are when they get out.

5 Fortunately, the Legislature got off to a good start. The House approved a reform bill, and the Senate is advancing a companion bill, that set up an evidence-based approach to reducing recidivism with a pilot project that tackles the process of entering someone into the criminal-justice system. The bills would require the Department of Corrections to create an assessment tool based on a wide range of data that would evaluate a person charged with a crime to help prosecutors, judges, correctional officials and parole officers consider the punishment and programming for that particular person that would most likely turn them away from returning to crime.

6 This system would be tested on a trial basis in Hillsborough, Pasco, and Pinellas counties. The pilot program would run for three years and be evaluated for effectiveness along the way.

7 Sen. Jeff Brandes, R-St. Petersburg, author of the Senate bill, told reporters this is part of "a deep dive into criminal-justice reform." To be certain, getting people who have been convicted of crime on to the right track from the start is a vital first step in attempting to reduce recidivism. And it would be an important part of Florida improving the outcomes of our criminal-justice system, not just for the benefit of ex-convicts, but for all Floridians.

Source: Adrian Moore and Sal Nuzzo. "Before, During, After Prison: How Florida Should Reform Criminal Justice." **www.jamesmadison.org/before-during-after-prison-how-florida-should-reform-criminal-justice/**. Used by permission.

QUESTIONS FOR REFLECTION

Considering Ideas

1. What problem have Moore and Nuzzo identified in the essay? Do they effectively convince the reader that the problem exists? Explain.
2. According to the authors, what are some of the reasons why extended prison stays do not work?
3. What do the authors propose as a potential solution for the problem? Do you think this solution will help? Why or why not?

Considering the Rhetorical Star

1. What is the *subject* of the article? Is the specific topic engaging? Why or why not?
2. Who is the intended *audience* for the piece? Explain.
3. What is the authors' main *purpose* (to inform, to persuade, to entertain, to express feelings) for the essay? Do they use a combination of purposes? How effective is this approach? Explain.
4. What writing *strategies* does the article reflect? How do these strategies affect the work?
5. What is the *design* of the piece? Is it effective? Why or why not?

Considering Writing Strategies

1. What is Moore and Nuzzo's claim. Where does it appear in the article? Is the placement of the claim effective? Why or why not?
2. What is the tone of the article? Identify several passages that reflect this tone.
3. In places, the authors intentionally switch to the first person point of view. Identify several passages that do this. Why effect does this approach have on the readers?

Writing Suggestions

1. Write a problem-solution essay suggesting how to reduce crime in your community.
2. Write a problem-solution essay offering one or more methods for rehabilitating prisoners. If you use research, be sure to document your sources using your instructor's preferred method. (See Chapter 14 for more details about documenting sources in the MLA and APA formats.)

Reading and Reflection PROBLEM-SOLVING WRITING

[preview] **ANDREA WOODS** is a staff attorney with the Criminal Law Reform Project and previously worked as an Equal Justice Works Fellowship attorney to implement bail reform litigation. She earned a Juris Doctor degree from Yale Law School. **PORTIA ALLEN-KYLE** is the Advocacy and Policy Counsel with the American Civil Liberties Union (ACLU) Campaign for Smart Justice. She previously served as an instructor at St. Aquinas College and at Rutgers University. Allen-Kyle earned a Juris Doctor degree from Rutgers University School of Law–Newark. The article that follows was originally published by the ACLU. Before reading the article, consider these questions: How effective is the criminal justice system in the United States? Is jail time the best punishment for most serious crimes?

America's Pretrial System Is Broken. Here's Our Vision to Fix It.

by Andrea Woods and Portia Allen-Kyle

1 Every year, millions of people are arrested, required to pay money bail they cannot afford, separated from their families and loved ones, or subjected to long periods of incarceration based on the mere accusation of a crime. This all occurs while people are presumed innocent under the law. Black and brown people, their loved ones, and those without the economic resources to thrive suffer the worst harms.

2 Yet while there is broad consensus that our money bail system is in dire need of an overhaul, difficult questions remain about how to best shape that reform. For instance, if we abolish money bail, will judges and prosecutors seek increased authority to jail people outright pending trial? This preventive detention could result in as many people—or more—languishing in jail without their day in court.

3 Further, what factors should judges consider when deciding to release or detain a person who hasn't been convicted? How much evidence must the government show before someone is put in jail awaiting further process? Can—and should—predictive algorithms based on criminal justice data play a role in these determinations?

4 The ACLU has wrestled with these questions considerably. We looked to the constitutional principles we fight for in our lawsuits every day, available empirical research, and guidance from our organizational partners and other recognized experts in the field. We co-hosted a gathering of interdisciplinary experts to explore civil rights concerns algorithmic risk assessment tools.

5 On Tuesday, the ACLU released, "A New Vision for Pretrial Justice in the United States," which describes our pretrial policy vision. We envision a country in which pretrial incarceration is all but eliminated, with at least 95 percent of all people in the criminal legal system released no later than 48 hours after arrest. We also demand adequate and robust protections for people going through the system and that for-profit actors be removed from this pretrial space.

6 Here is a big picture overview of our vision.

1. **Reduce the harms of the pretrial process.**
   7 Jurisdictions undertaking reform have to meaningfully move away from a "law and order" approach to a humanizing one. For example, when a person has work or family obligations, they should have the right to reschedule a court date without being punished. Moreover, we should evaluate closely

what we criminalize, decriminalize widely, and invest instead in community-based alternatives to incarceration.

2. **Eliminate pretrial profiteering.**

No one should make a living on the backs of 8
people being churned through the criminal legal system. We must completely abolish for-profit bail and for-profit pretrial supervision.

3. **Create a wide net of people eligible for mandatory and presumptive pre-booking release on no conditions.**

Even a day in jail causes tremendous harm and 9
negates, rather than promotes, the purposes underlying our bail system. And jurisdictions that have adopted pretrial reform are generally left with the subjectivity of judges' determinations about whom to free and whom to detain. Meanwhile, most people are likely to show up for court and pose no threat to public safety. Given these realities, we have prioritized diverting as many people as possible from jails in the first place.

4. **Facilitate speedy individualized release hearings—distinct from "detention hearings"—with necessary due process protections.**

If a person is arrested, they should proceed to 10
a hearing within 24 hours at which a judge can only impose conditions on her release, not order them jailed. Given the presumption of innocence and the fundamental right to liberty, everyone will be presumed to be released with no conditions, regardless of what they are accused of.

5. **Narrowly limit who is jailable before conviction.**

We cannot continue to assume someone is 11
dangerous and should, therefore, be in jail because they are charged with a serious crime. Detention should be the exception, not the rule. Courts should only be empowered to jail someone awaiting trial in rare cases where a person is accused of an extremely serious charge *and* the prosecutor files a motion establishing that pretrial jailing should be considered. People then need to receive a hearing, with public defenders available. There can be no shortcuts to this process.

6. **Ensure robust appeal rights and speedy trial protections**

A judge's decision to do anything other than 12
release someone outright should never be absolute. People ordered to stay in jail should be able to appeal their detention, and people released on conditions should be able to ask the court to reconsider those conditions.

7. **Do not allow actuarial algorithms to play a role in pretrial systems.**

The ACLU has significant concerns about 13
actuarial algorithms' potentially detrimental racial impact, lack of transparency, and limited predictive value. Not only do these tools not provide the specific, individualized information required to justify limiting a person's pretrial liberty, but the underlying racial bias presented in criminal justice data points makes it impossible to reconcile how existing tools operate with our vision of justice.

8. **Eliminate wealth-based discrimination.**

No one should be deprived of their liberty 14
or subjected to onerous conditions simply because they cannot obtain a sum of money. As is constitutionally required, any time bail or release conditions are considered, courts must undertake a careful examination of the person's ability to pay *any* amount.

This is a critical moment for advocates 15
to capitalize on the momentum surrounding pretrial justice and bail reform. However, it is critical to remain steadfast in our vision as we approach system change. Only through collective investment in all of the necessary components of reform can the United States have a fair and just pretrial system. We believe this better and more humane future is possible and will continue to fight towards this vision.

Source: Andrea Woods and Portia Allen-Kyle. "America's Pretrial System Is Broken: Here's Our Vision to Fix It," April 2, 2019. Used by permission of ACLU.

QUESTIONS FOR REFLECTION

Considering Ideas

1. What problem have Woods and Allen-Kyle identified in the article? Do they effectively convince the reader that the problem exists? Explain.
2. According to the authors, what are some issues related to the current pretrial system?
3. How do the authors propose to solve the problem? Do their suggestions seem viable? Why or why not?

Considering the Rhetorical Star

1. What is the *subject* of the article? Is the specific topic engaging? Why or why not?
2. Who is the intended *audience* for the piece? How do you know?
3. What is the authors' main *purpose* (to inform, to persuade, to entertain, to express feelings) for the essay? Do they use a combination of purposes? How effective is their approach? Explain.
4. What writing *strategies* do the authors use in the article? How effective are these strategies? Explain.
5. What is the *design* of the piece? Is it effective? Why or why not?

Considering Writing Strategies

1. What is the authors' claim? Where does it appear in the article? Is the placement of the claim effective? Why or why not?
2. What is the tone of the article? Identify several passages that reflect this tone.
3. The authors use headings for each section of the article. How does this organizational approach enhance the piece?

Writing Suggestions

1. Is the current criminal justice system in the Unites States fair? Write a problem-solution essay that identifies a specific problem with the legal system and offers one or more possible solutions.
2. Regarding those accused of serious crimes, Woods and Allen-Kyle state, "Detention should be the exception, not the rule." Do you agree or disagree with their assertion? Write a problem-solution essay suggesting one or more alternatives to jail for people who are accused of nonviolent crimes. If you base your proposal on research, be sure to cite any sources you use. (See Chapter 14 for more details about documenting sources in the MLA and APA formats.)

Reading and Reflection PROBLEM-SOLVING WRITING

xpixel/Shutterstock

[preview] **SUSAN GLASPELL (1876–1948)** was a Pulitzer Prize–winning playwright and best-selling fiction writer. She worked as a journalist for the *Des Moines Daily News* and was the founder and director of the Provincetown Players in Cape Cod, Massachusetts, for which she wrote 11 plays. She also wrote more than 50 short stories and nine novels. Many of her works focus on feminist issues. In the following play, Glaspell reveals the details of a murder investigation. The mystery, however, is not one of whodunit, but one of motive. Glaspell later transformed the play into a short story called "A Jury of Her Peers." If possible, read this play aloud with classmates or other people. Before reading, think about whether you feel that there is any situation in which it is okay for someone to cover up a crime. Under what circumstances, if any, would that option be acceptable?

Trifles by Susan Glaspell

CHARACTERS

GEORGE HENDERSON, *County Attorney*

HENRY PETERS, *Sheriff*

LEWIS HALE, *A Neighboring Farmer*

MRS. PETERS

MRS. HALE

Scene: *The kitchen in the now abandoned farmhouse of* JOHN WRIGHT, *a gloomy kitchen, and left without having been put in order—unwashed pans under the sink, a loaf of bread outside the breadbox, a dish towel on the table—other signs of incompleted work. At the rear the outer door opens, and the* SHERIFF *comes in, followed by the* COUNTY ATTORNEY *and* HALE. *The* SHERIFF *and HALE are men in middle life, the* COUNTY ATTORNEY *is a young man; all are much bundled up and go at once to the stove. They are followed by the two women—the* SHERIFF's *wife first; she is a slight wiry woman, a thin nervous face.* MRS. HALE *is larger and would ordinarily be called more comfortable looking, but she is disturbed now and looks fearfully about as she enters. The women have come in slowly, and stand close together near the door.*

COUNTY ATTORNEY [*rubbing his hands*]: This feels good. Come up to the fire, ladies.

MRS. PETERS [*after taking a step forward*]: I'm not—cold.

SHERIFF [*unbuttoning his overcoat and stepping away from the stove as if to mark the beginning of official business*]: Now, Mr. Hale, before we move things about, you explain to Mr. Henderson just what you saw when you came here yesterday morning.

COUNTY ATTORNEY: By the way, has anything been moved? Are things just as you left them yesterday?

SHERIFF [*looking about*]: It's just the same. When it dropped below zero last night, I thought I'd better send Frank out this morning to make a fire for us—no use getting pneumonia with a big case on; but I told him not to touch anything except the stove—and you know Frank.

COUNTY ATTORNEY: Somebody should have been left here yesterday.

SHERIFF: Oh—yesterday. When I had to send Frank to Morris Center for that man who went crazy—I want you to know I had my hands full yesterday. I knew you could get back from Omaha by today and as long as I went over everything here myself—

COUNTY ATTORNEY: Well, Mr. Hale, tell just what happened when you came here yesterday morning.

HALE: Harry and I had started to town with a load of potatoes. We came along the road from my place and as I got here I said, "I'm going to see if I can't get John Wright to go in with me on a party telephone." I spoke to Wright about it once before and he put me off, saying folks talked too much anyway, and all he asked was peace and quiet—I guess you know about how much he talked himself; but I thought maybe if I went to the house and talked about it before his wife, though I said to Harry that I didn't know as what his wife wanted made much difference to John—

COUNTY ATTORNEY: Let's talk about that later, Mr. Hale. I do want to talk about that, but tell now just what happened when you got to the house.

HALE: I didn't hear or see anything; I knocked at the door, and still it was all quiet inside. I knew they must be up, it was past eight o'clock. So I knocked again, and I thought I heard somebody say, "Come in." I wasn't sure, I'm not sure yet, but I opened the door—this door [*indicating the door by which the two women are still standing*], and there in that rocker— [*pointing to it*] sat Mrs. Wright.

[*They all look at the rocker.*]

COUNTY ATTORNEY: What—was she doing?

HALE: She was rockin' back and forth. She had her apron in her hand and was kind of—pleating it.

COUNTY ATTORNEY: And how did she—look?

HALE: Well, she looked queer.

COUNTY ATTORNEY: How do you mean—queer?

HALE: Well, as if she didn't know what she was going to do next. And kind of done up.

COUNTY ATTORNEY: How did she seem to feel about your coming?

HALE: Why, I don't think she minded—one way or other. She didn't pay much attention. I said, "How do, Mrs. Wright, it's cold, ain't it?" And she said, "Is it?"—and went on kind of pleating at her apron. Well, I was surprised; she didn't ask me to come up to the stove, or to set down, but just sat there, not even looking at me, so I said, "I want to see John." And then she—laughed. I guess you would call it a laugh. I thought of Harry and the team outside, so I said a little sharp: "Can't I see John?" "No," she says, kind o' dull like. "Ain't he home?" says I. "Yes," says she, "he's home." "Then why can't I see him?" I asked her, out of patience. "'Cause he's dead," says she. *"Dead?"* says I. She just nodded her head, not getting a bit excited, but rockin' back and forth. "Why—where is he?" says I, not knowing what to say. She just pointed upstairs—like that [*Himself pointing to the room above*]. I got up, with the idea of going up there. I walked from there to here—then I says, "Why, what did he die of?" "He died of a rope round his neck," says she, and just went on pleatin' at her apron. Well, I went out and called Harry. I thought I might—need help. We went upstairs, and there he was lyin'—

COUNTY ATTORNEY: I think I'd rather have you go into that upstairs, where you can point it all out. Just go on now with the rest of the story.

HALE: Well, my first thought was to get that rope off. It looked. . . [*Stops, his face twitches.*] . . . but Harry, he went up to him, and he said, "No, he's dead all right, and we'd better not touch anything." So we went back downstairs. She was still sitting that same way. "Has anybody been notified?" I asked. "No," says she, unconcerned. "Who did this, Mrs. Wright?" said Harry. He said it businesslike—and she stopped pleatin' of her apron. "I don't know," she says. "You don't *know?*" says Harry. "No," says she. "Weren't you sleepin' in the bed with him?" says Harry.

"Yes," says she, "but I was on the inside." "Somebody slipped a rope round his neck and strangled him and you didn't wake up?" says Harry. "I didn't wake up," she said after him. We must 'a looked as if we didn't see how that could be, for after a minute she said, "I sleep sound." Harry was going to ask her more questions but I said maybe we ought to let her tell her story first to the coroner, or the sheriff, so Harry went fast as he could to Rivers' place, where there's a telephone.

COUNTY ATTORNEY: And what did Mrs. Wright do when she knew that you had gone for the coroner?

HALE: She moved from that chair to this over here [*Pointing to a small chair in the corner*] and just sat there with her hands held together and looking down. I got a feeling that I ought to make some conversation, so I said I had come in to see if John wanted to put in a telephone, and at that she started to laugh, and then she stopped and looked at me—scared. [*The* COUNTY ATTORNEY, *who has had his notebook out, makes a note.*] I dunno, maybe it wasn't scared. I wouldn't like to say it was. Soon Harry got back, and then Dr. Lloyd came, and you, Mr. Peters, and so I guess that's all I know that you don't.

COUNTY ATTORNEY [*looking around*]: I guess we'll go upstairs first—and then out to the barn and around there. [*To the* SHERIFF] You're convinced that there was nothing important here—nothing that would point to any motive?

SHERIFF: Nothing here but kitchen things.

[*The* COUNTY ATTORNEY, *after again looking around the kitchen, opens the door of a cupboard closet. He gets up on a chair and looks on a shelf. Pulls his hand away, sticky.*]

COUNTY ATTORNEY: Here's a nice mess.

[*The women draw nearer.*]

MRS. PETERS [*to the other woman*]: Oh, her fruit; it did freeze. [*To the* COUNTY ATTORNEY] She worried about that when it turned so cold. She said the fire'd go out and her jars would break.

SHERIFF: Well, can you beat the women! Held for murder and worryin' about her preserves.

COUNTY ATTORNEY: I guess before we're through she may have something more serious than preserves to worry about.

HALE: Well, women are used to worrying over trifles.

[*The two women move a little closer together.*]

COUNTY ATTORNEY [*with the gallantry of a young politician*]: And yet, for all their worries, what would we do without the ladies? [*The women do not unbend. He goes to the sink, takes a dipperful of water from the pail and pouring it into a basin, washes his hands. Starts to wipe them on the roller towel, turns it for a cleaner place.*] Dirty towels! [*Kicks his foot against the pans under the sink.*] Not much of a housekeeper, would you say, ladies?

MRS. HALE [*stiffly*]: There's a great deal of work to be done on a farm.

COUNTY ATTORNEY: To be sure. And yet [*with a little bow to her*] I know there are some Dickson county farmhouses which do not have such roller towels.

[*He gives it a pull to expose its full length again.*]

MRS. HALE: Those towels get dirty awful quick. Men's hands aren't always as clean as they might be.

COUNTY ATTORNEY: Ah, loyal to your sex, I see. But you and Mrs. Wright were neighbors. I suppose you were friends, too.

MRS. HALE [*shaking her head*]: I've not seen much of her of late years. I've not been in this house—it's more than a year.

COUNTY ATTORNEY: And why was that? You didn't like her?

MRS. HALE: I liked her all well enough. Farmers' wives have their hands full, Mr. Henderson. And then—

COUNTY ATTORNEY: Yes—?

MRS. HALE [*looking about*]: It never seemed a very cheerful place.

COUNTY ATTORNEY: No—it's not cheerful. I shouldn't say she had the homemaking instinct.

MRS. HALE: Well, I don't know as Wright had, either.

COUNTY ATTORNEY: You mean that they didn't get on very well?

MRS. HALE: No, I don't mean anything. But I don't think a place'd be any cheerfuller for John Wright's being in it.

COUNTY ATTORNEY: I'd like to talk more of that a little later. I want to get the lay of things upstairs now.

[*He goes to the left, where three steps lead to a stair door.*]

SHERIFF: I suppose anything Mrs. Peters does'll be all right. She was to take in some clothes for her, you know, and a few little things. We left in such a hurry yesterday.

COUNTY ATTORNEY: Yes, but I would like to see what you take, Mrs. Peters, and keep an eye out for anything that might be of use to us.

MRS. PETERS: Yes, Mr. Henderson.

[*The women listen to the men's steps on the stairs, then look about the kitchen.*]

MRS. HALE: I'd hate to have men coming into my kitchen, snooping around and criticizing.

[*She arranges the pans under sink which the* COUNTY ATTORNEY *had shoved out of place.*]

MRS. PETERS: Of course it's no more than their duty.

MRS. HALE: Duty's all right, but I guess that deputy sheriff that came out to make the fire might have got a little of this on. [*Gives the roller towel a pull.*] Wish I'd thought of that sooner. Seems mean to talk about her for not having things slicked up when she had to come away in such a hurry.

MRS. PETERS [*Who has gone to a small table in the left rear corner of the room, and lifted one end of a towel that covers a pan*]: She had bread set.

[*Stands still.*]

MRS. HALE [*eyes fixed on a loaf of bread beside the breadbox, which is on a low shelf at the other side of the room. Moves slowly toward it*]: She was going to put this in there. [*Picks up loaf, then abruptly drops it. In a manner of returning to familiar things.*] It's a shame about her fruit. I wonder if it's all gone. [*Gets up on the chair and looks.*] I think there's some here that's all right, Mrs. Peters. Yes—here. [*Holding it toward the window.*] This is cherries, too. [*Looking again.*] I declare I believe that's the only one. [*Gets down, bottle in her hand. Goes to the sink and wipes it off on the outside.*] She'll feel awful bad after all her hard work in the hot weather. I remember the afternoon I put up my cherries last summer.

[*She puts the bottle on the big kitchen table, center of the room. With a sigh, is about to sit down in the rocking-chair. Before she is seated realizes what chair it is; with a slow look at it, steps back. The chair, which she has touched, rocks back and forth.*]

MRS. PETERS: Well, I must get those things from the front room closet. [*She goes to the door at the right, but after looking into the other room, steps back.*] You coming with me, Mrs. Hale? You could help me carry them.

[*They go in the other room; reappear,* MRS. PETERS *carrying a dress and skirt,* MRS. HALE *following with a pair of shoes.*]

MRS. PETERS: My, it's cold in there.

[*She puts the clothes on the big table, and hurries to the stove.*]

MRS. HALE [*examining the skirt*]: Wright was close. I think maybe that's why she kept so much to herself. She didn't even belong to the Ladies Aid. I suppose she felt she couldn't do her part, and then you don't enjoy things when you feel shabby. She used to wear pretty clothes and be lively, when she was Minnie Foster, one of the town girls singing in the choir. But that—oh, that was thirty years ago. This all you was to take in?

MRS. PETERS: She said she wanted an apron. Funny thing to want, for there isn't much to get you dirty in jail, goodness knows. But I suppose just to make her feel more natural. She said they was in the top drawer in this cupboard. Yes, here. And then her little shawl that always hung behind the door. [*Opens stair door and looks.*] Yes, here it is.

[*Quickly shuts door leading upstairs.*]

MRS. HALE [*abruptly moving toward her*]: Mrs. Peters?

MRS. PETERS: Yes, Mrs. Hale?

MRS. HALE: Do you think she did it?

MRS. PETERS [*in a frightened voice*]: Oh, I don't know.

MRS. HALE: Well, I don't think she did. Asking for an apron and her little shawl. Worrying about her fruit.

MRS. PETERS [*starts to speak, glances up, where footsteps are heard in the room above. In a low voice*]: Mr. Peters says it looks bad for her. Mr. Henderson is awful sarcastic in a speech, and he'll make fun of her sayin' she didn't wake up.

MRS. HALE: Well, I guess John Wright didn't wake when they was slipping that rope under his neck.

MRS. PETERS: No, it's strange. It must have been done awful crafty and still. They say it was such a—funny way to kill a man, rigging it all up like that.

MRS. HALE: That's just what Mr. Hale said. There was a gun in the house. He says that's what he can't understand.

MRS. PETERS: Mr. Henderson said coming out that what was needed for the case was a motive; something to show anger or—sudden feeling.

MRS. HALE [*who is standing by the table*]: Well, I don't see any signs of anger around here. [*She puts her hand on the dish towel which lies on the table, stands looking down at table, one half of which is clean, the other half messy.*] It's wiped to here. [*Makes a move as if to finish work, then turns and looks at loaf of bread outside the breadbox. Drops towel. In that voice of coming back to familiar things.*] Wonder how they are finding things upstairs. I hope she had it a little more red-up[1] up there. You know, it seems kind of *sneaking*. Locking her up in town and then coming out here and trying to get her own house to turn against her!

MRS. PETERS: But Mrs. Hale, the law is the law.

MRS. HALE: I s'pose 'tis. [*Unbuttoning her coat.*] Better loosen up your things, Mrs. Peters. You won't feel them when you go out.

[MRS. PETERS *takes off her fur tippet, goes to hang it on hook at the back of room, stands looking at the under part of the small corner table.*]

MRS. PETERS: She was piecing a quilt.

[*She brings the large sewing basket and they look at the bright pieces.*]

MRS. HALE: It's log cabin pattern. Pretty, isn't it? I wonder if she was goin' to quilt it or just knot it?

[*Footsteps have been heard coming down the stairs. The* SHERIFF *enters, followed by* HALE *and the* COUNTY ATTORNEY.]

SHERIFF: They wonder if she was going to quilt it or just knot it.

[*The men laugh; the women look abashed.*]

COUNTY ATTORNEY [*rubbing his hands over the stove*]: Frank's fire didn't do much up there, did it? Well, let's go out to the barn and get that cleared up.

[*The men go outside.*]

MRS. HALE [*resentfully*]: I don't know as there's anything so strange, our takin' up our time with little things while we're waiting for them to get the evidence. [*She sits down at the big table, smoothing out a block with decision.*] I don't see as it's anything to laugh about.

MRS. PETERS [*apologetically*]: Of course they've got awful important things on their minds.

---

[1] **Red-up** To clean or tidy up.

[*Pulls up a chair and joins* MRS. HALE *at the table.*]

MRS. HALE [*examining another block*]: Mrs. Peters, look at this one. Here, this is the one she was working on, and look at the sewing! All the rest of it has been so nice and even. And look at this! It's all over the place! Why, it looks as if she didn't know what she was about!

[*After she has said this, they look at each other, then start to glance back at the door. After an instant* MRS. HALE *has pulled at a knot and ripped the sewing.*]

MRS. PETERS: Oh, what are you doing, Mrs. Hale?

MRS. HALE [*mildly*]: Just pulling out a stitch or two that's not sewed very good. [*Threading a needle.*] Bad sewing always made me fidgety.

MRS. PETERS [*nervously*]: I don't think we ought to touch things.

MRS. HALE: I'll just finish up this end. [*Suddenly stopping and leaning forward.*] Mrs. Peters?

MRS. PETERS: Yes, Mrs. Hale?

MRS. HALE: What do you suppose she was so nervous about?

MRS. PETERS: Oh—I don't know. I don't know as she was nervous. I sometimes sew awful queer when I'm just tired. [MRS. HALE *starts to say something, looks at* MRS. PETERS, *then goes on sewing.*] Well, I must get these things wrapped up. They may be through sooner than we think. [*Putting apron and other things together.*] I wonder where I can find a piece of paper, and string.

MRS. HALE: In that cupboard, maybe.

MRS. PETERS [*looking in cupboard]:* Why, here's a birdcage. [*Holds it up.*] Did she have a bird, Mrs. Hale?

MRS. HALE: Why, I don't know whether she did or not—I've not been here for so long. There was a man around last year selling canaries cheap, but I don't know as she took one; maybe she did. She used to sing real pretty herself.

MRS. PETERS [*glancing around*]: Seems funny to think of a bird here. But she must have had one, or why should she have a cage? I wonder what happened to it?

MRS. HALE: I s'pose maybe the cat got it.

MRS. PETERS: No, she didn't have a cat. She's got that feeling some people have about cats—being afraid of them. My cat got in her room and she was real upset and asked me to take it out.

MRS. HALE: My sister Bessie was like that. Queer, ain't it?

MRS. PETERS [*examining the cage*]: Why, look at this door. It's broke. One hinge is pulled apart.

MRS. HALE [*looking too*]: Looks as if someone must have been rough with it.

MRS. PETERS: Why, yes.

[*She brings the cage forward and puts it on the table.*]

MRS. HALE: I wish if they're going to find any evidence they'd be about it. I don't like this place.

MRS. PETERS: But I'm awful glad you came with me, Mrs. Hale. It would be lonesome for me sitting here alone.

MRS. HALE: It would, wouldn't it? [*Dropping her sewing.*] But I tell you what I do wish, Mrs. Peters. I wish I had come over sometimes *she* was here. I—[*Looking around the room.*]—wish I had.

MRS. PETERS: But of course you were awful busy, Mrs. Hale—your house and your children.

MRS. HALE: I could've come. I stayed away because it weren't cheerful—and that's why I ought to have come. I—I've never liked this place. Maybe because it's down in a hollow, and you don't see the road. I dunno what it is, but it's a lonesome place and always was. I wish I had come over to see Minnie Foster sometimes. I can see now—

[*Shakes her head.*]

MRS. PETERS: Well, you mustn't reproach yourself, Mrs. Hale. Somehow we just don't see how it is with other folks until—something comes up.

MRS. HALE: Not having children makes less work—but it makes a quiet house, and Wright out to work all day, and no company when he did come in. Did you know John Wright, Mrs. Peters?

MRS. PETERS: Not to know him; I've seen him in town. They say he was a good man.

MRS. HALE: Yes—good; he didn't drink, and kept his word as well as most, I guess, and paid his debts. But he was a hard man, Mrs. Peters. Just to pass the time of day with him— [*Shivers.*] Like a raw wind that gets to the bone. [*Pauses, her eyes falling on the cage.*] I should think she would 'a wanted a bird. But what do you suppose went with it?

MRS. PETERS: I don't know, unless it got sick and died.

[*She reaches over and swings the broken door, swings it again. Both women watch it.*]

MRS. HALE: You weren't raised round here, were you? [MRS. PETERS *shakes her head.*] You didn't know—her?

MRS. PETERS: Not till they brought her yesterday.

MRS. HALE: She—come to think of it, she was kind of like a bird herself—real sweet and pretty, but kind of timid and—fluttery. How—she—did—change. [*Silence; then as if struck by a happy thought and relieved to get back to every day things.*] Tell you what, Mrs. Peters, why don't you take the quilt in with you? It might take up her mind.

MRS. PETERS: Why, I think that's a real nice idea, Mrs. Hale. There couldn't possibly be any objection to it, could there? Now, just what would I take? I wonder if her patches are in here—and her things.

[*They look in the sewing basket.*]

MRS. HALE: Here's some red. I expect this has got sewing things in it. [*Brings out a fancy box.*] What a pretty box. Looks like something somebody would give you. Maybe her scissors are in here. [*Opens box. Suddenly puts her hand to her nose.*] Why—[MRS. PETERS *bends nearer, then turns her face away.*] There's something wrapped up in this piece of silk.

MRS. PETERS: Why, this isn't her scissors.

MRS. HALE [*lifting the silk*]: Oh, Mrs. Peters—It's—

[MRS. PETERS *bends closer.*]

MRS. PETERS: It's the bird.

MRS. HALE [*jumping up*]: But, Mrs. Peters—look at it. Its neck! Look at its neck! It's all—other side too.

MRS. PETERS: Somebody—wrung—its neck.

[*Their eyes meet. A look of growing comprehension, of horror. Steps are heard outside.* MRS. HALE *slips box under quilt pieces, and sinks into her chair. Enter* SHERIFF *and* COUNTY ATTORNEY. MRS. PETERS *rises.*]

COUNTY ATTORNEY [*as one turning from serious thing to little pleasantries*]: Well, ladies have you decided whether she was going to quilt it or knot it?

MRS. PETERS: We think she was going to—knot it.

COUNTY ATTORNEY: Well, that's interesting, I'm sure. [*Seeing the birdcage.*] Has the bird flown?

MRS. HALE [*putting more quilt pieces over the box*]: We think the—cat got it.

COUNTY ATTORNEY [*preoccupied*]: Is there a cat?

[MRS. HALE *glances in a quick covert way at* MRS. PETERS.]

MRS. PETERS: Well, not now. They're superstitious, you know. They leave.

COUNTY ATTORNEY [*to* SHERIFF PETERS, *continuing an interrupted conversation*]: No sign at all of anyone having come from the outside. Their own rope. Now let's go up again and go over it piece by piece. [*They start upstairs.*] It would have to have been someone who knew just the—

[MRS. PETERS *sits down. The two women sit there not looking at one another, but as if peering into something and at the same time holding back. When they talk now it is the manner of feeling their way over strange ground, as if afraid of what they are saying, but as if they can not help saying it.*]

MRS. HALE: She liked the bird. She was going to bury it in that pretty box.

MRS. PETERS [*in a whisper*]: When I was a girl—my kitten—there was a boy took a hatchet, and before my eyes—and before I could get there—[*Covers her face an instant.*] If they hadn't held me back, I would have—[*Catches herself, looks upstairs where steps are heard, falters weakly.*]—hurt him.

MRS. HALE [*with a slow look around her*]: I wonder how it would seem never to have had any children around. [*Pause.*] No, Wright wouldn't like the bird—a thing that sang. She used to sing. He killed that, too.

MRS. PETERS [*moving uneasily*]: We don't know who killed the bird.

MRS. HALE: I knew John Wright.

MRS. PETERS: It was an awful thing was done in this house that night, Mrs. Hale. Killing a man while he slept, slipping a rope around his neck that choked the life out of him.

MRS. HALE: His neck. Choked the life out of him.

[*Her hand goes out and rests on the birdcage.*]

MRS. PETERS [*with rising voice*]: We don't know who killed him. We don't know.

MRS. HALE [*her own feeling not interrupted*]: If there'd been years and years of nothing, then a bird to sing to you, it would be awful—still, after the bird was still.

MRS. PETERS [*something within her speaking*]: I know what stillness is. When we homesteaded in Dakota, and my first baby died—after he was two years old, and me with no other then—

MRS. HALE [*moving*]: How soon do you suppose they'll be through, looking for evidence?

MRS. PETERS: I know what stillness is. [*Pulling herself back*]. The law has got to punish crime, Mrs. Hale.

MRS. HALE [*not as if answering that*]: I wish you'd seen Minnie Foster when she wore a white dress with blue ribbons and stood up there in the choir and sang. [*A look around the room.*] Oh, I wish I'd come over here once in a while! That was a crime! That was a crime! Who's going to punish that?

MRS. PETERS [*looking upstairs*]: We mustn't—take on.

MRS. HALE: I might have known she needed help! I know how things can be—for women. I tell you, it's queer, Mrs. Peters. We live close together and we live far apart. We all go through the same things—it's all just a different kind of the same thing. [*Brushes her eyes; noticing the bottle of fruit, reaches out for it.*] If I was you, I wouldn't tell her her fruit was gone. Tell her it ain't. Tell her it's all right. Take this in to prove it to her. She—she may never know whether it was broke or not.

MRS. PETERS [*takes the bottle, looks about for something to wrap it in; takes petticoat from the clothes brought from the other room, very nervously begins winding this around the bottle. In a false voice*]: My, it's a good thing the men couldn't hear us. Wouldn't they just laugh! Getting all stirred up over a little thing like a—dead canary. As if that could have anything to do with—with—wouldn't they laugh!

[*The men are heard coming down stairs.*]

MRS. HALE [*under her breath*]: Maybe they would—maybe they wouldn't.

COUNTY ATTORNEY: No, Peters, it's all perfectly clear except a reason for doing it. But you know juries when it comes to women. If there was some definite thing. Something to show—something to make a story about—a thing that would connect up with this strange way of doing it—

[*The women's eyes meet for an instant. Enter* HALE *from outer door.*]

HALE: Well, I've got the team around. Pretty cold out there.

COUNTY ATTORNEY: I'm going to stay here awhile by myself [*To the* SHERIFF.] You can send Frank out for me, can't you? I want to go over everything. I'm not satisfied that we can't do better.

SHERIFF: Do you want to see what Mrs. Peters is going to take in?

[*The* COUNTY ATTORNEY *goes to the table, picks up the apron, laughs.*]

COUNTY ATTORNEY: Oh, I guess they're not very dangerous things the ladies have picked up. [*Moves a few things about, disturbing the quilt pieces which cover the box. Steps back.*] No, Mrs. Peters doesn't need supervising. For that matter, a sheriff's wife is married to the law. Ever think of it that way, Mrs. Peters?

MRS. PETERS: Not—just that way.

SHERIFF [*chuckling*]: Married to the law. [*Moves toward the other room.*] I just want you to come in here a minute, George. We ought to take a look at these windows.

COUNTY ATTORNEY [*scoffingly*]: Oh, windows!

SHERIFF: We'll be right out, Mr. Hale.

[HALE *goes outside. The* SHERIFF *follows the* COUNTY ATTORNEY *into the other room. Then* MRS. HALE *rises, hands tight together, looking intensely at* MRS. PETERS, *whose eyes make a slow turn, finally meeting* MRS. HALE*'s. A moment* MRS. HALE *holds her gaze, then her own eyes point the way to where the box is concealed. Suddenly* MRS. PETERS *throws back quilt pieces and tries to put the box in the bag she is wearing. It is too big. She opens box, starts to take bird out, cannot touch it, goes to pieces, stands there helpless. Sound of a knob turning in the other room.* MRS. HALE *snatches the box and puts it in the pocket of her big coat. Enter* COUNTY ATTORNEY *and* SHERIFF.]

COUNTY ATTORNEY [*facetiously*]: Well, Henry, at least we found out that she was not going to quilt it. She was going to—what is it you call it, ladies!

MRS. HALE [*her hand against her pocket*]: We call it—knot it, Mr. Henderson.

Curtain

Source: Susan Glaspell, *Trifles*, 1916.

QUESTIONS FOR REFLECTION

Considering Ideas

1. How do the men and women differ in their separate investigations of Mr. Wright's murder? Why are their approaches so dissimilar?
2. How had Mrs. Wright changed since she was Minnie Foster 30 years ago? What do you suppose led to that change?
3. What problem do Mrs. Peters and Mrs. Hale face as they uncover the details of the investigation? How do they finally decide to resolve that problem at the end of the play? Do you feel that their resolution is justified? Why or why not?

Considering the Rhetorical Star

1. What is the *subject* of Glaspell's play?
2. Who is the intended *audience* for the play? Explain.

3. What is Glaspell's *purpose* for writing the play? Does she achieve her purpose? Explain.
4. What is the playwright's primary writing *strategy?* What other strategies does she use?
5. What is the *design* of the play? Is it effective? Why or why not?

Considering Writing Strategies

1. What is ironic about the title *Trifles?* Do you prefer this title or "A Jury of Her Peers," the short story version of the play? Why?
2. What analogy does Glaspell draw between the canary and Mrs. Wright? What is the significance of the cage in this analogy?
3. How does the writer appeal to the audience? Has she made you feel compassion for Mrs. Wright? Why or why not?

Writing Suggestions

1. In response to Glaspell's *Trifles,* write a proposal suggesting what Mrs. Peters and Mrs. Hale should do with the evidence they found. You might weigh the pros and cons of several possible solutions before making your final recommendation.
2. Write an essay proposing ways for women, or men, to deal with domestic abuse.

STUDENT WRITING

Note: The following paper documents sources by including APA style in-text citations and a References list (but omits a title page). Your instructor may require a different format for your paper. See Chapters 13 and 14 for details about citing sources using the MLA and APA formats. In particular, see the student paper in APA style on pages 411–417.

Combating Juvenile Delinquency

by Koray Easom

1 Adolescence is a tender age when children are making many changes in all aspects of their lives and transferring into adulthood. Without a smooth transition during vital pivotal moments, there may be concerns that arise for some children. Juvenile delinquency is a problem that the nation is constantly fighting to bring to a minimum. A lack of parental supervision, untreated mental health related issues, and peer pressure contribute significantly to juvenile delinquency in America; therefore, these issues must be addressed to help combat this problem.

2 From birth, parents usually have the greatest influence in a child's life. Parenting is the foundation on which a young child is molded into a respectable adult. Parental presence, influence, and guidance are among the most important factors for deterring delinquency. When children grow up in a home with both parents, they are far less likely to engage in delinquent behavior (Moynihan et al., 2005, p. 115). When a parent is absent from the home, the child misses out on that shaping. This is also the case for parents who are not absent but are too preoccupied with their own criminal acts. Youth who "live apart from their biological fathers are more likely to use illegal substances and to have early contact with police" (Moynihan et al., 2005, p. 123). A lack of parental supervision causes children to be left with no capable guardian to prevent delinquency leading to crime and drug use.

3 When going through vital stages of their lives and transitioning into young adults, it is extremely important for every child to have a strong relationship with at least one caring adult who will influence his or her decisions and actions in a positive light. Providing a child with a mentor can help to fill the gap when one or both parents are not present to help show children what behaviors are right or wrong. Organizations

such as Big Brothers and Big Sisters of America and Tuesday's Child can pair up children with positive role models who can help steer them toward becoming productive citizens. Some of the benefits of youth mentoring programs are "improved grades and reduced involvement in delinquent behavior" (DuBois, 2016). A teacher, coach, family member, or other adult can serve in that role as well. Even if a child has parental and other positive role models, to combat delinquency, one must also pay close attention to the child's mental state.

4 In addition to absent parents, untreated mental health-related issues can lead to troubled behaviors for children. According to the Substance Abuse and Mental Health Services Administration (2017), 50–70% of all youth brought into the juvenile justice system meet criteria for a mental health disorder. Many of these children end up in the system because they do not have easy access to mental health services in their communities and are not receiving the help they need. Even while in custody, most juveniles do not receive the proper care they need to get their mental health under control and eventually are let back into the community to fight the same mental health issues that contributed to their delinquency in the first place. Like adults, youth who are not receiving help with mental health issues have a hard time with decision making and truly comprehending right from wrong and end up acting out in a criminal or delinquent manner. But the mental health crisis does not end once the juvenile is brought into the criminal justice system.

5 Children need to be provided with a more effective approach to mental health, one that will lead to less juvenile delinquency and recidivism in the future. Mental health issues need to be handled by professionals in that field. According to the National Center for Mental Health and Juvenile Justice (n.d.), "93% of youth in detention reported 'adverse' events including accidents, serious illness, physical and sexual abuse, [and] domestic and community violence" and the "effective response involves community-based treatment interventions that engage youth and their families." Ideally, treating mental health issues with therapy and medication (if necessary) will help prevent children who have experienced adverse circumstances from entering the juvenile justice system. Even when positive role models are involved and proper mental health treatment is available where needed, there is still a possibility for juveniles to engage in delinquent acts, especially when being pressured by their friends.

6 Peer pressure contributes to many of the delinquent behaviors in which youth engage. Most juveniles continually seek acceptance from those around them. "Peers are among the most salient influences on an individual's behavior during the transition from childhood through adolescence" (Farrell et. al., 2017). During adolescence, children are seeking their own identity while they begin spending more time with their peers and become less involved with their parents. At this point in life, juveniles are influenced by their friends more than they will be at any other time in in their lives. Often juveniles turn to deviant behaviors in order to be a part of a crowd or scene in which they seek to fit in, or they feel the need to act in a deviant manner if their friends are doing so. This is a very unfortunate scenario that lands many children into the juvenile or criminal justice system. The powerful impact of peers during adolescence is supported by studies that have found links between peer factors and problem behaviors including gang involvement, aggression, drug use, and delinquent behavior (Farrell et. al., 2017). There is no question that peer pressure affects the decision making of those in their adolescence. Peer pressure, however, can be negative or positive.

7 Providing children an opportunity to be involved with peers who avoid negative behaviors and engage in positive ones can help to prevent juvenile delinquency. Most youth just want to be liked and accepted, and some will do whatever it takes to achieve the acceptance they seek. With positive peer pressure, youth are influenced to do things that will better themselves and their lives. Community- and school-based programs, such as Drug Abuse Resistance Education (D.A.R.E) and Gang Resistance Education and Training (G.R.E.A.T), can significantly help to prevent and reduce juvenile delinquency as well (Shoemaker, 2018, p. 124). Preventing drug use and gang involvement will go a long way toward reducing juvenile crime and violence. According to Impact Law (2019), the key components for juvenile delinquency prevention are education, recreation, community involvement,

parent-child interaction training programs, and bullying prevention programs. Recreational programs are a great deterrence for delinquency because they create a positive environment for youth where they can form bonds with healthy-minded adults and peers. This is something that will take the entire community, working together, to make a difference.

8 In summary, a lack of parental supervision, the presence of an untreated mental health issue, and negative peer pressure contribute significantly to juvenile delinquency in America. While juvenile crime is an ongoing problem in the United States, taking steps to combat this problem can help to reduce its impact. Providing children with better supervision and role models, treating their mental illnesses effectively, and placing them in environments where there is positive peer influence can help to solve the problem of juvenile delinquency in America. Using all three approaches in tandem will have the greatest impact on children who are at risk for committing crimes. The future of this nation depends on it.

References

DuBois, D. (2016, January 3). How does mentoring benefit youth? Let's count the ways. *The Chronicle of Evidence-Based Mentoring.* www.evidencebasedmentoring.org/how-does-mentoring-benefit-youth-lets-count-the-ways/

Farrell, A. D., Thompson, E. L., & Mehari, K. R. (2017). Dimensions of peer influences and their relationship to adolescents' aggression, other problem behaviors, and prosocial behavior. *Journal of Youth and Adolescence, 46*(6), 1351–1369. https://doi-org.prxkeiser.lirn.net/10.1007/s10964-016-0601-4

Impact Law. (2019). Juvenile delinquency prevention. www.impactlaw.com/criminal-law/juvenile/prevention

Moynihan, D. P., Smeeding, T. M., & Rainwater, L. (2005). *The future of the family.* Russell Sage Foundation.

Shoemaker, D. J. (2018). *Juvenile delinquency* (3rd ed). Rowman and Littlefield.

Substance Abuse and Mental Health Services Administration. (2017, September 15). Criminal and juvenile justice. www.samhsa.gov/criminal-juvenile-justice

QUESTIONS FOR REFLECTION

1. Identify the thesis. Is it effective? Why or why not?
2. Does the essay convince the reader that a problem exists? Explain.
3. Problem solving is the primary writing strategy for the essay. What additional writing strategies are used?
4. What possible solutions does Easom provide for the problem? Is the final solution convincing? Why or why not?
5. What additional solutions might help to solve the problem?

Activity Proposing Solutions

On your own or in small groups, identify three problems that you have experienced at home, school, or work. Brainstorm several possible solutions for each problem. Weigh the pros and cons of each possible solution, and determine which solution seems to be the most feasible. Be prepared to share your results with the class. This activity may give you ideas for writing a problem-solving essay.

Now that you have read one or more examples of problem-solving writing, it's time to write your own proposal. You may choose to write about one of the writing options that follow, the advertisement, the image, or one of the media suggestions. Additionally, keep your ears open for problems at school or work; you may hear a conversation that sparks your interest. You might also read through an online newspaper or magazine to find a problem that calls for a solution. Remember to keep track of any sources you use in case you need to cite them in your paper. Consider your rhetorical star and the qualities of effective proposal writing as you begin to compose your assignment.

Writing Assignment Options

Write a proposal about a problem related to one of the following topics. You'll need to narrow the topic to something you can reasonably cover within the scope of your assignment.

1. Managing time or money
2. Relationships
3. Teenage pregnancy
4. Drug or alcohol abuse
5. Drinking and driving
6. Divorce
7. Plagiarism or cheating on tests
8. Overcrowded prisons
9. Pollution
10. Poverty or homelessness

> ***ESOL Tip >***
>
> You may choose to propose a solution to a problem that exists in your culture or native country.

Multimodal Assignment

Using one of the readings, writing assignment options, or another topic, create a multimodal project using the problem-solving writing strategy and at least two or more of the options listed in Table 12.2.

Table 12.2

Multimodal Options		
Artifact	Images	PowerPoint
Artwork	Infographics	Prezi
Audio clip	Journal	Video
Blog	Montage	Website
Digital portfolio	Podcast	Wiki
Graphic organizer	Poster	Writing

(See Chapter 15 for more details about multimodal compositions.)

Interpreting an Advertisement

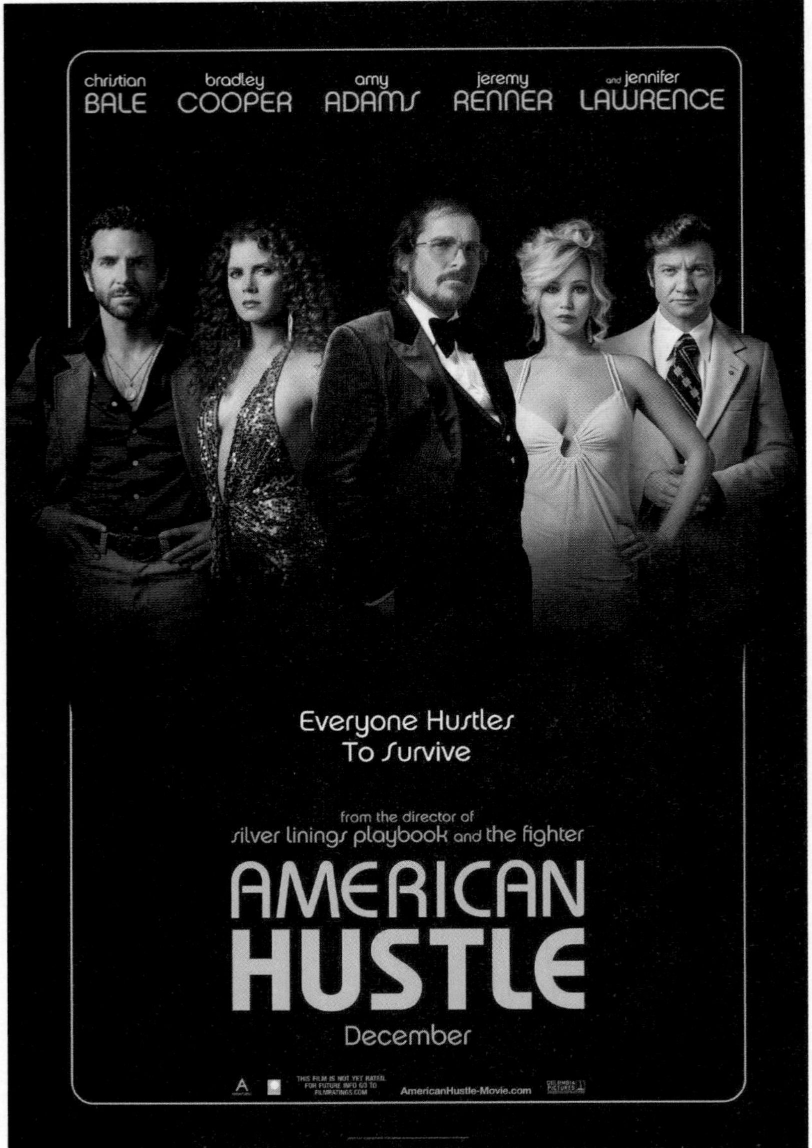

Annapurna Productions/Photo 12/Alamy Images

Who might be interested in the *American Hustle* advertisement? How do the images and text interact? What details catch your eye? Does the movie look appealing? Why or why not? Is the advertisement effective? Why or why not? Write a proposal related to the movie poster above or another crime movie you have seen. For example, you might propose a particular law that you believe should be in effect to help prevent people from being conned by scam artists, or you may propose a law that would punish those who have conned others. Remember to identify the problem and then propose one or more solutions to the problem.

Writing about an Image

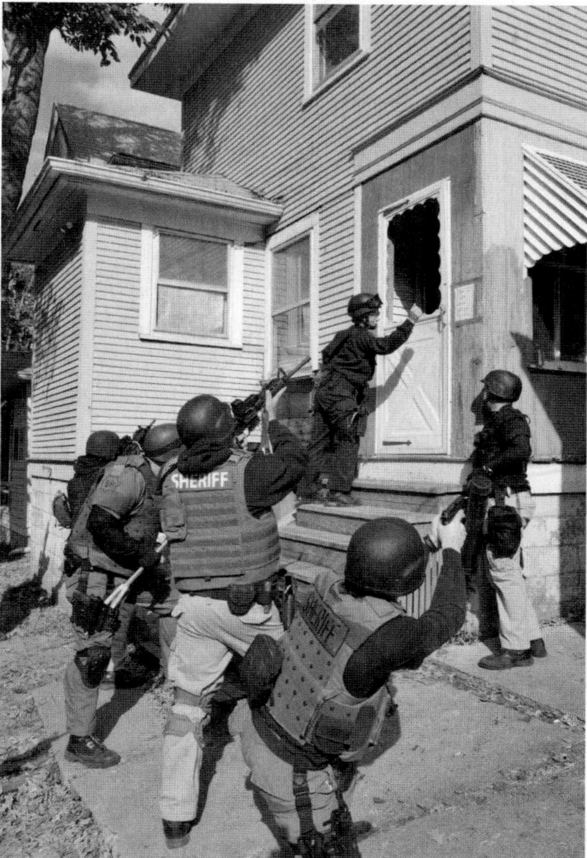

Aaron Roeth Photography

Write a problem-solving essay related to one of the images in this book or another source. What kind of crime has occurred? Could it have been prevented? What should be done about it? You may write about the image itself, or you may choose to write about something that relates to it. For example, you might write an essay about the first image in the chapter, which shows a courtroom and gun. Your essay would propose a solution for dealing with gangs and guns. Or you may choose to write about the image above, which depicts a drug raid, suggesting ways to help reduce the sale and use of illegal drugs in the United States.

Media Connection for Solving a Problem

You might watch, read, and/or listen to one or more of the suggested media listed in Table 12.3 to discover additional examples of problem solving. Exploring various media may help you to better understand methods for solving problems. You may also choose to write about one or more of the media suggestions. For example, you might watch the movie *Oceans 8* and propose alternate solutions for how the characters dealt with the problems they faced. Be sure to give credit to any sources you use in your essay.

Table 12.3

Media Chart				
Television	*CSI, NCIS*	*Sons of Anarchy, Criminal Minds*	*Law and Order*	*Homeland*
Film	*Widows* (2018)	*American Hustle* (2013)	*Ocean's 8* (2018)	*Joker* (2019)
Print/ E-Reading	*Conflict Resolution Quarterly* (magazine)	*Criminal Justice* (journal)	*Crime & Justice* (journal)	*Homeland Security Today* (magazine)
Internet	**www.msn.com/en-us/news/crime**	**https://nij.ojp.gov/library/nij-journal**	**www.cnn.com/specials/us/crime-and-justice**	**https://thecrimereport.org**
Music	"Please Man" by Big & Rich	"I Fought the Law" by Green Day	"Hurricane" by Bob Dylan	"Criminal" by Fiona Apple

Figure 12.1
The Rhetorical Star

12.4 Analyzing the Rhetorical Star for Solving a Problem

As you prepare to write your proposal, consider the five points of the rhetorical star (Figure 12.1). You might use some of the questions in the chart as you conduct your rhetorical star analysis.

Subject	Identify a problem that you have observed in your community, at home, or at work. The issue can be one you have witnessed or experienced firsthand or one that you have noticed in the media. For example, maybe you have heard that someone has been vandalizing apartments in your complex and want to urge someone to do something about it. Or perhaps you feel your credit card company is taking unfair advantage of you by charging outrageous interest rates and you want to do something about it.
Audience	Who will read your proposal? What will interest your readers about your subject? What do they already know about the problem? Why will they care about it? Are your readers experiencing the problem or contributing to it? Will the problem affect them in some way? Are they in a position to do something about the problem? Think about what kinds of details would be most appropriate to share with your audience. Appeal to the interests and needs of your specific audience and anticipate their potential responses to your proposal. For example, if you are writing about problems in your apartment complex, then your audience could be the landlord, supervisor, other tenants, surrounding community members, security personnel, and/or the police department.
Purpose	Think about what you are trying to accomplish through your proposal. Do you simply want your readers to have a better understanding of the problem and possible solutions for solving it? Do you intend for your audience to do something based on your proposal? Either way, your main goal is to convince your readers that a problem exists and offer a reasonable solution.
Strategy	Even if your primary goal is to propose a solution to a problem, you may decide to use additional writing strategies as well. For example, you might show the causes of the problem or the effects of allowing it to continue, you may compare and contrast what the situation will be like in the future if your solution is implemented or not, or you could decide to evaluate several possible solutions before persuading your reader that one particular solution is the best.
Design	What is the best format for your proposal? Should you write an essay or a newspaper article? Would a letter or an e-mail be appropriate? Could you post a flyer at work, on campus, or in the community? Also, what other design details might enhance your proposal? Using bullets, headings, photographs, or charts might strengthen your problem-solving essay.

12.5 Applying the Writing Process for Solving a Problem

After you have completed your rhetorical star analysis, follow the steps of the writing process (Figure 12.2) to compose your problem-solving paper.

1. **Discovering:** Once you have decided on a problem, you might try discussing the problem with a classmate or friend to get some ideas for solving it.
2. **Planning:** After you have chosen a topic, you might write out the problem and then make a list of potential solutions. Consider the pros and cons of each solution before choosing which one or ones to include in your essay. Use a graphic organizer (Figure 12.3) or create a cluster or an outline (informal or formal) to help you arrange your ideas.
3. **Composing:** Using your plan from the previous step, write a first draft of your problem-solving essay. Don't worry too much about grammar and punctuation at this time. Keep focused on explaining the problem and offering viable solutions. Use the qualities of problem-solving writing.
    1. Identify a problem and demonstrate that it exists.
    2. Appeal to your audience.
    3. State your claim (thesis).
    4. Propose a solution or several possible solutions to the problem.
    5. Organize your solution(s) effectively.
    6. Persuade your readers that your proposal is feasible.
    7. End with a call to action.
4. **Getting feedback:** Have at least one classmate or other person read your rough draft and answer the peer review questions on page 335. If you have access to a writing tutor or center, get another opinion about your paper as well.

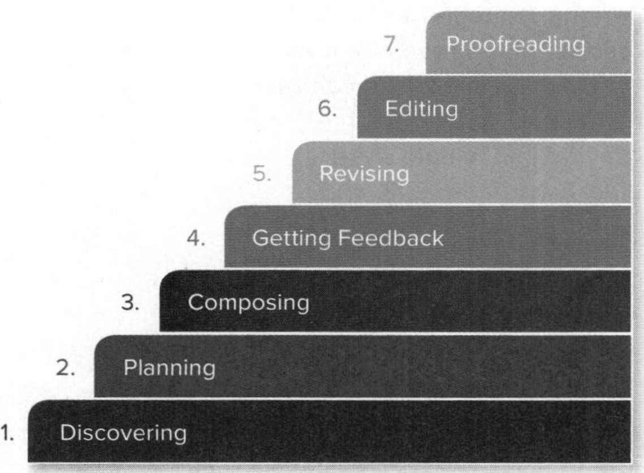

FIGURE 12.2 The Seven Steps of the Writing Process

Problem:

Solution 1

Pros	Cons

Solution 2

Pros	Cons

Solution 3

Pros	Cons

Conclusion:

Solving a Problem

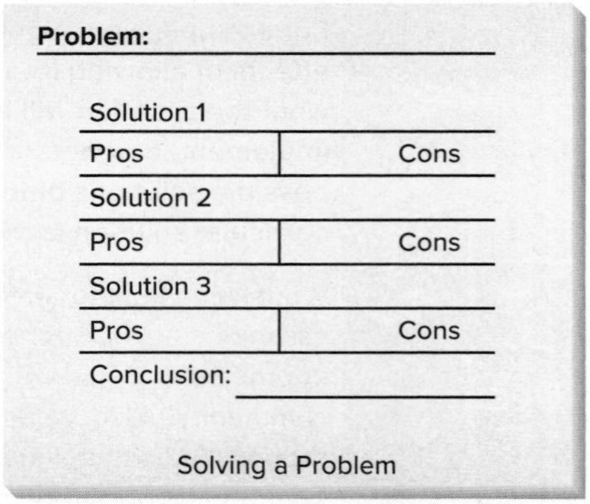

FIGURE 12.3 Graphic Organizer for Solving a Problem

5. **Revising:** Using all of the feedback available to you, revise your problem-solving essay. Be sure that your overall solution is reasonable and explained clearly. Add, delete, and rearrange ideas as necessary.
6. **Editing:** Read your problem-solving essay again, this time looking for errors in grammar, punctuation, and mechanics. Pay particular attention to your choice of words and tone. Also, keep in mind that there may be other possible solutions that would work, so you don't necessarily want to imply that your solution is the only viable one.
7. **Proofreading:** After you have carefully edited your essay, read it again. This time, look for typographical errors and any other issues that might interfere with the readers' understanding of your problem-solving essay. Make your final corrections.

PEER REVIEW QUESTIONS FOR SOLVING A PROBLEM

Trade rough drafts with a classmate and answer the following questions about his or her paper. Then, in person or online, discuss your papers and suggestions with your peer. Finally, make the changes you feel would most benefit your paper.

1. Has the author clearly identified a problem? What is it?
2. Has the author demonstrated that a problem exists?
3. How does the author appeal to the audience?
4. What is the author's claim (thesis)? Is it clear?
5. Has the author effectively supported the problem-solving essay? What kind of evidence is included?
6. Is the problem-solving essay organized effectively? Why or why not?
7. What is the strongest part of the essay?
8. Does the conclusion contain a call to action? Is it effective? Why or why not?
9. What kinds of grammatical errors, if any, are evident in the problem-solving essay?
10. What final suggestions do you have for the author?

Writer's Checklist for Solving a Problem

Use the checklist below to evaluate your own writing and to help ensure that your problem-solving essay is effective. If you have any "no" answers, go back and work on those areas if necessary.

- ☐ 1. Have I clearly identified the problem?
- ☐ 2. Have I demonstrated that the problem exists?
- ☐ 3. Have I appealed to my audience?
- ☐ 4. Have I stated a clear claim?

- [ ] 5. Have I proposed a reasonable solution or solutions?
- [ ] 6. Have I organized my proposal effectively?
- [ ] 7. Have I supported my solution in a convincing manner?
- [ ] 8. Have I included a call to action in my conclusion?
- [ ] 9. Have I proofread thoroughly?

CHAPTER SUMMARY

1. Use the problem-solving strategy to determine a solution to a challenging issue or situation.
2. Problem-solving writing is an important part of your education, daily life, and career.
3. Interpreting readings and images related to problems and solutions can help you to prepare to write a problem-solving essay.
4. Carefully analyze the rhetorical star before writing a problem-solving essay: subject, audience, purpose, strategy, and design.
5. Use these qualities when writing an effective problem-solving essay: identify a problem and demonstrate that it exists; appeal to your audience; state your claim; propose one or more solutions; organize your solution(s) effectively; persuade your readers that your proposed solution is feasible; end with a call to action.

WHAT I KNOW NOW

Use this checklist to determine what you need to work on in order to feel comfortable with your understanding of the material in this chapter. Check off each item as you master it. Review the material for any unchecked items.

- [ ] 1. I know what **problem-solving writing** is.
- [ ] 2. I can identify several **real-world applications** for problem-solving writing.
- [ ] 3. I can evaluate **readings and images** that reflect problems and solutions.
- [ ] 4. I can analyze the **rhetorical star** for problem-solving writing.
- [ ] 5. I understand the **writing process** for writing about problems and solutions.
- [ ] 6. I can apply the **seven qualities** of problem-solving writing.

Design elements: *Graduate Spotlight:* Ingram Publishing/AGE Fotostock

PART 3

Research Guide

Why Research Skills Are Essential

The chapters in Part 3 are geared toward helping you plan, write, document, and present a research paper or multimodal project. In the real world, you often conduct research when you want to know the answer to a question, even if you don't realize that is what you are doing. For example, if you want to know where to go to get your computer fixed without spending a fortune, then you might ask a friend who is a computer science major for suggestions. If you are looking for a job, you may go to **monster.com** or look in the classifieds section of your local newspaper for possible employment opportunities. If you want to know who the lead singer is for a new band, you can go online and conduct a Google search to find out whose voice it is that you keep replaying in your head. All of these activities require research of one type or another.

Being able to write an effective research-based paper or a multimodal project is an essential skill for college, the work world, and your personal life. You need to be able to gather pertinent information and put it together in a meaningful way. You also need to avoid plagiarism throughout the research process. That's one reason why documentation methods are so important.

If you panic when you hear the words *research essay,* you are not alone. The good news is that writing a research-based paper or a multimodal project can be a rewarding and worthwhile experience. The keys to success are choosing the right topic, planning your assignment effectively, selecting appropriate sources, and budgeting enough time to revise and complete the paper by the due date. You will probably spend more time on this assignment than any other you complete for your composition course. Therefore, you will need to get organized and make the most of your opportunity to learn and write about something new and interesting.

OVERVIEW of Part 3

Chapter 13
You will learn techniques for planning and composing a research paper.

Chapter 14
You will learn strategies for documenting a research paper using the MLA and APA formats.

Chapter 15
You will learn techniques for planning and delivering an oral presentation or a multimodal project.

CHAPTER 13 Planning and Writing a Research Paper

moodboard/Corbis

learning outcomes

In this chapter you will learn techniques for achieving these learning outcomes:

13.1 Discovering a Research Topic

The first step when you are conducting research is to find a suitable topic. To do that, you must understand your assignment. Read the instructions carefully and make sure you know what topics are acceptable and what your instructor expects from you. Ask questions to clarify any uncertainties you have. Your instructor may assign a topic or allow you to choose a topic to explore. If you do have an opportunity to select your own topic, make your selection carefully. You will spend a fair amount of time on your research assignment, so choose a topic that is interesting and meaningful to you.

Perhaps you would like to know more about your major field of study so that you can have a clearer understanding of what types of duties you will be expected to perform on the job. Maybe you have always wondered what it would be like to visit outer space or to go scuba diving. Your topic doesn't have to be stuffy or academic. If you choose a topic you genuinely want to learn more about, you will find the research process can be quite enjoyable. To find an appropriate topic, you can brainstorm ideas, skim through written sources, browse the library, surf the Internet, watch television, listen to the radio, or discuss your assignment with others.

13.2 Narrowing a Research Topic

After you have selected a topic, you will want to narrow it so that you can adequately cover it within the parameters of your assignment. For example, if you choose space exploration as your broad topic, then you might focus on how space exploration affects life on Earth. You can narrow that topic even further by focusing on how National Aeronautics and Space Administration (NASA) technology designed for space exploration can be used to improve everyday household items.

Similarly, if you decide to write about a hobby you would like to try, such as scuba diving, you might narrow your subject by focusing on what you would need to get started. Understanding the specific requirements for the assignment will also help you decide how to narrow your topic. Consider the length of the assignment, the number and type of sources you will need to use, and the due date when determining how to focus your topic.

13.3 Creating a Researchable Question

You can develop a research question to help guide you through the research process. Having a good research question can help you to focus your essay. Also, the answer to your research question can help you to develop a working thesis statement. An effective research question has enough depth to help you develop a thesis, but is narrow enough to fit within the guidelines of your assignment. Think about what you already know about your subject and what you would like to learn. Make sure that you don't already know the answer to the question and that you truly want to know the answer. You can always revise your question after you have begun your preliminary research.

Sample Questions

- **Too broad:** How has NASA affected the average American citizen?
- **Too narrow:** Has NASA affected the average American citizen?
- **Appropriate:** How has NASA's technology designed for space exploration helped to improve everyday household products?
- **Too broad:** What does scuba diving involve?
- **Too narrow:** What is scuba diving?
- **Appropriate:** What is required to begin scuba diving?

13.4 Writing a Preliminary Thesis Statement

Developing a researchable question can help give you a sense of direction for your research process, but it will not substitute for a clear thesis. As you begin the research process, you will need to draft a preliminary thesis, sometimes called a

Graduate SPOTLIGHT

©Karin L. Russell

Ashley Shannonhouse, Teacher

Ashley Shannonhouse has a BA degree in elementary education, and she teaches third grade in a public school setting. Here's what Shannonhouse has to say about the significance of writing in her career:

" In my career writing is important on a daily basis. I write letters and e-mails to parents providing them with details about what is happening at school and strategies for them to help their children to learn at home. Additionally, I write weekly newsletters to post on the school's website. I also write narratives to document students' growth throughout the year. One of the best ways for me to grow professionally is to keep current with the latest research in teaching methods. I read professional educational journals and research credible websites so that I can improve my knowledge base and provide my students with the best learning experiences possible. Every year I write a professional growth plan expressing my goals and comparing the new plan with my plan for the previous year. I am evaluated on my new plan, and it affects my raise for the following year. Overall, writing is critical to my career as an educator. "

working thesis. As with any essay, your research paper needs a thesis that includes your subject and an opinion. Having a working thesis will help you as you begin to select sources. You may decide to refine your original thesis later as you come across new ideas in the sources you find.

Sample Thesis Statements

- NASA has developed a number of high-tech devices for space exploration that have practical applications for everyday household products.
- The most essential requirements for becoming a scuba diver are purchasing (or borrowing) equipment, taking lessons, and getting certified.

13.5 Locating Library and Internet Sources

Finding the right sources for your topic is key to the success of your research project. For most research topics you will benefit from using a variety of sources, including books, periodicals, the Internet, and primary research. Learning how to conduct library and Internet research effectively will save you valuable time. Get started by visiting your library's website. Figure 13.1 shows the home page of a university's library.

FIGURE 13.1 Keiser University Library Home Page

Keiser University

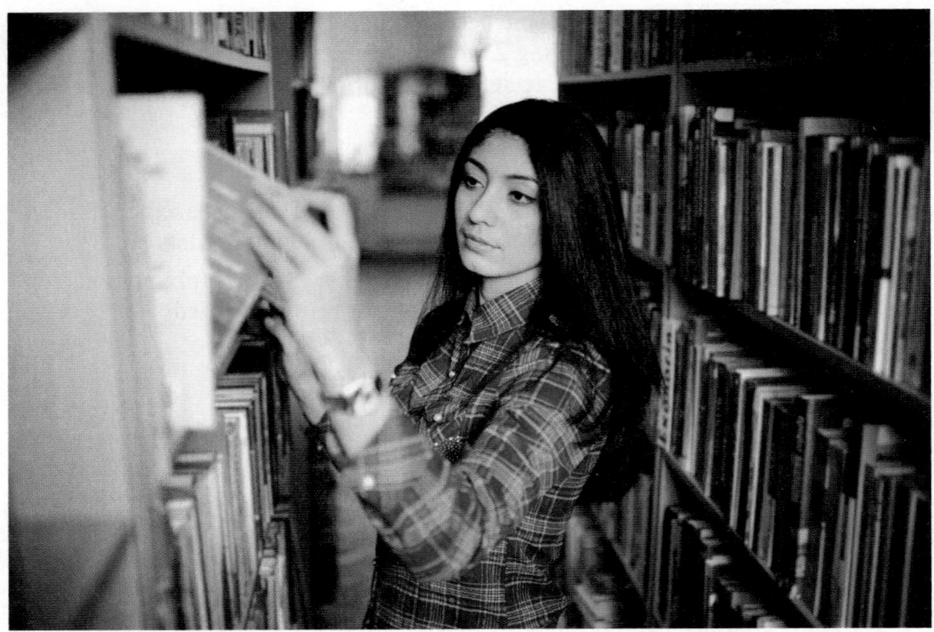

Evgeniy Kalinovskiy/Shutterstock

If you are not familiar with the library where you will be conducting your research, check to see if the library offers a workshop or tour that will show you how to find useful sources for your subject. You can also benefit from talking to a librarian. Reference librarians are information experts who can point you toward the authoritative sources that are most relevant to your topic. In addition to books, periodicals, and multimedia sources on your subject, your library also offers specialized databases and reference materials that will help you in the search process. As you learn more about the library, look for the following features:

Library Catalog

Library catalog An index of a library's holdings with specific information about each item.

A **library catalog** is an index of the library's holdings with specific information about each item. You can use the catalog to find books, periodicals, reference works, and audiovisual materials. You may also be able to determine if an item you need is on the shelf or checked out by another library patron. The library catalog is an excellent place to begin your research. Typically, you can search by title, author, or subject.

Keywords Significant words or phrases used to narrow a database search.

Type keywords into the catalog to find what you need. **Keywords** are significant words or phrases used to narrow a database search. Be careful to spell the words correctly, or you may not find anything that matches your topic. Also, you may need to experiment with different keywords until you find exactly what you need.

Use the words *and, or,* or *not* (known as Boolean logic) to help narrow your search (see p. 346 for more on Boolean logic). Print out or jot down important information about the sources that are relevant to your topic, such as the author, title, call number, and date of publication. Having that information will help you locate the source on the shelf.

As you locate the sources you found in the catalog on the shelf, look at nearby books to see if any of them are relevant to your topic as well. If a book you need is not on the shelf or is at another branch of the library, ask a reference librarian to help you locate the book. You may be able to obtain it using interlibrary loan.

Periodicals

Periodicals make good sources for research papers because they contain information that is precise and current. Magazine and newspaper articles tend to be more general than professional journals. They appeal to the average reader whereas journal articles usually go into more depth and are geared toward an audience that is knowledgeable in a particular field.

Current periodicals and newspapers are usually shelved alphabetically by title. Back issues may be bound and stored in the stacks or another area of the library. The online or print version of the *Reader's Guide to Periodical Literature* can help you to find relevant sources.

Databases

A **database** is a comprehensive, searchable collection of content that you can mine for articles and other sources related to your chosen research topic. Databases provide abstracts (summaries) of articles and often make the full text of articles available as well. See Figure 13.2 for databases that might provide useful sources on your research topic. Most college libraries subscribe to one or more databases such as ProQuest. A reference librarian can help you access the databases your library provides.

Database A comprehensive, searchable collection of content.

Reference Works

On your library's website, and in the reference area, you will find encyclopedias, dictionaries, almanacs, and other sources. Typically, reference works are not checked out, so they are always available to library patrons. Be careful not to rely too heavily on reference materials for your research. Instead, use these works as starting points for basic information about your topic.

While it is a popular reference work, *Wikipedia* is not a credible source for a research paper. Anyone can add, modify, or delete information that has been posted on a topic; therefore, there is no guarantee that the material is accurate. You may, however, use *Wikipedia* to find authoritative sources by reviewing the references at the end of an entry.

FIGURE 13.2 Keiser University Library Databases

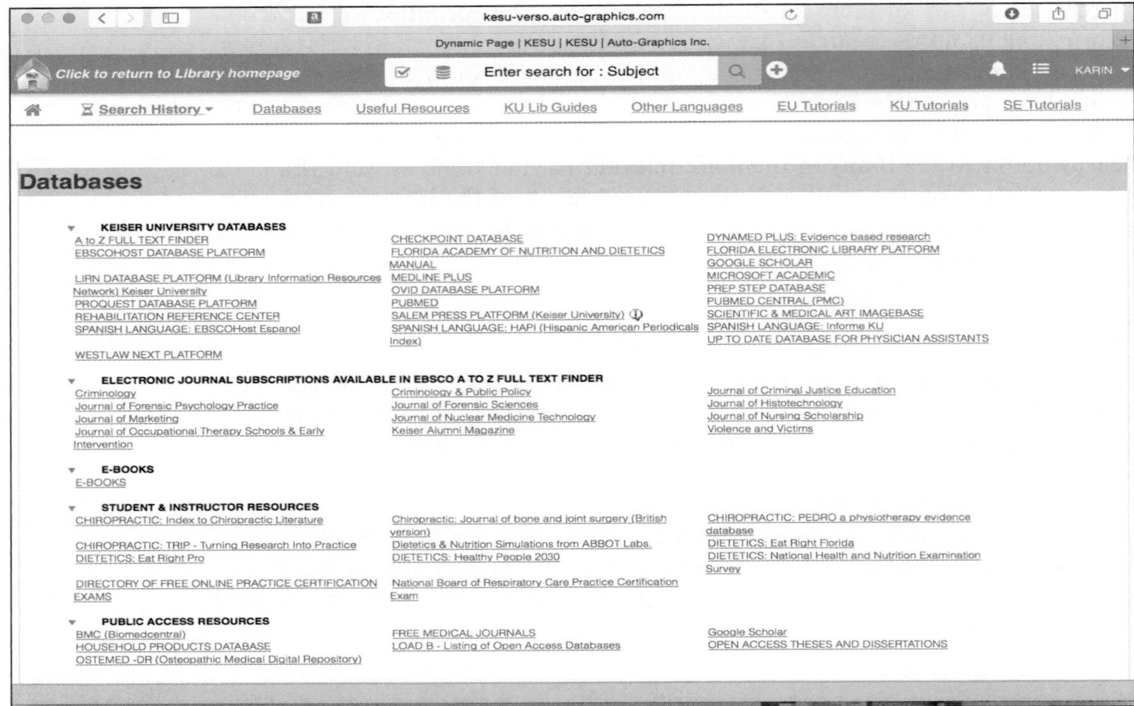

Keiser University

Internet Searches

The Internet is a valuable research tool. You can access a great variety of sources by using a **search engine** such as Google or Bing. Using a search engine will help you to sift through the billions of web pages to find what you need. For example, if you want to find websites that include information about NASA and household products, then you might try a search such as the one shown in Figure 13.3. Table 13.1 lists popular search engines.

Search engine A computer program used to locate information on the Internet.

Blogs and Social Media

Blogs and social media posts can add valuable perspectives to your research paper, but they are not necessarily the best sources for facts. As noted below, the quality of the content depends on authorship, so be sure to evaluate each source carefully. (See pp. 346–347 for advice on evaluating sources.)

Blogs A blog (short for web log) is a personalized online journal, a website or web page that the blogger updates regularly. Bloggers typically write in a conversational style that is less formal than, say, a news article. Blogs often feature advice and opinions. Businesses, organizations, and individuals can create blogs. Typically, almost anyone interested in the discussion at hand can post a comment to a blog.

FIGURE 13.3 Google Search Results for "NASA and household products"

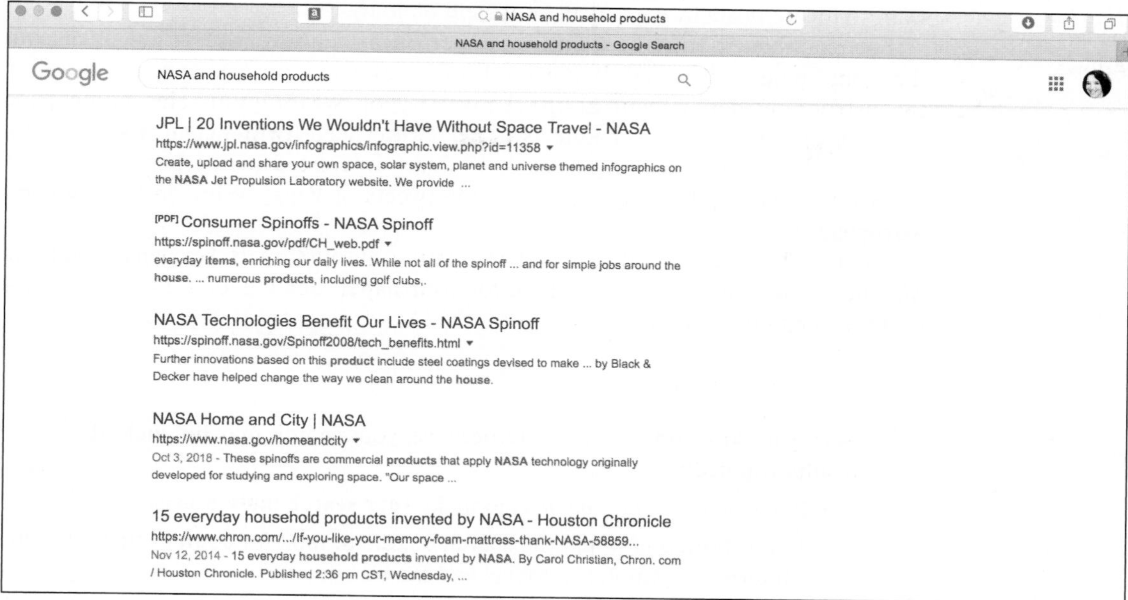

Google Inc.

Table 13.1

Search Engines	
Ask	**www.ask.com**
Bing	**www.bing.com**
Excite	**www.excite.com**
Google	**www.google.com**
Google Scholar	**scholar.google.com**
Lycos	**www.lycos.com**
MSN Search	**www.msn.com**

For example, *The New York Times* offers a blog called *The Daily* (**www.nytimes.com/column/thedaily**), which is also an app. *The Daily* is hosted by journalist Michael Barbaro who, each day, posts a twenty-minute audio file in which he summarizes and analyzes a significant news event or issue.

Using a blog post as a source is fine if you are certain that the author or publisher is credible. In addition to the *Times,* a posting on a blog hosted by a publication such as *Scientific American* (**blogs.scientificamerican.com**), or a government organization such as NASA (**blogs.nasa.gov/**) for example, is a good bet.

Social Media Facebook, Twitter, and Instagram are websites and apps that allow people to compose and share content and to interact socially. Posting on social

FIGURE 13.4 Web Page Navigation Arrows

media can be thought of as microblogging. For the purposes of research, you may want to locate posts by experts in your field of study.

For example, if you are writing a paper on astronomy, you might check out the home page and social media for Emily Levesque, an assistant professor in the astronomy department at the University of Washington. Her home page (**www.emlevesque.com**) also connects to her Twitter feed (**twitter.com/emsque**) where you can follow her research on stars. If you're interested in the perspective of a NASA astronaut, you might check out the tweets of Peggy Whitson (**twitter.com/astropeggy**).

As noted above, identifying and evaluating authorship is key when deciding on whether to use a post as a source for your paper. See Chapter 14 for guidance on how to cite these sources.

Tips for Searching the Internet

1. **Spell your keywords correctly.** Otherwise, your search may not yield the results you need.
2. **Use Boolean logic (*and, or, not*) to make your search more precise.**
   - Use the word *and* to tell the search engine to look for sources that contain both terms. Example: "phobias and famous people"
   - Use the word *or* to tell the search engine to look for any of two or more words. Example: "phobias or fears or aversions"
   - Use the word *not* to tell the search engine to exclude one or more words. Example: "phobias not obsessions"
3. **Click on hyperlinks to get more information.** If you see a highlighted word or a special icon, you can usually click on it to learn more information about the term.
4. **Use the back and forward arrows to navigate web pages.** For example, if you click on a hyperlink and want to return to the previous page, click the back button (see Figure 13.4). If you keep clicking the back button, you can get all the way back to your original search. This will allow to you go to another source without retyping your search term or terms.
5. **Bookmark or print out useful sources.** Keeping track of sources you may want to use in the future will save you time later if you decide to use them.

13.6 Evaluating Sources

You are likely to come across far more information on your subject than you could ever incorporate into your research paper; therefore, you will need to evaluate the sources you locate before choosing which are the most appropriate to use. The accuracy and credibility of your paper depend on your use of high-quality sources. Here are some tips for evaluating research sources:

1. **Author and publisher:** Is the author an expert in the field with the appropriate credentials? Is the publisher or website reputable? If you have doubts about

the reliability of the source, then you may want to investigate by searching for a biography of the author or the history of the publisher or sponsoring organization.

2. **Date:** Check to see when the information was published or posted on the Internet. If you are reporting on a famous study or historical event, then you may find that older sources are appropriate for your research paper. In other cases, you will need to have the most up-to-date information. New discoveries in science and technology are being made every day. If the information seems too old, then find a more current source.
3. **References:** Has the author documented his or her sources? Most reputable sources will include a bibliography to back up the information presented. If there is a list of sources, look to see if they seem appropriate. If no sources are cited, be wary of the information unless the author is an expert with the appropriate credentials.
4. **Bias:** While no information is 100 percent unbiased—all authors, including reporters, scientists, and other experts cannot help but share information through their own perspectives—it is helpful to ask the following questions: To what extent is the information objective and fair? Are there any overt biases or extreme views that make the source unreliable? For example, a website sponsored by a drug company may not be the most reliable source to use to determine if a particular drug is the best treatment for an illness. On the other hand, a source that is not necessarily objective may offer a point of view that you, as a writer, advocate. In that case, evaluate that source closely and consider using it.
5. **Effectiveness:** How useful is the content? Is it relevant to the specific areas you plan to cover in your research paper? Is it presented clearly and logically? Does the material seem accurate?

Activity Evaluating Sources

Locate an article or other source that is relevant to your research topic. Evaluate the source using the list above. Does it seem like a credible source for a research paper? Why or why not?

13.7 Taking Notes from Your Sources

After you have determined which sources will be the most useful for your research paper, you will need to begin reading them and taking notes. Taking effective notes from your sources is essential to successfully completing a research paper. You can take notes as summaries, paraphrases, or quotations. Whether you use a computer, a research journal, a legal pad, or index cards to keep track of your notes is your personal choice. You might want to make two columns, one side for your notes and the other side for your thoughts on why those ideas are relevant and where they might fit into your paper. Be sure to note exactly where you found the information by labeling it with the author, title, date, and page number or URL. Doing so will help you later as you draft your paper and document your sources.

Plagiarism The use of another's words or ideas without giving appropriate credit.

Anytime you use summarized, paraphrased, or quoted material in your paper, you must give credit to the original source(s) to avoid **plagiarism**, the uncredited use of borrowed material. Your instructor will let you know which system of documentation you need to follow in your final research paper. (See Chapter 14 for information on the MLA and APA systems of documentation.) If you add personal comments to your notes, be sure to include them in brackets [ ] so that you can distinguish your ideas from the concepts presented in your source materials.

Summarizing

Summary A condensed version of an original document using different wording.

When you write a **summary**, you condense ideas from an article, a chapter, or a passage, using your own words. Include the main ideas, but leave out most of the specific details and examples. Summarizing is useful in helping you manage large amounts of information. The following tips will help you to write a summary:

- Read the original work and make sure you understand it.
- Underline the thesis statement.
- Rewrite the thesis in your own words.
- Identify the main point in each paragraph.
- Rewrite main points in your own words.
- Put your rewrites together to create the summary.
- Review the original document to ensure that you have not changed the intended meaning or added anything in your summary.

The following is a summary of the essay "How Urban Myths Reveal Society's Fears," which appears on pages 107–109 in this textbook.

Sample Summary Although urban myths lack merit, they often catch the attention of the public. They represent our modern-day version of folklore because they combine unreal circumstances with everyday occurrences. People tend to believe urban legends because they tap into the fears that they have. Even though urban legends have been found to be completely false, some people will claim to have witnessed the incredible events that are portrayed through them. People may support these legends because the stories explain the unexplainable. Everyone who shares an urban legend has a hand in shaping it and takes ownership of its creation.

(Source: From "How Urban Myths Reveal Society's Fears," Neal Gabler, *Los Angeles Times,* November 12, 1995.)

Paraphrasing

Paraphrase A reworded version of a sentence or short passage from an original work.

When you **paraphrase**, you restate a sentence or passage from an original work in your own words. Unlike a summary, your goal is not to condense the original. Instead, your aim is to express the idea or ideas in the original sentences in your own way. As you paraphrase, change the sentence structure and word choice so that the new sentences are not too similar to the original, even though they express the same ideas. When you finish, highlight any words in your paraphrase that are the same as in the original document. You should have very few exact words. If you have several, reword them. Although it should be used sparingly, paraphrasing is useful when the original sentence or passage is complex or technical.

Sample Paraphrase

Original Passage. "Though urban legends frequently originate with college students about to enter the real world, they are different from traditional fairy tales because their terrors are not really obstacles on the road to understanding, and they are different from folklore because they cannot even be interpreted as cautionary. In urban legends, obstacles aren't overcome, perhaps can't be overcome, and there is nothing we can do to avoid the consequences."

(Source: From "How Urban Myths Reveal Society's Fears," Neal Gabler, *Los Angeles Times,* November 12, 1995.)

Inappropriate Paraphrase. Neal Gabler says that even though urban legends often originate with university students who are about to go into the real world, they are not the same as fairy tales because their terrors are not roadblocks on the way to comprehending, and they are not the same as folklore because they aren't cautionary. In urban legends, roadblocks are not overcome, and we can't avoid the repercussions.

Appropriate Paraphrase. According to Neal Gabler, many urban myths begin with students who are about to graduate from college and join the workforce. However, urban myths should not be confused with fairy tales because they do not provide a warning for the reader, and the results are inevitable.

Discussion. The inappropriate paraphrase follows the original passage too closely and uses exact words from Gabler's essay. The highlighted areas are exactly the same as in Gabler's essay, and the words in between are simply synonyms used to replace exact wording. Occasionally substituting a word with a synonym does not constitute an acceptable paraphrase. On the other hand, the appropriate paraphrase covers the main ideas presented in Gabler's original passage, but the sentence structure and word choice are unique.

Quoting

When you include a **quotation** in your paper, you take someone else's exact words and put quotation marks around them. Like paraphrasing, quoting should be used sparingly. Introduce a quote only when the original is particularly vivid or expressive or when you want to use an authority figure's exact words to add credibility to your paper. Be sure to carefully copy any quotes you use word for word. If you decide to leave out part of a sentence that you are quoting, then use an ellipsis (. . .) to show that you have

Quotation An author's exact words enclosed in quotation marks.

omitted words. However, do not alter the intended meaning of the author. Also, if you find an error (such as a misspelled word) in the sentence or passage you are quoting, include the Latin word *sic* in brackets right after the error to show that the mistake was the original author's, not yours, and that you copied the quote faithfully. (See Chapter 14 for examples of quoted material in the MLA and APA formats.)

Sample Quotation According to Gabler, "Though urban legends frequently originate with college students about to enter the real world, they are different from traditional fairy tales because their terrors are not really obstacles on the road to understanding, and they are different from folklore because they cannot even be interpreted as cautionary."

(Source: From "How Urban Myths Reveal Society's Fears," Neal Gabler, *Los Angeles Times,* November 12, 1995.)

Remember to follow the documentation method that your instructor requires any time you summarize, paraphrase, or quote material from a source. If you don't give appropriate credit to the source, then you are plagiarizing.

Discussion. When you use a quotation in your paper, you will often include a signal phrase to introduce the author's name at the beginning, as the example above illustrates: "According to Gabler. . . ." Another method is to include the author's name after the quote in a parenthetical citation. The MLA and APA formats require additional information to be included in the parenthetical citation as well. (See Chapter 14 for more information on citing sources in your paper.)

Activity Taking Notes

Choose a magazine or newspaper article, or use one provided by your instructor.

1. Write a summary of the article. Be sure to include the most important ideas and to put all of the ideas into your own words.
2. Write a paraphrase of two or three sentences in the article. Be sure to include every idea from the original source, but put the ideas into your own words.
3. Write a direct quote from the source. Introduce the author and/or title of the work, and use quotation marks around exact wording.

13.8 Conducting Primary Research

In addition to using the research of others, you can gather firsthand information about your subject by conducting **primary** or **field research**. Conducting a survey or personal interview is a credible way to supplement the information you find in the library and other sources. One benefit of conducting field research is that you can tailor it to yield the exact results you need. For example, in addition to using books and magazines about scuba diving, you might send out a survey to several divers, asking

Primary or field research Information collected firsthand from sources such as surveys, interviews, and experiments.

for their opinions about the most important things to know before beginning to dive. Similarly, if you are writing about a topic related to your major, then you may choose to interview an instructor in that program or a professional in your chosen field who works in your community.

Surveys

A *survey* is a questionnaire geared toward gaining information from people who are familiar with the subject you are researching. Surveys are useful for learning about the habits or opinions of a particular group of people. For example, you might use a questionnaire for a college-related topic, such as study skills or extracurricular activities. Check with your instructor to see if a survey is appropriate for your subject. Here are some tips for designing and conducting a survey.

1. **Clarify your purpose.** Make sure you know exactly what you hope to learn from the survey, and make your purpose known to the respondents. You might include a cover letter or note at the top of the survey explaining why you are conducting the survey and how you will use the information. For example, if you are writing a persuasive research paper about the benefits of being actively involved in student organizations, then you might mention to respondents that you will share the results with the school administration and that more extracurricular activities might become available as a result of their participation in your survey.
2. **Choose your participants carefully.** Decide who will be able to provide the best answers for your survey. Make sure your target audience is very familiar with the subject you are researching. For instance, if you are writing about student organizations, then you might invite some students who are involved in organizations on campus and some who are not. You might separate the responses according to those two criteria in your analysis. Also, make sure that your audience represents a fair sampling of the student population, in terms of gender, ethnicity, area of study, and so on.
3. **Set clear expectations for your respondents.** Be sure to give a reasonable deadline. Allowing a few days to complete the questionnaire should be enough. Also, make it easy for the participants to respond and let them know that you value their time and input.
4. **Design effective questions.** Make sure that your questions are clear and that they do not overlap. Before sending out your survey, test it with a few friends or colleagues. That way, you can modify your survey as needed. To prevent confusion, avoid using too many different kinds of questions. Two or three should be sufficient. Choose the type(s) of question(s) that will give you the best results for your subject (see Table 13.2).
5. **Compile and interpret the results.** Tally the results from the surveys that are returned to you and analyze their significance. Be sure to include information in your report that reflects all of the completed results, not just the ones that support the position you are taking in your paper. Also, you should include the raw data you receive as an appendix to your research paper so that your readers can review the information for

themselves. Keep in mind, the results you gather are merely the opinions of the respondents, so you can't necessarily assume that these results will hold true for college students in general, just for the ones you survey.

Note: Free online survey tools such as SurveyMonkey or Survey Gizmo make it easy for you to enlist respondents—and to gather, analyze, and share survey results.

Personal Interviews

Sometimes, conducting a personal interview can provide you with insights that are not available through other sources. You may find an expert on your subject who can answer specific questions that would be difficult to answer through your research. Here are some suggestions for planning and conducting a personal interview.

Table 13.2

Sample Survey Questions
• **True/False** I belong to an extracurricular student organization. ________True ________False
• **Rating System** Participating in a student organization helps the participants to strengthen their leadership skills. ________1. Strongly agree ________2. Agree somewhat ________3. Neither agree nor disagree ________4. Disagree somewhat ________5. Strongly disagree
• **Checklist** Check all that apply. Belonging to student organizations . . . ________ helps students to strengthen their leadership skills. ________ provides students with more scholarship opportunities. ________ impresses potential employers on a résumé. ________ takes away from valuable study time. ________ doesn't have any benefits. ________ isn't worth the effort required.
• **Multiple Choice** Choose one answer. How much time do you spend with extracurricular student organizations each week? ________ 0 hours ________ 1–2 hours ________ 3–4 hours ________ 5 or more hours
• **Open-Ended** How has belonging to an extracurricular student organization affected you?

1. **Clarify your purpose.** Make sure you know exactly what you hope to learn from the interview, and make your purpose known to your interviewee. Keep your interview focused on information that will be useful for your paper.
2. **Choose your interviewee carefully.** You may need to make several phone calls before you discover who would be the best person to provide you with the specific information you need for your paper. You may decide that someone in your community or at your college campus will be able to aid your research process.
3. **Determine how you will conduct the interview.** Whenever possible, a face-to-face interview is ideal. If you are able to schedule a meeting in person, then call ahead to make an appointment. If the interviewee is not available to meet in person, then schedule a call or an online chat, or conduct the interview by e-mail.
4. **Prepare your questions.** To ensure that your interview session runs efficiently, have 5 to 10 questions written out. The questions will help guide the interview. If you think you might get nervous during the interview, test your questions on someone before the real interview. Typically, open-ended questions work best. For example, if you are researching what it would be like to specialize in pediatric nursing, you might ask a pediatric nurse several questions, including the following:
   - What are the most rewarding aspects of being a pediatric nurse?
   - What challenges do you face on the job?
   - Would you recommend your area of specialty to someone just getting started in the nursing field? Why or why not?

Note: Sharing your questions with your interviewee ahead of your meeting may allow your interviewee to give more thoughtful responses.

5. **Be courteous to your interviewee.** Show up on time for the interview and dress appropriately. Also, tell your interviewee a little bit about what you hope to accomplish through the interview. Listen carefully and ask additional questions if you need the interviewee to clarify or expand on a point of interest. Be sure to thank your interviewee for taking the time to help you with your research project.
6. **Take thorough notes during the interview.** Even if you have a good memory, you will need to take copious notes during the discussion. Make sure to document the time and date of the interview as well as the interviewee's name and title. Additionally, write the answers to all of the questions you ask. If you would like to record the conversation, ask the interviewee permission first. Some people may be uncomfortable being recorded. If you are able to record the interview session, then you will need to go back and transcribe the answers later. Carefully documenting the entire interview will make it easier for you to include ideas from the interview in your research paper.

> *ESOL Tip* >
>
> You may be more comfortable taking your interview notes in your native language and transcribing them into English later.

Activity Conducting Primary Research

Develop and administer a survey and/or conduct a personal interview to gain information about your research subject. Follow the steps on the previous pages. Keep track of your raw data as well as your interpretation of the information you gain through your primary research.

13.9 Creating an Outline

After you have gathered all of your research notes, you will need to organize them into a logical sequence by drafting a preliminary outline. Determine the major points you want to cover in your paper and make sure that all of the points help to support your thesis statement. The outline will serve as the framework for your entire paper. You might begin with a topic outline and then expand it into complete sentences. Stay flexible as you begin drafting your paper. You may find that you can't get to everything on your outline, or that you need to include additional points to fully substantiate your thesis. If your instructor requires that you submit an outline with your final paper, then you will need to revisit your outline and make any necessary changes to ensure that your final outline reflects the organization of your final research paper.

Note: See pp. 27–29 for more details about developing an outline.

STUDENT RESEARCH PAPER OUTLINE

How Scared Are You?
by Neil Harris

Thesis: Although some people may think phobias sound silly or trivial, they are a frighteningly real phenomenon for those who suffer from them. Fortunately, with proper treatment, many people are able to live a reasonably normal life despite their phobias.

I. Description of phobias
   A. Categories
      1. Panic disorders
      2. Anxiety disorders
   B. Symptoms
II. Types of phobias
   A. Common phobias
   B. Strange phobias
   C. Ironic phobias

III. Treatment for phobias
   A. Relaxation and exercise
   B. Psychotherapy
      1. Changing view of phobia
      2. Exposure or desensitization
   C. Flooding
   D. Medications

13.10 Composing Your Research Paper

Following the preliminary outline you constructed, write a first draft of your research paper. Remember to consider your rhetorical star (subject, audience, purpose, strategy, and design) and follow the steps of the writing process (discovering, planning, composing, getting feedback, revising, editing, and proofreading).

As you compose your essay, you may combine the ideas in your notes from secondary sources as well as any primary research you may have conducted. Even though most of the ideas in your research paper will come from outside sources, you will want to make sure that your voice is the strongest in the paper. Use the research paper to support your own point on the topic. To do that, you will need to consider how all of the information you have gathered fits together. Keep in mind that a research essay is more than merely a string of quotes or series of facts. Choose your angle on the topic, and shape your paper to make it an original work.

A research paper follows the same basic structure as a traditional essay; however, you may need two or more paragraphs to fully develop each supporting point. Also, you must cite sources throughout your paper to indicate exactly where you have used primary or secondary research in your paper. As you **synthesize** (combine) ideas from your sources, be careful to note the author, work, and page number (or the website address) so that you know exactly where you obtained the information. Later, you can put source information into the specific format that your instructor requires, such as APA or MLA. (See Chapter 14 for documentation methods.)

Synthesize To combine material from two or more works to create something new.

STUDENT RESEARCH PAPER ROUGH DRAFT

Here is a portion of Harris's rough draft. You will notice that he chose to use numbers to keep track of his sources. Also, he covers his points in a different order in his draft than he does in his outline. He addressed these issues in later drafts.

How Scared Are You?
by Neil Harris

When confronted with a phobia, the individual 1
experiences what is in effect a panic attack. Symptoms include but are not limited to rapid heartbeat, high bloodpressure, dry mouth, nausia, and rapid breathing. "A phobia is a type of anxiety disorder"[4] grouped into two categories, panic disorder and generalized anxiety disorder (GAD). Panic disorders are "Recurrent episodes of unprovoked feelings of terror or impending doom"[2] while generalized anxiety disorder is "exaggerated worry about health, safety, money, and other aspects of daily life that lasts 6 months or more." GAD may be a response to a 24-hour news cycle and the times we live in. But panic disorders are very serious. Life activity condition phobias are grouped into three genres—specific, social, and agoraphobia. Specific phobias entail the individual being paniced by one trigger.[3] This phenomenon will be discussed later in detail. Social phobias or social anxiety disorder (SAD) is the fear of public situations. Individuals suffering from SAD will avoid public places. Some are worried about being embarrassed or calling attention to themselves.[1] Last, agoraphobia is a category in and of itself defined as "fear of having a panic attack in public,"[5] agorophobia is typically portrayed as fear to leave safe confines. People suffering from this disorder can progress to home confinement but are often observed with lesser degrees.

Stockdisc (Stockbyte)/Getty Images

Many well-known personalities deal with pho- 2
bias, which vary widely from normal to very strange. Some phobias were much more prominent in the past. Napolean Bonapart, Augustus Caesar, Julius Caesar, and Alexander the Great all suffered from ailurophobia or fear of cats. Others are more recent developments. Germophobia is the fear of germs. Howard Hughes, Howie Mandell, and Donald Trump are "GERMOPHOBES." Madonna shares her phobia with many dogs; brontophobia is the fear of thunder. The phobias can seem strange such as David Beckham's fear of disorder—ataxophobia. Anything out of place will drive him crazy. Billy Bob Thorton is terrified of antique furniture, called panophobia. There is nothing funny about clowns to Johnny Depp and Sean Combs who suffer from coulrophobia, the fear of clowns. Famous former Monday night football anouncers John Madden and Tony Cornheiser will not fly. Their fear of flying is called aerophobia. Marilyn Monroe suffered from agorophobia, the fear of open spaces, while Uma Thurman is claustrophobic, which is the fear of confined spaces.

Some people suffer from phobias that clash with 3
their characters. Roger Moore, who played James Bond 007 for years, is afraid of guns, or hoplophobic. The famous vampire novelist Anne Rice is acarophobic; she is afraid of the dark.[6] Sheryl Crow has one of the more common phobias called acrophobia, or the fear of heights. Odd phobias would include Nicole Kidman's lepidopterophobia or fear of butterflies and Christina Ricci's botanophobia or fear of indoor plants. But maybe phobias are there for a reason. Natalie Wood suffered from hydrophobia or a fear of water, which, sadly she drowned in.[2] By far one of the best phobias is hippopotomonstrosesquipedaliophobia which is the fear of long words. Linguists have their jokes too.[7]

Now you should be ready to get started on the first draft of your research paper. Chapter 14, "Documenting a Research Paper," addresses avoiding plagiarism and documenting your sources.

CHAPTER SUMMARY

1. Choose a research topic that is interesting and meaningful to you.
2. Narrow your topic to fit within the parameters of your assignment.
3. Create a researchable question to investigate.
4. Write a preliminary thesis statement to guide your research paper.
5. Locate appropriate library and Internet sources for your paper.
6. Evaluate your research sources carefully.
7. Take notes from your sources by summarizing, paraphrasing, and quoting the ideas presented in them.
8. If the project requires it or would benefit from it, conduct firsthand research through a survey or interview to supplement your library and Internet sources.
9. Create an outline to help you organize the ideas you want to include in your paper.
10. Compose a first draft of your research paper.

WHAT I KNOW NOW

Use this checklist to determine what you need to work on in order to feel comfortable with your understanding of the material in this chapter. Check off each item as you master it. Review the material for any unchecked items.

- ☐ 1. I know how to discover and narrow a meaningful **research topic.**
- ☐ 2. I understand how to create a **researchable question** and write a preliminary thesis.
- ☐ 3. I understand how to locate and evaluate library and Internet **sources.**
- ☐ 4. I know how to take **notes** from research materials by summarizing, paraphrasing, and quoting appropriately.
- ☐ 5. I know that I need to **document** all sources appropriately in my research paper.
- ☐ 6. I understand how to conduct **primary research** through a survey or interview.
- ☐ 7. I know how to create an **outline** for my research paper.
- ☐ 8. I know how to compose a first **draft** of my research paper.

Design elements: *Graduate Spotlight:* Ingram Publishing/AGE Fotostock

CHAPTER 14

Documenting a Research Paper

arek_malang/Shutterstock

learning outcomes

In this chapter you will learn techniques for achieving these learning outcomes:

14.1 Avoid plagiarism. *p. 359*

14.2 Determine when to cite or not cite a source. *p. 360*

14.3 Apply the MLA format for in-text citations, a works-cited page, and a research paper. *p. 362*

14.4 Apply the APA format for in-text citations, a reference page, and a research paper. *p. 389*

14.1 Avoiding Plagiarism

Would you walk into a store, take something off the shelf, and shove it into your backpack because you think no one is looking? That is unethical, right? Stealing someone's words or ideas without properly citing them is just as wrong. Many people cringe when they hear the word *plagiarism,* especially college students and English teachers. To understand how to avoid plagiarism, you need to be sure of exactly what it entails. According to the Merriam-Webster Online Dictionary, the four definitions for the verb *plagiarize* are as follows:

1. To steal and pass off (the ideas or words of another) as one's own.
2. To use (another's production) without crediting the source.
3. To commit literary theft.
4. To present as new and original an idea or product derived from an existing source.

All of these definitions represent serious forms of academic dishonesty. Go to **www.plagiarism.org** for additional details about plagiarism. The consequences for committing plagiarism at the college level range anywhere from failure of an assignment or the entire course to permanent dismissal from college. This problem goes beyond college, however. In the workplace, people can be terminated for plagiarism. However, there is no need to panic. If you learn the proper techniques for avoiding plagiarism, then you will have nothing to fear.

Basically, unless you are reporting commonly known facts or your original ideas, you need to document every source that you incorporate into your essay to avoid plagiarism. For example, if you are writing an essay on the effects of television violence on young children, and you want to include some statistics to support your thesis, then you will need to cite your source. Similarly, in a persuasive essay you may want to include a quote from a famous doctor about a new medical treatment for curing the common cold. To cite sources in some types of essays, your instructor may allow you to note the source in your paper with an informal citation, as the following fictitious examples illustrate:

Examples of Informal Citations

- According to psychologist Amy Telly, children who watch television for more than 50 hours per week are more likely to demonstrate violent behaviors at school than children who watch fewer than 25 hours per week.
- As Dr. Maverick stated in the introduction to his book *Killing a Cold* (2020), "*Incredicold* is the biggest breakthrough in cold treatment since the invention of the tissue."
- *Incredicold* is a new product that is taken orally, in gel or pill form, and that helps to relieve patients of nearly all of their cold symptoms (**www.incredicold.com**).

Citing sources in the ways shown above is appropriate for some writing situations. Your instructor may ask you to provide a copy of the original source(s) to be sure that you summarized, paraphrased, and/or quoted materials correctly

ESOL Tip >

Some countries do not emphasize plagiarism in academia as much as the United States. Be sure you know the correct documentation guidelines.

Library of Congress, Prints and Photographs Division

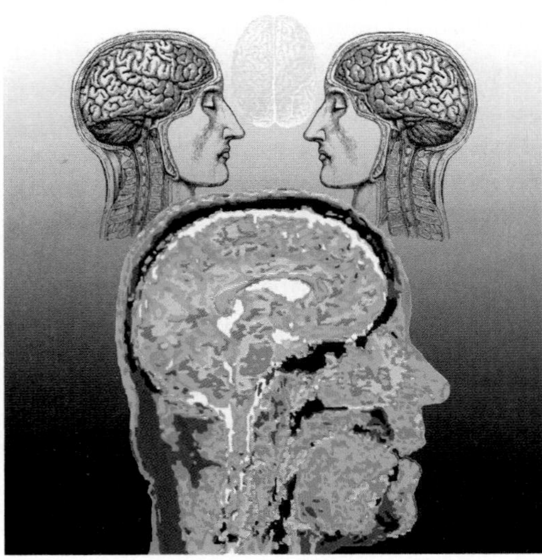

Brand X Pictures/PunchStock/Getty Images

(see Chapter 13 for more on note taking). However, if your primary assignment is to write a formal research paper, then your instructor will probably require that you follow the specific guidelines of the Modern Language Association (MLA) or the American Psychological Association (APA). The rules for each format are extremely precise, so follow the directions very carefully so that you document your papers correctly and avoid plagiarism.

14.2 Determining When to Cite or Not Cite a Source

As you gather information from various sources, you will need to know what needs to be cited in your paper. Using and citing sources accurately will add credibility to your paper.

What Doesn't Need to Be Cited?

1. **Common knowledge:** Common knowledge includes widely known facts that can be found in multiple sources. No one *owns* these facts. For example, the fact that George Washington was the first president of the United States is commonly known. Likewise, many people know that Betsy Ross sewed the first American flag.
2. **Personal experience:** If it is relevant, you may decide to incorporate your own personal experience into your paper. For example, if you are writing a paper about autism and want to include your sibling or child as an example, then you would not need to cite a source for that information. Ask your instructor if using a personal example is appropriate for your paper.

What Does Need to Be Cited?

1. **Direct quotes:** Anytime you use someone else's exact words in your paper, you must enclose the exact wording in quotation marks and give credit to the source.

2. **Facts that aren't common knowledge:** Even if you come across the same idea in several sources, it may not be considered common knowledge. For example, you may find several sources that explain how brain surgery is performed, but your average reader would probably not be familiar with the intricacies of that process. Think about what your audience is likely to know about your subject. If most people won't know about your subject, then cite your source. If you're not sure, cite it just to be safe.
3. **Opinions:** If you come across an interesting opinion in one of your sources and want to include it in your paper, then you must give credit to the original source. For instance, if you are writing a research paper for an economics course, you might cite an economist whose opinions about the state of the current economy help support your thesis.

Graduate SPOTLIGHT

Eric Osborn, eTime Administrator

©Karin L. Russell

Eric Osborn earned BA degrees in business administration and accounting. He is the system administrator and supervisor for the time and attendance system in the workforce management and planning department of eBay Enterprise. Here's what Osborn has to say about the writing he does in his career:

"At eBay Enterprise I am responsible for the overall system functions and setup of the time and attendance system. Communicating in writing is critical to my career. I communicate with over 3,000 employees regarding payroll and policies. Additionally, I write weekly summaries and reports, procedure guides for tasks related to my department, and proposals for changes to policies or procedures. For example, I recently convinced the management to provide additional training to new supervisors on the time and attendance system to better review and approve time cards. In my report, I documented cases where lack of approvals and reviews were causing loss of revenue and inaccurate pay to the employee. I also cited specific statistics to support my proposal. By implementing my proposal, eBay Enterprise will see better labor reporting, a gain in revenue, and happier employees with fewer pay inaccuracies. To make my reports believable, I must be thorough with my research and meticulous with my documentation. My overall goal is to propose written solutions to ensure that my company's operating expenses are cost-effective."

4. **Statistics:** Anytime you incorporate statistics into your paper, you must give credit to the originator. For instance, you might decide to include statistics from a reputable source to support your thesis that earning a college degree will lead to a higher-paying job.
5. **Original ideas:** Often authors who are experts in a given field will create original theories or ideas for their publications. Be sure to give appropriate credit to these authors and any others whose work you draw on. If you decide to write a paper about the theory of relativity for a science class, then be sure to mention Albert Einstein in addition to citing the sources you used to find the information.
6. **Studies and experiments:** If you are writing a paper for a behavioral science course, you might want to refer to a professional study or experiment. For example, in a psychology paper on sleep deprivation you might cite a landmark study to illustrate your main idea.

Basically, cite a source in your paper every time you present summarized or paraphrased material that isn't common knowledge or your original idea. If you are not sure whether you need to cite an idea in your paper, then you should be cautious and document the source. You are better off over-citing than under-citing. Also, you can check with your instructor if you are in doubt.

14.3 MLA Format

Many English and humanities courses use the Modern Language Association (MLA) format. The most up-to-date information about the MLA format is included in the 8th edition of the *MLA Handbook* (2016). You can find more information about the MLA format by going to **www.mla.org** and to MLA's style blog where experts frequently provide updates and respond to questions: **https://style.mla.org/category/behind-the-style/.** The MLA style of documentation requires that you cite sources in your text as well as on a *works-cited* page at the end of your paper. The following examples will help you to cite sources using the MLA format. You may also want to try using an electronic tool, such as **www.noodletools.com**, to help you correctly document your sources, but make sure that the source you use has incorporated the latest advice of the MLA.

MLA In-Text Citations

An *in-text citation,* also known as a *parenthetical citation,* shows the reader exactly where you have borrowed ideas from outside sources in your paper. When using the MLA format, you generally need to include the author's last name and the page number on which the borrowed material appears in the original source. Providing this information allows the readers to locate the correct entry on the works-cited page so they can find additional information about your topic if desired. You may include the author's last name in the text or in parentheses with the page number. If there is no author, use the title of the work. If there is no page number, such as for a website, omit that part. Vary the way in which you introduce sources in your paper to keep your writing fresh and to show how the idea from the source is connected to your point. Be sure to include the correct information and make it clear exactly what material comes from a particular source. The following examples show how to cite various types of sources in your text.

One Author

According to Li, tuning into our senses can help us to feel more connected to nature (15).

Tuning into our senses can help us to feel more connected to nature (Li 15).

Two Authors

Gordon and West suggest that successful people do not let their environment negatively affect them (62).

Successful people do not let their environment negatively affect them (Gordon and West 62).

Three or More Authors

Ma, Mateer, and Blaivas have observed that even though three-dimensional ultrasound technology can provide amazing images, it is currently not the best tool for making a diagnosis (25).

Even though three-dimensional ultrasound technology can provide amazing images, it is currently not the best tool for making a diagnosis (Ma et al. 25).

According to Bishop et al., image editors, such as Macromedia Fireworks or Adobe Photoshop, are useful for enhancing images in a document or web page (C22).

Image editors, such as Macromedia Fireworks or Adobe Photoshop, are useful for enhancing images in a document or web page (Bishop et al. C22).

Note: The Latin term *et al.*, which means "and others," shows that you have omitted all but the first author. Notice there is no period after ***et*** but there is one after ***al.*** You may list the authors by name in your text if you prefer (see the first Ma example), but always use *et al.* within the parenthetical citation and in the works-cited list. Also, the Bishop book includes section letters and page numbers.

Multiple Works by the Same Author

Novelists often include figurative language to create visual imagery for their readers, such as in the following sentence: "Their conversation is like a gently wicked dance; sound meets sound, curtsies, shimmies, and retires" (Morrison, *Bluest Eye* 15).

Authors also use descriptive language to help the reader feel the emotions of the characters, as in this excerpt: "Sweat poured from his temples and collected under his chin; soaked his armpits and the back of his shirt as his rage swamped and flooded the room" (Morrison, *Jazz* 141).

Some of the most successful writers begin with a shocking statement to immediately engage their readers, as in the following example: "They shoot the white girl first. With the rest they can take their time" (Morrison, *Paradise* 3).

Note: In addition to the author's name and page number, cite a shortened version of the title of the book to distinguish it from another book by the same author that you are citing in your paper. Place a comma after the author's name.

No Author

According to the book *The Workout Journal and Roadmap,* "Committing to specific action steps–workouts, meals, and more–on paper will help you head into the week with clear focus and motivation" (7).

"Committing to specific action steps–workouts, meals, and more–on paper will help you head into the week with clear focus and motivation" (*Workout Journal* 7).

Note: Use the first few of the words of the title in place of an author's name. The entry needs to match the beginning of the corresponding entry on the works-cited page.

Corporate Author

Children's Hospital Boston suggests that the parenting process becomes less demanding when a child enters school (277).

The parenting process becomes less demanding when a child enters school (Children's Hospital Boston 277).

Indirect Source

According to Budman et al., studies show that children who have Tourette Syndrome may experience "rage" attacks when they see a specialist at a clinic (qtd. in Chowdhury 61).

Note: Use this example if you want to use a quote or information you find in a source that was cited by a different author. Give credit to the original author of the material in your text and the source where you found the quote or information in your parenthetical citation.

Multiple Works

The most common side effect of having a Botox injection is droopy eyelids (*Botox Cosmetic;* Langdon 75).

Note: Use this example when you find the same information in two sources and want to cite both to add credibility to your paper. Cite each work the same way you normally would, and add a semicolon between the works in parentheses. In the above example, the first work is a website with no author or page number, and the second is a book.

Long Quote

Glave urges his readers to help do their part to save the planet:

> Do something. Do it now. Dream up your own Eco-Shed, Eco-Car, Eco-Boat, Eco-Garden, Eco-Concrete, Eco-Whatever, and start on it today. Sit right up front and take charge of the process. Stop thinking about what you have to give up, or whom you might tick off, and start thinking about what you'll gain. Each of us must earn our own green belt at our own pace. But believe me, once you begin punching and kicking in that direction, you won't ever look back. (248-49)

Note: For quotes that are longer than four lines, set off the entire quote from the text and begin it on a new line. Indent the quote one-half inch from the left margin and double-space it. Omit the quotation marks and place the final period before the citation.

Website/Source without a Page Number

In an Instagram post, Positivemindsetdaily says "What is coming is better than what is gone."

Note: Use a screen name when no author is listed.

Visuals (Photos, Maps, Charts, Posters. or Other Graphic Works)

The circa 1942 "We Can Do It!" poster, commonly referred to as "Rosie the Riveter," is an iconic symbol of World War II (Miller).

Note: J. Howard Miller is the maker of the poster.

Personal Communication (Email, Text Message, Letter, Interview)

Raising a toddler can be a challenge, especially when a parent is over 50 (Vining).

Note: This is a paraphrase from a phone interview with Ashley Vining that was conducted by the writer.

Literary Work

Poe shows his macabre side in the poem "The Raven" when the narrator says, "Ah, distinctly I remember it was in the bleak December, And each separate dying ember wrought its ghost upon the floor" (lines 1-2).

Note: For a novel, include the page number and chapter, like this: (Fitzgerald 43; ch 3).

Sacred Text

The creation of plants and trees is described as follows: "And the earth brought forth grass, and herb yielding seed after his kind, and the tree yielding fruit, whose seed was itself, after his kind; and God saw that it was good" (*King James Bible,* Gen. 1.12).

Note: The quote is from the book of Genesis, Chapter 1, verse 12.

MLA List of Works Cited

When using the MLA format, you must include a *works-cited* page at the end of the paper to fully document your sources. Literally, this means that you list any *work* you have *cited* in your paper. You may need to look at several examples of works-cited entries to find the exact format you need to document a research source (see Table 14.1). For example, if you need to cite the fourth edition of a book with

Table 14.1

—continued

Table 14.1 (*cont.*)

MLA Directory to Works Cited Examples
Other Sources: Overview, p. 380
Advertisement, p. 381
Personal Interview, p. 381
Broadcast Interview, p. 381
Sacred Text, p. 381
Legal or Historical Document, p. 381
Government or Business Document, p. 381
Work of Visual Art, p. 381
Music Recording (Song), p. 382
Spoken-Word Recording (Audiobook), p. 382
Television Show Episode, p. 382
Film, p. 382
Brochure or Pamphlet, p. 382

three authors, then you would need to look at the sample entries for "Book with Three or More Authors" and "Book in Edition Other Than the First." Generally, you will alphabetize the works-cited entries according to the authors' last names. If there is no author, begin with the title. Ignore words such as *a* and *the* when alphabetizing an entry by the title in the list of works cited.

Books Here is a list of the basic information you need to include for book sources using the MLA format. List the information in each works-cited entry in order, and follow the punctuation guidelines of the examples. You should be able to find all of the information you need on the title and copyright pages of the book. (See Figures 14.1 and 14.2.)

1. **Author:** List the author's last name, followed by a comma and the author's first name and middle name or initial as it appears on the title page of the book. Do not include degrees or titles, such as "PhD" or "Sister," with the author's name. If the book has more than one author, invert only the first author's name and include a comma between authors. If the author is unknown, begin with the title of the book.
2. **Title:** Italicize the complete title of the book. Use title case capitalization, which means that you capitalize every word except articles (words such as *a* and *the*), conjunctions (words such as *but* and *for*) and prepositions (words such as *to, from, for,* and *with*). If there is a subtitle, add a colon between the title and subtitle and capitalize the first word after the colon, even if it is an article, a conjunction, or a preposition. You may need to include additional information after the title, depending on the type of source you are citing. For example, you may be using an edition other than the first or one volume of a multivolume set. See the corresponding examples that follow.
3. **Publisher:** Include the full name of the publisher, omitting only business words such as *Company, Incorporated,* and *Limited.* For example,

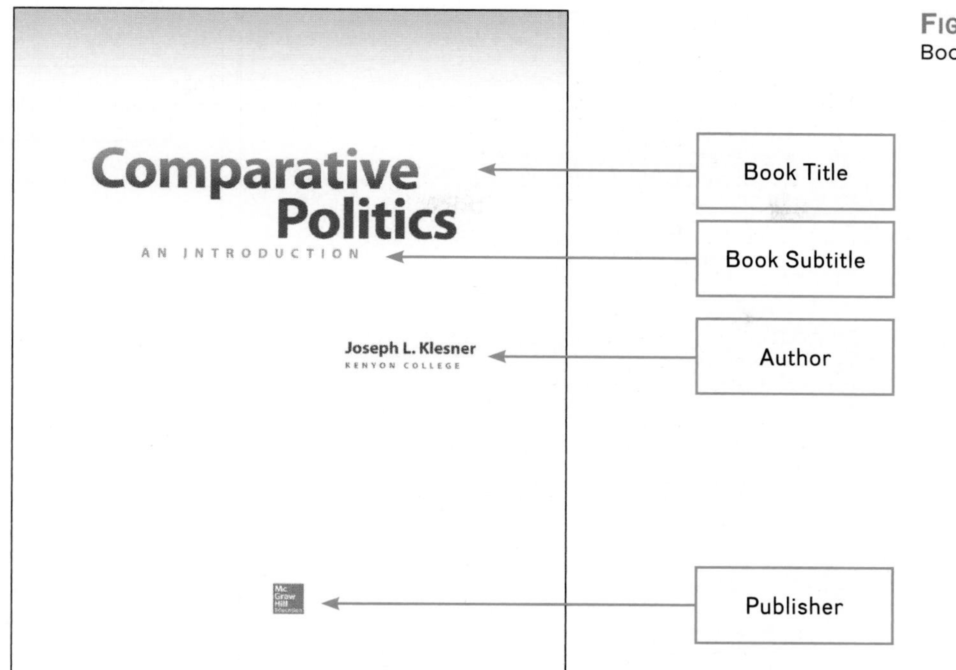

FIGURE 14.1
Book Title Page

W. W. Norton & Company simply becomes W. W. Norton. For university presses, abbreviate *University* as *U* and *Press* as *P*, but spell out *Press* in commercial publishers' names: U of Iowa P, but Penguin Press. If a parent company, division, and imprint are all listed, use the division name only. For example, if Macmillian (parent), Farrar, Straus and Giroux (division), and Faber and Faber (imprint) are listed, use Farrar, Straus and Giroux.

4. **Date of publication:** List the year. If the year does not appear on the title page, check the copyright page for the year. (See Figure 14.2.)

Sample MLA Book Citation

- Author's Last Name, First Name. *Title of Book.* Publisher, Year of Publication.

Book Example

Klesner, Joseph L. *Comparative Politics: An Introduction.* McGraw-Hill Education, 2014.

Book by One Author

Clegg, Brian. *Quantum Theory: A Crash Course.* Metro Books, 2019.

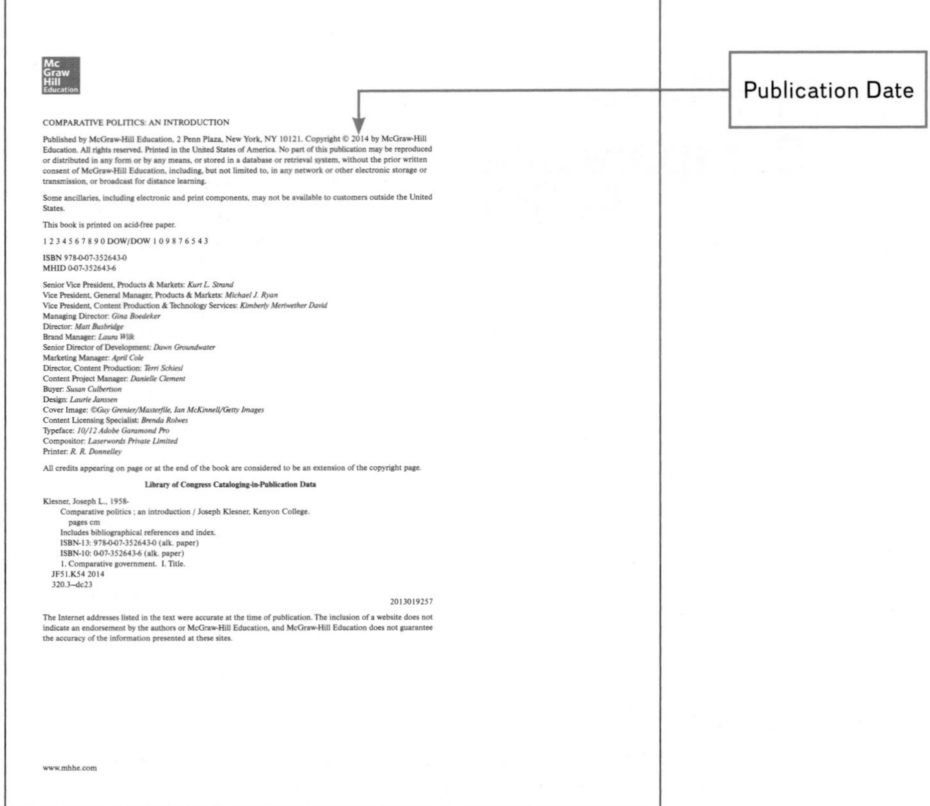

Mc Graw Hill Education

COMPARATIVE POLITICS: AN INTRODUCTION

Published by McGraw-Hill Education, 2 Penn Plaza, New York, NY 10121. Copyright © 2014 by McGraw-Hill Education. All rights reserved. Printed in the United States of America. No part of this publication may be reproduced or distributed in any form or by any means, or stored in a database or retrieval system, without the prior written consent of McGraw-Hill Education, including, but not limited to, in any network or other electronic storage or transmission, or broadcast for distance learning.

Some ancillaries, including electronic and print components, may not be available to customers outside the United States.

This book is printed on acid-free paper.

1 2 3 4 5 6 7 8 9 0 DOW/DOW 1 0 9 8 7 6 5 4 3

ISBN 978-0-07-352643-0
MHID 0-07-352643-6

Senior Vice President, Products & Markets: *Kurt L. Strand*
Vice President, General Manager, Products & Markets: *Michael J. Ryan*
Vice President, Content Production & Technology Services: *Kimberly Meriwether David*
Managing Director: *Gina Boedeker*
Director: *Matt Busbridge*
Brand Manager: *Laura Wilk*
Senior Director of Development: *Dawn Groundwater*
Marketing Manager: *April Cole*
Director, Content Production: *Terri Schiesl*
Content Project Manager: *Danielle Clement*
Buyer: *Susan Culbertson*
Design: *Laurie Janssen*
Cover Image: ©*Guy Grenier/Masterfile, Ian McKinnell/Getty Images*
Content Licensing Specialist: *Brenda Rolwes*
Typeface: *10/12 Adobe Garamond Pro*
Compositor: *Laserwords Private Limited*
Printer: *R. R. Donnelley*

All credits appearing on page or at the end of the book are considered to be an extension of the copyright page.

Library of Congress Cataloging-in-Publication Data

Klesner, Joseph L., 1958-
Comparative politics ; an introduction / Joseph Klesner, Kenyon College.
pages cm
Includes bibliographical references and index.
ISBN-13: 978-0-07-352643-0 (alk. paper)
ISBN-10: 0-07-352643-6 (alk. paper)
1. Comparative government. I. Title.
JF51.K54 2014
320.3–dc23

2013019257

The Internet addresses listed in the text were accurate at the time of publication. The inclusion of a website does not indicate an endorsement by the authors or McGraw-Hill Education, and McGraw-Hill Education does not guarantee the accuracy of the information presented at these sites.

www.mhhe.com

FIGURE 14.2
Copyright Page

Li, Qing. *Forest Bathing: How Trees Can Help You Find Health and Happiness.* Viking, 2018.

Langdon, Robert. *Understanding Cosmetic Laser Surgery.* UP of Mississippi, 2004.

Book by Two Authors

Gordon, Jon, and Damon West. *The Coffee Bean: A Simple Lesson to Create Positive Change.* Wiley, 2019.

Vernberg, F. John, and Winona B. Vernberg. *The Coastal Zone: Past, Present, and Future.* U of South Carolina P, 2001.

Note: Invert only the first author's name. The first author was listed on the book as F. John Vernberg.

Book by Three or More Authors

Ma, O. John, et al. *Emergency Ultrasound.* 2nd ed., McGraw-Hill Education, 2008.

Bishop, Sherry, et al. *The Web Collection.* Course Technology, 2004.

Wysocki, Anne Frances, et al. *Writing New Media: Theory and Applications for Expanding the Teaching of Composition.* Utah State UP, 2004.

Note: Use the Latin term *et al.,* which means "and others," to show that you have omitted all but the first author. Notice there is a period after *al* but not after *et* in the examples.

Book with No Author or Editor

The Workout Journal and Roadmap. St. Martin's Press, 2018.

Edited Book in a Series

Harris, Nancy, editor. *Space Exploration.* Greenhaven Press, 2005. Exploring Science and Medical Discoveries.

Note: If there are two editors, use the plural *editors.* The name of the series appears at the end of the entry. If there is an author, begin with the author rather than the editor.

Two or More Books by the Same Author

Morrison, Toni. *A Mercy.* Knopf, 1998.

---. *Paradise.* Knopf, 2008.

Note: Use three hyphens in place of the author's name for the second book (and subsequent books). Alphabetize the books on the works-cited page by the author and title. Ignore words such as *a* and *the* when alphabetizing the titles. Use the second word instead. In the examples above, *Mercy* comes before *Paradise* regardless of the word *A.*

Book in an Edition Other Than the First

Baker, Nancy L., and Nancy Huling. *A Research Guide for Undergraduate Students: English and American Literature.* 6th ed., Modern Language Association of America, 2006.

Book by a Corporate Author

Children's Hospital Boston. *The Children's Hospital Guide to Your Child's Health and Development.* Children's Hospital Boston, 2001.

Discovery Channel. *North American & Alaskan Cruises.* Insight, 2005.

Work with an Editor or Translator

Lutkewitte, Claire, editor. *Multimodal Composition.* Bedford/St. Martin's Press, 2014.

Beowulf. Translated by Seamus Heaney. W. W. Norton, 2008.

Note: Beowulf has no author.

Work in an Anthology

Poe, Edgar Allan. "The Raven." 1845. *The Norton Anthology of American Literature: Beginnings to 1865,* shorter 9th ed., edited by Robert S. Levine, W. W. Norton, 2017, pp. 688-91.

Note: An anthology is a collection of works selected by one or more editors. Use this example if you are citing an essay, letter, poem, short story, or other work that appears in an edited collection or compilation of works by different authors. "The Raven" was originally published in 1845, and it appears on pages 688–91 in the anthology.

Foreword, Introduction, Preface, or Afterword of a Book

Niles, John D. Afterword. *Beowulf,* W. W. Norton, 2008, pp. 213-48.

Note: Follow the author's name with the type of section.

Multivolume Book

LaBlanc, Michael L., editor. *Poetry for Students: Presenting Analysis, Context, and Criticism on Commonly Studied Poetry.* Vol. 10, Gale, 2001.

Note: This book has an editor rather than an author. The student consulted only volume 10 of this multivolume work.

Dictionary or Encyclopedia Article

"Italy." *The World Book Encyclopedia.* World Book, 2020.

Note: Use the word you looked up in the reference book as the title in quotation marks.

Printed Periodicals (Journals, Magazines, Newspapers) Here is a list of the basic information you need to include for periodical sources using the MLA format. List the information in each works-cited entry in order, and follow the punctuation guidelines of the examples. You should be able to find all of the information you need on the cover of the periodical and in the article itself. (See Figures 14.3 and 14.4.)

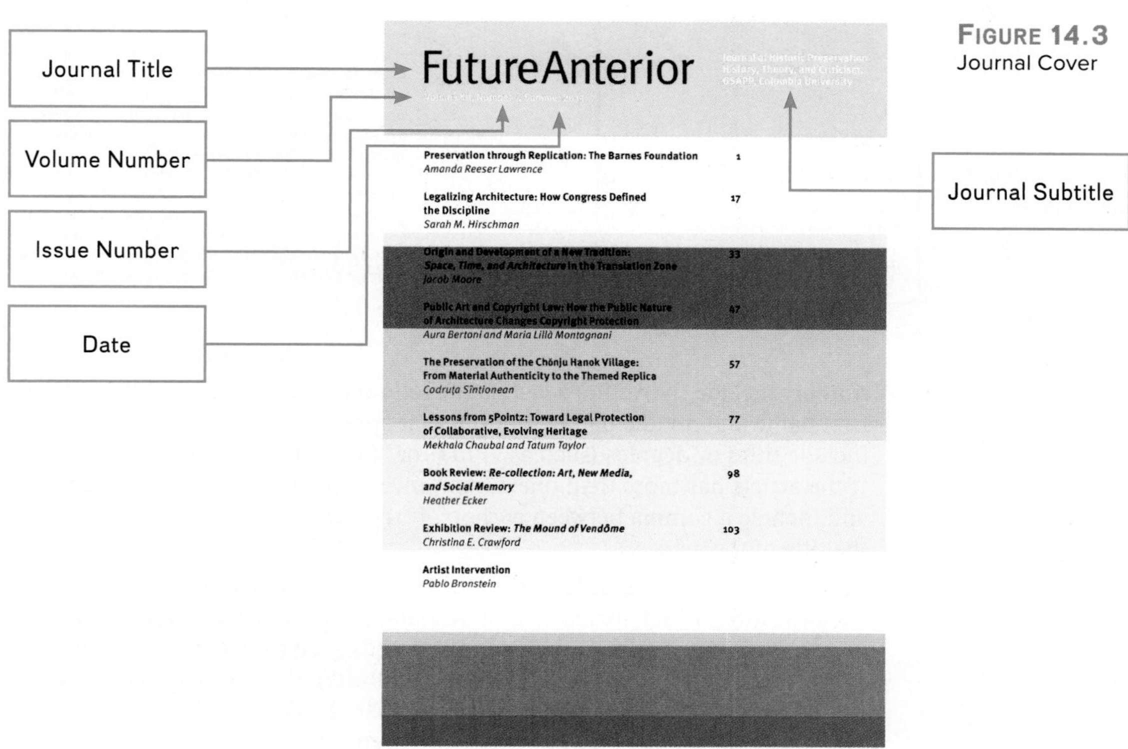

FIGURE 14.3 Journal Cover

FIGURE 14.4
Journal Article

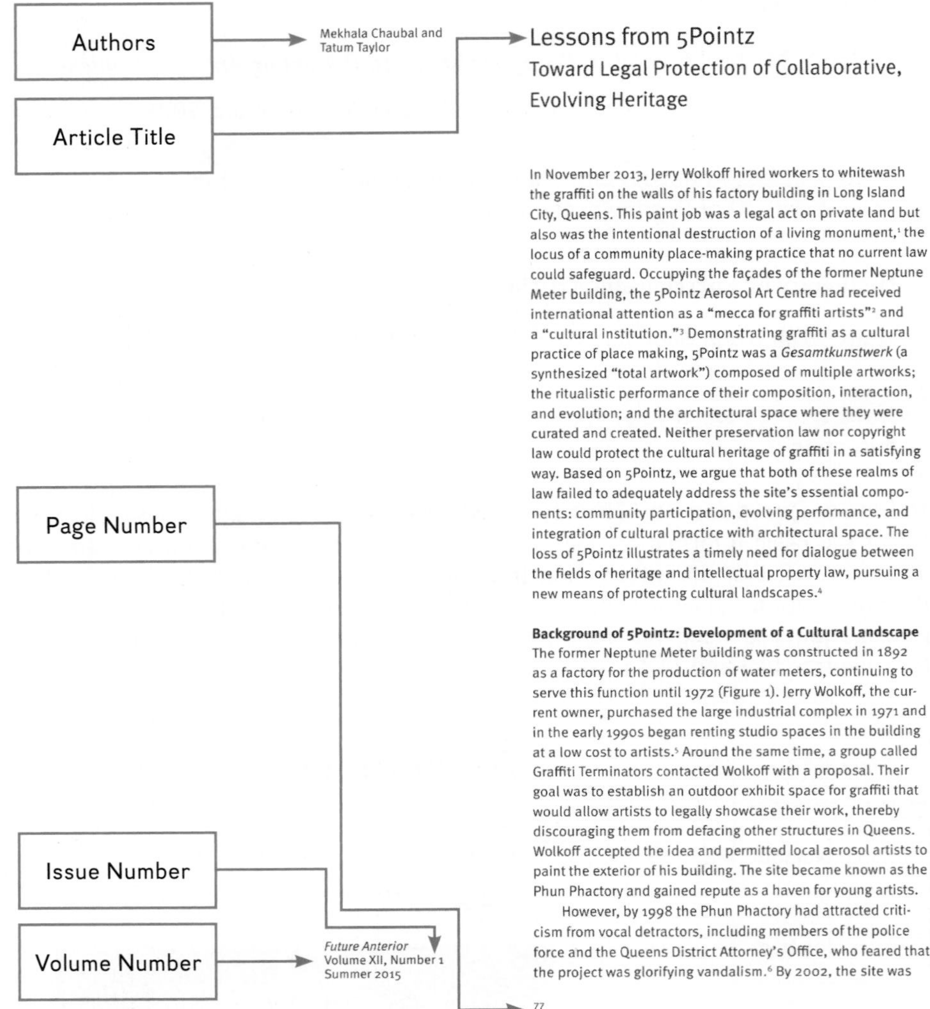

Mekhala Chaubal and Tatum Taylor

Lessons from 5Pointz
Toward Legal Protection of Collaborative, Evolving Heritage

In November 2013, Jerry Wolkoff hired workers to whitewash the graffiti on the walls of his factory building in Long Island City, Queens. This paint job was a legal act on private land but also was the intentional destruction of a living monument,[1] the locus of a community place-making practice that no current law could safeguard. Occupying the façades of the former Neptune Meter building, the 5Pointz Aerosol Art Centre had received international attention as a "mecca for graffiti artists"[2] and a "cultural institution."[3] Demonstrating graffiti as a cultural practice of place making, 5Pointz was a *Gesamtkunstwerk* (a synthesized "total artwork") composed of multiple artworks; the ritualistic performance of their composition, interaction, and evolution; and the architectural space where they were curated and created. Neither preservation law nor copyright law could protect the cultural heritage of graffiti in a satisfying way. Based on 5Pointz, we argue that both of these realms of law failed to adequately address the site's essential components: community participation, evolving performance, and integration of cultural practice with architectural space. The loss of 5Pointz illustrates a timely need for dialogue between the fields of heritage and intellectual property law, pursuing a new means of protecting cultural landscapes.[4]

Background of 5Pointz: Development of a Cultural Landscape
The former Neptune Meter building was constructed in 1892 as a factory for the production of water meters, continuing to serve this function until 1972 (Figure 1). Jerry Wolkoff, the current owner, purchased the large industrial complex in 1971 and in the early 1990s began renting studio spaces in the building at a low cost to artists.[5] Around the same time, a group called Graffiti Terminators contacted Wolkoff with a proposal. Their goal was to establish an outdoor exhibit space for graffiti that would allow artists to legally showcase their work, thereby discouraging them from defacing other structures in Queens. Wolkoff accepted the idea and permitted local aerosol artists to paint the exterior of his building. The site became known as the Phun Phactory and gained repute as a haven for young artists.

However, by 1998 the Phun Phactory had attracted criticism from vocal detractors, including members of the police force and the Queens District Attorney's Office, who feared that the project was glorifying vandalism.[6] By 2002, the site was

Future Anterior
Volume XII, Number 1
Summer 2015

77

1. **Author:** Include the author's last name, followed by a comma and the author's first name and middle name or initial as it appears on the article. Do not include titles or degrees (such as "PhD" or "Sister") with the author's name. If the article has more than one author, invert only the first author's name and include a comma between authors. If the author is unknown, begin with the title of the article.
2. **Title:** Put the complete title of the article in quotation marks. Use title case capitalization, which means that you capitalize every word except articles (words such as *a* and *the*), conjunctions (words such as *but* and *for*), and prepositions (words such as *to, from, for,* and *with*). If there is a subtitle, add a colon between the title and subtitle. Capitalize the first word after the colon, even if it is an article, a conjunction, or a preposition.

3. **Publication:** Italicize the title of the periodical and use title case capitalization.
4. **Volume and issue numbers:** If the periodical has volume and issue numbers, cite them both. For example, you would cite an article that appears in volume 10, issue 3, as vol. 10, no. 3.
5. **Date of publication:** Include as much information about the date as you can find on the journal, magazine, or newspaper. If you find the day, month, and year, list the day first, followed by the month, and the year, like this: 21 Apr. 2019. If you find just the month(s) and year, cite it this way: July-Aug. 2019.
6. **Page number(s):** List the inclusive page numbers of the article, not just the ones you used. If the pages are consecutive, write them this way: pp. 25-31. If the pages are not consecutive, then use a plus sign. For example, if the article starts on page 13 and then skips to page 26, cite it like this: pp. 13+. For a newspaper, include the section letter before the page number: p. A4. Follow the page number(s) with a period.

Sample MLA Periodical Citation

- Author's Last Name, First Name. "Title of Article." *Name of Periodical,* vol. X, no. X, Day Month Year, pp. X-Y.

Periodical Example

Barrow, Melissa A. "Even Math Requires Learning Academic Language." *Phi Delta Kappan,* vol. 95, no. 6, Mar. 2014, pp. 35-38.

Callaway, Ewen. "Siberia's Ancient Ghost Clan Starts to Surrender Its Secrets." *Nature,* vol. 566, no. 7745, 17 Feb. 2019, pp. 444-46.

Scholarly Journal Article

Black, Anne C., et al. "Advancement via Individual Determination: Method Selection in Conclusions about Program Effectiveness." *Journal of Educational Research,* vol. 102, no. 2, 2008, pp. 111-23.

DeVoe, Jennifer E., et al., "Uninsured Children and Adolescents with Insured Parents." *JAMA,* vol. 30, no. 16, 2008, pp. 1904-13.

Magazine Article

Lashinsky, Adam. "Apple: The Genius behind Steve." *Fortune,* 24 Nov. 2008, pp. 71+.

Scoles, Sarah. "There's No Space Like Home." *Popular Science,* Fall 2019, pp. 66-73.

Note: Use the complete date if it appears on the cover. Also, the "+" sign after the page number indicates that the article started on page 71 and continued later in the magazine with interruptions of advertisements and/or other articles.

Newspaper Article or Editorial

Tierney, John. "You Won't Stay the Same, Study Finds." *The New York Times,* 4 Jan. 2013, p. A15.

"Which Way to the Moon?" Editorial. *The New York Times,* 7 Feb. 2019, p. A30.

Note: The section number is included before the page number for newspaper articles.

Letter to the Editor

Kramer, Diane. Letter. *The Wall Street Journal,* 4 Jan. 2013, p. A12.

Electronic Sources Here is a list of the basic information you need to include for electronic sources using the MLA format. List the information in each works-cited entry in order, and follow the punctuation guidelines of the examples.

1. **Author:** Begin with the author's last name, followed by a comma, the author's first name, and a period. If there is no author, include the editor, compiler, narrator, or director of the work. If no name is listed, begin with the title.
2. **Article title:** Italicize the title if it is an independent work, and put it in quotation marks if it is part of a larger work. Use title case capitalization, which means that you capitalize every word except articles (words such as *a* and *the*), conjunctions (words such as *but* and *for*), and prepositions (words such as *to, from, for,* and *with*). If there is a subtitle, add a colon between the title and subtitle and capitalize the first word after the colon, even if it is an article, a conjunction, or a preposition.
3. **Website title:** Italicize the website name and use title case capitalization. Also include the edition or version you accessed if applicable.
4. **Publisher:** Include this information unless the publisher or sponsor is the same as the title of the website. If the publisher or sponsor information is not available, omit it.

5. **Date of publication:** Include the day, month, and year if they are available, like this: 15 Jan. 2015. Use the month and year or just the year if that is all that is available. If there is no publication date, omit it but include your access date.
6. **URL or DOI:** Include the Uniform Resource Locator (URL) or Digital Object Identifier (DOI) for the source. For URLs, omit *http, ftp, telnet,* and other prefixes, but retain the *www.* For DOIs, precede the DOI with *doi:* (no italics).
7. **Access date:** Include the day, month, and year you accessed the source only if the source is undated, likely to change, or likely to be taken down.

Sample MLA Electronic Citation

- Author's Last Name, First Name. "Title." *Website,* Publisher, Date of Publication, URL or DOI. Access Date (if needed).

Electronic Source Example

"Endeavour Crew Returns Home after 'Home Improvement' in Orbit." *NASA,* www.nasa.gov. Accessed 22 Jan. 2020.

Note: The article has no author, so the works cited entry begins with the title. Also, the article was not dated, so the student's access date is given.

FIGURE 14.5 Website Article

Tony Landis/NASA

Website (Entire)

National Geographic. National Geographic Society, www.nationalgeographic.com. Accessed 8 Feb. 2019.

Note: Include an author if there is one. Because the source is undated, MLA recommends providing the date the writer accessed it.

Website Article

Shute, Nancy. "Apes Have Food, Will Share for a Social Payoff." *NPR,* 3 Jan. 2013, www.npr.org/sections/thesalt/2013/01/03/168527985/apes-have-food-will-share-for-a-social-payoff.

Author Identified by Screen Name Only

Goldi1504. "Microsoft Service Helps Healthcare Organizations Develop and Deploy Virtual Assistants." *Reddit,* 7 Feb. 2019, www.reddit.com/r/technews/comments/ao3k8z/microsoft_service_helps_healthcare_organizations/. Accessed 12 Feb. 2019. Social media post.

Note: An access date is not a requirement, but for sources that can be easily edited, such as social media pages or posts or wiki entries, it is a good idea to include one.

Online Scholarly Journal Article

Nayar, Pramod K. "New Media, Digitextuality and Public Space." *Postcolonial Text,* vol. 4, no. 1, 2008, www.postcolonial.org/index.php/pct/article/view/786/521.

Note: When no page numbers are available, omit them.

Online Magazine Article

Fallows, James. "Be Nice to the Countries That Lend You Money." *The Atlantic,* Dec. 2008, www.theatlantic.com/magazine/archive/2008/12/be-nice-to-the-countries-that-lend-you-money/307148/.

Online Newspaper Article

Yin, Steph. "The Mirrors behind Rembrandt's Self-Portraits." *The New York Times,* 13 July 2016, www.nytimes.com/2016/07/14/science/rembrandt-old-master-optics-mirrors.html.

Online Encyclopedia or Dictionary; Wiki Entry

McNamee, Gregory Lewis. "Albuquerque." *Encyclopaedia Britannica,* 4 Apr. 2016, www.britannica.com/place/Albuquerque.

"Carpaccio." *Merriam-Webster,* www.merriam-webster.com/dictionary/carpaccio. Accessed 1 Feb. 2019.

"Robot." *Wikipedia,* en.wikipedia.org/wiki/robot. Accessed 10 Feb. 2019.

Note: Access dates are provided for the online dictionary and wiki examples because the sources are undated and, in the case of the wiki (and social media profiles), providing the access date is a good idea because wikis can be edited at any time, making them unstable sources.

Periodical Article from an Online Database

Glock, Sabine, and Carrie Kovacs. "Educational Psychology: Using Insights from Implicit Attitude Measures." *Educational Psychology Review,* vol. 25, no. 4, Dec. 2013, pp. 502-22. *Academic Search Elite,* doi:10.1007/s10648-013-9241-3.

Note: Follow the MLA guidelines for the type of source you are citing, and then add the database information and source URL or DOI to the end of the citation.

Online Audio Recording or Podcast

Sheeran, Ed. "Perfect." *Divide, iTunes* app, Warner/Asylum Records, 2017.

Note: Mentioning that you listened to this song on an app is optional.

Van Nuys, David. "Thriving in the Aftermath of Trauma." *Shrinkrapradio.* Episode 628, 31 Jan. 2019, shrinkrapradio.com/628-thriving-in-the-aftermath-of-trauma-with-ken-falke. Podcast.

Radio Program

Meek, Miki. "Before Things Went to Hell." *This American Life,* Produced by Ira Glass, episode 665, 11 Jan. 2019, WBEZ Chicago, www.thisamericalife.org/665/before-things-went-to-hell. Radio show.

e-Book (Novel)

Angelou, Maya. *Mom & Me & Mom.* Kindle ed., Random House, 2013.

Email, Text Message, or Letter

Record, Michael. "Using the Online Writing Lab." Received by the author, 20 Oct. 2019. Email.

Blog or Social Media Post

Strayed, Cheryl. "The Broken Horses of My Youth." *Facebook,* 30 Dec. 2018, www.facebook.com/cherylstrayed.author. Social media post.

PositiveMindsetDaily. "What is coming is better than what is gone." *Instagram,* 30 Jan. 2019, www.instagram.com/p/BITACGBH8Gr/?utm_source=ig_share_sheet&igshid=ID8geid5Cnx8.

Note: The access date and label of "Social media post" are optional for social media posts, which typically include publication dates. However, for social media pages and profiles, and for wikis, sources that can be easily altered, it's a good idea to include an access date.

***YouTube* Video, Online Movie or TV Show**

"The Problem with Museums." *The Origins of Everything*, PBS Digital Studios, 12 Nov. 2019, *YouTube*, www.youtube.com/watch?v=Av_3tGceTvs&t=62s.

Video Game, Online Game, or Software

Sugg, Darren. *Fortnite.* Epic Games, 2017, www.epicgames.com/fortnite/en-us. Video game.

Other Sources You may decide to use other types of sources in your research paper. Each type of source has its own unique format. Be sure to give readers enough information to be able to find the source if they so desire. Many of the MLA rules from previous examples apply to the following sources.

Advertisement

Apple iPad. Advertisement. *Wired,* Jan. 2019, p. 150.

AT&T. Commercial. CNN, 6 July 2019.

Personal Interview

Blush, Linda. Personal interview. 6 Jan. 2020.

Vining, Ashley. Telephone interview. 12 Dec. 2019.

Broadcast Interview

Sweeney, Alison. Interview by Ellen Degeneres. *The Ellen Degeneres Show,* NBC, WESH, 3 Jan. 2013.

Note: After the network, include the call letters of your local station.

Sacred Text

Holy Bible. New International Version, Zondervan, 2001.

Legal or Historical Document

California, Office of the Attorney General. *Proposition 65: Safe Drinking Water and Toxic Enforcement Act,* 1986.

Government or Business Document

The Constitution of the United States. 1987, National Archives, www.archives.gov/founding-docs/constitution.

Work of Visual Art

Bonnard, Pierre. *Before Dinner.* 1924, Metropolitan Museum of Art, New York.

Simmons, Laurie. *Walking House.* Photograph. 1989, Museum of Modern Art, New York.

Note: Include the current location of the artwork after the date of its creation.

Music Recording (Song)

Keys, Alicia. "Brand New Me." *Girl on Fire,* RCA Records, 2012.

Or, for a song accessed through an app:

Keys, Alicia. "Brand New Me." *Girl on Fire, iTunes* app, RCA Records, 2012.

Note: Begin the entry with the name of the artist or group.

Spoken-Word Recording (Audiobook)

Gore, Al. *The Assault on Reason.* Narrated by Will Patton, Penguin Audio, 2007. Audiobook.

Television Show Episode

"Little Girl Lost." *Cold Case Files. Amazon Prime* app, A&E Network, 27, Feb. 2017.

Film

No Country for Old Men. Directed by Joel Coen and Ethan Coen, performances by Tommy Lee Jones, Javier Bardem, Josh Brolin, and Kelly MacDonald, Miramax, 2007.

Or, if the film was accessed online:

No Country for Old Men. Directed by Joel Cohen and Ethan Coen, performances by Tommy Lee Jones, Javier Bardem, Josh Brolin, and Kelly MacDonald, Miramax, 2007. *Amazon Prime,* www.amazon.com/Country-Old-Men-Tommy-Jones/dp/B00BQPHZ6A.

Brochure or Pamphlet

Visitor's Guide to the Morse Museum. Charles Hosmer Morse Foundation, 2019.

Note: Include an author if there is one.

MLA Research Paper Formatting Guide

1. **Margins:** Use one-inch margins at the top, bottom, and sides of the paper.
2. **Heading:** Place your heading at the upper-left corner of your paper, one inch from the top and one inch from the left edge of your paper. Include the following information, double-spaced: Your name, your instructor's name, the course name and number, and the date in this style: 15 November 2015.
3. **Header:** Include your last name and the page number on every page of your paper in the upper-right corner, one-half inch from the top and one inch from the right edge of your paper.
4. **Title:** Center your title on the page, two spaces down from the date. Your title should be descriptive and, if possible, creative. Avoid italicizing, underlining, or boldfacing your title or putting it in quotation marks. Use title case capitalization.
5. **Text formatting:** Throughout the paper, use a 12-point font with a typeface that is easy to read, such as Times New Roman. Do not justify the right-hand margin of the text; the text should have a ragged (uneven) right margin. Double-space the entire paper, and indent each paragraph one-half inch. Leave one space between sentences. Do not include an extra space between paragraphs. Include in-text citations to indicate where you have borrowed quoted, paraphrased, and summarized ideas from your sources.
6. **Visual elements:** If you decide to include tables or illustrations, such as maps, charts, or works of art, in your paper, place them near the text in which you refer to them. Label the item Table or Fig. (short for figure) and consecutively number each one. In the body of the paper, where you refer to the table or illustration, write the following in parentheses: (see fig. 1). For a table, include the label above the table, with the table number and table title on separate lines. Place the source note below the table. For a figure, include the label and complete source information below the figure.

FIG. 1. Monet, Claude. *Villas at Bordighera.* 1884, Santa Barbara Museum of Art, California.

Note: Because you will include the complete source information with the table or figure, you will not need to duplicate it on the works-cited page.

Peter Horree/Alamy Images

STUDENT MLA RESEARCH PAPER

From Stigma to Status

by Margaret Rowland

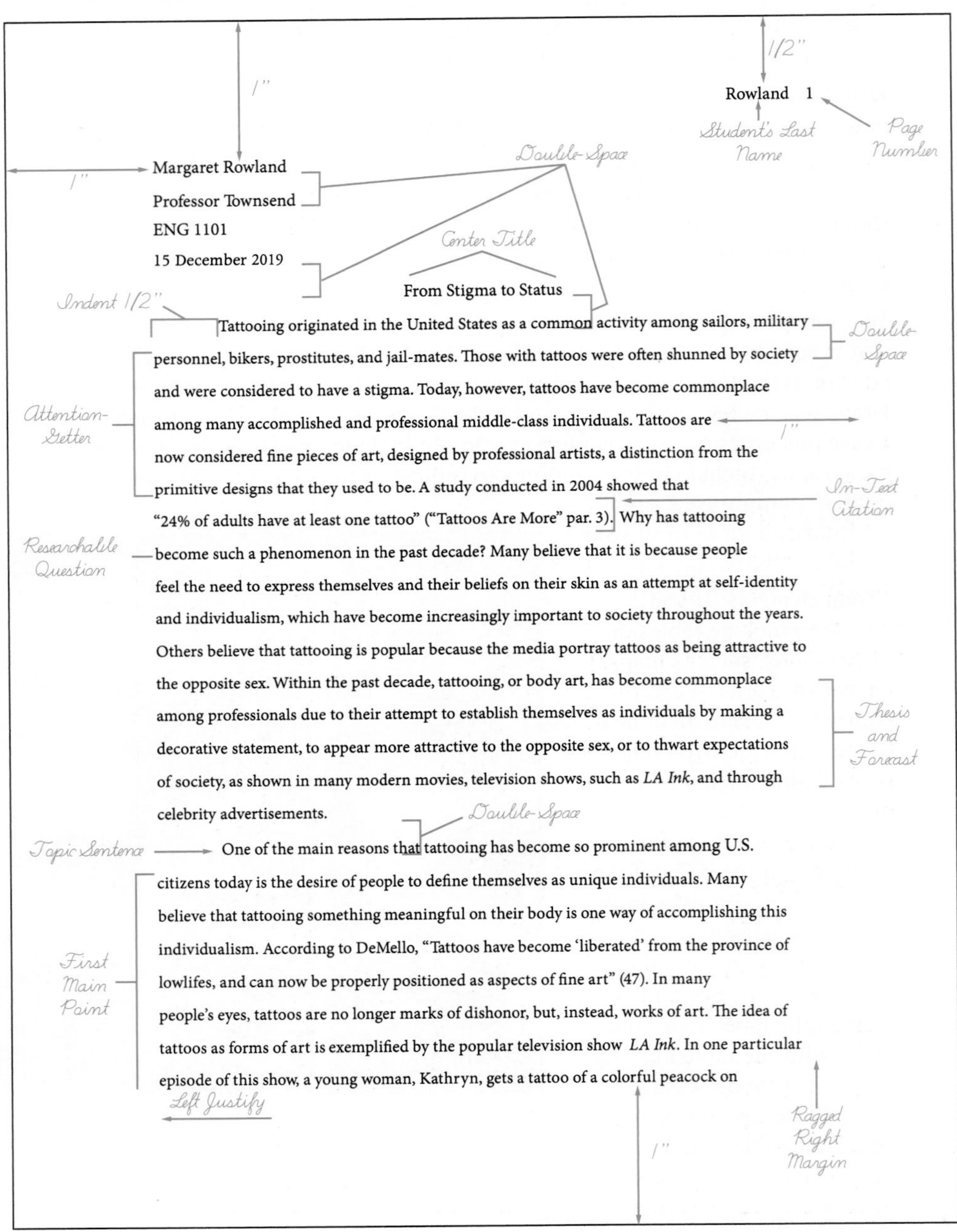

Rowland 1

Margaret Rowland

Professor Townsend

ENG 1101

15 December 2019

From Stigma to Status

Tattooing originated in the United States as a common activity among sailors, military personnel, bikers, prostitutes, and jail-mates. Those with tattoos were often shunned by society and were considered to have a stigma. Today, however, tattoos have become commonplace among many accomplished and professional middle-class individuals. Tattoos are now considered fine pieces of art, designed by professional artists, a distinction from the primitive designs that they used to be. A study conducted in 2004 showed that "24% of adults have at least one tattoo" ("Tattoos Are More" par. 3). Why has tattooing become such a phenomenon in the past decade? Many believe that it is because people feel the need to express themselves and their beliefs on their skin as an attempt at self-identity and individualism, which have become increasingly important to society throughout the years. Others believe that tattooing is popular because the media portray tattoos as being attractive to the opposite sex. Within the past decade, tattooing, or body art, has become commonplace among professionals due to their attempt to establish themselves as individuals by making a decorative statement, to appear more attractive to the opposite sex, or to thwart expectations of society, as shown in many modern movies, television shows, such as *LA Ink*, and through celebrity advertisements.

One of the main reasons that tattooing has become so prominent among U.S. citizens today is the desire of people to define themselves as unique individuals. Many believe that tattooing something meaningful on their body is one way of accomplishing this individualism. According to DeMello, "Tattoos have become 'liberated' from the province of lowlifes, and can now be properly positioned as aspects of fine art" (47). In many people's eyes, tattoos are no longer marks of dishonor, but, instead, works of art. The idea of tattoos as forms of art is exemplified by the popular television show *LA Ink*. In one particular episode of this show, a young woman, Kathryn, gets a tattoo of a colorful peacock on

1/2"

1"

1"

1"

First Main Point Continued

her arm to represent the strength of her mother who had recently been in a coma for two months and completely lost her memory. Kathryn was not a biker or involved in crime, but was an educated, middle-class individual who desired to make a statement about her mother's heartbreaking situation in the form of body art (*LA Ink—Peacock Tattoo*). In DeMello's article, "Not Just for Bikers Anymore," she quotes an individual who was interviewed about his decision to get a tattoo. He responded, "The power of the tattoo is in the ability to express individuality and in its permanence" (DeMello 41). Kathryn, from *LA Ink—Peacock Tattoo*, and this quoted individual share similar beliefs about tattoos and their meanings. Whether they are designed in memory of a loved one or to symbolize an important value or belief of the individual, tattoos are most commonly acquired for the purpose of making unique, decorative statements.

Topic Sentence →

Second Main Point

Another fundamental motivation for people in this country to get tattoos is the belief that they create sex appeal. A study of college students found that "almost three-fourths of the undergraduate women reported that they 'sometimes' viewed openly visible tattoos as attractive when on a man" (Horne et al. 1011). On the other hand, "58.8 percent of the undergraduate men viewed such visible tattoos as attractive when on a woman" (Horne et al. 1011). Therefore, men and women may get tattoos if they feel that they will add to their sex appeal. A large portion of this thinking has derived from the fact that many celebrities have tattoos, and, because celebrities are often seen as sex icons, common people believe that if they get tattoos then they will be appealing to the opposite sex as well (Horne et al. 1011). DeMello states, "Tattooing has moved from being a symbol of the outcast to that of a rock star, model, and postmodern youth, and with this shift in public perception has come a shift in meaning as well, as tattoo moves from stigma to status" (49). The idea that tattoos are sexy is exemplified in many modern movies, including *Wanted*. The most famous scene of this movie depicts Angelina Jolie getting out of a bathtub, completely naked, with large tattoos covering her back. Jolie seductively peers around her shoulder at the camera, an obvious attempt of the director to attract men with her tattoo-covered body (*Wanted*). Since the premier of the movie, this scene has become extremely famous. However, Jolie is not the only celebrity to endorse tattoos. Others, including David Beckham, Rihanna, Michael Jordan, and Gisele, have been pictured in advertisements that show

1"

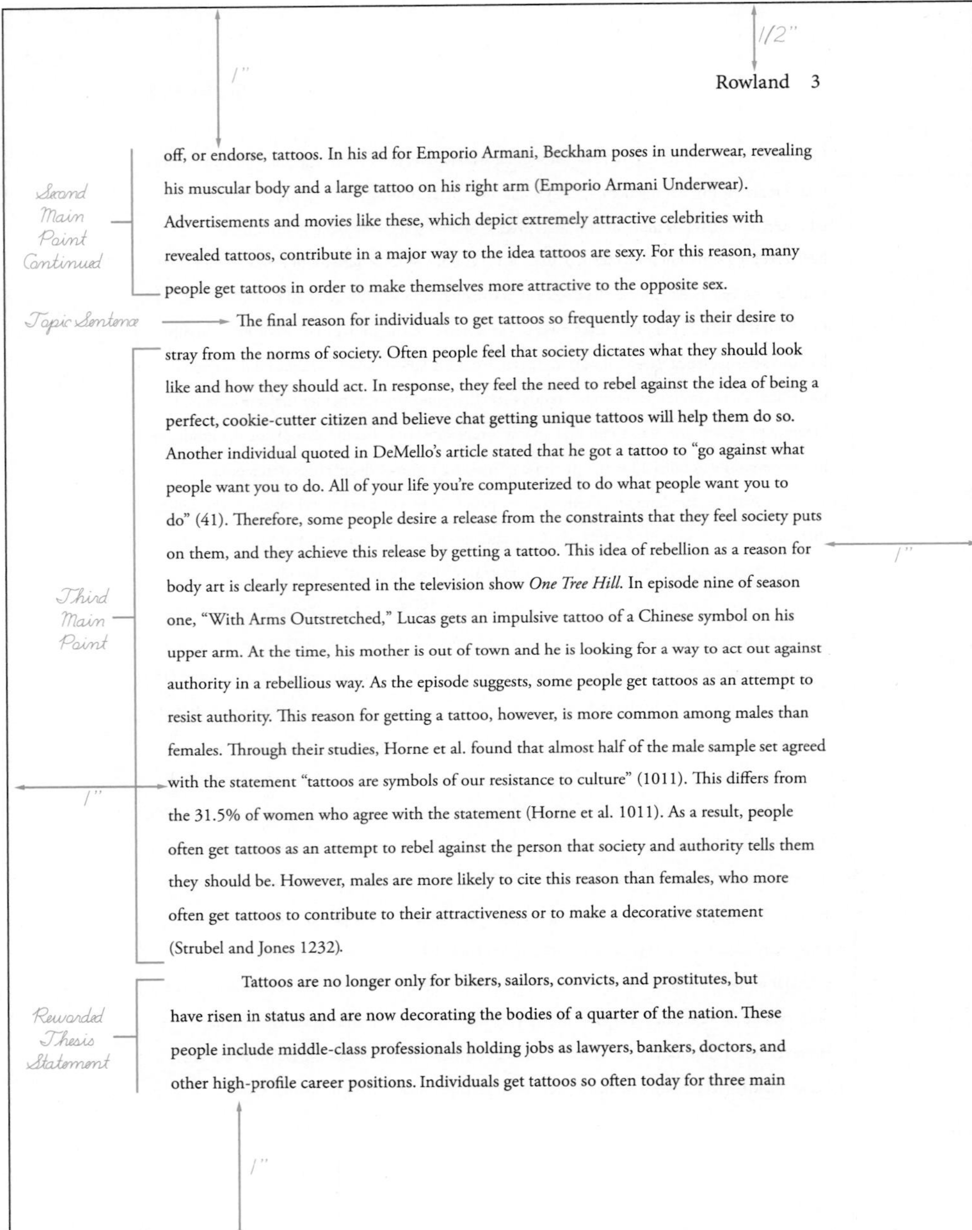

Rowland 3

off, or endorse, tattoos. In his ad for Emporio Armani, Beckham poses in underwear, revealing his muscular body and a large tattoo on his right arm (Emporio Armani Underwear). Advertisements and movies like these, which depict extremely attractive celebrities with revealed tattoos, contribute in a major way to the idea tattoos are sexy. For this reason, many people get tattoos in order to make themselves more attractive to the opposite sex.

The final reason for individuals to get tattoos so frequently today is their desire to stray from the norms of society. Often people feel that society dictates what they should look like and how they should act. In response, they feel the need to rebel against the idea of being a perfect, cookie-cutter citizen and believe chat getting unique tattoos will help them do so. Another individual quoted in DeMello's article stated that he got a tattoo to "go against what people want you to do. All of your life you're computerized to do what people want you to do" (41). Therefore, some people desire a release from the constraints that they feel society puts on them, and they achieve this release by getting a tattoo. This idea of rebellion as a reason for body art is clearly represented in the television show *One Tree Hill.* In episode nine of season one, "With Arms Outstretched," Lucas gets an impulsive tattoo of a Chinese symbol on his upper arm. At the time, his mother is out of town and he is looking for a way to act out against authority in a rebellious way. As the episode suggests, some people get tattoos as an attempt to resist authority. This reason for getting a tattoo, however, is more common among males than females. Through their studies, Horne et al. found that almost half of the male sample set agreed with the statement "tattoos are symbols of our resistance to culture" (1011). This differs from the 31.5% of women who agree with the statement (Horne et al. 1011). As a result, people often get tattoos as an attempt to rebel against the person that society and authority tells them they should be. However, males are more likely to cite this reason than females, who more often get tattoos to contribute to their attractiveness or to make a decorative statement (Strubel and Jones 1232).

Tattoos are no longer only for bikers, sailors, convicts, and prostitutes, but have risen in status and are now decorating the bodies of a quarter of the nation. These people include middle-class professionals holding jobs as lawyers, bankers, doctors, and other high-profile career positions. Individuals get tattoos so often today for three main

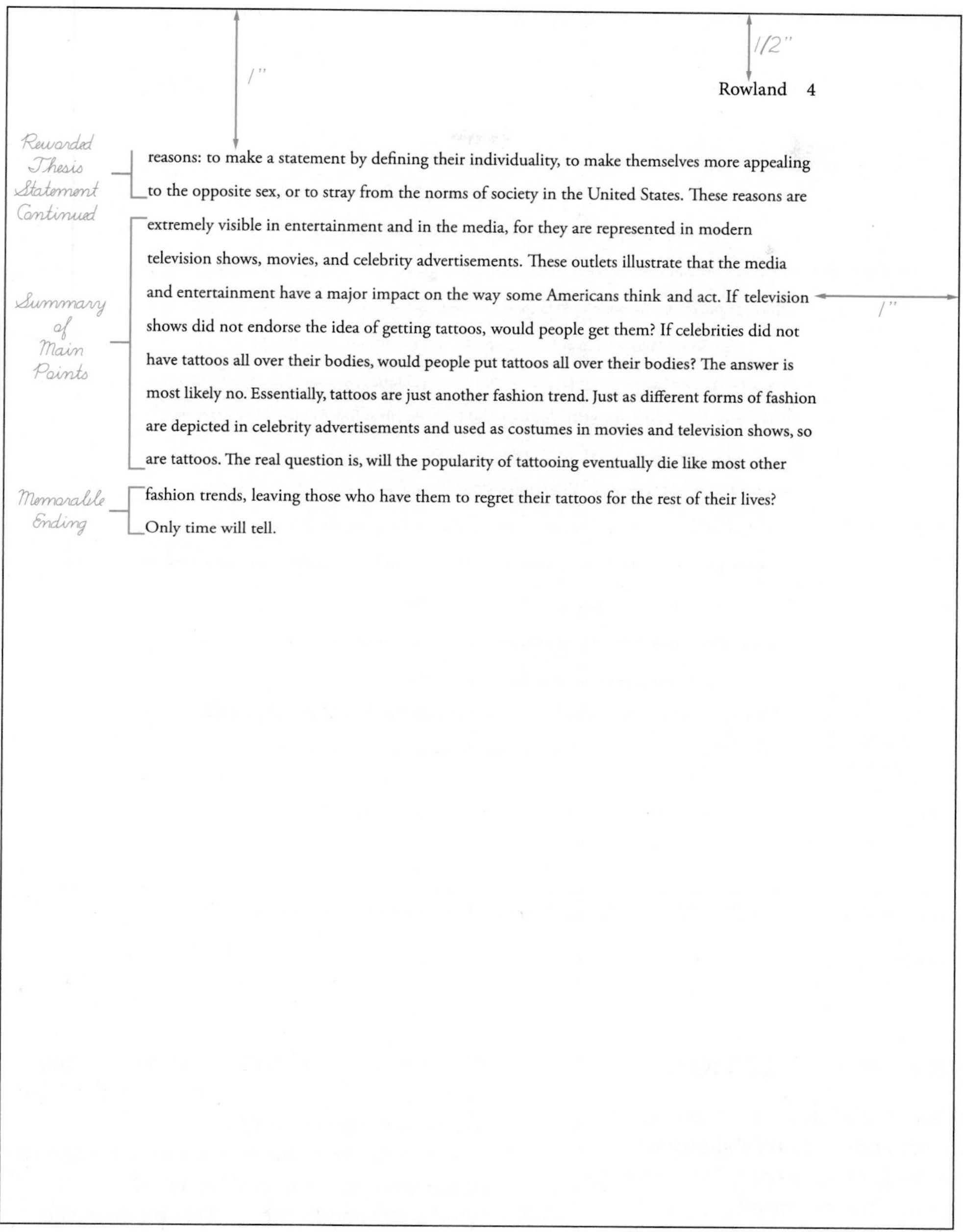

reasons: to make a statement by defining their individuality, to make themselves more appealing to the opposite sex, or to stray from the norms of society in the United States. These reasons are extremely visible in entertainment and in the media, for they are represented in modern television shows, movies, and celebrity advertisements. These outlets illustrate that the media and entertainment have a major impact on the way some Americans think and act. If television shows did not endorse the idea of getting tattoos, would people get them? If celebrities did not have tattoos all over their bodies, would people put tattoos all over their bodies? The answer is most likely no. Essentially, tattoos are just another fashion trend. Just as different forms of fashion are depicted in celebrity advertisements and used as costumes in movies and television shows, so are tattoos. The real question is, will the popularity of tattooing eventually die like most other fashion trends, leaving those who have them to regret their tattoos for the rest of their lives? Only time will tell.

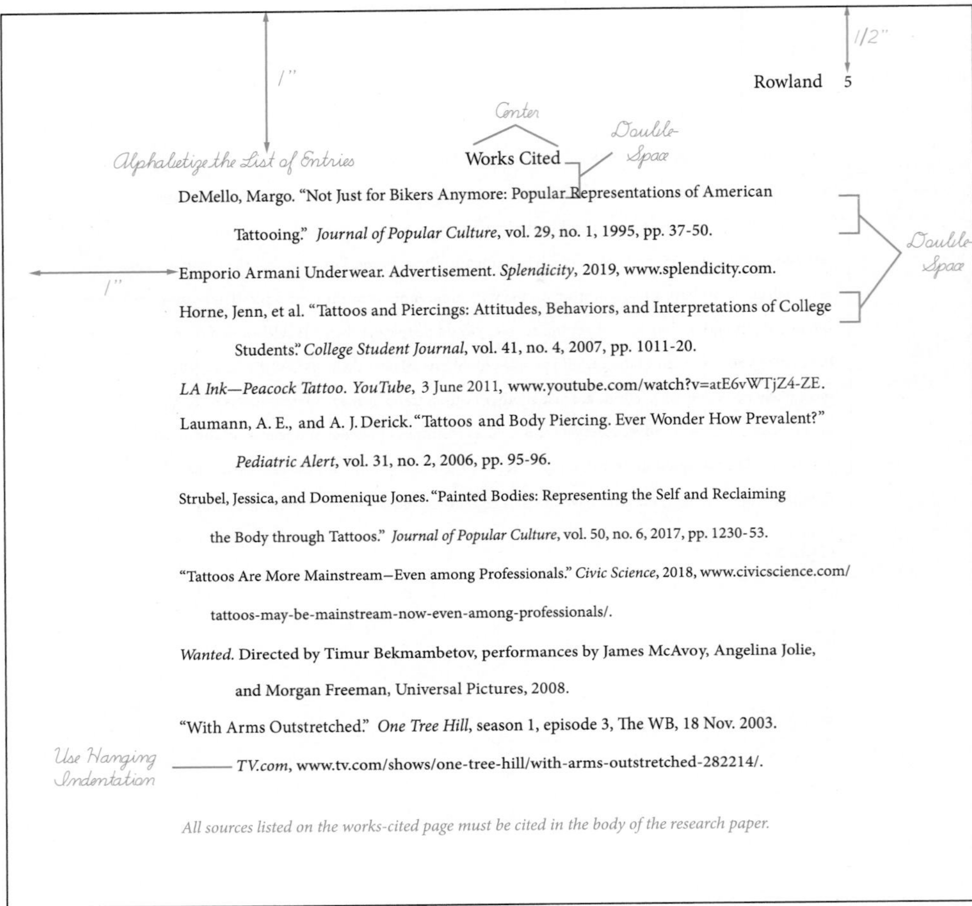

Works Cited

DeMello, Margo. "Not Just for Bikers Anymore: Popular Representations of American Tattooing." *Journal of Popular Culture*, vol. 29, no. 1, 1995, pp. 37-50.

Emporio Armani Underwear. Advertisement. *Splendicity*, 2019, www.splendicity.com.

Horne, Jenn, et al. "Tattoos and Piercings: Attitudes, Behaviors, and Interpretations of College Students." *College Student Journal*, vol. 41, no. 4, 2007, pp. 1011-20.

LA Ink—Peacock Tattoo. YouTube, 3 June 2011, www.youtube.com/watch?v=atE6vWTjZ4-ZE.

Laumann, A. E., and A. J. Derick. "Tattoos and Body Piercing. Ever Wonder How Prevalent?" *Pediatric Alert*, vol. 31, no. 2, 2006, pp. 95-96.

Strubel, Jessica, and Domenique Jones. "Painted Bodies: Representing the Self and Reclaiming the Body through Tattoos." *Journal of Popular Culture*, vol. 50, no. 6, 2017, pp. 1230-53.

"Tattoos Are More Mainstream—Even among Professionals." *Civic Science*, 2018, www.civicscience.com/tattoos-may-be-mainstream-now-even-among-professionals/.

Wanted. Directed by Timur Bekmambetov, performances by James McAvoy, Angelina Jolie, and Morgan Freeman, Universal Pictures, 2008.

"With Arms Outstretched." *One Tree Hill*, season 1, episode 3, The WB, 18 Nov. 2003.

——— *TV.com*, www.tv.com/shows/one-tree-hill/with-arms-outstretched-282214/.

All sources listed on the works-cited page must be cited in the body of the research paper.

Source: Rowland, Margaret, From Stigma to Status. Reprinted by permission of the author.

QUESTIONS FOR REFLECTION

1. Based on Rowland's introductory paragraph, what three main points does she promise to cover in the body of her paper? Does she follow through with her promise?
2. What supporting details and examples does she offer for her first main point? Are they sufficient? Why or why not?
3. What supporting details does Rowland offer for her second main point? Which details are the most convincing? Why?
4. Which ideas from the author's third body paragraph are most memorable? Why?
5. What is Rowland's thesis? Do you think she fully supports her thesis in the body of the paper? Why or why not?

14.4 APA Format

Generally, the American Psychological Association (APA) format is used for courses in the behavioral sciences. Additionally, some colleges have adopted the APA format for use in all subjects. The complete APA guidelines are explained in the 7th edition of the *Publication Manual of the American Psychological Association* (2020). Go to **www.apa.org** for more information about the APA format and to APA's style blog where an expert provides updates and answers questions: **https://apastyle.apa.org/blog/.** The APA style of documentation requires that you cite sources in your text as well as on a reference page at the end of your paper. The following examples will help you to cite sources using the APA format. You may also want to try using an electronic tool, such as **www.noodletools.com**, to help you correctly document your sources.

APA In-Text Citations

An *in-text citation,* also known as a *parenthetical citation,* shows the reader exactly where you have borrowed ideas from outside sources in your paper. When using the APA format, you generally need to include the author's last name and date for summarized and paraphrased information. For direct quotes, include the page number in addition to the author's last name and date. (If a source does not include page numbers, then skip them.) Providing this information allows the readers to locate the correct entry on the reference page so they can find additional information about the subject if desired. You may include the author's name in the text or in parentheses with the date. Either way, the date immediately follows the author's name. If there is no author, use the title. Vary the way in which you introduce sources in your paper to keep your writing fresh and to show how the idea from the source is connected to your point. Be sure to include the correct information and make it clear exactly what material comes from a particular source. The following examples show how to cite various types of sources in your text.

One Author: First Citation

According to Li (2018), tuning into our senses can help us to feel more connected to nature.

Tuning into our senses can help us to feel more connected to nature (Li, 2018).

APA Format

APA Format

APA Format

One Author: Subsequent Citation within the Same Paragraph

Li (2018) also suggests . . .

Note: If you cite the source again later in the paper, list the author's name and date again.

Two Authors

Gordon and West (2019) recommend that successful people do not let their environment "weaken" or "harden" them (p. 62).

Successful people do not let their environment "weaken" or "harden" them (Gordon & West, 2019, p. 62).

Note: Include the page number when you quote any words from the original text. Use an ampersand (&) between the authors' names in parentheses.

Three or More Authors

In their study, Ma et al. (2008) observed that even though three-dimensional ultrasound technology can provide amazing images, it is currently not the best tool for making a diagnosis.

Even though three-dimensional ultrasound technology can provide amazing images, it is currently not the best tool for making a diagnosis (Ma et al., 2008).

Note: For works with three or more authors, only the first author listed in the source is included, followed by "et al.," which means "and others." In your corresponding reference list entry, you will include the names of up to 20 authors

Multiple Works by Authors with the Same Last Name

J. E. Rivera (2018) and A. M. Rivera (2020) recommend . . .

N. D. Goldstein and Hertz (2019) and S. P. Goldstein and Michaels (2017) found . . .

Note: Include the initials to clearly distinguish the authors with the same last names. Omit the initials for authors with different names.

No Author

According to the book *The Workout Journal* (2019), "Committing to specific action steps–workouts, meals, and more–on paper will help you head into the week with clear focus and motivation" (p. 7).

"Committing to specific action steps–workouts, meals, and more–on paper will help you head into the week with clear focus and motivation" (*The Workout Journal,* 2019, p. 7).

Note: Use the first few words of the title in place of the author's name. The entry needs to match the beginning of the corresponding entry on the reference list.

Anonymous Author

Studies show that . . . (Anonymous, 2020).

Note: Use this only when the source lists its author as "Anonymous."

Corporate or Group Author

Children's Hospital Boston (2001) suggests that the parenting process becomes less demanding when a child enters school.

The parenting process becomes less demanding when a child enters school (Children's Hospital Boston, 2001).

Indirect Source

According to Budman et al. (as cited in Chowdhury, 2004), studies show that children who have Tourette Syndrome may experience "rage" attacks when they see a specialist at a clinic (p. 61).

Note: Use this example if you want to use a quote or information you find in a source by a different author. Give credit to the original author of the material in your text and the source where you found the quote or information in your parenthetical citation.

Multiple Works

The most common side effect of having a Botox injection is droopy eyelids (*Botox Cosmetic,* 2015; Langdon, 2004).

Note: Use this example when you find the same information in two sources and want to cite both to add credibility to your paper. Cite each work the same way you normally would, and add a semicolon between the works in parentheses. In the above example, the first work is a website with no author, and the second is a book.

Personal Communications (Email, Text Message, Letter, or Interview)

According to M. Record (personal communication, October 20, 2020) working with a writing studio or online writing lab tutor can help students significantly improve their research essays.

Note: Use the above format for personal emails, personal interviews, telephone conversations, and other forms of personal communication.

Long Quotation

Glave (2008) urges his readers to help do their part to save the planet:

> Do something. Do it now. Dream up your own Eco-Shed, Eco-Car, Eco-Boat, Eco-Garden, Eco-Concrete, Eco-Whatever, and start on it today. Sit right up front and take charge of the process. Stop thinking about what you have to give up, or whom you might tick off, and start

thinking about what you'll gain. Each of us must earn our own green belt at our own pace. But believe me, once you begin punching and kicking in that direction, you won't ever look back. (pp. 248–249)

Note: For quotes that are longer than forty words, set off the entire quote from the text and begin it on a new line. Indent the quote a half inch (about five to seven spaces) from the left margin and double-space it. Omit the quotation marks and place the final period before the citation.

Edited Quotation

"Dream up your own [eco-friendly project] and start on it today. . . . Stop thinking about what you have to give up . . . and start thinking about what you'll gain" (Glave, 2008, pp. 248–249).

Note: Use brackets around material that has been worded differently (but has the same intended meaning) and an ellipsis to indicate an omission. Use three dots for an ellipsis within a sentence and four dots for an ellipsis at the end of a sentence.

Website/Source without Page Number

"What is coming is better than what is gone" (Positivemindsetdaily, 2019).

Note: Use a screen name when no author is listed.

Visuals (Photos, Maps, Posters, or Other Graphic Works)

Starry Night (van Gogh, 1889) is the topic of many poems and songs.

APA References

When using the APA format, you must include a list of *references* at the end of the paper to fully document your sources. This means that you list any *work* you have *referenced* (cited) in your paper. You may need to look at several examples of reference entries to find the exact format you need to document a research source. (See Table 14.2 on page 394.) For example, if you need to cite the fourth edition of a book with three authors, then you would need to look at the sample entries for "Book with Three or More Authors" and "Book in Edition Other Than the First." Generally, you will alphabetize the list according to the authors' last names. If there is no

Table 14.2

author, begin with the title. Ignore words such as *a* and *the* when alphabetizing an entry by the title on the list of references.

Books Here is a list of the basic information you need to include for book sources using the APA format. List the information in each reference entry in order, and follow the punctuation guidelines of the examples. You should be able to find all of the information you need on the title and copyright pages of the book. (See Figures 14.6 and 14.7.)

1. **Author:** List the author's last name, followed by a comma and the author's first initial and middle initial (if you have it). Do not include degrees or titles, such as "PhD" or "Sister," with the author's name. If the book has more than one author, list the additional authors in the same manner as the first author, include a comma between authors, and include a comma and an ampersand (&) between the final two authors' names. If the author is unknown, begin with the title of the book.
2. **Date of publication:** List the year in parentheses, followed by a period.

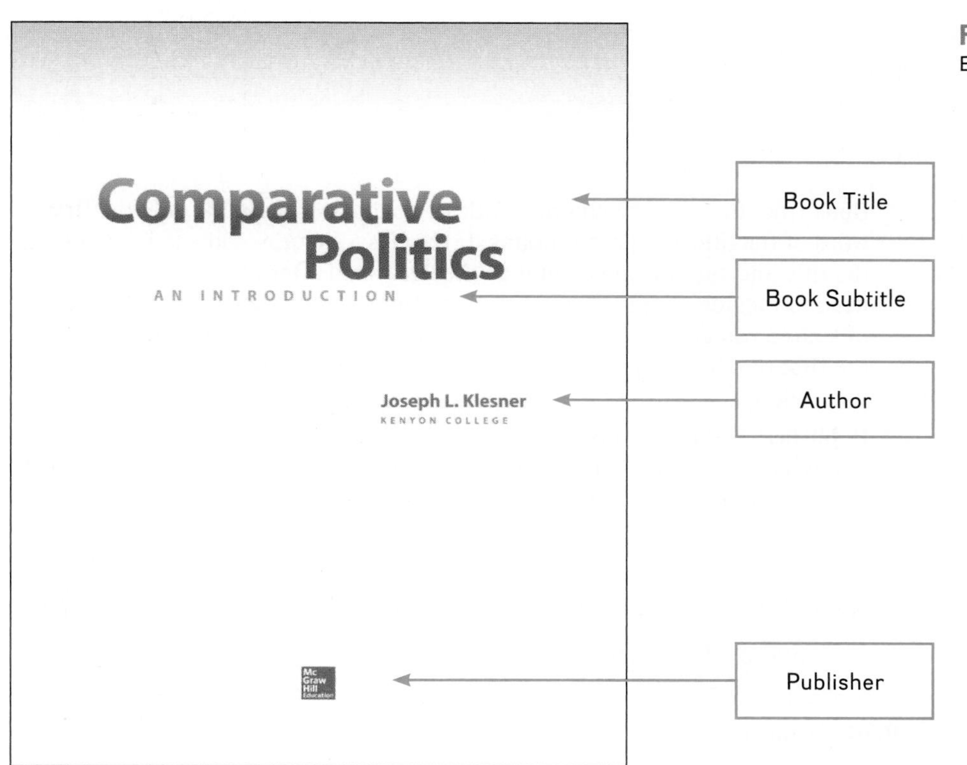

FIGURE 14.6 Book Title Page

FIGURE 14.7
Copyright Page

Mc Graw Hill Education

COMPARATIVE POLITICS: AN INTRODUCTION

Published by McGraw-Hill Education, 2 Penn Plaza, New York, NY 10121. Copyright © 2014 by McGraw-Hill Education. All rights reserved. Printed in the United States of America. No part of this publication may be reproduced or distributed in any form or by any means, or stored in a database or retrieval system, without the prior written consent of McGraw-Hill Education, including, but not limited to, in any network or other electronic storage or transmission, or broadcast for distance learning.

Some ancillaries, including electronic and print components, may not be available to customers outside the United States.

This book is printed on acid-free paper.

1 2 3 4 5 6 7 8 9 0 DOW/DOW 1 0 9 8 7 6 5 4 3

ISBN 978-0-07-352643-0
MHID 0-07-352643-6

Senior Vice President, Products & Markets: *Kurt L. Strand*
Vice President, General Manager, Products & Markets: *Michael J. Ryan*
Vice President, Content Production & Technology Services: *Kimberly Meriwether David*
Managing Director: *Gina Boedeker*
Director: *Matt Busbridge*
Brand Manager: *Laura Wilk*
Senior Director of Development: *Dawn Groundwater*
Marketing Manager: *April Cole*
Director, Content Production: *Terri Schiesl*
Content Project Manager: *Danielle Clement*
Buyer: *Susan Culbertson*
Design: *Laurie Janssen*
Cover Image: *©Guy Grenier/Masterfile, Ian McKinnell/Getty Images*
Content Licensing Specialist: *Brenda Rolwes*
Typeface: *10/12 Adobe Garamond Pro*
Compositor: *Laserwords Private Limited*
Printer: *R. R. Donnelley*

All credits appearing on page or at the end of the book are considered to be an extension of the copyright page.

Library of Congress Cataloging-in-Publication Data

Klesner, Joseph L., 1958-
Comparative politics ; an introduction / Joseph Klesner, Kenyon College.
pages cm
Includes bibliographical references and index.
ISBN-13: 978-0-07-352643-0 (alk. paper)
ISBN-10: 0-07-352643-6 (alk. paper)
1. Comparative government. I. Title.
JF51.K54 2014
320.3–dc23

2013019257

The Internet addresses listed in the text were accurate at the time of publication. The inclusion of a website does not indicate an endorsement by the authors or McGraw-Hill Education, and McGraw-Hill Education does not guarantee the accuracy of the information presented at these sites.

www.mhhe.com

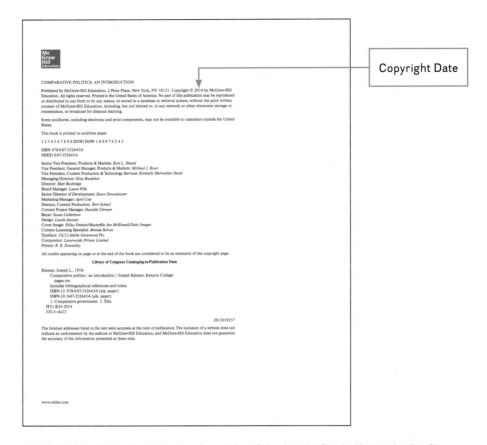

Copyright Date

3. **Book title:** Italicize the complete title of the book. Capitalize only the first word of the title and proper nouns. If there is a subtitle, add a colon between the title and subtitle and capitalize the first word after the colon. You may need to include additional information after the title, depending on the type of source you are citing. For example, you may be using an edition other than the first or one volume of a multivolume set. See the corresponding examples that follow.
4. **Publisher:** List the publisher's name in brief form. Omit terms such as *Publishers, Co.,* and *Inc.* If the author and publisher are exactly the same, list the word *Author* (not italicized), where you would normally list the publisher.

Sample APA Book Citation

- Author's Last Name, First Initial. Middle Initial. (Year of Publication). *Title of book.* Publisher.

Book Example

Klesner, J. L. (2014). *Comparative politics: An introduction.* McGraw-Hill.

Book by One Author

Clegg, B. (2019). *Quantum theory: A crash course.* Metro.

Langdon, R. (2004). *Understanding cosmetic laser surgery.* University Press of Mississippi.

Li, Q. (2018). *Forest bathing: How trees can help you find health and happiness.* Viking.

Book by Two Authors

Gordon, J. & West, D. (2019). *The coffee bean: A simple lesson to create positive change.* Wiley.

Vernberg, F. J., & Vernberg, W. B. (2001). *The coastal zone: Past, present, and future.* University of South Carolina Press.

Book with Three or More Authors

Ma, O. J., Mateer, J. R., & Blaivas, M. (2008). *Emergency ultrasound* (2nd ed.). McGraw-Hill.

Note: For books with three to twenty authors, include the names of all. If there are twenty-one or more authors, list only the first nineteen authors' names followed by an ellipsis (. . .) and the last author's name.

Book with No Author or Editor

The workout journal and roadmap. (2019). St. Martin's Press.

Note: The date goes after the title when there is no author.

Book with an Editor or Translator

Lutkewitte, C. (Ed.). (2014). *Multimodal composition.* Bedford/St. Martin's Press.

Note: Use *Trans.* instead of *Ed.* for a translator.

APA Format

APA Format

APA Format

Book in an Edition Other Than the First

Baker, N. L., & Huling, N. (2006). *A research guide for undergraduate students: English and American literature* (6th ed.). Modern Language Association.

Book by a Corporate Author

Children's Hospital Boston. (2001). *The Children's Hospital guide to your child's health and development.*

Discovery Channel. (2005). *North American & Alaskan cruises.* Insight.

Note: When a work has been created by an organization and also published by that same organization, present the organization's name as the author and omit any publisher information (see Children's Hospital example above).

Work in an Anthology

Poe, E. A. (2017). The raven. In R. S. Levine (Ed.), *The Norton anthology of American literature: Beginnings to 1865* (Vol. 1, Shorter 9th ed., pp. 735–738). Norton. (Original work published 1845)

Note: An anthology is a collection of works selected by one or more editors. Use this example if you are citing an essay, letter, poem, short story, or other work that appears in an edited collection or compilation of works by different authors. The editor is listed by first initial, middle initial (if known), and last name.

Foreword, Introduction, Preface, or Afterword of a Book

Niles, J. D. (2008). Afterword. In *Beowulf* (pp. 213–248). Norton.

Multivolume Book

LaBlanc, M. L. (Ed.). (2001). *Poetry for students: Presenting analysis, context, and criticism on commonly studied poetry* (Vol. 10). Gale Group.

Note: This book has an editor rather than an author.

Printed Periodicals (Journals, Magazines, Newspapers) Here is a list of the basic information you need to include for periodical sources using the APA format. List the information for each entry on the reference page in order, and follow the punctuation guidelines of the examples. You should be able to find all of the information you need on the cover of the periodical and the article itself. (See Figures 14.8 and 14.9.)

1. **Author:** List the author's last name, followed by a comma and the author's first initial and middle initial (if you have it). Do not include degrees or titles, such as "PhD" or "Sister," with the author's name. If the source has more than one author, list the additional authors in the same manner as the first author, include a comma between authors, and include a comma and an ampersand (&) between the final two authors' names. If the author is unknown, begin with the title of the article.
2. **Date of publication:** Include as much information about the date as you can find on the journal, magazine, or newspaper. If you find the day, month, and year, list the year first, followed by a comma, the month, and the day, like this: (2015, April 21). If you find just the month(s) and year, list it this way: (2014, July/August). Enclose the date in parentheses, followed by a period.
3. **Article title:** List the complete article title, capitalizing only the first word and proper nouns. If there is a subtitle, add a colon between the title and subtitle. Capitalize the first word after the colon.

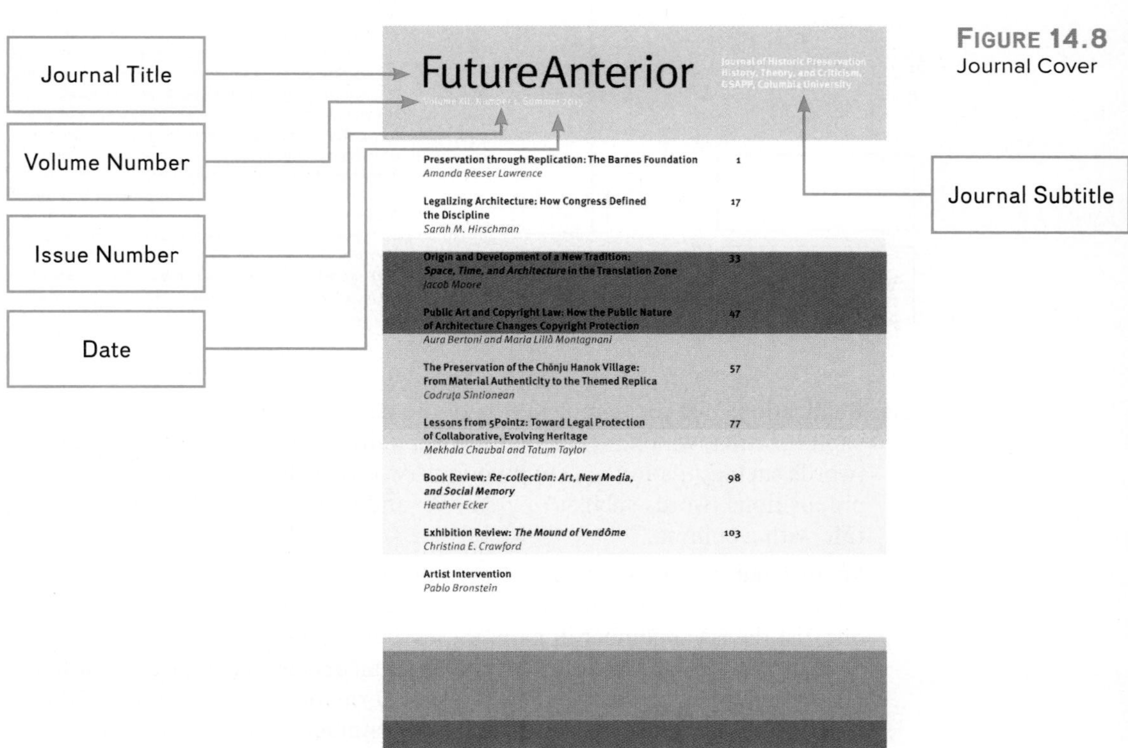

FIGURE 14.8 Journal Cover

FIGURE 14.9
Journal Article

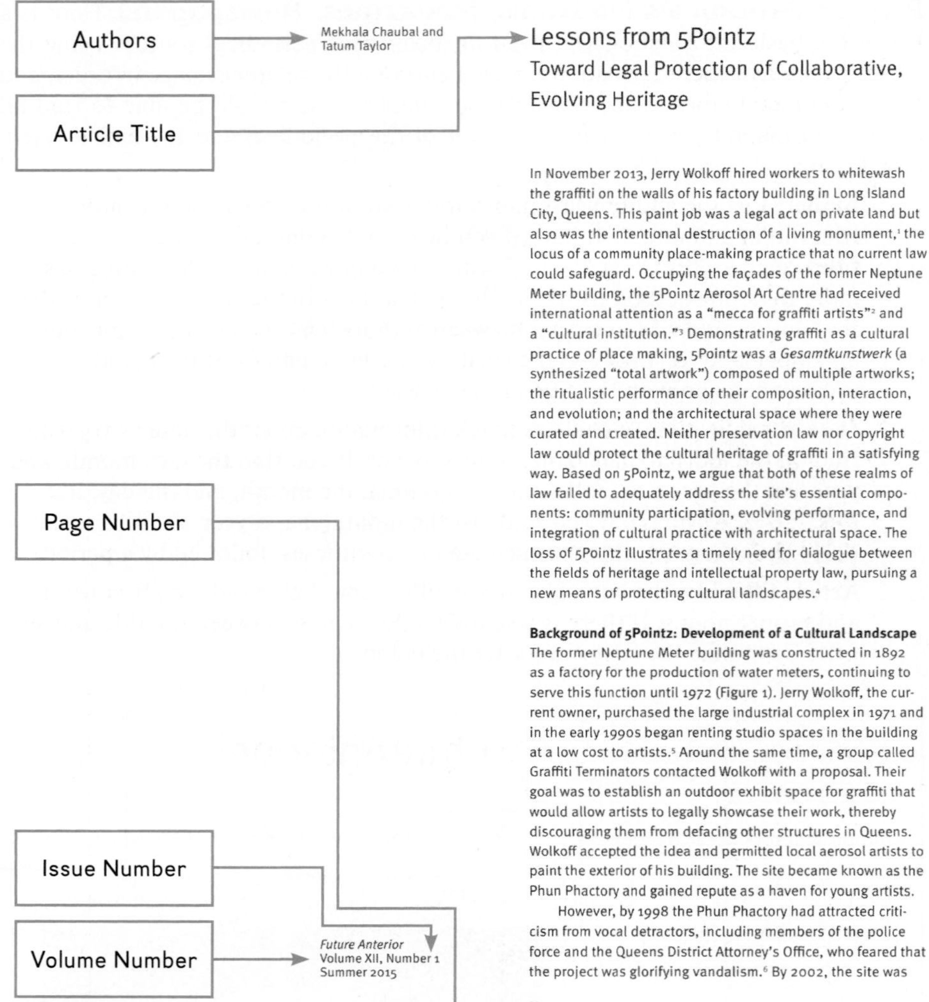

Mekhala Chaubal and Tatum Taylor

Lessons from 5Pointz

Toward Legal Protection of Collaborative, Evolving Heritage

In November 2013, Jerry Wolkoff hired workers to whitewash the graffiti on the walls of his factory building in Long Island City, Queens. This paint job was a legal act on private land but also was the intentional destruction of a living monument,[1] the locus of a community place-making practice that no current law could safeguard. Occupying the façades of the former Neptune Meter building, the 5Pointz Aerosol Art Centre had received international attention as a "mecca for graffiti artists"[2] and a "cultural institution."[3] Demonstrating graffiti as a cultural practice of place making, 5Pointz was a *Gesamtkunstwerk* (a synthesized "total artwork") composed of multiple artworks; the ritualistic performance of their composition, interaction, and evolution; and the architectural space where they were curated and created. Neither preservation law nor copyright law could protect the cultural heritage of graffiti in a satisfying way. Based on 5Pointz, we argue that both of these realms of law failed to adequately address the site's essential components: community participation, evolving performance, and integration of cultural practice with architectural space. The loss of 5Pointz illustrates a timely need for dialogue between the fields of heritage and intellectual property law, pursuing a new means of protecting cultural landscapes.[4]

Background of 5Pointz: Development of a Cultural Landscape

The former Neptune Meter building was constructed in 1892 as a factory for the production of water meters, continuing to serve this function until 1972 (Figure 1). Jerry Wolkoff, the current owner, purchased the large industrial complex in 1971 and in the early 1990s began renting studio spaces in the building at a low cost to artists.[5] Around the same time, a group called Graffiti Terminators contacted Wolkoff with a proposal. Their goal was to establish an outdoor exhibit space for graffiti that would allow artists to legally showcase their work, thereby discouraging them from defacing other structures in Queens. Wolkoff accepted the idea and permitted local aerosol artists to paint the exterior of his building. The site became known as the Phun Phactory and gained repute as a haven for young artists.

However, by 1998 the Phun Phactory had attracted criticism from vocal detractors, including members of the police force and the Queens District Attorney's Office, who feared that the project was glorifying vandalism.[6] By 2002, the site was

Future Anterior
Volume XII, Number 1
Summer 2015

77

4. **Publication:** List the complete title of the periodical in italics. Use title case capitalization, which means that you capitalize every word except articles (words such as *a* and *the*), conjunctions (words such as *for* and *but*), and prepositions (words such as *to, from, for,* and *with*). Follow the periodical title with a comma.
5. **Volume and issue numbers:** If the periodical has a volume number, list it in italics. If the periodical has an issue number, and each issue begins on page one, list the issue number in parentheses, but not italicized, immediately after the volume number. For example, cite an article that appears in volume 10 of issue 3 this way: *10*(3). Follow this information with a comma. If the periodical does not have volume and issue numbers, list the year followed by the month or season, like this: (2015, Spring).

6. **Page number(s):** List the inclusive page numbers of the article, not just the ones you used, like this: 25–31. If the page numbers are not continuous, list the specific pages for the article this way for magazines and periodicals, 6, 8, 12–14, and this way for newspaper articles, pp. B1, B4, B6–7. Follow the page number(s) with a period.

Sample APA Periodical Citation

- Author's Last Name, First Initial. Middle Initial. (Date of Publication). Title of article. *Name of Periodical, Volume*(Issue), Page(s).

Periodical Example

Barrow, M. A. (2014, March). Even math requires learning academic language. *Phi Delta Kappan, 95*(6), 35–38.

Callaway, E. (2019, February 17). Siberia's ancient ghost clan starts to surrender its secrets. *Nature, 566*(7745), 444–446.

Journal Article

Lleras, C. (2008, December). Race, racial concentration, and the dynamics of educational inequality across urban and suburban schools. *American Educational Research Journal, 45,* 886–912.

Roberts, K. T., Robinson, K. M., Stewart, C., & Wright, J. C. (2008). Integrated mental health practice in a nurse-managed health center. *The American Journal for Nurse Practicioners, 12*(10), 33–34, 37–40, 43–44.

Magazine Article

Penny, L. (2019, September). We can be heroes: How the nerds are reinventing pop culture. *Wired,* 50–59.

Scoles, S. (2019, Fall). There's no space like home. *Popular Science,* 66–73.

Newspaper Article or Editorial

Tierney, J. (2013, January 4). You won't stay the same, study finds. *The New York Times,* p. A15.

Koppel, N., Scheck, J., & Stecklow, S. (2008, December 19). Fast living, bold ambitions drove lawyer's rise and fall. *The Wall Street Journal,* pp. A1, A14.

Note: The section number is included before the page number for newspaper articles. Also, for newspaper articles, precede the page numbers with *p.* (for one page) and *pp.* (for multiple pages).

Letter to the Editor

Greenwood, D. (2019, February 1). A serious flaw in the Silver Line contract [Letter to the editor]. *The Washington Post.* 2.

Electronic Sources Here is a list of the basic information you need to include for electronic sources using the APA format. List the information in each reference page entry in order. Note that the various types of electronic sources require different information. Use the examples that follow as a guide. Generally, you will cite electronic sources the same way as print sources, but you will need to add enough electronic retrieval information to help your readers find your source.

1. **Author:** List the author's last name, followed by a comma and the author's first initial and middle initial (if you have it). Do not include degrees or titles, such as "PhD" or "Sister," with the author's name. If the source has more than one author, list the additional authors in the same manner as the first author, include a comma between the authors, and include a comma and an ampersand (&) between the final two authors' names. If there is no author, include the editor, compiler, narrator, or director of the work. If no name is listed, begin with the title.
2. **Date of publication:** List all of the available information you have about the date. If you find the day, month, and year, list the year first, followed by a comma, the month, and the day, like this: (2015, April 21). If you find just the month(s) and year, list it this way: (2014, July/August). Enclose the date in parentheses, followed by a period. If the publication date is not available, list *n.d.* in parentheses, like this: (n.d.). In such cases, and for online sources that can be easily edited, such as social media pages and profiles and wiki entries, include a retrieval date in your reference list entry.
3. **Article title:** List the complete article title, capitalizing only the first word and proper nouns. If there is a subtitle, add a colon between the title and subtitle. Capitalize the first word after the colon.
4. **Periodical information:** For online periodicals, list the title of the periodical (in italics) followed by volume (in italics) and issue number (in parentheses). Follow the same guidelines as you would for print periodical sources.
5. **DOI:** Some sources such as journal articles contain a digital object identifier (DOI), which is a set of numbers and letters that is unique to a particular

digital source. If the source you wish to document has a DOI, you must provide it, regardless of whether you accessed the source in print or digital format. Copy and paste the DOIs of your sources into your reference list. Do not include a period following the DOI link. ***Important:*** If a an online source does not have a DOI, then include its URL. The APA now requires that DOIs and URLs be presented as live links.

6. **URL:** Include entire URLs for online sources that do not provide a DOI. Copy the URLs carefully so that your readers can access the information if desired. Do not include a period after the URL. ***Important:*** The APA now requires that DOIs and URLs be presented as live links.

Note: For long URLs or DOIs (direct object locators), you have the option of providing a shortened version. To shorten a DOI, use the "shortDOI" service of the International DOI Foundation (http://shortdoi.org)). To shorten a URL, use apps such as Bitly (https://bitly.com/). Whether in full-length or shortened form, be sure to live link your URLs and DOIs so that readers can easily access your sources.

Sample APA Electronic Citation

- Author's Last Name, First Initial. Middle Initial. (Date of Publication). Article title. Periodical information. DOI or URL presented as a live link

Electronic Source Example

Endeavour crew returns home after "home improvement" in orbit. (n.d.). www.nasa.gov

Note: Include an author if there is one, and list the date immediately after the author. Do not include a period at the end of the entries that end with a URL.

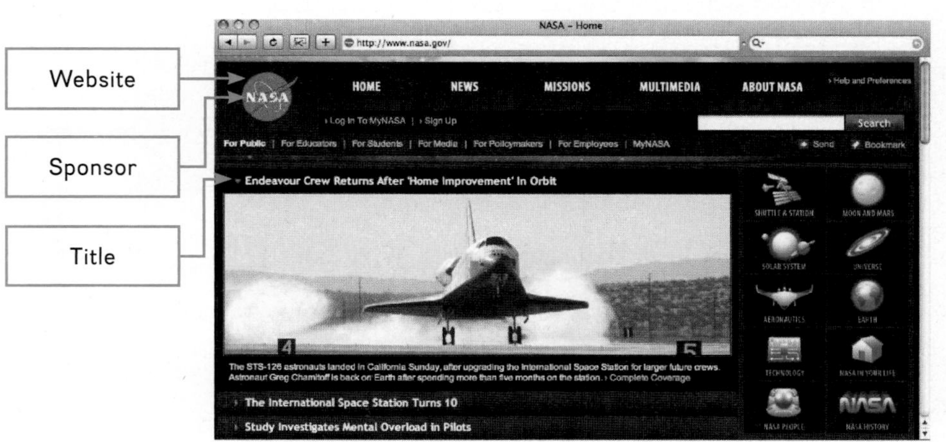

FIGURE 14.10 Website Article

Tony Landis/NASA

APA Format

Website (Entire)

National geographic. (n.d.). www.nationalgeographic.com

Website Article

Shute, N. (2013, January 3). Apes have food, will share for a social payoff. www.npr.org/blogs/thesalt/2013/01/03/168527985/apes-have-food-will-share-for-a-social-payoff

Online Journal Article with a DOI

Anderson, C. B., Hughes, S. O., & Fuemmeler, B. F. (2009). Parent-child attitude congruence on type and intensity of physical activity: Testing multiple mediators of sedentary behavior in older children. *Health Psychology, 28,* 428–438. doi: 10.1037/a0014522

Online Journal Article without a DOI

Nayar, P. K. (2008). New media, digitextuality and public space. *Postcolonial Text, 4*(1). journals.sfu.ca/pocol/index.php/pct/article/view/786/521

Online Magazine Article

Fallows, J. (2008, December). Be nice to the countries that lend you money. *The Atlantic.* www.theatlantic.com/magazine/archive/2008/12/be-nice-to-the-countries-that-lend-you-money/307148/

Online Newspaper Article

Chopra, D. (2013, January 4). Secrets to a better brain. *CNN.* www.cnn.com/2013/01/04/health/chopra-better-brain/index.html?hpt=hp_abar

Online Encyclopedia or Dictionary Article; Wiki Entry

Robotics. (2013). In *Encyclopaedia britannica.* www.britannica.com/search?query=robotics

Robot. (2019). In *Wikipedia: The free encyclopedia.* Retrieved February 10, 2019 from https://enwikipedia.org/wiki/robot

Note: For sources such as wikis and social media pages and profiles—in other words, sources that are meant to be easily edited and that by definition are unstable—provide a retrieval date as in the *Wikipedia* example above.

e-Book

Angelou, M. (2013). *Mom & me & mom* [Kindle]. Random House.

Blog or Social Media Post

Strayed, C. (2018, December 30). The broken horses of my youth. [Status update]. Facebook. https://facebook.com/CherylStrayed.Author/

Author Identified by Screen Name Only

Positivemindsetdaily [@positivemindsetdailly]. (2019, January 30). What is coming is better than what is gone [Photograph]. Instagram. www.instagram.com/p/BtTACGBH8Gr/?utm_source=ig_share_sheet&igshid=Id8geid5cnx8

Audio Recording or Podcast Episode

Sheeran, E. (2017). Perfect. On *Divide* Warner/Asylum. iTunes. https://itunes.apple.com/us/album/perfect/1193701079?i=1193701400

Van Nuys, D. (Producer). (2019, January 31). *Thriving in the aftermath of trauma* [Audio podcast]. www.shrinkrapradio.com/

Radio Program

Meek, M. (2019, January 11). Before things went to hell [Radio series episode]. In I. Glass (Producer), *This American Life,* WBEZ. www.thisamericalife.org/665/before-things-went-to-hell

APA Format

APA Format

APA Format

Video, Movie, or TV Show on the Web

PBS NewsHour. (2019, February 3). *Earth's most massive thing is struggling to survive* [Video]. YouTube. www.youtube.com/watch?v=pwHyEz0qSnA

Video Game, Online Game, or Software

Sugg, D. (2017). Fortnite [Video game]. Epic Games. epicgames.com/fortnite/en-us

Other Sources You may decide to use other types of sources in your research paper. Each type of source has its own unique format. Be sure to give your readers enough information to be able to find the source if they so desire. Many of the APA rules from previous examples apply to the following sources.

Advertisement

Wrigley's Extra. (2019, February). Give extra get extra [Advertisement]. *Better Homes & Gardens,* p. 9.

Note: Include volume and issue numbers if applicable.

Business or Government Document

U.S. Congress, House of Representatives, Committee on Homeland Security. (2017). *Securing American non-profit organizations against terrorism act of 2017.* Government Printing Office. https://www.congress.gov/bill/115th-congress/house-bill/1486

Legal or Historical Document

California, Office of the Attorney General (1986). *Proposition 65: The safe drinking water and toxic enforcement act.* https://oag.ca.gov/prop65

Brochure or Pamphlet by a Corporate Author

Charles Hosmer Morse Foundation. (2019). *Visitor's guide to the Morse Museum* [Brochure].

Motion Picture

Curling, C., & Meurer, J. (Producers), & Hoffman, M. (Director). (2010). *The last station* [Motion picture]. Sony Picture Classics.

Music Recording (Song)

Pearson, D., & Holden, G. (2012). Home [Album recorded by P. Phillips]. On *The world from the side of the moon*. Interscope Records.

Swift, T. (2008). Love story. On *Fearless*. Big Machine Records.

Note: The in-text citation for this source would look like this: "Love Story" (Swift, 2008, track 3).

Painting

van Gogh, V. (1889). *Starry night* [Painting]. Museum of Modern Art.

van Gogh, V. (1889). *Starry night* [Painting]. www.vangoghgallery.com/painting/starryindex.html

Note: If you viewed the painting online instead of in the museum, use the second example to enable your readers to view it as well.

Visuals (Photos, Maps, Charts, Posters)

Howard, M. J. (1942). We can do it! [Poster]. National Museum of American History. americanhistory.si.edu/collections/search/object/nmah_538122

Personal Communications (Email, Text Message, Personal Interview, Phone Conversation)

Cite personal communications in the body of your paper, but not on your reference page. For example, A. Vining (personal communication, December 12, 2019) suggests that . . .

Television Episode in a Series

Meyer, G., et al. (Writers). (2012). Gone Abie gone [Television series episode]. In M. Groening & J. L. Brooks (Executive producers), *The Simpsons.* Fox Broadcasting.

Sacred Text

APA requires only in-text citations for sacred texts, such as the *Holy Bible,* with no entry on the reference page.

APA Research Paper Formatting Guide

1. **Title Page:** Include the following information on your title page.
   a. **Page number:** Put this at the upper-right corner of the title page, about one half inch from the top and an inch from the right edge of the paper. The page number will appear on every page of your paper.
   b. **Title:** Center the full title of your paper about six lines below the running head. Your title should be descriptive and, if possible, creative. Avoid italicizing, underlining, or boldfacing your title or putting it in quotation marks. Use title case capitalization.
   c. **Your name:** Place your name, and any co-authors' names, double-spaced and centered below the title.
   d. **School:** Write your school name, double-spaced and centered below your name.

Note: Although not an official part of the APA format, your instructor may prefer for you to include his or her name and the due date as well. If so, include those on separate lines below the school name, double-spaced and centered on the page.

2. **Abstract:** The abstract is a brief (150- to 250-word) summary of your paper that will enable your readers to have an idea of what to expect in your paper. Center the word *Abstract* one inch down from the top of your paper. Avoid italicizing, underlining, or boldfacing the word or putting the word *Abstract* in quotation marks. Begin your abstract at the left one-inch margin, without indenting it. Your abstract should not be a copy of your introduction or conclusion. Ask your instructor if an abstract is required.
3. **Text formatting:** Throughout the paper, use a 12-point font with a typeface that is easy to read and as accessible as possible to all users. This may be a san serif font such as Calibri, or a serif font such as Times New Roman. Do not justify the right-hand margin of the text; the text should have a ragged (uneven) right margin. Center the title of your paper one inch from the top

of the first page, but not on subsequent pages. Double-space the entire paper, and indent each paragraph one tab space, about five to seven spaces. Do not include an extra space between paragraphs or between sentences. Include in-text citations to indicate where you have quoted, paraphrased, or summarized ideas from your sources.

4. **Figures:** If you decide to include graphs, tables, charts, maps, drawings, or photographs with your paper, place them at the end of your paper, after the references page. Label them consecutively, beginning with Figure 1. In the body of the paper, where you refer to the figure, write the following in parentheses: (see Figure 1). Include the label, a brief description, and the complete source information below the figure.

5. **References:** Your references page gives credit to your sources and provides your readers with a way to locate your sources. Center and capitalize the word *References* about an inch from the top of the page. Avoid italicizing, underlining, or boldfacing the word *References* or putting it quotation marks. Alphabetize the list of references according to the author's last name or the word that begins the entry, not including words such as *a* or *the.* Use hanging indentation, which means that the first line of each entry begins at the left margin and the second and subsequent lines are indented one-half inch, about five to seven spaces. Double-space the entire page, without including extra spaces between each entry. Follow the precise APA guidelines for each entry.

6. **Appendixes:** If your instructor asks you to include any additional material, place it after the references page. This may include interview notes, visual aids, or survey data you collected that would be awkward or distracting to include in the body of your paper.

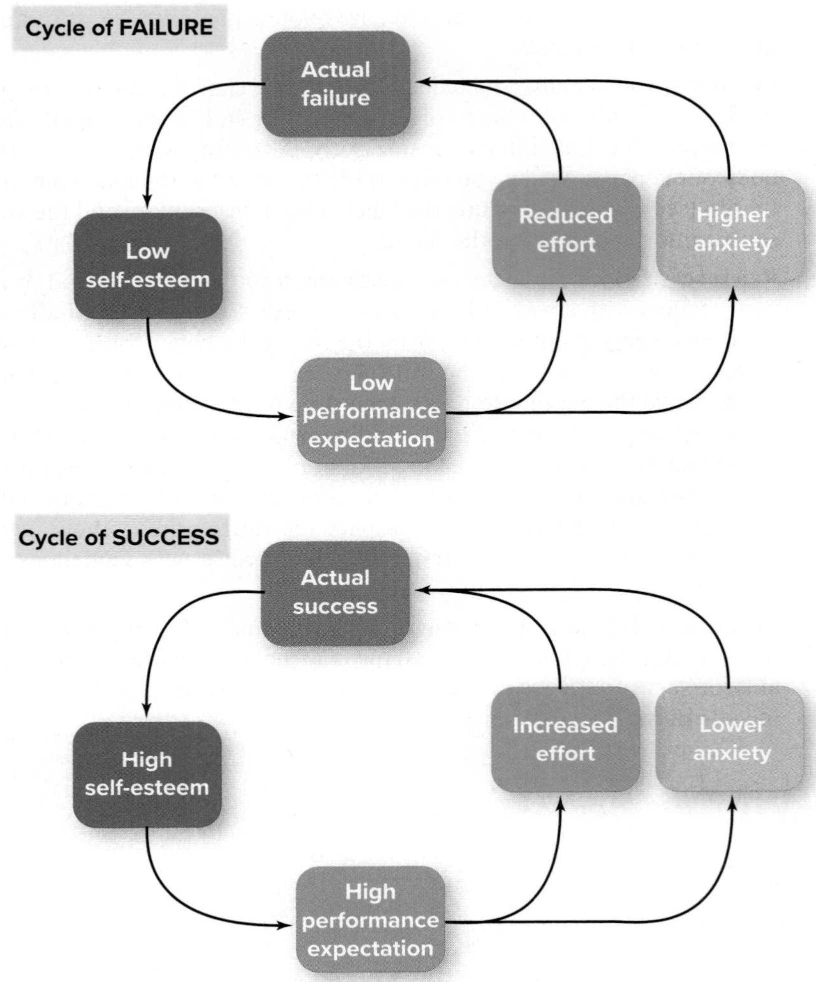

FIGURE 1 Chart comparing the cycle of failure to the cycle of success. Adapted from *Power learning* by R. S. Feldman, 2011, p. 75. Copyright 2011 by McGraw-Hill.

STUDENT APA RESEARCH PAPER

From Stigma to Status

by Margaret Rowland

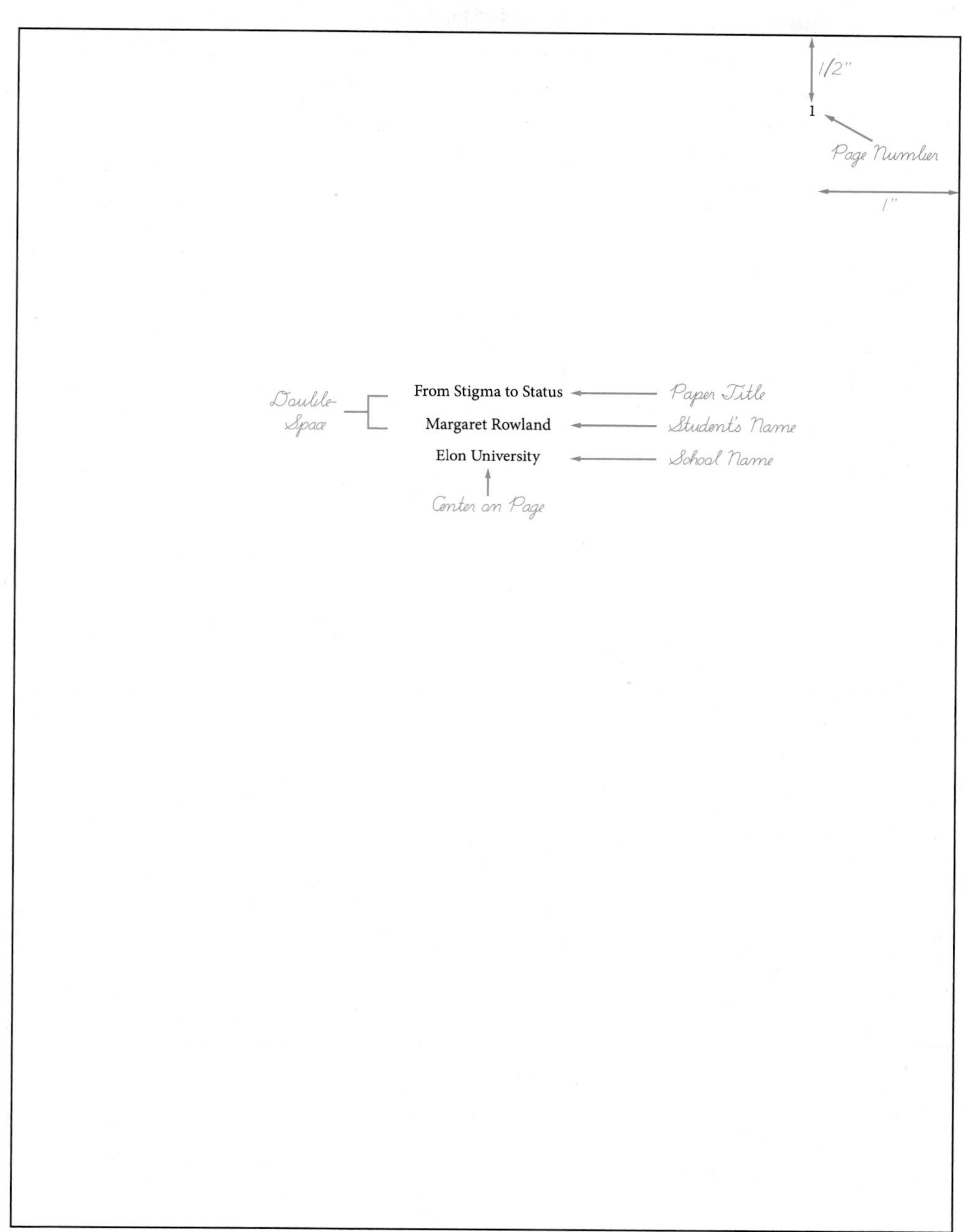

1/2"

1"

2 ← Page Number

Center

Abstract — Double-Space

1"

Tattoos have become a popular form of expression in the United States. Originally, tattoos were common among sailors, military personnel, bikers, prostitutes, and jail-mates. Now, however, the use of tattoos is increasing among professionals and other people. Why has tattooing become such a phenomenon in the past decade? Many people feel that it is because people who get tattoos want to express their individuality, appeal to the opposite sex, or rebel against the expectations of society.

Double-Space

Ragged Right Margin

Left Justify

The abstract is a short overview of the paper.

Note: If your instructor does not require an abstract, the body of your paper will begin on page 2.

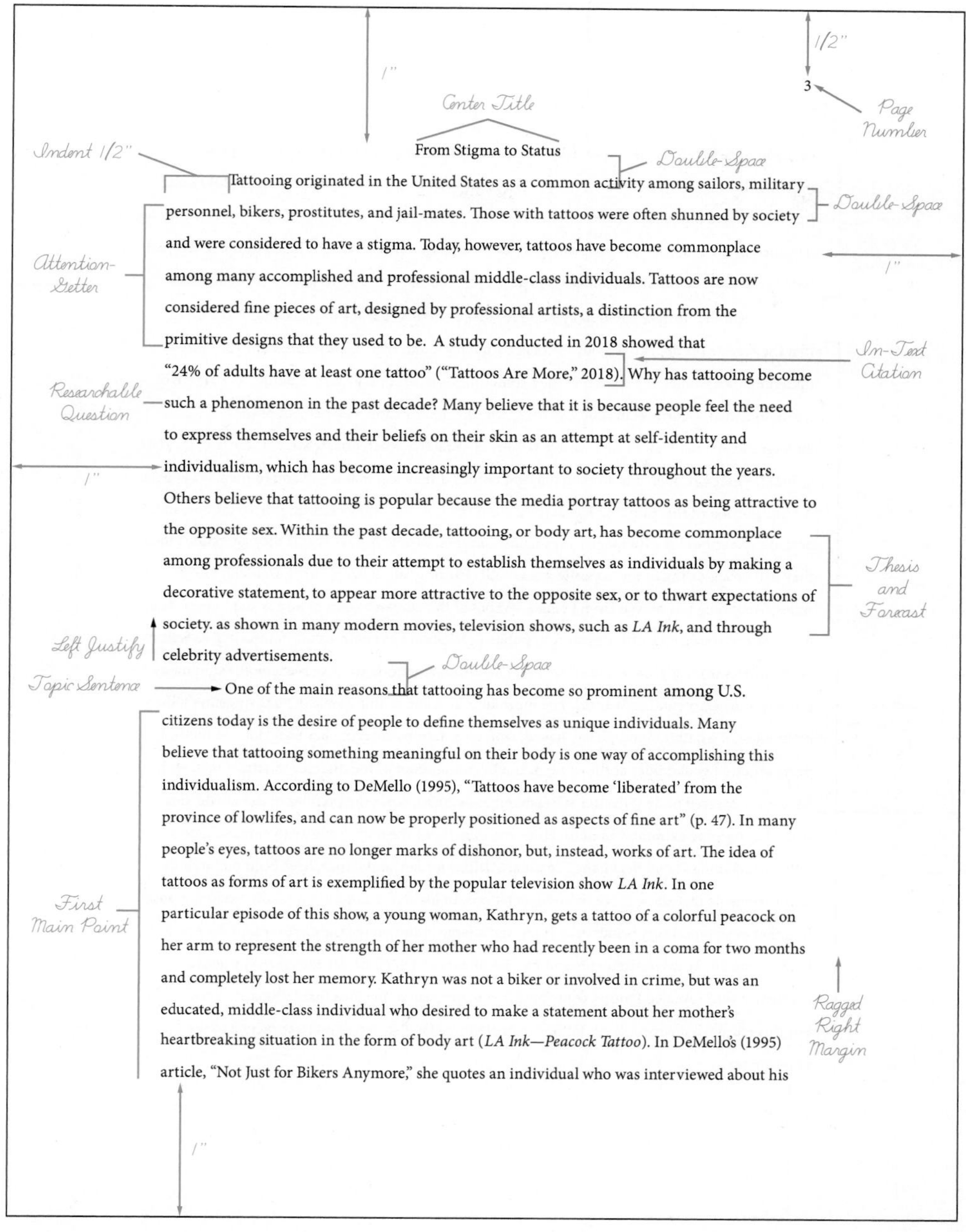

1/2"
1"
3
Page Number
Center Title
Indent 1/2"
From Stigma to Status
Double-Space
Tattooing originated in the United States as a common activity among sailors, military personnel, bikers, prostitutes, and jail-mates. Those with tattoos were often shunned by society and were considered to have a stigma. Today, however, tattoos have become commonplace among many accomplished and professional middle-class individuals. Tattoos are now considered fine pieces of art, designed by professional artists, a distinction from the primitive designs that they used to be. A study conducted in 2018 showed that "24% of adults have at least one tattoo" ("Tattoos Are More," 2018). Why has tattooing become such a phenomenon in the past decade? Many believe that it is because people feel the need to express themselves and their beliefs on their skin as an attempt at self-identity and individualism, which has become increasingly important to society throughout the years. Others believe that tattooing is popular because the media portray tattoos as being attractive to the opposite sex. Within the past decade, tattooing, or body art, has become commonplace among professionals due to their attempt to establish themselves as individuals by making a decorative statement, to appear more attractive to the opposite sex, or to thwart expectations of society. as shown in many modern movies, television shows, such as LA Ink, and through celebrity advertisements.
Double-Space
Attention-Getter
1"
In-Text Citation
Researchable Question
1"
Thesis and Forecast
Left Justify
Double-Space
Topic Sentence
One of the main reasons that tattooing has become so prominent among U.S. citizens today is the desire of people to define themselves as unique individuals. Many believe that tattooing something meaningful on their body is one way of accomplishing this individualism. According to DeMello (1995), "Tattoos have become 'liberated' from the province of lowlifes, and can now be properly positioned as aspects of fine art" (p. 47). In many people's eyes, tattoos are no longer marks of dishonor, but, instead, works of art. The idea of tattoos as forms of art is exemplified by the popular television show LA Ink. In one particular episode of this show, a young woman, Kathryn, gets a tattoo of a colorful peacock on her arm to represent the strength of her mother who had recently been in a coma for two months and completely lost her memory. Kathryn was not a biker or involved in crime, but was an educated, middle-class individual who desired to make a statement about her mother's heartbreaking situation in the form of body art (LA Ink—Peacock Tattoo). In DeMello's (1995) article, "Not Just for Bikers Anymore," she quotes an individual who was interviewed about his
First Main Point
Ragged Right Margin
1"

1/2"

1"

First Main Point Continued

decision to get a tattoo. He responded, "The power of the tattoo is in the ability to express individuality and in its permanence" (p. 41). Kathryn, from *LA Ink—Peacock Tattoo* (2011), and this this quoted individual share similar beliefs about tattoos and their meanings. Whether they are designed in memory of a loved one or to symbolize an important value or belief of the individual, tattoos are most commonly acquired for the purpose of making unique, decorative statements.

1"

Second Main Point

Another fundamental motivation for people in this country to get tattoos is the belief that they create sex appeal. A study of college students found that "almost three-fourths of the undergraduate women reported that they 'sometimes' viewed openly visible tattoos as attractive when on a man" (Horne et al., 2007, p. 1011). On the other hand, "58.8 percent of the undergraduate men viewed such visible tattoos as attractive when on a woman" (Horne et al., 2007, p. 1011). Therefore, men and women may get tattoos if they feel that it will add to their sex appeal. A large portion of this thinking has derived from the fact that many celebrities have tattoos, and, because celebrities are often seen as sex icons, common people believe that if they get tattoos then they will be appealing to the opposite sex as well (Horne et al., 2007, p. 1011). DeMello (1995) states, "Tattooing has moved from being a symbol of the outcast to that of a rock star, model, and postmodern youth, and with this shift in public perception has come a shift in meaning as well, as tattoo moves from stigma to status" (p. 49). The idea that tattoos are sexy is exemplified in many modern movies, including *Wanted*. The most famous scene of this movie depicts Angelina Jolie getting out of a bathtub, completely naked, with large tattoos covering her back. Jolie seductively peers around her shoulder at the camera, an obvious attempt of the director to attract men with her tattoo-covered body (Silvestri & Bekmambetov, 2008). Since the premier of the movie, this scene has become extremely famous. However, Jolie is not the only celebrity to endorse tattoos. Others, including David Beckham, Rihanna, Michael Jordan, and Gisele, have been pictured in advertisements that show off or or endorse tattoos. In his ad for Emporio Armani, Beckham poses in underwear, revealing his muscular body and a large tattoo on his right arm (Emporio Armani Underwear, 2019). Advertisements and movies like these, which depict extremely attractive celebrities with revealed tattoos, contribute in a major way to the idea that tattoos are sexy. For this reason, many people get tattoos in order to make themselves more attractive to the opposite sex.

1"

1"

APA Format

APA Format

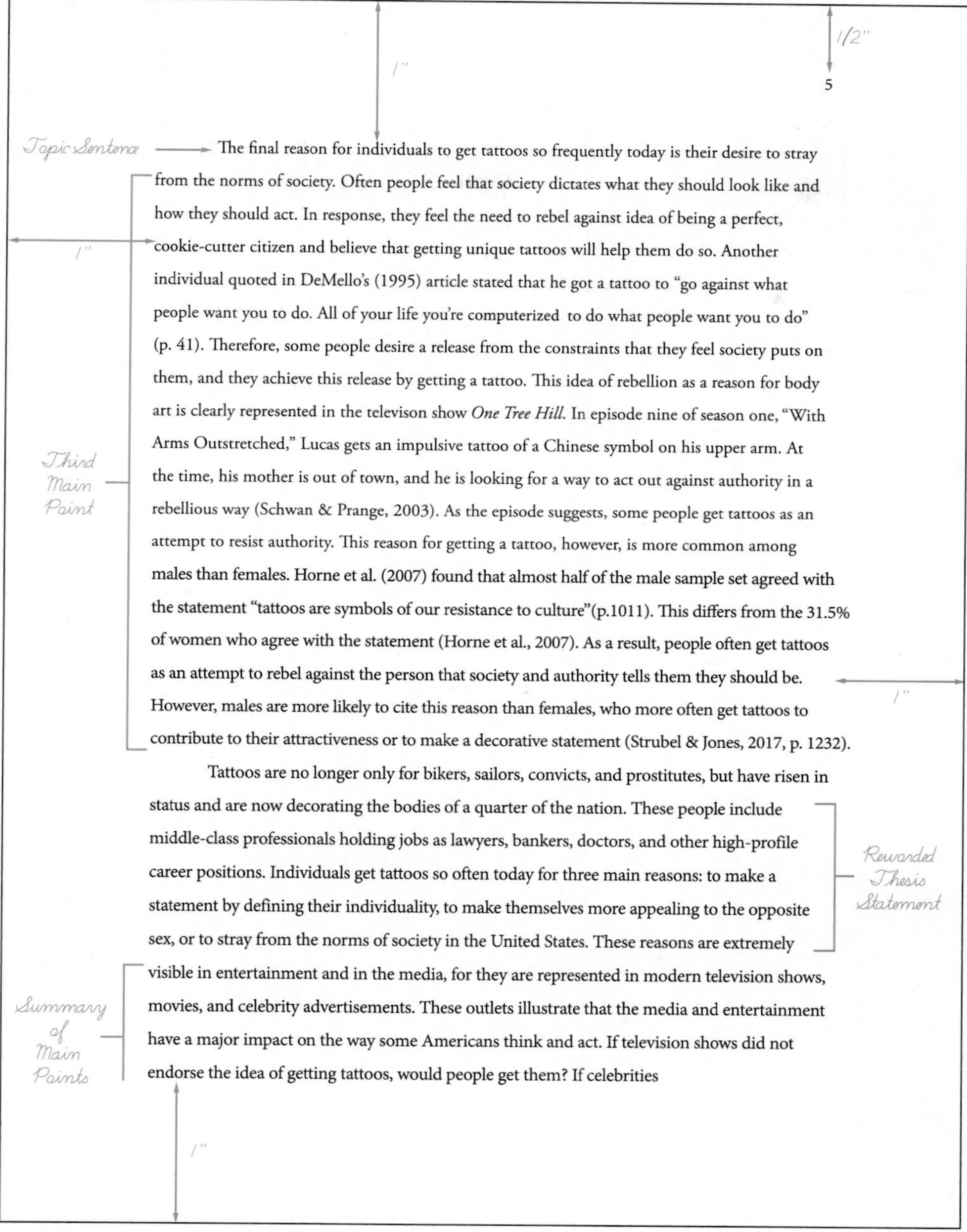

5

The final reason for individuals to get tattoos so frequently today is their desire to stray from the norms of society. Often people feel that society dictates what they should look like and how they should act. In response, they feel the need to rebel against idea of being a perfect, cookie-cutter citizen and believe that getting unique tattoos will help them do so. Another individual quoted in DeMello's (1995) article stated that he got a tattoo to "go against what people want you to do. All of your life you're computerized to do what people want you to do" (p. 41). Therefore, some people desire a release from the constraints that they feel society puts on them, and they achieve this release by getting a tattoo. This idea of rebellion as a reason for body art is clearly represented in the televison show *One Tree Hill.* In episode nine of season one, "With Arms Outstretched," Lucas gets an impulsive tattoo of a Chinese symbol on his upper arm. At the time, his mother is out of town, and he is looking for a way to act out against authority in a rebellious way (Schwan & Prange, 2003). As the episode suggests, some people get tattoos as an attempt to resist authority. This reason for getting a tattoo, however, is more common among males than females. Horne et al. (2007) found that almost half of the male sample set agreed with the statement "tattoos are symbols of our resistance to culture"(p.1011). This differs from the 31.5% of women who agree with the statement (Horne et al., 2007). As a result, people often get tattoos as an attempt to rebel against the person that society and authority tells them they should be. However, males are more likely to cite this reason than females, who more often get tattoos to contribute to their attractiveness or to make a decorative statement (Strubel & Jones, 2017, p. 1232).

Tattoos are no longer only for bikers, sailors, convicts, and prostitutes, but have risen in status and are now decorating the bodies of a quarter of the nation. These people include middle-class professionals holding jobs as lawyers, bankers, doctors, and other high-profile career positions. Individuals get tattoos so often today for three main reasons: to make a statement by defining their individuality, to make themselves more appealing to the opposite sex, or to stray from the norms of society in the United States. These reasons are extremely visible in entertainment and in the media, for they are represented in modern television shows, movies, and celebrity advertisements. These outlets illustrate that the media and entertainment have a major impact on the way some Americans think and act. If television shows did not endorse the idea of getting tattoos, would people get them? If celebrities

1/2"

6

1"

Summary of Main Points Continued

did not have tattoos all over their bodies, would people put tattoos all over their bodies? The answer is most likely no. Essentially, tattoos are just another fashion trend. Just as different forms of fashion are depicted in celebrity advertisements and used as costumes in movies and television shows, so are tattoos. The real question is, will the popularity of tattooing eventually die like most other fashion trends, leaving those who have them to regret their tattoos for the rest of their lives? Only time will tell.

1"

Memorable Ending

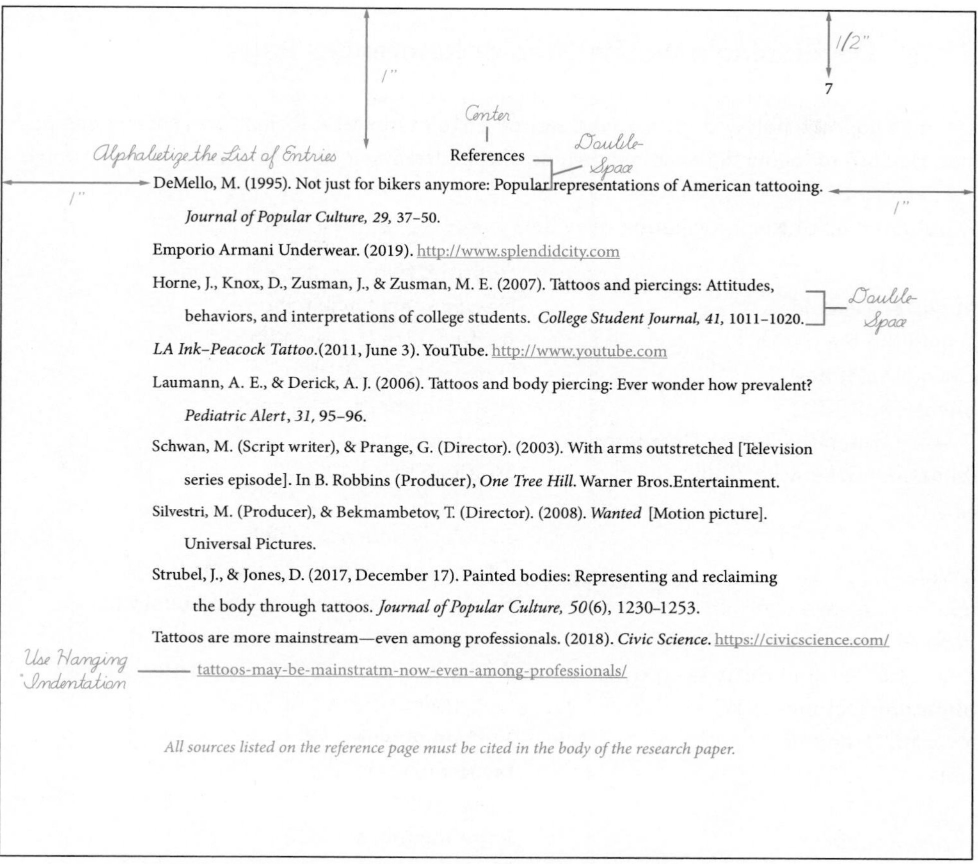
7

References

DeMello, M. (1995). Not just for bikers anymore: Popular representations of American tattooing. *Journal of Popular Culture, 29,* 37–50.

Emporio Armani Underwear. (2019). http://www.splendidcity.com

Horne, J., Knox, D., Zusman, J., & Zusman, M. E. (2007). Tattoos and piercings: Attitudes, behaviors, and interpretations of college students. *College Student Journal, 41,* 1011–1020.

LA Ink–Peacock Tattoo.(2011, June 3). YouTube. http://www.youtube.com

Laumann, A. E., & Derick, A. J. (2006). Tattoos and body piercing: Ever wonder how prevalent? *Pediatric Alert, 31,* 95–96.

Schwan, M. (Script writer), & Prange, G. (Director). (2003). With arms outstretched [Television series episode]. In B. Robbins (Producer), *One Tree Hill.* Warner Bros.Entertainment.

Silvestri, M. (Producer), & Bekmambetov, T. (Director). (2008). *Wanted* [Motion picture]. Universal Pictures.

Strubel, J., & Jones, D. (2017, December 17). Painted bodies: Representing and reclaiming the body through tattoos. *Journal of Popular Culture, 50*(6), 1230–1253.

Tattoos are more mainstream—even among professionals. (2018). *Civic Science.* https://civicscience.com/tattoos-may-be-mainstratm-now-even-among-professionals/

All sources listed on the reference page must be cited in the body of the research paper.

Source: Rowland, Margaret, From Stigma to Status. Reprinted by permission of the author.

QUESTIONS FOR REFLECTION

1. Based on the introductory paragraph, what three main points does Rowland promise to cover in the body of her paper? Does she follow through with her promise?
2. What supporting details and examples does she offer for her first main point? Are they sufficient? Why or why not?
3. What supporting details does Rowland offer for her second main point? Which details are the most convincing? Why?
4. Which ideas from the author's third body paragraph are most memorable? Why?
5. What is Rowland's thesis? Do you think she fully supports her thesis in the body of the paper? Why or why not?

Activity Developing a Works-Cited or References Page

Using the six fictitious sources below, create a works-cited page in the MLA format or a references page in the APA format. Be sure to follow the exact guidelines of the format you are using. Arrange your entries in alphabetical order.

Tip: You may not need all of the information provided.

Book
Title: all that glitters is gold
Subtitle: earning the big bucks
Author: Showmei Z. Money
Date of publication: 2020
Publisher: Greedy Green Publishing Company, Inc.
Place of publication: Greenville, South Carolina
Medium: Print

Magazine Article
Title: a computer can save your life
Magazine: today's computers
Authors: Joey T. Hacker and Betty Lynn Byte
Date of publication: October 2019
Page numbers: 10, 11, and 16
Medium: Print

Online Magazine Article
Title: justice for juveniles in Jamestown
Magazine: crimesolversareus.com
Author: Jamal J. Jolly
Date of publication: August 19, 2017
Page numbers: None
URL: www.crimesolversareus.com/juvenilesingreenville
DOI: 10.1234/0011-2233.45.6.789
Retrieval Date: January 14, 2020
Medium: Internet

Newspaper Article
Title: stray alligator terrorizes shopping mall
Subtitle: two shoppers injured
Newspaper: trivia tribune
Author: Liza L. Love-Lizzard
Date: July 27, 2018
Page Numbers: 4, 5, and 8
Section number: B
Medium: Print

Scholarly Journal Article
Title: best business practices
Subtitle: earn and keep good customers
Journal: universal business journal
Authors: Kiefer G. Consumer, Mario López Servicio, Fahad Al-Safar
Volume number: 6
Issue number: 3
Date: 2020
Page numbers: 14–15
Medium: Print

Website Document
Title: a healthier you
Subtitle: living life to the fullest
Author: Elsie B. Eatwell
Website: Living Well
Date of publication: April 23, 2018
Retrieval Date: March 25, 2021
Page number: none
URL: www.livingwell.org/ebeatwell/livinglife
Medium: Internet

PEER REVIEW QUESTIONS FOR A RESEARCH PAPER

1. Identify the thesis statement in the introduction. Is it clear and effective? Why or why not?
2. What are the author's main points? Are they fully developed? Explain.
3. What is your favorite part of the research paper?
4. Are any areas confusing? Explain.
5. Does the paper flow well? Which parts, if any, could be smoother?
6. Is the concluding paragraph effective? Why or why not?
7. What kinds of grammatical errors, if any, are evident in the research paper?
8. Are all sources clearly and properly documented in the text and on the works-cited or reference page? Identify any areas that need attention.
9. What final suggestions do you have for the author?

Writer's Checklist for a Research Paper

Use the checklist below to evaluate your own writing and help ensure that your research paper is effective. If you have any "no" answers, continue work on those areas as needed.

- ☐ 1. Does my introduction clearly state my thesis and give the reader an indication of the direction my essay will take?
- ☐ 2. Are my topic sentences and body paragraphs clear and well developed?
- ☐ 3. Have I fully supported my thesis with ample supporting details and examples?
- ☐ 4. Have I used a sufficient number and variety of sources in my paper?
- ☐ 5. Are all of my sources properly cited in the body of my paper according to the MLA or APA format?
- ☐ 6. Does my conclusion effectively summarize my main points and restate my thesis in different words?
- ☐ 7. Have I carefully proofread and revised my paper for sentence variety, word choice, grammar, and punctuation?
- ☐ 8. Does my works-cited or reference page include every source I cited in the text, and is it in the correct format?
- ☐ 9. Have I used the correct margins, line spacing, and other format issues required by my instructor and the MLA or APA guidelines?

CHAPTER SUMMARY

1. Avoid plagiarism by clearly citing sources you use in a research paper.
2. Follow the specific guidelines of the format your instructor requires you to use, such as MLA or APA.
3. Cite sources within your text and on a works-cited page (MLA format) or on a reference page (APA format).
4. Use the correct MLA or APA format for your entire research paper.

WHAT I KNOW NOW

Use this checklist to determine what you need to work on in order to feel comfortable with your understanding of the material in this chapter. Check off each item as you master it. Review the material for any unchecked items.

- ☐ 1. I know what **plagiarism** is and understand how to avoid it.
- ☐ 2. I understand what **sources** I need to cite in a research paper.
- ☐ 3. I know that I need to cite sources in the body of my paper as well as on a **works-cited** or **reference page.**
- ☐ 4. I know how to **cite sources** using the **MLA** or **APA** format.
- ☐ 5. I know how to **format a paper** using the MLA or APA guidelines.

Design elements: *Graduate Spotlight:* Ingram Publishing/AGE Fotostock

CHAPTER 15

Delivering an Oral Presentation or a Multimodal Composition

dotshock/Shutterstock

learning outcomes

In this chapter you will learn techniques for achieving these learning outcomes:

15.1 Planning a Presentation

Does the idea of giving an oral presentation make you nervous? You're not alone! Some people fear public speaking more than spiders, snakes, or even death. Fortunately, with careful planning and practice, you can become more confident and effective at giving oral presentations. This chapter is not designed to be a complete guide to public speaking. Your school may require that you take a separate speech communications course and read an entire textbook devoted to delivering speeches. This chapter, however, will give you a brief introduction to giving a research paper presentation in your writing class (or another class) in case you haven't taken a speech class yet. If you have already taken a public speaking class, this chapter will serve as a quick refresher.

You will have many opportunities to give presentations at school, on the job, and in your personal life. In other courses, your instructors may require you to give presentations based on course material or papers you have written. At work, you may need to give a presentation to supervisors, colleagues, clients, customers, or patients. Or you may need to say a few words to friends or family members at a special occasion or event, such as a wedding or a reunion. Regardless of what type of speaking engagement you face, you will benefit from preparing what you will say ahead of time. Planning a speech is very similar to writing an essay. For both you need to have an introduction, a body, and a conclusion.

Developing the Introduction

Similar to your research essay, the introduction of your speech should do three things: capture your audience's attention, state your thesis, and give a forecast of your main points.

1. **Gain your audience's attention.** The fact that you have an audience assembled in front of you doesn't guarantee that they will actually listen to you. Try beginning with a thought-provoking question, a relevant quote, a brief story or description, a shocking statistic, a surprising statement, or a comparison to help hook your listeners. For example, you might begin by explaining how to budget money with the question, "Have you ever wished you had more money to spend?" Your goal is to entice your listeners to want to hear what you have to say.
2. **State your thesis.** For a presentation based on your research paper, you may choose to use the exact thesis from your paper. Be sure your thesis covers the topic you are addressing as well as your overall opinion about it and that it isn't too wordy for your audience to remember. For example, the thesis might be, "If you effectively plan for your financial future now, you will reap the benefits for a lifetime." Memorize your thesis statement so that you can look right at your audience when you state it.
3. **Give a forecast of your main points.** Provide your listeners with a preview of what they will learn from your presentation. For instance, you might say, "There are three steps you can take to reduce your debt and improve your financial prospects. These three steps are . . ." Being clear about the main

points will also help your audience members to take notes if they need to. If you are using a research paper as the basis for your presentation, you can go through your paper and determine which points will be most interesting and relevant to the group. You may choose not to include every main point from your paper.

Developing the Body

In the body of your presentation, you want to give the audience what you promised in your forecast. Although you probably will not write out your main points word for word, you need to decide exactly what you will cover in your presentation. Use an outline or note cards to help you keep track of ideas you want to emphasize in your speech.

1. **Emphasize your main points.** Cover your points in a logical order. Give relevant details and examples to help you support your main ideas. If your presentation is based on a research paper, you do not need to include every example from your paper. Choose the ones your audience will find most interesting and useful. You can use the same strategies you learned about in Chapters 5–12 to organize your speech (see Table 15.1). Depending on your subject, you may focus on one particular strategy or combine two or more strategies to get your point across to your audience.
2. **Make transitions smoothly.** Determine your transitions ahead of time so that you don't forget to use them during your presentation. As you move from one point to another, use a transition to signal the change to the listeners. For example, you might use the transitions *first, second, third,* and *last* to help your audience keep track of your main points.
3. **Cite sources.** If you use words or ideas from an outside source, you need to mention the source to give appropriate credit to the originator of the material. For example, you might say, "According to Suze Orman, a financial expert who has her own television show, people need to spend below their means to get ahead financially." Omitting citations in a speech is just as unethical as leaving them out of a research paper. Work on incorporating your citations smoothly so that they don't interfere with the flow of your presentation. Another option, if you are using PowerPoint and/or visuals, is to provide your sources on a slide, as a works cited (MLA) or reference (APA) list to present at the end of your talk.

Developing the Conclusion

The conclusion of your speech serves the same purpose as the conclusion to an essay. You want to restate your main points and leave your audience with a lasting impression. Keep your conclusion short and interesting.

1. **Restate your thesis.** Remind your listeners of your thesis by restating it using slightly different words than the ones you used in the introduction.
2. **Summarize your main points.** Mention your main points again, but do not restate your specific details and examples. You might say something like, "Remember, the three steps for becoming more financially secure are . . ."

Table 15.1

Organizational Strategies	
Describing and Narrating	Tell a descriptive story about something that happened. Usually you will present the details of the event in chronological order, but occasionally a flashback can be useful. Be sure to cover who, what, where, when, why, and how. Also, use plenty of sensory appeal (sight, sound, taste, smell, touch) to help your audience envision what happened.
Dividing and Classifying	Divide a concept into groups with common traits or principles and explain the significant elements of each group.
Explaining a Process	Tell how something works or what something does. You may give step-by-step instructions so your listeners can perform the task or write an explanation so that your listeners are able to understand your subject.
Comparing and Contrasting	Show how two people, places, or objects are similar and/or different. Be sure to make a worthwhile point while doing this.
Explaining Causes and Effects	Examine how one event or situation caused another to occur, or determine the effects of an event or situation. Be careful to apply sound logic as you analyze causes and effects.
Persuading	Take a stand about an important or controversial issue, and convince your audience that your position is valid. Use research to support your main idea.
Evaluating	Make a judgment about your subject by determining how well it meets specific criteria that you feel are important for that subject.
Solving a Problem	Explain a problem to your audience and offer several solutions. You may evaluate each possible solution before persuading your listeners that one specific solution is best.

3. **End with a memorable statement.** Leave your audience with a final vivid thought. You might tell a brief story that relates to your topic or suggest a call to action. Another option is to end with a quote that fits with your overall purpose.
4. **Say thank you.** Saying "thank you" at the end of your presentation is courteous, and it provides a definite signal to your audience that your speech is over. Your listeners will know when it is time to clap and ask questions, if appropriate.
5. **Answer questions.** If you are in a situation where the audience will have an opportunity to ask you questions after your presentation, then you will need to be prepared. Try to anticipate the types of questions your listeners might have. Have your notes handy in case they might be helpful. It's all right if you don't know every answer. Be honest and say, "I'm not sure. I didn't research that particular area." Or you might answer, "That's a good question; I'll have to get back to you on that." Don't fake it.

Graduate SPOTLIGHT

Frank Ragozino, Medical Assistant

Frank Ragozino has an AS degree in medical assisting and is the lead medical assistant for a family practice medical center. Here's what Ragozino has to say about the importance of communication in his career:

©Karin L. Russell

"At the medical center where I work, having good oral and written communication skills is second only to patient care. Every day I talk to patients to learn about their conditions, symptoms, allergens, and so on. I have to listen very carefully to what they say so that I can communicate the information to the doctors and meet the patients' needs. I also have to be able to explain to a patient how to use an inhaler or glucometer or how to give an insulin injection. Additionally, as the lead medical assistant I am responsible for training new employees and student interns and explaining all of the aspects of becoming a medical assistant. Writing is another important skill I use while on the job. I have to carefully document everything that takes place when I see a patient. I have to use a lot of detail when writing on a patient's chart. This is important not only for the patient's health but also for the liability of the medical center. In my career, being able to communicate effectively orally and in writing is critical to the well-being of the patients."

15.2 Choosing Visuals

Visuals can be a true asset to any presentation. Choose your visuals carefully. Make sure that each one enhances your speech without overshadowing it. Keep your audience in mind as you decide which visuals are most appropriate for your presentation. (See also Section 15.5, Creating a Multimodal Composition.)

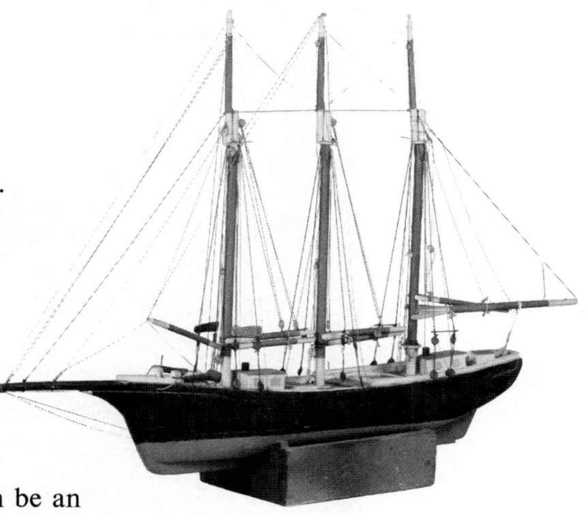

Ingram Publishing/SuperStock

Objects or Models

Sometimes a three-dimensional object or model can be an effective visual. Make sure it is large enough for the audience to see, but not so large that it would be difficult to bring to your presentation. For example, if you were giving a presentation about techniques used in sailing, a sailboat would obviously be too large for the room; however, a 1/18-scale model would be appropriate.

Posters, Flip Charts, and Whiteboards

You may find a poster board to be a useful visual for your presentation. You can use it to display photographs, drawings, maps, charts, graphs, timelines, or fairly small three-dimensional items. Writing words or drawing simple figures on a whiteboard or flip chart can be useful during your presentation, especially if you are soliciting responses from your audience. This method is appropriate only for small amounts of information. If the room is equipped with a smart board, use that because projected images will be large and easy to see. Face your listeners as much as possible as you write or draw.

Slides

Developing a presentation using PowerPoint, Keynote, Lotus, Adobe, or another software application can help you to give a smooth speech if you use it correctly. Be sure to write short sentences or phrases on each slide, and elaborate on them during your speech. Avoid making your slides too busy. (See Figures 15.1 and 15.2.) Choose images that relate to your topic and enhance your presentation. Also, choose transitions that are interesting but not overdone. Sound clips, movie clips, and other features can add pizzazz.

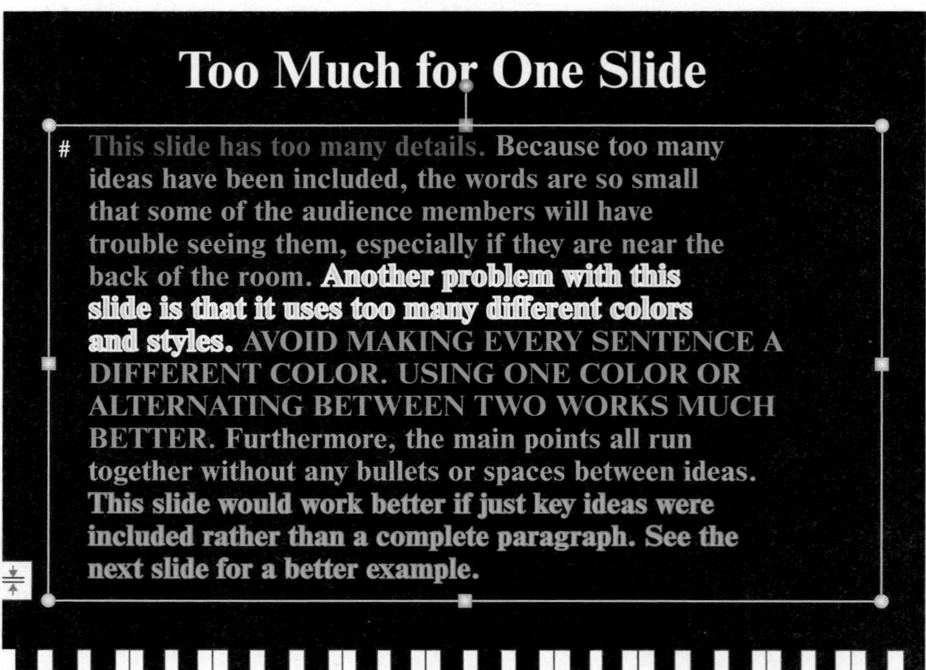

FIGURE 15.1 Inappropriate Slide

Appropriate Slide
Highlight key points.
Use short sentences or phrases.
Keep colors and styles consistent.
Use visuals to paint a picture.

FIGURE 15.2 Appropriate Slide

Video Clips

Depending on the type of presentation you are giving, you might find it useful to show a short video clip that relates to your topic. For instance, if your presentation is on scuba diving, you might show a one- or two-minute clip of divers exploring a coral reef. Similarly, if the point of your presentation is to give a review of a book you have read, you might show a brief YouTube or movie clip of a critical scene from the book that relates to one of your key points. If you are creating a presentation for an online class, you might design it to play automatically, so that your viewers don't have to click from slide to slide. For more on developing a digital presentation, see Section 15.5, Creating a Multimodal Composition.

Handouts

A handout may serve as a useful visual for your presentation, especially as a backup in case you have technical problems. If you create a handout, consider giving it out after rather than during your presentation. You don't want to unintentionally lose your listeners by diverting their attention elsewhere. Handouts should look professional and visually appealing. Be sure to proofread them carefully for content and grammar.

15.3 Delivering a Presentation

Comstock Images/Getty Images

1. **Get psyched.** Pump yourself up on the day of the presentation. Focus on positive thoughts. Visualize yourself giving a great presentation. Being a little nervous is fine and even desired because you will get a boost

of adrenaline to keep you going. It also gives you the opportunity to channel any nervous energy into enthusiasm for your topic. If your hands are a little shaky or sweaty, it's no big deal. You are probably the only person who will notice. Just before you get up before the audience, take a deep breath and try to relax. Look out at your audience and smile. Look at someone who smiles back as you begin your presentation.

2. **Use an outline or note cards.** You will probably be able to use an outline or 3-by-5-inch note cards to help guide you through the presentation. Some speakers prefer to access their notes from their tablets or smartphones. If you decide to do this, make sure your gear is charged ahead of time. Avoid writing out your entire speech word for word. Instead, use an outline or notes to help you keep track of the main points you want to cover. Include any quotes, statistics, and sources you want to mention so that you will give the correct information to your audience. Be careful not to rely on these tools too heavily. Spend more time looking at your listeners than at your notes.

STUDENT OUTLINE FOR A PRESENTATION

Texting While Driving

by Anita Jitta

Speech Goal: To inform my audience about the dangers of texting while driving.

Introduction

Hook: On November 2, 2019, my husband, Anthony, was driving home when a teenaged girl slammed into him with her car. What was she doing? She was texting while driving. Luckily enough, another driver saw what this girl was doing and decided to wait at the scene of the accident to be a witness when the police arrived. The teenager ended up receiving a citation for reckless driving, but the results could have been much worse, even deadly.

Thesis: Texting while driving is extremely dangerous and can lead to devastating consequences.

Preview: First, you will learn what happens when you text while driving. Second, you will learn how people feel about texting while driving. Finally, you will learn about what some famous people are doing to try to prevent drivers from texting while driving.

Body

I. What can happen when someone text messages and drives? According to DriversEd.com, 73% of American drivers admit to reading texts while behind the wheel; 54% admit to typing texts while driving.

II. How do people feel about texting and driving? The study by researchers, published in 2018 by *Risk Analysis,* brought about some interesting responses.

III. Who is against texting and driving, and what do they plan to do about it? State and federal legislatures are trying to change laws to help tackle this problem.

References

Drivers-Ed Staff. (2018, October 1). DriversEd.com survey reveals majority of drivers admit to distracted driving. DriversEd.com. https://driversed.com/trending/drivers-admit-to-distracted-driving/

Kitch, A. (2018, June). State and federal efforts to reduce distracted driving. *National Conference of State Legislatures.* www.ncsl.org/research/transportation/state-and-federal-efforts-to-reduce-distracted-driving.aspx

National Highway Traffic Safety Administration. (2019). Distracted driving. *NHTSA.* www.nhtsa.gov/risky-driving/distracted-driving

Oviedo-Trespalacios, O., Haque, M., King, M., & Washington. S. (2018). Should I text or call here? A situation-based analysis of drivers' perceived likelihood of engaging in mobile phone multitasking. *Risk Analysis.* doi: 10.1111/risa.13119

Science Daily. (2018, July 9). Majority of drivers don't believe texting while driving is dangerous. *Science Daily.* www.sciencedaily.com/releases/2018/07/180709120143.htm

U.S. Department of Transportation. (2019). April is national distracted driving awareness month. *Traffic Safety Marketing.* www.trafficsafetymarketing.gov/get-materials/distracted-driving

Note: The sources listed in the above outline are provided in APA format (according to the APA manual's seventh edition, 2020). Your instructor may request that you list your sources in the MLA format. If so, please see Chapter 14 for the exact guidelines.

3. **Speak clearly and enthusiastically.** If you are excited about your topic, your audience will be too. Vary your pitch and tone to emphasize important words and keep your listeners interested. Enunciate your words carefully so that your audience can hear each word. Also, make sure your pace is appropriate. Speaking too slowly will give your audience too much time to think about other things. However, if you speak too rapidly, your listeners might not catch everything and get frustrated.
4. **Communicate nonverbally.** In addition to listening to what you have to say, your audience will be paying attention to the nonverbal cues you display. Your clothing, poise, posture, movements, hand gestures, facial expressions, and eye contact all affect the message you are attempting to convey to your audience. You want to communicate an attitude of professionalism and confidence as you give your presentation. If you make a mistake or forget something, don't apologize or stop. Just pick up where you left off and keep going.
5. **Incorporate visuals.** Decide ahead of time exactly when and how you will show your visuals to enhance your presentation. Generally, you should display each visual only when you are talking about it. As you show each item, hold it up and away from your body so that everyone in your audience can see it. Avoid passing visuals around the room. You might even walk around the room so everyone can get a closer look. If you are using a PowerPoint or Keynote presentation, talk about each slide as you show it to your audience. Don't read your presentation from the slides. Instead, use the keywords on the slide to help you remember what to say.
6. **Have a backup plan.** As you are well aware, things don't always go as they are planned. What happens if the projector doesn't work the day of your presentation? What will you do if the computer freezes? Have a secondary

plan. Bring additional materials with you to ensure that you are able to give an effective presentation even if you experience a technological glitch. For example, write out some note cards in case your PowerPoint or Keynote presentation won't work.

7. **Practice your presentation.** Before the big day, practice delivering your presentation several times. If you can, assemble a small audience to simulate the experience as closely as possible. If no one is around, stand in front of a mirror. Explore different methods for using your visuals, note cards, hand gestures, and so on to see what feels most comfortable and seems to work best. You may even want to videotape or digitally record your presentation so that you can watch and critique yourself. Make adjustments as needed to smooth out your presentation. Also, time yourself to ensure that your presentation falls within the time requirements.

> *ESOL Tip* >
>
> Practice your speech for a native English speaker to ensure that your listeners will understand everything you say. For example, some non-native speakers pronounce *i's* as *e's*.

Presenter's Checklist

Use this checklist before you give your presentation to make sure that you are ready. Keep working on any items that don't yet earn a "yes."

- ☐ 1. Are my outline and note cards ready?
- ☐ 2. Are my thesis and main points clear and well organized?
- ☐ 3. Do I have the right number of details and examples to support my main points fully?
- ☐ 4. Have I planned how to make transitions from one point to the next?
- ☐ 5. Are my visuals useful and appropriate for the audience?
- ☐ 6. Do I have a backup plan in case something goes wrong?
- ☐ 7. Am I ready to give an enthusiastic presentation?
- ☐ 8. Have I practiced my presentation several times?

Comments:

Observer's Checklist

Use this checklist to evaluate someone else's presentation.

- ☐ 1. Were the thesis and main points clear?
- ☐ 2. Was the organization of the presentation effective?
- ☐ 3. Did the presentation flow well?

- ☐ 4. Was the speaker enthusiastic?
- ☐ 5. Were the visuals useful and handled well?
- ☐ 6. Did the presenter speak clearly and effectively?
- ☐ 7. Did the speaker look at the audience?
- ☐ 8. Were the presenter's posture and movements effective?
- ☐ 9. What suggestions do I have for the speaker?
- ☐ 10. What was the best part of the presentation?

Comments:

Activity Evaluating a Presentation

Go to **YouTube.com** and find Dr. Martin Luther King's "I Have a Dream" speech. Watch King's speech and evaluate it according to the observer's checklist. Write at least one paragraph explaining what was most memorable or inspiring about his famous speech. You may be asked to share your reaction in groups or with the class.

Note: Another famous speech could be used as an alternative. Additionally, **YouTube.com** has numerous student speeches to evaluate.

Activity Conducting Research for a Presentation

Using the ideas from a research paper you have written, plan and deliver a presentation.

1. Use your paper to develop an outline or note cards for your presentation.
2. Organize the introduction, body, and conclusion of your presentation.
3. Keep track of your sources so you can cite them as needed.
4. Prepare appropriate visuals for your presentation.
5. Be ready to answer questions from your listeners.
6. Pay attention to your nonverbal communication and time constraints as you practice delivering your presentation.
7. Relax—this is not a life-or-death situation!
8. Deliver your presentation.

15.4 Group Presentations

You will have many opportunities to participate in group presentations in school and at work. One of the benefits of working with others is that you gain the perspective of all of the participants. Follow these steps to ensure that your group presentation goes smoothly.

1. **Establish goals.** Everyone in the group needs to understand what the goals are and be willing to help achieve those goals. Keep your overall purpose in mind as well as the effect you want to have on the audience. The goals you develop need to be reasonable. You may want to set benchmarks for accomplishing specific tasks to ensure that you prepare an effective presentation and meet your deadline.
2. **Assign roles.** Each member of the group needs to have a particular role. For example, if your group has five members, then each person might take one of the following roles: leader, note taker, researcher, encourager, and harmonizer. The roles of the group members will vary based on the parameters of the assignment. The group members will also need to determine who is responsible for each task that needs to be completed before the presentation. While many details can be worked out together, each member may need to work on certain parts of the presentation away from the group.
3. **Participate in group meetings.** If you do not have an opportunity to meet with your group members during class, then you will need to establish meeting times. Find a time that works best for everyone in the group. If face-to-face meetings are impossible or inconvenient, then have virtual meetings via e-mail, teleconferencing, videoconferencing, or online threaded discussions. Everyone needs to cooperate in the meetings and contribute ideas for the presentation.
4. **Organize the group presentation.** Work as a team to organize the introduction, body, and conclusion of the presentation. Decide what each person will say and/or do during the presentation. Listen to everyone's ideas and be open to suggestions. If the group has trouble agreeing on a particular issue, then the group members can go with majority rule or work to come to a consensus. Be willing to compromise for the sake of helping the group to accomplish its goals.
5. **Practice the group presentation.** Practice your presentation before giving it. Have a dress rehearsal complete with visuals to make sure that everyone and everything is ready. Make sure your presentation flows smoothly and that everyone knows his or her part.
6. **Deliver the group presentation.** On the day of the presentation, everyone should show up prepared to do his or her part. If someone doesn't make it, then the other members need to step in and fulfill that person's duties. The group members need to show enthusiasm, communicate nonverbally, and incorporate visuals smoothly during the presentation. If someone makes a mistake or forgets something, keep going as if everything is fine.

Activity Planning a Group Presentation: Preparing a Sales Pitch

In groups of three to six, invent a realistic or futuristic product or service that you would love to see on the market. For example, maybe you would like to offer a vacation package to Pluto. How will your customers get there? What will they do for fun and relaxation once they arrive? Why is this vacation worth taking? Or maybe you would prefer to present a new product that will wow your audience, such as a robot that will clean your home from top to bottom while you are away or a chocolate bar that helps you to remember important concepts on test day.

Work cooperatively to develop a mini-infomercial to present to your live class or a magazine advertisement to present to your online class. Every member in the group needs to participate in the preparation and presentation of your sales pitch. For this one assignment only, you may invent the supporting details. Use the following guidelines for your sales pitch:

1. Grab your audience's attention with a catchy opening.
2. Describe the product or service and emphasize the benefits it will have to the consumer. You want audience members to be interested in your product or service so that they want to buy it.
3. Create testimonials, statistics, or other data to promote your product or service and convince your audience that your product or service is worth buying.
4. Display appropriate visuals to enhance your presentation.
5. Let your audience members know how much your product or service costs and what they need to do to get it. Do they need to call a 1-800 number, visit your store, or go online?
6. You might mention any disclaimers or side effects that the product or service may cause the consumer.

Note: Making up the data is appropriate only as an exercise. You should never invent support for a product or service that you are really selling because it is unethical.

15.5 Creating a Multimodal Composition

While words are often enough to capture your reader's attention and get your message across, sometimes it's appropriate (and even necessary) to communicate through additional modalities. A multimodal composition can be as simple as a paper that includes visuals or as complex as a research project in which you present to your audience a collection of written, dimensional, audio, and video creations. Often, a multimodal assignment for a writing class is accompanied by a written statement in which students explain their goals and evaluate their work. Some may also be accompanied by a research paper that includes all of the sources drawn upon to create the work.

When you create a multimodal text, you create meaning for your audience through two or more of the following modal elements:

1. Written/linguistic.
2. Nonverbal.
3. Visual/digital.
4. Audio.
5. Spatial.

1. Written/Linguistic Elements

The language that you use, whether spoken or written, is important to your composition. Considering your diction (word choice), syntax (arrangement of words), and morphology (sounds) are all part of linguistics. Be sure to match your language to your writing occasion and consider your rhetorical star: subject, audience, purpose, strategy, and design.

Writing Of course writing is the primary modality through which you communicate in assignments in your composition course. As you write your compositions, remember to choose an engaging topic that fits your purpose and falls within the constraints of the assignment set by your instructor. Consider your rhetorical star as you write: subject, audience, purpose, strategy, and design. (See Figure 15.3.)

Additionally, choose a writing strategy (or a combination of strategies) that works well with your topic: describing and narrating, dividing and classifying, explaining a process, comparing and contrasting, explaining causes and effects, persuading, evaluating, or solving a problem. Be sure to follow the steps of the writing process as well: discovering, planning, composing, getting feedback, revising, editing, and proofreading.

FIGURE 15.3
Rhetorical Star

Journaling Keeping a journal is a great way to document experiences or new learning over time. In college, an instructor may ask you to keep a journal of your intern or other working experience, field work, research project, or learning process. Unlike a personal journal, which may cover any topic, journaling for school (or the workplace) is more focused on a specific subject. For example, in a literature course, you may be asked to keep a journal of your responses to what you are reading. If you are working in a clinical setting for college credit, you may need to keep a journal of your daily experiences and reactions to those. Typically, a journal includes dated entries with a written explanation of events, concepts, or findings. Journals may be handwritten or digital, depending on the requirements of your instructor. You may be asked to review your journal entries at the end of the course or learning experience to reflect on your learning process.

2. Nonverbal Elements

When giving a presentation or recording a video related to your composition, you will need to consider how you communicate nonverbally to your audience through facial expressions, body language, and gestures. (See also Section 15.3, Delivering a Presentation.)

- **Facial Expressions:** When facing your audience, smile as you begin your presentation and make eye contact with members in the audience throughout. Looking around at different audience members is better than focusing on one person. Try to match your facial expression to the tone of your presentation. For example, if you are talking about something serious, such as abuse, your facial expression should either be neutral or a reflection of the seriousness of your topic. If you are giving information that might surprise your audience, you might raise your eyebrows.
- **Body Language:** Your body language, also known as *kinesics,* communicates a message to your audience beyond the words you say. Wear clothing that fits the occasion. Stand up straight and maintain good posture, but try to look natural. Consider what your arms and hands are communicating to the audience as well. Crossing your arms may make you look defensive or closed off. Having your arms up and exposing the palm of your hands from time to time can help you to look more open and relaxed. If you're standing behind a lectern, don't hang on to it.
- **Gestures:** You can emphasize important points in your presentation through head or hand gestures. Nodding, shaking your head, and tilting your head sideways or backward all communicate a message to your audience. Similarly, you can use hand gestures to help get your message across. For example, you can hold up fingers to show numbers when you count or move your hand with your palm facing up to indicate an audience member can speak or ask a question. Be aware of how your audience may perceive your gestures.

3. Visual/Digital Elements

Building a visual component into your presentation or other text helps you reinforce the message you are communicating to your audience. The typeface, layout and spacing, lines and shapes, images, colors, and backgrounds and borders that you choose affect your audience's experience and understanding.

Basic Visual Elements

- **Typeface:** If you are given a choice of typeface, choose one that fits with your purpose, audience, and the tone you want to achieve. For example, an APA paper requires Times New Roman because it is easy to read. If you are developing a flyer for a campus or workplace event, you might choose a more elegant font for a heading, such as *Apple Chancery.*

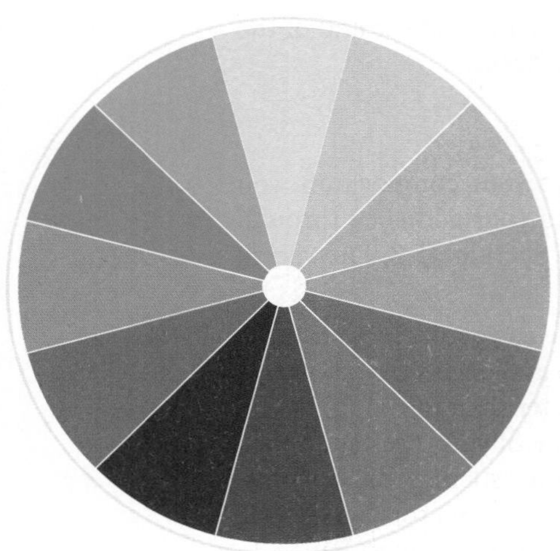

FIGURE 15.4
Color Wheel

- **Lines and Shapes:** These are useful for many types of documents, especially if you are including a graphic organizer, chart, or graph in your composition. Additionally, you might present some text in circles or rectangles to separate ideas and create visual interest. At times, depending on your audience and purpose you may want to use arrows, bullets, or other graphic features to emphasize certain concepts and add visual appeal to your presentation or other composition.
- **Colors:** Your rhetorical situation may require that you present your writing in a black font on a white background. At other times, though, you may have the option to add color to your text or background. As with images, make sure that the colors do not distract your audience from your message. Choose colors that complement one another without making your composition too busy. Consulting a color wheel can help you determine what colors work well together (see Figure 15.4). For example, opposite colors on the wheel, such as blue and orange, generally complement one another, and side-by-side colors, such as blue and green, tend to be visually pleasing, too. Be sure that the colors you choose for your typeface, background, or border look good with any images you choose.
- **Backgrounds and Borders:** Adding a background to your multimodal composition can make your project pop. You might include a light image, pattern, or color behind your text to increase visual appeal. As with other visual features, be sure the background doesn't overwhelm the text. Borders, such as lines, patterns, graphics, and so on, can be visually appealing as well. It's easy to add a background or border using Microsoft Word or PowerPoint. If you want more options, many templates with backgrounds and borders for Word and PowerPoint documents are available for free online (see Table 15.2). Again, choose a template that complements the content of your composition as well as any other visual elements you are including.

Table 15.2

Resources for Border and Background Templates
www.smiletemplates.com/backgrounds-textures/word-templates/0.html
www.all-free-download.com/free-vector/ms-word-background-design.html
www.free-powerpoint-templates-design.com
www.page-borders.com
www.bing.com/discover/borders-for-word-documents

Types of Visual Elements

- **Images:** You may use many different types of images, such as photographs, artwork, graphs, or charts, to add a visual element to your multimodal composition. Or, you might create an image to present as a freestanding composition. When including visual elements, choose images that illustrate for your audience an important aspect of your topic that would be difficult to describe fully in writing. Be sure that your images do not overpower your written text or other elements. When composing, it is a good idea to refer to the images in your written text so your audience will better understand your reason for including them. Also, if you use images that you did not create, be sure to cite your sources for them appropriately. (See Chapter 14 for more on citing visuals.)
- **Artifacts and Objects:** You may want to include one or more handmade or other types of objects to accompany your multimodal project. Or, you might create an object that is a composition in its own right. Depending on the parameters of your assignment, you may use a three-dimensional artifact or a photo of one to add a visual and perhaps tactile element to your project. For instance, if you are writing a process analysis essay about making pottery, you might present with it a bowl or other artifact made of clay if appropriate for the assignment.
- **Posters:** Even though digital formats have taken the place of more traditional methods of displaying concepts, a poster can still be a good way to present material to your instructor and classmates. Having a tangible representation of your ideas with written text, visual images, and even three-dimensional objects, as noted above, can be very effective. If you are taking your writing course on campus, your instructor might ask you to present your poster to your class or to display it in the classroom. For an online course, you may upload a photo of the poster, perhaps accompanied with an audio clip, for your instructor and classmates to see.
- **Artwork (Fine or Other):** You may want to include original or professional artwork, such as a drawing, painting, or clip art, to add context and visual appeal to your multimodal composition. Choose works that match your intended purpose and help create meaning for your audience. For example, you might include a sketch of a pyramid if you are writing about Egyptian history.
- **Graphic Organizers:** Using graphic organizers can help you to arrange your ideas during the writing process. They also provide your readers with a focused representation of your ideas. For example, if you were writing a paper about ideas that influence a person's health, your graphic organizer might look like the one in Figure 15.5. Graphic organizers typically feature boxes or circles and lines or arrows to show how ideas are related to one another.
- **Infographics:** The word *infographics* is a combination of the words *information* and *graphics.* Infographics can be a great way to provide your readers with a quick and easy way to understand the message you are communicating by combining statistics, written text, and visual components, such as clip art, charts, tables, graphs, and other visual material, as shown in Figure 15.6.

FIGURE 15.5 Graphic Organizer

Source: Smartdraw.com

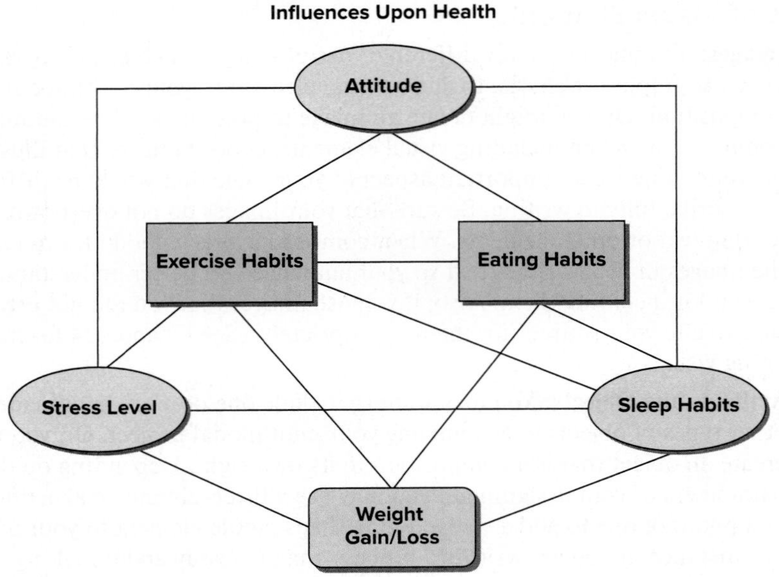

FIGURE 15.6 Infographic

Source: usaid.gov

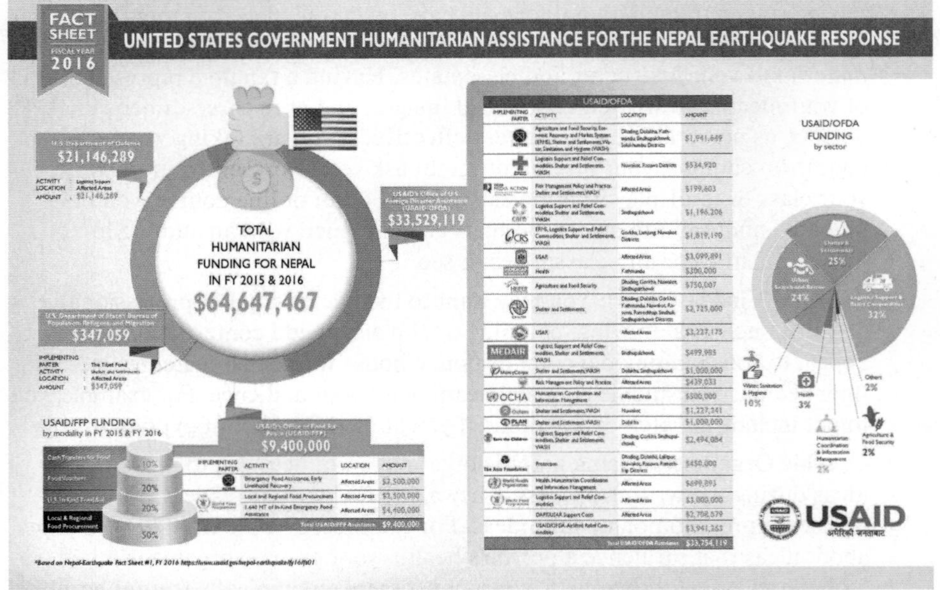

- **Videos:** You may choose to accompany your written composition with a video. Or depending on your assignment you might present a video that you've created as a freestanding composition. Using your computer, tablet, or cell phone, you can create a video of yourself, or you can make a video of something related to your topic (with or without your voiceover). If you are speaking, be sure to enunciate your words carefully and use a pleasant tone of voice. If you are filming yourself, be sure your clothing, posture, gestures, facial expressions, and tone of voice are appropriate for your subject. Depending on your project, it may be appropriate to supplement your writing with a YouTube video. Regardless of what type of video you use, make sure its length fits the occasion. A video that lasts from 30 seconds to a few minutes will often be enough to sufficiently convey your ideas.

Basic Digital Elements

- **Blogs:** You may choose to present your multimodal project as a weblog (blog). Typically, a blogger writes and posts regular updates about a particular hobby, career, or other subject. For example, you might create a blog related to your intern or extern experience, where you explain various aspects of the knowledge and skills you are learning. Blogs provide a great forum for including audio or video clips, images, and other media in addition to writing.
- **Digital Portfolios:** A digital portfolio is a computer-based collection of your material as you have developed it over time. Your instructor may require a digital portfolio, or you may choose to create one for a course or for employment purposes. You might choose to use one of the following free programs for your digital portfolio: Adobe Portfolio, Behance, Carbonmade, Cargo, Coroflot, Crevado, Dribble, Jobrary, PortfolioBox, or Portfoliopen. For example, you might create a digital portfolio when you are ready to search for a job. You can display your résumé, achievements, photographs, and other information pertinent to your specific career field.
- **Montages:** As part of a multimodal project, you may want to include a *montage,* which is a collection of digital photographs or video clips that are edited and pieced together. The skills needed for editing photos and videos are similar to the techniques used for editing a written composition. A montage can take on many forms. You might take a series of three or four still shots or video clips and arrange them to convey a message to your audience. Try different arrangements to see what works best. Free online applications such as Avidemux, Blender, DaVinci Resolve, Fotor, iMovie (for Mac), Lightworks, Montage Lite, Quick, Shotcut, and Splice can be helpful in developing your montage.
- **PowerPoints:** Microsoft PowerPoints can be a very effective way to help you get your message across to an audience during an oral presentation (see pp. 426–427); they can also stand alone as documents that you can share. Choose a pleasing template and a catchy title to display on the first slide of the presentation, along with your name, an image, and other relevant information. For the body of the presentation, include a variety of words, images, audio and/or video clips, and any other features that will enhance your presentation. Use short bulleted points rather than long explanations to highlight key concepts. Choose colors and fonts that are appealing without being overwhelming. Also, choose transitions between

slides that are smooth but not overdone. A PowerPoint presentation can also accompany a written composition depending on the assignment.

- **Prezis:** Like a PowerPoint presentation, a Prezi (or Prezi Next) presentation provides you with a method of sharing your words and images with your audience. While a PowerPoint presentation tends to be linear, progressing from the first slide in a set sequence until the last slide, a Prezi presentation typically begins with a visual representation of the entire project and then zooms in on key concepts before displaying the big picture again at the end. Go to **Prezi.com** to develop a presentation using a free educational account. Choose a template that fits your purpose and subject matter. Write key concepts and include images and charts or graphs where appropriate. As with a PowerPoint presentation, be sure to use only a few words per slide. See Figure 15.7 for an example of a Prezi slide.
- **Websites:** You will very likely be assigned to build or contribute to a website in school as well as in the workplace, so it's a good idea to get some practice in this skill. You will want to choose a layout that fits with your subject and is appealing for your audience. Choose the tools and functions that work best for you. For example, you might have an introductory home page, a place for an interactive discussion or blog, informative or instructional content, images, audio clips, videos, and links to other resources. If you use an image, an audio clip, or a video from a source, make sure you have the appropriate permission to include the material on your site. The following are free website builders that can be useful for your multimodal project: Doodlekit, emyspot, IM Creator, Jimdo, Moonfruit, GoDaddy, Mozello, SiteBuilder, Squarespace, Weebly, WordPress, and Zoho Sites.

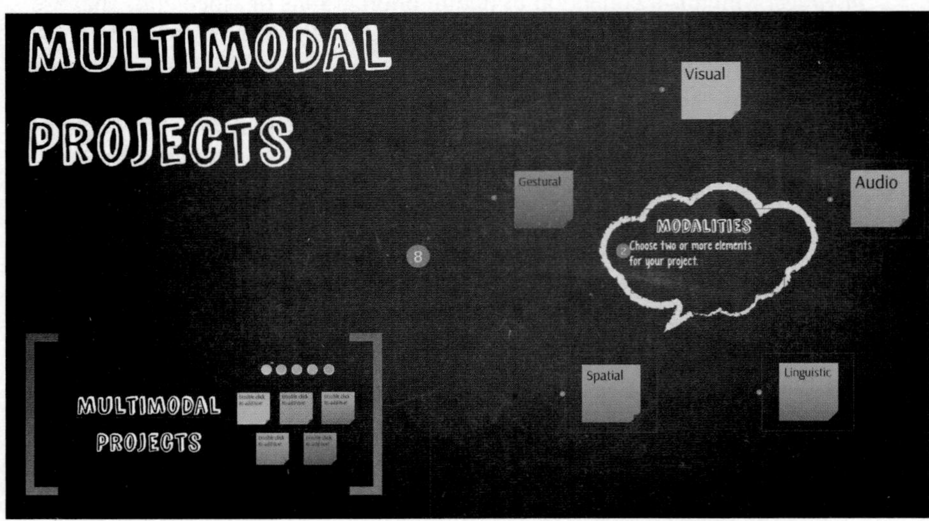

FIGURE 15.7
Prezi Slide

- **Wikis:** A wiki is an online system that enables multiple participants to add, structure, and edit content. The word *wiki* means *quick* in the Hawaiian language. Wikis can be a fast way to generate and access materials related to a specific subject. If your multimodal project needs to be interactive, developing a wiki can be very useful for constructing knowledge, sharing ideas and sources, and engaging with the material and your classmates. Some free wiki builders you may want to try are Google Docs, PBworks, Wikidot, and Wikispaces. You are probably already familiar with Wikipedia, the most well-known wiki. As a reminder, reading a wiki is a great way to get a quick answer to a question, but avoid using a wiki as a source for a research paper. You may, however, consult a wiki to find useful sources on a specific subject.

4. Audio Elements

Adding an audio component to your multimodal composition can enrich your audience's experience. You can use your tone of voice (*intonation*) to communicate another layer of your message. For example, if you are presenting an argument, your vocal intonation might be a bit urgent. If you are speaking about yoga or Zen practices, you might try a more soothing tone of voice. Additionally, you may want to play a music clip or sound effects or have ambient noise in the background during your presentation. If you are developing a PowerPoint or Prezi presentation, you might record your voice, an interview, or other sound bites to accompany your slides. You can edit your recordings using free, open-source audio editing software, such as Audacity (**Audacityteam.com**).

- **Audio Clips:** Including an audio clip can enhance your multimodal composition. You might include your own voice, a narrator's voice, music, sound effects, or other relevant sounds. Use sounds or voices that relate to your subject and help to set the tone of your project. For instance, if you are writing about a topic that takes place in another era or country, you might play music or a radio broadcast that reflects that time period or place. When recording your voice, be sure to speak clearly and at a moderate pace.
- **Podcasts:** A podcast is a digital audio file that can be shared and downloaded via computer or mobile device. The word *podcast* stems from a combination of the words *iPod* and *broadcast.* You can plan and record series of podcast episodes about a specific subject or research paper topic and upload them to a learning management system (class platform) or another website. Your instructor and classmates can download and listen to your podcasts at their convenience. Depending on where you post your podcasts, your listeners may be able to write comments to you regarding the content you have shared.

5. Spatial Elements

When considering the spatial components of your composition, look at the size of the paper you are using, the size and location of any photos or graphs you're including, the line spacing (single or double are most popular), the use of white space, the alignment of texts and visuals, and the overall visual organization. Images that are too large may be overwhelming, and images that are too small may be difficult to see. Having enough white space on the page can help your document to look less busy. Be sure to check that you don't have odd shifts in alignment of your written text or images. Try moving the text and visuals around to see what will be most visually appealing to your audience.

Multimodal Options		
Artifact or Object, p. 437	Images, p. 437	PowerPoint, p. 439
Artwork, p. 437	Infographics, p. 437	Prezi, p. 440
Audio clip, p. 441	Journal, p. 434	Video, p. 438
Blog, p. 439	Montage, p. 439	Website, p. 440
Digital portfolio, p. 439	Podcast, p. 441	Wiki, p. 441
Graphic organizer, p. 437	Poster, p. 437	Writing, p. 434

CHAPTER SUMMARY

1. If you plan carefully, you can become more confident and effective at giving oral presentations.
2. Organize your presentation with a clear introduction, body, and conclusion.
3. Carefully design your visuals, such as objects, models, posters, flip charts, whiteboards, media presentations, video clips, and handouts, to enhance your presentation.
4. When you deliver an oral presentation, think positive thoughts, use an outline or notes, speak clearly and enthusiastically, communicate nonverbally, and incorporate visual aids smoothly.
5. Always have a backup plan in case your equipment fails during your presentation.
6. Practice, practice, practice your presentation before delivering it.
7. When planning to deliver a group presentation, establish goals, assign roles, work cooperatively, and organize the presentation effectively.
8. Multimodal compositions include two or more of the following modalities: written/linguistic; nonverbal; visual/digital; audio; and spatial.

WHAT I KNOW NOW

Use this checklist to determine what you need to work on to feel comfortable with your understanding of the material in this chapter. Check off each item as you master it. Review the material for any unchecked items.

- ☐ 1. I know how to plan and develop the **introduction, body, and conclusion** of an oral presentation.
- ☐ 2. I can choose and **prepare visuals** for an oral presentation.
- ☐ 3. I understand how to deliver an oral presentation using an **outline or note cards.**
- ☐ 4. I can plan and deliver an effective **group presentation.**
- ☐ 5. I can develop an effective **multimodal composition** using two or more of the following modalities: written/linguistic; nonverbal; visual/digital; audio; and spatial.

Design elements: *Graduate Spotlight:* Ingram Publishing/AGE Fotostock

PART 4

Editing Guide

While you may not need to worry about style, grammar, punctuation, and mechanics when you send a text message to a friend or write a note to yourself or a loved one, most academic and career-related writing occasions require that you follow the conventions of standard American English. When you write a report for your instructor or boss, a letter to a client or patient, or an e-mail to a co-worker, you need to take a few minutes to edit it carefully before you submit or send it.

Others will judge you on how well you write. If your document is filled with errors, the recipients will question your credibility and the content of your message.

As you edit your documents, pay particular attention to your sentence structure, word choice, grammar, punctuation, mechanics, and spelling. Being adept at following the conventions of the English language will help you to communicate your message clearly to your audience and achieve success in your personal, academic, and professional life.

This guide is designed to make it easy for you to find answers to questions you may have about proper sentence structure and diction. It will help you edit your writings for grammar, punctuation, mechanics, and spelling. Activities are included throughout to help with comprehension.

OVERVIEW of Part 4

A. Editing Sentences

Fragments

Sentence fragment A group of words that cannot stand on its own because it lacks one or more elements of a complete sentence.

Most academic and professional writing situations require that you write in complete sentences. A complete sentence must contain a subject and a verb and express a complete thought. A **sentence fragment** is a group of words that cannot stand on its own because it is lacking one or more of the elements of a complete sentence. Often you can correct a sentence fragment by adding a subject or verb or by connecting it to another sentence.

FRAGMENT: Is fun and relaxing.
REVISED: Camping is fun and relaxing.
DISCUSSION: The fragment lacks a subject.

FRAGMENT: Especially on a hot day.
REVISED: Going to a lake is refreshing, especially on a hot day.
DISCUSSION: The fragment lacks a subject and a verb.

FRAGMENT: While I was driving to school today.
REVISED: While I was driving to school today, I saw a red car with yellow flames painted on it.
DISCUSSION: The fragment has a subject and verb, but it does not express a complete thought.

Activity Editing for Sentence Fragments

Revise the following sentences to eliminate sentence fragments.

EXAMPLE

Fragment: Many students have strengths and weaknesses in different areas. Especially in subjects such as math and English.

Revised: Many students have strengths and weaknesses in different areas, especially in subjects such as math and English.

1. Many colleges offer tutoring services. For students who need to strengthen their skills in math or English.
2. Because he has good math skills. Hector tutors other college students.
3. He enjoys helping others. And feels good about himself after each tutoring session.
4. Even though Hector is very strong in math. He sometimes needs help with his writing.
5. Hector is grateful that he benefits from the tutoring services. Offered at his college.

Run-Ons and Comma Splices

A **run-on sentence,** also known as a *fused* sentence, occurs when two complete sentences (*independent clauses*) run together without a proper punctuation mark or a comma and coordinating conjunction. A **comma-spliced sentence** occurs when two complete sentences are joined improperly with just a comma.

Run-on sentence Two independent clauses that run together without a proper punctuation mark or a comma and a coordinating conjunction.

Comma-spliced sentence Two independent clauses that are joined improperly with just a comma.

RUN-ON SENTENCE: Sara likes to exercise before going to work Enrique prefers to exercise after work.

COMMA-SPLICED SENTENCE: Sara likes to exercise before going to work, Enrique prefers to exercise after work.

To revise a run-on or comma-spliced sentence, try one of these five methods:

1. Separate the sentences.

   REVISED: Sara likes to exercise before going to work. Enrique prefers to exercise after work.

2. Combine the sentences using a comma and a coordinating conjunction. A **coordinating conjunction** is a word that joins words or independent clauses that are equal and shows how they are related. Figure 1 provides the seven coordinating conjunctions and an easy way to remember them.

   REVISED: Sara likes to exercise before going to work, but Enrique prefers to exercise after work.

Coordinating conjunction A word that joins words or independent clauses that are equal and shows how they are related.

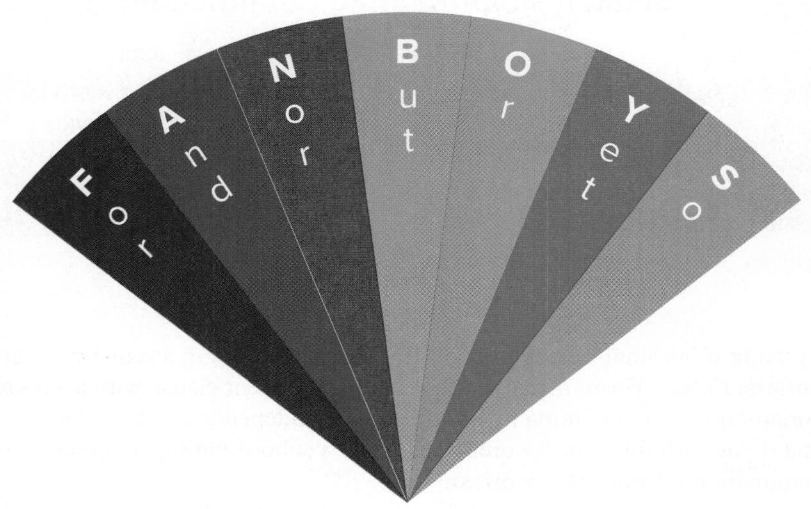

FIGURE 1 The Seven Coordinating Conjunctions (FANBOYS)

3. Combine the sentences using a semicolon. Use this method only if the sentences are fairly short and are similar in content and structure.

   REVISED: Sara likes to exercise before going to work; Enrique prefers to exercise after work.

Conjunctive adverb An adverb that serves as a transition between two independent clauses.

4. Combine the sentences using a semicolon and a conjunctive adverb. A **conjunctive adverb** is an adverb that serves as a transition between two independent clauses.

Common Conjunctive Adverbs			
accordingly	furthermore	meanwhile	similarly
also	hence	moreover	still
anyway	however	namely	then
besides	incidentally	nevertheless	thereafter
certainly	indeed	next	therefore
consequently	instead	nonetheless	thus
finally	likewise	otherwise	undoubtedly

Subordinating conjunction A dependent word that helps to show the relationship between the ideas in two independent clauses.

REVISED: Sara likes to exercise before going to work; however, Enrique prefers to exercise after work.

5. Combine the sentences by using a subordinating conjunction. A **subordinating conjunction** is a dependent word that helps to show the relationship between the ideas in two independent clauses.

Common Subordinating Conjunctions			
after	as though	if only	until
although	because	now that	what(ever)
as	before	provided (that)	when(ever)
as if	even if	since	where(ever)
as long as	even though	so that	whether
as much as	how	though	which(ever)
as soon as	if	unless	while

Try using subordinating conjunctions in different places in a sentence to emphasize different ideas. If you introduce the first independent clause with a subordinating conjunction, add a comma before the second independent clause. Do not use a comma if you introduce the second clause with a subordinating conjunction unless the conjunction introduces a contrast.

REVISED: *Although* Sara likes to exercise before going to work, Enrique prefers to exercise after work.

REVISED: Sara likes to exercise before going to work, *even though* Enrique prefers to exercise after work.

Activity Editing for Run-On and Comma-Spliced Sentences

Revise the following sentences to eliminate run-ons and comma splices. Try different methods to see which one works the best to correct each run-on or comma splice.

1. Watching movies is a popular way for people to unwind movies provide an escape from reality.
2. Some people prefer action adventure movies, others prefer comedies.
3. Action adventure movies are exciting they keep the audience riveted to their seats.
4. Good comedies are hilarious, they can keep the audience laughing from start to finish.
5. It's fun to watch movies in the theater watching them at home can be entertaining too.

Mixed Constructions

If the first part (subject) of a sentence doesn't fit logically with the second part (predicate), the sentence has a **mixed construction.** Using mixed constructions can confuse readers.

Mixed construction Occurs when the subject of a sentence does not fit logically with the predicate of the sentence.

MIXED:	The best career field for me is becoming a nurse.
REVISED:	Nursing is the best career field for me.
DISCUSSION:	A nurse isn't a career field, but nursing is.
MIXED:	The reason I want to be a Web designer is because I am good with computers.
REVISED:	I want to become a Web designer because I am good with computers.
DISCUSSION:	Avoid using the construction *the reason . . . is because.*
MIXED:	The fact that I got a new computer is why I'm so excited.
REVISED:	I'm so excited because I got a new computer.
DISCUSSION:	Avoid using the construction *the fact . . . is why.*
MIXED:	The chefs, although they created delicious dishes, but were not awarded a prize by the committee.
REVISED:	Although the chefs created delicious dishes, the committee did not award them a prize.
DISCUSSION:	Avoid using the construction *although . . . but.*

Activity Editing for Mixed Constructions

Revise the following sentences to eliminate mixed constructions.

1. The best car I could ever hope for is driving a BMW.
2. The reason I like BMWs is because they are luxurious cars.
3. The fact that my friend Kenny loves his BMW is why I am so interested in getting one.
4. Because BMWs are fast is what makes them fun to drive.
5. The reason I want to get a used BMW is because new ones are too expensive.

Faulty Parallelism

Parallelism Occurs when similar ideas in a sentence are expressed in a similar grammatical manner.

Parallelism occurs when similar ideas in a sentence are expressed in a similar grammatical manner.

Ideas in a sentence that have the same level of importance are parallel and, therefore, should be expressed in parallel grammatical constructions. When sentence elements such as nouns, verbs, and phrases are parallel, sentences flow more smoothly.

PARALLEL NOUNS:	Laura bought a hotdog, a pretzel, and a soft drink at the concession stand.
PARALLEL VERBS:	On the weekends I enjoy bicycling, hiking, and fishing.
PARALLEL PHRASES:	He drove the car around the tree, across the sidewalk, and into the lake.
NOT PARALLEL:	Whether she is with a patient, drawing blood, or administering a shot, Kathie is always a professional.
REVISED:	Whether she is helping a patient, drawing blood, or administering a shot, Kathie is always a professional.
NOT PARALLEL:	Marcello needs to write his résumé, fill out an application, and he should apply for a job.
REVISED:	Marcello needs to write his résumé, fill out an application, and apply for a job.

Activity Editing for Faulty Parallelism

Revise the following sentences to give them parallel structure.

1. The local hospital offers employees good salaries, flexible hours, and it offers meals that are inexpensive.
2. Employees who work on the top floor go down a hallway, through a lobby, and then they ride an elevator up to get to their station.

3. Employees spend much of their time helping patients, writing charts, and they also develop procedures.
4. Patients are very satisfied with the personnel, treatment, and they are also pleased with the facilities at the hospital.
5. The hospital is raising funds to update the cardiac and pediatric facilities, and it is also raising funds for updating the oncology facilities.

Active and Passive Voice

Many instructors prefer that you use the active voice when writing essays. When you write in the **active voice,** the subject performs the action in the sentence. When you write in the **passive voice,** the subject receives the action in the sentence.

Active voice Occurs when the subject performs the action in the sentence.

Passive voice Occurs when the subject receives the action in the sentence.

PASSIVE VOICE: The award was won by the best writer in the class.

ACTIVE VOICE: The best writer in the class won the award.

DISCUSSION: Placing the subject up front emphasizes the subject of the sentence.

Writing in the active voice is more direct and less wordy. However, occasionally you may want to use the passive voice, especially if you need to emphasize the recipient of the action, don't know who performed the action, or prefer not to say who performed the action.

ACTIVE VOICE: James broke the copy machine.

PASSIVE VOICE: The copy machine is broken.

DISCUSSION: Is it necessary for everyone to know who broke the machine? If not, the passive voice has a friendlier tone and is more tactful.

ACTIVE VOICE: Someone hired Veronda immediately after her interview.

PASSIVE VOICE: Veronda was hired immediately after her interview.

DISCUSSION: If you do not know who hired Veronda, then using the passive voice is appropriate.

Activity Revising for Active or Passive Voice

Revise the following sentences by changing the passive sentences to the active voice and the active sentence to the passive voice.

1. The job fair was hosted by Star University.
2. The graduates were invited to attend the job fair by the career placement director.

—continued

Activity Revising for Active or Passive Voice (*cont.*)

3. Most of the graduates were recruited by well-known employers in the area.
4. Some of the recruits were given signing bonuses by their new employers.
5. Unfortunately, Susan lost some of the completed job applications.

B. Editing Words (Diction)

Diction A writer's or speaker's choice of words.

As you edit your documents, pay attention to your choice of words, also known as **diction.** You want to select words that create the most precise and accurate image in the minds of your readers. You also want to choose words that will not offend your readers. Using good diction will help you to communicate your message more clearly to your audience.

Denotation and Connotation

Denotation The dictionary definition of a word.

Connotation The meaning of a word, including the attitudes and feelings people associate with the word.

Denotation refers to the dictionary definition of a word; **connotation** refers to all of the meanings of a word, including the attitudes and feelings people associate with it. For example, a surgery and a procedure have similar denotative meanings; however, the term *surgery* has more negative connotations than the term *procedure.* Similarly, while *residence* and *home* have similar definitions, *home* has warmer connotative feelings. Keep in mind that not all readers will have the same connotative meanings for words.

As a writer, you want to be sure to choose words that will suggest the right connotative meaning to your readers. This doesn't mean that emotionally charged words are inappropriate or ineffective. You just want to be sure that you evoke the desired emotions from your readers. For instance, the terms *childish* and *childlike* have similar denotations. However, saying someone is *childish* has more negative connotations than saying someone is *childlike.* If your goal is to illustrate how immature a particular adult is, then *childish* might be the correct term to use.

Activity Interpreting Connotations

Explain the connotative differences for each set of words.

1. worker, grunt, employee
2. smart, brainy, intelligent
3. artificial, fake, counterfeit
4. educate, train, drill
5. sip, guzzle, slurp

Jargon and Slang

Jargon is the specialized vocabulary that people connected to a particular career field, group, or interest use. **Slang** is similar to jargon, except that jargon tends to be formal, and slang tends to be informal and nonstandard. Professionals in the legal, medical, computer, education, and business fields use vocabulary that is specific to those areas. Likewise, athletes, musicians, surfers, and video gamers use terms that are specific to their interests.

Jargon Specialized vocabulary that people connected to a particular career field, group, or interest use.

Slang Informal, nonstandard vocabulary that people connected to a particular career field, group, or interest use.

Jargon and slang can be acceptable when writing for an audience whose members share the vocabulary of the field. For example, a professional in the health care field may use medical jargon in an e-mail to a co-worker. As long as the writer and recipient of the message understand the terminology, effective communication can take place.

However, if your audience might not understand the vocabulary of a particular field, then you are better off using terms that are more generic or standard. For instance, if you write a flyer for patients with instructions for practicing a stretching technique at home, then you will need to explain the key terms or replace the jargon with more common terms.

JARGON: When Deveney bought a new PC, she nuked her old one.

REVISED: When Deveney bought a new personal computer, she deleted her directories without saving her individual files.

SLANG: The dude was totally barnwalling on the gnarly wave.

REVISED: The surfer was exhibiting poor technique on the treacherous wave.

Activity Revising to Avoid Jargon and Slang

Replace the italicized words with standard terminology.

1. I *totally blew off my* history assignment.
2. Adam *Christmas treed* his psychology test because he didn't bother to study.
3. The new math instructor is a *nut case.*
4. I need to *catch some Z's* before the *monster* test tomorrow.
5. The student who sits next to me in biology class is *da bomb.*

Clichés

A **cliché** is a worn-out expression. While it may have once been original and fresh, by now it has been used so many times that it has lost its impact. Avoid using clichés because they make your writing sound dull and uninspired. Instead, take the time to find a more interesting way to express your ideas.

Cliché A worn-out expression.

CLICHÉD: Employees who *stab their co-workers in the back* rarely find success on the job.

REVISED: Employees who *betray their co-workers* rarely find success on the job.

Clichés to Avoid	
above and beyond the call of duty	green with envy
add insult to injury	hard as nails (or as a rock)
back stabber	in my wildest dreams
black as night	last but not least
bright-eyed and bushy-tailed	last straw
busy as a bee (or a beaver)	Life is like a box of chocolates.
cold as ice	like taking candy from a baby
come hell or high water	not the sharpest tool in the shed
cool as a cucumber	older than dirt (or the hills)
cream of the crop	on top of the world
cried like a baby	over the hill
crystal clear	skating on thin ice
Don't burn your bridges.	skeleton in the closet
dry as a bone	slower than molasses
dumber than a box of rocks	stick out like a sore thumb
easy as cake (or pie)	sweet as syrup (or honey)
few and far between	That's the way the cookie crumbles.
first and foremost	too little too late
free as a bird	tried and true

Activity Editing to Avoid Clichés

Write five complete sentences, each including a different cliché. Revise each sentence by replacing the cliché with fresh, original language. Keep the intended meaning of the cliché as you revise.

EXAMPLE

Clichéd: The executive was as *cool as a cucumber* when she delivered her presentation.

Revised: The executive was *calm and poised* when she delivered her presentation.

Note: Pairs or small groups of students may trade sentences to revise.

Biased Language

As you revise your writing, look for biased language that you may have inadvertently used. **Biased language** reflects an unfair assumption or prejudice about someone. Be sensitive to gender, culture, and age as you choose your words. You don't want to stereotype people or be condescending toward them.

Biased language Reflects an unfair assumption or prejudice without cause.

Gender Bias

One way to eliminate bias in your writing is to avoid words that unnecessarily refer to gender, also known as **sexist language.** Sometimes you can avoid or correct sexist language by making the subject of the sentence plural.

Sexist language Words that unnecessarily refer to gender.

SEXIST: A nurse should treat *her* patients with kindness and respect.

REVISED: Nurses should treat their patients with kindness and respect.

DISCUSSION: Men and women can be nurses. Unless you are referring to a particular nurse, leave the sentence gender neutral.

Sexist Language	Gender Neutral Language
chairman	chair/chairperson
chicks/girls	women
male nurse	nurse
fireman	firefighter
mankind	humankind/people
mailman	mail carrier
policeman/lady cop	police officer
stewardess/steward	flight attendant
waitress/waiter	server

For people who do not identify as male or female—and who do not want to be described as *she, he, her,* or *him*—one option is to reword your sentence to avoid using any pronoun at all.

GENDERED: *She* is a fan of arachnids, of tarantulas in particular.

REVISED: *Jordan* is a fan of arachnids, of tarantulas in particular.

DISCUSSION: In this case, Jordan, a nonbinary, gender-fluid person, does not wish to be described as a *he* or a *she.* One way to avoid the gendered pronouns *he* or *she* is to reword the sentence by including the person's name, as shown above.

Another way to avoid using gendered pronouns when referring to nonbinary, gender-fluid individuals is to use the singular *they.* The use of *they* as singular pronoun has come into practice recently and is recognized by such style guides as *The Chicago Manual of Style* and the *Publication Manual of the*

American Psychological Association, and by dictionaries including America's oldest, *Merriam-Webster.*

GENDERED:	Kit, a gender-fluid megastar, surprised *his* audience by announcing the end of *his* tour. *He* had finally cut ties with *his* record label.
REVISED:	Kit, a gender-fluid megastar, surprised *their* audience by announcing the end of *their* tour. *They* had finally cut ties with *their* record label.
DISCUSSION:	In this case, Kit a nonbinary, gender-fluid person does not wish to be described by a gendered pronoun. To avoid this, writers can replace *him* with the singular *they,* and *his* with the singular *their,* as shown above.

Cultural Bias

Culturally biased language stereotypes people positively or negatively. Assuming someone has a particular attribute because of his or her culture is unfair and can be offensive. Consequently, you'll want to avoid using culturally stereotypical language in your writing.

STEREOTYPICAL:	Natsumi is very hardworking because she is Japanese.
REVISED:	Natsumi is very hardworking.

Age Bias

Identifying someone's relative age can be useful, but you should do it in a dignified way. Avoid using language that is insulting or condescending toward people.

INSULTING:	The old geezer who lives next door invited me to watch the big game with him.
REVISED:	The retired firefighter who lives next door invited me to watch the big game with him.

Activity Revising to Avoid Biased Language

Identify and revise the biased language in the following sentences.

1. A member of the armed forces should be commended for serving his country.
2. The chick who was hired to replace my boss is intelligent.
3. Because she is Italian, Nancy is a great cook.
4. Like most black people, Rick is a terrific basketball player.
5. The punk who lives across the street won an award for his science project.
6. The old hag would like a refund for the defective merchandise.

Wordiness

Including unnecessary words is tiresome for the reader and can make a text hard to understand. Often you can tighten a wordy passage by substituting a single word for a long phrase or by taking out words that are repetitive or don't add meaning to a sentence. You want to be as clear and concise as possible.

WORDY: It seems to be true that much of humankind enjoys having pets, such as felines or canines, around to help alleviate feelings of emptiness or loneliness.

CONCISE: Many people enjoy having cats and dogs around to keep them company.

Wordy	Concise
arrive at a conclusion	conclude
at a later point in time	later
at this point in time	now
bear a resemblance to	resemble
due to the fact that	because
in many cases	often
in the near future	soon
in this day and age	now
on a weekly basis	weekly
persons of the male gender	men
provide aid for	help
purple in color	purple
small in size	small
without a doubt	certainly

Activity Revising to Avoid Wordiness

Revise the following paragraph to make it clearer and more concise. You may eliminate words and phrases and combine sentences as you revise.

There is little doubt that technology has changed the way that people can communicate with other people who are male or female, young or old. Because computers used to be so large in size that they took up an entire room, very few people had access to computers. Additionally, computers used to be extremely expensive; therefore, very few people could afford to own them. Due to the fact that computers have become smaller in size and less expensive, computers are readily available to a wide range of people. Desktop computers and laptop computers are quite common these days. People use them to make phone calls, send text messages, and e-mail other people

—*continued*

Activity Revising to Avoid Wordiness (*cont.*)

with whom they want to communicate. Also, in today's day and age, many adults, teenagers, and children have smartphones that they carry around with them in their pockets, purses, backpacks, or briefcases. They can use these phones to call, text message, and e-mail their friends, family members, and co-workers. One can only imagine how computers will continue to affect communication in the near or distant future.

C. Editing Grammar

Pronouns

Pronoun-Antecedent Agreement

Pronouns Words that replace nouns.

Antecedents Nouns that pronouns refer to.

Pronouns (words that replace nouns) need to agree with their **antecedents** (the nouns they refer to) in number and gender.

Use singular pronouns to refer to singular nouns; use plural pronouns to refer to plural nouns.

SINGULAR: The stethoscope was on the floor because *it* fell off the table.

SINGULAR: Each of the patients received *his or her* lunch at noon.

SINGULAR: Everybody in the lobby was waiting to see *his or her* loved one.

PLURAL: The hazardous materials containers were removed because *they* were full.

Note: Some indefinite pronouns, such as *everybody, anybody, each,* and *everyone,* seem plural, but they are really singular. Therefore, you will need to use a singular pronoun to refer back to those words.

Nouns and pronouns can be feminine, masculine, or neutral.

FEMININE: Carmen was thrilled because *she* got an extra shift at the hospital.

MASCULINE: John was happy because *he* passed the RN exam.

NEUTRAL: That building is older than *its* neighbors.

Collective nouns can be singular or plural, depending on how you use them. Therefore, you may use a singular or plural pronoun with a collective noun. (See pp. 462–463 for more on collective nouns.)

SINGULAR: The band received an award for *its* performance.

DISCUSSION: The band is used singularly as one unit that won one award.

PLURAL: The band are tuning *their* instruments.

DISCUSSION: The band members are acting individually rather than as one unit.

Note: You can say *band members* to clarify that you are using the collective noun in a plural manner.

Pronoun Reference

A pronoun needs to clearly refer back to a noun (*an antecedent*). Typically, a pronoun will refer back to a preceding noun that matches it in number and gender, if applicable. Sentences need to clearly identify who is doing what to whom.

UNCLEAR: The patient received a call from his brother, but he wasn't happy about it.

REVISED: The patient wasn't happy about the call he received from his brother.

DISCUSSION: The first sentence does not clarify who is not happy. Is it the patient or the brother?

UNCLEAR: Lucinda had facial plastic surgery six weeks ago, and it already looks better.

REVISED: Lucinda had facial plastic surgery six weeks ago, and her face already looks better.

DISCUSSION: The first sentence implies that Lucinda's face looks better, but the pronoun actually refers back to the facial surgery. Saying that the facial plastic surgery looks better does not make sense.

UNCLEAR: It is a nice facility.

REVISED: The facility is nice.

DISCUSSION: The word *it* does not refer to anything. Sometimes a sentence can start with the pronoun *it* if the word *it* refers to a noun in a previous sentence.

EXAMPLE: The new outpatient clinic opened yesterday. It is a nice facility.

Pronoun Case

Pronouns can be subjects, objects, or possessives.

Pronoun Types

	Subjective	Objective	Possessive
First person singular	I	me	my, mine
First person plural	we	us	our, ours
Second person singular	you	you	your, yours
Second person plural	you	you	your, yours
Third person singular	he, she, it, who	him, her, it, whom	his, her, hers, its, whose
Third person plural	they, who	them, whom	their, theirs, whose
Nongendered, nonbinary first person singular or plural	I	me	my, mine
Nongendered, nonbinary second person singular or plural	you	you	yours
Nongendered, nonbinary third person singular or plural	they	who	their, theirs, whose

Subjective pronouns perform the action in a sentence.

SUBJECTIVE PRONOUN:	*She* is going to see a nutritionist.

Objective pronouns receive the action in the sentence or are part of a prepositional phrase.

OBJECTIVE PRONOUN:	The nutritionist gave *her* a diet plan.
OBJECTIVE PRONOUN:	Between you and *me,* I am having trouble with my diet.

Possessive pronouns show ownership.

POSSESSIVE PRONOUN:	The diet plan from the nutritionist is *hers.*

Using the correct type can be tricky at times, especially when a sentence has a compound subject or object, makes a comparison, includes an appositive, or uses *who* or *whom.*

Compound Subjects and Objects When the subject is compound, eliminate the double subject to figure out which pronoun to use.

SINGLE SUBJECT:	*I* donated blood.
COMPOUND SUBJECT:	My mother and *I* donated blood.
SINGLE OBJECT:	Dr. D'Alessandro gave a list of exercises to *me.*
COMPOUND OBJECT:	Dr. D'Alessandro gave a list of exercises to Todd and *me.*

Comparisons Using the correct pronoun when making a comparison is essential to getting the correct message across to your audience. Choosing the correct type can be difficult because sometimes words are implied rather than stated. To find the correct pronoun, mentally add the missing words.

COMPARISON:	Kristin likes Denny more than *I* [like Denny].
DISCUSSION:	The sentence means that Kristin likes Denny more than I like Denny.
COMPARISON:	Kristin likes Denny more than [she likes] *me.*
DISCUSSION:	The sentence means that Kristin likes Denny more than she likes me.

Appositive A word or phrase that renames a noun or pronoun.

Appositives An **appositive** is a word or phrase that renames a noun or pronoun. Eliminate the appositive to determine which pronoun to use.

APPOSITIVE:	We *Floridians* like not having to wear a coat in the winter.
DISCUSSION:	*Floridians* renames *we. We* like not having to wear a coat in winter.

Who and Whom Use *who* as the subject of a sentence. Use *whom* as the object of a sentence.

SUBJECTIVE PRONOUN:	Dennis wants to know *who* is going to the party.
OBJECTIVE PRONOUN:	For *whom* did Michelle buy that gift?
TIP:	The word *whom* often appears in a prepositional phrase: to whom, for whom, with whom.

Activity Choosing Correct Pronouns

Choose the correct pronouns for the following sentences.

1. Each of the participants received (his or her/their) certificate.
2. Patti and (I/me) will ride together to the show.
3. Melissa gave the box of chocolates to Liza and (I/me).
4. (Us/We) college students need to stick together.
5. (Who/Whom) is going to donate money for the charity?

Verbs

Subject-Verb Agreement

Singular and Plural Subjects The subject and verb in a sentence need to match (agree). A singular subject needs to have a singular verb; a plural subject needs to have a plural verb.

SINGULAR SUBJECT AND VERB:	The *guitar player is* amazing.
SINGULAR SUBJECT AND VERB:	The *sound* from the speakers *is shaking* the entire arena.
DISCUSSION:	The subject in the sentence above is *sound,* so the verb is singular. The word *speakers* is in a prepositional phrase, so it does not affect subject-verb agreement.
PLURAL SUBJECT AND VERB:	The *speakers are* shaking the entire arena.
DISCUSSION:	In the sentence above, *speakers* is the plural subject of the sentence, so the verb is plural.

Compound Subjects When two or more subjects are combined, the subject is compound. Compound subjects joined by the word *and* are usually plural, so the verb needs to be plural.

COMPOUND SUBJECT: *Ashley* and *Jenny are* hosting the event.

DISCUSSION: Ashley and Jenny are separate subjects, so the verb is plural.

Sometimes, however, the word *and* appears as part of a singular subject, so the verb needs to be singular.

SINGULAR SUBJECT: *Rock and roll is* one of my favorite types of music.

DISCUSSION: Rock and roll is one subject, so the verb is singular.

Compound subjects joined by *or, nor, either . . . or,* or *neither . . . nor* are singular. Therefore, the verb needs to be singular.

SINGULAR SUBJECT: *Mark* or *Gregg is* going to advance to the next race.

SINGULAR SUBJECT: *Briana is* not going to give up, nor *is Natalie.*

SINGULAR SUBJECT: Either *Ellen* or *Margaret is* going to win the contest.

SINGULAR SUBJECT: Neither *Fred* nor *Jorge* displays bad sportsmanship.

DISCUSSION: The sentences above refer to each person individually, not collectively, so the subjects and verbs are singular.

Collective Nouns Collective nouns have a singular form. However, the verbs that go with them can be singular or plural depending on how writers use them. Below are some examples of collective nouns.

Collective Nouns		
audience	faculty	majority
band	family	pack
choir	group	swarm
class	herd	team
committee	jury	tribe

When you use a collective noun, consistently treat it as singular or plural in a passage. If you are referring to the collective noun as a single unit, use a singular verb.

SINGULAR COLLECTIVE NOUN: The *jury is* undecided.

DISCUSSION: The jury, as a whole, is not ready to make a decision.

If you are referring to the collective noun as a group of individuals, use a plural verb.

PLURAL COLLECTIVE NOUN: The *faculty have* moved into their new offices.

DISCUSSION: Here, the sentence refers to all of the members of the faculty as individuals with separate offices.

Sometimes you are better off clarifying the collective noun to avoid sounding awkward.

AWKWARD:	The committee were excited about completing the proposal.
REVISED:	The committee members were excited about completing the proposal.

Indefinite Pronouns *Indefinite pronouns* refer to an unspecific number of subjects. Indefinite pronouns can be singular, plural, or varied (singular or plural depending on the context). You need to determine whether the indefinite pronoun is singular or plural in a particular sentence to make sure that the verb agrees with the subject.

SINGULAR INDEFINITE PRONOUN:	*Everyone is* thrilled about the new policy.
VARIABLE INDEFINITE PRONOUN (SINGULAR):	*Most* of the lasagna *is* very cheesy.
VARIABLE INDEFINITE PRONOUN (PLURAL):	*Most* of the employees *are* hardworking.
PLURAL INDEFINITE PRONOUN:	*Many* of the cupcakes *have* been eaten.

Indefinite Pronouns

Singular	Variable (Singular or Plural)	Plural
anybody	all	both
anyone	any	few
anything	more	many
each	most	others
either	none	several
everybody	some	
everything		
neither		
nobody		
no one		
nothing		
somebody		
someone		
something		

Inverted Subject and Verb Determining subject-verb agreement can be tricky if the verb is inverted (comes before the subject). Make sure that the verb agrees with the subject of the sentence, rather than another word that is closer to the verb.

INVERTED SUBJECT AND VERB:	Sitting in the courtroom *were two suspects.*
DISCUSSION:	The subject (*two suspects*) is plural, so the verb (*were*) needs to be plural as well.

Separated Subject and Verb Determining subject-verb agreement can be tricky if the verb is separated from the subject.

SEPARATED SUBJECT AND VERB:	The *lawyers,* waiting for the judge to arrive, *are* exhausted from the lengthy trial.
DISCUSSION:	The plural subject (*lawyers*) needs a plural verb (*are*).

Activity Editing for Subject-Verb Agreement

Identify the subject of each sentence. Choose the verb that agrees with the subject.

1. The music coming from the instruments (is/are) melodic.
2. Lori and Megan (was/were) hoping to attend the concert.
3. Frank, who is one of the guitar players, (is/are) the lead singer.
4. Waiting patiently backstage (is/are) Vicki and Jill.
5. Everyone attending the concert tonight (is/are) going to get a free CD.

Regular Verbs

With regular verbs, you can simply add *-d* or *-ed* to the infinitive (base) form of the verb to change the tense. See the examples below.

Regular Verbs

Infinitive	Past Tense	Past Participle
arrive	arrived	arrived
earn	earned	earned
graduate	graduated	graduated
receive	received	received
walk	walked	walked

Irregular Verbs

Many verbs in the English language are irregular. The chart that follows includes some of the most common irregular verbs.

Irregular Verbs		
Infinitive	Past Tense	Past Participle
arise	arose	arisen
be	was, were	been
become	became	become
begin	began	begun
bind	bound	bound
bite	bit	bitten
buy	bought	bought
catch	caught	caught
choose	chose	chosen
come	came	come
dig	dug	dug
drink	drank	drunk
drive	drove	driven
eat	ate	eaten
forbid	forbade	forbidden
freeze	froze	frozen
get	got	gotten
give	gave	given
go	went	gone
grind	ground	ground
grow	grew	grown
have	had	had
hide	hid	hidden
hold	held	held
lay (to put or place)	laid	laid
lay (to recline)	lay	lain
mistake	mistook	mistaken
pay	paid	paid
proofread	proofread	proofread
ride	rode	ridden
ring	rang	rung
rise	rose	risen
see	saw	seen
seek	sought	sought
set	set	set
sing	sang	sung
speak	spoke	spoken
swear	swore	sworn
think	thought	thought
throw	threw	thrown
wring	wrung	wrung
write	wrote	written

Linking Verbs

Linking verbs show existence and explain what something is, was, or will become. Linking verbs connect the subject of a sentence to a *complement* (a word that renames or describes the subject).

LINKING VERB: Laura *is* a media specialist.

LINKING VERB: Ryan *seems* distracted.

Linking Verbs			
Forms of the Verb *Be*		Verbs That Can Function as Linking Verbs	
am	is	appear	remain
are	was	become	seem
being	been	feel	smell
were	be	grow	sound
		look	taste

Adjectives and Adverbs

Adjectives and Adverbs

Adjectives Words that modify nouns or pronouns.

Adjectives and adverbs are modifiers, words that describe or *modify* other words. **Adjectives** are words that modify nouns or pronouns.

ADJECTIVE: Scott is *intelligent.*

DISCUSSION: The adjective *intelligent* modifies the noun *Scott.*

ADJECTIVE: She is *pretty.*

DISCUSSION: The adjective *pretty* modifies the pronoun *she.*

Adverbs Words that modify adjectives, verbs, and other adverbs.

Adverbs are words that modify adjectives, verbs, and other adverbs. Adverbs often end in *-ly* and tell *how.*

ADVERB: The chili is *especially* good tonight.

DISCUSSION: The adverb *especially* modifies the adjective *good.*

ADVERB: The chef worked *diligently* on the new recipe.

DISCUSSION: The adverb *diligently* modifies the verb *worked.*

ADVERB: Julie smiled *very* sweetly.

DISCUSSION: The adverb *very* modifies the adverb *sweetly.*

The following adjectives and adverbs often cause problems for writers: good/well; bad/badly; real/really. Remember, adverbs often tell *how.*

Good and Well

Good and *well* are commonly confused words. *Good* is an adjective (or sometimes a noun) and *well* is an adjective or adverb, depending on the context.

ADJECTIVE:	The sushi is *good.*
ADVERB:	The chef prepared the sushi *well.*
ADJECTIVE:	Gina feels *good* about the exam.
ADVERB:	Gina performed *well* on the exam.
DISCUSSION:	Use *good* when you use a linking verb and *well* when you use an active verb.

Bad and Badly

ADJECTIVE:	The bananas have gone *bad.*
ADVERB:	Marge used the *badly* bruised bananas for banana bread.
ADJECTIVE:	The *bad* dog went to obedience school.
ADVERB:	The dog behaved *badly* in class.

Real and Really

ADJECTIVE:	These pearls are *real.*
ADVERB:	Rhonda worked *really* hard to make the necklace.
ADJECTIVE:	The *real* problem is that we have too many choices.
ADVERB:	We are *really* confused about all of the choices we have.

Note: Real = genuine

Comparatives and Superlatives

Comparatives are adjectives and adverbs that compare two items. *Superlatives* are adjectives and adverbs that compare three or more items. Usually you can make comparative and superlative forms be adding *-er* and *-est, more* and *most,* or *less* and *least.*

BASE ADJECTIVE FORM:	Toby is a *cute* puppy.
COMPARATIVE FORM:	Toby is *cuter* than Roofus.
SUPERLATIVE FORM:	Toby is the *cutest* puppy in the litter.

Avoid doubling comparatives and superlatives.

INCORRECT: Jack is the *most sweetest* boy I know.

REVISED: Jack is the *sweetest* boy I know.

Comparatives and Superlatives

Adjective or Adverb	Comparative Form	Superlative Form
big	bigger	biggest
desirable	less desirable	least desirable
expensive	more expensive	most expensive
fascinating	less fascinating	least fascinating
good	better	best
pretty	prettier	prettiest
rapidly	less rapidly	least rapidly
unusual	more unusual	most unusual
wonderful	more wonderful	most wonderful

Activity Using Adjectives and Adverbs

Choose the correct word or words for each sentence.

1. Tamika works (good/well) with her group mates.
2. Marco wanted to fire the (bad/badly) employee.
3. William tried (real/really) hard to finish the report on time.
4. John is the (more/most) gifted of the two students.
5. Ava is the (better/more better/best/bestest) swimmer on the team.

Dangling and Misplaced Modifiers

Dangling Modifiers

As you write, you need to make sure that your modifiers clearly describe something specific that is stated in the sentence. Otherwise, you might create a *dangling modifier* and confuse your readers.

DANGLING MODIFIER: While driving south on I-95, an iguana ran in front of his car.

QUESTION: Was an iguana really driving the car?

REVISED: While Pat was driving south on I-95, an iguana ran in front of his car.

DISCUSSION:	The revised sentence clearly explains that Pat was driving the car.
DANGLING MODIFIER:	While talking on a cell phone, Pat's car swerved and missed the iguana.
QUESTION:	Was the car talking on the cell phone?
REVISED:	While talking on a cell phone, Pat swerved his car and missed the iguana.
DISCUSSION:	The revised sentence clearly explains that Pat was talking on his cell phone.

Misplaced Modifiers

Misplaced modifiers occur when they appear too far away from the words they describe.

MISPLACED MODIFIER:	The reckless driver almost angered every other driver on the road.
REVISED:	The reckless driver angered almost every other driver on the road.
DISCUSSION:	The first sentence suggests that the driver may not have angered any of the drivers.

MISPLACED MODIFIER:	Tammy threw the Frisbee for the dog still dressed in her nightgown.
REVISED:	Still dressed in her nightgown, Tammy threw the Frisbee for the dog.
DISCUSSION:	The first sentence suggests that the dog was wearing a nightgown.

Activity Revising for Dangling and Misplaced Modifiers

Revise the following sentences to eliminate dangling and misplaced modifiers.

1. The exquisite food was prepared by chefs ranging from lobster bisque to tuna tartar.
2. The jury took a lunch break still undecided about the guilt of the suspect.
3. Worried about spreading germs, an antibacterial soap dispenser was installed near every entrance to the hospital.
4. Susan bought a cell phone for her daughter with broken buttons.
5. Getting ready for Sullivan's grand opening, the jewelry was displayed in glass cases.

D. Editing Punctuation

Commas (,)

Some writers place commas wherever they might pause as they are speaking; however, that approach doesn't always work. Learning the following comma rules will help prevent you from confusing your readers.

Introductory Phrase or Clause

Use a comma to set off introductory material in a sentence.

EXAMPLE:	*After she got to the grocery store,* Diane realized that she had forgotten her purse.
EXAMPLE:	*According to her son,* Diane often forgets things.
EXAMPLE:	*For instance,* one time Diane forgot to bring her running shoes to a marathon in which she was competing.

Nonessential Phrase or Clause

If you can omit a phrase or clause in a sentence without changing the meaning, the phrase or clause is nonessential and should be enclosed in commas. Essential phrases and clauses should not be enclosed in commas.

NONESSENTIAL:	Juanita, *who is my friend's cousin,* loves listening to music.
DISCUSSION:	The main point of the sentence is that Juanita loves listening to music. The italicized clause doesn't change that.
ESSENTIAL:	The song *now playing on the radio* is one of Juanita's favorites.
DISCUSSION:	The reader wouldn't know which song is Juanita's favorite without the italicized phrase.

Interrupters

Use commas to set off words that interrupt the flow of a sentence. Interrupters can occur at the beginning, middle, or end of a sentence.

EXAMPLE:	*Of course,* Steve may want to choose his own pizza toppings.
EXAMPLE:	We are having tilapia, *one of my favorite foods,* for dinner tonight.
EXAMPLE:	The mayor had a snack attack on Saturday, *according to the local newspaper.*

Items in a Series

Use commas to separate three or more words, phrases, or clauses in a series.

EXAMPLE: Jamal loaded many items into his backpack, such as *clothes, food,* and *water.*

EXAMPLE: The dog chased the squirrel *around the tree, over the log,* and *into the house.*

Before Coordinating Conjunctions

Use a comma before a coordinating conjunction (*for, and, nor, but, or, yet, so*) that separates two independent clauses. (See FANBOYS on p. 447.)

EXAMPLE: I was hoping to bring Bryan to the concert, *but* he wasn't feeling well.

EXAMPLE: Emma got elected president of the Student Government Association, *so* she is likely to develop some new leadership skills.

Note: Do not use a comma to separate words or phrases joined by a coordinating conjunction.

EXAMPLE: Elaine's clothing is simple *but* stylish.

Conjunctive Adverbs

Use commas to set off conjunctive adverbs, such as *however, furthermore,* and *therefore.*

EXAMPLE: Dave was, *however,* more experienced than James.

EXAMPLE: *Therefore,* Dave got a promotion.

Adjectives

Use commas to separate adjectives if they modify (describe) the same noun and have equal emphasis.

EXAMPLE: It is a *hot, sticky* day.

EXAMPLE: The *cool, refreshing* ocean waves are the perfect remedy for the heat.

TIP: If you can replace the comma with the word *and,* then you need a comma. If not, leave the comma out.

EXAMPLE: Brad was sitting in the *red lifeguard* booth.

DISCUSSION: You would not say it was a *red and lifeguard* booth, so leave out the comma.

Dialogue

Use commas to separate dialogue from the speaker. You do not need commas to separate indirect quotations.

EXAMPLE: Ann Marie exclaimed, "I see a shark in the water!"

EXAMPLE: "It's just a dolphin," replied Brad, "so you have nothing to fear."

EXAMPLE: Brad told Ann Marie that she had nothing to fear.

Direct Address

Use commas to set off a direct address.

EXAMPLE: Children, please be quiet.

EXAMPLE: Please, Randall, I need your advice.

EXAMPLE: Here, kitty, I have a treat for you.

Titles or Degrees

Use commas to set off a title or degree that comes after a name.

EXAMPLE: Curtis Counter, CPA, does my taxes each year.

EXAMPLE: Neil Healer, MD, is a great physician.

EXAMPLE: One of my favorite teachers was Eric Illuminator, PhD.

Addresses and Dates

Use commas to separate items in addresses and dates.

EXAMPLE: I enjoyed visiting the French Quarter in New Orleans, Louisiana.

EXAMPLE: He was born on November 30, 2002.

Activity Correcting Comma Errors

Add commas as needed to the following sentences.

1. After Nessa finished her salad she wanted a piece of dark chocolate.
2. Carlos who lives next door bought a new boat last week.
3. Susan stocked her medicine cabinet with aspirin cough drops and cold medicine.
4. Heather was looking for a bargain so she shopped at a discount store.
5. Stewart is however a talented singer.
6. Geoff dreaded entering the damp musty cave.
7. Debbie shouted "You're the best friend ever!"
8. Ladies please be seated.
9. I have an appointment with Glen Martin DDS to get my teeth whitened.
10. Lisa visited San Francisco California on August 25 2019.

Semicolons (;) and Colons (:)

Semicolons (;)

Independent Clauses Use a semicolon between two main clauses if the conjunction is left out and if the clauses are closely related in content and style.

EXAMPLE: Sally likes vanilla caramel ice cream; Gale prefers chocolate ice cream.

Conjunctive Adverbs Use a semicolon before and a comma after a conjunctive adverb that joins two independent clauses. (See p. 448 for a list of common conjunctive adverbs.)

EXAMPLE: Sally likes vanilla caramel ice cream; however, Gale prefers chocolate ice cream.

Items in a Series with Commas Use semicolons to separate items in a series when commas are present within one or more of the items.

EXAMPLE: Some of the most exciting cities to visit are London, England; Paris, France; Rome, Italy; and Athens, Greece.

Colons (:)

List of Items Use a colon after a main clause (complete sentence) to introduce a list of items.

CORRECT: When going on a Caribbean cruise, always pack the following items: a bathing suit, a bottle of suntan lotion, and a book to read.

INCORRECT: When going on a Caribbean cruise, always pack: a bathing suit, suntan lotion, and a book to read.

CORRECT: When going on a Caribbean cruise, always pack a bathing suit, suntan lotion, and a book to read.

DISCUSSION: If what precedes the list is not a complete sentence, then a colon is not needed.

Explanation or Emphasis Use a colon after a main clause when what follows it explains or emphasizes the subject in the main clause.

EXAMPLE: Maggie is going to school for one reason: to get a better job.

Quotations Use a colon to introduce a quotation after a main clause.

EXAMPLE: Oscar Wilde, a Victorian playwright, had an interesting view of himself: "I am so clever that sometimes I don't understand a single word of what I am saying."

Salutations Use a colon to follow the salutation of a business letter or formal correspondence.

EXAMPLE: Dear Ms. Snider:

Activity Editing for Colons and Semicolons

Add colons and semicolons to the following sentences as necessary. Note, not every sentence needs a semicolon or colon added.

1. Fred is going hiking Julie is going shopping.
2. Tina wants to get a new job furthermore, she expects higher pay.
3. Pete and Barb have one expectation of their vacation relaxation.
4. For the cookout, Rose is going to buy chips, potato salad, and soft drinks.
5. My father always gave me this advice "Never give up on your dreams."

Quotation Marks (" ") and (' ')

Double Quotation Marks

Exact Words Use a set of double quotation marks to enclose the exact words that someone spoke or wrote.

EXAMPLE: Malcolm X once stated, "Education is our passport to the future, for tomorrow belongs to the people who prepare for it today."

Titles of Short Published Works Use quotation marks to enclose the title of essays, articles, book chapters, poems, and short stories.

EXAMPLE: "Annabel Lee" is a powerful poem by Edgar Allan Poe.

Note: Do not place quotation marks around your own title in your essay. If you refer to your essay in another document, such as in the cover letter for a portfolio, then use quotation marks.

Emphasis Use double quotation marks around a word or phrase that introduces a concept that might be unfamiliar to readers or when a word or phrase is used ironically, satirically, or as unfamiliar slang. Do this sparingly. You may use italics for this purpose as well. Be consistent with how you emphasize words in a particular document.

EXAMPLE: The word "textese" refers to the informal language favored by those who send text messages.

Single Quotation Marks

Use a set of single quotation marks to enclose a quote within a quote.

EXAMPLE: Carol recalled, "I once heard an instructor say, 'A prepared student is a passing student.' "

Note: The single quotation mark at the end of the quote within a quote goes inside of the double quotation marks.

Activity Editing for Quotation Marks

Add quotation marks to the following sentences as needed.

1. Michael's mother once exclaimed, I brought you into this world, and I can take you out of it!
2. For an extra thirty dollars, explained the dental hygienist, you can have a flavored fluoride treatment.
3. In class we read a student essay called Adrenaline Rush.
4. People assign different meanings to the word love.
5. My friend said, I thought I had received a bad grade on my paper until my instructor exclaimed, Yours was the best in the class!

Ellipses (. . .)

Omission from a Quote

An *ellipsis* is a series of three dots (periods) used to show that something has been intentionally omitted from a quotation. An ellipsis may occur at the middle or end of a sentence, but not at the beginning. Be careful to not change the intended meaning of the original sentence or passage.

ORIGINAL SENTENCE: The future graduates lined up at the ceremony, eagerly anticipating the walk across the stage, the handshake with the school president, and the roar of the crowd when the degrees are conferred.

EXAMPLE: "The future graduates lined up at the ceremony, eagerly anticipating . . . the roar of the crowd when the degrees are conferred."

EXAMPLE: "The future graduates lined up at the ceremony, eagerly anticipating the walk across the stage, the handshake with the school president, and the roar of the crowd. . . ."

Note: Use four dots instead of three if the ellipsis ends the sentence.

Incomplete Thought

Use an ellipsis to indicate an incomplete thought.

EXAMPLE: This year we are working to pay off the car and the boat. Next year we hope to . . . well, we will worry about that later.

Apostrophes (')

Possessives

Use an apostrophe to show possession (ownership) for nouns and some indefinite pronouns. (See p. 463 for a list of indefinite pronouns.)

To show possession, add an apostrophe and an *-s* to singular nouns or indefinite pronouns that do not end in *-s.*

EXAMPLE: The teddy *bear's* eyes are green.

EXAMPLE: My *sister-in-law's* recipes are delicious.

EXAMPLE: *Everyone's* paychecks have grown a little this year.

EXAMPLE: Nicholas received an extra *week's* pay for his unused vacation.

To show possession, add an apostrophe and an *-s* to a singular noun that ends in *-s.*

EXAMPLE: The *bus's* passengers are all looking out of the windows.

EXAMPLE: *Carlos's* motorcycle is parked in the garage.

To show possession, add just an apostrophe (but no *-s*) to a plural noun that ends in *-s.*

EXAMPLE: The protesters' signs are insulting to the spectators.

Note: Do not use an apostrophe with a possessive pronoun, such as *its, his, hers, whose,* or *theirs.*

Contractions

Use an apostrophe to indicate where letters are missing in a contraction.

EXAMPLE: *I've* never seen a sunset that beautiful before.

Common Contractions	
are not	aren't
do not	don't
has not	hasn't
have not	haven't
he will	he'll
I will	I'll
is not	isn't
it is or it has	it's
she will	she'll
should not	shouldn't
that is or that has	that's
we are	we're
we have	we've
we will	we'll
who is or who has	who's
you are	you're

Missing Letters or Numbers

Use an apostrophe to indicate where numbers or letters are missing.

EXAMPLE: Gurmeet graduated in the class of *'12.*

EXAMPLE: The polite country boy said, "*Ma'am,* I am going *fishin'* today."

Note: Apostrophes can be used in a quote to reflect a speaker's dialect.

Activity Editing for Apostrophes

Add or delete apostrophes as needed in the following sentences.

1. The kicker said to the reporter, "Ive been playin football my whole life."
2. The coaches hearts were racing as the football soared toward the goal post.
3. The quarterback couldnt believe he had thrown the pass so far.
4. The fans cheered when the team won it's final game of the season.
5. Jimbo Fisher, the Florida State University coach, resigned in 17.

Hyphens (-) and Dashes (—)

Hyphens (-)

Adjectives Use a *hyphen* to combine two or more words that serve as a single adjective preceding (but not following) a noun.

EXAMPLE: Shakespeare is a *well-known* playwright.

EXAMPLE: The playwright Shakespeare is *well known.*

EXAMPLE: Simon loves *chocolate-covered* pretzels.

EXAMPLE: Simon loves pretzels that are *chocolate covered.*

Note: Do not use a hyphen with *-ly* adverbs: quickly eaten dessert.

Compound Numbers Use a *hyphen* with compound numbers.

EXAMPLE: Judy is *thirty-three* years old.

EXAMPLE: The *two-year-old* boy was returned safely to his parents.

EXAMPLE: Trent ate *three-fourths* of the pizza.

Prefixes Use hyphens with the following prefixes: *all-*, *ex-,* and *self-*.

EXAMPLE: The spa treatment package is *all-inclusive.*

EXAMPLE: He and his *ex-wife* get along remarkably well.

EXAMPLE: The business owner was a real *self-starter.*

Dashes (—)

Create a *dash* with two hyphens, or use the dash character if your word processing program has one. Use a dash to create emphasis; to illustrate a change in direction; or to replace parentheses, semicolons, colons, or commas. Use dashes sparingly, so they do not lose their intended effect of creating interest for your readers.

EXAMPLE: The storm is drawing near—where are the children?

EXAMPLE: Jennifer told me—much to my dismay—she is not going to attend Joey's recital.

EXAMPLE: I know why Salvatore did not show up to work today—although I wish I didn't.

Activity Editing for Hyphens and Dashes

Add hyphens and dashes to the following sentences as needed.

1. My father in law is going to help us repair our stone covered walkway.
2. Kevin's exroommate is getting a well deserved letter in the mail.
3. The triplet six year olds each ate one third of the birthday cake.
4. Joy won the lottery how amazing!
5. Holly's landlord that rat has given her only two weeks to move out!

Parentheses ( ) and Brackets [ ]

Parentheses ( )

Use *parentheses* to set off a comment you want to include in or after a sentence when the comment may be relevant to the main point but is not essential to the reader's understanding of it.

EXAMPLE: My favorite actor (who happens to be from my hometown) is starring in a Broadway play.

EXAMPLE: I'm going to see a Broadway play starring my favorite actor (who happens to be from my hometown).

EXAMPLE: My favorite actor is starring in a Broadway play. (He happens to be from my hometown.)

Note: If the parentheses enclose a complete sentence, the period goes inside the parentheses. If the sentence appears in parentheses within another sentence, however, it does not begin with a capital letter or end in a period.

Use parentheses to set off numbers or letters in a list of items.

EXAMPLE:	Follow these three rules if you are on fire: (1) stop moving, (2) drop to the floor, and (3) roll around to extinguish the flames.

Use parentheses for in-text citations in research papers that follow the guidelines of the Modern Language Association or the American Psychological Association.

MLA EXAMPLE:	"Eating dark chocolate makes us feel better" (Rich 65).
APA EXAMPLE:	"Eating dark chocolate makes us feel better" (Rich, 2019, p. 65).

Brackets [ ]

Use *brackets* to indicate that you have modified or added a letter, word, or group of words to a direct quote.

ORIGINAL:	Eating dark chocolate makes us feel better.
MLA EXAMPLE:	According to Rich, "[Consuming] dark chocolate makes us feel better" (65).
APA EXAMPLE:	According to Rich (2019), "[Consuming] dark chocolate makes us feel better" (p. 65).

Use the word *sic* enclosed in brackets immediately after an error in a direct quote. This lets your readers know you are aware of the error and that you quoted it exactly as it appeared in the original.

EXAMPLE:	According to Dr. Smock, "An elegant black dress is flatering [*sic*] on most women."
DISCUSSION:	The writer used [*sic*] to acknowledge that Dr. Smock misspelled the word *flattering.*

E. Editing Mechanics

Capitalization

Titles

Capitalize the titles of articles, books, poems, plays, songs, brochures, and so on. Capitalize all main words, but not articles (*a, an, the*), prepositions (*to, from, in*), or conjunctions (*and, but, or*). Always capitalize the first word of a title as well as the first word after a colon, even if it is an article, a preposition, or a conjunction.

POEM:	"Because I Could Not Stop for Death"
SONG:	"If I Had a Million Dollars"
BOOK:	*The Travel Book: A Journey through Every Country in the World*

Names

Capitalize the names of specific people, characters, and animals:

Dr. Wigelsworth	Professor Davis	Pastor Calhoun
Judge Crawford	Aunt Mary	Grandpa Chuck
Batman	Snow White	Miss Piggy
Fido	Nellie	Fuzzball

Note: Do not capitalize words that are not part of a proper noun, such as the professor, the judge, and my mom.

Capitalize name brands.

Coca-Cola	Doritos	Godiva

Regions, Locations, Buildings, and Monuments

Capitalize specific regions, but not directions.

Mitch is from the Midwest.	Drive north on I-95.

Capitalize geographical locations, buildings, and monuments.

Austin, Texas	Paris, France	Ocala National Forrest
Pacific Ocean	Lake James	Jetty Park
World Trade Center	Eiffel Tower	Statue of Liberty

Seasons and Events

Capitalize events but not seasons.

The Spring Fling is next week.

My favorite season is summer.

Capitalize historical events, documents, and movements.

Civil War	Declaration of Independence	Renaissance

Language, Ethnic, and Religious References

Capitalize nationalities, languages, and ethnicities.

American	Spanish	Asian
Greek architecture	Hispanic culture	Japanese cuisine

Capitalize religions, religious books, religious followers, religious holidays, and words referring to God.

Christian	Jewish	Muslim
Methodists	Holy Bible	Torah
Easter	Yom Kippur	Buddha
Allah	Jehovah	the Trinity

Courses

Capitalize language courses and complete course names.

French	English 1101	General Biology II

Note: Do not capitalize general subjects: psychology, math, and biology.

Activity Editing for Capitalization

Edit the following sentences for capitalization errors.

1. Terrence loves to visit mount dora every Spring.
2. My sister-in-law amy is looking forward to taking psychology II and calculus.
3. My friend shalerie, who is from france, loves to eat yoplait yogurt.
4. The famous dr. oz wrote a book called *you: the owner's manual: an insider's guide to the body that will make you healthier and younger.*
5. One of professor tiffany's favorite songs is called "single ladies."

Abbreviations

Abbreviations in School Papers

Do not use these abbreviations in your papers for school:

&	b/c	co.	dept.	Eng.
Fri.	gov't.	Prof.	thru	w/o

Titles and Degrees

Abbreviate titles that appear before names:

Dr. Goldstein　　Ms. Gibson　　St. Thomas

Abbreviate titles and degrees that appear after names:

Frieda Walker, PhD (or Ph.D.)　　Charles Rowland, Jr.　　Ed Ellis, DDS (or D.D.S.)

Acronyms

Generally, spell out a name before using an abbreviation:

EXAMPLE: The Children's Home Society (CHS) is a good organization.

Some familiar acronyms are nearly always abbreviated:

EXAMPLE: The FBI is working with NASA and IBM.

Times and Dates

For exact times, use uppercase or lowercase abbreviations for A.M. (a.m.) and P.M. (p.m.).

EXAMPLE: The rocket is scheduled to launch at 6:51 A.M.

EXAMPLE: The fundraiser lasts from 7:30 p.m. until 1:00 a.m.

Do not abbreviate days or months in formal writing.

EXAMPLE: You are invited to attend the Rose Gala on Saturday, August 20.

Place Names

Spell out names of places except in addresses.

EXAMPLE: Laurie visited Rochester, New York, during her vacation.

EXAMPLE: Mail the payment to 555 Generic Street, Rochester, NY 55555.

Numbers

Spell out numbers for the following situations:

- One- or two-word numbers, such as four, thirty-three, six million.
- Numbers beginning a sentence.

  EXAMPLE: *Two hundred and ten* people participated in the self-defense workshop.

  EXAMPLE: The self-defense workshop drew *210* participants.
- Numbers forming compound words.

  EXAMPLE: The *seven-year-old* boy gave *one-half* of his toys to charity.
- Times using *o'clock.*

  EXAMPLE: I was up writing a paper until *three o'clock* this morning.

Use numerals for these situations:

- Exact times and dates.

  EXAMPLE: The show starts at 6:30 p.m.

  EXAMPLE: Graduation will take place on May 23, 2019.
- Numbers with three or more words.

  EXAMPLE: Nico and Leslie invited 425 guests to their wedding.

  EXAMPLE: The meeting room will hold 1,250 attendees.
- Addresses.

  EXAMPLE: Marsden lives at 444 Apple Lane.
- Money and percentages.

  EXAMPLE: The bake sale raised $695.50.

  EXAMPLE: According to the survey, 78% of the students voted for the new policy.
- Numbers in a series or list.

  EXAMPLE: Melony still needs to work on problems 2, 5, 7, and 11.

Activity Editing for Abbreviations and Numbers

Edit the following sentences for errors with abbreviations and numbers.

1. The science dept. just received funding for three hundred and twenty new microscopes.
2. Doctor Snow is hosting a seminar on Thurs., Feb. tenth at 2 o'clock.
3. Sandra is looking forward to her trip to San Francisco, CA on May fifth.
4. Prof. Smith, Doctor of Philosophy is hosting a field trip for 20 students.
5. Jared & Josie are going to the visit the gov't building in Tallahassee, FL at three p.m.

Italics and Underlining

Italics and underlining are equivalent. Use italics when typing on a computer, and use underlining when handwriting.

Emphasis

Italicize or underline words you want to emphasize in your writing.

EXAMPLE: The word *hate* can be so destructive.

Note: You may use quotation marks for this as well. Be consistent with how you emphasize words in a particular document.

Titles of Longer Works

Italicize or underline titles of books, plays, newspapers, magazines, works of art, CDs, movies, television shows, and websites.

EXAMPLE: I read a book called *The History of Art* that featured van Gogh's painting *Starry Night.*

Foreign Words

Italicize or underline foreign words that have not become common in the English language.

EXAMPLE: When Paul spilled his cup of coffee, he said, "*C'est la vie.*"

EXAMPLE: Marcella is going to eat a burrito with salsa for lunch.

DISCUSSION: The words *burrito* and *salsa* have become common in the English language.

Activity Editing for Italics and Underlining

Identify words in the following sentences that need to be italicized or underlined.

1. The show The Voice has attracted a lot of attention during the last several years.
2. The word plagiarism scares many novice writers.
3. Brett graduated magna cum laude.
4. I'm hoping to see the Mona Lisa when I'm in France.
5. I read an article about a serial killer in USA Today.

F. Editing Spelling

Commonly Misspelled Words

While the spell checker on your computer may help you to identify some misspelled words, you still need to proofread all of your papers before submitting them. Otherwise, you may end up with some spelling errors that could cause your readers to think you are careless.

You may remember a couple of spelling rules from your younger days, such as "use *-i* before *-e* except after *-c*" or "drop the *-y* and add *-ies.*" You will find an extensive list of spelling rules at The Purdue Online Writing Lab: **http://owl.english/purdue.edu/owl.**

Knowing the rules can be useful; however, you have probably already realized that the rules have many exceptions. If you are not sure how to spell a word, look it up in a dictionary or go to **http://dictionary.reference.com.**

You also can study a list of commonly misspelled words, such as the following. Many of the words are irregular or are spelled differently than they sound. Watch out for these words as you edit your writing.

Commonly Misspelled Words			
absence	conscience	harass	occasionally
acceptable	conscientious	height	occurrence
accessible	conscious	hierarchy	pastime
accidentally	consensus	humorous	prejudice
accommodate	convenience	hypocrisy	privilege
accuracy	criticism	ignorance	probably
achievement	criticize	immediately	questionnaire
acquaintance	deceive	incredible	receive
acquire	definitely	intelligence	recommend
a lot	disappoint	interest	reference

amateur	disastrous	jewelry	relevant
analyze	discipline	judgment	restaurant
apparent	efficient	knowledge	rhyme
appearance	eligible	leisure	rhythm
argument	embarrass	license	ridiculous
believe	environment	loneliness	schedule
boundary	exaggerate	maintenance	separate
business	exhilarate	maneuver	sergeant
calendar	existence	medieval	successful
category	experience	memento	tendency
cemetery	familiar	millennium	thorough
changeable	fascinate	miniature	through
collectible	foreign	minuscule	truly
characteristic	gauge	mischievous	vacuum
column	grammar	misspell	villain
committed	grateful	necessary	weird
conceive	guarantee	noticeable	writing

Activity Editing for Misspelled Words

Identify and revise the misspelled words in the following sentences. Each sentence has two misspelled words.

1. Writers should proofread for grammer and mispelled words.
2. Dave is eligable for a garanteed student loan.
3. Cindy is an amature guitarist who plays with great acuracy.
4. The employee tried to acomodate the customer who had alot of complaints.
5. Raul was greatful for the raise he recieved.

Homonyms

Homonyms are words that sound the same but are spelled differently. Watch out for these homonyms as you edit your writing. If you use the wrong word, you will likely confuse your readers.

Homonyms	Examples
accept—to receive or approve **except**—to take out or exclude	Many local hospitals *accept* interns. Everyone has voted *except* Trisha.
affect—to change or influence **effect**—the result or outcome	His decision *affected* everyone in his family. The counselor had a positive *effect* on her.

continued

Homonyms	Examples
allowed—permitted **aloud**—spoken	Monica *allowed* Shannon to borrow her car. Troy read the example *aloud* for the class.
allusion—an indirect reference to **illusion**—a fantasy or deceptive appearance	The rap song makes an *allusion* to a Greek play. Jim created the *illusion* of always studying when he was really reading a magazine.
already—by now **all ready**—fully prepared	Minh has *already* studied for the test. Jessica was *all ready* to give the presentation.
all together—all in one place or time **altogether**—completely	Let's go for a ride *all together.* Susan is *altogether* responsible for her bills.
appraise—to determine the value **apprise**—to tell or notify	The ring was *appraised* for $2,000. She was *apprised* of the status of her request.
cite—to refer to, to give an example **sight**—vision, something to see **site**—a location	John *cited* Benjamin Franklin in his paper. The Statue of Liberty is an amazing *sight.* The *site* for the new student lounge is perfect.
coarse—rough **course**—path of travel	The exterior paint was very *coarse.* He is on the right *course* to success.
complement—to complete, a counterpart **compliment**—to praise	The curtains *complement* the window. Anna received a *compliment* on her new outfit.
confidant—someone to confide in **confident**—self-assured	Jordan was Edward's best friend and *confidant.* Sue was *confident* she would pass the exam.
conscience—moral right or wrong **conscious**—aware of one's feelings	Bob followed his *conscience* and told the truth. Susan was not *conscious* of her depression.
discreet—confidential or tactful **discrete**—distinct or separate	They were *discreet* about their relationship. They kept their finances *discrete.*
elicit—to bring out **illicit**—illegal	The essay *elicits* feelings of compassion. He was arrested for selling *illicit* drugs.
every day—happening daily **everyday**—ordinary	I ride my scooter to class *every day.* Riding my scooter to class is an *everyday* event.
fair—impartial, evenhanded **fare**—payment	The instructor's policies are *fair.* Trent paid his cab *fare.*
faze—to stun **phase**—part of a sequence	Vicki was *fazed* by the news of her award. Jill started a new *phase* in her life.
its—possessive of *it* **it's**—contraction of *it is*	The dog wagged *its* tail. *It's* time for the show to start.

Homonyms	Examples
lead—a heavy metal **led**—past tense of *to lead*	Sidney suffered from *lead* poisoning. The millionaire *led* a good life.
loose—not securely attached **lose**—to fail to win or keep	The door handle was *loose*. Shaquanda didn't want to *lose* her scholarship.
principal—head of school, main **principle**—a general rule or truth	The administration's *principal* goal is student success. You can't go wrong if you follow this *principle*.
stationary—not moving, fixed **stationery**—writing paper	Kevin rode a *stationary* bike in the winter. Tanisha loves to send letters on pretty *stationery*.
than—comparison **then**—at that time or after that	Francesca is taller *than* Maria. First we'll work, and *then* we'll play.
their—possessive form of *them* **there**—in or at that place **they're**—contraction of *they are*	It is *their* decision to make. Please put the book over *there* on the shelf. I hope *they're* not late for the meeting.
to—toward **too**—excessively or also **two**—the number 2, a couple	I'm going *to* the library. Sasha is *too* hungry to think straight. Amy has *two* papers to write next week.
who's—contraction of *who is* **whose**—possessive of *who*	*Who's* attending the conference in Arizona? *Whose* presentation did you like best?
your—possessive of *you* **you're**—contraction of *you are*	*Your* positive attitude will take you far. *You're* likely to get a great job after graduation.

Activity Editing for Homonyms

Identify and revise the incorrectly used homonyms in the following sentences.

1. Angelica blushed when her boyfriend paid her a complement.
2. Your not going to be able to attend the seminar next week.
3. Terry is more skilled at designing Web pages then Jake is.
4. Bruce was confidant that he would get a promotion soon.
5. Misty was careful to sight her sources in her paper.

Glossary

A

Active voice Occurs when the subject performs the action in the sentence. 451

Adjectives Words that modify nouns or pronouns. 466

Adverbs Words that modify adjectives, verbs, and other adverbs. 466

Antecedents Nouns that pronouns refer to. 458

Appeals Persuasive strategies used to support claims. 241

Appositive A word or phrase that renames a noun or pronoun. 460

Argument A communication in which writers or speakers present a position/make a claim with the goal of convincing their audience to agree with their view—or to at least consider its validity. 238

Audience People who will read or hear the message. 5

B

Biased language Reflects an unfair assumption or prejudice without cause. 455

Brainstorming Writing whatever comes to mind about a topic. 18

C

Causal analysis Analyzing reasons and results. 210

Claim A debatable assertion. 240

Cliché A worn-out expression. 453

Comma-spliced sentence Two independent clauses that are joined improperly with just a comma. 447

Conjunctive adverb An adverb that serves as a transition between two independent clauses. 448

Connotation The meaning of a word, including the attitudes and feelings people associate with the word. 452

Coordinating conjunction A word that joins words or independent clauses that are equal and shows how they are related. 447

Criteria Principles or standards used to evaluate something. 276

Critical thinking Interpreting ideas and reflecting on them. 69

D

Database A comprehensive, searchable collection of content. 343

Denotation The dictionary definition of a word. 452

Design The genre, format, length, and appearance of a message. 10

Diction A writer's or speaker's choice of words. 452

E

Essay A group of paragraphs related to a particular subject. 57

F

Forecast Helps the reader predict the main points. 59

Freewriting Unstructured writing for a set amount of time. 20

G

Graphic organizer A visual representation of an abstract idea. 25

J

Jargon Specialized vocabulary that people related to a particular career field, group, or interest use. 453

Journal A place to keep track of thoughts and feelings. 21

K

Keywords Significant words or phrases used to narrow a database search. 342

L

Library catalog An index of a library's holdings with specific information about each item. 342

Listing Making a list about ideas related to a specific topic. 19

Logical fallacies Occur when someone draws a conclusion not based on sound reasoning. 83

M

Mixed construction Occurs when the subject of a sentence does not fit logically with the predicate of the sentence. 449

Multimodal Using more than one modality to communicate an idea. 433

O

Outline A blueprint of the divisions and subdivisions in a paper. 27

P

Paragraph A group of sentences related to one idea. 52

Parallelism Occurs when similar ideas in a sentence are expressed in a similar grammatical manner. 450

Paraphrase A reworded version of a sentence or short passage from an original work. 348

Passive voice Occurs when the subject receives the action in the sentence. 451

Plagiarism The use of another's words or ideas without giving appropriate credit. 348

Primary or field research Information collected firsthand from sources, such as surveys, interviews, and experiments. 350

Pronouns Words that replace nouns. 458

Proposal A plan put forward for consideration by others. 301

Purpose Reason for writing. 7

Q

Quotation An author's exact words enclosed in quotation marks. 349

R

Rhetoric The art of communicating effectively through writing or speaking. 5

Run-on sentence Two independent clauses that run together without a proper punctuation mark or a comma and a coordinating conjunction. 447

S

Search engine A computer program used to locate information on the Internet. 344

Sentence fragment A group of words that cannot stand on its own because it lacks one or more elements of a complete sentence. 446

Sexist language Words that unnecessarily refer to gender. 455

Slang Informal, nonstandard vocabulary that people related to a particular career field, group, or interest use. 453

Strategy Approach to writing that best serves your purpose and audience. 10

Subject A general concept, such as health, technology, or crime. 5

Subordinating conjunction A dependent word that helps to show the relationship between the ideas in two independent clauses. 448

Summary A shortened version of an original work including only the main ideas and using different wording. 71, 348

Synthesis A combination of ideas from different sources to form a new whole. 71, 355

T

Thesis Identifies the main idea of an essay. 23, 57

Tone The mood or feeling a writer or speaker is trying to create. 6

Topic sentence States the main idea of a paragraph. 53

U

Unity Ensures every idea relates to the overall thesis of the essay. 60

V

Visual literacy The ability to read and interpret a variety of visual texts. 76

A

B

C

D

E

F

G

H

I

J

K

L

M

N

O

P

Q

R

S

T

U

V

W

Editing and Proofreading Marks

Use these editing marks to help you as you edit and proofread documents. Also, your instructor may use them when grading your papers.

Mark	Meaning
ab	abbreviation
ad	adjective problem
adv	adverb problem
agr	agreement problem
ambig	ambiguous wording
’ over ^	insert apostrophe
appr	inappropriate language
awk	awkward expression
cap ≡	capitalize
case	case error
⊐ ⊏	center horizontally
⊔ over ⊓	center vertically
◯	check this
choppy	choppy style
^ with ,	insert comma
:	insert colon
coord	faulty coordination
cs	comma splice
(delete mark)	delete
d	diction
dev	develop idea more
dm	dangling modifier
d neg	double negative
ds	double-space
doc	documentation problem
frag	sentence fragment
gen	be more specific
gram	grammatical error
inf	too informal
irr	irregular verb error
^	insert
ital ___	italicize or underline
lc	use lowercase
logic	not logical
mm	misplaced modifier
nc	not clear
nonst	nonstandard language
num	numbers error
¶	new paragraph
//	not parallel
omit	omitted word
pass	passive voice
⊙	insert period
pro ref	pronoun reference
“ ” over ^ ^	insert quotation marks
rep	too repetitive
;	insert semicolon
ro	run-on sentence
shift	shift in tense or person
⁀	close space
# over ^	insert space
(*sp*)	spelling
ss	sentence structure
stet	let it stand
sub	faulty subordination
support	add more evidence
t	wrong verb tense
thesis	thesis
ts	topic sentence
trans	weak transition
tr ⊓⊔	transpose
vary	add variety
voice	inconsistent voice
w	wordy
wc	word choice
wo	word order